# THE MOUNTAIN ARAPESH

# THE MOUNTAIN ARAPESH
## VOLUME III
### Stream of Events in Alitoa

## MARGARET MEAD

AMERICAN MUSEUM SCIENCE BOOKS
Published for The American Museum of Natural History
THE NATURAL HISTORY PRESS
Garden City, New York
1971

This volume of *The Mountain Arapesh* was originally published as *The Mountain Arapesh*, Part III: *Socio-Economic Life* and Part IV: *Diary of Events in Alitoa*. Anthropological Papers of The American Museum of Natural History, Vol. 40, part 3, 1947.

Library of Congress Catalog Card Number 68–11800

# PREFACE TO THE AMERICAN
# MUSEUM SCIENCE BOOK EDITION

This is the third and last volume in the republication of
the monograph series on the Mountain Arapesh, the New
Guinea people among whom I worked in 1931–32. Today
the pace of change is so rapid that change has been registered in the interval between the new preface to the first and
to this third volume.

Several years ago Anthony Forge, a fellow anthropologist
who was working among the neighboring Abelam, visited
Alitoa, where he found only two old men looking after a few
pigs. The rest of the people had moved down to the coast
and were living in various coastal villages. When Volume I,
*The Record of Unabelin*, was published, I did not even know
whether Unabelin still was alive.

Later, in 1967, when I was on my way to the Sepik River,
I met in Wewak (the district capital) Saharu, who had been
the smallest member of our household staff in 1932. He told
me that Unabelin had died and that the people of Alitoa
were living in many different places. He himself had come to
consider Waginara as his home village. Some younger Arapesh, who were working in Wewak, were delighted to claim
me when I greeted them in their own language. But the
village described in detail in this volume is no more. It
seemed to me then that the Arapesh—my name for them,
because they had no name for themselves—would vanish as
a group and that no one of their children's children would
know that a people described long ago by an American anthropologist were their ancestors.

At present, no matter how far into the modern world any
people have moved from an isolated and primitive past, it
is uncertain how they will view the record of that past. Often

they prefer a new myth to the actuality painstakingly set down by an anthropologist two generations ago. Their rejection is in accord with the new spirit that is abroad in the whole world; it expresses their awareness of a new reciprocity between those who learn and those who teach, those who are patients and those who seek to cure them, and those whom an anthropologist studies and the anthropologist himself.

In the past the anthropologist did indeed respect the people whom he studied and accepted as colleagues those among them who had curiosity and intellectual interest. The Arapesh described in this record of a seven-and-a-half-month residence in their village were my friends and colleagues in an enterprise that meant a great deal to me and that would, I hoped, illuminate our understanding of human behavior. During those months we depended deeply on one another. But when all was said and done, our motives remained a mystery to them. Why should we have come so far into such a poor and remote mountain country where food was scarce and living meager? Why did we ask so many questions and watch so persistently when, in the end, we would go away forever? The intellectuals among them—Unabelin with his luminous curiosity, Mindibilip with his sensitive linguistic ear, and Gerud who combined helping to cook our meals with trance seizures at suppertime—enjoyed our stay. But they had no purpose for themselves other than survival. To this we contributed a little as we dressed their sores and in emergencies supplemented their diet.

When I left Alitoa and during the thirty-five years before I met Saharu in Wewak, I thought of the Arapesh as we had known them. I had little sense that what we had done ever would be valued by them unless, by chance, one of their descendants generations later might become a social scientist. They had contributed to us far more than we could contribute, in those days, to them. It is this one-sidedness that has led many peoples to rebel against the anthropologists who recorded their past, especially those peoples, like the American Indians, who find their present lives unsupportable. Then, in 1968, I received this letter:

St. John's College
Camperdown
Sydney University
*9th August 1968*

Dear Dr. Margaret Mead:

Your book, *Sex and Temperament in Three Primitive Societies*, has come into my hands.

It so happens that I am a tribesman from the "Arapesh." I am currently studying law in Sydney University.

I wish to congratulate you on your accurate record of my tribal life. Much of what you recorded is still true today, although as you know, much has changed.

Whether the change is something better, I cannot say. I could tell you much more about my tribe, now, although I fear this letter may never reach you. It might get lost in post.

If it does reach you, may I ask if it is at all possible to publish the book in paperback. I imagine the book is out of print now.

My village (Wantogik) is only a few miles from Dagur village, 7–8 miles from Karawap plantation. It is high up on the hills. Wishing you my very best wishes in many years ahead of you,

*Yapubi Wab* (Good Night),
Bernard Mullu Narokobi

It was hard to believe.

How was it that one of the Arapesh—a people who had had such a light hold on any form of cognitive style—should have come further than any individual among the Manus, who had moved as a group into the modern world in the years between our first study of them, in 1928, and the beginning of our restudy, in 1953?

The fact is, the Arapesh did not move as a group. Instead, as Bernard Narokobi explained in his next letter, four men from one village had moved ahead—he to Sydney University and the others to the University of Papua-New Guinea. This was another piece of valuable information on the different

ways people can move from one period in human culture
to another. The Manus changed as a group, transforming
their culture and preserving their society as they changed.
The Arapesh underwent no such group transformation, but
single individuals, less tightly bound within a coherent culture, were able to move further more rapidly.

When I answered Bernard Narokobi's letter, I also sent
paperback copies of *Sex and Temperament Among Three
Primitive Peoples* and *The Record of Unabelin* (Volume I
of this series). Soon after, I received his reply:

                                        St. John's College
                                        . . .
                                        *12th November 1968*

Dear Dr. Mead:

What a great surprise to receive a letter and the books.
Without doubt, this is my most pleasant of surprises. The
day was brilliant; summer brightening up and heat gaining
momentum, no doubt to prepare me for the beloved Arapesh
mountains, soon.

I had been studying the law of easements, mortgages and
covenants since nine in the morning. Whatever relevance a
claim against obstruction of a natural God-given element of
sunshine through a defined window, to the mountains, I know
not. But I believe it's good fun trying to learn new things for
their own sake. Being exhausted, I got home at six. What
should I find, but a surprise. Thank you most kindly.

As my examinations are few days away, I will be brief in
this letter. I know, too, you are a busy lady and so I will say
only a few things. Perhaps I may be permitted to write to
you again.

Frankly, when I wrote, your name was like a legend or a
dream about some great person. I thought you might have
long left our world. I got this impression partly from the fact
that the book *Sex and Temperament* . . . looked well worn
down by students, poor sense of judgment on my part, no
doubt! I saw Professor Elkin of Anthropology Department
in Sydney and he gave me your address.

There are no other Arapesh students in Sydney University and as far as I am aware, anywhere else outside Papua-New Guinea University. I think there are three attending the Papua-New Guinea University. By some strange occurrence, these three are all from my village (pardon my parochialism in these days of great outcry for unity). And even more strange, one is my first degree cousin—my mother's brother's son, one second degree—son of my mother's brother through another marriage, I believe, and third is somehow related, I dare not narrate relations without charts after good counsel from my elders! Two are challenging Science and one is doing Arts. To be more boastful, my fourth cousin, actually brother in the tribal sense, will be finishing his medicine after six years next year, at Papuan Medical College in Port Moresby.

I find law difficult but exciting. If good fortune comes my way, and of course I have to work for it! I should finish my law studies in 1971. I may then go to the bar in New Guinea as an advocate. If my results are good enough, I wish to teach law.

This Christmas, a couple of Australian friends of mine will come with me to stay with my people for two weeks. One is a barrister, and he is very dear to me. He is like my father. He is Mr. W. T. Prentice, and indeed it was at his suggestion that I wrote to you. He and mother, Mrs. Prentice, read your book with great interest. I believe some of your books on New Guinea should be made compulsory reading in some New Guinea Tertiary institutions. Your books on Manus Island, *New Lives for Old* and *Growing Up in New Guinea* are prescribed texts in first year (preliminary) at Papua-New Guinea University.

I trust this letter will find you in good health and in preparation for Christmas eve.

Wishing you happiness now and always, *iapupi wabigep.*

Sincerely yours,
Bernard Narokobi

When I was ready to write the new preface for this volume, I cabled for permission to reproduce the two earlier letters. This was the reply:

International House
University of Sydney
New South Wales
*13/5/70*

Dear Margaret:

It was so thrilling and joyous to receive your telegram and to know you are publishing more on my tribe. I pray God that what you write may shed light on the world. I am writing a novel based on legends and day to day living of life in my village with some of my own imagination. I am writing at the rate of one page a week, so I figure it may take a couple of years. I will then write to different publishing houses and ask for help. I wrote a play last year in Pidgin for a literary competition conducted by PNG University. I was very happy to receive first prize. But I must tell you too that not many students bothered trying. I was the only New Guinea student studying in Australia who submitted one. The theme is the betrothal of a young girl to be married, but she has the calling to a convent to become a nun. This is a new concept and she has trouble convincing her parents. In the play I tried to bring out the present day cultural clashes. If you are interested, I can try and send you a copy.

Regarding my letters to you in 1968. I am not sure what I wrote then. I never thought my letters would one day be requested for publication. I do not think I said anything derogatory. In any case, even if I did, it was history, so you are free to publish them, with or without my name as it pleases you.

. . .

Now I must tell you about some of my clansfolk. Nearly all our *takuiens* or the big men are dying. Peter Simogren has gone to Cape Hoskins in Talorea and many people went with him to cultivate oil palm. It is promising. When I told my people of you in 1968 Christmas Home, old men remembered bearing you on a stretcher up the hills from Banak, between Karawap and Dagua. Some said they were small boys then.

I am happy to tell you, our tribe now has quite a number of students at Papua-New Guinea University. Two of my cousins, sons of my mother's brothers, are nearing their science degrees. A third cousin is doing second year arts and two more cousins, all from the same village, begin their preliminary year for Medicine and Science next year. My cousin, but brother in traditional sense, who was studying medicine when I last wrote, has finished his studies. He is finishing his residence. I am making slow progress too. I am in my fourth but second last year in law.

My immediate ambition is to apply for a scholarship to come to United States and study Constitutional Law. I will see the Dean of law school towards next year. I hope then to return home and either teach law at University or join the civil service.

I am telling you about the tribe, not because I am unduly proud of it but because I feel you are entitled to know about it. The more I think about values my tribe hold, the more often I return and live in the village, and the more I see of the Western Way of life, the more convinced I am of this. There is something in my tribe that is noble and worth knowing by the world at large. I therefore encourage you and pray that your work may be more widely read and talked about.

Whenever I get the opportunity here in Australia, I tell the people of my tribe. I feel now that I can feel proud of my tribe and at the same time feel I belong not only to Papua-New Guinea, a nation to be, but to the world community at large.

I long to meet with you. But I guess I'll never have the privilege of shaking your hands. I will remember you and pray for your good health and wide publication of your works.

If what I write here is different in tone or taste to what I wrote two years ago, it is because I have evolved in spirit and intellect. I feel I am a fuller being now, though still as powerless and longing for something better in human aspirations to higher ideals of love and understanding. My heart yearns for union with nature, with my traditional background and Western conditioning. I think it is possible. If therefore it is possible for one man, it can be possible for a number and so a nation could be born, composed of different elements, all combining in diversity to form a national integration.

Trusting this letter reaches you remaining in good health,

> *Wabigep,* your Arapesh friend,
> Bernard Narokobi

It is appropriate that now, in 1970, more than half of the preface to this volume, the last in the republished series, should be written not by the ethnographer, but by an Arapesh who is an aspiring author.

I have made as few changes as possible in the text of this volume. The plates have been expanded from four to eight. The word *gens,* used in the 1930s for a patrilineal clan, is now archaic, a usage introduced by Robert H. Lowie that failed to take. Pidgin English is now spoken of as Neo Melanesian. I have added later publications by Dr. Fortune and myself, particularly those on the Arapesh.

> MARGARET MEAD
> New York
> *June 1970*

# PREFACE TO THE ORIGINAL EDITION

This is the third and fourth of a series[1] of papers on the culture of the Arapesh people of the Sepik-Aitape District of the Mandated Territory of New Guinea. These people were intensively studied by Dr. R. F. Fortune and myself from December to August, 1931–32. For the comparative discussions I have drawn upon our subsequent field experience among two tribes of the Sepik River basin, the Mundugumor and the Tchambuli, and upon the collections from the regions anterior to the Arapesh and the Sepik River, which are now in the Museum. My part of the investigation was undertaken in regular pursuit of my duties in the American Museum and was financed by the Frederick G. Voss Anthropological and Archaeological Fund. Therefore, I owe particular thanks to The American Museum of Natural History, and especially to Dr. Clark Wissler, for the opportunity to make this two-year expedition to New Guinea.

Dr. Fortune's work was conducted under a grant from the Social Science Research Council of Columbia University. Collaborating throughout the expedition, we were able to share, and so considerably reduce, our expenditures, so that my thanks are due to Columbia University and to the Frederick G. Voss Anthropological and Archaeological Fund of The American Museum which financed our respective researches. In regard to my field researches, my major thanks are due to Dr. Fortune, for the partnership that made it possible for me to work with people more uncontaminated and inaccessible than I could have reached alone, for cooperation in the field in the collection of ethnological materials upon which parts of this paper draw, for analysis of the phonetically difficult Arapesh language, and for accounts of parts of the men's esoterica and of events and ceremonies which

[1] Mead, 1938; 1940.

occurred outside the village of Alitoa. Furthermore, Dr. Fortune made two long trips into the interior to obtain the Plains
Arapesh and Abelam collections, organized and supervised
their packing and transportation, and cooperated in the routine collecting at our field sites.

For preliminary orientation in the selection of a field, which
finally resulted in the choice of the Arapesh region, I am
indebted to Dr. Briggs of the University of Sydney who had
made a survey trip in this region some years previously. For
orientation in the relationship between the cultures I studied
and neighboring cultures, I am indebted to Mr. Gregory
Bateson and Mr. E. W. P. Chinnery. For administrative en-
dorsement, I have to thank the Department of Home and
Territories of the Commonwealth of Australia. For assistance,
encouragement, and hospitality on the part of members of
the Government, I am indebted to His Honor, then Acting
Administrator, Judge Wanless, to His Honor Judge F. B.
Phillips, to Mr. Chinnery, then Government Anthropologist,
to Mr. T. E. McAdam, and to the late Mr. Macdonald. I am
especially indebted to the late Mr. M. V. Cobb of Karawop,
and to Mrs. Cobb, who offered me the most extensive hospitality and permitted me to use Karawop Plantation as a
base throughout the Arapesh work. This section, as part of
the projected single monograph on the Mountain Arapesh,
was completed in April, 1936. When it became clear that
the monograph would have to be issued in sections, I made
a few necessary revisions in the cross references and took
the opportunity to revise the initial discussion of methodology
in the light of my subsequent experimentation with more pre-
cise field methods in Bali. Owing to changes in publication
plans, the beginning of the war found it still unpublished,
and during the war the paper shortage made publication impossible. It stands, however, as completed in 1936, without
any additional theoretical illumination from my field work
subsequent to that date. Bibliographic reference to some
work published since 1936 has been included.

MARGARET MEAD
New York
*October, 1945*

# CONTENTS

# LIST OF ILLUSTRATIONS

*Plates*   (*following page 256*)

*Text Figures*

# Part I:  Socio-Economic Life

---◇---

## METHOD OF PRESENTATION

This is the third publication in a series on the culture of
the Mountain Arapesh, originally designed to be issued as a
single monograph. The most relevant geographical considerations and methods of work for each particular section have
been described in those sections to which the reader is referred for such details. These papers represent an experi-
ment in method of presentation, an attempt to solve a number of presentation problems: how to present the material
so that students wishing to use it at different levels of ab-
straction and generalization may do so without impediment;
how to satisfy this first demand and yet keep the illustrative
detail close enough to the discussion so that its particular
relevance to any point is not lost; what orders of materials
should be presented together; what type of presentation best
represents the peculiar form and emphases of Arapesh culture. No one of these problems has been permitted to
dominate the others, but the clarity of the arrangement has
been considerably obscured by the conditions which necessitated breaking the monograph up into a series of separate
publications. According to the original plan, the order was
to have been as follows: the culture area, the place of the
Mountain Arapesh as an importing culture in that area, their
domestic material culture and everyday life, followed by a
section devoted to the details of the material culture. (This
plan was carried out except for a shift in the order, so that
the discussion of the place of the Mountain Arapesh in this
culture area became a conclusion for the first paper.) The
sections following were then to be: the supernaturalism of

the Mountain Arapesh; a general discussion of the main emphases, and a set of supporting materials, dealing with particular forms, rituals, and myths. Then, leaving the statement on supernaturalism and omitting details of actual events or individual variations in behavior, I planned a general discussion of the socio-economic structure, to be followed by the details of socio-economic forms, kinship terminology, property rights, etc., in their formal aspects and by the bulk of the illustrative material on the functioning of the culture, and finally, by a diary of events in the village of Alitoa from January 28, 1932, to August 16, 1932, and an analysis and summary treatment of them. This plan was necessitated partly by considerations of economy and partly by the forms of Arapesh culture. It would have been possible to follow the more conventional usage and illustrate the discussions of sorcery with examples of sorcery, of kinship, with instances of individual kinship behavior, and of feasts, with the details of a feast. But this method has two great disadvantages. An event as complicated as a quarrel between kindred in which sorcery is invoked after a feast is in progress has many facets: the time, its position in a sequence of other quarrels, sorcerizings, and feasts, and the actors' personalities are all significant. All the details classifiable, for purposes of analysis, as economic or religious behavior are part of a unit to which any illustrative use of an event does violence. Secondly, any partial use of an event to illustrate first one type of discussion, then another, necessarily makes for much repetition. The *Diary* presentation is designed to obviate all these difficulties. Every event on which I have detailed material is presented in its proper sequence and context only once, and specific theoretical discussions may be referred to it.

When it became necessary, however, to break up the monograph, I found that while the section on supernaturalism could stand without the illustrative materials from the *Diary*, that on the socio-economic structure could not. The fact that it could not is, I think, a significant statement about Arapesh culture. In the section on supernaturalism I was dealing with aspects of Arapesh culture in which the forms were most congruent with the ethos and in which a statement of the forms adequately conveyed the ethos of the behavior of those whose activities embodied these forms. But there is far less agreement in the socio-economic forms; the data upon which my generalizations are based are not myths, or clichés, or pieces of ritual, but the way in which actual individuals act. Arapesh socio-economic forms, in conventional outline, differ very little from forms widespread in this area: gentile hamlets combined into localities; dual organization governing feasting and initiation; a kinship system stressing economic and ceremonial obligations to the mother's brother's line; hereditary partnerships acting as pivots for the ceremonial economic life; a loose political organization without formal leadership in which personality, as expressed in various forms of socially dominant behavior, gives temporary leadership— all of these are familiar enough in the Sepik-Aitape District. But the Arapesh in everyday life have so re-interpreted these formal emphases that an examination of the forms does not in any way give an adequate picture of actual conditions.

In previous publications[1] I have tried to deal with this problem under the concepts of the "ideal pattern" and "subversion of the ideal pattern" in which the statement of the "subversion" was abstracted from an account of what identified individuals actually had done, as placed in opposition to the articulate statements of what carriers of that culture should do. When the ideal pattern is close enough to actual practice so that any deviation from it is noted and commented upon, rationalized, or deprecated, this subversion concept is relevant. But when every individual is, as a matter of course, acting very differently from the way in which the articulate forms suggest he should act, and when such action is not accompanied by any sense of deviation and requires no rationalization, the concept of subversion becomes useless.

The difficulty here also impinges upon the difference between explicit and inexplicit aspects of culture,[2] but it is not identical with it; the difficulties of recording and generalizing are the same, whether the inexplicit aspects of the culture do or do not conform to the articulate pattern; but there the similarity ends. So a culture may present an almost consistent

[1] Mead, 1930b; 1934a.
[2] Mead, 1933b, pp. 1–15.

picture between articulate forms and actual practice, with such deviations as occur mainly referable to the idiosyncratic personality or situation of the deviators; or the number of deviations may be large, the deviators may actually be in the majority, but the conduct itself may still be defined in terms of the degree and way in which it differs from the articulately approved behavior (as the Mundugumor do in matters of cross-generation marriage,[3] or the present-day "Antler" tribe treat premarital intercourse for girls[4]) or the conduct may differ from the articulate norm and definite articulate ways of accounting for, and regularizing, these deviations may exist (as in Manus when the rule that children of cross-cousins should marry has been given an additional, but quite articulate, subversive phrasing, that cross-cousins should be the persons who make the arrangements, for the marriage of other than the children of cross-cousins[5]). Or, instead of a legal fiction, there may be a ritual taking formal account of the deviation, as among the Maori[6] where, to the formal statement that the eldest son inherits, is added the ritual prescription that the inheriting son must rise and bind his father's corpse, so that if the eldest has not the requisite personality, a younger son performs the ritual and becomes the inheritor of his father's position. Or adjustments may be made between articulate formulation and actual practice which take the form of exoteric and esoteric phrasings, serving the interests of particular groups (as among the Omaha in which the democratic phrasing that the vision and so membership in the religious secret societies are open to everyone is contradicted by an esoteric phrasing in terms of hereditary membership, and acompanied by a mechanism of declaring the vision of the non-hereditary visionaries to be invalid[7]).

Various sorts of deviation occur among the Arapesh. For example, the Arapesh say, "Boys must be initiated before they enter the *tamberan* house," a phrasing in which they agree with the widespread *tamberan* practices of the area.

[3] Mead, 1935b, chapt. 11.
[4] Mead, 1932a, chapt. 10.
[5] Mead, 1934a, pp. 316–317.
[6] Tregear, 1904, pp. 150–151.
[7] Fortune, 1932b, chapt. 3.

But when Dr. Fortune confronted them with the presence of Gerud, an uninitiated boy, in the *tamberan* house, they said in substance: "He is too big to be excluded. There has been no initiation for a long time. If no Beach people are present to criticize, and if no Cassowary, who is likely to become angry,[8] is present, we let big, uninitiated boys in, so that they can help with the music and share in the feast." Here is a deviation from the articulate rule, which would not be given spontaneously to the ethnologist. But, if he happens to observe it, the people recognize it as general practice; they can articulate it and are willing to admit that they act in terms of such a rule. They do not find it necessary to insist that they are obeying the more widespread rule, but merely to stipulate that it is better that no self-appointed guardians of orthodoxy be present. If the Mountain people present an orthodox front to the Beach people, it is a front upon which everyone is perfectly agreed, an articulate and approved form of social hypocrisy. In the investigation of any people who have a reason for being ashamed, in the eyes of another section of the community, of other communities, of government, or of the white man, the task of ferreting out such secondary phrasings as these is always present.

For the benefit of the women the phrasing of the *tamberan* cult is different from that given to the men. I had hung up a carving purchased from a Bonaheitum man, who had said explicitly that it was not a *tamberan* and could be seen by women. Then one day Ombomb of Alitoa told me that he had ordered his Wihun wife to keep their female child out of the house as long as that carving hung there. "But they said it is not a *tamberan*," I objected. "Not here, but my wife comes from Wihun where it is a *tamberan;* if some of my child's maternal relatives should hear that she had seen it, they might kill her by sorcery." Now this was a slip. Ombomb realized this as soon as he had said it, for the official version to women is that the mere sight of a *tamberan* is enough to produce illness and death. Within the men's group

[8] A reference to the fact that occasionally a hereditary Incisor (the Cassowary) is said to become infuriated by the presence of an uninitiated boy and attack him on the spot.

it was also known that men found it necessary to preserve the prestige of their death-dealing sacra by recourse to a little sorcery. Here again there was no subversion of an ideal pattern, but merely two versions, differentially serving the interests of one group in the community.

Another type of deviation from articulate cultural phrasing does not fall under these heads. It is this type, so common in Arapesh social life, which makes the formal treatment of this aspect of Arapesh culture so difficult. Arapesh gardening may be taken as an example. The formal phrasing is that a man gardens on his father's land, protected by his ancestral ghosts, under the eye of his gens ancestor. The actual circumstances are that gardening units are formed in the loosest sort of fashion. The individuals who garden together are bound together by a diversity of individual ties: A owns the land, or has made a temporary exchange of his owned land for another's; B, his brother-in-law, joins him, and B is joined by *his* mother's brother, C, who brings along *his* second wife's child, D, etc. Now this situation might be handled in different ways. Some cultures would abandon the phrasing that a man always gardens on his own land; some would invent legal fictions by which all the men who gardened together were regarded as brothers; others would invent rituals by which yams grown on another man's land were exchanged for yams grown by others on one's own ancestral lands. Still other cultures might articulately recognize that the old phrasing was no longer adequate and invent new names and new rituals to suit these new constellations of workers. In any of these cases, a presentation of the formal statements, the clichés, rituals, etc., would give a picture of the culture without recourse to individual instances of behavior. It would be enough for us to have a formal statement of what was done.

But the Arapesh do none of these things. When asking for a formal statement about gardening, one is merely informed that a man or a group of brothers garden on inherited land. Analysis of the actual behavior of any group of Arapesh men reveals that they do nothing of the sort. But there are no intermediate terms between the formal statement which is not a description of behavior and the actual behavior which is oriented, not in terms of convenient legal fictions or adaptive rituals but in terms of inarticulate attitudes of warmth, helpfulness, and gregariousness. The Arapesh do not subvert one form by another or a set of forms of the same order, but rather by a shift of emphasis, a change in ethos. It is as if the culture obeyed one set of formulations in one dimension and a different one in another dimension. From such contradictions comes the fact that the ceremonial hazing in the *tamberan* house, formally cruel and bullying, is felt to make "the initiates grow," and is assimilated in feeling to all the other pleasant parental growing activities in the culture, or, the practice of infanticide which is formally ruthless, but actually felt to be an adjustment to the strength of the women and the resources of the people to do their best for children. There is no formal plea that the beating with nettles is for the boys' good, which is a legal fiction to bring a cruel ceremony in line with a beneficent phrasing of life; the contrast is between a form and actual phrasing which implies cruelty, and an attitude, a way of performing an act, which belies it. But in order to derive a full understanding of the way in which Arapesh actual behavior modifies, distorts, and completely changes the formal phrasings of the culture, it is necessary to record and analyze a large amount of individual behavior. Only then can we understand that institutional behavior can be habitually rendered innocuous through the existence of personality standards which negate their formal intent but are present in full force, to be invoked by all the individuals whose personalities have assumed the typical Arapesh mold. In the *Diary* it will be seen how the actual sorcery forms—cruel and arbitrary enforcements of one man's will against another—are still present, ready to the hand of the antisocial man. What we have to record, therefore, is no subversion of one form by another, but the continuing, inexplicit, inarticulate subversion of the intent explicit in a form by the actual intent of the individuals whose behavior embodies that form. In order fully to appreciate this subversion, it is always necessary to know, not only what was done, but *who* did it. No illustration which does not include the known personality of the actors is an adequate comment on the functioning of Arapesh life. A mere statisti-

cal statement of the number of men gardening alone or quarreling with their wives or engaging in brawls in their lifetime
is an insufficient amount of data. Suppose, for instance, that
I state that in 100 anecdotes of quarrels over women, 30 per
cent emphasized that some blood was shed in the course of
the quarrel. But further analysis shows that 29 of those anecdotes came from one man, and 20 referred to the activities of
a single gens, dominated by a particularly violent and quarrelsome man, while the other 70 anecdotes were taken from
many different individuals' accounts, and involved a great
many different gentes. Suppose, furthermore, we have supporting evidence to show that the informant on the 30 cases
of bloodshed tended to regard the tiniest scratch as a major
wound and exaggerated the violence of any situation in all
contexts. Immediately the whole value of my evidence, which
looked so neat in statistical form, is changed.[9]

So in a question like sorcery, we have such cultural formulations as: "When you fall ill, look about for someone whom
you have angered, and follow his Path to the Plains, where
you will find the sorcerer smoking your exuviae," which
plainly implies sorcery, sustained by payment to the sorcerer,
by close relatives near home. We have, furthermore, day-
by-day behavior implying deep trust and affection for close
relatives, an articulate preference in favor of marrying daughters near home, where there will be no fear of sorcery, a belief that affinal ties and quarreling are antithetical, and ad-
monitions to children that they are always safe with relatives
and need never fear sorcery there. We actually have statistically large numbers of cases where near relatives, blood
or affinal, are accused of or claim the practice of sorcery
against their kin, when their private feelings or interests are
outraged. Faced with these discrepant data—first, a sorcery
form particularly adapted to use by near relatives for the
avenging of private wrong and no socio-political institutions
designed to outlaw such behavior; second, a belief, orally
expressed and daily acted upon, that within the circle of
one's kin one is absolutely safe and protected; and third, a

[9] This is a very specific type of objection to statistical statements.
If we wish to know what proportion of a community follows a preferred marriage form, for instance, they are valuable and necessary.

large number of instances of sorcery practice within the kin group—we could say the first is the truth as proved by the third, and the second is a rationalization, an unwillingness to admit the truth. If the second were actually a rationalization of an unpalatable truth, then the third would be the proof which we need, that is, as between two formulations, one of which contradicts the other. If they are of the same order, a recourse to statistics will demonstrate which is a statement upon which people really act and which is a cover statement. But if the first and second are *not* of the same order, if the first represents an institution which is formally accepted but nevertheless incongruent with the ethos of the people and that ethos is expressed in the second, then further data are to be sought, not in a mere enumeration of *how many* individuals put the first into practice and *how many* act upon the second, but rather in *which* individuals put the first into practice and follow the second. Only by a detailed examination of the actors as well as the acts can we hope to arrive at any understanding of the dynamics of this type of complicated situation.[10]

Other forms of discrepancy must also be mentioned, although they are less important. The Arapesh value patrilocal institutions to such an extent that whenever possible patrilineal or patrilocal phrasing will be used. So when Walawahan went to live in Ahalesimihi, people said, "It is nearer his hereditary gardens," not "It is his wife's place," which was the real reason why he had gone. So Wabe, when he went to live in the place of one of his wives, in Alipinagle,

---

[10] For this reason among the Arapesh anecdotes about unknown persons who are dead or belonged to a distant locality are poor data about the actual facts concerned, although they are good data on the personality and attitudes of the informant who relates them. Unless the anecdotal material is sufficient to give an adequate picture of the personality of the actor—and to do this a number of different anecdotes about the same person, in which consistency is displayed, as over against other actors in anecdotes told by the *same* informant, or a number of informants' accounts of the same person, are needed—it is not comparable with material on the behavior of known individuals which is the type of material upon which this monograph is based.

said he went there to plant trees for an Alipinagle child whom he meant to adopt.

In a few cases, also, the discrepancy between practice and formulation may be referred not only to the Arapesh ethos but to the Arapesh eidos.[11] Therefore the Arapesh use of kinship terminology, with a constantly shifting point of view in which a set of full siblings may be called by a whole series of incomparable terms, one viewed as a sister's child, the second as a brother's daughter-in-law, the third as a sister's co-wife, may be regarded as an aspect of Arapesh ethos, involving the way in which they delight in identifying themselves with others, or equally illuminating, may be referred to Arapesh eidos, as involving their tendency to regard each instance as isolated and existing *in vacuo*, without reference to a wider frame of reference. In either case, the actual use of kinship terms, as distinct from the usage given when a genealogy is used as the basis of collection, plays complete havoc with the formal system and its basic premises.

We may say then that among the Arapesh we find several kinds of cultural discrepancy between articulate forms and actual practices:

1. Local subversion of a more widely distributed pattern which is, however, articulately recognized and merely regarded as a matter to be guarded from critical foreign comment, e.g., the usage in regard to the admission of uninitiated boys into the *tamberan* house.

2. Contradictory formulations which serve the interests of a section of the community, e.g., the adult men's view of the magical powers of the *tamberan* objects compared with the tale they tell the women.

3. Discrepancies in practice which are felt to be subversive of a form to which the people give allegiance, so that they have to be rationalized, e.g., the refusal to phrase matrilocal residence as such.

4. Usages which may be referred to the eidos of the Arapesh such as their habit of thinking in terms of particular instances, e.g., the lack of consistency in kinship usage.

[11] In the use of these terms I am following the definitions given by Bateson, 1936, pp. 118 and 220.

5. The great mass of contradictory usage which may be referred to the ethos, which is maintained by the personality type standardized by the culture, and not by articulate forms, and which is not articulately recognized, e.g., gardening habits. (In these instances, when an Arapesh follows a form which is correct, but betrays in so doing an attitude which is antithetical to the ethos, the Arapesh condemn him, but do not articulately disallow the form that he uses.)

Because of these considerations, the record of what identified individuals actually did in identified contexts is absolutely essential documentation for any discussion of socio-economic functioning, and the discussion cannot be separated from the *Diary*, as it was reasonably possible to separate the sections on the forms of supernaturalism. But to follow my original scheme: a general discussion of socio-economic functioning, a section on particular forms, and then the *Diary* as the main mass of supporting material, is impractical in terms of publication possibilities. I have, therefore, adopted the following compromises. There will be no general summary discussion here, but the reader who wishes such a preliminary orientation is referred to Chapter 1 of *Cooperation and Competition among Primitive Peoples*, 1937, and to Chapter 2 of *Sex and Temperament*, 1935. The second part of the projected treatment of such a subject as kinship has been drastically cut. I give only the bare forms necessary to follow the details in the *Diary*. Only in this way do I feel that the peculiar demands of this section of the Arapesh material can be met.

The *Diary* itself is preceded by a discussion of specially relevant methods and only one further method, other than those discussed in Part II, need be referred to here, and that is the method of random sampling in kinship (below, pp. 34–35).

One further aspect of Arapesh culture remains to be presented, the culture as seen through the eyes of a single individual, under the title *The Record of Unabelin*. This is not a life history but an attempt to illustrate the relationship between a known personality and a known culture, with annotated verbatim material.

As previously stated in the introduction to this series of reports on the Arapesh,[12] certain considerations relevant to the material culture, such as details of the way in which artists paint their bark panels, have been postponed for a publication on the entire collection, the chief emphases of which were sketched in Part I of this series.

[12] Mead, 1938, pp. 147–152.

# THE SOCIAL STRUCTURE

## THE LOCALITY

The locality as a cluster of associated gentes is a concept which is only implicit in Arapesh terminology. There is no word for locality. There is, in fact, no word for any place larger than a *wabul*, residence place, and larger areas are referred to vaguely by suffixing *igen*, a suffix meaning "place," to words like "river." So the whole Plains area is referred to as *waribisigen*, river, or the place of people of the river. That the idea of a locality is incipiently present is shown in three ways: first, although there is no general term, certain place names refer to whole localities, although very often this is merely extended reference and the name is also that of the chief hamlet of the locality; second, there are collective words, sometimes, but not usually, derivatives of the locality name, referring to all of its inhabitants; third, there are names of *marsalais* which are called out at feasts as a kind of shouted emblem of the locality. Locality boundaries are recognized, usually in the form of streams, cliffs, or other natural barriers. Fishing rights are conceived as belonging to all the members of a locality. (These contrast with hunting rights which are phrased as gens owned.) Theoretically, sorcery rather than a fight should settle quarrels within the locality. This is, however, more of a theory than practice. If sorcery has been used to avenge sorcery, an informant will explain that it is because it is within the locality, but actually informal, irregular fights do occur within a locality.

There are many indications that the locality is really an enlargement of the ideal village, around which cluster a number of small hamlets, with all ceremonial life centered in the village. Such an ideal locality would be divided into two parts: one half would contain a number of gentes clas-

sified as *iwhul,* tabooing the *kumun* (hawk, P. E.[1] *terugau*)
and the other a number of gentes classified as *ginyau,* tabooing the *kwain* (the black and red cockatoo, P. E. *kolekol*).
The feasting village would have a large *tamberan* house
with two ends exactly alike, each door being surmounted by
the enlarged gable called a *map.* Each important man in
one half of the village would have a hereditary feasting
partner, a *buanyin,* in the other half. Because of the prohibition against marriage of cross-cousins this village and hamlet
unit would not, however, be self-contained. Therefore, if
wives were exchanged between the two divisions in one generation, in the next generation they would have to be obtained elsewhere, thus establishing ceremonial and economic
ties outside the village. But it is also supposed that only one
half of the village would engage in an important economic
activity at one time and would be regarded as the "trunk"
(*bauwanag*), while the other moiety would act as "dog"
(*nubat*) and "vomit" back the food deposited with it by the
"trunk." Each moiety would have a portion of the residence
ground of the village and an *agehu,* or feasting plaza, within
the village, where ancestral stones would be arranged. Meanwhile, outside the village, each gens would have a hamlet
where its members built their dwelling houses and stored
their yams, planted fallow garden lands, sago patches, and
hunting land on which the gens members hunted.

The possibility of such a scheme of reference as this, so
symmetrical and formal, can be derived only from a detailed
examination of the history of hamlets and of gentes, and of
the way in which localities have become enlarged, have split,
or have consolidated. Usually there is no *tamberan* house
with two doors, one for each moiety. Instead there are very
small, undistinguished *tamberan* houses with one door, the
property of one gens, located in the gens hamlet, or the part
of the feasting village which that gens now treats as if it
were its *sho'ubeli wabul,* its "small place," or gens hamlet.
An example of this is Balidu's *tamberan* house in the Walinuba section of Alitoa village, No. 32, on village plan (Fig.
1). No. 13 on the plan was once used as a *tamberan* house

[1] Pidgin English.

by the gens of *Uyebis*. Although there may be a large feast-ing village, the scarcity of level ground seriously constricts its extension; the difficulty of getting firewood and water makes it unpopular with the women; the poverty of the people makes building a large *tamberan* house an enormous, and seldom engaged in labor; and finally, the ground plan of such a village is not strong enough to hold the people to-gether in large groups when the economic conditions and their own ethological preferences are continually causing them to scatter.

However, various gestures are made toward keeping some semblance of this form, and the nature of these gestures de-pends upon the concepts of the moieties and of the gentes which the people possess. Before discussing the moieties fur-ther, it will be more orderly to discuss the gentes and then return to the dynamics of the social situation, as it affects the arrangement of groups within localities and villages.

## LINKED LOCALITIES

I have previously discussed at some length the Roads into which a series of hamlets running north and south between the Beach and the Plains were joined. Tabulation of the paths of individual men, their hamlet membership, and the mem-bership of the hamlets in localities, showed that actually each Road could be discussed as a series of linked localities stretching from the Beach to the Mountains bordering the Plains, within which the diffusion of small trade objects and large dance complexes and the transfer of sorcery exuviae took place. The formation of gift friendships across these linked locality or Road cluster lines was resisted much more strongly; fighting was more likely to take place between lo-calities belonging to different Roads; marriages between ham-lets which belonged to different Roads were regarded as having higher political importance. So, from the standpoint of a social analysis, it is possible to speak of four effective social units, but the Arapesh themselves do not think of them in this way. Instead, an Arapesh thinks of his own paths, of the Road along which the big dance complexes enter, and of the fact that one locality after another, as he ap-

proaches the Beach, are parts of his Road. When he speaks
of the *Lahowhin* Road, he thinks of Alitoa's tie to Liwo,
Liwo's tie to Bugabihiem, Bugabihiem's tie to Umanep, etc.,
down to Sublamon. These Roads are essentially cores, along
which localities cluster; the borders are vague, a given hamlet may desert one locality and so desert a Road; the localities
involved never act as a complete unit; but one or two localities and individuals from others will participate in some
event. Fights amounting to a sort of informal warfare, the
only type of warfare which the Mountain Arapesh knew,
could take place between parts of the Road, but there were
always strong sanctions against it, because of the outstanding
feast plans. When the old men would say, "Do you want
sorcery and quarreling, or talk of pigs and feasts?" they referred primarily to the two possibilities which were always
present in the linked localities, because they were the organized routes for the distribution of exuviae and the resulting
recriminations, as well as the organized routes for the feasts
which accompanied the distribution of the dance complexes.
But the actual existence of the linked localities, so vaguely
conceptualized, was invoked oftenest in hostility or fear of
hostility. It was the Plainsman, threatening because he was
not given part of the feast, who commented at length upon
the fact that the hamlet in which he stood was part of his
Road, which he always traveled, or the peacemaker, fearing
the outbreak of hostilities, who spoke of the feastmaking
practices of the Road and how superior they were to quarreling and sorcery.[2]

[2] This is characteristic behavior when there is danger or fear.
Then the Arapesh think collectively; then group membership is substituted for individuality and an expected group behavior substituted for the importance of individual ties. The contrast in their
attitudes towards Beach and Plains shows up clearly here; one hears
repeatedly of *waribim,* the Plainsmen, but very seldom is the word
*yausim,* Beachmen, used; instead, one hears "men of Sublamon,"
"men of Maguer"; oftener still, the hamlet is substituted for the
locality name, which is always the case when people from nearer
home are mentioned. So in peace times, and among themselves,
they speak less of the *Lahowhin* Road; but when Liwo is angry
and threatening to desert in a body and import their next *tamberan*
by the *Shemaun* route, then it is that the names of the two sets of

Although individuals follow their paths under the assurance of sanctuary, nevertheless there is no sanction against fighting along the Roads. Rivalry may develop between two localities parallel to one another, as between Kobelen and Umanep; there may be accusations of sorcery between such localities and threats of reprisal. Because fighting is forbidden within so many individual paths, there is less likely to be fighting, that is all; the Road *qua* Road carries no sanction against it.

## LOCALITY NAMES

Locality names are known only within a narrow range; beyond that, main village names are substituted for them, if they are mentioned at all. In Alitoa, the Beach inhabitants are merely classified together as Yausim; similarly in Maguer, all the Mountain villages beyond Alitoa are classified as Mideamin. This is as excellent an example as can be found of the Arapesh custom of thinking from a point outward and never looking at themselves as a whole. Plains villages are merely given village names and lumped together as *waribim*. Alitoa call Bonaheitum locality *kwainagil,* the name applied to Alitoa itself by the beachward villages. This is the only duplication of a locality term which I found. For the distant villages, the ending *im,* men of, or *ibis,* people of, is simply added to the village name. So the people of Kobelen are called by the Alitoa people *'Obelenim.*

## TERMS USED IN ALITOA

| Main Village, "Big Place" | People of the Locality of which it is Chief Village |
|---|---|
| Wihun | Masuenibis |
| Boinam | Iluhaimebis |
| Numidipiheim | Mawelibini |
| Dunigi | Lawaginebis |
| Liwo | Otoiengou |

linked localities, on whose intermediate border Liwo stands, are mentioned.

| Hamisuk | Wahewlibim |
|---|---|
| Nugia or Malis[3] | Winyegibis |
| Ybonimu | Yabuim |

# THE GENS SYSTEM

## The Gens

Each Arapesh belongs to a very small named local gens. This is a more accurate statement than to say that the Arapesh are divided into gentes, as an Arapesh never conceptualizes it in this way. The word for gens, *awhilap*, is hardly ever used; whether I should ever have found it without the help of the pidgin English "pigeon," the word for clan or gens, derived from the Melanesian bird totemic practices, I do not know. When I made the census, however, as I recorded the names of adult males, I asked, "What pigeon?" and so received at once the local gens proper names, *Toto'alaibis, Kanehoibis*, etc. The gens is a definitely genealogical concept, and it is very seldom that the members of a gens cannot trace their immediate patrilineal relationship to one another. A definite concept of the origin of new gentes by splitting is symbolized in the story of the eldest brother who tears his G string into strips and gives a piece to each of the younger brothers, each of whom then founds a gens which carries the order of birth term, so *Labinem*, the men of the second brother, *Dibatua'am*, the men of the fourth brother, etc. These are the only recurring gens names of which I have any record. The less analytic people regard them as related, but most well-informed people realize that the name merely means a gens which split off from another gens by following the fortunes of a younger brother. Sometimes old relationships are preserved between now separate gentes, as when the gens of *Toto'alaibis* of Alitoa is said to be

---

[3] Not on map, as not on Government map.

related to the gens of *Uyebis,* and descended from a marriage between a *Uyebis* man and a woman from the locality of Dunigi. Disappearing gentes may join forces with another gens, and if they happened to belong to a different moiety the distinction between the two may be preserved for some time. The custom of remembering the genealogies of mothers as often as fathers may also serve to distinguish two family lines within one gens. Membership splits and amalgamations of gentes are both preserved, sometimes in shared participation in *marsalai* places. Ideally, a *marsalai* place is a dangerous spot located on the gens-owned hunting land and inhabited by a gens-associated *marsalai,* embodied in a specific animal or reptile, with a definite name, around which gather the ghosts of the gens dead and their wives. Actually some *marsalai* places are divided in half, one half said to belong to *iwhul,* and the other to *ginyau,* each moiety being represented by one or more gentes. This suggests the preservation of either gens splits or of gens amalgamations in the *marsalai* allocations.

In the locality there is a ranking gens whose members retain the hereditary right to act as Cassowaries in the initiatory ceremonies. The use of the term rank here is slight overstatement, but it is the gens whose members are felt to be privileged above the others by heredity. Special efforts will be made to prevent this gens from dying out; if the male children are few and unpromising, new male children will be given to it for adoption. Gens members who exercise their hereditary right as Incisors taboo cassowary meat.

The dividing line between a true family line and a gens is very tenuous. The Arapesh always tend toward the family line concept and away from the more collective concept implied in the gens. House sites within the gens hamlet are individually owned, descend from brother to brother, or from father to brother, and may be lent or given to relatives outside the gens. Similarly hunting rights tend, in one generation, to be exercised by only one or two men. These men, especially if they be brothers, may bequeath them, informally by right of usage to a sister's son. Sago patches and palm trees are all individually planted and individually bequeathed to the next generation. Thus, while there is a con-

cept of a gens hamlet, gens garden land, gens hunting bush,
and a gens *marsalai* place, all of these are subject to the tendency towards family line ownership and either temporary or
permanent alienation to matrilineal and affinal kin. One exception is the *marsalai* place which displays a different tendency, to become more and more generalized in ownership,
until in time it becomes the *marsalai* place of an entire
locality.

The emphasis on individual ties rather than upon collective
activity makes it possible for all these tendencies to find expression. So a man invites his brother-in-law to garden with
him, or to share his house in the hamlet, or to hunt with him.
He is not asking his brother-in-law to join his gens; it is a
transaction between two individuals, but some dozen such
transactions a year serve effectively to break down the residential, gardening, and hunting unity of any of these theoretically gens-owned, territorially based groups.

There are no gentile totems, but there are gentile omens,
called *saginin*, which, if seen in dreams, betoken the death of
a member of the gens.[4] In a village in which there are only
child-of-gens members of a gens whose omen is seen in a
dream, the death of one of these is augured, if the omen is
dreamt by someone else. If, however, a man or woman sees
in a dream the omen of his or her mother's gens, then the
death of a cross-cousin member of the gens is forecast. These
omens are continually confused with idiosyncratic *marsalais*,
such as the phosphorescent rat of Yapiaun which is also the
omen of the Yapiaun gens of *Biegelipim*, and with various
manifestations of *kumun* and *kwain*, the special birds of the
moieties which bear their names.

Some gentes also have old heirlooms called *ginyau*, which
may take the form of any particularly handsome and rare
import, an ax, a spear, a large ring, etc. If preserved long
enough, they assume an aura of sanctity and can be handled
only by gens members who must wash their hands carefully
afterwards. Whether the association between such heirlooms
and the moiety name *ginyau* is more than an original coincidence, it is impossible to say. Some people say that all peo-

---

[4] Mead, 1940, p. 436.

ple who are *ginyau* can touch a *ginyau*, but this is not generally believed. I did not find any instances of *iwhul* gentes which had *ginyau* heirlooms, but as we shall see later, gentes frequently change their *iwhul-ginyau* alignment so this is hardly significant. These *ginyau* are principally important as offering a very pallid version of the complicated clan relic collections which form the basis of the *pwivu* meal among the Iatmül.[5]

Members of a gens are sometimes regarded collectively when there is a question of sister-exchange or near sister-exchange in marriage, but here the same practice also leads to equating all the members of a large village or of an entire locality. The idea of exchanging women exists in a very loose form among the Mountain Arapesh; true sister-exchange occurs rather seldom, and there is more of a desire to find some way in which a return can be claimed to have been made than there is a desire for an actual return. The most elaborate legal fictions are continually resorted to so that members of different gentes or different villages can claim that one marriage may properly be regarded as a return for another. This cannot therefore be regarded as a gens function, but rather as one of the ways in which the fiction of gens unity subserves another fiction, that of the exchange of women.

## GENS NAMES

Gens names are all local, with the exception of those derived from the order of birth terms, *labin, bwahein, nyumia, asho'en,* and *dibatu'a.* Ideally, as is also shown in the myths, as when all the gens of *Suabibis* is derived from Suabi, the termination *ibis* (the ending for the gender which contains clustering things like eggs and areca nuts) is added to the ancestral name or order of birth term, to indicate members of both sexes. The ending *im* indicated men of, and *iel,* women of. Actually, many of these terms have become somewhat altered phonetically so that *am* as well as *im* occurs. *Ehas,* the plural ending for mixed gender, ordinarily used for ag-

[5] Bateson, 1932, especially pp. 427–429.

gregations of men and women, may also be used. Derivative
gentes, especially those with order of birth term names, are
spoken of by the parent gens as *mbulieneshap,* the edge of
the G string, illustrated by the legend of Suabi in which he
tears his G string up for his younger brother.[6]

Personal names are supposed to be gens owned. The general feeling is that other gentes should not be allowed to have
them, although this feeling tends to be expressed in terms of
places rather than of gentes. Every effort is made not to
duplicate names among the living, especially the names of
men, because of the danger of sorcery misfiring. Women's
names are not so important. To name a child after some
maternal relative is felt as a slightly outrageous thing to do,
as the name should rightly remain in the patrilineal line. If,
however, the child so named lives near by there is very little
feeling. But if an Alitoa woman marries in Wihun and names
her children after her male relatives, there is some annoyance, and people hurry to use the names before the Wihun
people take them all away. At the same time, once a name is
taken in this way, nothing can be done about it. Two people
cannot have the same name at the same time, so if a man
gives his own name to a child, he himself must take a new
one. There is no such close association between names and
gens ownership as is found on the Sepik River. No names at
all are definitely associated with the mother's gens. If people
are questioned as to why so few of the genealogical names
occur in the present generation, they reply, "Our women
have married abroad and scattered the names about in other
places." I compared 187 names known in Kobelen, Dakuar,
Maguer, Umanep, and Waginara and found that only 43 occurred elsewhere in the five villages. Of the 43, 23 were
women's names. As women are believed to be less liable to be
sorcerized, there is a little less feeling about duplicating
women's names among the living. Women's names are also
more similar than men's, with a tendency to recurrence of
such endings as *aijo* and *to'a.* Men's names, on the other hand,
show enormous variability; they do not conform to the gender

[6] See "The tale of Suabi" in Mead, 1940, p. 367.

or any other recognizable pattern, and range from two syllables to five and six.

Legends were sometimes sources for names for large rings, or for *ginyau*, such as stone axes or spears; place names in legends especially could be drawn upon. Pigs and dogs had special names, and the names of pigs were used as children's lullabies.


## THE MOIETIES

In discussing the Arapesh ideas about moieties, it is first necessary to say that if one had never heard of such a concept, or did not know that moieties were common in the area, their own ideas are so confused that it would be extremely difficult to untangle them. At first only one positive clue appeared. As soon as we arrived I began to hear comments about the "half belong *tultul*"[7] and the "half belong *luluai*."[8] These pidgin phrases were new to me, and I have found it a very safe rule that the appearance of a new pidgin phrase usually heralds a new native concept or institution. However, inquiry merely revealed that the people were divided into two halves and one half helped the *tultul* and the other the *luluai*. This division seemed to correspond to no further reality. Then gradually the following concepts emerged:

1. Everyone is either *kumun*, hawk, or *kwain*, cockatoo, by birth, and must always taboo the respective birds.

2. Some people belong to *iwhul* and some to *ginyau*, which are concerned with making feasts. *Iwhul* talks at night and *ginyau* at dawn. When *iwhul* gives a feast, they can call *ginyau*, dog, to help them.

3. If a man is *iwhul*, his *buanyin* is *ginyau*.

4. All *ginyau* taboo *kumun* (hawk) and all *iwhul* taboo *kwain* (cockatoo).

5. When *iwhul* die, they sleep on a bed and breath leaves

---

[7] Government-appointed interpreter.

[8] Government-appointed executive constable for the village or locality.

their bodies by way of their little fingers and their big toes. When *ginyau* die, they stand up, open their mouths, the spirit emerges in one gasp, and they fall dead.

6. If a man in a gens has an heirloom, that gens is *ginyau*.

7. When the *kumun* people eat meat they eat it bloody, as does the hawk; when the *kwain* people eat meat they eat it dry.

8. When the *kwain* people make speeches, they talk a long time as does their bird, when the *kumun* people speak, they speak briefly.

9. *Kwain* and *kumun* had some relationship to making a *tamberan* house with one or two gables, but no one knew exactly what.

10. Occasionally, the group affiliation of a man's mother would be mentioned. So the children of *ginyau* mothers were said to be able to talk at dawn also.

11. At initiation *kumun* belong to one line and *kwain* to another.

So there appeared to be a dual division, with two names, one set translatable, and the other referring to bird taboos of a totemic character. Informants tended to interchange the words *iwhul* and *ginyau* with *kwain* and *kumun*, as if they were strictly synonymous. However, further investigation of the present alignments of gentes, individuals, and localities showed that this was by no means so. There appeared to be two further, less explicit concepts:

1. Being *kumun* or *kwain* was an attribute of birth which could not be changed, even by gens amalgamation.

2. Every group of people consisting of two or more gentes should be divided for feasting purposes into an *iwhul* and a *ginyau*.

It will readily be seen that these two concepts are incompatible. The Arapesh operate with both and continually confuse the issue by reequating the two types of division. So Kobelen and Umanep, once said to have been parts of the same locality, split into two localities. This left Kobelen all members of *kumun* and Umanep all members of *kwain*. Each locality then redivided into *iwhul* and *ginyau*, for the purpose of local feasting reciprocities. However, the old idea of two birds associated with two halves again reasserted itself, or so it seems from the accounts, and each moiety in Kobelen took a hawk emblem, *iwhul* took the *wholowhepin* hawk and *ginyau* took the *genakaben* hawk. An equally illuminating instance comes from the hamlet of Ahalesimihi. Two members of the disintegrating gens of *Kanehoibis*, named Nagawe and Naushe'e, live in Ahalesimihi and are now usually accepted as members of the gens *Diboaibis*, the gens of Manum, Silisium, and Amambut, all three of whom are *kwain*, while Naushe'e and Nagawe are *kumun*. Now, say the Arapesh, whether in time *Diboaibis* becomes *kumun* or *kwain* depends on which of these men have the most children.

Liwo shows a double division. Once said to have been a part of a locality of which Bugabihiem was the other part, Liwo is now all *kumun* and Bugabihiem all *kwain*. But Liwo is further divided into two named groups, each of which contains an *iwhul* and a *ginyau* division.

A further complication is found in that in initiatory ceremonies the *kumun* and *kwain* groups are seated separately. On the whole, it seems safest to say that the Arapesh have two moiety sets which function differently, but which they tend to equate loosely and confuse. Whether these two moieties were originally one, whether possibly they were imported at quite different periods, or whether one was imported and one developed within their own social system, it is impossible to say. Very occasionally, the invocation of the *kumun-kwain* membership of mothers to explain contradictions, as when two *buanyins* both belong to *iwhul*, gives the faintest hint of a possible matrilineal emphasis. This would be given no weight at all were it not that moieties named after the hawk and the parrot are a common Melanesian matrilineal institution and occur even on Wogeo and scatteringly along the Wewak coast. The Arapesh stubborn insistence upon inheritance and lack of flexibility in handling the *kumun-kwain* concept might be due to the importation of this matrilineal concept by a people who would then have been unable to handle it.

# THE KINSHIP SYSTEM

## THE KINSHIP TERMINOLOGY

The Arapesh kinship system is exceedingly simple and highly characteristic for the area. Some of the terms are shared, not only with the people of the Sepik River, but also with the peoples of the islands along the coast. At present there is no way of ascertaining the direction of the borrowing, although two points are of special interest: the plurals of Arapesh kinship terms are irregular[9] and do not fall into any Arapesh system of noun classes. A few anomalous affinal terms might be correlated with some form of cross-cousin marriage, an institution occurring on the other bank of the Sepik, but of which there are no other direct indications among the Arapesh. The system is essentially the same, although there are some dialectical differences and a shift of a term or so between Beach, Mountain, and Plains. Also, on the Beach, kinship terms are used very extensively to the exclusion of personal names; in the Mountains only certain kinship terms of address are substituted and then not entirely for personal names; and in the Plains, informants and Mountain observers report the use of names and the nonemployment of kinship terms as terms of address. The principal vocabulary differences fall in the terms used for sibling order. These differences will be recorded when that set of terms is discussed.

The system includes a special terminology for the mother's gens and for the children-of-gens, and a rather full complement of affinal terms. As has been mentioned earlier, it is used with the most extraordinary irregularity, and this irregularity is facilitated by the lack of differentiated behavior as suitable for different relatives.

Although there is a wealth of special ceremonial behavior between mother's brothers, sister's sons, and between cross-cousins, the everyday behavior of these relatives is not dis-

[9] For full discussion, see Fortune, 1942, pp. 6–45.

tinguished in any way. From observation of a group one would never be able to learn the relationship between any two members, whether it was blood or affinal, or whether they were merely well acquainted, although most distantly related. In a region where avoidances and preferential marriages, with their resulting specialized behavior, are so common, this is the more striking.

It will be realized that this system is not complete. Many possible terms are missing, and many would be derived doubtfully from the terms given. From the discussion of the way in which the Arapesh actually handle this system, it should be abundantly clear to the reader that it would be unjustifiable to expect to find a system covering all the categories of relatives which happen to be named in other kinship systems. It also raises the question of the meaning of such a term as completeness when applied to an anthropological report of a kinship system, as distinguished from the use of the term completeness when applied to the actual native terms. A well-informed Omaha adult can extend the kinship terminology systematically to every member of the tribe, because the idea of systematic extension is present in the culture. A well-informed Arapesh can do nothing of the sort. If he is presented with a schematic diagram, he can work from point to point, arguing one link at a time, and the result might be a very complete kinship chart covering all the possible relationships on a cross-cultural check list. The ethnologist who wasted his time forcing such an acultural procedure on his informant might come back with a complete kinship terminology which would be quite meaningless. The question whether there exists in any culture a set of kinship categories which could be extended indefinitely should be sharply distinguished from the question whether such categories ever would be extended. A term such as father's father's sister's daughter's daughter is completely meaningless to the Arapesh; unless the woman in question has been reclassified into some more relevant relationship, they would not apply any kinship term to her.

# THE TERMINOLOGY

## CONSANGUINEOUS TERMS

| | | As a Term of Address |
|---|---|---|
| *Remote Ancestors* | | |
| *walagainin* | Ancestor, great great grandfather, if used with specific references | |
| *popueen* | Ancestor or great grandfather | *popueen* |
| *Second Ascendent Generation* | | |
| *babu'en* | Grandfather and all men of second ascendent generation; husbands of all women called *babu'e'* | *babuen* |
| *babu'e'* | Grandmother and all women of second ascendent generation; wives of men called *babu'en* | *babue'* |
| *wa'en* | Father's mother's brother alternate to *babu'en* | *wawen* |
| *First Ascendent Generation* | | |
| *yain* | Own father; used like own father | *yain* |
| *ya'en* | Father's brother; all men whom father calls brother, and husbands of all women whom mother calls sister | *ya'en*; used by a child to a stepfather who is a father's brother |
| *yamo* | Own mother; never used for other than own mother, except with intent to substitute | *yamo* |
| *ama'e'u* | Mother's sister; all women whom mother calls sister, wives of all men whom father calls brother | *ama'e'u* |

| | | |
|---|---|---|
| *ma'e* | Father's sister; all women whom father calls sister, mother's brother's wife | Not used as a term of address and seldom used at all; descriptive terms like *yain*, *anani*, *mohowhi*, my father his sister, are likely to be substituted |
| *wai'en* | Mother's brother, mother's brother's son; all men whom mother calls brother | *wauwen* |

### Ego's Generation

| | | |
|---|---|---|
| *mahonin* | Brother, w.s.; sons of all men called *ya'en* | *mahowhin'* |
| *mahowi'* | Sister, m.s., and daughter of all men called *ya'en* | *mahowi'* |
| *asho'en* | Elder brother, m.s, and all sons of men called *ya'en*, older than ego | *ashoen* |
| *asho'e* | Elder sister, w.s., and all daughters of men called *ya'en*, older than ego | *ashove'* |
| *awanin* | Younger brother, m.s., and all sons of men called *ya'en*, younger than ego | *awanin'* |
| *awauwi'* | Younger sister, w.s., and all daughters of men called *ya'en*, younger than ego | *awauw'* |
| *wauen* | Mother's brother's son | *wauen* |
| *mehinen* | Father's sister's son | *mehinen* |
| *mehini'* | Father's sister's daughter, m.s. | |
| *amí'e'u* | Mother's brother's daughter, b.s. | *ama'e'u* |
| *babuen* | Father's mother's brother's daughter's son | *babuen* |
| *babu'e'* | Daughter | *babu'e'* |
| *balahan* | Mother's father's sister's son's son | *balahan* |

# THE TERMINOLOGY—*Continued*

## CONSANGUINEOUS TERMS

RECIPROCAL TERMS USED BETWEEN CHILDREN OF CROSS-COUSINS

| | |
|---|---|
| *nigawik* | Father's sister's daughter, w.s. |
| *niganin* | Father's sister's son, w.s. |

*nigawik*
*niganin*

### First Descendent Generation

*niganin*
Son, b.s., brother's son, m.s., sister's son, w.s.; sons of all men whom man calls brother and all women whom woman calls sister

*nigauwi'*
Daughter, used as above

*mehinen*
Sister's son; son of all women called *mohowhi'*, m.s.; brother's son, son of all men called *mahonin*, w.s.

*mehini'*
Sister's daughter; daughter of all women called *mahowhi'*, m.s.; brother's daughter; daughter of all men called *mahonin*, w.s.

### Second Descendent Generation

*balohan*
Grandson; male children of all members of first descendent generation, as given above

*baloho'*
Granddaughter; female children of all members of first descendent generation, as given above

## AFFINAL TERMS

### First Ascendent Generation

| | |
|---|---|
| *ya'en* | Husbands of all women whom mother calls sister |
| *amae'u* | Wives of all men whom father calls brother |
| *ma'e* | Wives of all men whom mother calls brother |
| *ana'olin* | Husbands of all women whom father calls sister |
| *ana'oli'* | Father-in-law |
| | Mother-in-law |

### Own Generation

| | |
|---|---|
| *laminen* | Husband |
| *ulohowhi'* | Wife |
| *mahonin* | Brother-in-law |
| *mehen* | Brother-in-law |
| *ashoe'n* | Husband's elder brother, w.s. |
| *asho'e* | Husband's elder brother's wife |
| *awanin* | Husband's younger brother |
| *awawi'* | Husband's younger brother's wife |
| *asho'e* | Wife's elder sister; wife of a *mehinen* who is older than ego |
| *asho'en* | Wife's elder sister's husband |
| *awauwi'* | Wife's younger sister; wife of a *mehinen* who is younger |

*mewhen*
Wife's brother sometimes called *mahonin*

## THE TERMINOLOGY—*Continued*

### AFFINAL TERMS

| | |
|---|---|
| *awanin* | Wife's younger sister's husband |
| *megan* | Husband's brother's wife |
| *megani* | Brother's wife, w.s. |
| *ma'e* | Wife's brother's wife |
| *amá'en* | Husband's sister's husband |
| *'ashin* | Child's spouse's father |
| *'ashi'* | Child's spouse's mother |
| *mehen* | Brother's wife's brother |

#### *First Descendent Generation*

| | |
|---|---|
| *nigauwin* | Son-in-law; also applied to sister's daughter's husband |
| *mehi'* | Daughter-in-law; also applied to sister's son's wife |

## METHODS OF RECKONING EGO'S POSITION

Although there is no differentiated kinship behavior in Arapesh, examination of choice reveals some preferences. When an individual could choose one of two or more routes to emphasize, blood terms were chosen in preference to affinal terms, and any term which specified the mother's brother-sister's child relationship was always preferred above the others. This preference was manifest not only in direct choice, but also when the kinship term was established by "helping," the peculiar Arapesh mechanism for establishing relationships wherever the actual relationship is vague. Helping can take three forms: first, it can mean simply that "when I count my relationship to so and so, I count it through my father," thus I "help my father." Second, it can mean, "when I count my relationship to so and so, I take over my brother-in-law's term, i.e., if my brother-in-law calls him 'brother-in-law' I also call him brother-in-law." Third, it can mean, "I don't know what to call her, but I call her co-wife 'daughter,' so I will classify her with her co-wife and call her 'daughter' also." For the first, the phrase "think about" is sometimes substituted, so "I think about my father and from that standpoint I use such a term." Usually when parents are taken as the point of reference the kinship terminology follows genealogical rules, and a man calls "brother" the son of a man whom his father calls "brother." This does not follow for stepparents, uncles, etc., where ego may take up the same position as the member of the last generation, and join his uncle in calling a man "brother-in-law" rather than calling this affinal contemporary of a member of the last generation "father-in-law." Because of this habit of arbitrarily aligning oneself with a member of another generation, the perfectly formal usage by which the mother's brother's son is called *wauwen,* reciprocal, *mehinen,* is interpreted by the Arapesh as the second form of "helping." They say of their mother's brother's sons' usage, "We help our fathers and we call them *wauwen* also."[10] Below I give a series of examples to show

[10] This type of reinterpretation of a formal point is often very revealing and can also prove to be a matter of great confusion. The Mundugumor identify, in name and social position, a man and

the endless contradictions and confusions which result from
this willingness to shift one's point of reference to that of
another person's. In our method of collecting kinship systems,
based upon first recording a genealogy, we assume that the
individual has a fixed position, allotted to him by birth or
adoption, and that he will continue to maintain this position.
When Arapesh kinship is collected from this point of view,
a perfectly consistent picture is obtained. The informant is
first asked to give a genealogy; with the genealogy written
out, he is interrogated on the terms he uses. In such cases
no anomalies occur; brothers and sisters are classified as
members of one generation, etc. The investigator who was
content with checking over the terminology on a set of different genealogies with a number of different informants, and
finding it always consistent and congruent with well-known
forms of kinship reckoning would leave the Arapesh, igno-
rant of one of the most dynamic aspects of their attitudes
toward social relationships—their willingness, nay delight, in
alignment with other persons. The Arapesh always wishes to
use a kinship term, if possible; he thereby creates a warm
and reliable tie; men whom he calls by any kinship term are
his friends; women whom he calls by any kinship term can
be trusted not to seduce or betray him. But he implements
his desire to establish relationship by a willingness to abrogate
his own position, in a generation, in a gens, or in a genealogical constellation, and take on, temporarily, the position of
another.[11]

---

his mother's father, and a woman and her father's mother. As a
result an individual applies own generation terms to the members
of the grandparent generation. The Mundugumor have phrased this
formal point as a part of the joking-relationship which obtains between a man and his maternal grandfather, "I joke with my grandfather and I call his brother 'brother,' and so discontinue the practice when the grandfather dies."

[11] I strongly recommend that no matter how neat and consistent
the results obtained from genealogies may be they should never be
regarded as an adequate exploration of a kinship system. The investigator who stays many months in one village and speaks the
language will of course come to know everyone's genealogical relationship to everyone else and can check on divergencies in usage by
attending to everyday interrelationships. But if kinship terms are

### ILLUSTRATIONS TO SHOW CHARACTERISTIC
### SHIFT OF POSITION

The terms that Ombomb gave spontaneously when confronted with a series of households are tabulated below. When asked to give kinship terms in accordance with a genealogy, he gave them perfectly consistently. Here he was asked by households, which were arranged at random but which still gave him more form than is necessarily present when an Arapesh decides on what relationship path he will use.

### OTHER USAGES REFERRING TO OWN GENS

Further light is thrown on the relationships between a man and his own gens by the attitudes toward various types of adoption. The Arapesh recognize three types:

1. Adoption of children when a man marries a widow whose husband was not closely related to him. Such children are called by him, and if they remain with his gens, by his brother, *tuanahes*. This term is never used by a man who inherits a widow and her children in the ordinary operation of the levirate and it is never used by a woman. Here the tie is that of foster-fatherhood in which fostering under unusual conditions and no considerations of gens rights or of gens strength are involved.

2. Adoption of a child when it is formally given by one gens to another, to maintain gens strength. Such a child is called *gwai'oyen*. Only male children are given in this way. Usually rings are paid for such children, but sometimes they

---

not used as terms of address and relationship behavior lacks any specific and distinguishing character, this day-by-day check may not prove very fruitful and more systematic methods will be necessary. The use of random selections of persons, arranged alphabetically or in some other way which obscures their genealogical and residential interrelationships, is then a very useful and quick method, and a situation is set up experimentally which is analogous to the confrontation of the native by one individual at a time toward whom he must take up a kinship position.

| NAME | RELATIONSHIP TO OMBOMB | TERM USED | REASON GIVEN |
| --- | --- | --- | --- |
| Kule | Father's brother's son's son | *niganin*, son | Genealogical reason |
| Ilautoa | (Wife of Kule) | *mohowhi'*, sister, m.s. | Because she belongs to the gens of *Kweyenahas*, which belongs with his mother's gens of *Kanehoibis* |
| Naguel | (Son of Kule and Ilautoa) | *mehin*, sister's son | Note here that he prefers the vague classificatory claim to Ilautoa to the close gens claim to Kule |
| Soatsalamo | (Wife of Kule) | *ama'e'u*, mother's brother's daughter | Because she comes from Wihun and all of Wihun are his mother's brothers, etc. This is more distant than his tie with *Kanehoibis* through his own mother |
| Walipin | (Child of Kule and Soatsalamo) | *balahan* | Because he is the child of a *niganin* |
| Silisium | Member of a distant gens | *mahonin* or *mehen* | Because his father's brother's daughter, now dead, married a brother of Silisium who is also dead |
| Ya'umen | (Wife of Silisium) | *ma'e* | ? |
| Cowais | (Son of Silisium and Ya'umen) | *mehen*, brother-in-law | Helps his gens brother, Sinaba'i, who is married to Gowais' sister |
| Imau | (Daughter of Silisium) | *mehini'*, sister's child | Because his father's brother's daughter married her father's brother |

Note that Imau was grown before Sinaba'i married the sister, and Ombomb retains earlier term for her, but shifts his terminology for her younger brother. But now note, when it comes to the brother of Silisium, Manum:

| | | | |
|---|---|---|---|
| Manum | (Brother of Silisium) | *mehen* or *mahonin* | Because he helps La'abe, his father's brother's son, whose sister (Homendjuai) is married to Manum |
| Homendjuai | (Father's brother's daughter of Ombomb, wife of Manum) | *mahowhi'*, sister, m.s. | But note that he did not count his relationship to Manum through her, but through her brother who is a gens brother and lives in his village |
| Maginala | Father's sister's son | *mehinin awani'* | Genealogically correct<br>Helps his own Dunigi wife. Note this correct terminology for the wife of a younger cross-cousin, but he does not invoke it |
| Wife of Maginala (who is from Dunigi) | | | |
| Children of Maginala | | *balahan*, grand-children | |

are given to settle a quarrel,[12] and occasionally a child is so
given in adoption in return for an *alapwen*.

3. Adoption of a child which is returned in payment to the
men of the gens to which the child's mother's former husband
belonged. Such a child is called an *alapwen* and, in a sense,
straddles both gentes. Arapesh comment upon the behavior
of *alapwen* is significant of their attitude towards gens relationships. An *alapwen* is likely to grow up to be wild and
ungovernable; he has two sets of fathers; if one disciplines
him, he goes to the other set; he always has two places and
he can never be kept in order. It is significant that although
Arapesh children spend a great deal of time with various relatives other than their parents, this is not regarded as a refuge
from parental discipline, always light and gentle, except in
the case of *alapwen*. Descendants of an *alapwen* are called
*awalahen* (pl. *awalahem*) by the descendants of the *alapwen's* blood relatives.

As an illustration of the *alapwen* institution, a man of
*Dibatua'am* gens of Alitoa married a woman of *Madjubatim*
gens, of the locality of Numidipiheim. He died. She married
a man of the *Toto'alaibis* gens of Alitoa, to whom she bore
Yelehiu, who was then given back to *Dibatua'am* gens as an
*alapwen*. Here he had sons, Ulaba'i, Nyelahai, and Yabinigi.
These men are called *awalahem* by the men of *Toto'alaibis*,
the descendants of the brothers of the father of Yelehiu.
Yelehiu returned to *Toto'alaibis* a foster son, Inoman, whom
he acquired by marriage with Inoman's widowed mother.
Inoman was spoken of as a return for Yelehiu and also as a
*gwai'oyen*.

*Gwai'oyens*, as well as *alapwens*, tend to straddle two
gentes, but whereas in the case of the *alapwen* it is he himself who maintains both sets of relationships, the *gwai'oyen*
becomes more completely identified with the gens of his
adoption, but his children will call the members of his
adopted and his own gens both by own gens terms.

Adoption in the case of *gwai'oyen* is most often phrased
as a generous act on the part of the parents who give up the

---

[12] See *Diary*, the settlement of Sinaba'i's adultery with Menala
by the promise of Aimau to Wabe, Menala's former husband
(p. 180).

child, "We saw that those people were few; there would be no one beneath their trees in the next generation. So we gave them a child." It is always said in this way, even though several rings are usually paid for such a child, who will be marked as a young pig or dog is marked for its future "parents."

## EXTENSION OF KINSHIP TIES TO OTHER COMMUNITIES

The Arapesh do not extend their kinship relationships along lines based upon the logic of genealogical connections, but rely upon various forms of "helping" specified individuals.

Instead of following out genealogical ties to individuals in other communities, the Arapesh adopt various contemporary ties with other villages upon which they can generalize. So the men of Alitoa would say, "All the men of that locality are our brothers-in-law, because one of them has married our sister." Or a man may look at an entire community through an identification with an hereditary trade friend within it. Occasionally some former tie becomes institutionalized so that a kinship term, used in this general vague fashion, will be applied to a whole locality by invoking the past. But it is significant that in no case are these logical extensions of strict genealogical relationships; some tie between two individual members of the two communities, either a contemporary tie or a past tie, is seized upon and very loosely generalized.

## THE TWO MAIN CLASSES OF KINSHIP

### DEFINITION OF CLASSES

Although it introduces a slightly clumsy phraseology, I shall use, to describe these two sets of relatives, the term Class One for ties based upon ties of direct descent and same sex links, and Class Two for ties based upon opposite-sex-links. In the first group are included father's parents, mother's parents, father, father's brother, mother, mother's sister, brothers (m.s.), sisters (w.s.), sons, daughters, and grandchildren, and their spouses. In the second group are

included, mother's brother, father's sister, sister (m.s.), and
brother (w.s.), wife's brother and wife's parents, husband's
parents, husband's sisters, and their spouses and children. It
will be seen at once that one very important assumption is
made here; a man and his wife are equated, and he therefore
shares with her her sibling-of-opposite-sex relationship to her
brother, whom he may speak of as *mahonin,* sibling of opposite sex, just as he takes over her sibling-of-the-same-sex relationship to his wife's sisters, and she takes over his siblings-
of-the-same-sex relationship to her husband's brothers. In this
way matrilineal and affinal relationships are subsumed under
one feeling tone, without any necessary resort to such explanations as that the brother-in-law is the mother's brother of
the son, and, therefore, the father, by virtue of identification
with the son, regards his brother-in-law as a maternal relative.
It is necessary to assume only two points: first, that the Arapesh regard differently all relationships which are counted
through a sibling of opposite sex, and second, that husband
and wife are equated and take over each other's kinship
terminology and behavior. Every marriage between a sibling
of the same sex and a new affinal relative endows ego with a
whole set of relatives who fall into Class One, and every marriage between a sibling of opposite sex endows ego with a
whole set of relatives of Class Two.

### CLASS ONE RELATIONSHIPS

Within all Class One ties, only one complementary[13] principle, the principle of age, operates, whether expressed as a
generation point or as a seniority point within a generation.
The elders are bound to cherish and guard, advise and help,
feed and shelter those younger than themselves. The
younger ones are charged with heeding the advice of their
elders, caring for them in their old age, performing tasks
which they are no longer strong enough to perform. In every
sibling relationship, no matter how close together in age the
brothers are (I have no instances of twins), there is a shadow

---

[13] Throughout this discussion, I shall adhere strictly to the definitions of complementary, symmetrical, and reciprocal behavior given
by Bateson, 1935.

of this parent-child relationship; the elder and younger terms
are always used; there is no term which merely means sibling
of the same sex and is not qualified by the elder or younger
significance. When children are very young, the order-of-
birth terms are often used, so a mother says to her child,
"See, the first sister eats her soup and the second sister sits
and does not eat," or "The second sister goes and gets firewood and the first sister sits at home." This emphasis upon
seniority carries with it no onus, but merely a coloring of affect; in some ways the elder is a little more solicitous for the
younger; in other ways the younger is a little more solicitous
for the elder. This mutual solicitude is forever exemplified in
what may be called the "cross-generation taboo," which
each generation must observe for the sake of the next. Because of the early age of death (very few men live to see
adolescent grandchildren) these "cross-generation taboos"
might be mistaken for taboos between the young and the old.
But an examination of the *bonah* and *shaloh*[14] food regulations shows that the division of food is postulated on a three
generation basis, in which children and their grandparents
are grouped together as against the parent generation which
is conceived as being in an active state of reproductivity.
Children before adolescence share with men and women past
the climacteric, which the Arapesh define as occurring when
the eldest child reaches adolescence, one state of vulnerability, as over against the intermediate generation. There is no
reflection of this grouping together of alternate generations
in the kinship terminology (however, it is a very widespread
and highly institutionalized practice on the Sepik River,
where the cross-generation taboos are also found); without a
knowledge of the very slightly conceptualized food divisions,
one would be tempted to say that the Arapesh did not share
in any way in the area tendency towards the identification of
alternative generations.

The cross-generation taboos apply between adjacent generations, as between parents and young children only. The
parental taboos are most strongly in force during the conception, gestation, and lactation periods when they must pre-

[14] Mead, 1940, pp. 401 *et seq.*

serve the child rigorously from any contact with their own
sexuality. These taboos fall into abeyance after the child is
weaned or has learned to walk and talk. (Arapesh parents
always associate these two; the child must be nursed until it
can walk and talk, which is equivalent to saying, it must be
protected from its parents' sexuality until it can walk and
talk, i.e., until it is strong.) Now comes a period when there
is a minimum of tension between the parent and child generation; the parents can again engage in sex activity without
fear of injuring the child; the child shows, as yet, no signs of
springing sexuality which heralds the parents' old age and
ultimately their death.[15] But with the onset of puberty, the
situation is reversed; it is now the parents who are in a vulnerable state—the climacteric—and the children who may en-
danger them. Before marriage, the taboos which the young
people observe are of two types: first, taboos against stepping
over any object which will come into close contact with a
parent's body, over a carrying bag, a lime gourd, a plate of
food, the cooking stones, etc.; and second, taboos against
working sago which the parents or any member of the parents' generation will eat. Parents may work sago for their
adolescent children, but their adolescent children may not
work sago for them. After the young peoples' marriage, the
taboos deal specifically with any contact between the sexual
life of the young and the bodies of the old. So the young wife
must be careful not to dry tobacco for her mother or her
mother-in-law on the fire beside which she and her husband
have slept, which is supposed to have taken on some of the
heat of intercourse. It should be noted that it is not intercourse, in general, which is regarded as dangerous, either to
the young infant or the man or woman at the climacteric,
but, specifically, the sex activity of the parent or of the child.
A child may sleep with an aunt who is leading an active
sexual life, and middle-aged people do not need to watch
all the food they eat, in terms of what kind of fire heated it.
Finally, the last expression of this cross-generation taboo

[15] The hostility of the parent generation to the emerging sexuality of the child generation can, I believe, often be assigned to fear;
as the child waxes in potential sexuality, the strength of the parent
wanes.

comes with the prohibition that the mother may not see her daughter's child born lest she go blind, i.e., lest she become entirely senile, for which blindness is the common symbol.

When these taboos are mentioned, they are almost always commented upon in connection with active services rendered by one generation to the other; the father will say, "I worked sago, I planted yams, I hunted game, I abstained from intercourse, that you might be strong." The young girl, commenting upon her relationship to her parents-in-law,[16] says, "I help my mother-in-law; I get firewood; I pare taro; I fetch water; I go to the gardens; I am careful not to dry her tobacco at the fire beside our bed." The taboo stresses the danger which was guarded against, but the oral emphasis is upon the positive cherishing care which is given by one relative to another. If children are disobedient or lazy the parents will remember, with some disgruntlement, the taboos they kept and the efforts they made that those children should grow; in moments of anger these will be cast up against them, but this seldom occurs. Almost always the emphasis is upon the mutual helpfulness rendered by one relative to another, and the cross-generation point is not stressed.[17]

But aside from these few taboos which guard each generation at its moment of danger from the adjacent generation and from the slight extra deference allotted to seniority, there is no complementary behavior between these relatives which I have classified as Class One. The father hunts and gives meat to his child; the child hunts and gives meat to the parent; brothers hunt for and give meat to each other. Only in the initiatory system is there some slight echo of comple-

---

[16] Note that here is another case of complete husband and wife identification, in which the parents of one spouse become effectively the parents of the other.

[17] In connection with these cross-generation taboos, it is interesting to note that where they occur among the Mundugumor the onus is reversed; parents must not eat of the food which their children have first eaten or they will grow old and die, i.e., the individual is required to keep taboos to preserve his own health against the danger which others bring to it. This is the case also with the Mundugumor taboo during lactation; if the parents have intercourse it is the father, not the child, who suffers.

mentary behavior when the elder brother's line makes the younger brother's line run the nettle gauntlet, but here the phrasing is that the initiation is for the benefit of the younger ones and so the one-sided hazing element is practically removed.

Other evidence of the symmetry of the brother-to-brother relationship is found in the lack of taboos in regard to the treatment of one brother's wife by another and the lack of any formalized avoidance or respect behavior between brothers. There is neither the Mundugumor taboo against friendly conversation between brothers, nor the Iatmül taboo against quarreling between brothers, nor the Tchambuli taboo by which father and eldest son, and eldest brother and next brother, are always on terms of embarrassment.

The Arapesh possess the idea of primogeniture, but make very slight use of it. The eldest son will very often have the largest post-initiatory feast made for him, but this is said to be done not because he is the eldest, but because the moment of his initiation marks his father's retirement as an active participant in the community life. One who has been an important man, has given numerous feasts and made many *abullus*,[18] will sometimes, just before he retires, make a little extra splash. He may build a larger house than he has built before, and then assigning that house to his son, start him off particularly well. He may betroth two wives for his eldest son, especially if this eldest son has shown the necessary personality traits to become a leader.[19] For a leader in the community needs strong, intelligent, hard-working wives; if a man succeeds in playing such a role, with the help of only one wife, people comment upon her special abilities. So, also, if a man is angry with one of his wives, his brothers will discuss the matter in relation to his need of able wives, if he is to discharge his obligations.[20] Additional light is thrown on the

[18] Mead, 1940, pp. 427 *et seq.*

[19] For a discussion of the Arapesh standards of personality and the way in which future leaders are chosen and trained, see Mead, 1935b, pp. 27–28.

[20] See *Diary* for the account of the argument presented to Baimal when he and Amito'a, his able wife, quarreled, of how helpless he would be with only Alaijo, his less able wife, to help him (p. 402).

unimportance of primogeniture by the fact that the eldest son, even the son for whom two wives have been chosen, may then be given away in adoption, or be chosen to carry the inheritance of a different gens than his own.[21]

Such contradictions as these serve to blur any strong competition between eldest son and younger sons. The only indication of suppressed competitiveness and aggression is the extreme guilt felt by some younger brothers if they become involved with their elder brothers' wives. I found no parallels for this guilt among elder brothers, perhaps because all of the little girls who are brought into the gens are felt to belong first to the father, who assigns them to his sons, and then perhaps most strongly to the elder brother who helps the younger brothers meet their marriage obligations. If an elder assigns to a younger brother a girl for whom he has paid and who was intended for him, without the young people's having made any moves in that direction themselves, the younger brother seems able to accept her without any sense of guilt.[22] This point should be borne in mind later when the equivalence of husband and wife is discussed in more detail.

In connection with parent-child and brother-brother relationships, it is necessary also to discuss the regulations in regard to competition for women and the levirate. In this entire area, one of the most potent causes of quarreling is the unresolved rivalry over women. This becomes most disruptive in those communities where rivalry is permitted between fathers and sons, or at least between the members of the two genera-

[21] So Matasues, the eldest of the four *Toto'alaibis* brothers, was given to the gens of *Uyebis*. And Balidu gave Badui, his eldest and most promising son, for whom he had built a big house and given a big feast and betrothed two wives, to carry on the name and care for the trees of the vanishing *Hamiebis* gens, while the younger brother, less energetic, less intelligent Pidjui, was to remain as his father's heir.

[22] See below, cases of Silisium's affair with the wife of his elder brother Manum (p. 396); Nyelahai's taking the betrothed of his younger brother Yabinigi (p. 185); Kule's affair with Ilautoa, his elder brother's betrothed, and his elder brother's resignation in his favor, and Kule's habit of kleptomania (p. 160); Bischu's assignment of his betrothed to Wena, his gens brother (p. 176).

tions, so that fathers and sons are symbolically, if not actually, rivals. The Arapesh insistence that a man is old, ready, and glad to retire when his first child reaches puberty successfully disposes of this possibility in most cases. In fact, the practice of child betrothal advances the age at which the father thinks not of his own possible further marriages but of his sons'. Consequently, many men of 35 are already turning all of their energies to find wives for their young sons. With this narrow period of maturity, during which sex activity is regarded as appropriate, there is no great need to institutionalize the junior or senior levirate. In Arapesh conception, it is always the older brother who dies first and the younger brother who succeeds him and takes over the care of his wife and children. As a man is conceived of as dying in his late prime, his younger brothers will necessarily be the ones who are strong enough to take on the extra care of his wife and children. Arapesh reasoning runs both ways: if a man is to carry a heavy burden of social participation, he must have a very strong wife, but also, if he is to care for two wives, clear their ground and bring up their children, he must himself be strong. Polygamy is not regarded as a proof of one's strength as compared with others, but rather as a kind of economic challenge which only the able will accept.

With the very thorough regulation of inter-generation competition for women, the early retirement of middle-aged men, the emphasis upon the protective character of the levirate, the relationship of polygamy to social responsibilities, there would be hardly any quarreling over widows in Arapesh, if death always struck when the Arapesh believe it should, and if they did not so loosely extend their classification of which relatives may inherit to include cross-cousins and maternal parallel cousins. Death interferes in two ways; if the betrothed husband of a young girl dies, she may then, no longer disciplined by the years of dependence upon her slightly older husband who has fed her, prefer a different brother from the one who has been selected for her. This is irregular and may produce some slight altercation. If a man's children all die, he may not reach the retired list quite as young as he should, and so remain in the field after he has more power than is usual.[23]

In painting this very Utopian picture of brother-to-brother attitudes, it is necessary to emphasize that this is the cultural picture, postulated by the Arapesh on their conception of human nature as unaggressive and responsive. In spite of the educational system, which is remarkably efficient in disciplining divergent temperament to its emphasis, all Arapesh are not unaggressive and mild, lacking in jealousy or possessiveness. But nevertheless, the culture contains no regulations which allow for jealous and possessive behavior, such as the avoidance rules between parents and sons or between brothers on the Sepik River. In its formal regulations the culture assumes friendliness, non-competitiveness, and mutual helpfulness between brothers. Any other attitude toward a brother is an occasion for wonder and disapproval on the part of the community—in consequence, a cause of guilt and shame to the unfortunate individual who displays such un-Arapesh feelings.

In conclusion, it should be understood that maternal parallel cousins are included in this conception of relatives through a sibling of the same sex. These also are called brothers, and their fathers are called by the same term as that applied to father's brothers.[24]

[23] This was the case with Nyelahai, all of whose children, except one puny runt of about 12, had died. So Nyelahai, confused in this as in everything else, had from the Arapesh point of view overstepped the age bounds, although not the fraternal bonds, in marrying the girl for whom he had paid for his younger brother. Mead, 1935b, pp. 119–120.

[24] My realization of the importance of this dichotomy of relatives in Arapesh came in response to a problem raised by Ruth Benedict. There seemed to be abundant evidence for the origin of classification of extra-gens parallel cousins with gens brothers and cousins, in America, in the practice of the sororate. But this same type of classification is also very common in Oceania, and the sororate is not. In considering this problem, I replied at the time that I felt that this classification had to be assigned to a different basis in Oceania, and that this probably lay in the great difference between ties through siblings of the same and of opposite sex, a situation which is also determinative among the Dakota in North America. This is an excellent illustration of the fruitfulness of cross-culture-areal comparisons in the dynamics of kinship systems.

I shall postpone the discussion of women's kinship attitudes, as they are so largely determined by the marriage arrangements.

If we turn now to the Class Two relationships, we find these carry the special aura of the mother's brother tie. Here it is necessary to remember several points. The special warmth of this tie cannot be attributed in Arapesh to an extension of a warmer attitude toward the mother than toward the father, an explanation which fits so many primitive cases so perfectly,[25] because among the Arapesh there is no differentiation either in the ethos of men and of women[26] or in the attitude of a man towards his own or his sister's child.[27] Nor, in a society in which ties between individuals of all categories of relationship are so readily substituted for gens loyalties, can the emphasis on the mother's brother tie be attributed to a desire to maintain a tie between the mother's gens and the child of gens. Among the Tchambuli, the sisters' sons of a gens form a compact group; they work together for the men's house of their mothers' brothers; they all carry names given them by their mothers' brothers' gens; and the perpetuation of this collective tie to the mothers' gentes is of the greatest importance to the society. But among the Arapesh, a man cannot tell one offhand who the sisters' sons of his gens are; he is not even accustomed to name the women of his

[25] Cf. Radcliffe-Brown, 1924.

[26] For the articulation between the role of the mother's brother and a highly differentiated male and female ethos, see Bateson, 1936, chapt. 6.

[27] It is necessary not to confuse the type of differentiation between *male* and *female* ethos, with the differentiation between *maternal* and *paternal* ethos which is characteristic of South Africa. Among the Iatmül, through sibling-of-opposite-sex identification, the mother's brother acts ceremonially like a woman and the father's sister acts like a man. Among the Ba Thonga and the Valenge, however, each individual possesses two roles, so a man is stern to his own son and gentle with his sister's son, and a woman is gentle with her own daughter and stern to her sister's daughter. The kinship behavior is primarily a comment, not on a contrasting sex ethos, but upon contrasting parental roles. Junod, 1927; Earthy, 1933.

gens who are married abroad. He does not think in any such collective gens-determined way. A third possible reason for stressing the mother's brother tie would be the presence of cross-cousin marriage. We have seen that there are two or three slight indications of such a marriage in the Arapesh terminology. Although it may never have obtained at any time among the Arapesh, we might argue that the importance of the mother's brother relationship had been imported from some region where this marriage did obtain. It is necessary to remember that while none of these various strong determinants of a mother's brother tie in a patrilineally organized society, i.e., contrasting parental attitudes, contrasting ethos for the sexes, importance of the child of gens to the maternal gens, or marriage with the mother's brother's daughter, obtains in Arapesh, they all do obtain in surrounding regions, which share much of the same terminology and usage. It may fairly be argued that the formal origin of this usage is extra-Arapesh.

The Arapesh formulation which validates the mother's brother tie is based on their conception of "blood" and their theory of impregnation and conception. All of the child's blood comes from the mother; his father contributes semen and sometimes a soul, but not blood. Brothers and sisters share the same blood; therefore, the blood of the sister's son and the blood of the mother's brother are one. When the child is born, the father buys the child from the mother's brother, he "pays for the blood." The child then becomes his, and if a girl, he can control any bride price which is paid for her. However, the blood of the child remains the concern of the mother and mother's brother. The infant's nose and ears can only be pierced by the mother or the mother's sisters; boils must be cut by the mother's brother; the pubescent girl is scarified by the mother's brother. Finally, whenever a man is wounded, he must pay his mother's brother for the blood which he has spilled. When a man beats his wife, he may be called upon to pay her brothers, if any of her blood has been shed. When a woman dies, her children finally pay for her blood, to her brothers. Curiously enough, in the ritual shedding of blood at incision, the importance of the mother's brother disappears, although in so

many parts of the area, it is he or his surrogate who does the
cutting or dresses the wounds of the novice (Tchambuli,
Iatmül, Mundugumor). Here in Arapesh he performs no such
function; the old men all contribute blood for the novices
to drink, i.e., they become mothers and give birth to the
child, and the Cassowary, who is the surrogate of the entire
male group, performs the operation. But afterwards, again,
the Arapesh youth must make a feast and pay his mother's
brother for the shed blood. This is the core, the theory of the
mother's brother relationship; it is preserved in terminology
and in the details of the *rites de passage;* it provides the form
of the mother's brother observances. Therefore, theoretically,
all observance, all ceremony, goes from sister's son, or from a
brother-in-law in his child's name, to the mother's brother.
The mother's brother has an inalienable right in the child
which is being inevitably violated during the birth, growth,
and finally the death of that child. From this point of view,
the whole mother's brother relationship may be regarded as
a price paid for the preservation of patrilineal institutions by
a people who retain beliefs which are in some respects more
consistent with mother-right.

Before proceeding further with the discussion of the
mother's brother relationship, it may be well to describe
briefly just how vigorously patrilineal institutions are maintained among the Arapesh.

### THE BASES OF ARAPESH MARRIAGE

It will be remembered that in the Arapesh theory of conception, the father's role during the first six weeks to two
months of gestation is to *feed* the child. After the child is
born, he establishes his claim to it in two ways, by paying
the mother's brother for the blood and by continuing to feed
it. His effective paternity is connected with his ability to find
game and grow yams. If a child is orphaned and the mother
returns home to her brothers and they feed the child, they
come to stand to the child as fathers. If the child's paternal
kin wish to regain it, they must pay for the food which has
grown it. Marriage falls into this pattern. Before a girl has
reached puberty, while she still lacks part of her growth, all
of her growth in fact which is conceived to bear directly upon

reproductivity, the father of an adolescent boy some years her senior takes her into his household and he and his son, her future husband, feed her and grow her. The young husband "makes the body of his wife," just as the father "makes the body of his child." When the girl is grown, she belongs to the patrilineal household into which she is betrothed more thoroughly than do her husband's sisters who have been grown in the households of their betrotheds. Every attempt is made to stabilize the marriage, invoking the same kind of tie which binds a father to his child. If the original husband dies, the wife remains to marry one of her husband's male kin, who cares for her and for his brother's children. If she marries elsewhere, as is often the case among as individual-istic a people as the Arapesh, who do not arbitrarily insist upon the observance of rules, the first child she bears is called an *alapwen* (see above, p. 38) and stands in a special rela-tionship to members of the gens who grew his mother. When a woman dies, she is not buried by her brothers on their land, but by the men of her husband's gens on the land of her hus-band's people.[28] There is a further point about the solidarity of the marriage tie which can be quoted to demonstrate the successful patriliny of the Arapesh; this is the attitude to-wards divorce. In so many societies, marriages can be broken merely by the wife returning to her brother, who shelters her, protects her against her former husband, and provides her with a base from which she can find a new husband. But among the Arapesh this is not possible, for no man will betray his brother-in-law by aiding his sister against him. As a result, all shifts in marriage arrangements must be phrased as abductions, even when arranged by the brothers of the disgruntled wife, and at least a show of a fight has to be made afterward. So two principal ways in which matri-lineal claims are likely to interfere with those of the father, the claims which the maternal kin make upon the children and in the security which is given to a woman by her kin instead of by her husband, are eliminated here. Dobu, with its extreme matriliny, demonstrates both forms of interference

[28] This stands out in such marked contrast to the complete rift in the marriage tie which occurs when a dead woman's kin take possession of her body in Dobu. Fortune, 1932a, p. 11.

and also an interference with residence, while Manus and Samoa show only the latter type.

In this connection it is of interest to consider the Arapesh attitudes toward incest. It follows, from the above definition of the parental roles, that there are two types of brother-sister relationships, depending upon whether one emphasizes the common blood tie through the mother, or the common feeding tie through the father. Now a boy's own sister is sent away from home when she is small, sometimes as young as seven or eight years old, and she becomes a part of another household, and is herself a tie which now unites her brother to that household. It is of sisters, in this connection, that the Arapesh think when they recite their aphorism forbidding marriage with your own sisters, your own mothers, etc.,[29] and add the permission to marry "other men's sisters and other men's mothers." It is of such sisters they think when questioned about incest. "No, we do not marry our sisters. We marry other men's sisters." When I could get no better answer and no illustrations of incest, I sent the young men to ask the old men what they would say to a man who wanted to marry his sister, and the replies were almost identical, "What? Do you not want brothers-in-law? If you marry another man's sister and another man marries your sister, you have two brothers-in-law. If you marry your own sister, you have none. With whom will you visit? With whom will you talk? With whom will you hunt? Are you mad, not to want brothers-in-law?" Now note here the emphasis, not "Are you mad to want to sleep with your sister," but "Are you mad not to want to use her to establish warm ties with other men?" Actually, I did not collect a single instance of incest among the Arapesh; a few men had once heard of a case in another tribe, but that was as close as they had come to it.

Now let us place beside this the parental attitudes toward boys and girls. If too many girls are born, they will not be allowed to live because the people prefer boys, "who will stay at home with their parents," to girls, "who will marry and go far away." A man who has daughters expects to scatter them abroad, to form new ties for his sons, and for their children. A man who refuses to let his daughter or his sister marry is regarded as anti-social and subject to group sanctions.[30] (See below, the case of Maginala's sister, p. 191.) So from the time she is a baby, a little girl is regarded by her brothers and her father as a pathmaker who is going far away from them, who is only theirs for a little while, until she goes away to be grown by a different set of males. The blood tie through a woman binds one to other males, but guarantees no close and continuous relationship to the woman herself. The Arapesh have no brother and sister taboo; brothers and sisters are warm and affectionate toward each other, but from childhood on they simply see very little of each other.

Now let us consider the other type of siblingship, children of a common father who has fed them. The sister is abstracted early from this type of relationship. She is replaced by another small girl, whom the father and all one's brothers also feed, whom one feeds oneself, and who becomes, not a blood sister through birth, but a feeding sister through nurture. For whereas blood ties are established only indirectly and through the help of women, feeding ties can be established directly by men themselves. In his ties to his blood sister, a man is dependent upon events which occurred long before his birth, but in his attitudes to the girls who are betrothed to the men of his family, he can take a positive, independent, and from the Arapesh point of view, male role. For his blood sister, he uses the reciprocal "sibling of opposite sex" term *mohowhi'*, but for his elder brother's wife he uses *asho'e'*, literally "older female sibling of the same sex as myself," and for his younger brother's wife he uses *awauwi'*, "female younger sibling of the same sex as myself," or to put it another way, he identifies his brothers' wives with his brothers, with the siblings who remain in the home and share the food of the household, that common food which establishes ties more binding than blood, ties that survive even after death. It is here that the Arapesh equivalent of incest occurs, when a man sleeps with the betrothed or the wife of his younger or older brother. This is never a matter for a fight; it is in

[30] Mead, 1940.

the family; it is not very important; the principal shame falls
upon the younger brother who has taken his elder brother's
wife. It is felt to be a kind of bad but explicable behavior,
not necessarily to be countenanced by a formal rearrangement of the marriage, but always and most significantly "in
the family." So, in a sense, it may be said that viewed from
the inside, from the emotional organization of the Arapesh
themselves, what looks like firm and well-institutionalized
patriliny is in reality a kind of adoption in which the young
wife becomes at once the child and the sister of the husband
group, and that this is in part responsible for the sense of
safety, of lack of passion, and therefore of lack of danger,
which attends intercourse with a wife of this type.

Viewed from the standpoint of their solution of a problem
which must be met by every primitive people organized
along kinship lines, namely, the balance between maternal
and paternal ties and their effect upon marriage, authority,
and descent, we can say that the Arapesh have made specific economic and ritual compromises with the recognized
legal claims of the maternal kin, and so have been able to
consolidate marriage along patrilineal lines.

To return now to the Class Two relationship and its actual
meaning for the Arapesh. To them, the mother's brother relationships are not ties to mother's gens, but rather ties to
individuals beyond the borders of one's own family. They
are ways in which highly personal relationships may be kept
warm and the routes through which one may involve oneself
or involve others in ceremonial activity. If we can take the
various relationships which fall under this heading, we can
see how this works out. When one is born, the mother's
brothers are already there, personal and separate from the
mass of kindred, distinguished by their special delight in saying *mehinen,* sister's son. Here there is no need to emphasize
the tie to the mother; the mother's brother is presented to
the child as given. As the child grows older, he also learns
that there are contemporaries who call his father *wauwen,*
and whom he can call *mehinen,* and thus single them out.
These are his father's sister's children, but again he pays
very little attention to this tie through their mother. His
mother's brother has sons whom he also calls *wauwen.* He

calls their sisters *ama'e'u,* the term he uses to his mother's sisters. Finally, he is taught to call the children of his parents' cross-cousins, his own age mates, either *balahan* or *babuen,* grandchild or grandfather. These two latter terms are used more extensively by growing boys than by any other portion of the population.

A great deal has been written about these "out of generation" terms which are such a common phenomenon all over the world. But whether their origin in a particular case be in a special form of marriage, in a form of secession, or in a failure to distinguish generations among the members of the same sex in either the maternal or the paternal clan, it is always necessary to consider the content which this explicit extension of terms has for the individuals who use it, especially the children. No formal category which successfully disposes of a word under the definition "women of father's gens regardless of generation," as can be done for the word *patiyeyen* in Manus, can obscure the fact that the child learns that wherever the word also has a fairly specific content, like father, mother, grandparent, or aunt or uncle, it is being "used in another sense." The misapplication, or wider extension of terms, itself such a formal derivative of the nature of kinship reckoning and the limited possibilities therein, provides a framework for varying psychological content in different cultural settings.

## THE EMOTIONAL TONE OF CLASS TWO TERMS

Among the Arapesh, the child learns that all of these terms, *wauwen, mehinen,* and the grandparent-grandchild terms when used to his contemporaries, are something special, something that he and the person addressed can feel glad about. All his relatives are good to him, all feed him and cherish him, but those to whom he uses these terms also enjoy him and treat him more personally. If the formal demands of the system are examined, the mother's brother is defined as one to whom the sister's child is always owing something, a one-sided relationship which does not carry any specially pleasant implication. But in real life, individuals seek out their *wauwen* as enthusiastically as they do their *mehinen.* Whenever possible, this relationship is claimed and is distinctly felt to be a symmetrical rather than a complementary relationship. This symmetry can be attributed to the fact that all *wauwen-mehinen* relationships, whether between mother's brothers and sister's children or between cross-cousins, are perpetuations of the brother-in-law tie which is felt as warmly symmetrical. One Arapesh explained the term *mehinen* as being an abbreviation of *mehen-batauwin*, invoking an inadmissible linguistic form; the correct form would have been *mehen ananin batauwin*, brother-in-law, his child, but the form *mehinen* is not a "sister's child" but a "brother-in-law's child." Marriage which, to a large extent, severs the effective tie between a little girl and her brothers just as thoroughly cements a new tie between her brothers and her husband and her husband's brothers. These ties are new, special, and can be relied upon to provide warm, stimulating, outside contacts. With a brother-in-law, one hunts, one gardens, one travels, one sleeps. The story of Agilapwe,[31] in which the man, enraged at his wife's elopement, attacks and pursues his brother-in-law is typical. The wound is not only that his wife has left him, but that the tie with his brother-in-law is thereby outraged.

In describing any sort of ceremonial relationships, such as payment of rings after an accident or after death, or the ceremonial presents of game, the Arapesh always classify affinal relatives together as *wauwen* and *mehinen*. This might of course be explained in terms of an old cross-cousin marriage, but it may be equally well attributed to the identification of husband and wife.

The frequent inclusion of *mehinen*, where they do not belong structurally, is a further attempt to make this relationship, formally one-sided, symmetrical.

In order to understand just how striking is this skewing of the real structure, it is necessary to consider particularly the death payments. When a man dies, his mother's brothers, if alive, and otherwise their sons, have a right to special payment of rings. If this payment is not forthcoming, the mother's brother and his wife can assume special mourning to shame the delinquent executors of the dead. There is no rubric

[31] Mead, 1935b, pp. 159–160.

under which a *mehinen* has any rights to receive property
at such a time. Yet when an Arapesh describes a funeral
payment, he always stresses the payment of rings to *wauwen, mehinen,* and *buanyins.* (We shall see later how the
*buanyin* is a generalized surrogate of the *wauwen-mehinen*
relationship.) It takes the most minute analysis finally to discover that what happens at a death is that the *wauwen*
of the dead is given rings for that occasion, and simultaneously, the *mehinen* are repaid by the executor for the last
rings which he formerly received from them at some other
death when he was *wauwen.* But the fact that one is a payment and the other is a repayment is ignored. If no repayment is due to the *mehinen* on any count, he is just given
a small ring anyway, because he is a *mehinen,* and payments
are being made to everyone in the *wauwen-mehinen* category. (See below, pp. 500–502.)

So if we return to our original suggestion that Arapesh
kinship terms could be divided into two categories, we find
these to be, first, relatives united through same sex and direct descent ties and, second, this special cluster of relatives
who spring from the brother-sister relationship, reinterpreted
as the brother-in-law relationship, with all it connotes of new
ties and outside stimulation of activity. Every Arapesh community is continually oscillating between marrying their
daughters abroad and establishing new and exciting ties but
running the risk of sorcery, and marrying them at home and
becoming ingrown, turned in upon itself, and lacking in excitement.[32]

[32] In actual content, it may almost be said that these two classes
of relatives correspond in Arapesh feeling to the self and the non-
self, and that Class One has as its base a combination of incestuous
and homosexual implications in which the wife is identified with the
trusted brother, as one of the same sex siblings who remains at
home, while Class Two contains all that the Arapesh know of a
heterosexual, non-incestuous tie. The fact that the homosexual attitude is attached to a member of the opposite sex and the heterosexual attitude to a member of the same sex does not invalidate this
assumption about the psychic attitudes involved. In this connection
it may be remembered that no overt homosexuality occurs among
the Arapesh, and that all heterosexual expression which is outside
the warm, domestic tie with the long-accustomed wife is felt as exceedingly dangerous and is much feared. The own sister becomes

This attitude shows up particularly in regard to the prohibitions about marriage. Formally, the children of parents
who use brother and sister, cross-cousin, or two-generations-
apart-child-of-cross-cousin terms to each other are not allowed to marry, nor may a man marry a woman whom he
calls either aunt, daughter, or niece, nor may a woman marry
a man whom she calls father, or mother's brother, or nephew.
But in actually deciding upon eligibility for marriage, the
children of related men are allowed to marry, if the mothers
have come from far distant places, because the marriage
will not then too greatly constrict the life of the next generation by cutting down on the number of new affinal relatives. This attitude is quite explicit, and the possible intermarriage of young children is discussed in these terms.

But it is possible to lay too much emphasis upon the Arapesh desire for new relatives and new experiences and to
underestimate their fear of strangers and of distant places,
especially their fear while these new bonds, so desirable to
possess but so dangerous to forge, are being cemented. Always, when a marriage at a distance is being discussed, sorcery is mentioned. At home, on the other hand, there is said
to be no risk of sorcery, which is not accurate but is a fair
statement of Arapesh feeling about the matter. Now the
brother-in-law does, in a sense, represent to the Arapesh the
stranger within the gates, the stranger whom he wishes and
yet fears to love, to whom he entrusts his sister, his own
blood, with some apprehension. This attitude is implemented
with the mother's brother's curse, a curse which functionally
in Arapesh is the power which a man wields against his sister's
husband and his sister's husband's children.

### KINSHIP CURSES

This cursing power must be understood against the wider
Oceanic background where it occurs in so many diverse
forms, as a sister's curse and a child of sister's curse in Samoa,
as the father's sister's curse and the cross-cousin's curse in
Manus, etc. The fact that, here in the Sepik-Aitape District,

---

very early the stranger woman, who lives at a distance, with whom
there is a tie, but no longer continuous reassuring domesticity. Her
husband, the brother-in-law, shares in this exciting, dangerous tie.

it is brother and child-of-brother who curse sister and child-of-sister does not mean that this is necessarily a different institution. Both forms of curse stem from the idea that the ghosts of the immediate ancestors are amenable to the prejudiced requests of one descendant against another, and how closely these two, the brother's curse against the sister and the sister's curse against the brother, are bound together is evidenced by the fact that among the Arapesh themselves we find the father's curse, the brother's and the elder sister's curse, with the brother's curse extended over his sister's children. The mother can also participate in the removal.[33] Just as the child of sister's curse in Manus may be interpreted as a sanction against the male line by the disinherited female line,[34] so the brother's curse in Arapesh is a sanction which prevents the brother-in-law from making off with the sister and failing to become an effective brother-in-law, which was the only reason that he was permitted to marry the sister. The Arapesh phrase it that if the sister has no children as yet and the brother is angry at the sister's husband, then the sister herself will sicken and never bear children; if she has already had children they will sicken or die. The causes of such cursing are usually cited as failure to make affinal gifts or to make payments. Actually, however, when these payments are examined, they are found to be very slight. The real failure is the failure to feel and, therefore, to act like a brother-in-law, the failure to cease to be a stranger. When this occurs, the Arapesh revert to the childhood attitude toward strangers as persons to be magically harmed and invoke the curse. And it is significant that the curse is phrased as an inimical act against the brother-in-law, as punishment for his derelictions and delinquencies, and never as a result of a quarrel between brother and sister, as the sister's curse is phrased in Samoa.[35] Only when the *mehinen* is full grown and fails to act with warm responsiveness toward his

[33] For a discussion of the way in which the dichotomy between relative and stranger is developed in young children and later becomes operative in sorcery practice, see Mead, 1940, p. 414; 1935b, chapt. 4.

[34] Fortune, 1935, chapt. 3.

[35] Mead, 1930b.

*wauwen* is the mother's brother's curse invoked; usually it
no longer involves sterility and death of children, but instead
is reassimilated to the curse which an elder brother or elder
sister can put upon a younger sibling, the curse which makes
him lazy, without ambition, and unable to find game.[36]
Here it is merely part of the family pattern for keeping the
young in line, by calling in the ancestors to help, if necessary. This latter curse merely consists in talking aloud and
rather formally to the immediate ancestors. The curse can
be removed in the same way. But the curse of the brother
against his brother-in-law's wife can be removed only by a
ceremonial encircling of her head with bark and fire tongs,
which ritually removes it. With their customary casualness,
the Arapesh leave one bad gap in their theory; the curse
may be removed by a different mother's brother than the
mother's brother who put it on. So unless there is family
solidarity, it may prove quite ineffective. As it is so much
more an expression of personal disappointment and affront
than it is any sort of effective social sanction for the collection of debts or enforcement of obligations, this is not very
important.

## FURTHER DISCUSSION OF THE HUSBAND AND WIFE
RELATIONSHIP AND WOMEN'S KINSHIP ATTITUDES

We have seen how husband and wife are identified in the
use of kinship terms, how a woman classifies herself with
her husband in the terms which she uses to his brothers and
their wives and how a man behaves similarly toward his
wife's sisters and their spouses. Furthermore, we have seen
how the direct-descent-own-sex-sibling terms predominate[37]

[36] See below (pp. 503–504) for a series of illustrations of the
occasions on which the curse was used. The details of the ritual,
see Mead, 1940.

[37] I am perfectly aware that the taking over of a spouse's kinship terms is a very common mechanism in many parts of the
world. I do not, for a moment, argue that it need have the same
significance everywhere that it occurs. It is, however, probably fair
to say that some sort of equivalence between spouses is always postulated, when one uses the terms of the other. This can be seen particularly in the greater tendency of these equivalent terms to appear

within the patrilocal community, and we have described how the little girl, betrothed long before puberty, is absorbed into her husband's family, is fed and grown there, until she becomes one of them. The strength of this tie is proportional to the length of her stay with them, and to how small she was when she came.[38] Between a man and his brother's betrothed there is always the greatest warmth and comradeliness. Together, the adolescents of a household, which includes most often a set of brothers and their betrothed wives, plus the sisters who have been betrothed near home, go to work sago or gather ferns for cooking meat. A man and his sister-in-law may go crabbing together at night with no more suspicion of possible intrigue than is felt if a brother and sister among ourselves share a dwelling. In the little patrilocal group, the girls who are married-in outnumber the sisters who are either home on short visits or who have been betrothed to near relatives. They set the key, so that, in time, these few sisters who have been kept within the group in this anti-social way take on somewhat the affect of the girl who is married-in, who is being grown by the residence group. This attitude is increased by the fact that the husband of the sister who is betrothed near home is already a close relative; he is not a newly acquired brother-in-law offering new possibilities and excitement, but just someone who has always been regarded as a relative. As the women grow older, the distinctions are made, not between the women who have married-in and the one or two who have remained, but between the wives of men who have always belonged and the wives of men who themselves were reared and fed elsewhere and so are regarded as partial strangers.[39]

---

in terms used to and by the next descendent generation, that generation which has come to identify closely together aunts and their spouses and uncles and their spouses.

[38] See Amito'a's speech to Me'elue, p. 415.

[39] See below, p. 164, in the gens of *Toto'alaibis*, the wives of La'abe were treated a little distantly by the other women. In a quarrel they might be reminded that La'abe hardly belonged to *Toto'alaibis* anyhow because he had lived most of his boyhood in Wihun and had been grown there, *therefore his wives were strangers*. It was, of course, the quarrelsome Amito'a who herself had come to Alitoa only some seven years before as a mature woman,

From the time that a little girl is betrothed, she leads a double life which centers more and more in her husband's group, and tends to attenuate to formal visits to her own group.[40] This, of course, is a function of the distance she has been betrothed; if it is only in the next hamlet, and the two hamlets are already in close and continuous relationship, her betrothal may make very little change in her life, the parents-in-law with whom she now sleeps at night may be an older couple who have often cared for her as a smaller child. But this is the less usual case; the pattern relationships of women are postulated upon a marriage outside the group and about a day's walk away. The little girl lives in her new home exactly as she did in her old home; she sleeps with her parents-in-law or with another sister-in-law who is also not old enough for the consummation of marriage; she helps the women of the household about their work; she laughs and jests with all the young people of the village. When there is a feast at home, or some special garden is being harvested, her parents will send for her; she will go home for a few days, work with the women, carry up firewood or help with the harvest, play with the babies at home instead of with the babies at her new home, and then go back again. Perhaps her young husband and others of his kin will come to get her, and her brothers and he will talk together. When she menstruates for the first time, her brother will come ceremonially and perform the fire circle ceremony[41] and seem a little bit more of a stranger than he has ever seemed before, just as her young husband also assumes a special role as he feeds her the post-menstrual meal[42] which gives him power over her health. From the time that her first child is born, she belongs very firmly and finally in her affinal group. As a rule, when she is delivered, no

who made this point, but the other, milder women agreed with the accusation, the wives of La'abe were stranger than was Amito'a, the wife of Baimal, who had lived all of his life with the gens of *Toto'alaibis.*

[40] The only exception to this is in two betrothals for one son where one girl remains with her parents. See below, p. 156.

[41] Mead, 1940, p. 420.

[42] Mead, 1940, p. 419.

woman of her own kindred is present; instead, the wives of her husband's brothers, or very occasionally a nearby sister of her husband, assists her. Her husband's brothers send their wives to attend her, and her husband's brothers bring food for the child. When the ceremony of naming the small yam fruits[43] is performed, they are all named after the children of her husband's hamlet. If it were not for the intrusion of death, this picture of complete absorption would never be disturbed. Even if death came in the orderly fashion in which it is expected, taking the father before the son and the elder brother before the younger, it would not be upset. When a woman became a co-wife, she would, except in the very rare cases where a boy had been betrothed to two girls at once, have already lived in the group for many years. She would have had children of her own and would have known her husband's younger brother's wife as being closer than a sister. Such combinations, a young wife whom a man has grown and a second inherited wife who comes in much later, are eminently peaceful. The wives alternate in caring for the children or in cooking the meals; while one wife goes to the garden, the other prepares food at home; they share one house, and their voices are not raised in altercation. This in fact is so like the picture of the relationship between the wives of different men who live in the same hamlet that it is hardly distinguishable. Many times in the morning, all of the women of a small hamlet will gather together, at the invitation of one, to share some tidbit of *oshogu* grubs or sago just brought from a feast. They sit about, chattering happily, in great amity.

When death interferes, however, and a young man dies just before the consummation of his marriage, let us say, then the whole balance is disturbed. The bereaved girl, ready for marriage, belongs to the gens; they have grown her. She must be given to some member of it. If she is given to someone younger than her dead betrothed, there are various disadvantages; he is probably too young and early indulgence in sex is believed to stunt his growth. Furthermore, he may already have a betrothed wife and this will involve

43 Mead, 1940, p. 415.

more rearrangements.[44] But if she is given as a second wife to an elder brother of the deceased, then all of the orderly interrelationships based on the theory that the first wife will be the younger and more attractive, the second wife, a tried worn mother of several children, are upset. She challenges the security of the first wife, in a way in which the first wife has not been led to believe that she will ever be challenged, and quarreling results; the husband may have to build two houses because the two women will not stay together in one. Each will cook a meal for him and try to attract his attention. From the Arapesh point of view all this is very bad and thoroughly undesirable.

A far more extreme difficulty results when a woman of the Plains runs away and marries a Mountain Arapesh, and almost every locality contains some half dozen such women. Throughout this part of New Guinea, the coast and the banks of the rivers represent the superior culture, where manners are more cultivated and costumes more elaborate, and the women run away from the crudities of their own culture to find a husband nearer the Beach. This is the native phrasing. Additionally, among the Arapesh, the difference in ethos between the Plains and the Mountains is important. Some of the dominating, vigorous Plains women prefer Mountain men, gentler, more acquiescent, as husbands. So occasionally a Plains woman finds her way into a Mountain village, or, working on the same Beachward principle, a Mountain woman finds her way into a Beach village, and demands permission to stay there. A variety of motives operate to make the Mountain people accept her, although they know that trouble will follow in her wake. Women are valuable, very valuable, and they are the nearest to group property

---

[44] Such rearrangements took place when Sagu's husband died and she insisted upon marrying Maigi, who suddenly left her younger sister Kumati, nearly at puberty, again an unbetrothed girl. Kumati had been at home with her father Balidu more than is usual for a betrothed girl, and when he now had to consider all over again giving her up to strangers, he was hostile and negativistic. She had become absorbed into the category of "women whom we have fed and whom, therefore, we will keep." See Balidu's speeches on the subject made to the men of Ahalesimihi (below, p. 292).

which the Arapesh have. This woman, cowering in the menstrual hut of one of the hamlet wives, where the old woman
found her, is tall and well grown; she should be able to work
and bear children. In time her relatives will come and make
friends and this means a new link with the Plains, made ef-
fortlessly and with minimum danger. There is, additionally,
the spice of adventure involved in marrying a Plains woman;
she is more highly sexed than a Mountain woman; this endangers one's hunting and yam growing, and still—there are
personalities among the Arapesh to whom it appeals. Also
a Plains wife will very often succeed in driving away a Mountain wife who has been there before her. A Mountain man
who has a wife, long betrothed, fed by him and his group,
has great difficulty in bringing himself to divorce her. But
he may not like her; she may be sickly or stupid or unattrac-
tive. This is a way of getting rid of her with less public cen-
sure. Sometimes also, taking in a Plains woman may solve
a different sort of problem, as when the stupid Dunigi
woman with her two children was held fast by the mother of
Ulaba'i and married to Gobonarra, a ne'er-do-well with whom
no Mountain woman would stay and over whose defecting
wife one scrap with a Liwo man had already ensued (see
pp. 156 and 329). Gobonarra was a young man, he needed
a wife; if his relatives refused to get him one this was a matter of reproach; if they did get him one, she would undoubtedly run away and then there would be trouble. A glance
at this woman, who had been foolish enough to come en-
cumbered with children, was sufficient. She would stay with
Gobonarra; she would have no place to go; let him marry
her, who was undoubtedly a fugitive from justice anyway.
And soon afterwards they heard that her husband had died,
and she probably had been suspected of having sorcerized
him.

So between the rearrangements which result from death
and the consequences of Plains marriages, the Arapesh marriage picture is far more confused than their formulations
would lead one to believe. For instance, there is no word
for co-wife. The terminology continues to assume only the
levirate as a basis for polygamy and the continuance of the
use of the term *asho'e'* for the inherited wife of the elder

brother. But in spite of these pitfalls to the complete and permanent absorption of the betrothed wife into her husband's gens, which is the Arapesh ideal, most women do become ultimately so absorbed. An unusual case was that of Ulaijo, of the Alitoa gens of *Dibatua'am*. She had been married in Wihun. After her husband's death she had returned to her brothers Nyelahai and Ulaba'i, and finally had settled down as a co-wife to her sister Baijo, whose husband Aden lived and worked in close association with his wife's two brothers. Consequently, her adolescent son had been brought up in Alitoa, and there had been a certain amount of hard feeling on the part of his paternal relatives in Wihun. Sometimes, if a woman was very attractive and took a great interest in her husband's affairs, it followed that, as a widow, she played a more important role, and the playing of this role, as a surrogate for her husband, might lead her back into more contacts with her own gens. Perhaps no other single instance could better document the completeness with which a woman becomes part of her husband's group and a passive link between her brothers and her husband, than this fact that she may resume an active role, if her husband dies, and she must take *his* place in helping *her* brothers.[45]

So throughout her life an Arapesh woman never plays a single formal or ceremonial part, except as the wife of her husband, and in those cases usually only in his absence. Except for her services as midwife and child's nurse to her husband's brothers' wives and as an assistant mourner in the ceremonies attending the purification of the widow of her husband's brother, she has no other special duties beyond those of day-by-day helpfulness and sympathy. But if the father is away, the mother can remove the curse which he may have put on the head of one of their sons. And if the husband is absent from home, his wife can act for him in relation to his trade friends. If, however, an only daughter inherited a trade friend from her father, this friend will be taken over by the daughter's husband.

It now becomes clear, I think, why the father's sister, *qua*

[45] Such roles were played by Nalaijo, the eldest sister of Ombomb, and by the mother of Ulaba'i. See below, pp. 250 and 174.

father's sister, plays so slight a role in Arapesh. For the father's sister to play a role, we must have identification between the brother and sister and a contrast in some way, either between the ethos of the sexes or between the paternal and maternal roles, which can give her a clue for behavior. In Arapesh, however, the identification is not between brother and sister, but between husband and wife, with the proviso that it is always best for men to assume all formal roles. The only existing present tendency in Arapesh which might make some development of the father's sister's role a possibility is the great emphasis upon the mother's brother and the way in which these two relationships make a symmetrical contrast to one another. So, twice, the more structurally minded of my informants answered, when asked, "And who would scarify a girl if she had no mother's brother?" "The father's sister." But when I pursued this, I found that it was merely a hypothesis, based upon formal logic.

## OTHER SOCIAL RELATIONSHIPS

The Arapesh view of social relationships is congruent with his conceptions of kinship. He calls by some kinship terms all of those whom he can trust. Similarly, anyone who cannot be classified in some way, through identification with a series of intervening human links, as a blood or affinal connection, is potentially an enemy. His willingness to accept a great number of links, to identify himself with his mother's younger brother's brother-in-law, if need be, makes it possible for him to extend this circle enormously, to include at times whole distant localities, and always a number of hamlets in the localities which are contiguous to his own, while beyond these borders, sanctuaries among strangers, lie the homes of his trade friends. Now, just as kinship, real or most imaginatively imputed, divides the whole world into friend or potential foe, so his two conceptions of kindred—Class One and Class Two types—also pattern his other formal relations upon which his socio-economic life is based.[46]

[46] This dependence upon kinship patterns for politico-economic forms is characteristic of the Oceanic area and is found in Poly-

## The *Buanyin* Relationship

The *buanyin* relationship is an institutionalized exchange relationship which is hereditary in the male line. *Buanyins* are always males, they must be members of different gentes, and they should be members of gentes which are ranged on opposite sides of the dual organization, *ginyau* and *iwhul*. Although theoretically every man may have a *buanyin*, actually one son or nephew of a big man will take over some male heir of the big man who was the *buanyin* of his father, and the lesser members of the gens of each will cluster about these two leaders, and help with the active prosecution of this one *buanyin* relationship. If none of the immediate heirs of a big man shows any signs of becoming a leader, a more remote heir or even a sister's son may be chosen.

The *buanyin* relationship is very definitely patterned on the Class Two kinship relationships, i.e., those ties formed from an opposite-sex sibling tie. The phrases "all the mother's brothers, all the sister's sons, all the brothers-in-law, all the *buanyins*" or "give it to a mother's brother, or a sister's son, or a brother-in-law, or a *buanyin*" continually recur in the description of ceremonial economic obligations. Furthermore, the *buanyin* relationship may be said to reflect these Class Two relationships in the following ways: First, it is conceived as ceremonial and special; the smallest piece of meat given to a *buanyin* is a formal matter. Second, two *buanyins* are never identified with each other, although they themselves may carry the burden of identification. On the other hand, brothers are frequently identified with one another. Third, children of *buanyins* call each other *buanyin*

nesia, Melanesia, and New Guinea. For specific discussion, see Hocart's series of papers on its importance in Fiji (*Man*, London, 1915–1918); Gifford, 1929; Mead, 1930b, pp. 139–146; and 1934a, pp. 310 *et seq.* It is probably impossible to lay too much emphasis upon this fundamental social mechanism of the Oceanic area, contrasting as it does with that other equally fundamental social mechanism, the assertion of the locality principle which Lowie has emphasized in his *The Origin of the State*, 1927, and which Elkin, 1935, feels is so important for an understanding of Australian social institutions.

again, not brother. Fourth, when a *buanyin* is used as a link in a chain of identification, the chain always ends in a Class Two relationship, e.g., the mother's brother. For example, if A's *buanyin* B has a sister's son, C, who is wounded in a scrap, B, as mother's brother, has the right to call for the payment of blood, and A, as C's mother's brother's *buanyin*, may also make such a claim, and in some cases does. Also, when a man has outraged the feeling of the community and it is desired to invoke the *tamberan* against him, either his mother's brother or his mother's brother's *buanyin* or his own *buanyin* may set this mechanism in motion. Fifth, the obligations to a *buanyin* are the same as those to Class Two relatives, ceremonial presents of food, especially of meat.

But the *buanyin* relationship serves several other purposes as well. First, it serves as a training ground in self-assertiveness for the heirs of big men who have been chosen by their elder male relatives as fit for leadership because their "ears and throats" are both open, i.e., because they can both learn and give out what they have learned. Such boys are taught that the lack of aggressiveness and competitiveness, appropriate in their relationships to all other individuals, are not required in their relationships to their *buanyins;* instead that assertive and aggressive behavior is actually appropriate. *Buanyins* are permitted, indeed expected, to insult each other ceremonially. One is expected to inquire about the economic standing of the other, mock at his pigs, decry his yams, and demand that he be up and doing. Second, it channels all these feelings of aggressiveness and competitiveness into narrow, socially guarded grooves, and so permits their exercise for the benefit of the society, without the disruption of the mild helpfulness characteristic of the bulk of Arapesh social life. The Arapesh do not phrase it this way; they insist that all men are unaggressive and that because leaders need a modicum of aggressiveness, they must be forced to develop it, and that early practice in dealing with a future *buanyin* is a good way for a youth to develop this modicum. Third, it is the one place where a heavy emphasis can be placed upon symmetrical behavior.

A digression here is necessary. In analyzing Arapesh behavior in terms of the concepts of competition and cooperation, we found that the Arapesh must be characterized as "helpful" rather than as cooperative, a distinction which was developed by May Edel in analyzing her Bachiga material.[47] According to our definition, cooperation was the sharing of a common end, in which the end was the essential goal; helpfulness was the direction of the activity of two or more persons towards an end conceived as belonging to only part of the group, whom the others helped. Here, for all of those who help, the relationship to the co-worker is primary and to the goal secondary. So, among the Arapesh, a man directs his energies to helping his brother garden, helping his father's brother build a house, helping his cross-cousin give a feast. Each goal is conceived of as one person's, who reaches his goal through the response of others to his need for assistance. All the emphasis of Arapesh daily life is upon this endless responsiveness to the needs of others and an extreme modesty in stating any needs of one's own.

At the same time, there is apparent in Arapesh ethos a great premium upon symmetrical behavior: the need to repay a good or a bad deed, ultimately to balance out the women married into one group by repaying the same number of women, the requirement that there should be two moieties who can continually repay each other. This theme of exact recompense either of good or of evil permeates every aspect of Arapesh culture. It is a favorite folklore theme; it crops up continually in their interpretation of natural phenomena, the northwest monsoon returns the southeast monsoon; if one blew strong, the other will blow strong. The moon attempts to return the brilliance of the sun, so a fair day means a fair moonlight night. And when we first lit our Tilly lamp, the moon's brilliant rising a half hour later was immediately interpreted as an attempt to return that light. In the peacemaking ceremony, a ring is exchanged for each blow given. Throughout all of this, the emphasis is always upon restoring a balance which has been disturbed; the minute equilibrium is restored, the debt paid, the rescuer recompensed; everyone is satisfied. The Arapesh have no feeling for the endless series of exchanges of revenges which characterize feud cultures,

[47] Mead, 1937a, chapter on the Arapesh.

nor have they any interest in permanently worsting another, nor in repaying a debt with interest. To make it exactly even, that is enough. This type of symmetry may be understood as one expression of responsiveness; every stimulation from outside produces a lack of balance, and the responsive individual moves to restore that balance, which is to him a state of well being.

The very curious institution of *ano'in,* which the Arapesh conceive of as vaguely related to the *buanyin* relationship, may be considered here also. The *ano'in* is a very poorly conceptualized relationship; informants will say, yes, everyone should have an *ano'in* the way everyone should have a *buanyin,* but most peoples' *ano'in* lines have died; *ano'ins* are inherited, and your father's *ano'in's* son is your *ano'in,* and when you meet him you can joke with him; people of the same sex born on the same day are *ano'in;* a girl and boy born on the same day are *ano'in* and should marry each other; *ano'ins* never meet, each one sits in his place and each hears what the other does; children of *ano'ins* should marry. A survey of *ano'in* relationships did not prove any more enlightening; one point seemed quite clear, that almost everyone's *ano'in* must be dead. Only by the examination of past history and conditions under which new *ano'in* relationships were formed did I finally introduce any order into this apparent chaos. The concept *ano'in* seems to mean vaguely "rival" or "competitor," with the notion that children born on the same day have in some way been matched against each other by that fact. I have only two cases of these common birthday *ano'ins;* in one, the boys were simply told that they could always joke with each other as much as they liked (a very slight privilege where easy joking is permitted everywhere); in the other, a man invoked his right to a girl born on the same day, as a way of cutting a Gordian knot in a marriage tangle.[48] A real *ano'in,* however, is someone with whom one has come into violent and unsuccessful competition, as in a fight between two communities over a woman. The man who is worsted, if he already stands in no ceremonial relationship to the leader of the other party, may say, "From now on,

[48] E.g., the marriage of Monau and Budagiel.

he and I are *ano'in*. He may stay in his place and I will stay in mine. I will plant yams. He can plant yams. I will raise pigs. He can raise pigs. I will give feasts. He can give feasts. We will each watch the other," setting up a lifetime of long-distance rivalry. So these *ano'in* relationships serve as a channel through which an aggressive and temporarily defeated man may declare his feelings of rivalry and institutionalize them. The strength of such feelings may be judged by the fact that if, when such a relationship has continued for years, one man dies, the death of the other is sought by sorcery, as the natural course for the vengeance to follow. So one of the two old *ano'in*, who posture at each other, one from Umanep, the other from Kobelen, would say, "Just let him try to sorcerize me. Just let him try! My Plainsmen friends are numerous and they will know on whom to avenge my death." Such relationships may theoretically become hereditary, but as their only apparent function is to permit strong and disgruntled individuals to express hostility at a distance, it is not surprising that most *ano'in* lines are dead. But it is significant that the Arapesh in discussing them tend to confuse them with the *buanyin* relationship, and it throws light upon the extent to which the *buanyin* relationship is recognized as channeling hostilities.

To return now to the way in which the *buanyin* relationship permits an emphasis upon symmetrical behavior. In the obligations to the mother's brothers, and to relatives-in-law, the phrasing is one-sided; a man has continuing obligations to his mother's brother and to his wife's brother; it is true that these payments are returned, but the return is almost extralegal, as it were, an informal concession to the desire for symmetry. And the symmetry is never quite established, so that, when a bride price is paid, each ring is repaid with one of the exact size and value, *except* the two or three rings given to the bride's parents. Where one side of the payment is compulsory and the other optional, as in the feast which a man demands of his sister's son after his initiation, there is always a slight strain, for the creditor can never openly push his claim. So after the great feast which Balidu gave in Badui's name to his Wihun mother's brothers (p. 275), he had to shrug and say: Who knew whether there would be any repayment. Oh, perhaps, if his brother-in-law was given a pig soon, he would bring it. That would be good, for then he, Balidu, would be able to distribute the pig among all those who had helped him. But one never knew. And this nonchalance masks a very real anxiety, because the man who has just given such a feast, the return for which at any given date is, in fact, very uncertain, is himself hounded by his own urge to repay at once those who have helped him give the feast, but he has no means of doing so, except through the return feast.

What a relief then to be able to turn to one's *buanyin* and openly dun him, charge him with laxness, laziness, bad management, and every other economic crime on earth, to make a bundle of coconut leaf riblets, each one representing a piece of meat one has given one's *buanyin,* a debt which has not been returned. Here the anxious entrepreneur can stamp and scream and abuse to his heart's content, and without any guilt whatsoever, for this is how *buanyins* are supposed to behave. In good weather *buanyins* stand some distance apart and shout at each other, but as the publicity of their accusations, rejoinders, and cross rejoinders is an important part of the proceedings, if it is necessary to conduct an important conversation in rainy weather, one has the amusing experience of seeing two men sit down side by side in a small house and shout at each other as if they were a block apart.

The *buanyin* institution permits more choice and more matching of strengths than is possible between affinal relatives and mother's brothers and sister's sons; it is a way in which actual economic ability can be ceremonially utilized so that men are not always ceremonially opposed to others who are weaker than they. This factor is not, however, as important among the Arapesh as it is for the Manus, where the substitution of the economically effective *vis-à-vis* for the *vis-à-vis* who is given by the kinship arrangements is very essential.[49] The *buanyin* does serve very definite economic functions among the Arapesh. He acts as a pivot in the organization of intra-community feasts, and through him

[49] Mead, 1934a, p. 315.

also unexpected kills may be economically banked and then called in later as domestic pigs. I shall discuss these aspects of the *buanyin* relationship at greater length later. But the greatest function of the relationship lies, I believe, in the channeling of aggressiveness and in the outlet it gives for resentments and annoyances for which no overt expression is permitted and which tend to culminate in the Class Two relationships.

The relationship of *buanyins* to intermarriage is not clear. Throughout this entire area we have these peculiar ceremonial friendships (the Iatmül have eight different types) which almost always approximate to the mother's brother, affinal pattern, rather than to the brother pattern.⁵⁰ There is no definite formulation among the Arapesh upon the subject. They will tell you that *buanyins* are different from relatives, but I have instances to show how closely the two types of ties, through marriage and through *buanyin* relationship, interact.

When all the descendants of the *buanyin* of Madjeke, himself the leader of *Suabibis*, proved unequal to the task of meeting the sons of Madjeke, Polip and Unabelin, Whoiban, the coming leader of the other division of Liwo and already a brother-in-law of Polip and Unabelin, began to assume the role of *buanyin* also, and to be spoken of as a *buanyin*. During his lifetime the two relationships, that of brother-in-law and of *buanyin*, would supplement each other, and then, if the heirs remained *buanyins*, the *buanyin* relationship would, people said, predominate. Aden and Balidu were two prominent *buanyins* of Alitoa, representing the two divisions of the village of Alitoa. Aden had been ill for a long time with a bad yaws sore; he had fallen into arrears, and relations between the two *buanyins* were not very friendly. Now the daughter of Balidu's brother was betrothed to the younger brother of Aden, who was away at work, and when the quarrels waxed louder than either side could bear,

⁵⁰ For a discussion of the way in which these relationships fit into various types of kinship patterns, see Bateson, 1936, chapt. 15. The ceremonial friendships of the Banaro are also a peculiar development of this same tendency to crystallize out and render hereditary some aspect of kinship behavior. Thurnwald, 1916.

people would murmur, "Ah, when that marriage is consummated, then they all will be relatives again." (See below, p. 417.)

## TRADE FRIENDS

The Arapesh share the institution of the hereditary trade friend, not only with all this part of Oceania, but also, in some of its aspects, notably the initiate's Road, with Australia. But whereas in so many parts of New Guinea these trade friendships cross head-hunting boundaries, this is not so among the Arapesh. The path is always conceived of as leading toward the Beach, toward the sea, the source of all delightful things. Although the path is associated with sanctuary, it is sanctuary from hunger and cold, and less often from physical attack or sorcery. The home of a trade friend represents food and warmth in a land where traveling is a chilly, hungry business. Although many of these trade friendships are believed to have originated in intermarriages, once established they fall into the brother-to-brother pattern of Class One relationships. There is no accounting, no recrimination, no dunning, but a general, casual helpfulness, a gift-giving friendliness. It is also possible to make an immediate identification with a trade friend. If one comes to live for long in his village, one "helps" him, and calls every person in the village by the term which he uses to them, and one is so called in return.[51] There is not, as in so many places, any taboo upon intermarriage between the children of trade friends; here the argument that "true, their fathers call each other brothers, but they come from distant places" would be regarded as quite sufficient. The Arapesh do not feel the need of protecting their daughters from seduction which seems to lie at the root of this rule in so many places. On the other hand, the young man calls the wife of his father's trade friend, "mother" and he has no fear that she will seduce him in order to sorcerize him, or that she will catch up a little of his saliva as he sleeps.

[51] See below, p. 128, for Maguer and Kobelen boys' adjustment in Alitoa.

## LEADERSHIP

The Arapesh lack any concept of rank, hereditary authority, or organized leadership. Their very simple concept of a "big man" is of one who has been the leader in a series of small events. The larger the number of events in which he played the principal part, the bigger man he is. His ability to play this part is conditional upon several things: First, early recognition by his relatives that he has ability and, therefore, a slightly different training, which includes the early assignment of a *buanyin*, early requirement that he entertain and deal with his father's gift friends, and the continual informal verbal insistence that some day he will be a big man, some day he will be able to "talk." The abilities which are so signalized in a boy are intelligence, energy, and a willingness to assume responsibility, to "take his father's place" in emergencies. Second, his successful inauguration and carrying through of a series of economic events the success of which is dependent upon such variable matters as yam crops and the growth of pigs. Third, the successful exercise of judgment in crises. The man who has been able to smooth over difficulties, say the diplomatic word, or quote a suitable precedent when trouble was impending is one who is likely to be classified as a big man, if he has also played the necessary economic role. However, no amount of tact and exercise of tact alone will earn him more than the appellation of one whose talk brings peace. Fourth, the ability to give a good display of aggressive anger when necessary. To be successful, this ability must be almost entirely histrionic and foreign to the man's character. The really violent man stands much less chance of becoming a big man; if he does become one, he is less respected and has a more circumscribed leadership role because people do not trust him.[52]

The role of the big man is definitely patterned upon the role of the elder brother, who inaugurates economic plans

[52] Cf. Nyelahai, in Mead, 1935b, p. 147.

for the others and can call down the anger of the ancestral ghosts upon the dilatory, who vetoes violence and advises when any action is safe. In return, his younger relatives look up to him, boast about his achievements, help him with his activities. As theoretically each gens would have such an older brother, and each such big man would have in his *vis-à-vis* gens another big man, his *buanyin,* it is obvious that there is no sense of a leader, but merely of a balancing of strength among the leading elders of socially opposed groups. The fact that the position is so fluid, that it has no name and need not be filled, means, however, that many gentes have no big man at all, and very often no sort of internal leadership. This condition is one of the chief contributing causes of the dissolution of a gens, for the weak men in it will turn to their relatives in other gentes for leadership and guidance. Continual turning to them will lead to more intensive economic cooperation and probably closer residence; the hamlet which is the residential unit of the weak gens will break down, and the gens itself dissolve. Sometimes a man of ability will, however, be left almost entirely alone, as the last of a disappearing gens. In this case, he may ally himself closely with the gens of his maternal kin, or of his brothers-in-law, and rise to some importance in either group, for every Arapesh group is quick to push into leadership anyone who shows any ability for it.[53]

## TRANSMISSION AND SPONSORSHIP RELATIONSHIPS

The relationships within which an individual learns a new technique, a new charm, or a new piece of ritual fall among the Arapesh into two categories. First, there is the simple relationship between a member of the parent generation and

[53] Such was the case of Aden, virtually alone in his gens and the child of an intra-group marriage, who had himself married sisters. He was a man of some importance, but only by virtue of his close association with his two brothers-in-law, Ulaba'i and Nyelahai, was he able to maintain his *buanyin* relationship with Balidu. See *Diary,* p. 170, and Mead, 1935b, p. 85.

a member of the child generation within which cultural
knowledge is handed down, without ceremony, without payment, and most informally; and second, there is the relationship between one who has performed an act before and one
whom he formally initiates into the performance of a similar
act. Within this second pattern falls the help which a woman
who has just successfully borne a child gives to the next
woman who has a child; the help which a man who has had
a child gives to the new young father; the assistance rendered
the man who has killed, by the others in the community who
have taken human life, etc. All these services are regarded
as slender links in a chain of tradition which can by no
chance be generalized and taught to the young as a group,
but which depend entirely upon the individual who has experienced the situation before inducting the next participant
into it. It is partly owing to this custom that the Arapesh feel
that the preservation of their tradition, of the knowledge of
the right way to do things, to be safe, is always in such great
jeopardy. "Suppose there was no one who had married a
widow before, then who would know what to do, and how to
escape the danger?" they say. "Without our old men who
have done all of these things, where would we young men
be?" The extreme casualness and privacy of these small bits
of ritual in Arapesh also contribute to this sense of fragility,
for unless an individual has actually participated as a principal
in such a ceremony, there is absolutely no guarantee that
he will ever have witnessed it at all. To all such sponsors,
the midwife, the sponsor of the new father, the sponsor of
the novice in the initiatory cult, the sponsor of the man who
makes his first *abullu*, the sponsor of the homicide, rings or
meat are paid by the one who has been led safely through
the hazardous new experience. All such experiences are periods of taboo and danger, and the payment is made in return
for guidance rendered at a critical time. No new tie is established between an individual and his or her sponsor. There
is no name for the relationship and no continuing obligation,
but rather the sponsor is always sought among those to whom
one already has fast kinship ties, a brother, a father's brother,
for a man, and usually a husband's brother's wife for a

woman.[54] So this extra teaching, this extra guidance, moves along the tracks laid down by kinship.

There is one further form of transmission relationship, that between two "trunks," two organizers of an inter-village exchange, in which some ceremonial complex changes hands. These men are called *gabunyan* and the relationship is complementary; the leader of the purchasing village makes payments to the leader of the selling village, which are regarded as never to be returned and as a function of the asymmetrical character of the relationship.

[54] See below, p. 504, for examples of sponsorship in Alitoa.

# THE ECONOMIC STRUCTURE

## THE POSITION OF THE ARAPESH IN THE AREA

In an earlier section[1] I have discussed the position of the Arapesh in the complicated network of the diffusion of material and nonmaterial traits which characterizes this area and have also given some account of the simpler techniques which they know and practice. They are already identified as an importing people living in a very meager environment, with poor garden land, a slender supply of game, a scant stock of sago, and poor, thin domestic pigs—a people who depend upon trade with neighboring groups for their tools and utensils. It is necessary also to realize that the Mountain Arapesh have only a single possession which is of the slightest interest to anyone, that is, they inhabit the trade route from the Beach to the interior. Their land is so poor and precipitous that the inhabitants of the richer level land of Beach and Plains would not live there, if they could; their yams and taros are notoriously small, their sago poor. They are not in the slightest danger from outside attack from aggressors who wish to take their lands away from them, or sack their houses for their handful of Tridacna shell rings and a few strings of shell money; there are no head-hunting peoples near them, people to whom a head is a head, and to whom therefore the mild and unaggressive Mountain Arapesh would offer excellent prey. But the Plainsmen do value highly the right to walk easily from the Plains to the sea, to obtain Beach trade. Conversely, the Beach values the trade with the interior upon which they depend especially for net bags, some feathers, and tobacco. And this the Arapesh control, not for the seemingly obvious reason that they inhabit all the land between Beach and Plains, but because their territory is the only inhabited area between Beach and Plains, with a great unin-

[1] Mead, 1938.

habited tract of bush to the south of them, because people of this area do not know how to travel through uninhabited country. This is explained partly by the nature of the bush, which is most inhospitable and unlikely to offer a full meal to the wanderer, and partly because of their lack of portable nourishing food. The Plains people have very little sago, the only portable food in this area; when they travel, they have to carry yams and taro as food. With the low standard of load size, the frequent impracticability of taking the habituated women with them, and the desire to carry tobacco for trade, a heavy load of food is regarded as a great handicap, and a line of hamlets where food can be found is felt to be absolutely essential.

The Arapesh have sufficiently capitalized this single economic advantage, their position in a trading constellation, so that without any surplus of natural and manufactured articles of their own, they are able to draw on the outside world, not only for their minimum requirements of tools and utensils, but also to some extent for luxury in the form of dance complexes. Or perhaps it would be more correct to say that this advantage has been capitalized for them; outside peoples have forced them by trade inducements, by threats of sorcery, to use it. So in their relationship to the outside world the Arapesh occupy a defined position in which the outsiders are perfectly willing to have them remain in possession, are indeed anxious that they should do so, and offer them definite trading advantages in return.

Second, we find, in investigating the Arapesh dependence upon the outside peoples, that their dependence is all long-time dependence. Throughout this whole area of Oceania, an important distinction can be made between the trade procedures and general economic organization of those communities living in continuous day-by-day dependence upon their trading partners in other communities, and those which are from the standpoint of food, areca nut, tobacco, and building material—the essentials of this area—self supporting, and depend upon outside trade only for tools, utensils, ornaments, currency, etc. In communities of the former type—Manus, Tchambuli—the whole rhythm of the economic life is keyed to meet outside demands. The individual learns to think of his control over the circumstances of his life largely in terms of material things; if he has the fish or the sago, his trading partner will sell, otherwise his larder is empty. The festivities of such a trading group have a kind of external quality, dependent as they are upon trade relations with outsiders who are not actually involved.

In an Arapesh community, however, months could pass without a single gift being received from the outside, before anyone would feel the pinch of poverty. Spear heads would break and new bamboo heads be cut and lashed on the shafts; arrows would be lost, and simpler, less elaborate arrows be substituted; adze haftings would fall apart and be replaced by clumsy local haftings. Pots would break and the supply would become gradually restricted; people would carry them about, because they would no longer have enough to leave a large pot in each of a household's dwellings; net bags would wear out, and more carrying would be done in packets made of *limbum* palm sheath. The bamboo water carriers from the Plains would gradually crack and break, and women would carry more and more water in clusters of coconut shells. There would be a gradual constriction of life; tools and utensils would become duller, scarcer, and more crudely fastened and hafted; inferior substitutes would be used, a few more women might learn to net bags, men might become a little more adept at cutting spear heads, but the whole process would be very gradual and it might be two or three years before a genuine scarcity of tools and utensils forced the attention of the Arapesh upon their state.

As far as we know, such events as this do not occur; I have merely made the reconstruction to suggest the difference between the Arapesh type of economic dependence and that of either a fishing people like the Manus or a solely agricultural people like their trading partners, the Usiai, or, also the dependence of a people who live by the export of manufactured objects, like the pot-making Manus of Mbuke, to whom the sudden termination of trade relations would mean not only an immediate scarcity of food, but a decided rearrangement in their way of life. Because neither of these conditions obtains among the Arapesh they are, on the whole, unconscious of their economic dependence upon the outside world and regard it as mainly intrusive; the Beach is intrusive because it offers such tempting luxuries, the Plains is intrusive in its blackmail demands for sorcery payments. Their own land and the way of life of their ancestors provide them with food, house building material, clothing, and areca nut, and it is their main task in life to settle down and cultivate it. I have stressed this matter of attitude in some detail because, from the standpoint of an external economic analysis, the Arapesh are a dependent people, dependent for their most important tools and utensils upon trade. But any such statement is misleading if it is not qualified by their own view of their dependence as a weakness of the spirit rather than a need of the flesh.

## THE EFFECTIVE ECONOMIC UNIT

I shall use this term to describe the limits within which the presence of economic resources—in the case of the Arapesh, mainly food, but for a people like the Eskimo, fuel and clothing would be included—can be mobilized. Definite limits are in most communities set to such mobilization. And for any society it is always fair to ask, Where do these limits lie? In Samoa the matter is quite clear; in times of great scarcity, the village became the unit, and people from other villages, no matter how closely related, were forbidden to come and deplete the village store of food. But when this same question is asked about the Arapesh, the extraordinary network of individual economic ties immediately comes to light. It is possible to find the answer by starting from a central point, as is always the case in analyzing Arapesh material. To stand aside and attempt a bird's-eye view of the whole is always distorting. For example, from an exterior view, one might say the amount of food in a Plains village will never be the concern of a Mountain village, and cite Alitoa's relation to Biligil and Kaboibis. This would be correct. All Biligil and Kaboibis could starve without anyone in Alitoa raising a hand. But then one comes to Dunigi. Three Dunigi women are married into Alitoa, immediately changing the whole picture; Alitoa men would attempt to send food to their affinal relatives. It is possible to say only that the effective economic unit in Arapesh is a constellation based on two principles, blood and affinal ties on the one hand and common residence on the other. The center of such a unit is a group of close kin, who also garden, hunt, and work sago together. Such a group is continuously economically interdependent, an interdependence reinforced by the prohibition against eating one's own kill and the obligation to get meat to Class Two relatives. Within such a constellation, which almost always includes several hamlets and may include half a locality, there is a strong central pull. The members of the group try to hold it together; they try to persuade brothers-in-law to garden with them and to dissuade their own number from gardening with distant brothers-in-law. If one of the group deserts almost entirely to live at too great a distance, it will be resented; men will grumble about him and be dilatory in fulfilling their obligations toward him. Each small group works on the axiom that there are never enough people for the land and the trees; if there were only plenty of people, children would also be plentiful. Every man, therefore, who deserts his home group and goes away to a distance—say to a hamlet a half day's walk away—endangers that state of comfort which it is just possible to maintain if everyone stays close together and works with his own group. At first sight, it may seem an obvious contradiction that a people with such poor land and a quite inadequate food supply should think that they can solve their food problem by greater concentration of population. In judging this, however, one must remember that the proposed concentration consists of 15 men instead of five, and that the distances which it is necessary to walk to enlist the help of these same individuals, if they insist upon living at a distance, play a very large role.

If, for instance, Yabinigi leaves Alitoa and gardens with his sister's husband in Wihun, it means that if Alitoa relatives want to share his yam crop, which they still have a right to do, they have to send their wives to Wihun to carry home bags of yams. The bags which they carry cannot be as heavy as for a shorter carry; the journey requires a whole day. If they need Yabinigi's help to fence or clear a garden, it is a long way to send for him, he may not get there in time, and return trips to help him with his gardens also take time. Furthermore, it is impossible to discharge as many other obligations on the way, since Yabinigi no longer lives in a close cluster of relatives to each of whom he owes some different obligation. So Nyelahai, Yabinigi's elder brother, puts a curse on Yabinigi's hunting, in the hope that it will bring him back again. But later, when there is some suggestion (see below, p. 435) of giving back to Yabinigi the wife to whom he was originally betrothed and whom Nyelahai took for himself, then Nyelahai, one of the two big men of Alitoa, threatens to break his house, break his rings, cut down his trees, and himself leave Alitoa forever, and the plans are hastily stopped. True, they would like to have Yabinigi back, but they can far less afford to lose Nyelahai.

It now becomes intelligible why the final resort of anyone annoyed with his own close relatives and neighbors is to threaten to destroy his own property, his foothold there, and cease to work with them forever. This is a loss which no Arapesh community faces with equanimity. They are as anxious to maintain the size and strength of their group as if they were needed, not for peace, but for aggression against other communities.

To diagram the effective economic unit then, one would have to diagram this central group, this cluster of most of the gens members of two or three gentes, with their most closely related brothers-in-law and mothers' brothers and cross-cousins, who habitually garden, hunt, and work sago together, and who continually exchange food, especially meat, informally. Out from each member of such a group would go their most important Class Two ties, sometimes reaching into several other localities. Each one of these ties, the direction of which was shared with another member of the central group, would be not only doubled but quadrupled in intensity, because of the Arapesh habit of helping other relatives. In the analysis of Alitoa below (p. 204) I have attempted to sketch in the ties which brought members from other hamlets to Alitoa, in order to give some picture of this economic constellation. Although geographical continuity is important, it is not determinative; an accusation of sorcery, a theft of a woman, a broken marriage, may alienate two hamlets which are very close together. If there are only two strong ties between two hamlets, as, for instance, one consummated marriage and one betrothal, if the marriage breaks under circumstances of suspicion and conflict, the betrothal may also be summarily severed, and all close contact, which means also all economic contact, between those two hamlets may lapse for several years. Then, gradually, some older tie will be resumed; cross-cousins will begin to hunt together or help each other at feasts, new betrothals will be set in motion, and with them, new informal and formal food exchanges will get under way. Therefore, the economic unit of interchange of food and services which centered in Alitoa in 1931 has undoubtedly changed several times since then.

In order to picture the dynamics of this unit more clearly and to show how the helpfulness of one man to another is enlisted, we can now look at the way in which the Arapesh plan their work, at the way in which they themselves see the disposition of their time and effort.

## PLANNING WORK

About one third of a woman's time is consumed with the daily routine for which she is continuously responsible, whether she is in her own or a relative's house; carrying water and firewood, preparing and cooking food (even if some other woman gets it from the garden) are her daily tasks. They vary greatly from day to day, when preparations for a feast are in prospect, when the family lives in one of its own houses or in one of the larger hamlets on the outskirts of which firewood is very scarce, etc. Because of the scarcity of firewood and the distance from the garden, the men realize that it is (and it is so regarded by the women) a definite imposition to ask the women to live for long in one of the large hamlets. Therefore, a special acknowledgment of their service is always made to the assistants in the feast which follows any ceremony. With a third of her time devoted to routine, another third is devoted to the extra toil which devolves upon her in connection with any special activities, such as sago working, meat smoking, entertainment of visitors, etc., which are organized in relation to some male undertaking, either her husband's or one of his kin, much less often one of her own male kin. The bulk of a woman's special obligations are towards her husband's gens. During childbirth a woman is cared for and fed by her husband's mother, husband's father's brothers' wives, and husband's brothers' wives, not by her own female kindred. It is only at very large feasts that women go home to help their own gentes. All this, however, is regulated by no hard and fast rules, but rather by temporary alignments: if a father-in-law and son-in-law work in close cooperation, the daughter will often be at home helping her mother, etc.

Men have no such simple routine tasks. Care of the children while their wives are away in a taro garden comes the nearest to being a fixed duty, but is dependent upon the ages of the children; small infants and children over three or four are able to accompany the mother. The father is responsible for no single item of the routine of daily life. This makes the man a free agent who plans his own activities. However, not more than one ninth to one tenth of the average man's time is taken up with activities for which he is the chief initiator or planner. Under such activities may be included clearing and fencing a taro patch for his wife, when it is either made on his land or he takes the principal responsibility; making a yam garden under the same circumstances; going on a hunting trip which he initiates; visiting a trade friend; working his own sago; or building a house of his own. In all these activities, except trading where he may sometimes but not very often act alone, he is assisted by others who assume nearly equal responsibility. Yet there is usually a shade of difference—at least three quarters of the houses are spoken of as belonging to one man rather than to two or three related men, and about half of the gardens are designated by the name of the man who has assumed the maximum responsibility. This difference expresses various degrees of assertiveness and also the characteristics of different residence groups. So the group of three brothers, of whom Baimal was the senior, always initiated activities in pairs; it was the house of Baimal and Kule, the hunting of Baimal and Alis, etc. On the other hand, when Balidu, the oldest member of the gens, built a house, it was known as his; when others made a garden with him, it was still designated as his garden.

Also, some men took a more active interest in one activity than another: a given man would initiate many trade activities, but little gardening, and the native terminology of ownership followed these lines. A few very assertive men might actively initiate or plan one half of the work in which they engaged, while the least enterprising members of the group simply tagged along and initiated nothing at all, not even one taro patch for their wives.

A great proportion of the time of the average man is spent in responding to the economic requirements of other people's plans: helping a brother work sago, a cousin build a house, a brother go hunting, a brother-in-law fence, planting yams in another man's garden, helping another man clear a patch of ground in which both their wives would plant taro, going on trading expeditions with others. This major dependence upon the initiative of others requires a very special adjustment on the part of the man, which, except for the lack of routine, is more nearly analogous to the usual woman's role in economic life than it is to the man's more usual role in primitive or civilized society.

Let us compare the Arapesh woman's view of life with that of the man. She carries in her head a groundplan of necessary activities for which she is responsible, which falls into two parts: daily tasks and her share in special undertakings. She has taro planted in a number of places, which she must weed, harvest, and replant. Her husband may direct her activity here if she is stupid, but more usually she makes her own plans, either taking or making an opportunity to go to her garden as often as is necessary.

But paralleling these known activities are a series of unpredictable demands—to accompany her husband 5 or 10 miles in any direction to which he is called to take part in someone else's enterprise, or to go as one of a group of carrying or sago-working women upon some special business. She must get her own work done in between these claims.

Although the man's picture of his future days contains no routine, nevertheless it contains a thread of necessary tasks of activity which he must initiate, a thread which runs through an extensive number of claims which will be made upon his time by others. The prevailing attitude towards one's own work is the usual one of a housekeeper mother in our society: it must get done somehow in the intervals between other and more exacting claims. Here again, there is great variation according to personality; some people will pigheadedly continue with their own plans and insist, by so doing, that others abandon their own plans to help them. There are those who chafe under the claims of others to which they are trained to respond, and feel a continual anxiety because their own work is not attended to. Some respond with such alacrity to the demands of others that they neglect anything which they initiate themselves. The final scheme of work in any Arapesh community depends upon the equilibrium between these different attitudes. Occasionally, unsocial people, especially men, succeed in settling down on one piece of ground and insisting upon young relatives and connections coming and helping them, planting with them, and receiving nothing except their cooperation on the spot in return. Such people benefit by the willingness of the vagrants who are always ready to undertake a day's journey to help with a more distant project, to get rid of more insistent claims nearer home.

It will readily appear that in any one man's life there is continual conflict between a number of claims—his own plans and the divers ones of his associates. Nor are the claims upon two men identical, because each has a different set of affinal relations and close cooperating male kin. It is not always possible for a brother to know just what obligations another brother is carrying. Furthermore, accident plays a far greater role than does relationship. A man is more likely to help another with his home because they have just been helping still another man work sago than because he is his brother or his cousin. Actual blood relationship or habitual helpfulness are invoked in cases of conflict, as when someone has great difficulty in getting labor.

The custom of planting in several gardens, planting coconuts on other men's house sites, and giving one's pigs to relatives to feed also provides a multitude of semi-impersonal reasons for walking about and becoming involved in other people's activities.

To make the whole point more concrete, let us take an individual case, a man of 30, with two wives, and the considerations which motivate him:

1. His own:

A year from now he is giving a feast for which he will need many yams; he has a major yam garden planted which must be periodically tended.

A trade friend, four localities distant, has promised him a piglet from his pig's next litter. The pigs will be born in the next month, and he must be on the spot within a few weeks to claim the little pig—a three-day trip at least.

He wants to build a new house for his feast; instigating the work and assembling the meat to feed the workers will fall upon him.

One of his wives is going to need a new patch in which to plant her taros, and it is really his turn to take the initiative in cultivating a piece of land. At least, none of the others who might be doing this are doing it.

He has been designated as "dog"[2] for a cousin's friend; this means working some sago due in about a month.

Six months ago his trade friends from the Plains came through and he gave them plates. He really should go and receive the pots they have promised him.

2. Activities which others to whom he is obligated have under way, of the same nature, houses which are planned, started, or nearly complete, gardens prospected, hunting trips upon which they have asked him to accompany them.

3. Activities of others about which he does not know in detail, which are dependent upon their participation in the plans of a third set of individuals.

4. Accidents which have economic repercussions—births, deaths, killing a pig in the bush, etc., fires, destruction of fences and gardens by storm and floods.

5. Events in which he will participate at a slight profit, e.g., when an important man has a *garamut* made for him and everyone helps drag it to a village or when someone has a good enough yam crop to celebrate an *abullu*.

Time and place are the two considerations which princi-

2 "Provider of feast food." See p. 112.

pally determine his choice. If he has been helping one relative with sago, and a relative a mile away is building a house, he is more likely to wind up that day at this building than if there is a house building with equal claim on his time, but 10 miles from his present location. Or if he spends the night in a hamlet where someone is building a small house, the house-builder may the next day discontinue his work and go off to help someone work sago; the newcomer, without any statement of intentions, spends the day working on the house. The needs of a brother who is building a large house will be borne continually in mind and as he passes through the bush, he will cut a bundle of rattan for him, or a bundle of thin sticks to use as lathes; his brother's wife needs bark for cord —there is some near that fence which needs mending in his uncle's yam garden. Under this continuous institutionalized responsiveness to the activities of others, his memory of his own desires runs as a thread of anxiety in those individuals whose personalities find this form of unintegrated unplanned response distasteful. But whether individuals like it or not, this continual responsiveness, with its reciprocal dependence upon assistance of others, is the order of economic life in Arapesh society.

Furthermore, such habits have profound reverberations in a lack of interest in time, place, schedules, in an enormous plasticity of response and a corresponding weakness of sustained purpose. It has often been claimed that housework produces a kind of special occupational disease in women so that the woman who has spent 15 to 20 years responding to the multiple desires of a number of dependent individuals is unfitted for sustained effort. So it is interesting to note that Arapesh men who exhibit so many of the character traits which western society has considered as typically feminine are required to act in the same nonegocentric responsive way in which we have traditionally required our women to act.

About a third of the time of both sexes is taken up with walking about and resting after the ardors of the journey. The time which a less mobile people would have free for various arts and handicrafts is thus disposed of very thoroughly. The woman who has carried 70 or 80 pounds on her head is content to sit with folded hands and nurse her baby. She does not restlessly look for weaving or beadwork. This attitude towards all sedentariness as a complete rest period is well expressed in the idiom "tomorrow we will sleep in the village," i.e., we will remain at home all day and do nothing. Perhaps as much as the lack of patterns for artistic achievement, this exacting mode of life, in which the man who sits down is almost always a tired man, is responsible for the low development of handicrafts among the Arapesh. And the poor diet is in turn responsible for part of this weariness. But a greater responsibility can be laid to the social habits which make it necessary to be everlastingly trekking from one end of a locality to another.

## INDIVIDUALITY OF ECONOMIC UNITS

If the full implication of this casual organization of economic effort in response to the expressed and unexpressed requests of 10 to 20 relatives of different categories be fully realized, it will be easy to see that among the Arapesh there are actually as many economic units as there are fully effective male adults. Like the European sib, each man defines his own position, and when affinal relatives are added, no two men, not even two brothers, have the same position. The ease with which one man identifies himself with another, takes over another's affinal obligations or *buanyin* ties, complicates rather than simplifies the situation, because it is completely unpredictable and is determined by accidents of residence, friendship, and temporary association which are not subject to any systematic classification. If, for instance, one makes the generalization that if brothers do work together, that is, if one of them has not definitely aligned himself with some other gens group in some other hamlet, the economic units on which they depend are likely to be very similar, one is immediately faced with endless variation, depending upon the compatibility of temperament among the brothers, whether they follow preferential occupations which complement each other or not, whether their wives come from the same place, related places, or widely distant places. And a circumstance which makes one set of brothers draw closer together may push another pair, of different personalities, further apart.

So in the gens of *Toto'alaibis*, Baimal, Kule, and Alis made a fast trio, in which Baimal and Alis hunted while Kule gardened and traded. They always worked in pairs. Two of the brothers shared a house; the wives were all fast friends, and everyone brought up the children. Within this firm little group, one man's obligation was another's, the brother-in-law of Kule was also, very strongly, regarded as the brother-in-law of Baimal. It was not that they did not help other people and make small gardens with others, but their main interests lay in their little hamlet of Mogiligen located far out in the bush, near good hunting territory. Another economic constellation in *Toto'alaibis* was represented by Balidu, the big man of the gens, and Sumali, his slightly younger brother. Balidu was a gardener *par excellence*, and his one wife was a fine pig raiser. Sumali was a hunter, restless, irritable, acquisitive, talkative, very restive under his elder brother's superior position. He had gone off to the bush and established himself, working with Aden and Nyelahai, in a garden on Aden's land which was near Sumali's hunting bush, rights to which he had inherited from his mother's brother who had belonged to Liwo. Sumali came in to Alitoa, in which the Walinuba half belonged to *Toto'alaibis*, only when he had to; he presented game to his brother with as much formality as if he were presenting it to a stranger. After Aden and Nyelahai tired of gardening at such a distance he was left alone with Gobonarra, his four young sons, and the occasional help of his Ahalesimihi brothers-in-law. Ombomb and La'abe, the other adult males in *Toto'alaibis*, both without own brothers in the gens, vacillated, gardening with Balidu, helping Baimal and Kule, and going off to work with Wutue, an old man of *Uyebis* gens, who was the father's brother of Ombomb. La'abe, who was a double parallel cousin of Ombomb, accompanied him on these expeditions to his work with his real gens; La'abe also worked with the Ahalesimihi men who were his brothers-in-law, where he again met Sumali, although Sumali was a senior member of his own gens.

I realize that it is tedious and difficult to follow such a mass of remote detail as the gardening behavior of this small group

of Alitoa males, but so unformalized, so unsystematic, is Arapesh behavior that in any attempt to state the rules which
govern their economic behavior one is immediately driven to
concrete cases.

I shall now try to state Arapesh economic conditions under
the more customary rubrics, of "property," "currency," and
"feast organization," in the hope that this preliminary statement will have sufficiently prepared the reader for the very
unsystematic way in which these would-be systematic concepts must be handled. It will be apparent throughout, I
think, that the Arapesh formal concepts do not differ nearly
as much from the concepts of surrounding peoples, or even of
primitive peoples in other parts of the world, as does their
practice. The basis of their economic life—that one owes certain informal services to gens relatives and others who live as
gens relatives within the residential group, and that one owes
more formal economic services to affinal and extragens relatives, to formally inherited feasting partners within the locality, and to hereditary trading partners in distant places—
sounds simple and usual enough. So also, when their conception of property is examined, we will find that their ideas on
the subject are quite clear; they understand ownership and
inheritance rights over things and rights over persons. It is
only when it comes to practice, to the use they make of that
property, that the individuality of their economic behavior
becomes apparent. With exactly the same set of formal requirements concerning property rights, kin cooperation, and
cross-gens obligations, it would be possible to set up a society
in which each man guarded his rights from every other man,
rendered such services as were required by custom in a meager and unwilling fashion, and waited always for threat or
goad to hurry his cooperation. The reason that Arapesh economic life presents no such picture seems to be a matter of
ethos; where cooperative societies rely upon organized formal
rules which will make the interest of the group primary and
the interest of the individual secondary,[3] the Arapesh have
none of these. Formally, we have a society in which narrow
kin claims, the father planning for his own children, the de-

[3] Mead, 1937a, pp. 458 *et seq.*

mand for meat from affinal kin under a threat of magically spoiled hunting, prevail. There is here no firm and well-integrated social structure which insures collective economic effort and orderly cooperative participation in group tasks. This will be seen again and again in the course of the *Diary;* when a man of aberrant but strong personality chooses to resist the prevailing ethos, to refuse to accept the inexplicit standards of mutual helpfulness and friendliness, he can always find all the formal support for his unhelpful behavior ready to hand. He can find magic to spoil his neighbor's hunting, a curse to render barren his sister for whom his brothers-in-law do not pay meat, a sorcery technique by which the exuviae of his relatives can be handed over to the Plainsmen. The social forms are ready for the individual with a harsh, jealous, possessive nature to utilize aggressively.

It is for this reason that it is so exceedingly difficult to give an accurate picture of the economic life of the Arapesh as a group; the communities are so small, three or four aggressive and uncooperative men, more or less, may make all the difference. Even from the outside, localities could be seen to differ. Maguer men seemed a disgruntled and meager lot; right next to them, Kobelen was a hearty, happy locality group, and it was almost possible to recognize a Kobelen man by his well-fed look, and to suspect a Maguer man in one who was weedy and hungry looking. This difference is in itself significant and suggests that the haphazard friendly give and take of the typical Mountain village has a high survival value. Where food was so very scarce and the hope of getting meat so fleeting, the individualistic forms of the better endowed Oceanic societies would be less adequate. We have seen how they were modified in work habits, how the Mountain people preserved the theory of the large village, ceremonially organized about a plaza, but actually scattered to live in small hamlets. In the same way they have preserved social forms which are more rigid and more effective in maintaining barriers between gentes than in breaking those barriers down, but they have developed a type of social personality, an ethos, which sets a premium upon a type of individual helpfulness despite their social forms.

## PROPERTY AND INHERITANCE

The formal economic system is based upon private property in land and everything existing upon it, game animals, trees, herbs, minerals, etc., and in the right to use it for gardening, hunting, or residence. All land is owned, even the steep declivities at the edges of inhabited sites and the quicksands and torrents inhabited by *marsalais*. Ownership is individual, not gentile. There is, strictly speaking, no gens-owned land, except the *marsalai* place and that is said to be owned by the *marsalai*. However, if two or three members of a gens own adjacent land, the aggregated individually owned lots may be spoken of as belonging to a gens. Only males can own land. While land may very occasionally be given a woman, it becomes the property of her husband or her sons. The same rule applies to sago and palm trees. Certain rights over land, the only very definite ones being fishing and transit rights, are vaguely conceived as belonging to a locality. These may be said to be rights of all members of a locality with regard to boundaries rather than rights over definite stretches of land, all of which are already individually owned, that is, they have a right to expect that members of other localities will not trespass without invitation within their boundaries.

Land assigned to different purposes is classified as follows: hunting territory (*balam*); sago land (*balot*); potential garden land (*bo'onap*); garden land in use (*dubarig*); house site (*aleb*); a number of contiguous house sites, not so large as a hamlet (*buluwelu*); hamlet site (*sho'ubeli wabul*); village site (*debebili wabul*); plaza of a hamlet (*agehu*); *marsalai* place (*walinagenum*).[4] A steep place adjacent to a residence site used for latrines, menstrual seclusion, and birth, is spoken of as *dewag;* the whole of the steep sides of a village is called a *yawigenum,* a bad, that is, steep place, while

---

[4] Note that the suffix *-igen* or *-agenum* corresponds to no substantive form; it can be used in the same way as is a terminal of a noun class, but there is no such class.

the entire level land of the hamlet is spoken of as *yapugenum,* a good, i.e., level place.

Among these various classifications of use, every piece of land in the Arapesh country is named and owned. All trees are owned, either as part of the soil on which they grow in the case of forest trees, or separately, if they are planted trees, coconut palms, areca nut palms, or sago palms.

There is no word for owner; instead, the possessive personal pronoun is used with the appropriate noun class ending. So Ombomb's house would be rendered, Ombomb *ananit ulipat,* Ombomb, third person, masculine gender, suffix referring to noun class of words ending in t, *ulipat* which is house. Separable and inseparable possession such as occur in Melanesian languages are not distinguished. A man's name, his land, his wife, his G string, his exuviae, his soul, the food he has eaten and is going to eat are all simply *anan*—plus the appropriate noun class ending.

In personal property, each individual owns what he himself has made, purchased, or been given. This applies to a woman as well as to a man. A woman owns all the pots, tools, utensils, and ornaments which her own kin gave her when she married; she also owns anything she may specifically purchase with the fruits of her own work: a pot traded for a net bag or tobacco she has grown. Children own anything they have made, small game they have killed, and objects assigned to them by adults, such as palm trees, wooden bowls, sago clumps, etc. In spite of this highly individualized ownership, there is felt to be a slight claim exercisable under the head of relationship. So, if a coconut dropped from a palm tree belonging to Amambut, which was, however, planted close to the house of La'abe, Amambut's brother's daughter's husband in Walinuba, and La'abe wanted the coconut palm picked up and brought into the house, he would send his little daughter to get it, if his wife was away, remarking loudly, "Go and pick up the coconut from the tree of your grandfather." This was explicit legalistic behavior, very much in the public eye. Relatives who were on good terms with one another could enter each other's houses and borrow tools and utensils freely, but this right was exercised only where the good terms were genuine be-

cause of the fear that anyone who entered the house of another in his absence might be accused of having purloined
some article which contained material which would be used
for sorcery.[5] So strong was this precautionary measure that
no other protection was needed against trespass; houses were
barred with a simple piece of wood fastened across the door,
and valuables were left inside. Theft was unknown,[6] and
only close and friendly persons would risk entering the house.

Property, in addition to being individually owned, can be
disposed of individually, in certain accepted ways. Legally,
a man may give a piece of land, a coconut tree, a hunting
territory, or a sago patch to anyone he wishes. This freedom
of testatorship is considerably reinforced by the custom of
disposing of all possessions of importance long before death;
a great deal of a man's property is disposed of in early middle age, assigned to real and adopted children, and spoken
of subsequently as theirs. Consequently, even if a man dies
quite young, he has virtually no property to dispose of. This
custom precludes quarrels among the heirs. The will of the
father in distributing his lands and trees as he pleases is reinforced by his presence and the sanctions which lie behind
his paternal authority.

The actual disposal of property is subject to certain nega-

[5] See below, Sauwedjo's accusations against Me'elue, p. 414.
[6] The only thefts I found among the Mountain Arapesh were
those which were secondary to the expression of some form of emo-
tion. Most of them might be classified under the heading of individual pathology, which is, however, in the case of sorcery practices,
raised to the level of culturally institutionalized behavior, but so
also are the childhood attitudes which lie behind it. Mead,
1935b, chapt. 4. The other types of stealing which occur are:
killing a pig known to belong to another under pretense that its cut
ears could not be seen, as revenge for its trespassing; pathological
stealing, such as that practiced by Kule, who seemed to be reenact-
ing his theft of his brother's wife (see below, p. 160), or that of the
young relative of Agilapwe who stole my matches when I refused
to buy from him, carrying off another man's wife for someone
else's use or at someone else's behest. In all these cases, stealing is
symbolic behavior and not directed towards real material ends; even
in the case of the trespassing pig, the owner was subsequently invited to come and collect his pig which had been killed "by mistake," and the perpetrator of the misdeed gains nothing but
satisfaction.

tive rules which, in contrast to the formulated rights and privileges, express the Arapesh ethos, their feeling about the relationship between a man and the property which he happens to inherit or acquire in any way. The most important of these negative rules forbids the use of one's own mother's or sisters' own pigs and own yam surplus. To this should be added the prohibition against a hunter's eating his own kill, interpreted by the Arapesh as an admonition to give the meat to others, just as the preceding set of prohibitions carries, by implication, the insistence that mothers, sisters, pigs, and yams should be given to others.[7] Large trees on one's land cannot be cut down without a special request being made of the ancestors to whom the land really belongs. In Arapesh feeling, as expressed in a hundred small acts and attitudes, land belongs to the ancestors, and the present generation merely lives on it. As the father assigns all of the good tools and weapons every day to his half-grown sons, but continues actually to use them himself, so the ancestors permit that it be said that this land belongs to one or another of their living descendants, who must exercise his right with care. He must address his ancestors and actually ask permission before cutting down trees, especially breadfruit trees, under penalty of supernaturally imposed sanctions, wind and rain which will knock down his house or devastate his garden. Here one comes directly upon an articulate contrast within the Arapesh formulations, the land belongs to Balidu, Sumali, and Baimal, but if they are to make any use of it, they must ask permission of their ancestors.

Whereas the sanction which lies behind the requirements concerning female relatives, pigs, yams, and one's own kill are mainly social—for the man who disregards these prohibitions suffers primarily a diminution of his social ties, a social ostracism, a branding as an *alomato'in*, a refusal of permission

[7] In connection with the hunting prohibition, it is interesting to note that the Mundugumor possess a similar prohibition. A hunter may not eat his own kill or it will spoil his magic. This taboo functions in Mundugumor to prevent much hunting because if one hunts one must give the game away; if one ever eats from the pot in which that game has been cooked, one's hunting magic is spoiled; by hunting one becomes vulnerable to the malice of others, ergo, it is better not to hunt.

to participate in important ceremonial[8]—the sanctions which protect land from trespass from all living persons, including, be it noted, the putative owners, are all supernatural. Gardens and hunting grounds are guarded along their boundaries by ghostly ancestors who watch and punish any failure to observe their rights in the gardening and hunting land, with wind, rain, and with particularistic failure—as by blinding the eyes of the trespassing hunter so that he fails to see game. So no man finds it necessary to defend his rights to land which belongs to the ancestors who are quite capable of defending their own rights.

Every man has garden land and a house site. If his father's lands were not sufficient for all of his father's sons, some other relative will assign a plot to him. Some unused house site is always available or a new hamlet can be built, and because of the custom of doubling up for gardening, a great part of the gardening land is always unused. Some men have no hunting land, for if no one of a man's sons shows any interest in or aptitude for hunting, his hunting land may pass to a brother's or sister's sons. This is particularly likely to happen if he himself is a good hunter, for then he will seek some avid young apprentice among his male relatives to whom he can bequeath his hunting lore and magic. His grandsons, if any one of them wishes to hunt, will in turn have to find an uncle or a cousin, hunt with him, learn from him, and ultimately inherit his rights. Coconut and sago palms are also somewhat unevenly owned; some fathers are more industrious than others in providing for their sons, or a family line may suddenly narrow down to one descendant who then inherits a great many palms. Palms are the nearest approach to capital; an Arapesh man who has plenty of sago may ask some other relative to cut it for him, as their joint contribution to some feast, but he is thereby not relieved of working for the feast, only relieved of working sago. Coconuts are almost entirely reserved for feasts and mothers of new born babies, and so individual ownership of them is virtually meaningless.

In contrast to these non-possessive attitudes towards land

[8] In the case of the yams, a man's ability to grow yams will suffer if he eats from yams descended from his own *abullu* seed.

and game, the Arapesh have a marked sense of ownership about anything into which they have put work. This applies particularly to children or women whom they have grown, pigs they have grown, and also to houses they have built or for which they have hunted and grown food to pay others to build. Here pride in achievement and admiration of the amount of hard work one has put into the task combine to give a strong possessive tinge. Most of the quarrels, which sometimes even lead to fighting between different hamlets, arise from disputes over a pig or a woman. Quarrels between individuals arise when a man who has fed the grandmother of a pig claims but does not receive one of the grandchildren or the return payment for one of the grandchildren; or, when the maternal kin of a child who have reared it demand payment for its growth from the paternal kin who wish to reclaim it; or when a woman remarries outside the gens which has grown her and the new husband fails to recompense the gens. The recompense demanded is always small, a couple of rings, a small piece of pig, a plate or so; its value is symbolic rather than actual for it serves in no way to meet the actual expenditure of food over which the quarrel ostensibly rages. But as growing things is the proudest deed of an Arapesh, he becomes angry at any act which throws into doubt his having grown some thing or some person. If another man carelessly marries his brother's widow and makes no payment, this is equivalent to saying, "I don't believe that your gens invested much food in her anyway, therefore I owe you nothing." And the failure to send a little piece of the feast from the pig's grandchild is equivalent to denying the hard work involved in feeding the pig's grandmother. The extent to which these apparently economic quarrels are symbolic is clearly demonstrated in a study of the reconciliations, the way in which the most fantastic equivalences will be accepted as having compounded the dispute.[9] So what appears to be at first sight a contradiction between the Arapesh casual attitude towards land, trees, and tools, and their strenuous insistence upon rights in women and pigs, is seen to be not really a contradiction at all. They themselves assume

[9] See below, the way in which Amito'a was regarded as a return for Tapik (p. 329).

no responsibility for the land, the trees, the tools, and they cannot therefore be wounded in their sense of achievement in regard to them. They are part of the land which will take its own revenge. But growing is the only achievement which they know, the ability for which they limit their sexual desires and control their aggressiveness, the ability for which they have tabooed and sacrificed and labored, and any act which attacks that attacks a vital point.

Because of the general lack of possessiveness about things, there are very few rules in Arapesh about trespass, or length of tenure, or usage. I found no rules about the selection of trees, for instance. A man cuts trees for house building on his own land; if there are none on his own land, he expresses his need and one of his associates gives them to him. In hunting, the man who saw the game had the first claim upon it.

## THE EFFECT OF INHERITANCE

Because there is so little fixed capital among the Arapesh and so little of that can be used in any way to the advantage of the owner, inheritance has very little to do with a man's future position. By charting the importance of the men of the last generation in terms of the attitude towards the bones and the records of their feasts, I did find that the sons of a strong man stood a better chance of being strong men than the sons of a weak man or of a man who had died young. But they stood this chance because of the effect either of inherited ability or early training and example, not because of accumulated goods. If a father leaves his sons coconut trees, those trees are always tabooed for some feast. If he left him sago, that too must be cut to meet extra-household obligations. Houses fall to pieces in a few years and rings are dissipated for death payments. Any man can in a few years become as prosperous as Arapesh standards permit, if he is industrious, has hard-working wives, and makes fortunate working combinations among his relatives. As his gardens improve, his obligations increase, that is all.

On the other hand, a son is not in any way left handicapped by his father's debts. Obligations are usually shared by a number of near age mates who, when a man dies, will complete them. A young boy is under no special obligation to those who paid for his marriage; this is a small matter, in any event. He must help the men who fed him, but that includes most of the men of the community, and in helping them he is merely following the path which he will follow all through life.

## A Man's Immediate Economic Obligations

We may now turn from the Arapesh attitude towards property, towards ownership of things and persons, to the culturally standardized attitudes towards production and distribution. What are the economic obligations of an Arapesh man to produce? With the exception of the hunter, who often specialized considerably, these are very similar for every man. A married man among the Arapesh is expected to shelter his household, to build and keep in repair for them the necessary number of houses, which includes shelters in gardens and sago patches. He is expected to keep each wife in a separate house if his wives quarrel. He is not expected to build a house of any great proportions or beauty; indeed, he is not allowed to build such a house himself. All conspicuous house building has to be done by men who can afford to give feasts as they build. So the building of a large house, like the making of an *abullu,* is a device for distributing surplus to the community, a productive act expected of the prosperous. Young married men without children may, however, live with relatives, if the women get on well together. There is no hard and fast rule; a man is merely expected to house his family decently, that is, not to house quarreling persons together, nor leave the roof in such bad repair that everyone is rained upon at night. Where he gets his house is a matter of indifference; he may merely build with materials of a disused old house belonging to some relative[10]; he may share another man's house, although if he has children this is regarded as a sign of shiftlessness, if it is not compensated for by a large house somewhere else, to which he can invite others.

[10] As Ombomb did with Matasues' ground house, p. 221.

He is furthermore expected to make gardens and this includes the planting of taro and yams. An unmarried man, unless he is responsible for a widowed mother, will only plant yams and will assist his father or brother in preparing the taro patches on which the women will work. A married man is expected to account for yam planting himself and for taro patches for his wife or wives. Failure to do the former is regarded as improvident and lazy, but the man who fails to keep his wives' taro patches in good shape is failing in a definite duty.[11] For the Arapesh household depends for subsistence upon the day-by-day yield of the taro gardens. If it were not for the yams and sago which are distributed at feasts, people would be far more undernourished than they are, but it is failure to provide taro which threatens a household with actual hunger.

The most important aspects of gardening for which a man is responsible are clearing (by lopping off the branches and ringing the large trees and cutting down the small trees) and fencing and thereafter keeping the fences in repair. Failure to keep one's fences in repair is an omission for which other people are permitted to rebuke one; only the most violent man would dare to keep his fences in disrepair, because to him alone would people be afraid to speak. It is a good thing for a man to have pigs, but raising pigs is regarded as difficult. If a man's wife has no luck with raising pigs and if the pigs he places about with his relatives die, he is treated with pity rather than with moral condemnation. Hunting is regarded more as a definite art; only certain men have hunting magic and training. If a man with magic and ability endangers his hunting prowess by quarreling with people who are in a position to injure his hunting, i.e., people to whom he has previously given game (Class Two relatives), or engages in sorcery traffic which spoils his hunting, this is regarded as wrong and subject to public comment and disapproval from the old men.[12] But not to be in the habit of hunting is not reprehensible. A man makes his own G string,

[11] See *Diary,* La'abe and Bischu's comment upon Ombomb's failure to provide for Me'elue's taro gardens, p. 418.

[12] See below for attitude towards Bischu (p. 175).

as does a woman her aprons, and the question of clothing is not considered a matter of economic duty.

Maintaining trade connections is again an optional undertaking. The man who meets a few such obligations, he who makes perhaps three or four trips a year, to his Beach friends and his Plains friends, and so keeps himself supplied with tools and utensils, is regarded as admirable. A greater interest in trade, one which makes a man so neglect his planting that his yams sprout in the yam house, and he plants only two crops in three years, is not quite good. It is not to be placed beside the solid contributions of gardening, hunting, and pig raising.

These basic economic activities are the ones in which a man engages for the sake of his own household, as if each household were a separate and independent unit. And it is worth noting that with the exception of building very large houses (which are not actually needed) all Arapesh techniques are adapted to single household living and do not rely upon the cooperation of larger groups of people. Actually a man alone or a woman alone would do quite well, technologically, for both men and women share a knowledge of most techniques; men hunt, but women collect small grubs and caterpillars; both sexes garden and cook; both prepare clothing; both make rope and string. The elaboration of economic obligations as between members of different households must therefore be regarded as being founded in the emphases of the social organization rather than in the dictates of the techniques themselves.

## Extra-Household Economic Obligations

Extra-household obligations may be divided into two groups, those which serve to strengthen ties between individuals or groups and which are therefore primarily sociological and only secondarily economic in function, and those which serve to redistribute within the group any surplus which may have accumulated and be temporarily in the hands of one of a few individuals. Very often one feast serves both functions.

All obligations to relatives, whether they be the informal

obligation to help a patrilineal Class One relative or the formal obligations to Class Two relatives, come under the first heading. They are primarily forms of validating ties. This is particularly so in the case of the *rite de passage* payments to Class Two relatives. The payments themselves are not important; it is what they stand for, the pledge of social solidarity between individuals, which is important.[13] When a *rite de passage* payment is made the occasion for a large feast—as for instance the Waginara feast to end mourning which was made the occasion of a great exchange of pigs —it may still serve the same purpose (p. 414). As in the small *rite de passage* feast, rings of exactly the same size are exchanged, and individuals thereby bound closer together, so in the enlarged *rite de passage* feast, pigs of exactly the same size are exchanged, and hamlets or even localities, through their representative participants, are bound closer together. In such cases there is very little extra distribution of food; the major emphasis is upon the exchange of equivalents, although in the large feast and in the small, social license is always given to consume more meat on the spot than would otherwise be permitted, as if it were said, "This society's safety has been enhanced today by this display of solidarity and it is, therefore, safe for us to eat some of our most cherished reserves, our pigs."

Before considering the second type of obligations, it is necessary to consider the question of surplus.

## FEASTS[14]

### DISPOSITION OF SURPLUS

Feasting, among primitive peoples, can very well be attacked from the standpoint of surplus. If, in regard to the economic functioning of any society we ask, "Is there a sur-

[13] See below, a series of *rite de passage* payments illustrating how very scant is the amount of property involved (pp. 284, 290, 292, 297).

[14] Mead, 1938, pp. 216–219.

plus, and if so, who gets it?"[15] we find that feasting, taken in its widest sense, as the use of food for ceremonial rather than merely routine subsistence, is a first consideration. We come first to the distinction between ceremonial economic games which are played almost entirely with surplus and those which are part of the every day routine life of the community. Such a contrast can be drawn between the feasting of the Northwest Coast, with the great destruction of oil and the interchange of unused blankets, and the typical Oceanic exchanges of economic goods which are subsequently consumed in an ordinary manner. In the Northwest Coast, the ceremonial economic life can be construed as a way of using surplus, as an essential in the equilibrium of a competitive rich society, which has already permitted individual ownership and accumulation to threaten its stability. From this point of view, all ceremonies of display and exchange in which more is consumed, either in pure destruction, in conspicuous waste, or in forms no longer of immediate subsistence value to the society, may be regarded as the consumption of surplus goods. If, on the other hand, the ceremonial exchanges, in spite of their pomp and display, are merely ways in which the ordinary necessary food supply is distributed in various bizarre or special ways, then such tribute to a chief or other ceremonial exchange of food is not consumption of surplus. The feast or its equivalent is a form of distribution serving other than economic ends, perhaps, as it bolsters prestige, establishes ties between families or clans, or validates claims to position. If we compare, for instance, the noonday feast during village work in Samoa, to which some household contributes a pig, which is then cooked ceremonially by the young men's organization and eaten by the whole group, with the presentation of a thousand fine mats at a great marriage ceremony of a Samoan high chief, we have the contrast. In the village feast, the food which the sum total of the households of the village

[15] This question was proposed to me as primary by Dr. Erich Fromm when I was attempting to organize the material on *Cooperation and Competition,* and I have found it of the greatest usefulness in probing the dynamics of a society. Mead, 1937a, pp. 487–488.

would have eaten separately was merely eaten ceremonially and in such a way that it was possible for everyone to have a share of one pig without the waste which would have ensued in a community with no means of keeping meat, if each household had killed a pig. But in the matter of the fine mats, time and effort which might have gone into necessities, but which were not needed because there were already sufficient, go into their plaiting. Aside from being stores of value they have no other usefulness than conspicuous consumption. Here we are dealing with surplus.

After so much emphasis has been laid on the very low standard of living of the Arapesh, on the insufficiency of food for minimum nourishment, it may seem ridiculous to inquire whether they have a surplus. But this depends entirely on the definition of surplus. If we define surplus as wealth which is created after all the necessary demands of the human body for food, warmth, and shelter have been met, according to some external standard based upon sciences like dietetics, then the Arapesh have no surplus whatsoever. Every Arapesh is undoubtedly undernourished. The entire resources of the community are not adequate to raise the standard of living until each one is properly nourished. But if, instead, we examine the situation from within, we find that the Arapesh do have a surplus. From their point of view, they do have wealth, in the form of food and the things which will purchase food, i.e., rings, tobacco, feathers. They can devote these to uses over and above the daily nourishment of the body. This surplus is consumed in purchasing dance complexes from the Beach and in buying immunity from death from the Plains. In both cases wealth leaves the community in a ponderable form which might have been converted into food and returns in a form which, in the case of dance complexes, can only partially be converted into food, and in the case of the imponderable, immunity from sorcery, purchased from the Plains, can never be reconverted into food. Neither the Plains nor the Beach peoples make any returns here; year after year the pigs of the Mountains are carried down to the Beach; rings and knives go into the Plains and imponderables are received in return.

If then we ask, "If there is a surplus, who gets it?" our

question reverts to the Arapesh Mountain communities. Who consumes the imponderables, the dances, the costumes, the songs, which come from the Beach? Here we see that this expenditure is actually socialized so that instead of the food which paid for the dance becoming part of the bodies of all the members of the society, the dance and its properties become the possession of all. When it is over, the big man who, as the "trunk," organized the purchase, has nothing except the slight prestige of having brought his people successfully through the purchase of a dance which will give them several hours of delight. The exigencies of the coastal trading peoples, working within a framework of localized trade which permits the sale of imponderables, have produced a situation which drains off part of the resources of the Arapesh people, but although this actually impoverishes them, it has not changed the social emphasis among themselves.

When we discuss the purchase of immunity and return to health from the Plains, it is again a question of an individual life, valuable to his community, being purchased by a drain upon his own resources or those of his brothers and associates. When a sorcery search party goes into the interior to find and bribe the sorcerer, a number of people, relatives or associates of the sick man, give several days for the trip, straining their trade relationships, perhaps contributing rings to the bribe, to buy back for the group the life of a "good man." If the sick person is old or infirm or chronically diseased, no such group effort is made; an individual relative may exert himself if he wishes, but the concerted efforts of the group are reserved for the man who is of value to it.

Now when we discuss feasting among the Arapesh, we can place it within this context—the feasts which are the means of collecting a surplus to be paid to a Beach village for imponderables which will again be socialized, the intra-village feasting which is a mechanism for distributing necessary foods in ways serving other than purely economic ends because they cement kin ties and provide for various sorts of social solidarity, and the distributions which are ways of socializing the surpluses of individuals. Such feasting may also be said to serve an economic end because the non-economic ends for which the feast is ostensibly organized, the validation of an initiation, validation of a hamlet's prestige, validation of a marriage, etc., all serve to mobilize energies in the collection and pursuit of food which might otherwise lie dormant. If Arapesh economic activity is closely scrutinized, it is found that only taro and greens are regarded as having been planted to meet the everyday demands of the people. Sago working, hunting, pig raising, yam gardens—all of these meet the demands of feast occasions. Without these extra foods, no single piece of which is ever wasted at a feast, the people could not survive in even as badly nourished a state as they do. Feasting with its non-economic overtones remains the mechanism through which they actually do the work to produce the food.

There is a great deal of confusion in the discussion of primitive economics and the insistence either that very simple peoples, like the Eskimo, are entirely governed by economic considerations, or that wealthy people, like the Trobrianders, are moved by quite other considerations. If the problem be approached through an examination of how much of what the people produce is a surplus and how much is essential —in their own terms—to the basic needs of life, then one may further examine the mechanisms by which the necessary wealth is mobilized to meet these fundamental needs. It will then undoubtedly be found that there is a great difference between cultures in the extent to which purely economic motives, that is, the desire for the means of survival (under which should be included freedom from outside attack), are blended with non-economic and insurance motives which are to a great degree cultural artifacts or attitudes acceptable only to certain types of character formation. It may furthermore be argued that at the very lowest range of subsistence, where there is no surplus, there is also less free energy to devote to the elaboration of such non-economic motives as display, prestige, validation of moral worth, and the like. But it may also be argued that once a mere minimum of free energy has been turned to such an elaboration of cultural motives, the society has reached a further integration which makes it possible for it to utilize more fully its unchanged natural resources.

The relationship between Arapesh working groups and the yam consumption of the Arapesh is a case in point. We have seen[16] how the Arapesh had altered the traditional yam-planting methods of the area so that the harvest was staggered, and there were yams all the year round. While this practice has not necessarily influenced either the number or the quality of yams produced (for while it may well have done so, because the extra stimulus provided by working in a group may have resulted in better gardening, it is even more possible to argue that this is more than compensated for by the forays of pigs into unguarded gardens), it may very well have been economically beneficial in its effect on the way in which the yams were utilized in the Arapesh diet. A yam-dependent people will eat yams until they are consumed, and then undergo a miserable period of hunger, eked out with poor substitutes. The Arapesh have spread their combination of yams and less nourishing foods over the entire year. Aside from the beneficial results of the absence of a starvation period, from the standpoint of nutrition, this may actually be a more economical use of the same quantity of yams.

The concentrated hunting drives which precede a feast for which meat must be obtained are far more productive than the Arapesh everyday habit of "walking about in the bush to find game." Lackadaisical individual hunting has been transformed into a much more purposeful activity by the pressure of a motive which is non-economic in content, although it may be strictly economic in function.

If we once realized that there are no such things as economic facts, but only economic aspects of facts, that a feast may be economic from one point of view, religious from another, and aesthetic from a third, we would be able to abandon at one stroke a great deal of purposeless controversy about primitive economics.

## MECHANICS OF FEAST ORGANIZATION

Among a people who live on such a narrow margin as the Arapesh, the giving of any large feast is very difficult and

[16] Mead, 1938, pp. 212–223.

entails a great deal of preliminary planning, tabooing of coconuts, marking of pigs, special planting of gardens, building
up credit with gift friends, etc. The man who undertakes to
organize any feast, either one of the large feasts on the *rite
de passage* pattern, or an inter-locality purchase or exchange
or repayment for initiation, must assure himself of adequate
and reliable help from many others. He does this in two ways:
by relying on the help of his close relatives and the close
affinal kin of his close relatives (in other words, on the people
who have encouraged him to undertake extensive economic
operations in the first place), and second, by establishing
formal ties with a group of members of the opposite dual
division (ideally), who will formally undertake to help him,
and who will formally participate in the honors of the feast,
while his close relatives who help him informally will participate only informally.

The principal of such a feast is called the "trunk" (*bauwanag*), and the men whose help he formally requests and
secures are called the "dogs" (*nubag*). The "trunk" gives
three feasts, the *abi'at*, the *tapa'as nubat*, and the *dah*. At
each of these, he kills one or more pigs, serves coconut croquettes, the feast food, and distributes some raw food—yams,
coconuts, and sago. How the return on these feasts is to be
made will depend upon the further distribution. If only one
or two men accept the whole feast, each time it is made,
they will be obligated to return pigs upon which they have
no further claim, as their share of the preliminary feasts is
supposed to equal one pig. Alternatively, they may each redistribute the sections of the feast to some four or five people,
and so spread the obligation among a number of people,
who are then obligated to put a pig in the final exchange,
for which, however, they must receive a pig in return. I
have called this type a chain feast, because the food first
passes along a whole chain, establishing the obligation. The
pig then comes back along the same chain, and ultimately
the return for the pig, after all the pigs have been assembled
in one place, as at the Waginara feast (see below, p. 414),
follows along the same chain. The former system, the simple
dog feast in which the "dog" returns as vomit (*gogwilis*)
just what he has received, is used for the smaller *rite de*

*passage* feasts, and for the purchase of dance complexes and other imponderables, when, of course, no repayment in pigs can be expected. The chain type of preliminary feast is an elaboration of the dog feast and is used in the post-initiatory feast organization,[17] and in the preparation of large intra-locality exchanges.[18]

In the *Diary* I have given exact descriptions of the feasts which I saw and the distribution of the food there. The statement of the above pattern was derived from studying these examples and from discussions with informants. But I found that it was impossible to get reliable information about any complicated economic transaction that I did not witness. Even then, it was necessary to know all of the participants to follow fully what happened. Accounts of future events and accounts of what had taken place only yesterday were equally unreliable. Reconstructing events which had taken place even within the last few months was equally hopeless. It is therefore quite possible that I have missed some significant aspects of these various feasting patterns. The only safeguard that I had was that I did not collect any isolated pieces of information which failed to check with the pattern as outlined here.

## FORMS OF EXTRA-HOUSEHOLD ECONOMIC TRANSACTIONS

As the Arapesh make no distinction between payments, presents, and feasts, all being classed together in feeling so that a feast to a mother's brother is called a payment for blood, for instance, it is possible to classify together all these different forms. They are:

1. Simple payments, typically of cooked food garnished with meat, made to Class One relatives or persons who temporarily assume a Class One status, in return for small services rendered or about to be rendered, either informally as in

17 Aden's, p. 213.
18 Ombomb's, p. 281.

building a fence, or more formally as to the midwife, the sponsor in an *abullu* ceremony, etc.

2. Payments to Class Two relatives, typically rings and un-cooked meat, accompanied by a small feast, in response to situations in which the Class Two relative was conceived as having a right to demand these payments—betrothal, first menstruation, childbirth, scarification of a girl, initiation of a boy, death, battle wounds, or loss of dignity through insult, the giving of an *abullu*. Repayments of these.

3. Payments which are concerned with clinching a bargain or establishing future obligations, typically rings or pieces of uncooked meat, as payment to a gift friend for a pig or pay-ment for a child which is to be adopted or payment of a ring to a *gabunyan* in another village. Here the gift friend, the friendly helpful person at a distance, is the prototype *vis-à-vis*. In transactions between close relatives the procedure be-tween gift friends is imitated slightly, while the procedure for *gabunyans*, contracting heads of a prospective ceremonial exchange between two localities, is virtually identical with that of gift friends, but on a larger scale.

4. Payments of food, cooked or uncooked, which establish a future obligation to assist in contributing to a large feast. These solicitory feasts have several variants, but the most typical is that in which a leader, a "trunk," calls a series of other men "dogs," and makes them a series of feasts, in re-turn for which they contribute a pig, sometimes outright, sometimes only against a return payment of another pig of the same size. The major distinction between the return of these solicitory feasts and the help which a man renders his close relatives, both Class One and Class Two, is that the payment of food which is accepted as establishing a binding obligation is accepted formally. The recipient runs around the display shouting *gugu gugu*, as much as to say, "I accept your challenge."

5. Payments to *buanyins* which have to be returned in kind and more or less on call, typically large pieces of wild game, or pigs, sometimes accompanied by a small feast.

## PAYMENTS FOR SMALL SERVICES

It would be possible to say that everything in Arapesh is paid for, that a man does not perform the simplest service for another, nor a woman cook a meal for her husband's brother's wife, without a payment. For helping with building a house, for scarifying a niece, for helping build a fence, for every single special service of this sort, pay must be given. Although this would be a perfectly accurate statement, it would do gross violence to the spirit in which these payments are made in Arapesh. Among a commercially minded people like the Manus, it is possible to say that transactions even between brother and sister are all commercial, strictly accounted for; the more intimate transactions take their pattern from the market place. Among the Arapesh, the opposite is true: the more distant relationships with trade friends take their pattern from the interrelationships between relatives. These are not commercial but ceremonial and symbolic. The type of Arapesh payment for small services can be found in the *baik* feast which is made by the men of a hamlet for the women who have helped them during the feast, who have carried the firewood, water, and cooking leaves, who have carried the taro and yams, and who have borne the brunt of the cooking. When the feast is over, the men will give a special small feast, garnished with meat, to their own wives, their mothers, and sons' wives. And this is done in no spirit of accounting, but out of courteous consideration for the labors of the women.

This feast may be taken as the prototype for all payments which are not part of the regular feast organization scheme, nor payments to Class Two relatives or to *buanyins*. They are typically made to Class One relatives and most often to members of one's own gens. When Class Two relatives help a man build a house or fence a garden, they do so, *qua* brothers, and lay aside their other forms of relationship. And so in all such formal helpfulness, when a man builds a small house or a large house, when his wife has a child, when his daughter menstruates and must be painted and cared for, he makes a small feast of meat. Also when a man exorcises someone who is ill from a disease of which he owns the exorcism, he is paid, sometimes with a small feast, or at least with areca nut and tobacco which are regarded as smaller denominations of food. The significant thing about all these payments is that rings are never used; food and areca nut and tobacco, and always cooked food, may be used in this way, within the group, for courtesy payments.

When new magic or new divinatory practices are imported, they are sometimes paid for to a member of another tribe. For a time, the new Arapesh user will demand a fee; but sooner or later this tendency wears down, and the man who exercises his magic finds that he must exercise it out of helpfulness and for courtesy fees only. This type of payment also carries no coercion with it. If one's child is sick and one thinks it is from the yam charm of one's cousin, one asks him to come and charm. If he comes, he is given a courtesy payment, but he may refuse to come just as he would refuse any other request *for help*.

Behind these small payments also lies the prohibition against people's feasting themselves; all meat should be given away to Class Two relatives or to Class One relatives with whom one is on a formal, *quasi* Class Two relationship. But if there are others of one's own group there, working, helping one cut or thatch or fence, then a feast is justified. The own group—the self—is transformed into two parts; the brother who is working for one is not quite the same as the brother who is identified with oneself, and so, at such a feast, meat can be eaten without guilt. The symbolism here is very much that of the individual who permits himself a treat of some forbidden sweet because he has made some other propitiatory payment to his conscience.

## PAYMENTS TO CLASS TWO RELATIVES

All *rite de passage* payments, the payments which are primarily concerned with validating and consolidating affinal and matrilineal ties, are made to Class Two relatives, and the prototypes of this payment are the ring and uncooked meat. There are substitutes for the ring. Strings of shell money, shell ornaments, dogs' teeth, and, today, knives and money may be used, but behind them lies always the concept of the ring. With very few exceptions (pp. 118–120), these rings are always returned with rings of equal size and finish and beauty, and there is absolutely no gain to either side in the transaction. The payments of meat are also returned, although without the articulate symmetry which places the given ring beside the returned ring to show how perfectly they match.

It may be said, however, that conceptually, Class Two payments are not returned. A man talks of the rings he paid for his son's wife, to his son's mother's brother, for the birth of each child, to his mother's brother when he was wounded, and which he pays as death payments, as if none of these had ever been returned. But this is because he wishes to claim recognition for his virtue, for his energy in initiating the payments. There is no virtue in having made a return on such payments. The Arapesh do not, as do the Manus, boast of having paid their debts. Repayment of rings and meat is the normal and natural behavior for the good man, and a dilatory failure to repay is just as congenial behavior to the cantankerous and intractable man, such as Agilapwe. Only in the licensed quarrels between *buanyins* is the matter of repayment ever discussed. The habitual defaulter, the man who accepts rings in payment for a female relative and then "sends them about all over the place" instead of repaying them, will only be upbraided, when he himself by more bad behavior brings down the storm (see p. 293).

Actually, in most of these Class Two exchanges of valuables, one relative is merely trusting another, showing his appreciation of the tie between them, working to make it stronger, in full knowledge that he will lose nothing thereby. And when men object to their sister's marriage because she has not been properly paid for, it is because they object to their brother-in-law's cavalier behavior, not that they hope to make any profit out of the transaction.

Stated formally, we may say, a man must pay rings to Class Two relatives on the following occasions:

| Occasion | Payment Made to | By |
|---|---|---|
| 1. Betrothal of his wife<br>*Ei sabo'mo eshauh*<br>(I put a net bag on her head) | Girl's father | Boy's father |
| 2. When the girl reaches adolescence<br>*ne natalu* | Young husband | Brother-in-law<br>Wife's brother |
| 3. When a child is born<br>*shi sulupa alalagi*<br>(They pay for the cord and afterbirth) | Husband | Wife's brother |

Here one ring for a boy and two rings for a girl are kept by the wife's relatives. This is to pay for the blood of the child. There is a greater payment for the girl, because otherwise there can be a claim such as that made by Agilapwe (see p. 293) when her marriage payment comes in.

4. At death

For a child, the payment is made by the father to the child's mother's brother; for a man, by his surviving brothers and sons to the mother's brothers or mother's brother's sons of the deceased; and for a woman to the brothers or brother's sons of the deceased. The rings paid on this occasion and the payment itself are spoken of as *gaba,* but of the payment for a woman they say *sha abalik.*[19]

These are the only payments which are inevitable in terms of the normal maturation of the individual. Even here, if there are no close Class Two relatives alive, the death payments may be omitted, which shows clearly that this set of payments is conceptualized as the right of actual individuals who stand in a definite relationship to the maturing individual, the woman of their gens and her children. There is no sense here that there must be a death feast to honor the dead, or a payment for a child in order that its birth may be legal-

---

[19] For samples of such payments, see below, p. 500.

ized. Nor is the familiar ancestral sanction of angry ghosts who disapprove of economic laxness in general present. If there are living relatives who have a right, they must be paid.

Important men, with yams and pigs and affairs of moment, become involved in an elaboration of these payments to their Class Two relatives, of two sorts:

1. The simpler payments of one or two rings, and a small feast, which accompany the performance of the *rites de passage*, may be enormously complicated by:

a. Formally invoking the help of other persons to make a large showing, by giving a series of solicitory payments.

b. Inviting the presence of the *tamberan* with all the additional ceremony and feasting which goes with the presence of the *tamberan*.

2. By taking advantage of the provision that all shed blood or the reception of any other wound, including an insult received in public, must be paid for to the matrilineal kin. This provision has its roots in the idea of shedding blood which belongs to the mother's gens, so that only a maternal kinsman can shed blood, and all other blood must be paid for. It has been used as the basis of a system by which the mother's brothers and cross-cousins, and their *buanyins* through identification with them, can demand heavy payments from any prominent man who suffers physical or social injury. Here again the elaboration proceeds by:

a. Involving other persons than those immediately concerned, particularly *buanyins*.

b. Invoking the *tamberan* in cases of insult, so that the whole male group of the community becomes involved and the victim has to feast the *tamberan*.

That this payment to the mother's brothers and their sons is a pattern which lies ready to the inventive is demonstrated by the fact that mother's brothers are now beginning to demand payment from a man who makes an *abullu*. He has shed no blood and has not been debased or insulted; he has, in fact, just been honoring himself. But the coincidence of the Ring Exorcism ceremony, usually associated with *rites de passage*, has apparently suggested to some inventive mind that here again the mother's brothers could initiate a demand for payments.

With the exception of the one or two rings left with the parents when a wife is paid for, and the rings paid for the child, and sometimes one ring left with each true mother's brother at a death, all of the rings and meat of these payments to Class Two relatives are returned. The phrasing is: "When a man dies, we pay the mother's brothers, the sister's sons, and the *buanyins*." Upon examination it is seen that when a man dies, payments are made to his mother's brothers and mother's brother's sons, and to their *buanyins*, and repayments are made to the sister's sons and their *buanyins*, in return for payments received—as mother's brothers, on some previous occasions.

Let us consider what happens when A, the husband of B, dies. Their son, C, makes payments to B's brother, D. When D dies, his son, F, not only makes payments to his mother's brother, E, but also must make return payments to C, for the payments C made to D when A died.

In the case of the death of an important man, the *buanyins* of both D and E may be involved.[20]

At their simplest, these payments to Class Two relatives are symbolic, a way of proclaiming the seriousness with which matrilineal and affinal ties are regarded. They represent hardly any strain economically, but a failure to make these payments can produce an enormous amount of bad feeling, distrust, and suspicion, which in turn has its reverberations in accusations of sorcery and failures in everyday relationships.

Economically, their chief importance is in providing a pattern upon which the more elaborate exchange functions to redistribute temporary surplus accumulated in the hands of one individual.

[20] See below for accounts of individual *rite de passage* payments: the payment for the wife of Anop (pp. 284–291), the payment for the wife of La'abe (pp. 292–294), a series of sample transactions at death (p. 500).

## FORMS OF EXTRA-HOUSEHOLD RETAINING FEES

The payments to clinch a bargain which cannot be completed on the spot again have a range from the very simple payment of a ring, a pot, or a net bag to a gift friend to "mark" a pig or a dog from one of a litter, up through the undertaking of a series of elaborate mutual relationships which may take years to consummate. They all, however, have the same pattern, the first slight payment which establishes the relationship, then the intermediate payments which extend over time. If the payment is for a pig, first there will be the ring, then the delivery of the little pig, and after it is grown, if it is a female, a return gift of one of its litter; if it is a male pig, a return from the feast in which it is finally butchered. When the transaction is of the grand type in which one locality purchases a dance complex or a new form of *tamberan* from another locality, the same pattern is followed. For each locality there is a principal, who acts as "trunk," as organizer of the preliminary feasts in his own locality, and contracts with the other principal, his *gabunyan*, to make the necessary payments. The *gabunyan* of the purchasing locality pays a ring, which is not returned, and sometimes a pig also. Then sometimes there are a few intermediate exchanges, culminating either in the great feast in which the complex is purchased, or else in a great exchange of pigs and coconuts, an *aubik*, or a feast of yams, a *pala'a*.

This pattern could be further extended so that, in the case of a great initiatory ceremony, the locality of the initiation acted as a kind of "trunk" with contracting *gabunyans* in every locality from which the novices came. Aden's feast was a feast in a series of this sort (see p. 213).

The internal arrangements in each locality were, of course, enormously complicated in these large feasts, but the fundamental relationship between the main principals remained the same. And it is interesting to note that the two types of purchase between gift friends which follow this pattern are of pigs and dogs on the one hand and of magic which will be tried out extensively before it is paid for on the other. And between localities the payments are either for future pigs or for the purchase of an imponderable, a dance complex or a new *tamberan*. In both latter types, the purchaser meets an unknown price; he makes anxious presents for these imponderables and hopes that the seller will be satisfied.[21]

## ECONOMIC RELATIONSHIPS WITH *Buanyins*

The form of the *buanyin* relationship, its approximation to Class Two relationship with a possibility of taking over any of three forms of Class Two relationships, mother's brother, sister's son, or brother-in-law, has been discussed above (p. 68) as has its function in channeling aggressiveness and providing one relationship in which dunning is permitted (p. 73). The economic function of the *buanyin* is, however, principally as a banker of unexpected kills of large game or unexpected presents of domestic pigs or game. In many respects the Arapesh have a hunting economy. The typical *rite de passage* feast is given by a man "when he has found meat." Even a larger feast, like a *balagasik* or an *abullu* feast, is deferred until "those who have gone into the bush find meat." But upon this very simple economic pattern which could not support large scale feasting has been laid a feasting pattern which is suited to domestic pigs. The domestic pig is the basis of most Oceanic planned feasting; in a few places replaced by dogs—Tchambuli—or by particularly reliable types of fishing. With pigs it is possible to plan far ahead, to undertake obligations and to meet them. The dog feasts and chain feasts and the intralocality feasting for which they are a preparation are all based upon the domestic pig. Yet the Arapesh have a very few pigs, and actually the meat that garnishes any feast is at least a third wild game. For weeks together, the meat that garnishes the plates of everyday meals is sometimes bits of smoked wild game. Between feasts, no pigs are eaten.

*Buanyins* represent a way in which a hunter, or the relative of a hunter, can bank a large kill of a bush pig, a casso-

---

[21] Ombomb's feast, p. 281, was a preliminary in a series given to meet obligations for an exchange which he had undertaken with Belagomini of Wihun as his *vis-à-vis*.

wary, a tree kangaroo, and later demand that this large kill be returned in kind or in a domestic pig. As the Arapesh are primarily trappers, they have slight control over when they will kill large animals, especially bush pigs and the domestic pigs that are always getting caught in their traps. If there is no Class Two relative who needs meat at the moment, then this large kill can be given to the *buanyin*, who cannot refuse it and who can be dunned for its repayment.

The *buanyin* relationship represents historically, I think, a fusion between the economic *vis-à-vis* patterns of Melanesia and the ceremonial friend patterns of New Guinea, and here, on this borderline between domesticated pigs and hunting reliance, plays a special role.

Typically enough, feasts made to *buanyins* are called *yapwigewek*, which is the term also applied to feasts between villages at which pigs are fastened but not cut. The exchange element is here stressed in the terminology.

I saw several small payments between *buanyins*[22] and heard discussions of obligations between them, but I did not see a feast. At a feast for a *buanyin* the *buanyin* himself does not eat but distributes the food among his helpers, and there is the peculiar feature of the hidden basket of food that the wife of the giver presents secretly to the wife of the receiver, which makes the difference between the good and bad *buanyin*, carrying out to the end the picture of commercial accounting and grudging generosity which is typical of *buanyins*.[23]

Only an enterprising man can maintain the demands of an active *buanyin* relationship. Similarly it offers great possibilities to an enterprising man, because by identifying himself with his *buanyins* in their claims on their Class Two relatives he may become involved in many more transactions, and in the end make many more feasts, by which honor is earned.

[22] See below, pp. 359, 395, 423, 441.
[23] This gift in the *serlau* basket is analogous to the *musui* payment in Manus, the payment made at night for which there need be no future accounting.

## THE ECONOMIC FUNCTION OF THE MOTHER'S BROTHER RELATIONSHIP

By virtue of their very one-sidedness, which the Arapesh take so much trouble to render nugatory, the mother's brother relationships, being understood in the wider connotations in which they have been discussed above (p. 49), have very definite economic functions. Whenever an event occurs in the life history of the individual, the mother's brother has a right to make a demand. Until a child is born the relationship between brothers-in-law is mainly symmetrical, except for the ceremony at first menstruation when the brother brings an elaborate present of weapons, pots, and baskets to his sister. But this is, at least in part, a newly introduced ceremony and is usually construed as a return for rings and meat which have been paid for the girl, although most of these have also been repaid in kind. From the time that a betrothal is undertaken, a continuous exchange of meat is set up between the two families, both informally as hunting luck or a share of feast brings them a bit of meat, and more formally as each is bound to help the other whenever any ceremony is afoot. But with the birth of the first child comes the payment to the mother's brother of two or three rings, and not of any great importance. The payment for the girl's scarification feast is equally slight, but the real events to which the mother's brother's rights act as a stimulus are the post-initiatory feasts for an adolescent boy and to a lesser extent the payments after a death. Although these are always phrased as a right of the mother's brother, they are always repaid in kind, and so it may be said that this mother's brother's right acts as a kind of trigger to the sluggish affinal exchange system, which is already kept working slowly by the prohibition against eating one's own meat, and the admonition to give this meat to mothers' brothers, sisters' sons, relatives-in-law, and *buanyins*. The unease, the possibility of hurt feelings and recriminations which lie in these fragile new affinal relationships, is shown by the fear of hunting spoiling magic, which also crops up in these relationships.[24] One is continually giving meat to one's affinal relatives and one fears that they will not consider that one has given enough. It is probable also that the men who resent most this continual economic drain on their own hunting efforts will be the ones to project this hostility upon their affinal relatives most easily, and believe that they have acted hostilely towards them. What individual cases I have of such accusations would bear this out.

So we have the Arapesh mechanism for widening domestic ties through the inclusion of affinal relatives and the ties between them and their children, the economic obligations which express and validate these ties, the suspicion and fear which go with all forming of new ties with strangers, the implementing of this fear with the mother's brother's curse and the bone binding hunting magic, and finally, the mother's brother's demands acting as the spur to special economic activities, just as the ties to affinals and mother's brother play continually into the system of informal game distribution.

In conclusion, it may be said that the Arapesh have, with some difficulty, combined the feasting mechanisms and the display exchanges which are more congruent with a better food supply with their meager resources in such a way as to stimulate production and completely socialize its results. The men who act as "trunks," as the leaders in economic undertakings, contribute a little more than other people, from their greater energy and resourcefulness. The man who makes an *abullu* adds to the supply of seed. The vigilant hunter adds to the supply of meat consumed by the whole community. The heaped-up food that is assembled for a feast is redistributed over two or three localities, until each member of 20 or 30 households has a little wisp of meat and a few extra croquettes. It is a truism that people always return from a feast hungry. This is not because there is any virtue in being hungry. The Arapesh do not, as do the Trobriand Islanders, parade a false modesty on the subject. Every man speaks fondly of the one time in his life when he had enough to eat, when he was inside the initiatory enclosure. For boys who are

[24] See Wabe's attitudes towards his affinal relations, in Mead, 1935b, p. 148.

being initiated, for the nursing mother, it is possible for a few weeks to collect enough food. Otherwise, the feasting, the exchanging of pigs and game, the husbanding of sago that is to be displayed on the plaza, or the yams that are to be built in an *abullu* are all gestures in the face of a great poverty. Because without the gesture there would be even less to eat, they honor those who assume the onerous task of organizing these feasts and call them "big men."

# Part II: Diary of Events in Alitoa

———◇———

## THE FUNCTIONING OF AN ARAPESH COMMUNITY, JANUARY 28 TO AUGUST 16, 1932

### SETTING UP THE HOUSEHOLD

In discussing the functioning of the village of Alitoa, which will be considered as a center of social activity since it cannot actually be called a unit, it is necessary to elaborate on the conditions of field work and the relations of the ethnologists' household and the local inhabitants. We are shifting here from a discussion of behavior patterns in which the actual behavior of named individuals is cited in illustration to a consideration of the behavior of a given group of individuals at a given period of time. As a background for the first part[1] of this report, it would have been adequate to state that the work was conducted in the native language, that informants were used to such and such extent, that they were in certain ways typical or atypical of the cultural emphases, that texts were collected in such and such instances, etc. However, such a statement of research methods is inadequate when the sociology of a native community is under consideration. We must allow not only for the eruption into a small, meagerly self-sufficient mountain community of two white people, intent upon studying it in detail, but also for their native household, each member of which also introduces new complications. Failure to make such allowance gives rise to various fantastic research plans, such as the longitudinal study of a

[1] Mead, 1938.

group of primitive children over a period of 10 years or so. If such a plan were carried out, it would be necessary to recognize that the presence of the investigator would continually alter the situation in which the native children were studied and render it increasingly atypical. The investigator is unable to discount at the time a great deal of the alteration which he brings with him, but it is possible that some part of it may be scientifically discounted in the final analysis.

When Dr. Fortune arrived in Alitoa in December, 1931, it was with the expressed intention of penetrating farther inland to the village of Naiyamikum, of which we had seen many photographs, through the courtesy of Dr. Briggs of Sydney University. Dr. Fortune had gone into the Arapesh country without personal boys. In the village of Umanep, he acquired two boys, Mindibilip of Maguer and Kaberman of Kobelen. During a short period of illness in Umanep, he made a preliminary sketch of the grammar of the language and discovered a rare linguistic ability in Mindibilip. Mindibilip and Kaberman had both been away to work for Mr. Davis, a plantation owner on "Wallis"[2] Island. They both spoke pidgin English, Mindibilip with greater fluency. After a day or so, at their instigation, two more boys were added to the household: Saharu, the "brother-in-law" of Kaberman, also of Kobelen; and Biagu, a cross-cousin of Mindibilip, also of Maguer. A man of about 25, who had had many years' experience working for the white man on Matty Island, who was a native of Umanep, and the husband of two wives, was also engaged as a shoot boy. Saharu, who was barely the size of a nine-year-old although he must have been about 13, was sent down to me at Karawop to become my personal boy.

Dr. Fortune arrived in Alitoa accompanied by Kaberman, Mindibilip, Biagu, and the shoot boy. All the hamlets between Alitoa and the Beach had turned out to carry our stores in; it had taken some 140 men to carry them so far. But the message which had been sent ahead to the more inland villages for more carriers brought a delegation of only 20 men from Wihun. As the map[3] shows, this is scantily populated

[2] Arapesh term for Valif and Tendanye Islands.
[3] Mead, 1938, Fig. 2.

country; furthermore, the inhabitants of the more inland hamlets are less willing to work for the white man than are the Beach people. A survey of the transportation situation made it seem virtually impossible to penetrate farther inland. Dr. Fortune began to negotiate with La'abe, the *tultul* (Government-appointed interpreter), in regard to building a house in Alitoa. He had been a night in the village, and the boys had already renewed old ties. Kaberman was a titular brother-in-law of La'abe; Mindibilip found gift friend brothers in the children of Sumali. The boys could vouch for the fact that Dr. Fortune was strangely interested in their language and customs, more concerned that his carriers were both well fed and well paid than with exacting the last ounce of strength from them.

The situation in Alitoa was favorable. There was actually room for a house, as an old *tamberan* house had recently been torn down on the site where our house was finally built. The *tamberan* house had been destroyed because there had been too much sickness attributed to exuviae secreted in the sacred flutes in it and in the wild taro growing on the hillside, which sloped sharply away from the site. This vacant house site was available, unkempt, but possible. But when the subject was broached to the Alitoa men, they demurred because they were planning to give a big feast in a few weeks. Good, said Dr. Fortune, he would like to see that feast. But, they countered, they would be very busy preparing for it, they had no time to build houses. However, after some argument, permission was given. Dr. Fortune told the 20 men from Wihun that they were to stay and help build the house. The site was measured. It extended from two of La'abe's areca palms on the northern boundary to Aden's house wall on the southern, including all the available space; in fact, in width it was to extend some 20 feet from the path through the village to the edge of the cliff. Temporarily, an unused house, which had once served as a *tamberan* house as well as a house where pig magic was elaborated (No. 13, Fig. 1), was put at Dr. Fortune's disposal. Here he placed all the stores in charge of Mindibilip and the shoot boy, and Dr. Fortune, Kaberman, and Biagu returned to Karawop. A week later, Dr. Fortune and myself, Kaberman, Saharu, and Biagu and the rest of our

stores arrived in Alitoa, which we found in a seething turmoil
of activity. The house frame was up; the floor was being laid;
a fence, with two gates for the path to keep the pigs out, had
been built around the central section of the village, half of
which our house now occupied. Everywhere groups of men
were seated sewing thatch, while a large party worked on the
house itself. Mindibilip, fat, beaming, bumptious, a feather
in his hair and a very impressive new *laplap*, stalked about,
bullying and bombasting. The people of Alitoa had completely
accepted our coming and had enlisted the help of all the
surrounding localities, Liwo, Numidipiheim, and Wihun, assigning special tasks to each. The techniques of interlocality
cooperation, invoked when a large *tamberan* house is built
and novices from several localities are initiated, were being
used here. As no large *tamberan* house was built during our
stay, this is the only opportunity we had to witness such large-
scale cooperation. Dr. Fortune had left a good supply of rice
and meat which the proud Alitoans served each day to all the
helpers. The great nightmare of an Alitoa feast, the fear of a
food shortage, was lacking, and everyone was in high good
humor. We were temporarily installed in the old house which
sheltered our stores and from there we supervised the completion of the new house.

Here I also had an opportunity to witness the methods of
directing work in large groups. I would say to La'abe, who
acted as director while Ulaba'i, the *luluai*, who spoke no
pidgin supervised dispensing the food, "I want a wall of
*ponkol* (P. E.[4] sago palm branch stems) here." He would
agree and, turning, remark into the air at random, "A lot of
*ponkol* needed here to make a wall." Sometimes such a remark evoked an immediate response. Two or three men
would seize knives and set off for the *ponkol*. Sometimes
nothing happened, in which case in a couple of hours' time
he would repeat the suggestion, in the hope that it would
fall on different ears. Sooner or later the *ponkol* would appear. Men would come, work for an hour or so, put on a
railing or fasten a wall, and then disappear, never to return,
although they knew there was to be a feast at the end of

[4] All pidgin English terms are designated P. E.

the house-building and gifts for all who had worked, in addition to the daily issue of food. Everything was done casually, without accounting, without hurry. It is also interesting to note that later when we tried to make a few trifling improvements in the house or mend a piece of floor where the *limbum* palm planks had worn out, it was impossible to get anyone to do it. We had to rely entirely on our own boys. But when they built our house, they accepted the task wholeheartedly, working as they would have on an important house-building of their own, but because of the lack of worry about food, with far more continuous concentration. During this entire period of almost two weeks, the unruffled surface was disturbed only by a dispute between Aden, Nyelahai, and Sumali, in which Nyelahai turned out the contents of his basket to account for the rings therein and to insist that he had not paid for *wishan* against Sumali's house which had burned down recently. One large knife disappeared and Dr. Fortune replaced it. Henalian of Alipinagle put in a claim that he had fed the grandmother of the pig killed by our shoot boy for the house-building feast. This claim was also settled. The pig was cooked and the feast served at noon of the day in which we moved into our new house. From the end of the ridge pole, which had been handsomely decorated with a *map*,[5] as if our house were a *tamberan* house, hung the temporary decorations of shredded sago leaves. The people lifted up our boxes and deposited them on the palm floor and vanished, quickly and unostentatiously, until by four o'clock in the afternoon only a handful, the actual residents of Alitoa, were left. The women, headed by Amito'a, came, standing at a distance, for they were still shy of me. It was weeks before anyone dared actually to touch me. They made a long speech saying that they would now have to go to their distant gardens for food because all their supplies were exhausted. Then they also went away. The sun went down on our first night in the new house with Alitoa, the largest village of the Mountain Arapesh, absolutely empty, except for ourselves and our boys, all newcomers. Never again, not even when almost 200 men gathered to carry our stores out of the

[5] Mead, 1938, Fig. 29, p. 241.

country, did we see so large a congregation of people, and I did not see many of the individuals again for weeks.

There now remains to give some account of the personalities of the five of their own people whom we had brought among them, a matter which was in some ways of far greater importance to the people of Alitoa than we were ourselves.

The shoot boy from Umanep was a sophisticated, fluent work boy, who had been absent from his people too many years and of his Arapesh inheritance retained only a love of gardening, which he claimed had finally brought him back, although he had had a wife among some fishing people elsewhere. He brought one of his wives to stay with him in Alitoa and cook for the boys, but we saw very little of him and his discharge will be recorded early in the *Diary*.

Mindibilip (Pl. 1b) occupied the position of head boy for several reasons. He had been left in charge while Dr. Fortune was away. He was the master's boy. While the others engaged in menial work, he sat on a box and gave important information all day. Actually, he did not have the strength of character to be head boy. Consequently a good deal of friction between the boys arose, as Kaberman resented his bullying, ineffective attempts at authority. Mindibilip was prodigiously fond of eating. His demands for three meals a day and those well garnished and cooked to his liking were a constant source of irritation in the household, in which the other boys laughed at his greediness. He was really an extremely precocious infantile person, a bully, and a swaggerer whenever he was given power, cowed and sulky before a show of force, good humored whenever there was a large enough quantity of good food in sight. He had been initiated hastily, in a small family initiation in Maguer. His parents were dead; his nearest relative was a father's brother who was himself something of a clown and wastrel. He had no sisters and no betrothed wife. Furthermore, because of his paucity of relatives he knew that he would find it hard to get one, for in Maguer, so much nearer the Beach, the emphasis upon sister-exchange was much greater than in the Mountains. He took a purely intellectual interest in language, always experimenting with new, logically possible, but idiomatically inadmissible, phrasings. In his use of language, he was flexible, adaptive, inventive; he fitted a new word into the gender on which its consonantal ending gave it the best claim, instead of merely classifying it as a foreign word and, therefore, belonging to the gender for such words, which ended in *has*. His personality is particularly important because Dr. Fortune's recorded texts are all his versions, sometimes of tales which he did not know himself and had to hear first from someone else, but ultimately it was he who dictated them for recording. The fine details differentiating one Arapesh version from another, and a comparison between Unabelin's and Mindibilip's renderings leave no doubt as to the role played by personality here—all are his. I have an impression that he was particularly fond of cannibal stories.

Kaberman (Pl. 1a) was much less intelligent than Mindibilip, but possessed of a stronger, more dependable character. Short, stocky, indomitable, he would stand up to a blow with his head up. He was much less fearful of the supernatural and inclined to consider some of the supernatural warnings which he had received as mere deception on the part of the old men to keep the young men in order. He had a high temper and a higher obstinacy. Although he was given the important position of cook boy, he never felt that he was sufficiently appreciated. Mindibilip had to do no menial work and was the master's boy; Saharu was my personal boy. He was no one's boy, nor was he boss boy. While working on Wallis Island he had received some training in the practice of the *sagumeh* cult, but the only part which had made any great impression was the training in possession. He sometimes combined this practice with the behavior which is the mild native version of running amuck, and with ears and eyes allegedly "fast," would terrorize the other boys after dark. His outburst after he was bitten by the centipede upon his return from the Kobelen trip (p. 403) is also highly characteristic. His betrothed wife Lamein, Saharu's "sister," was about 11 years old.

Saharu (Pl. 2a), tiny, wiry, indefatigable, violent, was as intelligent as Mindibilip, but with a very different type of mind. His whole attitude towards his environment was to master it, not to adapt himself to it. His parents were dead and his relatives were worried because he was growing so slowly.

He was brought to Dr. Fortune with the request that we take him and "grow him" on white man's food. He spent about 10 days at Karawop plantation with me where, under the tutelage of other boys of his own language group, he could observe a white household, every detail of which he reproduced faithfully upon our settling in the bush. He soon came to dominate the household, for his was far the strongest will among the boys. When his tiny stature interfered with his getting what he wanted, he burst into violent temper tantrums. We took him with us up the Sepik, by which time he was actually directing the household and would occasionally engage in ethnological research of his own, as he had seen me do. Throughout our stay he maintained the attitude of a superior among yokels, sniffing and glaring at naked Plainsmen who came up on the veranda during meal times, but he made warm friends with the village children in the moments of hilarity which he permitted himself in the intervals between the meticulous exercise of his duties.

Biagu was a distant relative of Mindibilip and, as such, pretty much dominated by him. He was also parentless, a stupid, emaciated waif, covered from head to foot with *tinea imbricata.* He had early made the passive adjustment to *tinea;* the active adjustment is to grow fat and to over-compensate with activity (see below, the case of Madje, p. 171). He knew that he would never have the rewards of an ordinary clean-skinned man; he would never have a wife; he must expect the remnants of a life, and would in return, as *alomato'in,* accept only the minimum of responsibility. He did for us the jobs which no one else would have been willing to do. He spent half of his time on the road between Alitoa and Karawop or between Alitoa and Wewak; in the intervals he cooked the boys' food and did other odd jobs. He was cheerfully irresponsible and mildly dishonest; he did not return when he was told to; he dallied on the road and feigned sickness; he assisted Mindibilip in his periodic truancies, but all this behavior was guaranteed to him by his culture in recompense for outlawing him as a "ringworm man." His chief ties in the village were with the household of Sinaba'i, an old family gift exchange tie.

After only a few days in the village, Mindibilip complained

that there was too much to do. He proposed the addition of a local boy, whom he called "brother" through gift friend ties, Gerud, the nephew of Balidu, the big man of Alitoa, and the son of Sumali, the hunter.

Gerud (Pl. 2b) was slight, wiry, and engaging. When we accepted him, we thought he was about 16 years old, but later inquiries revealed that he simply had not grown fast enough and was probably about 21. Beneath the slender exterior was a fully matured character; he was wary, a hunter and pursuer of game, possessive as was his father, and fearful of any restraining hand. He was up at dawn to make the fire; he was the most active in any local expedition; he grated coconut or pared taro; he absolutely refused to learn any of the household arts as practiced in a white man's house. He also refused to learn any pidgin. He was the principal *sagumeh* diviner during our stay in Alitoa. This proved exceedingly useful, as all but one divination took place in the village, and we were always advised of them beforehand. Because awkward points were likely to arise in a divination— for instance, someone was likely to suggest that the shoot boy could get no game because of magic which another community had placed on his shotgun—we found it necessary to exercise some indirect control over these divinations as they affected us. During dinner, on evenings when divinations were scheduled, we would talk loudly in pidgin, which he understood well enough, of the matters which must not come up in the divination, if there were to be any more of them. This was quite successful. If the forbidden questions were asked, Gerud sidestepped them, thus providing indirect evidence of the way in which his mind was working during his alleged possession. He provided an important link with the local community where he was valued highly as a hunter and a diviner. His previous betrothed, Imale, had grown so much faster that she had been given to La'abe as a second wife; Gerud now had, in Liwo, a new betrothed wife who had not yet come to live with them.

Another shoot boy was added to the establishment, Yabinigi, the half brother of Nyelahai, the other big man of the community. Though not totally deaf, it took persistence as well as shouting to make him understand. He was, therefore,

robbed of one of the senses upon which the natives depend
in their search for game and was said to be a very indifferent
hunter by native methods. He had, however, been trained to
shoot and was a first-class shot. Saharu early got him under
control; it was he who gave him orders and explained to him
what he must do. If he failed to bring in any birds one day,
Dr. Fortune merely cut down his supply of cartridges the
following day. The silent insult worked perfectly. He was
wild, recessive, shy, but a tireless hunter and an excellent
pacemaker on a trip.

This, then, was the household we brought into the village.
All of them had ties there, Kaberman and Saharu to the
family of La'abe, the *tultul,*[6] Mindibilip to Sumali's household, Biagu to the household of Sinaba'i. Gerud and Yabinigi
belonged to the village itself. Only the shoot boy from
Umanep had no close ties there, and he shortly got into
trouble.

## RELATIONS WITH THE VILLAGE

After our house was built and our stores were brought in,
we were independent of the village, except for large-scale
carrying and for supplementary food for ourselves and the
main food for our boys. Our boys got firewood and water.
Communications with the coast were maintained through
Biagu and casual companions who accompanied him.

The boys' food presented the greatest problem. In order
to have fed our household on rice, two boys would have had
to have been constantly on the road, carrying back and forth,
a grilling and impossible demand to make. Yet to feed six
boys, the four[7] whom we had brought in and the two local
boys whom we had withdrawn from horticulture, made a very
heavy demand upon that small community. It was equivalent
to asking them to feed about 15 extra adults, because the rations which we gave our boys were more than double those of
an Arapesh adult. For those rations we had to have either

[6] Government-appointed interpreter.
[7] I ignore the Umanep shoot boy who left so soon.

yams and taro, or preferably sago, which was cheaper and lasted longer. We could buy yams and taros for beads, salt, or knives, usually in about 15- to 20-pound lots—a tedious business when the boys' ration for the day amounted to 42 pounds of tubers. But we found we could not buy sago, which was so much more satisfactory. Finally, after we had been there long enough to understand the situation, Dr. Fortune solved the sago problem by distributing pieces of pig, which our shoot boy occasionally killed, against future payments of sago. The people were hungry for meat and could not resist it. Offered a section of pig, they took it and were scrupulously honest in paying their debts. When we had 150 pounds of sago stored, we felt as if we had a year's income in the bank.[8]

We had brought about a four months' supply of food for ourselves. We stayed seven and a half months by supplementing our food supply with pigeons shot by our shoot boy, taro, pawpaws, maize, French beans, and the native greens. All these had to be bought in very small quantities, very often a pawpaw at a time, for a teaspoonful of beads or a tablespoonful of salt. Dr. Fortune kept all the purchasing in his own hands and it constituted a continuous and wearying interruption. Yet at the same time it provided a channel through which the European goods which we had promised to bring with us could flow into native hands without our actually paying for information. Our stock consisted of Japanese matches, Japanese razor blades, salt, tiny colored beads, small knives, plane blades, belts, pipes, mirrors, and cloth. For carrying jobs and for food, if the natives wanted it, we paid in money; usually, however, the transactions were well under a shilling, the smallest unit they knew, and the possession of money meant a long walk to a trade store. With one or two exceptions, we did not pay informants. Those men who helped us a great deal felt justified in asking for a can of meat during a feast. When the shoot boy was particularly lucky we would send an extra bird to Ombomb or Wabe or La'abe. Occasionally, Dr. Fortune paid specifically for charms, as that was the custom, and once or twice for legends. I paid one informant, Unabelin, who came from a fair distance away, on a piece-

[8] A boy's ration of sago is 2 to 2½ pounds a day, as compared with 1½ pounds of rice.

work basis. He would say, "If I talk for a day, can I have a belt or a mirror," etc., and I would agree. He had to come from a distance and he planned his time carefully. Otherwise all the information was given voluntarily by a people whom we managed to recompense in other ways for the trouble we caused them.

There was also the question of caring for the sick. Every native in New Guinea considers it to be one of the duties of any white man to bandage his sores. We kept a large supply of standard remedies on hand; almost every morning, except toward the end of our stay when the village was empty, I had a line of people with cuts, tropical ulcers, yaws sores, inflamed eyes, burns, *tinea, kuskus,* etc., and babies for cough medicine and castor oil. It is impossible to estimate such a thing, but I am inclined to think that the sickness rate was probably lower because of the presence of the castor oil bottle, on which the people depended heavily after feasts. They were unendingly grateful and appreciative for the dressing of wounds and sores. Treating an illness was always a ticklish matter. Sorcery was involved here and various native remedies, magical concoctions, and emetics were likely to interfere with the cure. Fortunately, we encountered no serious cases and the dispensary practice merely encouraged more people to come to Alitoa, to bring food to sell to us, and to stay and gossip, and so build up my knowledge of personalities and of the culture. The practice of this sort of first aid also gives the fieldworker very valuable insight into attitudes toward pain, expressions of sympathy, standards of self-control, and relations between parents and children. Furthermore, in a culture in which so many events hinge on the interpretation of illness and death, the information which one gains at such times is exceedingly significant.

One boon which the native always hopes to gain from a white man resident near him is preferential treatment from the Government, letters putting his case better than his native opponent from the next village can put it, and requests for special treatment. But the Government is jealous of its prerogatives and it does not behoove an anthropologist or any other white man to extend any such helping hand. Here again we were fortunate, as our natives were involved in few difficulties during our stay and so did not feel that we were withholding help which we could have given.

## METHODS OF WORK AND SELECTION OF EVENTS RECORDED IN THE *DIARY*

The village awoke about five and we ourselves were up before six. There were usually people in and about the house before breakfast, especially three small boys, Segenamoya, Dubomagau, and Nigimarib, who spent a great deal of time there. After breakfast, there was a dispensary group which occupied from 10 minutes to two hours, and sometimes people came to trade. In the *Diary* I have merely recorded significant trading parties from a distance, but the local people were also continually in and out, with a handful of food to exchange for some salt to season the morning's soup. These visits gave a chance for gossip, accounts of the day's plans, etc.

I spent a good part of the morning in the village, sitting with the people, playing with the children, watching some craft, or casually questioning about some event. When the village was empty I used the time to organize work so that the next time I caught Ombomb or Wabe with an hour to spare, I could make the best of it. An example of such preparatory organization would be a list of all the married women in the community; then, with informants, I would run through the history of their own or their husbands' previous marriages. Later, I would select all the marriages which had lasted, analyze them, choose those which seemed to be the exception to whatever tendency appeared, and these would become the object of a special intensive conversation when I could get an informant's attention. One could seldom count on more than 15 or 20 minutes of such attention, unless there was a definite task like telling a legend.

During the day I recorded everything which seemed significant. In the late afternoon I walked through the village, usually accompanied by children, and checked up on every house and its inhabitants, to find where they were and where they had been that day. Very often no one knew. As will appear in the *Diary*, people vanished for days, with no one actually in the village knowing their whereabouts. They sometimes had a rough idea and 10 minutes' calling would probably locate most of the absentees, but their neighbors were not certain of their movements.

The question of the choice of significant events may well be challenged here. The ones which I recorded were:

1. Presences and absences, until I got a good sense of the rhythm of life
2. Destination, when they left the village or point from which they had returned, when this was ascertainable
3. Shouted calls from neighboring villages
4. All rumors of important events in other villages
5. All speeches
6. All quarrels
7. Illness and accidents
8. Parties of strangers coming through
9. Bad crying fits on the part of children
10. Shifts in allegiance or residence
11. Announced plans
12. Ritual events
13. Economic events
14. Participation by members of this community in events in other communities, including expressions of opinion about them
15. Accidental disturbances, such as bad storms, epidemics, etc.
16. Actions on our part which upset the normal routine, e.g., sending off a load of carriers
17. Government demands which upset the ordinary routine
18. White people passing through
19. Births and deaths

The next question might be what proportion of each of these escaped my notice. I slept for an hour in the afternoon and unimportant events occurring during that time were likely to escape notice. A good many days I had some fever; then I roused myself only to take the *Diary* and to follow major events which created a stir or which the natives themselves considered important enough to tell about. For the time when I walked about the village I got more minute details than for the other hours. If, for instance, a woman went to her garden and left her baby, and I was out in the village during the hour she was absent, I knew that she had left the baby and with whom. If this occurred when I was busy elsewhere, I would never know it. I have included such details, whenever I have them, because they provide a kind of sampling.

The only path through the village led past our house, but people from either end could enter and leave without passing our house.

Perhaps the most serious defect is the absence of information as to which garden individuals were working in. I began taking the *Diary* when I knew very little of the language and the habits of the people and before I suspected how they dissipated their energies in diffuse gardening. The habit became established of answering to, "Where is so and so?" "Working on yams," or "Working on taro," and, provided it was the informant's own garden and not one in which help was given another, that was all I learned. Later, when I wanted more information, the pattern had been well established and I found it too cumbersome to try to break it at the risk of disgruntling the people who had taken cheerfully to my daily inquisitiveness.

I became such a familiar figure in the daily life of the village that no child cried or woman stirred when I came near them. Everything continued exactly as before, except perhaps for the tendency for people, especially the children, to cluster a little in the part of the village where I was. I have noted several times in the *Diary* when there were more people present than the occasion justified.

As a method of recording, I used an actual diary and for small, apparently isolated events, a series of small, dated, classified notes on slips. In the field I worked up separate treatments of such events as Gerud's various divinations. These three sets of data I have recombined in the record that follows, selecting from the isolated notes only those relevant to the stream of events, and from the longer treatments such matter as referred to the participation of persons, to the individuality of an event, excluding details of ritual behavior which lacked this significance. For example, in the treatment of the divinatory ovens, I give here only such data as are relevant to the narrative, who made them, and what tests were made, and what the results. The prescription for these ovens has already been recorded.[9]

## THE PLAN OF THE *DIARY* AND SUGGESTIONS FOR ITS USE

For the reader, a detailed presentation such as this is bound to be tedious and unmanageable. I have taken what steps I could to mitigate this. In footnotes, I give running comments on the significance of events and some retrospective references. There still remains, however, the problem of how the reader is to grasp the material at all, interspersed as it is with 200 unintelligible names. A thorough reading of Parts I, II, and III of this series of reports and of Part I of *Sex and Temperament*[10] is a prerequisite to understanding this record.

I shall present first a description of the locality, emphasizing particularly the village of Alitoa, those with actual residence claims within it, and their connections with other hamlets of the locality. Here I shall go from household to household, describing the main personages in each. This will be followed by a less minute listing of the inhabitants of the rest of the locality and a summary of the relationships of the locality and its constituent hamlets to the surrounding localities.

At the end of the *Diary*, I give a series of lists to which the reader can refer to refresh his memory without actually plowing through the text again. The most important list is the census, arranged by households, to which the guide list to persons at the end of the *Diary* will refer. There also is a list of gentes, of hamlets, of the affiliation of wives, etc. (pp. 479–481, 487 ff.).

The *Diary* itself runs from January 28 to August 16, 1932. There is a running table of contents of all *Diary* events, and at the end I give a sequence of events for future reference. Following this I give other cross-section materials which will

[9] Mead, 1940, p. 435.
[10] Mead, 1935b.

be intelligible only in the light of the *Diary*, such as a table of working affiliations, a sample list of ownership of trees, a list of whose bones had been kept from the last generation, a list of the ownership of magic, what herbs were planted in Alitoa, etc. Such static statements should be much more valuable against the dynamic background which has preceded them.

With this arrangement, use of the *Diary* should not be prohibitively difficult, although for any complete understanding of it the reader should memorize the names of the members of the households of Balidu, La'abe, Ombomb, Wabe, Ulaba'i, Aden, Sumali, Kule, and Baimal, for they occur and recur and space does not permit a qualifying phrase when each child or woman is mentioned. Frequent reference to the village plan (Fig. 1) will also make all the events more intelligible. There is a list of where photographs of any individuals who appear in the narrative may be found when these have been published.

## THE LOCALITY OF ALITOA

The locality of Alitoa has the largest population in the Mountain region. It is bounded on the Beach side by Liwo, on the northeast by Numonihi, on the east by Wihun, and on the southwest by Numidipiheim. It lies on the *Lahowhin* Road. The Alitoa village combined two hamlets, Alitoa proper, at the end of the village which faces the Plains, and Walinuba, through which the Beach road enters. The coconut trees in Alitoa are very high, and the numerous old ornamental shrubs planted there indicate that the village is very old. The people themselves feel it to be very old and localize the origin of the gens of *Uyebis*, whose original founder emerged from a bamboo, and the exploits of another mythical *Uyebis* ancestor, Walawahan, in the same spot. The road from the Beach climbs a steep hill at the Walinuba end, then passes straight through the village, which is located on a sway-back ridge, so that the central space, occupied by our house, was lower than either the Walinuba or the Alitoa ends.[11] There is a little rise of ground at the entrance to the village and here Balidu, the big man of *Toto'alaibis* gens, whose home hamlet is Walinuba, had built a large yam house, a small *tamberan* house for the initiation of his eldest son Badui, and a series of small houses for himself and his wife Yahalijo, for Badui, for their second son, Pidjui. Here also Maigi, the slender young husband of Balidu's daughter Sagu, had built a small house. Next to the *tamberan* house (Fig. 1, No. 32) stood a good-sized house, falling into disrepair, which belonged to Sumali, the younger brother of Balidu, who was primarily a hunter and spent very little time in the village. Balidu made his principal garden nearby and usually returned to the village with his household to sleep. This end of Walinuba represented not only his formal foothold in the chief ceremonial center of his locality, but also his *sho'ubeli wabul,* his small place, his hamlet. Sumali's house, on the other hand, was merely a foothold in the ceremonial place; he and his wife occupied it when they had to help Balidu, or bring in food or come to a feast. Maigi belonged to the gens of *Uneyehas,* who made their hamlet in Manuniki. Its clustered palms, even higher than those of Alitoa, can be seen as one looks eastward across the deep gorge which lies between. But Maigi spent most of his time with his father-in-law Balidu; he gardened with him and worked sago with his sons, and so this might almost also be said to be his "small place."

Before going further, we can examine the personalities in this, the dominant household of Alitoa, for Balidu was the eldest son of the eldest line of the gens of *Toto'alaibis.* He was, furthermore, a man of responsibility and standing, unquarrelsome, hard working, prudent. He was non-exhibitionistic and found it difficult to rouse the necessary display of rage in ceremonial hostilities and sighed with relief when these were over. He belonged to the type of personality which the Arapesh associate with gardening as a principal occupation; he lacked the dash of the hunter and the adventurousness of the man who makes many trading connections. He was a careful man, a "near" man for an Arapesh. He

[11] Mead, 1938, Fig. 15, which shows the plaza of the Alitoa end as it looked from the lower ground in front of our house.

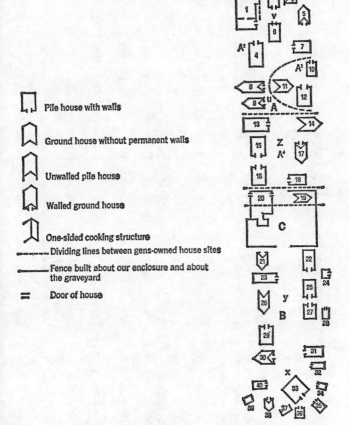

Pile house with walls

Ground house without permanent walls

Unwalled pile house

Walled ground house

One-sided cooking structure

----- Dividing lines between gens-owned house sites

——— Fence built about our enclosure and about the graveyard

= Door of house

Fig. 1. Plan of Alitoa village. (A) Alitoa; (B) Walinuba; (C) Section of ground assigned to us; (A¹ and A³) House sites belonging to the gens *Dibatua'am;* (A²) House sites of the gens *Uyebis;* (A⁴) House sites of the gens *Kanehoibis;* (B) House sites of the gens *Toto'alaibis;* (x) Plaza (*agehu*) of Balidu, Sumali, Baimal, and Kule; (y) Plaza of La'abe and Ombomb; (z) Plaza of Aden; (u) Plaza of Ulaba'i; (v) Plaza of Bischu, Wutue, Wabe, and Matasues.

## ALITOA HOUSE OWNERSHIP AND USE

| No. | House Type | Owner | Owner's Gens | User | User's Gens |
|---|---|---|---|---|---|
| 1 | Extra large pile house, without ridge spurs or projecting roofs; two side entrances, partition wall. Result of builder's experience of European architecture | Wabe | Uyebis, by adoption | 1a. Sinaba'i, as living quarters<br>1b. Wabe, on feast occasions | Dibatua'am<br>Uyebis |
| 2 | Very small, walled pile house | Wabe | Uyebis | Wabe and his wife Temos, and to store yams | Uyebis |
| 3 | Very small, unwalled pile house | Wabe | Uyebis | To store yams | |
| 4 | Medium-sized pile house, no decorations | Wabe | Uyebis | Wabe, for his wife Welima | Uyebis |
| 5 | Ground house with leaf walls | Wabe | | Wabe, as a cook house for Temos | |
| 6 | Large pile house, round roof projection | Wutue | Uyebis | Bischu and Wutue, very occasionally | Uyebis |
| 7 | Small pile house, no decorations | Bischu, brother's son of Wutue | Uyebis | Old, Bischu, only for feast entertaining | Uyebis |
| 8 | Very long, walled ground house | Matasues, brother of Wabe | Uyebis | Matasues, on occasional visits to Alitoa | Uyebis |
| 9 | Small, well-walled ground house | Bigalin | Uyebis | Matasues | Uyebis |

| No. | Description | Owner | | Use | |
|---|---|---|---|---|---|
| 10 | Small, walled pile yam house | Ulaba'i | *Dibatua'am* | Ulaba'i, for storing yams | *Dibatua'am* |
| 11 | Unwalled lounging house | Ulaba'i | *Dibatua'am* | For lounging by members of Alitoa half of village | *Dibatua'am-Uyebis* |
| 12 | Pile house, no decorations | Ulaba'i | *Dibatua'am* | Ulaba'i and both wives | *Dibatua'am* |
| 13 | Medium, walled pile house, decoration projection, and plates | Former *tamberan* house of Aden | *Kanehoibis* | Aden, only at feasts | *Kanehoibis* |
| 14 | Lounging ground house with no front and leaf walls | Aden | *Kanehoibis* | Aden, for his guests | *Kanehoibis* |
| 15 | Medium-sized, walled pile house, undecorated | Aden | *Kanehoibis* | Aden, for his wife Baijo | *Kanehoibis* |
| 16 | Small, walled pile house, undecorated | Aden | *Kanehoibis* | Aden, for his wife Ulaijo | *Kanehoibis* |
| 17 | Walled ground house | Madje, (unmarried brother of Aden) | *Kanehoibis* | Madje | *Kanehoibis* |
| 18 | Very small, walled pile house | Madje | | Madje, to store yams | *Kanehoibis* |
| 19 | Walled ground house | Aden | | Gobonarra | *Hamiebis* (mother's brothers of Aden) |
| 20 | Our house | Land owned partly by *Kanehoibis*, partly by *Toto'alaibis* | | | |

ALITOA HOUSE OWNERSHIP AND USE—*Continued*

| No. | House Type | Owner | Owner's Gens | User | User's Gens |
|---|---|---|---|---|---|
| 21 | Small, walled ground house with rounded ends | La'abe | | Used only for feasts | Toto'alaibis |
| 22 | Medium-sized, walled pile house, undecorated | La'abe | | La'abe, for his wife Imale | Toto'alaibis |
| 23 | Medium-sized, walled pile house, roofed with unworked sago leaves | La'abe | | La'abe, for his wife Imale | Toto'alaibis |
| 24 | Menstrual hut, cone-shaped, built of sago palm leaves | Wives of La'abe | Toto'alaibis | Both wives of La'abe, occasionally wives of Ombomb | Toto'alaibis |
| 25 | Large, walled pile house, undecorated | Ombomb (brother of Matasues) | Toto'alaibis | Ombomb, for his wife Me'elue | Toto'alaibis |
| 26 | Large ground house, with no front and leaf walls | Ombomb | Toto'alaibis | Built as a couvade house for Ombomb's wife and child | Toto'alaibis |
| 27 | Small, walled pile house, decorated | Ombomb | Toto'alaibis | Ombomb, his wife Sauwedjo, and for his yams | Toto'alaibis |
| 28 | Very small, walled pile house, falling down | Ombomb | Toto'alaibis | No longer safe for use | Toto'alaibis |
| 29 | Medium pile house, no decorations | Kule | Toto'alaibis | Kule and his brother Baimal, occasionally | Toto'alaibis |

| No. | House | | Owner | Use | |
|---|---|---|---|---|---|
| 30 | Small, walled ground house | | Kule | Baimal, during feasts | *Toto'alaibis* |
| 31 | Medium-sized, walled pile house | *Toto'alaibis* | Sumali | Sumali, occasionally | *Toto'alaibis* |
| 32 | Small, decorated walled pile house | *Toto'alaibis* | Balidu | *Tamberan* house, containing sacred flutes and *Toto'alaibis* | *Toto'alaibis* |
| 33 | Very large, decorated pile house | *Toto'alaibis* | Balidu | Balidu, for storing, and receiving visitors | *Toto'alaibis* |
| 34 | Small pile house | *Toto'alaibis* | Balidu | Balidu, as a regular cook house | *Toto'alaibis* |
| 35 | Small pile house | *Toto'alaibis* | Balidu | Balidu, as sleeping place for himself and wife | *Toto'alaibis* |
| 36 | Small pile house | *Toto'alaibis* | Balidu | Balidu, as sleeping place for his young sons | *Toto'alaibis* |
| 37 | One walled ground shelter | *Toto'alaibis* | Balidu | Built for Yahalijo at a feast | *Toto'alaibis* |
| 38 | Walled ground house | *Toto'alaibis* | Balidu | Balidu, as extra cook house | *Toto'alaibis* |
| 39 | Very small pile house | *Toto'alaibis* | Badui, eldest son of Balidu | Badui, whose pre-adolescent wife still sleeps with his parents | *Toto'alaibis* |
| 40 | Small pile house | *Uyenehas* | Maigi, son-in-law of Balidu | Maigi and his wife | *Uyenehas* |

planned the work of his little household carefully; he counted over his yams and weighed his obligations. He was senti- mental and a little sorry for himself; he was getting old; he had only daughters for oldest children; one of his daughters had married a boy of Bugabihiem, and the two of them had gone away to work for the white man and had never returned. Last year, he had Badui, his eldest son, initiated in a private initiation ceremony, as there were no plans for a large one on foot. Now he was preparing to give the *balagasik* feast to Honali and Nigi of Wihun, his double brothers-in-law, for his wife Yahalijo was their sister, and his own younger sister was married to Honali. With this feast he would retire. Al- ready as a sign that he was retiring, when there was any festivity he went about, shabby and unadorned. Threats of sorcery were no longer made against him but against his son Badui. When visitors came he sent Badui up to entertain them. He still went to his garden every day, but he was be- ginning to exercise the license of age. His *buanyin* was Aden, whose house was at the other end of the village. Quarrels, half real, half ceremonial, between the two were frequent. De- spite the slightly self-pitying tone which he was likely to take about himself, Balidu had been fortunate. He had had only one wife; his children were living, he had a thoroughly satis- factory eldest son; he had never killed a man or been involved in any serious fracas. He was a prudent, not extremely intelli- gent man of peace.

Yahalijo, his wife, was a gaunt, determined, hard-working woman, with a stronger will than her husband, who drama- tized his slight pompousness and pretended to take a great deal of notice of it. She, more than Balidu, took the re- sponsibility for the moral tone of the village. On a quiet warm evening when a good many members of the gens were sleeping in the village, one might hear either his voice or hers, raised in a slow, singing cadence of scolding, admonishment, and wonder at the ways of the younger generation. She got on very well with her daughter Yapul, who was married to Nagawe of Ahalesimihi, but she found Sagu, the younger daughter who was married to Maigi, impertinent and hard to understand. Her temper was higher than Balidu's and was matched by that of Nigimarib, her youngest son, with whom she occasionally came to blows. Here Balidu would interfere and merely prevent the small boy of nine from attacking his mother, while Yahalijo raged loudly. She had never permitted Balidu to have another wife, and everyone agreed that she had been equal to the task of being the wife of a big man. When she died, there would be a big funeral for her, people said, because she was the outstanding woman in the community.

Sagu, the eldest child at home, was a slight, high-breasted, trim little woman, shrewd and always happy in trading situations in which she would display her shrewdness. Her history had been somewhat unfortunate. She had been betrothed in Liwo, and her betrothed had died before she reached puberty. She had been given to his elder brother, who had committed one of the crimes most disapproved by the Arapesh—he had "stolen" her, that is, he had intercourse with her before she menstruated. That was the reason, people said, why her breasts would never slacken now, but would always remain small, high, and unwomanly. Soon afterwards, she had borne a puny baby which had died; then she had run away from her husband, who had another wife whom she disliked, and had come home to her father. He had then married her to Maigi's elder brother, who already had another wife. She had not been particularly happy here, and then, soon after, this second husband had died. Sagu had already had her personality distorted by this series of atypical experiences.[12] She had learned to value sex, even as she came to despair of having children. There was no need for her to evade her desires, so that her breasts would grow heavy and feed many children. She obviously was not meant to have children; that early sex experience had spoiled all that, had failed to loosen the chord which binds the breasts to the vulva. A second time a widow, she turned her eyes on her last husband's younger

[12] When an experience is said to be atypical, we can mean either that it happens to very few individuals in a culture, or that it is not supposed to happen to anyone, even though it may happen to many. Sagu's experience was not as statistically unusual as it was culturally unacceptable, but the fact that others have shared an equally interdicted fate does not necessarily reconcile an individual to it, if it is heavily enough condemned by the culture.

brother Maigi, a slim, yielding sprig of a boy, not yet mature enough for sex experience. And as she had been dealt by, so she dealt; she seduced Maigi, he became so enamored of her that he insisted upon marrying her despite the grave warnings of his elders that he would never grow to be a strong man. That was two years ago, and, true, Maigi was still a slim, adolescent-looking youth, following Sagu's determined little figure like a devoted shadow. They served as horrible examples to Alitoa's growing children; this was what happened to those who engaged in sex activities too early. So Maigi and Sagu came and went, between her father's garden and the garden of his father's brother in Manuniki. In a sense these two slender creatures who would never have any children were hardly regarded as people at all. Sometimes Sagu made trouble by her tale-bearing between the two hamlets; she loved to come and drive a hard bargain with us over her vegetables. Maigi sometimes joined our boys as they sang and played games together in the evening, but most of the time he worked soberly enough with his father-in-law and did as Sagu bade him.

Badui (Pl. 3a), Balidu's eldest son, was the delight of the whole village, so perfectly did he represent all that a young man should be. That he was the eldest son of the eldest son of the gens made it all the more delightful. If it had been Pidjui, Balidu's second son, nothing would have been expected of him. But Badui was tall, handsome, intelligent, deferential to older people, quick to "act in his father's place," careful of Sa'omale, his small plump betrothed wife, who had not yet reached puberty. Badui had never been away to work. His father had not wanted him to go; his obligations as the promising son of a big man had been pointed out to him and he had remained at home. He spoke very little pidgin. Where so many of the men of the half generation above him had been away to work, he stood out as a conservative, who, although only 18 or 19,[13] belonged more thoroughly to his society than did they, with their cosmopolitan experiences. Although born *Toto'alaibis*, Badui was destined by his father to carry on

[13] All ages are, of course, approximations.

the name and inherit the lands of *Hamiebis*, a gens which had died out. Its last representative had been Balidu's ward.

Pidjui, the worthless, shiftless, unreliable second son, was to remain *Toto'alaibis*. In this gesture, Balidu was entirely Arapesh. Pride of gens is not a value among the Arapesh, even though, with their formal valuation of seniority, it is convenient if the eldest son is also the ablest. But a greater value is the maintenance of vanishing lines and the sending of men to live beneath planted trees. So the eldest son, the pride of his father and of his gens, was assigned to carry on and renew a dying name.

Sa'omale was a shy little girl who had not yet reached puberty. She was a little more circumspect in this, her husband's village, than were the other girls of her age; she kept close to her mother-in-law and adored her tall young betrothed. A great deal of her time she spent with Kumati, Badui's younger sister, the peaceful progress of whose life had also been upset by the death of Sagu's second husband. Kumati, a skinny little girl of 11 or 12, had been betrothed to Maigi. When Sagu married him, she was returned to her father's house. No one considered letting her grow up and marry Maigi also; he obviously was not going to be equal to the task of supporting two wives, and there was slight chance that Sagu would tolerate a rival, even her own younger sister. So Kumati was back in her father's household, not quite belonging there; the young husband who had started to grow her was also there, but married to her sister. New proposals for her were now coming in to her father, who dallied over them in a high querulous voice, talking always of his daughter who did not return from the white man; why should he relinquish his last little daughter? Meanwhile, Kumati and Sa'omale worked together, helped Yahalijo in the gardens, teased Amito'a to dye special strands for new grass skirts for them, slipped about quietly in a secretive life of their own.

Pidjui, who was about 15, standing between Badui and Kumati, was unplaced and at loose ends. He had no betrothed wife; instead, Balidu had betrothed a second wife (the daughter of Silisium of Ahalesimihi) for Badui, which was perhaps one reason why he insisted that Pidjui was to be the inheriting *Toto'alaibis* son. As Badui was always correct, so Pidjui was always in the wrong; he did not know how to treat strangers; he did not help properly when there was work to do. Everyone in Alitoa had decided long ago that Pidjui would amount to nothing. Ever since he could remember, Pidjui had heard that he would amount to nothing. In a characteristic pose he leaned against any house post or palm trunk that presented itself, and did nothing, or teased Nigimarib, his youngest brother.

Nigimarib, a bright little urchin of about nine, showed every characteristic of the youngest child in a large family, who had been weaned very late (about four, people said) because there was no other baby. He clung to his father's side on every occasion; when alone with his brothers he was demanding and babyish; if his mother refused him anything, he flew into a rage. His overweening curiosity about the world was his salvation. Only a desire to roam the woods, to test a new toy, or stalk a strange bird in the company of his more independent cousins, tempted him away from his father. He was just beginning to wear a G string.

This, then, was the immediate household of Balidu, living in the series of small houses around his large house, where his yams were stored and his visitors entertained. Relations between him and his brother Sumali, whose house adjoined his, were a little distant. Sumali was a hunter by choice; he gardened only because every Arapesh man had to garden. As a boy, he had spent most of his time in Liwo with his mother's brother, who had taught him hunting magic and the practical techniques of trapping and trailing game. He was lithe, wiry, aggressive, voluble, impulsive, with a marked acquisitive streak. Although Gerud, his eldest son, was older than Badui, he had not yet been initiated. His eldest daughter Budagiel had, it is true, been grown up for a long while, but her first marriage, with Monau, her *ano'in*, had never been consummated. Budagiel might still be counted, somewhat tenuously, as an unmarried girl, and with Gerud uninitiated, Sumali still bedizened himself for feasts. With a wide new bark belt to hold his G string straight and a bird-of-paradise feather in his hair, none of the young men was smarter than he. With every exhibitionistic gesture, he made it clear that his doddering old brother Balidu might have retired, but that he, Sumali, had not. He was also one of the very few men in the locality who had ever killed a man, many years ago (see below, p. 209) in a quarrel over sorcery with Wihun. If there were talk of fights Sumali always had to be consulted; he was the man who had really had a fight and knew something about it, the young men would say with deprecatory looks. Furthermore, Sumali prided himself upon being stronger than the magic of the Plainsmen; for 15 years they had had a piece of his exuviae, stolen by a Plainswoman, and he had never been ill from it. Boastfully, he would remark that his exuviae had rotted away in the hands of powerless Plainsmen. When Balidu gave a feast, Sumali helped him by providing meat which was always presented with as much ceremony as if to a distant connection. And when people said of Balidu, "He can build a big house, he has meat," they did not add, "Because Sumali is his brother," but, "Because his son-in-law, Nagawe, has a good dog." Sumali had no hunting partners but his young sons. He had the reputation of always claiming "first sight," so that other people avoided hunting with him.

Winam, Sumali's wife, was an efficient, placid woman, the most fecund in Alitoa, the mother of eight living children. As a widow she had come into Sumali's house after the death of her first husband, to whom she had borne one son, Magiel, now away at work. She had found two childless wives in Sumali's house and had quarreled with both of them and run away to the distant hamlet of Malis[14] where she married. But a year later when she returned to visit her brothers in Ahalesimihi, they conspired with their erstwhile brothers-in-law, Sumali and his brother Balidu, who met her near a waterfall where her brothers had taken her. In the traditional way in which a woman is given over by her brothers to capture they "took her by the hand," and led her back. This time she stayed, but she drove the Wihun wife away; the other wife, the sister of Sinaba'i, died. This left her in sole charge. There she remained, to bear in steady succession: Budagiel, now a husky girl of 22, very weary of having an absentee husband; Gerud, who became our house boy and whose person-

14 Near Mowia on map, Mead, 1938, Fig. 2.

ality has already been described; Midjulumon, a weedy, alert youngster who tried hard to take Gerud's place; Bopugenon, a cheery eight-year-old, far more independent than his first cousin, Nigimarib; Ite'epe, a thin little girl of six or so; Moul, a sturdy four-year-old; and Eweluen, a baby at the breast.

This household presented the unusual picture of the large biological family, sufficient unto itself. Most of the time they lived in the distant "small place" of Malupit, on the property which Sumali had been granted by Aden in return for his taking on the responsibility of Gobonarra, Aden's worthless mother's brother. Gobonarra had a small house in Malupit, and he and his Dunigi wife and their two children also lived there. Gobonarra also had a tumble-down ground hut built on Aden's ground at the other end of Alitoa. Sumali got on well enough with Gobonarra, ignoring him and letting Winam see to it that at least Gobonarra's wife did some work. Sumali's household showed markedly the results of its restricted life; Budagiel was over-devoted to her father, accompanied him whenever he went on long trips, and was exceedingly unwilling to spend any time working on the gardens of her future husband with his elder brother Aden. Gerud also was remote and secretive, preferring hunting with his father to other activities; the two younger brothers preferred each other's company to any other. It is accepted in Arapesh that the men who choose hunting as a main profession are the less social, the less dependent, the more anxious to try out their own powers.[15] They lead more isolated lives and have a chance to impress the same way of life upon their sons.

The present members of *Toto'alaibis* gens were descended from three brothers, the eldest, Maulimen, had fathered Balidu and Sumali; his wife had been a Liwo woman, and so these two brothers looked towards Liwo for their Class Two kinship connections. Badui and Gerud were both betrothed to Liwo girls; Budagiel and Sagu had both been betrothed in Liwo, and the eldest daughter of Balidu was married in Bugabihiem, the village beachwards of Liwo. So, both in their parents' and children's generations, they were tied to

[15] However, even Sumali, for all his boastfulness, would say only that a tree kangaroo had got into his snare, not that he had caught a tree kangaroo.

Liwo. Through Balidu's marriage with Yahalijo of Wihun, and their sister's marriage with Honali, the brother of Yahalijo, they had close brother-in-law ties with Wihun. It was with Wihun that the biggest exchanges were made, as Balidu was the big man of the pair. On his own account Sumali took part in no extensive economic affairs, but through his marriage to Winam of Ahalesimihi, and the marriage of a parallel cousin to Manum, a brother of Winam, there were close ties between Sumali and Ahalesimihi. Both Manum and his brother Silisium gardened with Sumali and he with them. But while Sumali's relationship to Ahalesimihi was that of brother-in-law, Balidu's was that of father-in-law, through the marriage to Yapul to Nagawe. So while Sumali went and worked with his brother-in-law, Balidu remained at home and received help from his Ahalesimihi son-in-law and sent Badui with help and gifts to the household of Badui's other betrothed wife, a daughter of Winam's other brother, Silisium. This concludes the important extra-Alitoa ties of the two sons of Maulimen, the eldest of the three *Toto'alaibis* progenitors.

Baimal was the son of Balidu's and Sumali's elder brother, who had been dead for a long time. Baimal, who was only about 10 years younger than Sumali, had been too young to play much of a role when his father died and he succeeded to a kind of quiet, established position. He would never be a big man, although he had played his role in arranging several feasts, and he had made *abullus*. He was one of the most important men in the community, yet he was in no sense a leader. Slight, active, always bright-eyed and responsive, intensely masculine, rather than paternal, he was first and foremost an artist. Without any coherent tradition and without any rewards, his paintings showed genuine artistic ability. He had placed the onus of his masculinity upon his ability to paint and when he saw the minute water color copies which I had made of some damaged Plains paintings, he muttered, "Women, women, women," and left the village for a week. He took enormous pleasure in the beautiful Abelam paintings which Dr. Fortune brought back from the interior. When he was presented with a paint box with a full complement of colors, he took only those to which he was accustomed, and condemned the young men who used green and purple.

"They fight!" he said briefly. He even copied one of the paintings from the interior; in doing so he preserved the essential design but by altering the color and detail turned the dour hard lines of the Plains painting of a human being into a happy-hearted floral design.

Baimal was the eldest of six brothers, of whom the second, Bauwan, was dead, and the two youngest were away at work. He had one fairly large house in Alitoa, where the remaining three brothers and their wives stayed when they were in the village, but the trio spent most of their time in their hamlet of Mogiligen, where Baimal had built a fine large yam house. This was their hunting ground. The three brothers were good hunters. Alis, the youngest, devoted most of his time to hunting.

Baimal had been married four times. His first betrothed, an Alipinagle girl, died without reaching puberty. He was then betrothed to Ilautoa of *Uyenehas*, the sister of Maigi. Ilautoa had just reached puberty, when Kule, Baimal's third brother, returned from work, his skin shining with the well-fed, well-soaped look which distinguished the work boy from the village native. Kule had dash and charm, and Ilautoa took a great fancy to him. Baimal is reported to have shrugged his shoulders and said gently, "Well, perhaps I am too old for her. Let the young people marry." He later married a *Suabibis* girl from Liwo who died when her baby was born; the baby also died. This left him again a widower. Owing to the machinations of Aden and Ombomb, Amito'a, the rebellious wife of an old man in *Suabibis*, ran away to him. They had one child, Amus, a little girl of about five.

This marriage was one of the most tempestuous and highly charged marriages in Alitoa, and one in which it might fairly be said that the partners were in love with each other. Amito'a's (Pl. 6b) history had been a long and stormy one.[16] She had been betrothed to a boy who died, and had been inherited by his much elder brother; again death spoiled the Arapesh conception of orderly life. She had resented this elderly husband and in strictly sexual terms, for she, unlike most Arapesh women, was positively, aggressively sexed, and ar-

[16] For a summary account of Amito'a, see Mead, 1935b, pp. 149–153.

ticulately conscious of her desires. She continually quarreled with her husband; she attempted to strangle her first baby and objected to suckling it. She ran away to Kobelen, adopting the behavior pattern of the only violent women with whom she came in contact, the women of the Plains, but no one would accept her there. They were afraid both of breaking off friendly relationships with Liwo and of the women of the interior whose power to nullify a man's magic increases towards the Beach. Her brother, during a visit to her husband, returned her to him, where the quarreling resumed. Finally, with the help of Ombomb, who claimed her as a very distant sister, and Aden, she ran away to Alitoa and married Baimal and bore Amus, now about five.

Amito'a was Yahalijo's lieutenant among the women. She was a handsome, hard-faced, gaunt woman, with shrunken uneven breasts, possessing not a single semblance of softness. She was excitable, passionate, hot-tempered, violently defensive of all that she identified with herself. Walinuba was now hers; Balidu was her Big Man; what a wonderful Big Man he was! She was emphatic in her praises of her new hamlet and in derogatory remarks about that of the husband whom she had left. She was a good worker, vigorous, energetic, active. When she was in the village, life was always more exciting.

From his brother Bauwan, Baimal had inherited a second wife, Alaijo, a weak, limp creature, the mother of Minya, a thin, weak little girl, about four years older than Amus. Alaijo was the perfect example of the Arapesh ideal of what an inherited wife should be. They believe that her first marriage and child bearing should calm a woman into docility and submissiveness. Alaijo was so by natural endowment. Baimal was never tempted to leave Amito'a's side to pay any attention to her. She followed the pair about, or remained at home with the children, quietly, amiably. Only when any responsibility devolved upon her did she fall short; she was firmly convinced of her own unimportance and unwilling to make any efforts of any kind.

Amus was a sturdy, hot-tempered child, with the kind of personality which is most likely to develop in an only daugh-

ter among the Arapesh.[17] She was devoted to both parents;
Amito'a continually made her a pawn in the quarrels between them. If her father took her with him, Amito'a quarreled with him; if her father left her, Amus had a temper
tantrum. She was much more insecure than were most Arapesh children of her age, and if she wakened to find her
mother out of the house, would break into a storm of weeping. She dominated and terrorized Minya and insisted that
she was the older sister; Minya was too weak-spirited to dispute the ridiculous claim. Meanwhile, the two families lived
comfortably in one household, and the dominance of Amito'a
and her daughter was never disputed.

Kule (Pl. 3b), the third brother, had a disposition something like Sumali's, but modified by the different family constellations. He was also exhibitionistic and somewhat acquisitive, but he was more friendly and sociable than Sumali. He
was a mild kleptomaniac; from time to time, he compulsively
and meaninglessly stole something which he returned when
challenged. When we left Alitoa, he stole Dr. Fortune's purse,
but when we sent word in that it had better be produced,
Kule gave it up at once. He also had great difficulty in ever
returning any object that was lent to him, a blanket put about
him in illness, a knife lent him for some special task. He stuck
very close to his elder brother Baimal, to whom one felt he
was not completely devoted. Without a fuller history and
more searching analysis, it would be impossible to prove,
but I am inclined to think that Kule had never recovered from
the sin of taking his elder brother's betrothed wife. If Baimal
had fought him, called him names, demanded indemnity or
perhaps even the first child (for Baimal then had no children
and the first child of Kule and Ilautoa was a boy), this might
have assuaged his guilt. But Baimal had done none of these
things; he had simply shrugged his shoulders and said, "Perhaps I am too old for her. Let the young people marry each
other." It is certain that Kule was uneasy in life, and part of
his unrest had been communicated to his small son Naguel,
who had been weaned by the mud-smearing method which
has to be used if the mother becomes pregnant so soon that

[17] Mead, 1935b, p. 51.

the last child has to be weaned suddenly.[18] Here again, in hastening his wife's second conception, Kule had behaved badly. Yet no one suggested that he was or would become an *alomato'in*.[19] He was regarded as a very good man, a good hunter, a good gardener, who held up his end very well in the economy of the community. Later in the year, when he was very ill, the whole community was in turmoil over the possible loss (pp. 340, 341). He had become the doctor boy (the medical *tultul*) when his brother Bauwan died. Bauwan had succeeded Ombomb after he was disqualified through his jail sentence.[20] He had worked for the white man and spoke fair pidgin.

Ilautoa (Pl. 8b), the wife whom he had taken from Baimal, was an attractive, gentle woman, perhaps the most attractive woman in the locality.[21] She shared her grace and delicacy of feature with her brother Maigi. She had apparently quite simply fallen in love with Kule and did not share his guilt over leaving Baimal.[22] She was a fast friend of Amito'a's, and got on amiably and quietly with her own cowife Soatsalamo. Kule's preference for her was, however, so marked that she had no temptation to be jealous. She was very fond of Mausi, her little girl of four, the most charming child in the village, and seemed vaguely puzzled by Naguel's wanderings from home.

Kule had inherited Bauwan's younger wife Soatsalamo, a heavy, slightly morose, rather stupid woman who devoted all her time and thought to her plump baby boy Walipin, her son by Kule.

Alis, the youngest of the three brothers, was a frail, neurasthenic youth, always uneasy and worried. He believed he was dying from sorcery worked upon him by a Plains-

[18] Mead, 1935b, p. 38, for a discussion of this method.

[19] For a discussion of *alomato'in*, Mead, 1940, p. 352.

[20] Note the way in which the Government-appointed positions were already being fitted into a hereditary scheme. See above also, where these same positions had been adapted to the dual organization forms (p. 23).

[21] Mead, 1938, Fig. 13.

[22] Women are given so little social responsibility among the Arapesh that they are also largely freed from any burden of guilt over their own behavior.

woman who had seduced him in an attempt to get him to take her back to the Mountains with him.[23] He had run away from her and shortly afterwards she had died. This left him in the greatest danger, for he did not know where she had hidden his exuviae, which she doubtless had stolen; furthermore, if her relatives knew, they would never tell, as with the same logic which he was using, they would hold him accountable for her death. So Alis worried and pined and drank *ashup*, the ceremonial emetic, and begged for doses of castor oil. His young wife Taumulimen, the younger sister of Ilautoa, the wife of Kule, had had a mild case of *tinea* when she married him. This was spreading. The girl herself was becoming irritable under the perpetual anxiety. They very seldom came to Alitoa.

Alis had learned the practice of *sagumeh* divining which Gerud was now practicing with such success. He had introduced the use of his dead brother Bauwan as a control, a practice which Gerud still followed. But shy and inarticulate Alis had not made a success of divining, and when Taumulimen reached puberty he gave it up.

A fourth brother of Balidu and Sumali, Menyul, was a poor crooked creature, mildly foolish, and unutterably unreliable. He had married a woman of Numonihi who was as stupid as he, and was exceedingly lame, one leg being much shorter than the other. They had one puny child. The dominant members of *Toto'alaibis* had banished Menyul to the bush; he lived alone in the deep bush, where he raised a garden, cared for their pigs, and received scant attention. In the past, it was said, he was always getting involved in sorcery quarrels; whether he was guilty or not is not clear, but he was the kind of man who was always being accused of being a sorcerer, stupid and meaninglessly malicious in manner and obviously not happy. The Arapesh draw the obvious conclusion that unhappy people become sorcerers. This tendency to banish the less desirable members of the community into the bush appears repeatedly. Gobonarra was tucked away with Sumali in his very remote hamlet, never visited by strangers. Inoman and Nahomen, of whom we shall hear

23 Mead, 1935b, pp. 102–104.

later, were kept equally secluded. The feasting village is the place where strangers are received and where the impression of a community is given, where, furthermore, travelers pick up the theories about sorcery practice. It did not do to have men like Menyul and Gobonarra about, and they were told to stay in the bush, a prohibition which they obeyed somewhat indifferently.

The second brother had married two Wihun wives and had lived almost all of his life in Wihun. Two of his daughters had married in Numidipiheim and were never seen in Alitoa. One daughter was married to the *luluai*[24] of Wihun. Only one son, La'abe, had finally returned to take up his father's land in Walinuba. He had come back as a young man but had never been completely accepted as one of them; they always thought of him as belonging to Wihun; and he had the uneasy appearance of a bird who may at any moment take flight. Of his two full sisters, the eldest, Homendjuai, had married Manum of Ahalesimihi, and died. Manum had then married the younger sister, who had taken her eldest sister's name, and borne Manum a whole group of children. La'abe, slight, graceful, charming, petulant, with the melancholic, put-upon air of a man who has been given more responsibility than he actually is capable of discharging, depended very much upon his sisters. He had had no brothers of his own, and the fact that his father had lived in a village not his own had cut him off from his first cousins of *Toto'-alaibis*. He was easily irritated, but his anger melted away as quickly as it rose. He was a weak, lovable man, a good dancer, with delicately developed sensations. He would sit by the hour and play the hand drum to himself. I used him often as a rapid indicator of Arapesh response to some new situation which I wanted to pose, for where the average man would express disgust by a grimace, La'abe's whole body would recoil and register repugnance. His sexual potency was steady and reliable; he had no unmanageable aggressions to deal with within himself.

His marriage arrangements had not been fortunate. His

[24] In order to simplify somewhat the memory problem, I shall use the native official terms for members of other villages, a practice which the natives follow themselves.

father had died and he had gone away to work for the white man; then he came back to Alitoa to live without any betrothed wife. His sister Homendjuai was already married in Ahalesimihi. It was arranged that he should marry Lomaijo, a just pubescent girl who had been betrothed to the now dead brother of Nagawe. Lomaijo came to him at puberty; he had not grown her; she had not known him before. She was a frightened, insecure girl. In a quarrel over sago rights between the localities of Alitoa and Numonihi, a half-demented man had come upon her mother and sister and killed them. Such violence was unusual in Arapesh life and had perhaps left its mark upon her. At any rate, she was unstable, jealous, and very bad tempered. Twice she had publicly used obscenity to La'abe, the first time provoking the *tamberan* to come and demand a pig from him. She bore him two girls, Souato'a, who was now about five and Kamowon, about two.[25]

Then another set of circumstances were set in motion, further complicating the life of La'abe and Lomaijo. Gerud, the son of Sumali, La'abe's parallel first cousin, had been betrothed years before to Imale of Alipinagle hamlet. The betrothing had been perhaps a little careless; not quite enough difference in age had been allowed. Imale grew very rapidly and Gerud remained a slender adolescent. These are the cases which frighten the Arapesh and cause them to act quickly and without proper planning. Gerud was Sumali's treasured eldest son. If Imale grew up and she and Gerud slept together, Gerud's growth would be permanently stunted. Badui also did not have his growth. Sumali was in closer touch with La'abe through their common brother-in-law ties with Ahalesimihi than with the other *Toto'alaibis* lines; he proposed that La'abe should marry Imale and thus remove the danger from Gerud's path. After all, Lomaijo had borne him only girls and she was insubordinate—he had not grown her. Imale would not menstruate for another year, perhaps more, and La'abe would have a chance to contribute to her growth, i.e., to develop some submissiveness in her. So La'abe took Imale. When we came to Alitoa, he had been

[25] Mead, 1938, Fig. 16.

living with her for about a year, after growing her and putting her through her first menstruation ceremony. Lomaijo had disliked her from the first, and La'abe had built another house for her. Imale, a large, handsome, quiet woman, was better looking than Lomaijo. She did not bother to reciprocate her dislike, but instead followed La'abe about with cow-like eyes, and took a good deal of care of the children. Lomaijo was a slattern and careless with the children; Imale bathed and bedizened them. Souato'a spent most of her time with her father and Imale, paying very little attention to her mother. When La'abe went to Wihun or to the Beach, he took Imale with him and left Lomaijo at home to care for the children, the pigs, and the garden. Lomaijo was bitter and troublesome; La'abe was mildly puzzled by the tangle his affairs had gotten into. As it had been all his life, so it was now; he was surrounded by women—his sister in Wihun; his sister in Ahalesimihi, whose husband Manum was a dull, stupid man; two wives, and two daughters. La'abe sighed and beat the hand drum, or flew into occasional rages and chopped at his own areca palm trees. Neither wife wished to leave him, the usual Arapesh solution of such difficulties. So he scattered his energies; he fussed over the Government assignments which he received; he went to see now one sister, now another; he neglected his gardens and then complained bitterly when his crops were poor.

The last of the *Toto'alaibis* inhabitants of Walinuba was Ombomb (Pl. 5a),[26] the son of Pailit, the third of the three fraternal ancestors, the son of the youngest line. Ombomb was a proud, intelligent, vulnerable man, too ambitious for Arapesh standards, too careful of his own dignity, and exceedingly fearful lest either his dignity or his health be injured by others. His intelligence was too formal and structural for Arapesh methods of thinking; he found the greatest difficulty in reconciling the actual occurrences of everyday life with his mental formalized picture of life as it should be lived. He was the type of arrogant conservative who continually violates the will of the community while insisting that he is acting in a manner more orthodox than they. He

[26] Mead, 1938, Fig. 14.

was the youngest son, who had not been brought up by his father but by his eldest brother Wupale.[27] Wupale, 15 years older than Ombomb, had been a high-handed, hot-tempered man, who had gotten himself into a quarrel within his own community, in which spears had been thrown across the open space between Walinuba and Alitoa. He had broken his plates and his pots, torn down his house, and gone off to Wihun to live with the brothers of the dead wife, whose death he had accused his own community of causing. From his father, he had inherited hunting and garden land and coconuts; he gave these to his small brother Ombomb, who had then been just an adolescent boy, round-eyed with admiration of the exploits of his violent, contentious brother. For Ombomb, Wupale had also marked a young wife in Wihun.

Ombomb went away to work for the white man, accompanying his next elder brother Wabe, who was also violent, jealous, and vulnerable. When he returned he settled among the *Toto'alaibis,* where his young wife Me'elue was brought to be taken care of by his mother. Me'elue was covered with *tinea;* she was the thin type of *tinea* victim, and gradually succumbing to the disease. Ombomb did not like her; his pride was offended by the sight of her; furthermore, he was to become a big man some day, and how could he with a weak, puny wife? A girl from Liwo, who was within a few weeks of her first menstruation, ran away to him. He kept her, put her through her puberty ceremony, and started to live with her. By his account of the matter, her betrothed husband was quite willing to take rings in payment, but Kamil, the *tultul* of Liwo, insisted upon making a court case out of it. The whole group was taken to Wewak. The girl told Ombomb that the *tultul* had seduced her on the way. Ombomb reported this to the District Officer who returned the girl to her husband and jailed both Ombomb and the *tultul* of Liwo. The whole affair had given Ombomb a taste of the

---

[27] Ombomb's three older brothers had been given by his father to the parent gens of *Uyebis* which was becoming impoverished. The eldest, Abugil, had never returned from the white man's land, and the other two, Matasues and Wabe, lived in the other end of the village and will be described later.

role of the man to whom a woman elopes. Me'elue menstruated; he began to live with her. She bore him a child, a girl. His mother, who had five sons, sniffed at the birth of a girl, and went down to live in Moholigum, on the pretext that she was too old to live any longer in the village. Meanwhile, Ombomb outspokenly deprecated his *tinea*-covered, puny wife.

About two years later, two Dunigi women ran away and came to Wihun to find husbands. His cross-cousins in Wihun "held them fast," that is, detained and entertained them, and sent word to Ombomb to come and get one, as he was so dissatisfied with his present wife. He took one of these women, Sauwedjo (Pl. 8a), and Maginala of Alipinagle took the other. Sauwedjo was a lusty, slant-eyed woman, possessive and dominating. Ombomb was devoted to her; he built her a separate house and spent all of his time with her, taking her with him wherever he went. He hardly ever spoke to Me'-elue, except to give her orders.

Ombomb's economic position was peculiar. He was preparing to give the first of a set of feasts for collecting food for an exchange with Belal and Belagomini of Wihun, his *gabunyans*, in a transmission of new *tamberan* flutes. He was helped in this not so much by his fellow gens members, who were already completely occupied with helping Balidu and, to a slighter extent, Baimal, as by Bischu of *Uyebis*, his mother's sister's son, and by Matasues and Wabe, his own older brothers, who had been given to the gens of *Uyebis*. His main ties outside the community were with Wihun; his brother Wupale's wife and his first wife's brothers were Wihun. He was also beginning to build up ties of reciprocal relations with Sauwedjo's kin from Dunigi, although when he first married her there had been considerable hard feeling, and her former husband had died of sorcery.

Ombomb was also irritable over the situation with his two wives; he did not want Me'elue at all; he treated her abominably and in so doing he neglected the gardening for which she was responsible. He left her with Bischu and La'abe most of the time. This made them grumble; after all, she was Ombomb's wife and he should do his husband's share in her gardens; she was not, they pointed out, a widow, but Ombomb's wife whom he had fed and who had borne his child. If he went on like this there would soon be talk of sorcery, they said. Meanwhile, Ombomb talked a good deal; the man who couldn't keep two wives in order didn't amount to much; his wives didn't fight the way La'abe's did; if they did he would beat them. He was the kind of man who could keep two wives in order.

With all of his bluster, he was very easily frightened by the supernatural. When Dr. Fortune took him on a trip into the Plains, he fell seriously ill. He was so alarmed by the danger of giving Dr. Fortune the charms for protecting his gardens, that he first fell ill (from eating hornbill which our shoot boy had shot and he had been given in payment, for he said the charm had gone into the hornbill and both he and his wife fell ill), and then absented himself from the village for several weeks, lest he should be led into more danger.

He was fundamentally a confused person; he took seriously the parts of his culture which other people did not; the ethos of warm happy friendliness, a low amount of sexual specificity, and a general kindliness meant nothing to him. He was bored with his little girl, he valued sex highly, and he did not like other people. If magic was said to be dangerous, he thought it was dangerous. He could give a beautiful formal picture of his culture, but could never be relied upon to relate past events with any accuracy or cultural understanding, because the behavior of his fellows was largely unintelligible to him.

This concludes the members of *Toto'alaibis*. They fell, as a rule, into three little groups: Balidu and his household with Sumali, when he was there; Baimal and his brothers and their households; and Ombomb and La'abe, whose mothers had been Wihun women and whose wives worked closely together. When Kamowon and Yauito'a were younger, Me'-elue or Lomaijo had often suckled both of them. Ombomb and La'abe gardened together; they were both close associates of Bischu and were slightly alien in Alitoa. This alienation was more emphatic among the women, who fell into two groups; the women of Balidu's household and of Baimal's worked together and left the wives of La'abe and Ombomb rather out of it. That Imale, the wife of La'abe, was the sister of Welima, the wife of Wabe, Ombomb's brother, was a further tie between Ombomb and La'abe, and one which drew Imale more to the women of the other end of the village.

The Walinuba end of Alitoa presented a very orderly picture; it was presided over by Balidu, entirely inhabited by the closely related members of *Toto'alaibis,* including the two outlying hunting hamlets of Sumali and Baimal. Its extra-locality relations were represented by ties with Wihun and Liwo and with close ties also with Ahalesimihi and Manuniki within the locality.

When we cross the narrow no-man's land occupied by our house to the Alitoa end of the village, we find a situation as confusing as the Walinuba end was simple. This end belongs theoretically to the gens of *Uyebis,* the original gens of the Alitoa locality, who had come out of bamboos, and who were the hereditary Incisors in the initiation ceremonies and knew the strongest magic, that called *wunakau* which was put on the *tamberan* house. *Toto'alaibis* was regarded as an offshoot of *Uyebis,* from the marriage of a *Uyebis* man with a Dunigi woman. But it seemed as if *Toto'alaibis* had drawn off the strength of *Uyebis,* for in each generation there is a record of sending replacements (*gwai'oyen*) to maintain the strength of the gens.

The land ownership at this end of the village is so complicated that frequent reference to the village plan will be necessary (Fig. 1). Section 1, which included the houses now occupied by Aden, Madje, and Gobonarra, and also the land on which our house was built, all belonged to Balidu and Sumali. Aden had been invited to come and live there by Balidu, at the indirect instigation of Ulaba'i of *Dibatua'am,* whom Balidu called *awalahen* and who was Aden's double brother-in-law. But when people said that Aden of *Kanehoibis* gens was permitted to come and live on Balidu's land, they added, "Aden is the brother-in-law of Balidu"[28] and did

---

[28] This was a very far-fetched relationship. Owing to the return of Yelehiu, the father of Ulaba'i and the son of the brother of Balidu's father, to the gens of *Dibatua'am,* all his descendants were classified as *awalahem* of the members of *Toto'alaibis* gens and

not say "Aden is the *buanyin* of Balidu." It was this latter fact which made Aden's residence on Balidu's land exceedingly awkward whenever there was a *buanyin* quarrel.

Aden had built himself two small neat pile houses on this guest land. He had hardly any need of two houses, for his two wives got on perfectly together. His young half brother Madje, who was an *alapwen* to *Uyebis,* had also built a small pile house here, and there was a tumbledown ground house on the same piece of ground, built by the worthless Gobonarra, Aden's mother's brother.

Aden, was a delicate-featured, aristocratic-looking man who preferred the manipulation of trade to activities like gardening and hunting. He had a great number of trade friends. When, later, he built himself a new house outside of Alitoa, very close to the main road to the Beach, everyone was glad because it meant that fewer of the hated Plainsmen would be coming through the village. His was a secretive, ingrown personality, and people laid much of this to his peculiar relationship history. His mother and father had been first cousins; his mother had been a member of the disappearing gens of *Hamiebis.* Only two members of this gens were left, Gobonarra and his brother Kwanemit, who had gone to live permanently with his wife's people in Liwo. This left Aden with a very poor supply of maternal relatives. His father's sister had married Pailit, so that Matasues, Wabe, and Ombomb were all his cross-cousins, but they were within the immediate community. He had one sister, Ibanyos, who was married to Ulaba'i, the *luluai,* and two brothers: Monau, a full brother who was away at work and was betrothed to Budagiel, the daughter of Sumali, and Madje, who was, however, a doubtful asset. Monau, people said, might be the kind of man his father had been, for people still spoke of the father of Aden. But he had died when Aden was young and had not trained his son very well. People said of Aden that his ears were well open, but his neck was somewhat closed. He would never be a really big man. After the narrowing and restricting effects of his heredity, Aden should, in Arapesh theory, have mar-

---

also as brothers and sisters. Aden had married two of these descendants.

ried at a distance and into a very numerous gens. Instead
he had made a sister-exchange marriage and had married
Baijo, his sister's husband's sister. There was still, of course,
the possibility that some day he might take a second wife
from a distance, but this was obviated when Ulaijo, Baijo's
elder sister, widowed and, liking none of her husband's kin,
returned to Alitoa and married Aden. His situation was articulately recognized by everyone in Alitoa; he was a man
without relatives enough, who had married too close to home,
who lacked the means for expansive social life, and who,
instead of relatives, had only trade friends. And Aden, who
was not an old man, who was, in fact, less than 40 and perhaps as young as 35, smiled and patted the hair of his one
little daughter Sauisua, and said that for this basket of yams
he would like another small knife, the recognized means of
trading with the Plains.

When we reached Alitoa, he was just developing a bad
yaws sore on his foot which was in process of becoming
chronic. His two wives were a mass of fluttering, inept concern. Although they lived next door to us part of the time, I
never got a very definite impression of the personality of
either one. They looked very much alike; Baijo was still
suckling Sauisua. Aden gave some appearance of preferring
the company of the older, Ulaijo, but possibly only because
Sauisua was not yet weaned. The child, a thin, aggressive
little thing, tagged after either wife almost indifferently, or
begged food from her father. Perhaps it was due to Aden's
sore, that sore which played such a role in the community
life during the next few months; perhaps it was due to the
ingrown family, with its suggestion of incest. At any rate,
Aden's household, into which he would welcome the strange
Plainsmen who were his friends but not others, always gave
the impression of being embattled against a hostile world.
Polip and Unabelin of the *Suabibis* gens in Liwo were also his
cross-cousins and attempted to maintain the relationship, but
he was chilly about it and full of grievances. He was a cold,
intelligent, and not particularly likable man.

Madje, Aden's half brother, was a stout youth of about 18,
completely covered with *tinea*, to which he had reacted by
greater robustness than is usual for the average undiseased

Arapesh. Madje was the *alapwen* par excellence, to whom everyone could point as an example of how hard an *alapwen* was to discipline. His mother, who had been the wife of Aden's father and had borne Aden, later, as a widow, married Anouel of *Uyebis* and bore Madje. Madje was given back to the gens of *Kanehoibis*, the gens of Aden's father, as an *alapwen*. Because Anouel had been a *gwai'oyen* from *Toto'-alaibis* to *Uyebis*, Madje was said to belong to the three gentes of *Toto'alaibis*, *Uyebis*, and *Kanehoibis*. He was allowed to go very much his own way, to work when he chose, everyone realizing what he himself was only beginning to sense, that he would probably never be able to get a wife. His great energy and cheerfulness had somehow seemed to obscure the fate that awaited him; only in the months of our stay did it dawn upon him, that despite his energy in gardening, in building yam houses, in hunting, he would never have a wife. As he realized it his cheerfulness turned to sulkiness, and his energy to quite purposeful loafing, and people shrugged their shoulders and said what could you do with an *alapwen*.

The next section, Houses 8, 9, and 13 (Fig. 1), included two old house sites which had belonged to two *Uyebis* brothers, the fathers of Walawahan and Wena. Both of them had left Alitoa permanently to live in Ahalesimihi, returning infrequently to gather coconuts. Walawahan exercised the duties of a Cassowary Incisor in the initiatory ceremonies, but otherwise he maintained scant ties with Alitoa. The distant hamlet of Ahalesimihi was fast growing into a village, with representatives of several gentes living there. But the Alitoa people still regarded Ahalesimihi as a hamlet belonging to the gens of *Diboaibis*. So now these house sites, of men who had deserted *Uyebis* for Ahalesimihi, were spoken of as "belonging to *Diboaibis*." On the site of Walawahan's father's house stood the old *tamberan* house which was now used to house our boys, and Bischu had built a small, walled-in Messiah-cult ground house on Wena's land.

Ulaba'i of *Dibatua'am* gens, the *luluai* of Alitoa, occupied Section 3 (Fig. 1, A) on the opposite side of the ridge, and his site included the largest open space in the whole village; on this plaza he had built a small, unwalled shelter where people could sit and gossip during the heat of the day. Ulaba'i also had two pile houses, one for himself and his two wives and one in which he kept his yams.

Ulaba'i was a short, squat, incredibly tactless man, who always spoke pidgin when he should have spoken Arapesh and Arapesh when pidgin would have been much more appropriate. He had never worked for the white man, and his pidgin was very poor. He was inclined to strut a little, and to vary his strutting with self-pitying comments on his health and laments that now he had become an *alomato'in*. Unbelievable as it was, the people claimed that Ulaba'i had been an energetic and desirable citizen until an illness which had crippled all his bones with pain. He showed no signs of this now, beyond a general drooping of his whole person. It was impossible to tell how much his prestige had always been due to the cooperation of his elder brother Nyelahai. Certainly his two wives now bullied him to death, and his whole life was a feeble, futile effort.

Aden's sister Ibanyos was the wife to whom he had been betrothed as a boy; all her children had died. She was a tall, silent woman, very devoted to her brother, efficient at her work, and always busy with her hands. Everyone believed that she had wanted children; they pitied her as the victim of the mother's brother's curse. Her mother's brother, Kwanemit of *Hamiebis*, who had gone to Liwo, was given no ring from her marriage payment and so had cursed her. After two of her children had died, Aden, calling upon the immediate ghosts of his father and mother, ceremonially removed the curse, but she had no more children.

Whasimai, the second wife of Ulaba'i, had been married when she was an adolescent to the aging brother of Wamu'um, a mother's brother of Ulaba'i. She had taken a great fancy to her husband's sister's son and had run away to him and married him. Her former husband, as the mother's brother of her new husband, had cursed them, and one child had died. Then the former husband himself had died, and his brother Wamu'um had removed the curse.

Whasimai was a voluble, rather foolish woman, always more ready to sit and chatter than to work. As the mother of the children, Whasimai felt sufficiently superior to Ibanyos, so that she did not object to Ibanyos' domination of herself and Ulaba'i. The extreme good humor which prevailed between Ulaba'i's two wives was a matter for much joking, for the Arapesh regarded such an unusual state as only obtainable under conditions of complete dominance by one person.

Whasimai bore Ulaba'i three living children: Anyuai, aged about 10, who was betrothed and living in the home of her betrothed in Liwo; Segenamoya, aged six; and Nemausi, a child at the breast, who was between two and a half and three. Anyuai was a demure little girl, very grown up and conscious of her betrothed status, but still young enough to romp with her small brothers. Segenamoya, not yet wearing a G string and just emerging from babyhood, followed his father about in comical imitation of every gesture, and was a living bundle of curiosity.

Ulaba'i's mother had belonged to *Maliebis,* a gens of Numidipiheim; Whasimai also belonged to Numidipiheim, giving Ulaba'i double ties with that village.

At this time a sister of Ulaba'i, Maisoa, who had left a Numidipiheim husband who had not paid for her properly, was dividing her time between the households of Ulaba'i and Nyelahai. She was a dull, sluggish, very stupid woman.

Through his sister Ulaijo's former marriage, Ulaba'i had ties in Wihun, for she had been married to the brother of Wambibi, the *luluai*[29] of Wihun, the husband of La'abe's sister, and the *buanyin* of Balidu's brothers-in-law Honali and Nigi. After Ulaijo's husband died, Ulaijo brought her small son back to Alitoa, and her brothers Nyelahai and Ulaba'i fed him. When Wambibi claimed him, Nyelahai demanded rings in payment for his growth; when these were refused he cursed his sister's son. To remove the curse, Wambibi paid the rings and got the boy back. But this was long ago and now the *luluai* went often to Wihun.

As a small boy, Ulaba'i had been given as a *gwai'oyen* to a

29 It may be objected that whether or not a man held a Government appointment is of no consequence in the native social organization, but this would be, I think, a false purism. Men of some importance were usually given the positions, and the fact that they held them was felt to give them power and prestige by the other members of the community.

*Uyebis* man, the former husband of Winam, Sumali's present wife. The land upon which his houses now stood in Alitoa really belonged to Magiel, his foster brother, the son of Winam, who was away at work. This was the tie to *Uyebis* providing his foothold in the village, a foothold which he had developed more extensively since he became *luluai*. Just below the village he had a small hamlet site, Moholigum, where his family lived part of the time. This was the permanent residence of two old women, the mother of Ombomb and the mother of Anop, who were gens sisters and members of *Kanehoibis*.

Section $A^2$ (Fig. 1) had belonged to the father of Bischu, who had here a small house which he seldom used. On the Manuniki side Matasues had built a Messiah-cult ground house (No. 8) and Wabe a pile house (No. 9). On the rare occasions when he came to Alitoa, Bischu himself usually shared the dwelling house of Wutue, his father's younger brother. Bischu was a quiet, hairy man; soft black down lay over his rounded cheeks. He was good-humored, almost meditative, hated all strife and quarrels and was always likely to retreat to the bush in the middle of a ceremony. He had been a fine hunter, but in recent years his hunting had suffered, people said, because it had come into contact with sorcery. Bischu had more friends in the Plains and on the Beach than anyone in Alitoa, even Aden. Yet he was not a trader, but a very retiring hunter and gardener. Everybody trusted him and was fond of him, his friends as much so as his relatives. As a result, he was continually in demand to go into the Plains, now with one search party, now with another, looking for sorcery. In time, people sometimes accused him also of having been involved in sorcery transactions, especially jealous people like Wabe and Ombomb, who could not understand his mildness and his flight from fits of temper, for they knew he was no coward. In a fracas, Bischu would leap in, unarmed, seize the spears of the combatants and throw them away. He made not the slightest gesture toward conforming to the demand that able men should be big men. He lived very quietly, as the most private of private citizens, helping his relatives and tilling his garden. In hunting he had depended a great deal on his dogs, and their death was a great grief to him.

His wife Danue was a tall, full-breasted woman, who kept close to his side. As a very little girl she had been given to the *Uyebis* people to be grown; she had been so small that Ombomb and Wabe always called her "sister" (*mohowhi*). After she was grown a little, she had been assigned to Bischu, who already had a betrothed wife, Ma'omen of Wihun. When Ma'omen menstruated, Bischu took her as a second wife, but Danue objected so vigorously that he gave her up to his young cousin Wena, with whom she was now living in Ahalesimihi. Bischu never again tried to take another wife.

They had two children, Yabiok, a girl of four or so, and Anoan, a little boy of two. A second baby girl was born in January. Anoan and the new baby were a little close together for Arapesh standards. Anoan had had to be weaned by the mud method; he was unusually insecure and clung very closely to his father. However, people did not blame Bischu, but were inclined to think that a wife who felt so strongly about other wives might also be like a Plainswoman in other respects, too strongly sexed. Danue kept her own counsel.

Bischu's closest associate was Wutue, his father's younger brother. Wutue, a spry little man much older than he looked, was habitually spoken of as "the old man" by La'abe, Ombomb, Bischu, and the rest, who gathered about him more like children about a mother than like young men about an older one. Wutue had never been an important man. He was peaceful, shy, afraid of crowds, fond of his garden and of the silence of the bush. He used to seek out the most unfrequented parts of his garden land, and there the young men would go and garden with him. They always came to him in his sought-out fastnesses; he himself made no moves, but merely brooded over his gardens like a setting hen. His father had known many things; some of them he had taught Wutue who, among other strange arts, knew how to make bark belts with designs incised upon them.[30] No one else in all the Mountain country knew the art.

Wutue had first married a *Diboaibis* wife, who had died

[30] Mead, 1938, Fig. 60.

childless, and he then inherited the wife of his elder brother, with two small girls, Temos[31] and Sibowala. He later married Mela, of *Toto'alaibis*, who bore him three children; Shuisha, a girl of 11, Yanyibis, a boy of five, Ui, a boy of about two and a half. Sibowala was married in Wihun. Temos was married to Wabe whose Alitoa house stood opposite Wutue's on land which had belonged to the parents of Wutue and Bischu, but which had now been given to Wabe.

Mela was a quiet, dull woman, who disliked coming into Alitoa almost as much as her husband. All the time she was in the village she went about looking worried. Ui cried a great deal, perhaps in response to his mother's nervousness.

Two generations before, Anouel of *Toto'alaibis* had been given to *Uyebis* to replenish their decreasing numbers. But his wife had borne him only girls, so that again, in the next generation, Pailit of *Toto'alaibis* came to the rescue and sent his third son, Matasues, as a *gwai'oyen* to *Uyebis*. Later, Anouel's wife bore him a son, Anop, who was now a young man of about 20, while Matasues was coming to regard himself as an old man. Matasues had inherited the lands and the trees of Anouel, as if he were really the eldest son, but he took good care of Anop, paying for a wife for him and gardening with him.

Matasues had only the Messiah-cult ground house in Alitoa; he came up but seldom, and then rather ceremoniously. He was a gentle, bearded man, who had gone away during the German colonization to work for the white man, but the experience had made little impression on him; he had forgotten all of his pidgin long ago. He was very intelligent, and everyone deferred to his advice, but he made not the slightest attempt to emulate the proper behavior of a big man. His position as eldest brother in the *Uyebis* line which included his younger brother Wabe, also sent as a *gwai'oyen* from *Toto'alaibis*, and his foster brothers Anop and Madje seemed to weigh a little on his narrow shoulders; he discharged his duties anxiously, meticulously, but without enthusiasm. His voice was seldom raised, either in anger or

[31] Temos is described in Mead, 1935b, as the daughter of Wutue, to avoid further complications for the reader, but actually she was his brother's daughter, whose mother he married.

debate; he paid his debts; people spoke of him a little regret-
fully as one who might have made more of himself if only he
had tried. He was the *buanyin* of Nyelahai, the loud-mouthed
older brother of Ulaba'i. It would have been hard to find a
more incongruous pair of *buanyins*.

Matasues had two wives. Wahewai had been betrothed to
a Numidipiheim man who had another wife who took all the
food and made the new young wife very unhappy. Matasues'
elder sister Nalaijo, who was married into Numidipiheim,
conspired to help Wahewai escape and marry Matasues.
The Numidipiheim husband had threatened a fight and the
men of Alitoa had gathered at the river boundary, but their
opponents never came. Wahewai had borne him two boys,
Ashuga, now four years old, and Shu'ite, two.

Matasues' first wife, Minago'a of *Maliebis,* had originally
been betrothed to his elder brother Abugil, who had gone
away to work for the white man. Abugil was one of the two
Alitoa men who had remained permanently away from their
people. He was said to have advanced to the rank of store-
keeper on a plantation near Aitape and was highly valued
for his great intelligence. He returned occasionally to visit his
people; on one such visit he approved of Matasues' marrying
Minago'a, who was somewhat older than he. Minago'a had
borne Matasues two children, Una, now 10, and Anamen, a
boy, who was now five. She now looked like a very old
woman, with drooping, shrunken breasts, and a sour, thin
face. She had bitterly resented the advent of a second wife.

Wahewai was a jolly, robust woman, with a fine full figure showing no ravages from child bearing. She handled
Matasues and her children in the same gentle, ample way
and was always bustling and happy on the few occasions
when they came up to the village.

Una, the daughter of the elder wife, was the model little
girl of Alitoa. Whenever the question of good behavior or
desirable little girls arose, Una, slender, demure, infinitely
serious and watchful, was mentioned. She was always the
first to bring food to strangers, to put a pot on the fire, to have
a firebrand ready to light a cigarette. Una could already "take
her mother's place" in all things. And Una whose good habits,
one guessed, were mainly founded on her adoration for her

grave, gentle father, waited on him, and on all others almost as if they were he, and with a manner which was more his than it was that of her mother or her father's jolly other wife. When little girls were needed for carrying, she came up to Alitoa frequently, to work with Shuisha and Anyuai. She was betrothed to Magiel, Ulaba'i's foster brother, on whose land the house of Ulaba'i stood.

Wabe (Pl. 6a),[32] the next younger brother of Matasues and the fourth son of Pailit of *Toto'alaibis,* had been sent to *Uyebis* when he was a small boy, as a *gwai'oyen.* He had been brought up partly by his mother's sister-in-law, the mother of Anop, and partly by the mother of Bischu. He thought of Bischu and Anop both as younger brothers. Wabe possessed a more violent nature than did his brother Ombomb; he was more proud, more jealous, more possessive, and more afraid of any action which might bring defeat. He was a fine-looking man, with well-defined features, strong muscles, and no trace of the protruding belly which mars most Arapesh figures. When he had worked for the white man, he had been very successful, but in Alitoa there was no role for him to play. A piece of ground, $A^1$, had been given to him as his own, and a young wife, Welima (Pl. 7b) of the gens of *Banyimebis* of Alipinagle, the sister of La'abe's wife, had been marked for him. But although he had been given to *Uyebis,* there seemed no part within *Uyebis* that he could play. Who were the men of *Uyebis*? Wutue, a mild little motherly old man who liked growing and making things; Bischu, who preferred his solitary hunting and endless missions of conciliation to the Plains to more exciting affairs; Matasues, grave, anxious, and retiring. They remained at home, while Walawahan, a great stupid lout of a man, had gone off to Ahalesimihi, and Wena, who was taller than Wabe but also stupider, had joined him there. *Uyebis* was a marked contrast to *Toto'alaibis,* with its orderly hierarchy of descent and leadership, and Wabe had been born *Toto'alaibis.* His younger brother, reared not by the mealy-mouthed *Uyebis* people but by Wupale, their fire-eating elder brother, had been given a better chance in life and was indeed on his way

[32] For an account of Wabe, see Mead, 1935b, pp. 125–130, 148–149. For his photograph, see Mead, 1938, Fig. 94, p. 317.

to being a big man. Loudly Wabe disclaimed any desire to play any role whatsoever. He never had any luck anyhow; his hunting failed, his yams were few, his *buanyins* were dead. No, he would just help Ombomb a little, since Ombomb was foolish enough to give feasts.

Wabe's unfortunate marital affairs were partly responsible for his difficulties. While Welima was still a pre-adolescent girl, Wabe's cross-cousins in Wihun had persuaded him to help them in carrying off Menala, whose husband was not making a proper acknowledgement of his affinal obligations. Wabe had done so, seizing her in her brother's presence, as is customary in such collusive abductions. But Menala was stupid and unimaginative and could never forget that Wabe had carried her off by force. She distrusted and feared him, while he, who in helping her brothers rescue her from an unsuitable marriage had been acting with strict correctness, could not understand her resentment. She lived with him, but she remained afraid of his violence and yielded very readily to the advances of Sinaba'i, a mild widower who shared the other end of the house which he and Wabe had built together. Wabe had tied her up in the central plaza and had beaten her until she confessed. When the whole matter was smoothed over by Balidu's arbitration Menala was given to Sinaba'i, whom she so obviously preferred, with the proviso that their first child should come back to Wabe. In return Wabe received Temos (Pl. 7b), the "daughter" of Wutue, who had been betrothed to Sinaba'i.

Temos was a harsh, aggressive girl, not at all liked by her neighbors, who summed her up in the damning phrase, "she does not give to people." As a child she had been betrothed to Yauwiyu, a mentally deranged youth of Manuniki, but had been kept at home with Wutue until almost puberty. When she had finally been sent to her betrothed, she found him not only already provided with a Dunigi wife, who was greedy and disagreeable, but mentally unbalanced. She returned to Wutue, who then betrothed her to Sinaba'i, whom she had formerly called "father." Not yet adolescent, she now gardened with Sinaba'i and his ten-year-old daughter. Then came the scandal over Sinaba'i's intrigue with Menala, and Temos was transferred to Wabe, whom she had formerly called "cross-cousin." A second time another woman had come between her and a betrothed husband. In Wabe's house there was now the young Welima, a girl of about her own age, but of whom she had seen little, because Wutue lived so constantly in the bush. Temos and Welima reached puberty almost at once; Wabe made their puberty ceremonials close together. Temos hated Welima so much, and Welima feared Temos so much that Wabe had to build a separate house for each one, and then a third house for himself to escape from Temos' fits of rage and Welima's headaches and lamentations. Temos, however, usually won; it was she who accompanied Wabe most often; she was bitter and possessive and determined that this time things were going the way she chose.

Welima, much prettier and gentler than Temos, was confused and unhappy because of all these changes. She had attached herself to Menala, when she came as a co-wife, and she continued to be attached to her after the transfer was effected. She had been betrothed to Wabe for years and felt miserable over the way in which Temos ousted her from her rights as the betrothed wife, keeping Wabe all to herself and hardly letting Welima cook him a meal. When he killed game, the two fought over it until there was nothing left. Temos had miscarried. Both she and Welima had taken magic herbs so as to have no children. Wabe would remark with a twisted smile that it looked as if the only son he would have would be little Aimau, the crowing baby, child of Menala and Sinaba'i.

The last resident of Alitoa for whom we have to account is Sinaba'i. He belonged to *Dibatua'am,* but after the death of Pailit, his father had married the mother of Wabe. He was an extremely mild, friendly man, without any backbone at all—the kind of man who went to all the funerals, helped everyone with everything, and never succeeded in finishing even the very minor tasks which he attempted himself. He was endlessly garrulous, and taught me a great deal about the language because of his boring insistence upon saying the same things repeatedly. His interest in doing other people's work instead of his own never involved him in very extensive labor; the Arapesh voted him lazy; he neither got any meat nor did he raise enough yams to pay others to get it for him. In middle life he was living in half of a house on which Wabe had done most of the work, was married to Wabe's wife whom he had seduced under his nose, with a baby which would have to be given to Wabe. Yet he was not regarded as an *alomato'in*, he was too cheerful and likable for that; rather he was merely accounted as lazy and shiftless.

His marital history had been long and unsuccessful. He was first betrothed to a Numonihi girl, who disliked him because he was lazy and ran away from him before adolescence. Then he was betrothed to a Numidipiheim girl, who also ran away at adolescence. He then inherited a Dunigi woman, the widow of his elder brother, who bore three children, one of whom was dead, and died, leaving him a widower with two small children. The fact that Wutue was willing to let him marry Temos showed his despair of settling the intractable Temos down at a distance, for Sinaba'i would be no asset as a brother-in-law.

His daughter Miduain was a very ugly, good-humored, independent little girl of 11 or so, who was engaged to Sibaiyat, the son of Wamu'um, who was away at work, and spent much of her time working with the parents of her future husband. She was a shrewd, practical child, who had learned to make her father's improvident provision for them go as far as possible.

Her younger brother Dubomagau was about eight, a highly intelligent, sensitive little boy, gawky, underfed, eager for every new experience. He regarded his father as an incompetent and gave the impression of one who was already beyond his father's knowledge. He had a skeptical mind, a high degree of sensuousness, and a great interest in the details of his culture. His little basket, in which he guarded his finished bones or bandages from the Plainsmen, was never out of sight.

I have postponed discussing the affinal ties and gardening plans of these men because of the other complications involved. Aden had a garden of his own; he also gardened with Nyelahai and Ulaba'i. Until recently he had gardened at Malupit with Sumali. As we have seen, he had only the slightest of kinship ties with Liwo. Ulaba'i worked with Aden and

Nyelahai and maintained a small hamlet, Moholigum, at the
foot of the Alitoa hill, where Anop lived all the time. He also
maintained ties with Numidipiheim and Wihun, and now,
through Anyuai's betrothal, with Liwo. Wutue and Bischu
kept very much to themselves; it could be more accurately
said that La'abe and Ombomb were tied to them, than that
they acknowledged any ties to anyone. Each had a house
situated far in the bush, alone. Matasues worked principally
with a constellation of affinal kin, in a new faraway hamlet
called Kwobilisi. Here lived Wamu'um, the husband of
Matasues' dead sister, and his new wife, the mother of
Wena, with a brood of children. Here, because of Anop, also
worked Nahomen, the rather worthless father of Anop's
young wife, and Nahomen's younger brother Inoman. Inoman was the stepson of Yelehiu, the original *alapwen* from
*Toto'alaibis* to *Dibatua'am*, and had been given by Yelehiu
back to *Toto'alaibis*. Matasues' hamlet group was, therefore, a
curious constellation of the old, the young, and the unfit.
Wamu'um was an old man, too old to walk about any longer
to find rings, so that Wabe and Ombomb were beginning to
talk of the need of their finding a wife for Bunitai, Wamu'um's
adolescent son, the son of their dead sister. Bunitai was a
shy, retiring youth who had not yet been initiated, but who,
as had Gerud, had been surreptitiously smuggled into *tamberan* feasts when there were no onlookers from the Beach
present to criticize the unorthodoxy. Bunitai had just been
initiated into the *sagumeh* divination of the same type as
Gerud, and he was observing a three-month taboo period
after it, and had gotten very far behind with his gardening,
so that he seldom appeared in Alitoa.

Anop, who also worked with Matasues, was a fine, upstanding young man, older than Badui, and of very much the same
type, stable, reliable, a good hunter, and a steady worker.
He treated Matasues more as a beloved father than as an
elder brother; there seemed to be no rivalry between the
elder, who was the adopted but inheriting brother, and the
younger, who was the real son of his father. Anop had just
recently consummated his marriage with Yabenas, the fair,
blithe young daughter of Nahomen, and they were a gay and
happy pair, going about much together on small errands.

They divided their time between Moholigum and Kwobilisi. In Moholigum, Anop's sister Wadjubel stayed with the old mother of Matasues and Ombomb. Wadjubel was a full-grown girl, betrothed to a son of Amambut of Ahalesimihi, and had become a source of worry to all Alitoa as the months lengthened into years and her husband did not return to claim her.

Nahomen, the father of Yabenas, was a genuine *alomato'in*, lacking ambition, without any sense of social responsibility, a nerveless ne'er-do-well. He cut pigs for other people, a low, despised occupation. He was a widower; his wife had been the father's sister of Maigi. He had two younger children, Anim, a girl of 10, and Mi'a'inyu, a boy of three. He clung leechlike to Inoman who showed very much the same character. Inoman's wife Domau was an efficient woman whom everyone respected and who amply paid her way in the Kwobilisi group. She had been born *Uyebis* and had been adopted into *Maliebis*, so that whereas Inoman entered the Kwobilisi group through Nahomen, she was also related through her adopted ties with Wamu'um. They had three small children: Oiyale, a boy of 10; Gisoman, a girl of five; and a baby boy, Magi'a, of about a year and a half, who was still suckled.

Both Nahomen and Inoman had a bad reputation for sorcery practices. Both were said to purloin any bits of exuviae which came their way, out of a purely generalized malice. Poor, despised people, with no standards, what else would one expect of them, people said. So Matasues, in safely tucking them away in his faraway hamlet, to which strangers never came, was protecting the community from endless rows and accusations of sorcery which might have eventuated had either of the unsavory pair been about when parties of visitors came through. Both brothers were poor physical specimens; Nahomen, particularly, was only skin and bones; their intelligence was well below the average. They were very poor gardening partners; they were always slipping away and leaving Matasues in the lurch.

Although he actually had no house in the village, Nyelahai, the elder brother of Ulaba'i, and a quasi big man, should also be included with the Alitoa people. Nyelahai was too boast-

ful, too exhibitionistic, too bombastic, for Arapesh tastes. He
had been groomed for a big man, before people realized
that the traits displayed so readily were genuine parts of his
character and not merely appropriate public behavior.[33] He
was restless, uncomfortable in a role which he played too
well, and in which he could not understand his failure. He
took seriously the phantom rivalry allowed with other villages and tried to purloin the exuviae of potential *ano'in*. He
had had no luck in his marriages. His first wife, a sister of
Aden, had died childless; his second wife, a sister of Amambut of Ahalesimihi, had died, leaving him with only one living
child, a puny little creature who must have been 11 or 12,
but who looked six. The other children had died of convulsions. Then, from a Liwo maternal classificatory cousin he inherited a vigorous woman, much older than he, the grandmother of Badui's young wife, and an old virago. She was
almost enough older than Nyelahai to be his mother and
people said he took her only to keep his pigs. Then his eye
fell on the young betrothed wife of his half brother Yabinigi,
Natun of Wihun, the sister of Me'elue, the wife of Ombomb.
Natun disliked Yabinigi because he was deaf. Nyelahai married her against the tacit disapproval of the community which
continued to call her "Yabinigi's wife whom Nyelahai married." After he had married her and she had borne a puny,
ailing baby, Nyelahai found himself again involved in trouble
because of his deviation from his age group; he became
greatly attached to Natun's mother, who was nearer his own
age and a slim, well-preserved woman, but who was unfortunately not a widow. Nyelahai insisted upon calling her
*Yamo*, the word used only for "own mother," and spent a
great deal of time with her. His various marriages had therefore involved him only in confusion.

As long as Ulaba'i had been strong enough to work, with
his help and Aden's and the help of his cross-cousin Henalian,
Nyelahai had managed to put up a fair show. He and Ulaba'i
had built a small *tamberan* house in Moholigum and brought
the *tamberan* there. But, on the whole, he was a big man
with only a verbal role to play; his wives had nicknamed him

[33] Mead, 1935b, p. 147.

Nyelahai, "You walk about," because he was never still. He had made himself a separate little one-man hamlet at a place called Tereba and most of the time he refused to stay there. Yet the people clung to him, humored his bad tempers and his sorcery reputation; big men were scarce, Nyelahai was a sort of big man, his neck was open.

Beachward, across the gorge from Alitoa, were the cliffs of Manuniki where the coconuts were far taller and older than those in Alitoa. Manuniki had been the ceremonial village long before, it was said, and after that had remained the village of the gentes of *Kanehoibis, Uyenehas, Hamiebis,* and *Labinem.* But three generations before, the men of *Kanehoibis* had quarreled; the pig of one brother had littered the village and he had flown into a rage when the others rebuked him, and gone away forever to live in Ahalesimihi. Two descendants of this brother, Nagawe, the son-in-law of Balidu, and Naushe'e still lived in Ahalesimihi, but no longer had any gens relationship with the surviving members of *Kanehoibis,* Aden and his brothers. Of *Hamiebis,* only Gobonarra was left, and Badui cared for their *ginyau* and their lands. *Labinem* too had dwindled, until it was represented by only one man, Agilapwe, and his children. Of *Uyenehas* there remained only Belatau, the father's brother of Maigi, and his children, and Maigi himself. Maigi had had two strong elder brothers, one of whom had been married to the sister of Ulaba'i and Nyelahai, and one had been married to Sagu and Wasijo, the sister's child of Ombomb. Both were dead. People spoke of Manuniki as one might of a living charnel house. Situated high on the cliff, where the white parrots screamed in flocks over the winding path and gave notice of every approach, it was a home of baffled old age and anger. All about grew the dangerous wild taro roots, enough wild taro to give sores to everyone for miles about.

Belatau, or Saidoa as he was also called, was an old man, white-haired, stooped, no longer strong enough for journeying. He shared the fate of the few very old in Arapesh, that of exile from all excitement and festivity because he could no longer manage the roads. His first wife, a woman of Ahalesimihi, had run away from him without bearing him any children. Uwaidjo, his present wife, now an old woman too, came from the distant hamlet of Yapiaun, and had been betrothed to him as a child. They had a son over 20, a twisted, miserable youth, covered with *tinea*, and either stupid or numbed by misery (I never saw enough of him to be able to tell), and a small boy of 10, La'amen.

With them lived Agilapwe, whose pain-twisted face made him look much older than he really was. As it was, his father had married the mother of Aden and Anop. She had fled from him, back to the father of Anop, and then died, it was believed from Agilapwe's father's sorcery. Agilapwe's father had been a witch. Very probably Agilapwe was a witch also, but no one had ever had any proof of it. When he was still a small boy, a bad *framboesa* sore had come up on his leg and, after covering a space about 5 inches long, had become chronic. The people had given up looking for the hidden exuviae long ago. Agilapwe had been taken to the Government doctor to try arsenic injections; it was useless. This rather strengthened the people's belief that there was something wrong about him, for they had great faith in the power of arsenic injections over *framboesa*. He was an infuriated old man, living alone with an old pig keeper, an Alipinagle woman, the widow of a *Uyenehas* man, and three little children, a girl of eight, a girl of six, and a boy of four, children of his dead wife, the sister of Nyelahai. His first wife had been a *Kanehoibis* woman who had died childless. His second wife belonged to the gens of *Suabibis* in Liwo. She had run away from him,[34] and he had pursued her brother with a spear and badly wounded him. Safe in his parrot-patrolled eyrie, he had defied the revenge party which Madjeke of *Suabibis* had wanted to lead against him.

His third wife had been Talomen, the sister of Yabinigi and the half sister of Nyehalai. She was the mother of his children. He had inherited his present wife, or rather pig keeper, from his brother. With Agilapwe also lived Yauwiyu, an adopted son, a great bear of a man, who was generally accepted as mildly insane. Yauwiyu would not work, and wherever he heard the sound of drums beating, he was off to the dance. He suffered from an undiscriminating over-

[34] For a full account, see Mead, 1935b, pp. 159–160.

responsiveness. Yauwiyu had a Dunigi wife and through her Agilapwe kept up a brisk trade connection with the Plains. Yauwiyu, for all his unbalance, was sly and shrewd and was always threatening sorcery, if he did not get his own way. When the brother of Maigi died, Yauwiyu wished to marry Wasijo, his widow. Her mother's brothers, Wupale and Ombomb, objected. She quarreled continuously with Anone, Yauwiyu's Dunigi wife, and ran away to Wihun. Wupale announced his intention of supporting her in her refusal to return to Yauwiyu. Yauwiyu then announced that he had a piece of pepper root of Ombomb's, and chewed bandicoot bones of Kule and Badui, respectively, and that he would kill them all, if Wasijo was not returned. At the same time, Tapita, an old man of Alipinagle, was reported to have said that he had killed Bauwan, the brother of Baimal, and would presently kill Wabe and Kule too, if Wabe did not meet his affinal obligations better.[35] Ombomb and Kule summoned Tapita and Yauwiyu to Alitoa, accused them of their murderous intentions and beat them up, i.e., hit them ceremonially with switches. They added the touch learned from the white man, however, of stretching them over stones before hitting them. (This is the method of punishment known in pidgin English as *seleep bokis.*) After this aberrant behavior by Ombomb and Kule, Yauwiyu sent Ombomb's exuviae to his Dunigi father-in-law.[36] Yauwiyu also sent a

[35] This coincidence here is strictly typical. What probably happened was: Yauwiyu actually made the threat as reported. He was unbalanced and irresponsible enough to use sorcery threats openly. Then someone revived a rumor that Tapita was responsible for Bauwan's death, and Wabe and Kule, already frightened by Yauwiyu's threats, immediately began to worry, Wabe because he was involved in the Wasijo affair and had been dilatory in giving meat to Tapita, and Kule because he was being threatened by Yauwiyu and was the younger brother of the dead Bauwan. The two real situations, the recent death of Bauwan and the threats of Yauwiyu, were used to give verisimilitude to the phantasied additional danger. (This is, of course, a reconstruction of what happened before we arrived, but I have reconstructed the events congruently with Arapesh practice and the characters of the people involved.)

[36] Matasues went into the interior and paid one knife, one ring, and two wooden plates to bribe the sorcerer not to cook Ombomb's exuviae. At about the same time Sumali's house burned down. Matasues' expedition for Ombomb's exuviae was held responsible;

half-chewed bandicoot bone which Badui had eaten to some trade friends in the Nugum country. After this, the mother's brothers of Wasijo had had enough, and they sent her back to Yauwiyu.

Yauwiyu also periodically ran amuck. Ombomb was now plotting to persuade Wasijo to give him dog's dung soup, to cure him of his madness. But none of these methods, neither the old one of the dog's dung soup, nor the new one of flogging, could remove the menace of a man like Yauwiyu, with his bad-tempered, sore-ridden old adopted father, with his wife whose relatives' main traffic was in sorcery, and his own combined shrewdness and mental instability. Before such a combination, the responsible members of the community were helpless, as they were to control Agilapwe's trafficking in his wild taro patch.

Agilapwe, in spite of his infirmity, his bad disposition, and worse reputation, kept up a fairly lively relationship with some half brothers in Malis,[37] where his daughter was also married, and with the people of Alitoa proper. He was always present at ceremonial exchanges, making a fuss about something, but also taking his share of the obligating platters of food.

On the opposite side of Alitoa and a little farther away was the village of Alipinagle of the gens of *Banyimebis*. Long ago, in the time of La'abe's father's father, the people of Alipinagle had been enemies, and La'abe's grandfather had made peace by sending two women from Alitoa to marry in Alipinagle. They were sent freely, no return was ever asked for them, and peace reigned, although someone occasionally recalled the tale of how long ago, when there had been a death in Alipinagle, the Alitoa people had swarmed up the coconut trees and shouted with joy.[38]

Alipinagle was more closely allied to Wihun than to Alitoa,

he was believed to have taken a ring in at Nyelahai's behest to secure the firing of Sumali's house at the same time. However, no one, except Sumali, seriously believed that accusation.

[37] Near Mowia on map, Mead, 1937a; Edel, 1937.

[38] This is the obverse of the behavior of a friendly hamlet on the occasion of a death, when all rejoicing and all feasting must be stopped. The fear of such a death always hangs over any feast in Arapesh.

although the inhabitants now formally regarded Alitoa as their ceremonial center. It was a dying village, trying desperately to tempt new recruits to live there, and its present population was very mixed. At present, Henalian, the mother's brother of Ulaba'i, lived there, and Ulaba'i's mother lived with him. He was a pompous, blustery, lazy, insignificant man. He was a hereditary pig castrator. Here also lived Maginala, a cross-cousin of Wabe and Ombomb, with his two wives, one a Dunigi woman who had run away at the same time as Sauwedjo, Ombomb's wife, and one, from Boinam. With him lived Iwamini, the younger brother of Aden, who had been given as a *gwai'oyen* to the dying gens of *Banyimebis*. Iwamini was a gentle, delicate-featured youth, rather afraid of Aden, who had tried two or three years before to take his young betrothed wife, Yinauwhat of *Uyenehas*, away from him, and inclined to stay very close to Maginala's side. Maginala also had an unmarried sister of 18, Weamali, and a half brother, Ga'olin, who was a weak man, covered with *tinea* and unmarried. There was old Tapita, a disgruntled old man who had been born into the Ahalesimihi branch of *Kanehoibis*, and had married into Alipinagle, and after his wife's death had remained there. He had a Boinam wife and a child of three. Last, there was Wegul of Liwo, whose teeth were crooked and who was suspected of being a witch and said to know the magic by which the night was made to last twice as long when other people were weary of dancing. His mother, who now lived with him as a widow, had brought him home as a child, when she returned to her own village, and he had grown up there, with periodic returns to Liwo. Then he eloped with the wife of his cross-cousin Henalian, and the pair fled back to Liwo, where they remained for several years before returning to Alipinagle. Henalian had got out the *tamberan* against him. Wegul had three sons by a former Liwo wife, who was now in Liwo. In order to validate further their claim on Alipinagle ground, it was planned that they should be formally adopted: one, by Henalian, in return for his wife; the second, by Maginala, as a member of Alipinagle; and the third, by Wabe, to give him an Alipinagle child to bring up. In Alipinagle also there was one wife of Selalimi, the father of Welima; he had been born *Banyimebis*, but had moved to Ahalesimihi with his mother's brother, taking his one wife and three children with him, but his inherited wife, the widow Sa'i'o'o, a Wihun woman, had refused to go and remained in Alipinagle with her dead husband's child.

Alipinagle represented, though in less extreme form, the same tendencies as did Manuniki. It was a dying community, inhabited by various unfit and antisocial persons. Only Maginala was a really upstanding and reputable man, and although sturdy and reliable and a good hunter, he was not very intelligent, not nearly intelligent enough to unify the strangely assorted group of the old, the runaway, and the disapproved who constituted his community. He and Iwamini cooperated with their cross-cousins in Alitoa whenever possible; he also made the futile gesture of trying to keep his sister from marrying, in the hope of attracting at least one more good man to Alipinagle.

Beyond Alipinagle and even more closely allied to Wihun and Boinam in feeling was Yapiaun, the tiny hamlet from which the gens of *Biegilipim* had come, the gens to which the mother of Baimal and Kule and the mother of Lomaijo belonged. Yapiaun was really only a family hamlet, perched on the top of a hill with hardly room for a few small houses. Balili was the big man of Yapiaun, living there with his old father Sama'a, his brother Yamogwai, and Yamogwai's young Numonihi wife, and three wives of his own—one from Wihun, one from Numonihi, and one from Boinam. Balili was a shrewd, spry man; he had Baimal's lightness without his gentleness. In feeling, he belonged more with the Plains than with the Mountains; his attempts to emulate the imported feasting practices of the Mountains were feeble. Baimal and Kule, so indefatigable in maintaining their kin ties, always helped Balili and invited him to help them; it was through them that he came to Alitoa, or participated in affairs like the Kobelen purchase of the *shené*, to which he unexpectedly contributed a pig.

Ahalesimihi was the most distant, most prosperous hamlet in the Alitoa locality. Although people of Alitoa always spoke of it as a mere residential hamlet of the gens of *Diboaibis*, and insisted on assimilating to *Diboaibis* anyone who lived long in Ahalesimihi, actually it was almost a center in itself, with important affiliations with Wihun and Numonihi, and had as special a relationship to the Plains locality of Ilapweim as had Alitoa with Dunigi.

Nagawe, the son-in-law of Balidu, was the big man of *Diboaibis*. He was a tall, gaunt man, habitually silent, but able to make a good speech when necessary. He was a famous hunter and good organizer. Under his leadership Ahalesimihi had purchased the *tangeba* dance complex from Sublamon; in preparation for this ceremony they had called the people of Walinuba as dogs. The undertaking had been a little too ambitious, however, for the men of Sublamon had been so dissatisfied with the gifts received that they had taken away one of the masks.

Nagawe had two wives; the elder wife, Alo, who came from Yapiaun, had borne him two children, Anau, a boy now 10, and Malagi, now a girl of five. His second wife, Yapul, the daughter of Balidu, was so much younger than Alo and Nagawe that she seemed more like a daughter to them. She had two children, Maleheu, a girl of three, and Otamai, a boy about six months old.

With Nagawe worked also his nephew Wena, the tallest man in Alitoa. Wena's mother, now the wife of Wamu'um, was the sister of Nagawe, and Wena had given up all interest in his *Uyebis* lands near Alitoa, to live entirely close to his mother's brother. His young wife, Ma'omen of Wihun, had been betrothed to Bischu of *Uyebis*, who had given her to his young relative Wena.

With them worked also Walawahan, another *Uyebis* man, one of the men who actively exercised his hereditary right as Incisor in the *tamberan* ceremonies. His first wife had been an Ahalesimihi woman, and while she was still living, he moved to Ahalesimihi. She died and left him with two children, Sala'a, now a boy of 14, and Sauiadjo, a girl now 10. He was then a not particularly attractive widower, slow, unambitious, and not a very good provider. Nevertheless, Suamali of Wihun ran away to him, when the brother of Agilapwe turned her out because she had *tinea*. Walawahan took her in, and they now had an infant son.

With Nagawe worked also his brother Naushe'e, a slender, proud, aloof man who had quarreled with the people of Ahalesimihi years before and run away to his gift friends in Ilapweim. He had lived there many years and married an Ilapweim wife and had only recently returned to Ahalesimihi, with a three-year-old boy, Ame', and Moshesh, an infant boy. People looked at him a little strangely and spoke of him as an Ilapweim man now living in Ahalesimihi. He too had a strange, distant look in his eye, and when he was asked to paint bark paintings for us, painted over and over one intricate Plains design, the only one which he seemed to have learned.

All these men, Nagawe, Naushe'e, Wena, and Walawahan, were not *Diboaibis*, and yet were attached by permanent ties now to Ahalesimihi. Three of them had strong ties in Alitoa: Wena and Walawahan with the Alitoa side by birth, and Nagawe with Walinuba through his marriage with Yapul.

The other strong group in Ahalesimihi was headed by Silisium, the younger of two brothers, of whom the elder was Manum, the husband of Homendjuai, the sister of La'abe. Both were big, thickset men, who looked very much alike, slow, heavy, slightly overbearing. Yet there was no doubt in anyone's mind that Silisium was by far the more intelligent. Still, to do lip service to the theory of primogeniture, it was always said that such and such was done by Manum and Silisium together. The two brothers got on very well as a rule.[39]

Silisium had a Numonihi wife, Ya'umen, and four children: Gowais, a girl of 12, betrothed to Badui; Nautal, a girl of nine; Malipim, a boy of three; and an infant girl. He had formerly inherited a Numonihi wife from a mother's brother, but she had died childless. He marked another wife from Numonihi, but Ya'umen, who was regarded as something of a virago, drove her away.

Manum was first married to an elder sister of La'abe's,

[39] For the adultery which temporarily estranged them, see below, pp. 396–397, and Mead, 1935b, pp. 131–133.

named Homendjuai, who died soon after adolescence. He then married the younger sister Nigisiman, who changed her name to that of her older sister, Homendjuai. She bore him five children, all boys, the eldest of whom, Mai, was 14 and was betrothed to Amus, the daughter of Baimal. La'atowin was 11; Kubi, eight; Naipa'um, four; and Anuli, an infant. Homendjuai was a vigorous woman, one of whose breasts had hung atrophied while she had suckled her five sons from the other. She was bored and always a little impatient with her big stupid bear of a husband. He was the hereditary pig castrator for Ahalesimihi.

With Manum and Silisium worked Gabunyan, the son of a dead elder brother of Silisium and an elder sister of Sumali and Balidu, Nigilowe, who now, as a widow, lived with her son. He had a sprightly young wife, Malasamum of Wihun, whom he had grown.

Selalimi, the father of Welima and Imale, also lived in Ahalesimihi and worked with Manum and Silisium. He had inherited his present wife, Samanuai of Wihun, from a dead brother. They had three children, Iwatien, a girl of 12, Ilawen, a boy of seven, and Manawam, a girl of five. He also inherited a *Banyimebis* woman who died, childless, and a third widow, Sai'o'o of Wihun, who continued to live in Alipinagle, where Selalimi really belonged.

Amambut was the old man of Ahalesimihi, a close contemporary of Pailit. He had two wives, one inherited from an elder brother, and the other the widow of a Liwo man. They were mother and daughter. Amambut had first married the daughter, No'abis, by whom he had two children, a boy of 12 and a girl of four; then the mother had followed the daughter and he had married her too.[40] Amambut was the father's brother of Lomaijo, the wife of La'abe.

Amambut had always been a rather unimportant, disgruntled man. Years before, when Manola, the elder brother of Silisium, died, he had inherited one of his wives, because Ya'umen refused to let Silisium take her. This wife was a

---

[40] This practice had been initiated by another Ahalesimihi man in the previous generation. People were saying that soon this would be an Ahalesimihi custom.

*Kanehoibis* woman, the sister of the mother of Ombomb and Wabe, and also the sister of the mother of Anop. She had not wanted to stay with Amambut, who already had one wife, and she had been alienated by Tapita. But Pailit and the father of Anop and the rest of Alitoa disapproved of this shift and insisted upon her returning to Amambut. Tapita kept some of her exuviae and she eventually died, it was said, of sorcery. In the meanwhile, the shiftless Amambut did not fulfill any of his affinal obligations, and his affinal relatives complained about his lack of gratitude for the help that they had given him. The phrasing of this account, as I received it, is now interesting. "Amambut feared a quarrel. He stole a bandicoot bone from a meal eaten in his house by Ulaba'i and Wabe." This is treacherous and inadmissible sorcery practice, comparable to the behavior of Yauwiyu. Amambut sent the exuviae through a Wihun friend to Bauné of Biligil. When Wabe returned from work some six years after this had happened, he fell ill and word was sent to him through intermediaries as to the location of this bone. Wabe declared that he had confronted Amambut with the rumor and ordered him to go and make the sorcery cold. This was done without hope, however, and Wabe himself paid the blackmail, one ring, one plane blade, one knife, one tomahawk, and later another knife. For the same exuviae Ulaba'i has been blackmailed three rings and three knives. Amambut again represented a social liability in the community, taking unwarranted advantage of the institution of sorcery.

## MEN AWAY AT WORK AND WHITE CONTACT

As will have appeared from the previous listing of male inhabitants of Alitoa, the Mountain region has not been exhaustively recruited. The hamlets are so scattered that most recruiters prefer to go straight through to the more densely populated Plains. However, enough young men are away at work to have made a considerable difference in the social scene had they been present; their principal contribution

as absentees was to complicate the whole marriage problem.
A list follows:

| Name of Boy | Closest<br>Male Relative[41] | Where Working[42] |
|---|---|---|
| Subaiyat | Wamu'um | Salamoa |
| Bioyat | Amambut | Rabaul |
| Yanyibis | Amambut | Awar |
| Atuhibin | Amambut | Salamoa |
| Waisen | Amambut | Kavieng |
| So'openin | Anop | Salamoa |
| Monau | Aden | Kavieng |
| Sausa | Baimal | Salamoa |
| Baliat | Ulaba'i | Salamoa |
| Magiel | Ulaba'i | Salamoa |
| Yoipin | Ulaba'i | Kokopo |
| Nauwhi'u | Naushe'e | Rabaul |
| Loiyal | Maigi | (Left permanently and married a native near Awar) |
| Abugil | Matasues | (Left permanently and settled on a plantation near Aitape) |

The most significant thing about this list is the number
of young male relatives of Amambut who were away. Amambut at present occupies the position of a disgruntled and
unimportant old man, but it is possible that if even one or
two of his four absent relatives were back, the picture might
be quite different. Baimal had two brothers away, but two
at home made an adequate unit. Ulaba'i also lacks two potential helpers which may well have added to his economic
downfall.

In this connection it may be useful to review the working
experience of the men who now constituted the Alitoa population.

[41] Does not, of course, guarantee that there would have been
cooperation between them.
[42] This is merely the general area of work. Unless a boy has
come back to his village and returned to the same work place, his
relatives do not know his whereabouts more exactly.

OLDER GENERATION

| Matasues | Worked for a short time | Has forgotten pidgin |
|---|---|---|
| Aden | Carried off by a raiding recruiting party and escaped | No pidgin |
| Baimal | Carried off by a raiding recruiting party and escaped | No pidgin |
| Balidu | No working experience | No pidgin |
| Sumali | No working experience | No pidgin |
| Nyelahai | No working experience | No pidgin |
| Ulaba'i | No working experience | A little pidgin learned in the village |
| Wutue | No working experience | No pidgin |
| Bischu | No working experience | No pidgin |
| Kule | Indentured laborer and training as medical *tultul* | Pidgin |
| Ombomb | Indentured laborer and training as medical *tultul* | Pidgin |
| Wabe | Indentured laborer | Pidgin |
| La'abe | Indentured laborer on Government station | Pidgin |
| Sinaba'i | No working experience | No pidgin |

Maigi was the only one of the younger boys at home (Alis, Bunitai, Anop, Madje, Gabunyan, Badui, Pidjui) who had ever been away to work for a short time. Yabinigi, now our shoot boy, had worked for the Mission. Gerud was gaining a little experience and some understanding of pidgin from working for us.

The question arises how much the experience with the white man and the prestige, wider knowledge, and understanding gained thereby affected the interrelationships of the various men in the community. I am inclined to think that it altered the relationships between brothers to some extent, when the younger brother had been away to work and the elder had not, and undermined somewhat the elder brother's traditional authority. La'abe, by virtue of his having worked on a Government station and his presumed understanding of the ways of Government officers, was raised to a more important position, as *tultul*, than his personality entitled him to hold. Ulaba'i's continued retention of the title of *luluai*, after he had slipped so far down on the social scale, was an extra prop which he might not have had in former days. But relationships with the white man were so intermittent that the returned work boy had very little opportunity to demonstrate his superiority in dealing with him; the absence of traveling police boys also served to diminish the role of the returned indentured laborer. In an ordinary gathering of Arapesh men, it was impossible to tell, either by costume, bearing, or behavior toward their elders or to one another, which had worked for the white man and which had not— a very unusual state of affairs in New Guinea.

It is also necessary to ask how white contact had affected the functioning of Alitoa. When we follow the course of events there for a period of months, how much must be attributed to the immediate presence of our complicating household, or to the more diffuse effects of contact? In addition to the absence of young men and the disturbances in intra-group dominance and leadership resulting from some men's having worked and others not, there were, of course, other effects.

Fighting had been forbidden. The last interlocality murder, in which the mother and small brother of Lomaijo had been killed, had been severely dealt with by the Government. Several men had been imprisoned for it, and Amambut had gone all the way to Rabaul as a witness in the case. As the Arapesh were not head hunters and fighting was so slightly integrated into their social system, this did not result in a serious disarrangement of the social order, such as occurs in head-hunting societies like those of the Sepik River. But it did mean, no doubt, a certain lightening of tension; brothers were a little more cavalier in conniving with their sisters' elopements and not so harsh in insisting upon their return; perhaps a pig or so a year was killed which would not have been killed before. At the same time that tension was lightened among the Mountain people themselves, two new forms of tension developed: greater tension along the roads, which were losing their sanctions as the idea of the King's Highway developed, and a greater tyranny on the part of the sorcerers, who now walked unarmed among an unarmed people, where the power was all on their side. Formerly, although the sorcerer always carried his black magic with him, he nevertheless had to move warily—there was always the chance that he might be killed in spite of the fear of a sorcery vengeance. Now any such murder would be punished by the Government. This greater immunity of the traveling Plainsmen coincided with an increased demand for Beach goods, as the white man's goods, knives, tomahawks, and plane blades entered by way of the Beach. These two combined influences may well have resulted in accentuating the Plains drain upon the resources of the Mountains.

Economically, there were very few repercussions. Nothing the white man possessed, except knives and adze blades of which they obtained a good supply in trade from the Beach, had yet become an essential. Clothes were still a luxury and matches an item of display. It is true that an Arapesh's trading range had increased somewhat owing to the Pax Britannica. Alitoa men could now go along the Beach and into the hills of Wewak, trading for tobacco, and make better bargains than they had made before nearer home. The world was wider and its goods more numerous, but the center of life remained the same, as far as could be determined. The removal of the threat of violence always alters the life of a people, but it would be hard to find a group to which it made less difference than to the prevailingly peaceful Arapesh.

## INTERRELATIONSHIPS BETWEEN GENTES IN THE ALITOA CENTER

The hamlet center of Alitoa included its own dual division into *iwhul* and *ginyau*, at present aligned as:

| iwhul | ginyau |
|---|---|
| "The side of the *luluai*" | "The side of the *tultul*" |
| Uyebis | Toto'alaibis |
| Dibatua'am | Uyenehas |
| Kanehoibis | Hamiebis |
| Labinem | |

These relationships had changed frequently in history. *Toto'alaibis*, *Uyebis*, and *Uyenehas* are all three *kwain* and share a *marsalai* place, Buté; and *Hamiebis* and *Labinem* share a *marsalai* place, Uweíbun, and are said to have co-operated together in the past.

Sometimes an informant will give the *iwhul-ginyau* divisions as they existed for some big feast in the past, so the same informant will say:

One *ginyau: Toto'alaibis, Diboaibis, Uyebis,* and *Biegilipim*
Their *iwhul: Kanehoibis, Labinem, Dibatua'am, Suabibis*[43]

Also:

One *iwhul: Kanehoibis, Hamiebis, Diboaibis*[44]
Their *ginyau: Toto'alaibis, Diboaibis, Uyebis, Uyenehas, Biegilipim*

At present also there are splits. Maginala helps *Toto'alaibis,* while his brother Ga'olin helps *Uyebis,* etc. Nagawe helps *Uyebis;* Manum and Silisium help *Toto'alaibis,* etc.

Another way in which the various alignments are phrased is to state the main links between gentes or feasting divisions. So at present it could be said: Numidipiheim helps *iwhul,* called in by Nyelahai, or *Suabibis* helps *iwhul* called in by Aden.

Because of the possibility of a gens' splitting its allegiances so that some members help one side and some the other, the actual interrelationships between members of gentes are more important. They can be stated only as ties between pairs, thus:

### *Toto'alaibis* AND *Uyebis*

Two *gwai'oyen,* Matasues and Wabe
Winam, now married to Sumali of *Toto'alaibis,* was previously married to a *Uyebis* man, father of Magiel, so that children of Sumali have a half brother who is *Uyebis*
Una, the daughter of Matasues, is betrothed to Magiel of *Uyebis*

---

[43] This would refer to a special large occasion in which *Suabibis* cooperated with Alitoa, etc.
[44] This would indicate that *Diboaibis* split and certain men helped each side.

Temos of *Uyebis* is married to Wabe, *gwai'oyen* from *Toto'alaibis*[45]

## Toto'alaibis AND Dibatua'am

Through the *alapwen* relationship of Yeheliu, father of Nyelahai, all his children are *awalahem* to *Toto'alaibis*

Pailit married the widow of a *Dibatua'am* man, mother of Sinaba'i, so Sinaba'i was regarded as a half brother by the *Toto'alaibis* children of Pailit (father of Matasues, Ombomb, Wabe)

## Toto'alaibis AND Kanehoibis

The chief tie here was the intermarriage in the last generation between Muliwen of *Kanehoibis* and Pailit of *Toto'alaibis*

In the present generation there was the betrothal of Monau and Budagiel

Also Amito'a, wife of Baimal, had had a *Kanehoibis* mother and kept up her sense of *Kanehoibis* membership

## Toto'alaibis AND Uyenehas

These two gentes were bound together by a whole series of contemporary marriages and by the fact that *Uyenehas* was disappearing. The marriages were Kule to Ilautoa, Alis to Taumulimen, Sagu to Maigi's brother and then to Maigi (the contemplated betrothal of Kumati to a *Labinem* man who had become absorbed into *Uyenehas*)

## Toto'alaibis AND Hamiebis

The sister of Balidu had married a *Hamiebis* man and borne one son, Pidjui, whom Balidu had brought up and whose heir Badui was to be

An additional tie was the residence of Gobonarra on Sumali's land. As, however, there was no *Hamiebis* left, these ties merely served to reinforce the relationship between *Toto'alaibis* and Aden, whose mother had been *Hamiebis*

## Uyebis AND Dibatua'am

Ulaba'i had been adopted as a child by the father of Magiel, so that he was a *gwai'oyen* to *Uyebis*

[45] Note here that both of these *gwai'oyen* relationships had been taken advantage of to permit marriage which was functionally within the gens. In Wabe's case there had been some demurring because he was also related to Temos through his mother.

Anop's marriage to Yabenas, daughter of Nahomen, a *mahonin* of Yelehiu of *Dibatua'am*

The strongest ties, however, were through the *Toto'alaibis gwai'oyen,* who were themselves, through Yelehiu, closely allied with *Dibatua'am*

### *Uyebis* AND *Kanehoibis*

The main tie here was through the second marriage of Saluwen, who married first the father of Anop, and subsequently the father of Aden, and bore Madje, who was returned as an *alapwen* to *Uyebis.* This linked Anop, Madje, and Aden, and Matasues, who had been reared by the father of Anop, to Aden also

### *Uyebis* AND *Uyenehas*

There were no formal ties here at all

### *Uyebis* AND *Labinem*

No ties[46]

### *Uyebis* AND *Hamiebis*

No ties[46]

### *Dibatua'am* AND *Kanehoibis*

The ties between Nyelahai, Ulaba'i, and Aden had been reenforced by double sister-exchange. Ulaba'i had married Ibanyos, sister of Aden, Nyelahai's previous wife had been a sister of Aden, and Aden's two wives were sisters of Nyelahai and Ulaba'i. In a sense, Aden, the last of his *Kanehoibis* line (I am excluding from discussion Nagawe and Naushe'e who considered themselves completely cut off) was becoming absorbed into *Dibatua'am,* also a small and needy gens. Whether this absorption was complete would depend upon the role which Monau played, and whether Madje succeeded in establishing himself, and which gens he worked with, *Kanehoibis* or *Uyebis*

[46] The lack of ties here is mainly due to the small size of these three gentes. When a gens is disappearing, other gentes are wary of intermarriage. The result is likely to be the kind of incorporation in one other gens which had taken place in the case of *Uyenehas,* in their intermarriages with *Toto'alaibis.* When Belatau dies, Maigi will be probably classified as *Toto'alaibis* and there will be an end to the gens of *Uyenehas.*

### *Dibatua'am* AND *Uyenehas*

There were two ties here. In both one link was dead: the marriage of Welenue, the sister of Ulaba'i to the brother of Maigi, and the marriage of the sister of Maigi to Nahomen. These ties now survived mainly as irritating links with the past, and as unfortunate ties with Yauwiyu

### *Dibatua'am* AND *Labinem*

Only tie through Agilapwe's dead wife, who was the half sister of Nyelahai, full sister of Yabinigi

### *Dibatua'am* AND *Hamiebis*

No ties except through Aden's closeness to *Hamiebis*

### *Kanehoibis* AND *Hamiebis*

Aden's mother had been *Hamiebis,* and she, the dead Pidjui, the sister's son of Balidu, and her two brothers, Gobonarra and Kwanemit, had been the only survivors, so that before Kwanemit left, people already spoke of the two gentes as one, even to the extent of saying that Aden had married into his *own* gens

### *Kanehoibis* AND *Labinem*

The mother of Aden had married the father of Agilapwe, and Agilapwe, much older than Aden, had brought him up, thus making a close but rather quarrelsome tie

### *Kanehoibis* AND *Uyenehas*

The only tie here was through the marriage of Iwamini, *Kanehoibis gwai'oyen* to Alipinagle, to Yinauwhat of *Uyenehas*

### *Uyenehas* AND *Labinem*

These two gentes had lived side by side for a long time, and Agilapwe's present and fourth wife was the widow of a *Uyenehas* man. *Labinem* was generally spoken of as one with *Uyenehas*

This summary shows the major ties, adoption in the two forms, foster brotherhood, affinal ties, mother's-brother, sister-son, and cross-cousin ties, and common residence which weld gentes together. I have purposely omitted here a discussion of *buanyins,* just as I omitted a discussion of gift friends in the description of relationships between localities, because such ties are of a slightly different order.

This outline gives the structural interrelationships between localities, hamlets, and gentes, but of far greater importance was the question of what individuals embodied these relationships. Where the ties of men like Sinaba'i or Wutue were negligible, those of Balidu and Nyelahai were important. It will appear in the course of the *Diary* that there were two types of men whose ramified relationships affected the whole community: leaders, aggressive, intelligent, responsible men, who used these ties for socially valuable purposes, and the *alomato'in* and the mentally unbalanced who used their ties, especially with the Plains, for evil. It will be seen that the fact that Balidu, Honali, and Nigi were brothers-in-law, and so welded Wihun and Alitoa together, could be set over against the fact that the irresponsible, malicious Yauwiyu had a Dunigi wife and so kept open the paths of sorcery. This corresponds, of course, to the two uses to which the great roads can themselves be put, an extension of socio-economic ties, or an extension of sorcery practice. So it was also in the interrelationships between members of smaller groups.

The life of the whole Mountain people might be described as a continuous process of reaching out and withdrawal, and whether one temporarily triumphed over the other depended upon whether there were more Balidu's or more Yauwiyu's in the community.

In societies where kinship duties are sharply defined and well differentiated, the formal types of ties between gentes or between hamlets would be very important. In Arapesh, however, where all kinship ties tended to be honored in very much the same way, and where even the differences between Class One and Class Two ties were interchangeable, the number of ties and the personalities and social status of the individuals who embodied them were far more important. Any attempt to diagram the position of Alitoa would have to take these two factors into account, plus the relative strength, size, and importance of the various groups, gentes, hamlet clusters, and localities with which these ties existed. It is also important whether the group with which one's group is tied has other resources which do not draw on one's own resources at all. See below (p. 449), the case in which Bunitai was not invited to Aden's *garamut* hauling feast because the pig which *Suabibis* had given Aden had originally come from the gens of *Maliebis,* and Bunitai could not be invited to eat his own pig. On the other hand, *Suabibis* kept up many relationships with Suapali which did not drain Alitoa, except in the circumstances in which Suapali had drawn on Numidipiheim which had itself already drawn on Alitoa.

## INTERRELATIONSHIPS WITH OTHER LOCALITIES

In the course of discussing the members of the locality of Alitoa, their connections by intermarriages in this and in the previous generation with other localities[47] have been touched upon, but it may be well to summarize them here.

### TIES WITH THE PLAINS

#### To Dunigi

General ties between Alitoa, especially the gens of *Toto'alaibis,* and Dunigi as a whole due to old marriages five generations ago
Individual ties between Dunigi and Alitoa:

| | |
|---|---|
| Sinaba'i | Through previous wife |
| Yauwiyu | Through present wife, Anone |
| Ombomb | Through present wife, Sauwedjo |
| Maginala | Through present wife, Aga'amwi |
| (Gobonarra | Through present wife, Gulumen, virtually functionless) |

#### To Ilapweim

General ties between Ahalesimihi and Ilapweim
Individual tie between:

| | |
|---|---|
| Naushe'e | Through present wife, Weyal |

#### To Boinam

No general ties
Individual ties between:

| | |
|---|---|
| Maginala | Through present wife, Soasalamo |
| Balili | Through present wife, Halesiu |

[47] Mead, 1938, p. 156, for a map of the Arapesh country.

## To Ybonimu

No general relationship
Individual tie between:

| | |
|---|---|
| Tapita | Through present wife, Adule |

## TIES WITH THE BEACH

### To Kobelen

Alitoa, both *Toto'alaibis* and *Kanehoibis* strong general ties
Balidu was initiated in Kobelen

### To Sublamon (Magahine)

Ahalesimihi have strong general ties to Magahine
Gens of *Kanehoibis* has ties with Magahine

### To Waginara

No general ties
Individual ties because Bischu's father's sister was married there

## TIES WITH MOUNTAIN NEIGHBORS

### To Bugabihiem

General strained relationship, due to death of Pailit in previous generation which was attributed to his wife, a Bugabihiem woman
Individual ties between:

| | |
|---|---|
| Balidu | Through marriage of his daughter Bwa'o to a Bugabihiem man; but both were away at work |
| Sinaba'i | Had a Bugabihiem mother; she later married Pailit and was held responsible for his death. This tie never exercised in any way |

### To Liwo

History of many intermarriages and some recent clashes. Of these latter the most notable were: 1, the fight over Tapik (pp. 329–341) between Alitoa and Liwo proper; 2, the fight over Amito'a's elopement to Baimal, between Alitoa and *Suabibis*
It is customary to think of Liwo in two divisions:

1. *Aunyebimen,* which includes the gentes of *Labinem, Nyumeduakum, Ashue'bis,* and *Suabibis.* Of these *Suabibis* is the leading gens, and Alitoa usually spoke of this whole group either as "the *tultul's* division" or "all the people of *Suabibis.*" To this division belonged: Madjeke, Polip, Unabelin, Siakaru,

Kwanemit (the brother of Gobonarra), the brother of La'abe, the *tultul.* This division had formerly cooperated with the *ginyau* division of Alitoa and engaged in perennial controversies with *iwhul*

2. Now usually called Liwo, formerly *Iluwhibimen,* includes the gentes of *Whoibanibis* and *Dibatua'am.*[48] This group contained Whoiban,[49] the doctor boy, and *luluai,* Yelegen, Yelusha, and Ipagu, the brother of Amito'a. This division was traditionally on good terms with the Alitoa *iwhul*

Most important ties:

*Present generation*

    Through betrothal of Gerud to a girl of *Suabibis*

    Through betrothal of Anyuai to a boy of *Ashue'bis*

    Through marriage of Baimal with Amito'a

    Through betrothal of Badui to Sa'omale

    Through marriage of Nyelahai with Nyalamidju

    Through marriage of Maigi's sister to Polip

    Through marriage of Welenue, a sister of Ulaba'i, to Heagel of *Suabibis*

*Past generation*

    The mother of Balidu and Sumali had been Liwo

    A sister of the father of Balidu had married in Liwo and begotten Whoiban, and another sister had begotten the doctor boy

    A *Dibatua'am* woman had been the mother of Yelusha

    A *Kanehoibis* woman had been the mother of Madjeke of *Suabibis*

## To Suapali

Alitoa had no more relationship with Suapali than if they had belonged to different linguistic groups. Formerly, however, there had at least been clashes, but these had all the appearance of a completely inimical relationship. Nahomen's wife, the father of Maigi, and two children had been killed because they poached on the land of Suapali. This was spoken of as a completely alien event, as they might have spoken of relations with Suwein or the Nugum. More recently, the Suapali people had helped two Sepik boys domiciled among them to carry off Yabinigi's Wihun

[48] No relationship to the gens of the same name in Alitoa.

[49] In this analysis I include names only when they occur in some event, so that they have some significance beyond mere census giving.

wife. I never saw a single Suapali person all the time I was in the Arapesh country, yet the *Suabibis* people maintained continual close relationships with them. They were, however, on the *Shemaun* Road.[50] It was said that Suapali had once been friends with Alipinagle, until recently inimical to Alitoa themselves

### To Malis[51]

No general ties, but Agilapwe's father's other wife had belonged to Malis, and when her husband died she had taken two sons back with her to Malis. Agilapwe[52] had always maintained ties with these half brothers, and his oldest daughter had married in Malis, so there were regular interrelationships between Manuniki and Malis

### To Numidipiheim

Numidipiheim stood in a general friendly relationship to all the people of *Uyebis*, and *Dibatua'am* particularly, and were spoken of as friends of the *ginyau* division of Alitoa. A *Dibatua'am* man had moved to Numidipiheim and settled there. His sons, Manusa and his brothers, were sometimes spoken of as still members of the Alitoa *Dibatua'am* gens, sometimes as members of their mother's gens, *Suabibis*. Furthermore, the gens of *Maliebis*, originally Numidipiheim, was now coming to be regarded as belonging to Alitoa, as Wamu'um and his children were living permanently with *Uyebis*, and Henalian was domiciled in Alipinagle

*Ties in the last generation*
Mother of Nyelahai and Ulaba'i was *Maliebis*

[50] This does not necessarily preclude all relationships, for the hamlet of Malis was also on the *Shemaun* Road, and they kept up relationships through Agilapwe.

[51] This village was a little inland from Suapali. It is not marked on the Government map, and I have, therefore, thought it safer to leave it off the map previously published, Mead, 1938, Fig. 2, rather than venture a wild guess. It was somewhere near Mowia. Native comments are altogether too vague for even the sketchiest map making.

[52] Agilapwe was the last of his gens, which accounts for this anomalous disposition of two male children. It also accounts for the fidelity with which Agilapwe kept up his ties with his half brothers; he had very few relatives to depend upon.

Brother of father of Nahomen and Sinaba'i had moved to Numidipiheim

Nalaijo, eldest sister of Matasues, was married in Numidipiheim

*Ties in the present generation*
Wife of Ulaba'i
Both wives of Matasues
Sister of Ulaba'i married in Numidipiheim
Wife of Bischu
Sister of Anop, Nigat, married to Ombaligu
Sister of La'abe

## To Wihun

Ties with Wihun resembled very closely the kind of ties that Alitoa maintained with Liwo. The *iwhul* division of Wihun were traditional friends of the *ginyau* division of Alitoa and ceremonial enemies of the Alitoa *iwhul*. The converse was also true. Thus in spite of many intermarriages, the ceremonial hostility engendered by the many feast and exchange obligations which they involved sometimes reinforced the sense that the Wihun people were, after all, strangers, members of another locality

There had been an actual fight with Wihun within the present generation. A Wihun man had been accused of causing the death of Yelehiu, the father of Nyelahai, by sorcery. Wupali (then still living in Alitoa), Abugil (Matasues' oldest brother), Nyelahai, Sumali, and Sinaba'i had gone prepared to demand an explanation. There had been a real fight, in which Abugil wounded a man, Sumali killed a man, and Wupali a child by accident. In the past generation Wihun had purchased the right to wear clothes from Alitoa and also purchased the sacred flutes. Only a few years later, Wupali helped his Wihun brother-in-law in an attempt to regain a *Uyebis* runaway wife who had run away to Liwo. After the clash which ensued he moved to Wihun

*Ties in the last generation*
Mother of Anop
(Mother of La'abe) his father was domiciled in Wihun

*Ties in the present generation*
Sister of Balidu and Sumali, married to Nigi
Wife of Balidu
Wife of Kule
Wife of Ombomb
Wife of Nyelahai

Wife of Sema'a
Wife of Gabunyan
Wife of Selalimi
Wife of Wena
Wife of Wegul
Sister of La'abe
Sister of Yabinigi
Sister of Ulaba'i ( Ulaijo now a widow and remarried to Aden )
Wupali's domicile in Wihun
There is a slightly greater preponderance of Wihun women
coming towards the more civilized Alitoa

## To Numonihi

Alitoa stood in almost as distant a relationship to Numonihi as to
Suapali. Only the accident that the people of Ahalesimihi were
more closely connected prevented as absolute a breach, and there
had been a murderous quarrel between them and some Numonihi
people about six years before, in which the parents of Lomaijo
and the wife of Amambut had been killed over a question of
sago poaching[53]

One woman, Madjuamal, the crooked-hipped, was married from
Numonihi to a *Toto'alaibis* man, Menyul, but as he had no status
and she was discounted, this marriage had no social repercussions.
It had been a runaway marriage in which the woman was never
pursued, like the marriage of the stupid Dunigi woman Gulumen
to Gobonarra

But Numonihi were on much closer terms with the Ahalesimihi
through the marriage of Silisium, an important man, to Ya'umen
of Numonihi[54]

Ahalesimihi were also planning a big interlocality feast with
Numonihi[55]

Midway between relationships between localities or ham-

[53] The parallel here between Suapali and Numonihi is striking.
Both are localities on separate roads. Numonihi belonged to the
Road of the Setting Sun, and there is a persistent defense of locality
rights with far more vigor than occurs along the same Road. When
similar troubles over property rights arise along a Road, they take
the form of sorcery, not of open fighting. The only open fighting
that occurs along the same Road is over women, an intracommunity
matter.

[54] It was to Numonihi that Silisium ran away when he quarreled
with his brother (p. 396).

[55] See *Diary*, p. 520.

lets in localities (because it can never be said with justice, except for the large dance complex purchases, that the relationship is actually interlocality) stand the relationships between villages or, more properly speaking perhaps, hamlet centers. Four such hamlet centers functioned in Alitoa:

Alitoa, including the hamlets of Moholigum, Kwobilisi, Mobilinigum, Manuniki, Malupit, and Mogiligen

Alipinagle, which contained only isolated gardens and the one-man hamlet of Nyelahai's, Tereba

Ahalesimihi, including the hamlets of Amambut and Selalimi, of Nagawe and Wena, and of Silisium and Manum

Yapiaun, now shrunk merely to a three-man hamlet, but still regarded somewhat as a separate center

Disproportionate in size as these four hamlet centers were, relationships between them took on a semi-formal quality lacking within any one of them, and intermarriages had to be considered more seriously.

I will list here merely the ties between Alitoa and the others:

### To Ahalesimihi

Marriage of Balidu's sister Nigilawe (widowed)

Marriage of La'abe's sister Homendjuai to Manum

Marriage of Manum's sister Winam to Sumali

Marriage of Balidu's daughter Yapul to Nagawe

Betrothal of Silisium's daughter Gowais to Badui

Betrothal of Baimal's daughter Amus to Mai, son of Manum

Marriage of Lomaijo, "daughter of Amambut," to La'abe

Residence of Wena in Ahalesimihi, and marriage of Wena's mother, who was the sister of Nagawe, to Wamu'um

### To Alipinagle

In the last generation peace had been made with Alipinagle by the marriages of two *Toto'alaibis* women, who were not returned, and the sons of one of these marriages, Maginala and Ga'olen, stood therefore in a special helping relationship to Alitoa

Adoption of Iwamini into Alipinagle and his marriage with Yinauwhat of Manuniki

Residence of Henalian in Alipinagle, taking with him his wife of *Dibatua'am*

Marriage of Wabe with Welima, and his insisting upon regarding her as Alipinagle, because her father actually belonged there although he had lived for years in Ahalesimihi. Wabe's intended adoption of one of the children of Wegul, himself adopted into his mother's place

## To Yapiaun

Yapiaun seems, despite its great distance, to have been on good terms with Alitoa longer than had Alipinagle
Present ties:

  Former marriage of a Yapiaun woman who became the mother of Baimal, Kule, and Alis, who kept up close relations with their cross-cousins

  Marriage of Uwaidjo into *Uyenehas*. She was now married to Belatau

# THE RECORD OF EVENTS

## Introduction

When we settled in Alitoa we were told that preparations for a feast were under way. These preparations were resolved into three separate feasts: a feast given by Aden as a preparation for a grand Magahine[56] feast which would conclude all the payments connected with his initiation in Magahine some 15 years before; a *balagasik* feast to be given by Balidu to his brothers-in-law, Honali and Nigi, in his son Badui's name; and a preliminary feast to be given by Ombomb to his close associates, preparatory to collecting a large amount of food for an intralocality feast with Belagomini of Wihun, in concluding the purchase of the long flutes by Wihun. All three feasts had been scheduled well ahead to take place some time in the next two months, when the special gardens which had been planted for them were harvested and the necessary pigs and game collected.

I began to keep a detailed diary on January 28, the day before Aden gave his feast. Before that time, I was not conversant enough with the personalities and the culture to keep an intelligent record. There had been no outstanding events.

[56] A division of Sublamon.

However, the half ceremonial, half real hostility between Aden and Balidu, with covert accusations about the burning of Sumali's house, and the origin of Aden's sore, which was getting worse, were in the air. On January 21 our cook boy, Kaberman, had enlivened the general dullness of life by eating a little bone dust and putting on an exhibition of possession. This was in the middle of the night and we did not hear about it until afterwards. On January 24 a party of Waginara people, a man, his wife, two children, two widows, carrying salt water and a dog, went through on their way to Wihun. They were gift friends of La'abe's and stopped in his house for food. The dog had been marked as a puppy and was now being carried inland to the people who had marked it. The party returned the next day, again stopping at La'abe's.

## ADEN'S CHAIN FEAST[57]

JANUARY 28: During the afternoon the Numidipiheim people who were to be the principal recipients of the feast appeared, also a delegation of Liwo people. Polip and Unabelin of *Suabibis* brought game to Aden, their cross-cousin; Tangowa, the husband of Anyuai, the daughter of Ulaba'i, and his father brought game to Ulaba'i. Agilapwe, Matasues, Henalian, and Yauwiyu also helped Aden. The feast was to be of the chain type, in which the pigs contributed must come back along the lines of participants and do not become the property of the organizer of the feast, as in the dog type of feast (see p. 112). It was organized in two stages: Aden was to give to Nyelahai and Ulaba'i and Matasues and Wabe; they, in turn, were to enlist their connections. They were merely intervening links and would have no right to the pigs coming back along this chain. These were to be sent to Magahine, and the return pigs would again go back along the chain.

The village was crowded; all the visitors slept in the Alitoa end of the village. During the early evening, there were

[57] For convenience of reference I have introduced subheads so that particular events can be followed through the *Diary*.

speeches of ceremonial hostility, tinged with reality. It was already known that Aden had not yet secured a pig for the feast, but had only small game to garnish his yams and sago. His younger brother, Iwamini, had in desperation finally been sent to the Beach, with a large ring and a specially good plate to try to buy one, but he had not returned. The Numi-dipiheim men made scathing speeches about a previous attempt of Aden's to fasten a pig which had died on the way. (This meant Aden had either copulated with his wives, or cut a banana stem; people suspected the former as Aden had the most uxorious reputation in Alitoa.) This was followed by speeches between Aden and Nyelahai concerning the route of the pigs; whether they should be carried from Numidipiheim directly to Liwo, as Aden wished, or brought through Alitoa, as Nyelahai wished. These were loud ceremonial speeches which did not and were not meant to reach any conclusion. They merely defined a situation which could be argued about in the future.

JANUARY 29: The morning dawned cold and rainy; the crowded village roused, cross and uncomfortable. The houses had been crowded, some people had had to sleep far from any fire; others had slept under trickles of water from inadequately thatched roofs. The usual early morning feast dish, a very thin sago soup into which particularly bright green leaves had been cut in large pieces, was served to everyone. This soup was merely a gesture toward feeding the visitors; actually it left them hungry. As people walked about in the damp, trying to get warm on empty stomachs, the speech-making immediately turned to sorcery. First came a discussion of the house burning, terminating with Nyelahai's shouting formally to Aden: "There is someone sick in Mogili-gen.[58] We had better not walk about in the Plains, among our Plains friends, or we will be accused of that illness also."

Manusa, the *tultul* of Numidipiheim, now took occasion to "make court"[59] against the two wives of a Numidipiheim

[58] This was Taumulimen, the wife of Alis. See below, February 4.
[59] This is the modern version of an old custom of facing people publicly with their delinquencies and demanding an explanation. Nowadays, if there is any excuse for his participation, one of the

man, the elder of whom had been inherited from a cross-
cousin, and had run away. Manusa demanded an explanation
of the quarrel between the two wives which had caused the
new wife to run away. The women sat, sulky, far apart, and
at first refused to say anything. Finally, the first wife said
that the inherited wife stole her food and that, anyway, she
had called her "mother" and was ashamed to have her for
a co-wife.[60]

At noon it was known that Iwamini had not been able to
buy the pig. This news was shouted across the hill tops.
Shortly afterwards, Balidu, in a great rage, beat the large
*garamut* in front of his *tamberan* house, shouting angrily because he had heard that Aden's side were saying that he had
worked magic to keep Iwamini from finding a pig. As Balidu
beat the *garamut*, someone at the Alitoa end of the village
called out the name of one of Balidu's ancestors. This was a
double insult. Balidu made a long speech. Aden made a brief
reply, saying that it was a woman's gossip and untrue. Finally,
Balidu, staff in hand and still very much on the defensive,

Government appointees is likely to conduct the proceedings. This
is, I believe, the only genuine innovation.

[60] This is the only occasion upon which such a point was ever
made among the Arapesh, and I am inclined to regard it as a *tour
de force*, an unusual way of stating that she felt her co-wife belonged in the last generation and should not be married to her
husband.

An attempt to learn further details of this quarrel was not very
successful. Both women had a number of children, and there had
been considerable altercation about the payments for the widow.
The final version was that four rings and two pigs had been paid
by the new husband to the brother of the dead man, and he was
now claiming restitution. Further details of the cause of the quarrel
between the two women revealed that the son of the inherited wife,
a boy of 15, had killed a phalanger and brought it home to his
mother. The two women ate the meat; when their husband came
home they gave him only greens with his taro. Then the two women
quarreled and the second wife ran away. (This account is culturally
unintelligible. It is introduced here as a sample of the kind of information one receives at the beginning of field work. However,
one illuminating comment was made by Unabelin, who remarked,
"Of course, the second husband had paid for her; otherwise, if he
tried to beat her, the wife would say, 'My first husband grew me
and paid for me, you got me for nothing, so how dare you beat
me!'")

marched up through the village to Aden's part of the village and admitted that the tale had been brought by Sagu, Maigi's wife, who had been over at Manuniki and heard the gossip. Aden again denied it and peace was restored.

In the afternoon it cleared for a little while, and the feast was spread out in the plaza. Aden sat on one side and took no part, but whether this was owing to his sore or to the etiquette of this kind of feast, no one would say definitely. The feast was all arranged at once: bowls of sago croquettes, smoked game, a small amount of uncooked sago, and a small pile of yams. After all the food was spread out, the four men who would fasten pigs for the final feast ran around the pile shouting.[61] These four men were all from Numidipiheim: Mahes, Manigowa, Manusa, and Wamu'um (who now gardened with Matasues but is a member of the *Maliebis* gens of Numidipiheim).

The food exchanges were actually phrased as follows:

| FROM | TO | PLACE | RELATIONSHIP |
|------|----|-------|--------------|
| Wabe | Amau | Numidipiheim | Sister's son |
| Wabe | Wamu'um | (ex-Numidipiheim) | Dead sister's husband |
| Wabe | Ombomb | Walinuba | Brother who has been adopted into *Toto'alaibis* |
| Matasues to Nyelahai to Manusa | | Numidipiheim | Classificatory brother of Nyelahai gone to live in Numidipiheim |
| Aden | Wajai | Numidipiheim | Classificatory brother-in-law of Aden |
| Nyelahai | Wapinol | Numidipiheim | Husband of sister Maisoa, temporarily separated |
| Ulaba'i | Malitiwen | Numidipiheim | Classificatory brother-in-law |

Then followed a series of redistributions of this food which were too rapid to be followed without a knowledge of the

[61] This shouting is called *Ha bo walum*, "they kill the mud hen." The reference is not known.

personalities involved. After some of the coconut croquettes had been consumed on the spot, the visitors packed up the feast in their net bags and set off for home, and quiet descended upon the village. (End of Aden's Feast.)

## LA'ABE'S HARVEST

JANUARY 30: La'abe was preparing to harvest his yams and spent the day searching the bush for the proper herbs. The ceremony was to be performed by Ombomb, who was one of the few people who knew any yam magic.[62] Dr. Fortune accompanied him and reported how exceedingly casual and unimportant the whole affair had been. In the evening everyone left in the village gathered in our house, at loose ends after the feast. A Dunigi man, a relative of Matasues' wife, came to sell net bags to us.

The center of interest was really the harvest on Bischu's land, some of which was to help with Ombomb's feast and some with Balidu's. This interest was, however, interspersed with the other preparations for the feasts, sago working, hunting, and arrangements with people of other places. For the next 10 days, however, this harvest, which I have called La'-abe's harvest, was the focus for activities.

La'abe had the largest share of yams planted in this garden. However, he had been unfortunate, because both of his wives had menstruated, serially, and the two days' avoidance required of the husband had lengthened into four days. This yam garden was situated on Bischu's land and was worked by the following people:

Bischu, whose land it was.

Ombomb, who worked there with La'abe, his father's brother's son. His was also the yam magic for the group; this he had inherited from Wupali.

La'abe, mother's sister's son of Bischu.

Ulaba'i, *awalahen* of Ombomb and La'abe.

Wutue, father's brother of Bischu.

The harvest period extended from January 30, the day after Aden's feast, through the next week, during which time they

[62] See list of magic owned in Alitoa, p. 485.

were helped by a large number of relatives whose wives also carried away large net bags full of yams. They were helped by Sinaba'i, acting as a brother of Ulaba'i, by Wupali, the elder brother of Ombomb, and his elder son. The sisters of La'abe came from Numidipiheim and Wihun. Ombomb finished first on January 31.

JANUARY 31: That night Ombomb tried to organize a dance. La'abe was angry at the others for going ahead without him. He looked very sour over Ombomb's attempt to organize a dance on this evening. Ombomb, Badui, Pidjui, Maigi, and Gerud, however, dressed up with a little finery and held a small, dismal dance. They spent most of the evening singing a song from the *midep,* a dance for which La'abe was organizing the purchase from Kobelen. This was additional bad behavior because it is not good form to sing a song of a dance which is still in process of being paid for. This made La'abe angrier than ever. They phrased this dance, however, finally as preparatory to going hunting and working sago.

FEBRUARY 1: Harvesting continued as before. Baimal appeared with face painted and feathers in his hair, because he was thinking of the fact that later he was going to make a feast. He importuned Dr. Fortune to bring his shotgun and come to his hunting bush to shoot.

FEBRUARY 2: Harvesting still going on. Party of Dunigi Plainsmen went through on their way to the Beach for salt and lime.

FEBRUARY 3: The immediate personnel of Alitoa was occupied as follows:

Away at work:

Ulaba'i and household, except Segenamoya, planting taro.

Bischu and household harvesting yams.

Wutue and household harvesting yams.

Matasues and household harvesting yams.

Wabe and Temos helping Bischu.

Aden and his two wives planting taro in their newly made garden.

Madje helping Matasues.

Balidu and Baimal gone to Liwo to discuss feast arrangements with affinal relatives, the relatives of Sa'omali, wife of Badui.

Maigi and Sagu and Sa'omali working sago for the feast.

Yahalijo, Pidjui, Kumati, and Nigimarib working in taro garden.

La'abe and Souato'a at the yam harvest.

Menala and her baby gone to Ahalesimihi.

In the village:

Welima, wife of Wabe, Segenamoya, the six-year-old son of Ulaba'i, with her.

Sinaba'i, Dubomagau, and Miduain.

Ombomb and Sauwedjo, entertaining the father and brother of Sauwedjo who had come to discuss sago arrangements for Ombomb's feast.

Visitors:

Wupali with his wife and children passed through Alitoa on his way to Liwo.

Ombomb's affinal relatives from Dunigi.

In the harvest place itself there were present during the day of February 3 the following persons:

Ulaba'i, his two wives, his sister, his mother, and child Nemausi, planting taro.

La'abe, Imale, and Souato'a.

Me'elue, the wife of Ombomb, and her child, completing the carrying of Ombomb's harvest, while he stayed in the village to entertain his other wife's relatives.

Anop and his wife, helping with Ombomb's harvest. Anop was Ombomb's sister's son.

La'abe's sister from Wihun and her daughter.

Wabe and Temos, helping Bischu, adopted gens-brother.

Bischu, Danue, and their two children.

Wutue, his wife, and three children.

The wife of Belagomini of Wihun, Ombomb's *gabunyan* in the coming feast, during the day came to collect some sago which Ombomb owed her husband. Twenty-six people slept in the harvest grounds that night in two small ground houses.

FEBRUARY 4: Present in village:

Whasimai, wife of Ulaba'i, and Segenamoya and Nemausi. She came up from the garden early in the morning with a load of yams.

Welima. With her was Wadjubel, sister's daughter of Ombomb. She and Welima brought firewood and stored it under Ombomb's house for the coming feast.

Sinaba'i went in the late afternoon to fence his garden. Dubomagau refused to go. In the absence of her betrothed husband, Miduain left for Kwobilisi to help plant in the garden of her father-in-law, Wamu'um.

Events during the day:

Mc'clue brought up the remainder of Ombomb's yams and stored them in the house.

The wife of Matasues came up to fetch the Dunigi affinal relatives of Ombomb and took them down to Kwobilisi. (It seems that Ombomb's two visitors had been members of a party which had included two important Dunigi men who had gone to stay with Matasues, who through his brother Ombomb's tie with Dunigi was in the process of cementing a special gift friendship with them. A fifth member had been a gift friend of Agilapwe with whom he had gone to visit Agilapwe's daughter who was married in Malis. Now the party was collecting to return to Dunigi.)

La'abe came up during the day and expressed himself very freely to Kaberman[63] on the subject of his attitudes toward the harvest. He bitterly resented the others' having finished their harvesting ahead of him, while he was kept out of the garden by his menstruating wives. Furthermore, he was very disappointed at the size of his yam crop. Many yam holes had no yams in them. Obviously, they had walked about, into someone else's garden.[64]

The daughter of Silisium, who had just been betrothed to a Liwo cross-cousin of Sinaba'i's, came back from Ahalesimihi with Menala, Sinaba'i's wife. (She was a great hulking girl, whose original betrothal had been broken off. She was now betrothed, full grown, to a man whom she didn't know, who

---

[63] It is doubtful whether he would have talked as freely to anyone in the village, or if he had done so that any other confidant than Kaberman would have told us what he said as fully as did Kaberman, for our boys were already vying with each other as informants.

[64] La'abe belonged to the type of personality which is sometimes produced by being required to play a role which is superior to one's ability. Consequently he was always in a blue funk and always blaming others for his misfortunes.

was away at work. She was miserably embarrassed, more embarrassed than any other Arapesh girl whom I ever saw, and ran away if anyone mentioned her husband.)

Winam, the wife of Sumali, and the baby were here, while Sumali and Budagiel, with a mother's brother of Sumali's from Liwo, have gone on a trading trip to Dakuar.

About noon Ombomb announced that he was going to build a ground house for use at his feast. He went up and started to tear down the old Messiah-cult ground house which Matasues had built in the Alitoa end of the village. It seems that Ombomb had previously built this for Matasues when everyone was planning to take refuge in Alitoa from the coming flood of hot water.[65] He carried the pieces of the house down to a vacant lot across from the house in which he lived with Sauwedjo, but across the road, on La'abe's side. This had been the site of the house of Bauwan, Baimal's brother, who had died five years before and it had not been occupied since. Ombomb built his house alone, while Sauwedjo, Welima, and Wadjubel gathered firewood.

## Dance to Conclude Ombomb's Harvest

Meanwhile there was desultory talk of a dance that night. A survey of the available hand drums in the village revealed a great shortage of tympanums. Kule went off to try to borrow a hand drum. Just at dusk the sago-working crowd of young people (Maigi, Pidjui, Badui) returned with hand drums which they had borrowed. They announced that they meant to dance and began at once to dress. The originators of the dance, Ombomb, Kule, Badui, Pidjui, Maigi, Alis, Gerud, and Yauwiyu (who had no reason for being there, but who always scented a dance at a distance and turned up), all put on quite similar costumes: new G strings streaked with red paint, bustles of bright red croton leaves, big bunches of ornamental leaves stuck in their armbands, a large bunch of leaves hanging down the back by a string around the neck, shell ornaments on breast and back, and hair fastened in a

[65] An account of this threatened deluge, a typical culture contact cult, will be given in *The Record of Unabelin*. Mead, 1949a.

knot, or in imitation of a knot, bound with a fresh bark band, secured with flying "fox" bones at intervals, and surmounted with one long bird-of-paradise feather. Red paint was used generously on the hair and spread over the arms and legs without any definite design. In the center of Balidu's plaza the men danced in pairs and trios with hand drums in their hands. The women and children, at first only Ilautoa and her children, Naguel, Mausi, and Sagu, and the children of Balidu and Sumali—all of whom had now gathered in the village—danced. Sinaba'i returned with two Dunigi visitors, and danced, while one of his visitors went to sleep and one sat down in state with Balidu. Gradually all the women and children in the village joined the dance. But it was noticeable that the people who belonged to the "other half," that is, the Alitoa half of the village, came late and went home early. It was not their dance.

Our boys all marched up in single file, also decorated alike, wearing pairs of white feathers arranged like horns, white lines of paint on their faces and red *laplaps* with a band of white cloth under their belts. But they had no hand drums and so had to dance, in pairs, hand in hand, around the outside with the women and children. They demurred over this a long time. Biagu[66] looked particularly ashamed at taking the women's role, while Mindibilip brazened it out by introducing masculine side-steps in his dancing.

The women were not so elaborately dressed as the men; they wore extra shell ornaments and red or white *laplaps* over their own heads, or over the heads of the babies they carried on their shoulders. There was a preference for dancing with babies; a woman would drop out and sit down by the fire burning on one side of the plaza, casting a very faint light on the dance, but someone else would take the baby and go on dancing. The carried children, one hand fast in the hand of the dancing elder, fell asleep and bobbed back and forth in time to the music. Sometimes the woman raised the child's two hands in time to the music. The women and children danced in pairs, hand in hand, or paired with the rear dancer holding on to the front dancer's arms. Most of the women and

[66] Note that Biagu was already marked as a potential *alomato'in*.

children danced badly, losing step and bumping into each other. The central nucleus of male dancers, intent upon the posturing in pairs or trios, paid no attention to the fringe of women and children. It was so dark that virtually nothing could be seen.

In the middle of the dance, Temos, Imale, and La'abe's sister's daughter from Wihun came up, laden, from the gardens. They did not join the dance. About two o'clock the dance was stopped by a downpour of rain, but everyone who had still been dancing stayed up all night, in conformance with the rule that if a dance is really a dance, it should be kept up until dawn. Inside their houses they continued to sing dolefully until dawn.

FEBRUARY 5: The next morning they all appeared, still dressed up but tired and fidgety, without any idea of what to do next. Ombomb started to work on his new house, put in about six posts, arranged the rafter sticks, and then said that would do for the day and went and sat down inside his house and began to sing softly to himself.


## TAUMULIMEN'S ILLNESS

Meanwhile, the rumor came that the sickness of Alis' wife was increasing, and Maigi, Alis, and a small sister's son from Ahalesimihi who had just turned up went off to bring her to Alitoa so that I could look after her.[67] Ill as she was, she walked all the way, supported by the young men. She had been constipated for a week and sorcery was feared, although everyone suspended judgment. Meanwhile they speculated upon the probable source of the sorcery, if it were sorcery. It seems that Taumulimen had been originally betrothed to a brother of Yabinigi, who died while he was away at work. Nahomen wanted her for Yabinigi, but she objected because

[67] This is one of the cases which complicates the record. I could get only contradictory answers as to whether the wife of Alis was brought in solely so that I could give her castor oil, or whether she would in any event have been brought to the central hamlet of the gens. I am inclined to think the former was the case, as I could get no formulations about going to the mother hamlet in illness or death.

of his deafness. Kule, who was married to her sister, paid for her for his younger brother Alis. But Nahomen was still angry; if her illness were aggravated, it would be in the direction of Nahomen that they would look.[68]

I gave Taumulimen castor oil. Alis took advantage of this to get some castor oil for himself to wash away his chronic state of being sorcerized.[69] Both of them were lodged in the house of Kule and Baimal and cared for by Ilautoa.

\* \* \*

Present in the village during the day:

Ombomb.

Sinaba'i, wife, two children, and their Ahalesimihi visitor.

Ulaba'i, Ibanyos, Ulaba'i's sister, and children. Whasimai had gone down to the garden to bring up the cooking pots which they had been using there.

Madje was back lounging in Ulaba'i's house.

Wadjubel was alone in the house of Wabe.

Household of Kule, taking care of wife of Alis.

Pidjui, alone of the Balidu household, remained in the village, doing nothing.

FEBRUARY 6: Taumulimen was better in the morning. Maigi and Kule left for their work, but Ilautoa remained to look after her, and Alis stayed with her. It was said that she would not wash until she was quite well.[70]

Homendjuai, the sister of La'abe, and Yapul, the daughter of Balidu, had been in La'abe's garden helping with the harvest. They came up early in the morning and spent the day in the village with their children. Each had a nursing infant and they sat and suckled their children all day.

[68] Note the amount of trouble which is caused by the unfit. Yabinigi's deafness and consequent unavailability as a husband in a community which insisted upon treating him as normal were continually causing trouble. Nahomen was a low-grade moron, malicious and anti-social, but he was allowed to function in the social system and so took revenge when he was balked. See below, his behavior in connection with Yabinigi's Suapali wife (p. 456).

[69] For a description of Alis' state, see above, p. 161, and Mead, 1935b, pp. 102–104.

[70] In the negotiations over sorcery the phrase, "In two days he will wash" means, "In two days he will be well again."

## La'abe's Quarrel with His Wife (1)

Early in the morning, Lomaijo went down to the garden. She had gone down the day before and carried up yams, this being the first day that she was free from the taint of menstruation and so able to enter the garden. Imale and La'abe had remained in the garden. When she went down this morning, she found that La'abe and Imale had eaten all of the sago which his sister had brought him from Wihun, when she came to help with the garden. Lomaijo scolded La'abe for having eaten up the sago.[71] La'abe retaliated by saying that he was going to set off at once for Dunigi to get some pots which his gift friend there had promised him.[72]

Lomaijo immediately objected, adopted a moral tone, and told La'abe that it was his duty to stay here and work sago for the feast. He insisted that he was going. She lost her temper completely and told him that if he did go he would eat only the faeces of the Plainsmen. This was evil talk which meant bad luck and lack of food on the journey.[73] La'abe, declaring that he would burn the mouth that talked so evilly, seized a fire stick, hit her mouth, chin, throat, and chest with it and, in the struggle, also broke open a boil on her arm. In retaliation she broke a large cooking pot which belonged to him. She came back up to the village, carrying her child and crying, and came into Kule's house, where Taumulimen was lying ill. In the house were Ilautoa, Taumulimen and Alis, Sagu, Yapul and her children, Homendjuai and her children,

[71] That is, for having eaten the sago with Imale, and, in terms of Arapesh thinking, for having preferred Imale to herself, by staying with her in the garden. Note that Imale's menstruation had been over for three days now, and she and La'abe had been together, while Lomaijo had not only missed the yam harvest, but had also incurred La'abe's reproaches for menstruating at such an inopportune time.

[72] This was equivalent to saying, "I not only have stayed with Imale while we ate up the sago, but I now propose to go off on a three or four day trip, upon which I will, as is my custom, take Imale."

[73] This type of evil talk could also bring the *tamberan* cult down upon La'abe so that he would have to pay a pig as a fine.

Kaberman's little wife who had been staying with Lomaijo, and myself.[74] She sat down and told the tale. Ilautoa alternately consoled and scolded her. Between her *Gi ha, Gi ha* (alas, alas) and her affectionately pronounced "Sister-in-law! Sister-in-law!" she said that Lomaijo should not have gone to the garden this morning, she had no work there. Her work was finished yesterday. Lomaijo countered this accusation with the statement that La'abe was in a bad temper anyway. He was cross about his small yam crop, and about her menstruating, and about the others starting without him to harvest, and about that first dance when they had sung the *midep* song, and about the dance the other night without him. After Lomaijo had had her fill of exhibiting her wounds, and after I had dressed them, she went to her own house, accompanied by Homendjuai who stayed overnight with her. La'abe remained in his garden with Imale.

\* \* \*

Present in the village:

Wabe and Temos.

Sinaba'i, Menala, and visiting daughter of Silisium and two children.

Ulaba'i, Whasimai, her brother from Numidipiheim, and sister of Ulaba'i. Two Bonaheitum visitors arrived late last night and have now gone, one to Liwo. His mother came with them, and returned this morning to Alipinagle where she was staying with Nyelahai.

Lomaijo, Homendjuai, and her four children.

Ombomb and both his wives, and three Dunigi affinals.

Alis, Taumulimen, Ilautoa, Mausi, Naguel, and a small cousin from Ahalesimihi.

Pidjui and Nigimarib.

Away at work:

Aden and wives still making new garden. Ibanyos helping her brother Aden.

Welima had gone to help her father Selalimi harvest in Ahalesimihi.

---

[74] This large crowd was due more, I think, to my presence, than to any desire to attend upon Taumulimen. People used to complain that a crowd tended to gather wherever I went in the village.

Bischu and Wutue were planting taro.
La'abe and Imale, in his garden.
Balidu and Yahalijo, harvesting.
Kule, Badui, and Maigi working sago for the feast.


### MAGUER SORCERY DELEGATION (1)

In the evening three men from Maguer arrived, on a sorcery hunt. They were inquiring about the exuviae of Idupihi, the father of Tamapua, one of them who had a bad sore. Their reasons for suspecting internal not Plains sorcery were various. There are only three places where such sores were produced, in Alitoa, in Bugabihiem, and in Waginara. Furthermore, the sick man had seen Alitoa in a dream; they knew that Nyelahai was angry with him, because of a pig which he had gotten from inland and had not shared with Nyelahai. They stayed with Ulaba'i overnight, he acting for his brother Nyelahai as their formal host.

\* \* \*

During the night, Alis, Ilautoa, Pidjui, and Nigimarib got up to urinate. The two boys thought they saw a ghost and screamed. This awakened the rest of the village, who merely laughed at them. The fear of ghosts is very weak among the Mountain people.


### MAGUER SORCERY DELEGATION (2)

FEBRUARY 7: The Maguer delegation sat about in a desultory fashion, looking cross and suspicious. They had Ulaba'i's wife call out to Nyelahai to come up and talk to them and answer their charges, and then they sat down to wait for him to come. Ulaba'i then entertained the Maguer visitors with his wife.

\* \* \*

Sinaba'i and his household went to cut sago.
Wabe and Temos, with Shuisha, the daughter of Wutue, came up to the village and went back again to work with Bischu and Wutue, planting taro.

## LA'ABE'S QUARREL WITH HIS WIFE (2)

La'abe came up early and stalked about the Walinuba plaza and then returned to his garden. Lomaijo finally put on a big net bag and went down to carry up more yams, leaving Kamowon with Lamein (wife of Kaberman).

(End of La'abe's harvest and La'abe's quarrel with his wife.)

* * *

In Ombomb's household: Me'elue left for Bischu's garden. The Dunigi visitors left and were told to bring their contribution of coconuts in six days. Nebe'uma, a mother's brother's daughter of Ombomb, married in Liwo, arrived to ask him to get her a cooking pot. The fat mother of Sa'omali, the widow of the former *luluai* of Liwo, came with her.

Kule, Maigi, and Badui and their wives came back from cutting sago, their eyes red and inflamed, their cheeks drawn and thin. (The Arapesh method of cutting sago while sitting down seems to result in getting a lot of it into the eyes; at any rate, men who have been cutting sago always return with bloodshot eyes and a look of strain.)

Alis and Taumulimen remained all day in the house of Kule.

Maginala and Iwamini of Alipinagle passed through here on their way back from Boinam and stayed an hour or so to gossip.

Balidu and his wife were in the garden.

Some Umanep people came up with the wife of our Umanep shoot boy, but stayed with him and did not claim hospitality in the village.

## MAGUER SORCERY DELEGATION (3)

FEBRUARY 8: Nyelahai did not appear. The next morning, the Maguer delegation, full of muttered threats, went back. The *luluai* and his sister accompanied them and went on to Magahine to get a small pig which had been promised him.

* * *

Wabe and Temos were in the village all day. Wabe put a few finishing touches to his yam house, and Temos got firewood.

Ombomb and Sinaba'i worked sago, helped by Lomaijo, Sauwedjo, and Menala.

La'abe, Imale, and Souato'a started for Wihun. La'abe intended to go on to Dunigi to get those pots which were owed him, leaving Imale and Souato'a in Wihun with his sister.

Kule returned for the night and went away again in the morning. Alis and Taumulimen still sat about idly, although she was practically well.

Balidu's household were all in the garden.

FEBRUARY 9: The previous night the only people who slept in the village were: Wabe and Temos, Madje, the two wives of Ulaba'i and their children; Ombomb and Sauwedjo, Lomaijo, Lamein, and Kamowon, Alis, Taumulimen; Naguel and Mausi, the two children of Kule, Nigimarib, the youngest child of Balidu, Kule, and Ilautoa.

During the day, Wabe completed his yam house. Welima, just returned from Ahalesimihi, Temos, Shuisha, the daughter of Wutue, and Wadjubel helped him crinkle the fringes of sago leaf to decorate the house.

Madje helped Ibanyos in fencing the garden of Ulaba'i.

Ombomb, Lomaijo, Sauwedjo, Lamein, and Menala worked sago with Sinaba'i.

Balidu harvested yams, helped by Yapul, Naushe's wife, Honali, Gerud, Maigi, and his own wife and children.

Gobonarra, Baijo, the wife of Aden, and her little girl Sauisua came up to the village, and reported Aden very ill and likely to die.

Kule and Ilautoa, now joined by Kule's other wife, Soatsalamo, who had been in Mogiligen, were still working sago. They returned toward evening. Ulaba'i and his sister returned from Magahine without the pig, which had not yet been born.

## VISIT OF NUGUM POTTERS

FEBRUARY 10: A party of about nine Nugum visitors arrived with pots to sell. They were gift friends of Ulaba'i and sat about with him all day, holding an informal market. A kind of general discomfort reigned in the village. People would go and hunt out a ring or a string of shell money, look at it, put it away again, get out another, and offer it to the potters, who would perhaps refuse it. Very little trade was actually accomplished. The Nugum also had with them a large number of delicate little chains[75] which they specialized in making, but the Arapesh refused to pay the price they asked for them. Everyone went about muttering that there were too many Nugum all at once and that they overcharged for everything.

The Nugum were a thin, not particularly well-dressed group. As pubic coverings they wore little cornucopias of fresh green leaves fastened to a string around the waist. Their hair was stretched straight back from their foreheads and confined in halo-like, wickerwork circlets.[76] None of them spoke pidgin. No one in Alitoa was very anxious to act as an interpreter, so, aside from some numerals and a very meager vocabulary, we got nothing from them. They were suspicious and unresponsive. They left for the Beach early in the afternoon.

\* \* \*

Disposition of villagers during the day:

Wabe and both his wives went to his yam garden.

Matasues was said to be making a new yam garden.

Wutue and Bischu were working on their new taro garden.

Madje helped Ibanyos in her garden and stayed in the village overnight preparatory to going to Karawop for us in the morning.

Ulaba'i, his two wives, his sister, and his children were all in the village.[77]

[75] Mead, 1938, Fig. 52.
[76] Mead, 1938, Fig. 50a.
[77] It will be apparent how much more cohesive this household was than most of those in which there were two wives. This was

Balidu and his helpers were still digging yams, but Budagiel, daughter of Sumali, was in the village all day, with her little sister Ite'epe and her mother's sister's daughter from Liwo. This woman, who had an eighteen-month-old, very ailing child, was having difficulties with her husband, the doctor boy of Liwo. His second wife, a Bugabihiem girl, was originally betrothed to the husband of Balidu's absent daughter Bwa'o (both she and her husband were in Rabaul). The new wife was enamored[78] of the doctor boy and had been trying to expel the former wife. The former wife, a dull, heavy, rather self-pitying woman, was now living with the father of the doctor boy, who took her part.[79]

Ombomb and Sauwedjo stayed about all day doing nothing. Me'elue was with Bischu.

Kule and Ilautoa also stayed in the village resting. Alis and Taumulimen were still there.

Kule's children went back to Mogiligen with Soatsalamo, Kule's other wife.

Lomaijo also did nothing except care for her child all day.

FEBRUARY 11: Ombomb and Sauwedjo again went to work sago with Sinaba'i and returned in the evening.

Budagiel brought word that Sumali was preparing to harvest his smaller yam garden, and Lomaijo, taking Lamein and the baby, went to help him. Manum and his sons and Gobonarra were helping Sumali. Budagiel and Ite'epe also returned to the harvest.

Baimal, his wives, Amito'a and Alaijo, Minya and Amus,

---

due to the great friendliness of the two wives and the unquestioned dominance of Ibanyos.

[78] This is one of these cases complicated by the indentured labor situation. The girl had grown up, in her betrothed husband's absence, without the usual discipline and affection of the betrothal period, and had, as her first sex experience, a romantic encounter with a man from another place. It will be noted how a single culturally disapproved condition leads directly to a series of difficulties.

[79] This is a familiar situation in which some other male relative of the husband of the abused or neglected wife takes her part and gives her shelter. It is, of course, the logical result of the absorption of the wife into her husband's group and the disapproval of interference by members of her own blood group.

his two little daughters, Kule, Ilautoa, and Maigi returned from working sago.

Soatsalamo and Sagu had been sent to get yams from Balidu's harvest.

Mausi and Naguel and the wife of the doctor boy of Liwo spent the day with Alis and Taumulimen.

Balidu and his family were still in their garden. They had now been joined by Wabe and both his wives. There had been a big delegation of Ahalesimihi women there to get yams because Nagawe and his group would not be harvesting yams for four months more.

Ulaba'i and Ibanyos went to work on a new garden, which Ulaba'i was making with Aden, and Whasimai with her baby went to the old garden to weed.

Bischu and Wutue were still working on the new taro garden.

Wena and his young sister came through on their way to see their mother who was married to Wam'um and lived with Matasues at Kwobilisi. Wena's wife had just had a new baby, and he was going to receive food from his mother because she was an old woman with a tertiary yaws sore and could not go to him. He expected to receive yams from her as Ahalesimihi's yams were low.

A cross-cousin of Bischu's came from Waginara, looking for Bischu. Maginala, who had come to Alitoa with Wena, left with the Waginara man to accompany him to Bischu's garden. This was after they had called out for Bischu and waited in vain for him to appear. No one knew what the Waginara man wanted, but they suspected that it had something to do with sorcery or a pig.

Amito'a left for Liwo to visit her brother. Alaijo went with her and they left Minya and Amus with Baimal.

In the evening *garamuts* sounded, accompanied by explanatory calls summoning all *tultuls* and *luluais* to Wewak.

FEBRUARY 12: The day was full of comings and goings. It began early in the morning with a temper tantrum of Amus' because her father had refused to take her with him to work. Both her mother and her mother's co-wife Alaijo were away. He finally took both the little girls with him to work sago.

Early in the morning Taumulimen washed; she and Alis set off for their bush hamlet. Since she had responded to the castor oil, there had been no more talk of her having been sorcerized, although Alis had talked a good deal about his own sorcery state, and tried to get various kinds of medicine from me.[80]

Kule now planned that all of them should return to their bush hamlet to hunt for Balidu's feast. He sent Soatsalamo and Mausi and the baby ahead. He, Ilautoa, and Naguel stayed, it was said, to get firewood and follow the next day. Then Kule got the idea of turning his ground house (Fig. 1, No. 30) around so that the smoke of cooking would not blow into the faces of the visitors seated on Balidu's plaza. This ground house would be needed during the feast days. He pulled it down and set up the framework again during the day.

Ombomb went to work sago early in the morning, but came back before noon and shouted for Miduain to come up and get some yams for her family. She came up. Sinaba'i and his wife and child came soon after.[81] Dubomagau had joined our shoot boys at dawn.

Two young men from Boinam, the sons of Balidu's gift friend in Boinam, appeared. After shouts, Badui came up from the garden to receive them. Maigi and Badui's young wife who cooked for the visitors accompanied him.[82]

Early in the morning Ombomb had seen Wabe, who at Bischu's request had joined him in going to the Plains with the Waginara man on a sorcery investigation. It was publicly

[80] The tendency for one sorcery event or fear to initiate discussion of others is very pronounced. So Kule had occupied the time while he waited for Taumulimen to be brought in from the bush, partly by telling me that he suspected Nahomen was responsible for all this, and partly by remarking that Aden would probably try to work some sort of harm to Balidu's feast in revenge for his own feast's having been so poor.

[81] Ombomb had been working sago with Sinaba'i and so was in a position to know how his larder stood.

[82] Balidu was consistently retiring and turning over all of his responsibilities to Badui. It is interesting that Sa'omali, not yet adolescent, who could not cook for Badui, could nevertheless function socially as his wife in the entertainment of visitors.

said that Wabe and Bischu had gone to the Plains to look for dogs to mark. They were planning to go by Bonaheitum, to Biligil and Kairiru, and return by Dunigi, sleeping there the next night with Ombomb's affinal relatives (February 13) where they would be met by Ombomb and his wife who would return with them.

Ulaba'i's brother-in-law from Numidipiheim came to see him. Whasimai, the Numidipiheim wife, stayed about all day. Ibanyos went to get pepper leaves for the visitor.[83]

### RETURN OF THE MAGUER SORCERY DELEGATION (4)

Just as Ulaba'i's brother-in-law left, the Maguer sorcery delegation appeared again. They had told people whom they met on the way that they were going to accuse Agilapwe. This news had been shouted about so that Maigi, representing Agilapwe, arrived in the village almost at the same time they did. They were received by Ulaba'i, whose wives called out for Nyelahai, but without any hope that he would come. The sick man was Nyelahai's gift friend, his father having been the gift friend of Yelehiu. Nyelahai was so angry with the Maguer people over the pig and their previous insinuations that he refused to come up and entertain them and this fell to Ulaba'i.[84] One of the Maguer young men was entertained by Badui because he was a classificatory sister's son of Nigi, Badui's mother's brother, and Badui helped Nigi and called him "sister's son" (*mehinen*) also.

Agilapwe arrived late and slept in the house of Ombomb who called him *babu'en*.[85] There were no public speeches during the evening, just low-voiced inquiries, a kind of preliminary skirmishing. Baimal returned late from working sago,

[83] Notice that it is not the sister who waits on the brother, but the wife who waits upon her husband's brother-in-law. This feeling is so strong that a different wife from the one who is the link between the two men may be asked to perform the service.

[84] This is the sort of thing which Ulaba'i was always having to do; for all his economic laxness, he was in no danger of being classified as an *alomato'in*.

[85] "Child of father's maternal cross-cousin" in this case, and not grandfather.

and Me'elue came up with a net bag of yams from Ombomb's share of Wabe's patch in Balidu's garden.

## MAGUER SORCERY DELEGATION (5)

FEBRUARY 13: In spite of the presence of the Maguer delegation, Ulaba'i began to prepare to go to Wewak, to answer the Acting District Officer's summons. Ombomb was also anxious to be off to Dunigi to meet Wabe and Bischu. This meant that the hosts of the Maguer complainants and the host of Agilapwe were both in favor of hurrying the proceedings in general, in addition to their dislike of all talk of sorcery. In the morning there was a formal talk in the plaza, the Maguer men making their accusations. The sick man had dreamed that he saw a deceased friend of Agilapwe handing him a piece of a G string.[86] They added that everyone knew how thoroughly "hot" and pestilential the wild taro patch of Manuniki was, and, further, that Agilapwe's own sore pre-dated the death of the Maguer man who was accused of having given him the piece of G string.[87] Agilapwe angrily returned their charges and announced that he had no piece of G string. Furthermore he did not intend to venture into the wild taro patch in search of any such piece which someone else might have placed there, because he was afraid that the wild taro would make his own sore worse.[88] To this the Maguer people retorted that Agilapwe had probably gotten his sore in the first place by putting exuviae into wild taro.[89] Finally, in a great histrionic burst

[86] This dream had been reinforced by the statement of the sick man's daughter that she had witnessed this transaction.

[87] This was a rhetorical insinuation that Agilapwe had contracted his own sore when he attempted to sorcerize the Maguer man. Agilapwe's sore actually dated back to his childhood.

[88] This was also rhetoric; no one believed that this would happen.

[89] This is far more extreme talk than would be risked, as far as we know, in the Plains. But to send a search party to the Plains is to threaten an established and approved practice in the land of the enemy. On the Beach and in the Mountains, sorcery in any form was severely disapproved; furthermore, the Maguer people were among their own people. In accusing Agilapwe in this way they were assured of a good deal of public feeling on their side, as the

of anger, Agilapwe gave the Maguer men some tobacco and told them to take it to the Maguer sick man to smoke. If his body should become hot, it would prove that the piece of G string was somewhere in the Manuniki taro patch and Agilapwe would search for it. He finished his speech by remarking that the Maguer people did not seem to have any very serious intentions about rings.[90] The Maguer people accepted the tobacco, with no very good grace, left two rings with Ulaba'i, and departed. Ulaba'i gave them to Sinaba'i to keep while he went to Wewak. But then Ombomb came up to that end of the village and said that he would give them to Agilapwe, his *babu'en*.[91] He took them back to Agilapwe who was still at his house. Agilapwe flew into another histrionic rage, saying that he did not want the rings, he had not hidden the exuviae, he was not responsible, and wanted nothing to do with it. He then took the rings and stamped out of the village.

Ombomb said cynically to us that in about a week Agilapwe would go and look at that sore to see the chances of its healing. If it looked as if it would heal, he would produce the piece of G string and keep the rings, but if it did not

---

people of Alitoa were themselves tired of that wild taro patch in Manuniki and the search parties which it brought there. They had rooted out most of the wild taro on the slopes of Alitoa itself, and they did not see why Agilapwe should not do the same.

[90] When an accusation like this is made, rings are always left with the accused, to be kept if the sick person recovers, to be returned if he does not. They are supposed to be thrust upon him. Agilapwe's remark was very bad form, suggesting that he planned to profit from the other's sickness. At the same time, it fitted with his representation that he was an innocent man with a sore himself, unfortunately in possession of an incriminating taro patch, and that he should therefore be recompensed for all of these searching labors which were being thrust upon him.

The custom of forcing rings on the custodian of the sorcery place is paralleled in Mundugumor where rings are given to the men whose *marsalai* is suspected in a case of *marsalai*-caused illness. In Mundugumor rings are said to be given so as to influence the *marsalai* and are returned after the illness is over, even if the patient recovers.

[91] This type of stress on such a remote relationship as a second cousinship lays special emphasis upon the warmth of the relationship.

look as if it would heal, he would return the rings and say that he had been unable to find it.[92]

Ulaba'i then left for Wewak with the *tultul* of Numidipi-heim. Whasimai went to get her daughter Anyuai and bring her back to help with the taro planting. Ibanyos took the two children, Nemausi and Segenamoya, and went to help Gobonarra, her mother's brother, in Malupit.

Ombomb and Sauwedjo left for Dunigi to keep their appointment with Wabe and Bischu. They took Miduain[93] with them to help them carry back the dry coconuts which the Dunigi people were to give them.

Maigi and Sagu went to Liwo to see Maigi's sister. Maigi had remained in the village overnight to support Agilapwe, who had gone to sleep in Ombomb's house instead of Maigi's.

Kule and Baimal stayed in the village all day. It was rainy and cold. Baimal's two wives got back late in the afternoon.

Sinaba'i and his wife also remained in the village and did nothing all day.

FEBRUARY 14: The next day dawned stormy and cold again. Kule and Ilautoa left for Mogiligen, leaving Naguel with Baimal, who, with his two wives, went to work sago. Gerud went to Malupit to see his father and returned late

---

[92] This type of cynicism was characteristic of Ombomb, who was always able to reduce his own and other people's motives to the most self-interested terms. Nevertheless, confusion is shown even here, because even he does not suggest that Agilapwe would forge the piece of G string; he assumes that Agilapwe has a piece of G string, and rather admires the old man for his iniquity, but that he will only return it if the sore shows signs of healing. If the sore should not heal, the man will die and people will know that it was really Plains sorcery which was ultimately responsible. Ombomb assumes that Agilapwe will be too canny to take any payment for a cure of which he is not certain. It is worth noting that Agilapwe did not do anything of the sort. He simply sat growling in Manuniki and let the Maguer people make the next move.

[93] This is a characteristic Alitoa arrangement. As a rule, Ombomb did not have a great deal to do with Sinaba'i, but for two or three days he had been helping Sinaba'i work sago for the feast, then he found the household needed yams and gave them some, and now, in turn, Sinaba'i lets him take Miduain along to help with his carrying. So one piece of helpfulness or cooperation is likely to lead to a whole series.

in the afternoon, bringing his small brother Bopugenon and Manum's son Mai back with him.

Temos, Shuisha, and Yanyibis came up to the village and went down again.[94]

At dusk, two Magahine men, armed with spears, hurried through on their way to Dunigi. Finding the house of Ulaba'i, their gift friend, closed, they went on and stayed at Aden's place.

Ombomb got back late with Sauwedjo, Miduain, three Dunigi men, his father-in-law and two brothers-in-law, and three Dunigi women, the wives of the two men and an unmarried daughter of a sister of Sauwedjo who was unclothed, carrying loads of dried coconuts for his feast. Wabe and Bischu came with them and went immediately to the latter's garden.

## DANCE TO CONCLUDE BALIDU'S HARVEST

Balidu and his household came up and announced that the harvesting of the yam garden was finished. In honor of the completion of this harvest, Baimal's finishing his sago working, and Ombomb's return from Dunigi with the dried coconuts, the young men put on a very small dance. Ombomb, Madje, Badui, and Pidjui dressed up. Baimal put on armbands and danced a little. Manum's sons did not participate. The Dunigi visitors and Balidu went to sleep and only the women of the Walinuba end danced.[95]

\* \* \*

The other end of the village was empty except for Madje. Yahalijo and Kumati had stayed down in the garden, for

[94] Very often I can only report that someone came up to the village and left it. This is because no one else knew why the absentee made the trip, and it was impossible to check these points days later. Usually the trips are made either to bring food, or to get food or utensils, or to carry a message. In this case, Temos probably came up to see if there had been any news of Wabe.

[95] This little dance is typical. It was cold and rainy and only the very young or those directly involved felt it necessary to dance. To dance throughout the cold wet night was an obligation, not a pleasure.

their part of the harvest was not yet over. Lomaijo, Lamein, and the baby came back late from Sumali's harvest which was also not yet over.

FEBRUARY 15: Wabe had returned to the village late the night before and quarreled with his two wives, accusing Temos in particular of a series of small defections. He brought back with him the adolescent son of a Bonaheitum friend, and a dog, the gift of this friend, so his sorcery hunting trip into the Plains had not been wholly unprofitable.

Welima and Wadjubel carried up yams for Wabe's garden. Wabe sat about and sulked. Temos sat at some distance from him, but never let him out of sight of her possessive eyes. Wabe was disgruntled about his Plains trip; the sorcery search had been fruitless. He still had the two rings given him by Bischu's *mehinen* to pay for the exuviae, but he had found no takers. A Dunigi friend had also given him a ring. Presumably, most of his disgruntlement was due to his quarrel with his wives, because, on the surface, his Plains trip had been profitable enough. He sat and commented to us on the meagerness of his yam crop. Everybody's yam crop was no good, because of the Messiah-cult the year before which had made everyone's planting late. Bischu, La'abe, Ulaba'i, Matasues, Kule, and Balidu had built the new style ground houses, with the sago bark walls to withstand the flood, all together here in Alitoa. He, Wabe, had not wanted to do that and he had gone and awaited the flood in Alipinagle.[96] Finally, in the late afternoon his anger burst out into accusations against our Umanep shoot boy, to whom he had given two cartridges to shoot birds of paradise. The shoot boy had used the cartridges, but told him that they had misfired. Wabe came to us with a long tale of the number of fine feathered birds the shoot boy had shot, the way in which he used them as bribes, and the accusation that he was trying to seduce Wadjubel. We examined the shoot boy's net bag,

[96] This remark is significant in the light of Wabe's subsequent disgruntled departure for Alipinagle. Today, when he is angry with his wives and discouraged with his crops, his feeling turns against his own place, and he regards Alipinagle, the home of his wife's mother's people, as safe, and recalls the time when he took refuge there in an emergency.

found several secreted cartridges there, and discharged him, as he was obviously going to be a sore spot in our relations with the community. He left at once with his wife.

La'abe returned from his Plains trip with Imale and Souato'a, bringing Daulap, the fourteen-year-old son of his sister, with him. La'abe brought back two cooking pots given him by his Dunigi friends. He brought word that Ombomb's Wihun parents-in-law needed yams. Ombomb called out for Me'elue to come up from Bischu's garden and sent her off with her child and a load of yams to Wihun. She went all alone.[97] Her net bag held 50 pounds of yams and she would have to carry Yauwito'a who weighed another 30, a good part of the way.

Ombomb's Dunigi guests remained in his house. The women were very shy and could not be persuaded to come outside at all before noon. When they did emerge they sat with averted heads, staring into space. The men sat under the house with Ombomb, chewed areca nut, and talked without embarrassment. Miduain was still living in Ombomb's household and helping to entertain the visitors.

Baimal and his wives were working sago, and so were Sinaba'i and his wife. Matasues and Anop were also reported to be working sago.

Whasimai returned from Liwo with Anyuai and a puppy whose mother had just died from a nasal hemorrhage.[98] She stopped to collect her two younger children from Ibanyos.

Balidu, Badui, Pidjui, and Nigimarib stayed in the village the previous night. This morning Badui put the old thatch

[97] Although it is quite safe for women to journey about alone in Arapesh country, usually neither men nor women, except in emergencies, made so long and laden a trip alone. It was typical of Ombomb's callous disregard of Me'elue, towards whom he felt increasingly guilty, that he should send her alone, so heavily burdened.

[98] All the dogs in Alitoa were dying from a mysterious epidemic which had come from the direction of Aitape. This accounted for the great interest in new puppies. We tried to persuade people to keep the dogs isolated, but to no avail; when we left there was not a single old dog left in the whole Mountain region. When we reached the Yuat River the epidemic was just arriving, overland.

back on Kule's house which he had started to rebuild several days before. Maigi and his wife came back from Liwo; Sagu cooked for the household.

Two of Manum's small boys arrived and stayed in Balidu's house with Pidjui. Sumali and Manum were harvesting; the children of the two households were running about together.

Two Boinam men brought pawpaws to us to sell and news that the dog disease epidemic had spread to Boinam.

At night everyone who was in the village danced, although with less dressing up than for the dance two weeks ago. Wabe was the most energetic of the participants; part of the time he danced a kind of solo leap frog in the center of the ring, a dance which he had learned when he was away at work.

Aden, Ulaijo, and Sauisua came up, leaving Baijo in the garden. This was the first time Aden had been in the village since his feast. He took no part in the festivities at the Walinuba end.

During the night, there was a sudden gale. Ulaba'i's small lounging shed, situated in the center of his plaza, blew down.

FEBRUARY 16: After the dance of the night before, everyone was tired and captious. Mindibilip ran away. Dr. Fortune sent Ombomb after him, announcing that unless he was persuaded to come back we would ourselves leave Alitoa at once.

The remnants of the *luluai's* little house lay forlorn in the center of the village, as people began to scatter to their tasks.

The Dunigi relatives of Ombomb went home. Sauwedjo and Miduain went to her taro garden. Lomaijo went down to the garden, prepared to sleep there with Kamowon, while La'abe and Imale with Souato'a stayed here.

Balidu stayed here all day, entertaining his wife's cross-cousin and two of the cross-cousin's sister's sons from Wihun. Maigi, Sagu, and Badui assisted him.

Baimal and his two wives were still working sago.

Sinaba'i and his wife and children were in Moholigum, fencing.

Wabe, his two wives, and Wadjubel sat about and did nothing.

Aden remained in the village, keeping Sauisua and sent

Ulaijo down to relieve Baijo who came up. Madje was still there.

The wind which knocked Ulaba'i's house down was laid to Behebil, the great *marsalai*, because Iwamini had cut some sago there without pronouncing the proper propitiatory phrases. This was the only offense which gossip would uncover, but its connection with Ulaba'i was never further explained. Iwamini was, after all, only his brother-in-law and living in another place.

Ibanyos returned from helping Gobonarra; she, Whasimai, and the children were at home all day.

At sundown, La'abe, Imale, and Souato'a went down to La'abe's garden.

Yahalijo came up, with all the young people of Balidu's household, including Badui's Ahalesimihi betrothed who had been helping with the harvest. Yapul was here also.

FEBRUARY 17: Without any special event to focus life, people scattered about diverse tasks. The necessary main harvesting for the feasts was over; a good deal of the sago was worked. An interval of hunting would have to intervene before the date for the feast could be set.

La'abe came up from his garden to receive his brother-in-law, the *luluai* of Wihun, Wambibi, who was accompanied by his son Daulap, and Ulaijo's son, who had come to talk about a coming exchange of pigs. He had been harvesting small yams and brought some with him. On the way, he met Agilapwe and Yauwiyu, who had come up to sell things to us. Agilapwe and Wambibi are *ashin* (contracting *vis-à-vis* parents-in-law). Agilapwe returned again to the village with Wambibi and spent the night here also.

Baimal sent Alaijo back to Mogiligen to get greens; he, Amito'a, and Amus went to work sago.

Ombomb's two wives were both there, each sleeping in her own house.

Maigi and Sagu left for Manuniki with Yauwiyu, and took Naguel with them.

In the afternoon, Balidu grilled Wadjubel on the intentions of the shoot boy, but finally dismissed the whole matter as children's gossip.

FEBRUARY 18: A tempestuous, rainy day. Balidu was here

all day, Yapul and her baby with him. The two wives of Ombomb remained in the village all day. Wambibi stayed here all day; and in the evening he and Balidu sat in La'abe's house, and shouted to each other for an hour about the big pig which Balidu would fasten for Wambibi later on. This speech-making was ceremonial and meant for everyone to hear. Baimal and his wife returned late from working sago.

In the other end of the village, Sinaba'i and his wife and Ulaba'i's family came back, and Ulaijo went away and returned with one of Gobonarra's children.

FEBRUARY 19: (The sample of behavior during one hour was taken on the morning of this day, and can be placed in this context. See below, p. 521.)

## BEGINNING A NEW *Garamut* (1)

Wabe was preparing to make a new *garamut*. To do this he had summoned two sister's sons from Numidipiheim to help him. They arrived this morning. With the son of his Bonaheitum friend, he went off to the bush with them to work on the *garamut*.[99] This was said to be a *garamut* which he can beat later when he gives a pig to Aden as a return in the chain feast of January 29. Temos, Welima, and Wadjubel went down to Moholigum in the morning.

Ibanyos, Ulaijo, Anyuai, Nemausi, and Sauisua went to plant taro. Baijo was in Aden's garden and Whasimai stayed there, so that Nemausi and Sauisua, neither of whom is weaned, were both deprived of any suckling for the day.

Balidu, Badui, Kumati, and Nigimarib here, while Sa'omale and Yahalijo were in the garden.

La'abe and Imale went to work sago in Sumali's sago clump. Souato'a and Daulap stayed here.

Sauwedjo went for greens.

Baimal, Amito'a, and Amus rested all day.

Aden was here, but sent Ulaijo and Sauisua back to his garden.

[99] Making a *garamut*, like building a decorated house, is a task for which one must ceremonially enlist the help of others. In this case, the Numidipiheim men were more skilled carpenters than Wabe. Numidipiheim is a plate-making center.

Wambibi and Ulaijo's son left.

About noon, Ombomb returned with Mindibilip. Sauwedjo was away and Me'elue rushed to cook for him.[100]

Ulaba'i returned from Wewak and his sister came up to meet him. She came from Moholigum where she had been staying with Nahomen.

FEBRUARY 20: Anop came up late the night before to tell Welima, Wadjubel, and Temos to go down and get the sago which he and Matasues had been working. He stayed part of the morning. Temos went to get wood early.

## THE NEW *Garamut* (2)

Wabe returned after a night spent in a temporary shelter in the bush with the *garamut* makers.

Welima and Wadjubel went to help Whasimai work in the old garden of Ulaba'i. The children stayed with Ibanyos and their father. In the afternoon, Whasimai came back and the entire household set out for the new garden, planning to spend two days in Moholigum. Aden has also returned to his garden. At dusk, Wabe took food to the *garamut* workers and returned after dark. Iwamini came over in the afternoon and stayed in Aden's house overnight.

* * *

## BIRTH OF BISCHU'S BABY (1)

News came that Bischu's wife had borne a baby girl in the new garden. Me'elue was there already. Ombomb also went down. The new mother was also cared for by the wife of Wutue, but Me'elue, young, timid, having borne only one baby herself, acted as midwife.

* * *

Baimal, Amito'a, and Badui worked sago all day. Amus was with them. Alaijo returned laden with taro and greens from their garden, for Baimal's household to eat while they are working sago.

Badui was here alone all day. Yahalijo, Kumati, Nigimarib,

100 Mead, 1935b, p. 114.

and Sa'omali were in the garden. Pidjui and Naguel were in Manuniki with Maigi.

Kule, Alis, Sumali, and Nagawe were in the deep bush, hunting in preparation for the feast. Ombomb planned to join them, going direct from Bischu's garden.

FEBRUARY 21: About 10:30 in the morning, Mr. E. W. P. Chinnery, then Government Anthropologist, on a special inspection tour in the Wewak District, arrived. He brought with him a detachment of carriers from the next village. The *Diary* for the next three days is sketchy. The village life was complicated by the presence of the carriers. I was paying much more attention to discussing surrounding areas with Mr. Chinnery, who at this time very helpfully put at our disposal all the notes he had taken in other parts of the District.

## BIRTH OF BISCHU'S BABY (2)

Wabe sent Temos with food for the wife of Bischu. The child was born two days ago but this was the first that Wabe had heard of it.

The two days of strict couvade just over,[101] Bischu came up with Yanyibis to get coconuts for the nursing mother to drink.[102]

\* \* \*

Aden came back with Baijo, Sauisua, and the little daughter of Gobonarra.

Ulaba'i came up to report to Mr. Chinnery. Ibanyos, Maisoa, and Segenamoya came with him. Whasimai stayed in the garden.

La'abe came over to report to Mr. Chinnery and returned to Manuniki where he and Maigi, Imale, Sagu, and Pidjui

[101] When previously born children have lived, the length of the couvade is shorter for subsequent births. It is felt a man who has had two or three children who have lived should "know how to have children," consequently, he does not need to take such precaution as a new or hitherto unlucky father.
[102] This is the only non-feast use to which the rare and precious coconuts are put in Arapesh.

were working Sumali's sago, while Sumali himself hunted for the feast.

Balidu and Yahalijo were here all day. Nagawe came to see his father-in-law, Balidu, about meat for the feast.

Baimal, Amito'a, and Amus were here, taking a day off from the sago working. Alaijo and Minya have returned to Mogiligen. Balili and Yamogwai, Baimal's cross-cousins from Yapiaun, were here to inquire about the feast.

FEBRUARY 22: Seeing that we were fully occupied and also being anxious to avoid any chance jobs as carriers or messengers to the Beach, most of the people left.

Matasues, who came up the night before with Wahewai, stayed here part of the day with his Numidipiheim cross-cousins.

## THE NEW *Garamut* (3)

Wabe returned from the *garamut* making and reported that they had heated the stones for hollowing out the *garamut* and decorated it. Now it would remain unwatched in the bush, until the water dried out. Then he would have to find meat for the craftsmen.

\* \* \*

## BAIMAL'S QUARREL WITH AMITO'A (1)

Baimal and Amito'a had a violent quarrel because Amus cried to go with her father and Amito'a objected. In the midst of the quarrel, Amus fell on the path and became thoroughly enraged, but Amito'a received the only bad wound, a blow on the arm from the handle of Baimal's ax. He also reproached her because all her children had died and said that Amus was afraid of her because of her high temper. Amus ran away to Alaijo in Mogiligen and did not return until after dark with Alaijo and Minya. No one took very much interest in the quarrel, remarking that it was their own affair. They came and exhibited their scars to us, Baimal more tearful than Amito'a. Then Amito'a, sulking, sat outside her house for a while, announcing that Amus was undoubtedly lost forever in the bush[103] and that she was sick of marriage, and intended to return to her brother in Liwo.[104]

\* \* \*

Ulaba'i and Ibanyos were here, entertaining his brother-in-law from Numidipiheim and the brother-in-law's gift friend from the Nugum.

Miduain was here with Sauwedjo.

Sinaba'i and his family were here.

Budagiel and Bopugenon were said to have joined La'abe to help work their father's sago.

FEBRUARY 24:[105] Ulaba'i's brother-in-law and the gift friend are still here.

Iwamini's wife Yinauwhat came to stay with Aden[106] while Iwamini carried for Mr. Chinnery.

[103] It was a good two hours' walk to Mogiligen where Amus, who was five at the most, took refuge with Alaijo, her father's other wife.

[104] For the background of Amito'a's life, see Mead, 1935b, pp. 149–153.

[105] Our dating system had become dislocated during our first few days in Alitoa and I found I was a day behind. The sequence of events remains accurate, however.

[106] This was indicative of a healed quarrel. Yinauwhat had originally been betrothed to Monau, another younger brother of Aden and Iwamini, who had remained with his own gens, while Iwamini had been given to the *Banyimebis* gens of Alipinagle. When Monau stayed away for such a long time and Yinauwhat grew up, the usual problem developed of what to do with a full-grown, betrothed girl whose husband was absent. Iwamini's betrothed meanwhile had grown up too fast and been given to someone else. Iwamini and Monau were near in age; it was logical that she should be given to Iwamini, except that Maginala, Iwamini's adopted elder brother, would have to pay for Iwamini's wife, while Aden had paid for Yinauwhat, helping Monau. Aden, although he already had two wives, wanted to take her for himself, but here the entire community intervened. This is the only instance I have of this sort, but the feeling is very strong against events which would set the members of one generation against the younger generation over women. The only analogous case is Nyelahai's marriage to Natun, Mead, 1935b, pp. 119–122. But here several circumstances prevented the interference of the community, even though they disapproved. Nyelahai had no wife of child-bearing age, but only his old pig keeper; he had had very bad luck with his children dying; Yabinigi, to whom Natun was betrothed, was deaf and she did not

Wabe went to cut sago while his wives were carrying up the sago which Anop and Matasues had cut before.

FEBRUARY 25: Late last night, the mother of Me'elue and a ten-year-old daughter came from Wihun to bring areca nut to her daughter. Both Ombomb and Me'elue were absent; Ombomb was hunting and Me'elue taking care of Bischu's wife. Me'elue's mother slept in Ulaba'i's house, rather than sleep with Sauwedjo, her daughter's co-wife. She calls Ulaba'i "daughter's husband," including him with Nyelahai, who has married her other daughter, Natun. She left the areca nut in her daughter's house and left early in the morning before Ombomb returned.

Ombomb returned from several days' hunting with Kule and Alis. Taumulimen had accompanied them to smoke the meat. They had gotten three tree kangaroos, which were now in Mogiligen, being further smoked to preserve them for the feast. Ombomb was very gay over his hunting success and had fastened a number of red leaves in the front of his hair band. He sent Welima to Moholigum to look after a garden there. Sinaba'i, Wadjubel, Miduain, and Dubomugau went to Maguer to visit gift friends, one of whom had been among the Maguer sorcery delegation. Menala and Temos spent a lazy day, each in her own house.

Ulaba'i and his household were away, fencing.

Yesterday, the *tultul* of Kobelen, the elder "brother" of our boy Saharu, came up with two young children. He stayed overnight with La'abe and returned to Kobelen today taking Lamein, the little betrothed wife of Kaberman with him. La'abe returned to his sago working, taking Souato'a with him. Lomaijo and Kamowon remained in the village.

Baimal and Amito'a and Amus are resting again. Alaijo and Minya have again returned to Mogiligen for food and to look after the pig.

---

want to marry him. Even here, although no one intervened, disapproval was expressed in the continued description of Natun as "Yabinigi's wife whom Nyelahai took."

This old quarrel over whether or not Aden should take a third wife, instead of letting Iwamini have her, crops up again later, in one of Gerud's divinatory hunts for hidden exuviae. See below, p. 419.

Wabe, Madje, Maginala, Iwamini, Badui, and our boy Biagu left for Karawop as Mr. Chinnery's carriers.

FEBRUARY 26: Wutue, Bischu, and their wives and children were at Bischu's sago grounds, working sago. Wabe started to cut this sago several days ago. Ulaba'i was still fencing. Aden was planting taro. Bischu and Ombomb's taro was planted.

Sinaba'i and his party returned from Maguer, where they received only one packet of sago from their friends. On the road, Sinaba'i met his cross-cousin, whose younger brother was to marry the widowed betrothed of Sinaba'i's dead son. This girl, the daughter of Silisium, spent several days recently with Sinaba'i's wife. (See above, p. 220.) Sinaba'i's cross-cousin complained that the girl refused to stay in Liwo with her unknown new betrothed's strange kin. This conversation Sinaba'i reported to Balidu.

La'abe, Imale, Maigi, Sagu, Kumati, Pidjui, and Budagiel were working sago at Sumali's clump. Naguel and Bopugenon were there also.

Balidu was back in the village alone. Yahalijo and Sa'omali were in the garden. Yapul had been in the garden with her mother and just returned today to Ahalesimihi.

Me'elue just returned from taking care of Bischu's baby. Ombomb paid no attention to her, but spent the day instead inside his house with Sauwedjo.

In the evening, Balidu made a public speech, speaking in the low scolding voice of admonishment, not in the high aggressive voice of ceremonial speech-making to *buanyins.* He commented upon the news that Sinaba'i had brought back, upon how bad it was for Silisium's daughter not to be in the household of her betrothed, and upon the evils of these girls growing up with their husbands away at work.[107]

---

[107] Note that Balidu's connection with this whole matter was very slight. The girl had once been betrothed to Sinaba'i's son; Sinaba'i was a distant classificatory "brother," belonging to a *wabulip,* i.e., a gens of the same village. Furthermore, the girl had been visiting recently in Alitoa, in Sinaba'i's house. But Balidu's speech was merely a matter of taking any text to preach a sermon on a subject which, with Budagiel and Wadjubel roaming about without husbands, he had very much on his mind.

FEBRUARY 27: The women of the village started seriously carrying firewood for the coming feast. Sauwedjo, Wadjubel, Welima,[108] and Miduain piled theirs under Ombomb's house. Amito'a piled her own in the newly rebuilt ground house, which Badui had finished for Kule. Temos and Menala piled theirs under Wabe's house.

Lomaijo was menstruating and had gone off by a back road[109] to get firewood. She had taken the baby with her.

Balidu and Baimal built a small half-section ground house for Balidu's sister Nalaijo to use when she came to the feast. Amus had a temper tantrum because her father refused her his pipe and went off with Nigimarib to his mother's garden.

Ombomb and Sinaba'i cut up the firewood which the women brought.

Yabenas, the wife of Anop, and Aden's sister's daughter, from Numidipiheim, came up, also carrying firewood.

Me'elue went back to work sago with Bischu.

In the afternoon, Gobonarra and his wife came and slept here. Her daughter was still at Aden's garden. Sinaba'i went to his garden. The whole party, including Daulap, La'abe's sister's son from Wihun, who had been working sago at Sumali's patch, came back, their work finished. They had worked 12 large packets, a maximum of about 250 pounds by the usual Alitoa standards of packet size. Our carriers

---

[108] Observe how often Welima cooperated with Ombomb. Welima was not only his brother's wife, but she was La'abe's—his closest cooperating relative—wife's sister. Welima often came to La'abe's place to help Imale. This brought her in close touch with Ombomb. It was far oftener Welima than Temos who helped him or whom he took it upon himself to order about.

[109] There are certain little-traveled, poor tracks called the "little roads" on which menstruating women, men who have meat which they wish to conceal from others, and those bent on sorcery traffic travel. The association here is interesting.

A menstruating woman was not required to remain in the *sho'wet*, the menstrual hut; she simply was not allowed in the village houses or in the gardens. This means that the menstrual hut was her only shelter from sun and rain. She was, however, permitted to travel about on these unfrequented paths, gathering firewood or materials for clothing. She could not gather foodstuffs of any kind.

who had gone down with Mr. Chinnery called from Liwo
for help with the things they were bringing back. Ombomb,
Baimal, Kaberman, Gerud, and Sinaba'i went to help them.

In the evening, Amito'a delivered a long scolding tirade
addressed to Temos, on the theme of helping Bischu. Why,
she demanded, must it always be Me'elue, who had a small
unweaned child, who had to climb up and down the mountain sides, carrying and helping Bischu? If Bischu needed
more help, why could not Temos, who was his "sister," go
instead of the more distantly related Me'elue? Why did her
little *mehini'* (brother's daughter)[110] have to be exposed
to all the rain and cold?[111] Temos did not answer.

FEBRUARY 28: Baimal and Badui finished rough thatching
the walls of their rebuilt ground house with leaves. Amito'a
went down to Balidu's garden to get a load of food, and
then she, Baimal, Badui, Amus, and Naguel set off for
Mogiligen.

Lomaijo and Imale were both menstruating. Imale spent
half the day getting firewood and the other half making an
apron. La'abe hung about and did nothing, while Budagiel[112]
cooked for him, for Imale,[113] and the children.

Ombomb went out shooting with Yabinigi. Sauwedjo had
breakfast with Menala and Wadjubel and Miduain in Sinaba'i's house. Then they all went off to carry up some of

[110] Ombomb and Amito'a were very distantly related, but, having married into the village, Amito'a always stressed this relationship to the full.

[111] This tirade, although directed at Temos, and phrased as concern for the health of little Yauwito'a, Me'elue's small child, was
really an indirect expression of community disapproval of Ombomb
and a typical Arapesh method of showing it. It was not Temos, following well enough in her husband's interests, who was responsible
for Me'elue's overworked, neglected state, but Ombomb himself.
Amito'a delivered her harangue at the top of her voice from the
Walinuba end of the village, and Ombomb and Sauwedjo were
supposed to benefit by every word.

[112] Note that Budagiel was with La'abe, while he worked her
father's sago; she now returned with him and in turn assisted in his
household.

[113] Lomaijo, having borne two children, cooked for herself, over
her little fire in the *sho'wet*.

Ombomb's taro.[114] They had a feast of *oshugu*, (edible caterpillars) which had been found by Menala.

Maisoa, who had been staying over at Aden's, came into the village and joined Ibanyos, who had just come up from the garden with Segenamoya, to get taro rhizomes to plant. All three went back to the new garden. Whasimai, Anyuai, who is still here helping her mother plant taro, and the baby all came up and slept in the village.

Welima came back with her father's other wife and two of her father's children. They all helped her carry firewood, went with her for water, and then returned to Ahalesimihi. Welima also brought a little pig of Ombomb's up to the village to care for it there. His mother had previously been looking after it. Meanwhile there was talk of a dance that night. Bunitai came up with Madje. They spent the day lounging in Sinaba'i's house. Welima fed them.

Wabe worked sago, with Temos, Me'elue, Bischu, and Wutue. This afternoon Wabe and Temos returned to the village. Bischu, Wutue, and their families went back to their new gardens. Me'elue went to Moholigum to stay with Ombomb's mother.

Yapul, who had come the night before, was still at Balidu's. Sagu, who had just bathed after menstruation, Maigi, and Yauwiyu came back from Manuniki. Yauwiyu came because he had heard that there was to be a dance.

We sent Sinaba'i and Anop to the Beach on an errand.

After a great deal of indetermination, they finally decided to have a dance to celebrate La'abe's completed sago working. Ombomb, Yauwiyu, Yabinigi, Gerud, and Mindibilip danced until dawn.

MARCH 1:[115] Everyone was cross and befuddled after the dance, and the village was full of crying children.

[114] Note that because they were all going to carry for Ombomb and formed a formal work group, they could eat these caterpillars which Menala had found, but only if Sauwedjo, who lived at the other end of the village, was included in the meal.

[115] Note that I forgot, in making this diary, that 1932 was a leap year. As the exact dates are of no possible importance I shall choose the lesser evil and retain the dating scheme that I used; otherwise, there are likely to be many errors and confusions in cross-referencing from one set of notes to another.

Wabe went to work sago at dawn, instructing Temos to meet him at the sago clump. Instead, she went for firewood and returned to the village. Later she joined Me'elue to help carry Bischu's taro up.[116]

In the afternoon, Temos returned, bringing Bischu's four-year-old daughter Yabiok with her. She kept the child for the night.

Sinaba'i was away on a mission for us. Menala got firewood. Miduain and Whasimai took care of her baby. Whasimai suckled him a little, much to Nemausi's annoyance, but without enthusiasm. Anyuai and Nemausi were also here all day.

Ombomb made a small feast for the women who had helped his wives carry firewood. He used for this a pair of pigeons which we had given him, shot by our shoot boy. To the feast came Menala, Whasimai, Wadjubel, Miduain, and Welima. He had made coconut and taro croquettes and served the feast inside the house, in style.[117]

Budagiel and Bopugenon[118] went back to Sumali's hamlet.

Yapul came over again; with Sagu and Kumati she went down to the gardens to bring up taro. Yahalijo, returning with them, found that Ulaba'i's pig had gotten into a bundle of greens seed, which she had left in a ground house, and eaten up some taro buds[119] which she had tucked away

[116] This was the only formal attention which she paid to Amito'a's harangue of two nights before.

[117] This custom of giving small repayment feasts for services contributed within the group preparing for the feast is one of the reasons why the problem of getting enough food together in one place is so onerous.

[118] If Budagiel had been married, she would have gone about quite freely without a chaperoning child; she tried to follow the usual Arapesh custom and do this anyhow. But Balidu, whenever he met her, was accustomed to ask her casually who was with her, so she had begun to take Bopugenon, her favorite small brother, with her from place to place. So the Melanesian custom of the child chaperon was developing spontaneously, in response to a different type of situation from that for which the Melanesians usually employ it.

[119] *Bagi, bagihas,* the type of taro which keeps as do yams and can be replanted from the small buds which develop on the periphery of the main tuber.

inside the bundle. She made a furious row about this, working all the time to gather up the scattered remains of the dried greens. Bitterly she reproached Ulaba'i, who was not in the village, for having failed to blind the eyes of his pig and so allowed it to become a dangerous menace to everyone's possessions. Then she returned to her garden with the younger women.[120]

Lomaijo had bathed after menstruation and went down to carry up taro from Bischu's garden. Imale was still in her menstrual hut and La'abe was taking care of the children.

In the late afternoon, Wadjubel made Menala a pair of aprons.

Aden and Baijo came up in the afternoon and opened their house.

Nagawe was said to be hunting with Sumali.

Sinaba'i and Anop returned with a line of Liwo and Bugabahien carriers bringing out extra cargo, mostly trade goods, from Dakuar.

## ECONOMICS OF BALIDU'S FEAST[121] TO HONALI AND NIGI SAGO WORKING

| Clump Owned by | Worked by | Worked for |
|---|---|---|
| Balidu | Balidu, Kule, Maigi, Kumati, Sagu, Sa'omale, and Gowais (Badui's other betrothed wife), Ilautoa, Yapul, and Soatsalamo | Balidu |
| Matasues | Matasues, Anop, Madje, the two wives of Matasues, Yabenas | Matasues |
| | Carried by Temos, Welima, and Wadjubel | |

[120] Nothing further was ever said about this. Yahalijo had left the seed in an unprotected place, knowing that Ulaba'i's unblinded pig was in the village.

[121] As Ombomb was preparing to give a feast at the same time, some of his preparations are tangled with Balidu's in this account, as no one was very sure at this stage just which foods would be assigned to which feast.

| Sinaba'i | Ombomb, Sinaba'i, Sauwedjo, Me'elue, Menala, and Miduain | Sinaba'i and Ombomb |
| Bischu | Wabe, Bischu, Wutue, Bunitai, Temos, Mela, Me'elue, Tapita (a mother's brother of Wabe), and Tapita's wife from Alipinagle | Bischu and Wabe |
| Sumali | La'abe, his sister's son from Wihun, Maigi, Pidjui, Imale, Budagiel, Sagu, and Kumati | La'abe and Sumali |
| Gabunyan, son of brother of Silisium and sister of Balidu | Baimal and Amito'a | Baimal |

## TARO CONTRIBUTIONS

| FROM THE GARDENS OF | CARRIED BY | FOR |
|---|---|---|
| Balidu | Yahalijo, Yapul, Kumati, Sagu, Sa'omale, and Ano'a | Balidu |
| Ombomb | Sauwedjo, Me'elue, Miduain, Menala, Wadjubel, Welima | Ombomb |
| Manum (Ahalesimihi) | Budagiel, Lomaijo,[122] Welima,[122] and Wadjubel | La'abe (his brother-in-law) |
| Wabe | Temos, Welima, and Wadjubel | Wabe |
| Bischu | Me'elue, Lomaijo, and Temos | Bischu |

Taro carrying was not yet completed

[122] Both Ahalesimihi women married in Alitoa.

## CONTRIBUTIONS OF DRY COCONUTS

| PALMS OF | CARRIED BY | FOR WHOM |
| --- | --- | --- |
| Sauwedjo's Dunigi relatives | Sisters-in-law and sister's daughter of Sauwedjo, escorted by father and brothers of Sauwedjo | Ombomb |
| Ceremonial friend in Magahine | Baimal and La'abe | Baimal and La'abe |

Matasues, Balidu, Bischu, and Wabe contributed dry coconuts from their own trees

## HUNTING

Sumali, Kule, Alis, Ombomb, Baimal, Badui, and Nagawe

## FIREWOOD

This was being stacked by all the women in the village under the houses of Balidu, Kule, Baimal, Ombomb, and Wabe

## NEW HOUSES

Ombomb had built a large new ground house and Balidu two small shelters. Kule had rebuilt a ground house

### BALIDU'S FEAST SERIES: SUMMARY OF FEAST PREPARATIONS AS SEEN MARCH 1 (1)

He was informally assisted by Ombomb, Bischu, Baimal, Kule, Alis, Wabe, Matasues, and Anop.

This analysis represents the informal contributions of the immediate groups involved, and has very much the appearance of work in a large household. The formal contributions from outside helpers come later.

MARCH 2: Aden spent the day making a pair of coconut leaf mats. Sauisua, who came up in the early morning with Ulaijo, played around him. Baijo and Ulaijo made a trip to the garden to bring up miscellaneous supplies, taro and greens, and Ulaijo returned that night to the new hamlet.

a

b

(1) House staff. (a) Kaberman; (b) Mindibilip

(2) House staff. (a) Saharu; (b) Gerud

a

b

(3) Alitoa personalities. (a) Badui; (b) Kule, wearing woman's skirt for a dance

a

b

(4) Alitoa personalities. (a) La'abe, facing, playing sacred flute;
(b) Nyelahai and his son

a

b

(5) Deviants. (a) Ombomb; (b) Agilapwe

a

b

(6) Deviants. (a) Wabe; (b) Amito'a

a

b

(7) Alitoa women. (a) Sagu and a visiting child; (b) Wabe's two wives: Temos with dog, Welima seated

a

b

(8) Alitoa women. (a) Sauwedjo, Ombomb's Plains wife with her new baby; (b) Ilautoa, pregnant wife of Kule, and Mausi

Wabe, Temos, Welima, and Yabiok went to get taro. Temos[123] and Yabiok returned first, while Wabe and Welima did not get back until evening.

Sinaba'i and his whole household went to work in his taro garden; returned at nightfall.

Ulaba'i's family was away in the garden; Ibanyos, Maisoa, and Segenamoya returned late at night.

La'abe and Ombomb stayed in the village all day and did nothing, while their four wives went to get taro from an old garden. Imale returned the earliest with all the children and played with them for the next hour. When Lomaijo returned, La'abe set off to see Manum in Ahalesimihi about some taro.

Alaijo and Minya came in carrying taro for Baimal, which they stored in his house. They reported that Baimal had left the day before for Yamil in the Plains to get areca nut for the feast. They themselves returned to Mogiligen.

Yahalijo, Sagu, Kumati, and Yapul[124] came up bringing taro. Sagu, Kumati, Maigi, Pidjui, and Nigimarib stayed here overnight. Maigi had shaved his head.

Madje and Wadjubel were here all day and slept in Wabe's house.

MARCH 4: In the morning there was a false alarm that the District Officer might be coming, distracting everyone from their normal pursuits. It even brought Bischu and Wutue and their families up to the village. Wutue and his family

[123] Note that since the quarrel, Wabe has been paying much less attention to Temos, who follows him about with hungry eyes. Her bringing Yabiok up, in spite of the fact that she was not particularly fond of children and that they were not fond of her, was probably an attempt to mask her isolation.

[124] Yapul's frequent presence at her mother's was due to several circumstances: (1), during the preparations for a feast, a daughter goes home, if she can, to help somewhat; (2), she was so much younger than Nagawe that he tended to treat her more as he would have someone betrothed to a son, or as a daughter; (3), Nagawe himself was absent from home most of this time, hunting for the feast, and so, although they were separated, he and his wife were really engaged in similar economic activities; (4), she had an older and responsible co-wife who was quite capable of looking after the household, and who usually kept Yapul's three-year-old girl, for whom the long walk would have been too great, whereas Yapul could not have carried her and the baby both.

stayed overnight. Nahomen and his two children also stayed. Nyelahai took Segenamoya home with him. Naguel came back with Ilautoa and stayed with Sagu. Wabisu, the ten-year-old adopted daughter of Wamu'um, stayed with Sinaba'i. Anim, the eleven-year-old daughter of Nahomen, stayed with Ulaba'i. Keali, the daughter of Wamu'um, stayed with Ombomb, her mother's brother. Yabinigi killed a pig and we tried to trade it for sago, that is, give it away and hope for a return in sago, but got only about 50 pounds promised. All of Balidu's dry coconuts were piled up in cylindrical formation around a palm tree, by Pidjui, Gerud, Midjulumon, Bopugenon, and Nigimarib. Miduain, Imale, and Kumati made aprons. Ombomb fitted a new spear point to a spear.

MARCH 5: The normal routine was more or less regained, but the village was unusually full.

Bischu and his family, including the new baby, went to work sago.

Wutue and his family sat about and did nothing. They have no sense of belonging in Alitoa and always act as if they were visitors.

Ulaba'i had scratched his arm badly; he spent the morning sitting in the middle of his plaza with a look of histrionic agony on his face.[125] He kept announcing that he was going to Aden's place to see Nyelahai, but before he started, his Magahine gift friends arrived bringing areca nut. Ulaba'i then sent word up to the Walinuba end to ask Yapul if Nagawe was in Ahalesimihi and announced he would go to see him the next day and get some tobacco. He sent her a spray of the new areca nut which he had just received. Ibanyos and Welima, who had gone to Alipinagle the night before to get taro, from the garden of Welima's father's Ali-

---

[125] This is the regular behavior for someone with a slight illness or wound. By so exhibiting their misery they receive the maximum number of sympathetic exclamations, murmurs, and groans from the passers by. The extraordinary responsiveness of the Arapesh to another's misery is very marked. I once described to a group how I had caught my hand in a closing box; they recoiled, moving their bodies as if in pain, although it was obvious that the hand which I exhibited to them was not injured. They were reacting so strongly to the account of my previous pain, not to any spectacle of mutilation or even hurt.

pinagle wife, returned, also bringing taro from Ibanyos' garden.

Wabe went to see his gift friend in Waginara and came back late at night with only a very small spray of areca nut.

Temos, Menala, Miduain, and Wabisu got cooking leaves[126] and firewood.

Sinaba'i also got some leaves and then went to bed with a light attack of malaria. Bunitai[127] and Madje sat about and did nothing all day.

Balidu was in the village all day. In the afternoon he climbed a coconut palm that belonged to Wutue, the nuts of which Wutue was contributing to the feast. Balidu did this saying that the palm was too high and dangerous for the young to climb.[128]

Ombomb made a long bonneting mat of coconut palm leaves which both wives had gathered, in order to mend the leaking roof of the little *tamberan* house. Maigi and Pidjui brought in a lot of big firewood for the feast logs on the plaza. Maigi then helped Ombomb with the thatching.

Kule's two wives and the two youngest children arrived to stay in the village. Kule and Baimal were reported to have gone into the Plains to buy a pig. This superseded the earlier account that Baimal had gone alone to get areca nut.

The wife of Gobonarra, Midjulumon, Bopugenon, and the two eldest sons of Manum brought taro, and went back again immediately.

La'abe sent Imale off to Alipinagle where she was to sleep the night and get an early start for Wihun the next morning, in order to bring back taro from La'abe's sister. Lomaijo returned from carrying a load of taro, to find that La'abe had taken a large plate of hers which she had purchased with a tin of meat given her by one of her relatives, and put it in

---

[126] Leaves for serving food, for covering cook pots, and for seasoning pig.

[127] Bunitai was observing a sort of taboo period, after having learned the new *sagumeh* divination. Madje's laziness was due to his slowly dawning understanding that he would probably never have a wife anyhow, so what did it matter.

[128] Wutue was almost as old as Balidu, but as he was contributing the nuts, it was an act of courtesy on the part of Balidu to provide at least for gathering them.

Imale's house. This was thoroughly thoughtless and bad behavior on the part of La'abe, considering the state of Lomaijo's feelings about Imale. It would never have aroused anger except in someone whose feelings were already exacerbated. In a great rage Lomaijo shouted that this was unpardonable, that Imale had brought no proper household contributions, that her parents were poor and gave her nothing, that perhaps she had better copulate with her father, and then he would give her some things, that she, Lomaijo, did all the hard work of the household, and that Imale was petted and spoiled.

Welima was in Imale's house. She took it upon herself to answer on behalf of her sister, returning Lomaijo's obscene insults. Ombomb came down the hill just then and told Welima to go home and mind her own business, which she did. Lomaijo continued to scold at the top of her voice, but no one paid any attention to her. That night La'abe and Souato'a slept in the house of Imale, and Daulap, La'abe's Wihun sister's son, and the baby slept with Lomaijo.[129]

## BALIDU'S FEAST (2)

MARCH 6: Most of the local preparations for the feast were completed, and a general air of anxious expectancy pervaded the village. In the morning, Temos, Wabisu, Miduain, and Welima collected still more firewood. Sinaba'i, still ill, sat about in the plaza.

Wabe, La'abe, Bunitai, and Madje went down to help Bischu work a last lot of sago, returning late in the afternoon.

Ulaba'i and Aden harvested a small yam garden, with Nyelahai acting as magician. Nyelahai and all of Ulaba'i's household and Yabenas returned to the village in the late afternoon.

---

[129] Daulap did not feel at home in Alitoa, although he had been here most of the time for nearly a month. He was still shy and given to temper tantrums. He had set up a strong friendship with Lomaijo, however; they made common cause in their misery and when Daulap had a bad temper tantrum Lomaijo came out publicly and gave him food.

Ombomb worked on a new coconut husker[130] and Me'elue brought up more taro.

Nahomen went back to Kwobilisi.

Naushe'e, the son of Silisium, and the daughter of Manum came from Ahalesimihi to sell us food, paying no attention to the feast preparations which were under way.

Anone and Wasijo, the two wives of Yauwiyu, brought up taro to Ombomb.

At dusk, Baimal and Kule returned from the Plains village of Yamil, with two Plainsmen and two small nude girls. The Plainsmen had helped them carry back a small live pig, for which they paid 10 rings. The others had said that they would dance when Kule and Baimal got back. Everyone who belonged in the village was now there except Imale who had not yet returned from Wihun. But Kule and Baimal were too tired to dance. Nyelahai, playing the role of stimulating *buanyin,* acting as Ulaba'i's brother, stood up at the other end of the village and shouted, "You there! You called us Dog! You have got a pig! Why don't you dance? All this time you have been dancing about nothing. Now that you have a pig, you don't dance!" And much more to the same effect. But everyone was genuinely tired. As Wabe remarked, "There are not enough good men (i.e., unweary men) to dance; if we dance we will dance like sick men, like over-ripe bananas."

MARCH 7: At dawn, Balidu started off the ceremonial skirmishing with Nyelahai, each speaking from the far ends of the village. Two of Balidu's pigs had run away into the bush, and he had been putting food out in a distant place to tempt them back. Nyelahai's pig had eaten the food. Very probably he had also eaten the pigs, as it was obvious that he did not eat his own pig which was always prowling about in this village.

This was a covert reference to the pig's eating Yahalijo's taro buds. Nyelahai answered by saying, "Were Balidu's pigs little ones that he could hope to kill and eat, and conceal the fact? No, they were big pigs." (It is interesting to note that when ceremonial hostility is demanded, real grievances

[130] Mead, 1938, Fig. 76c.

tend to emerge. This corresponds, I believe, with some of
Moreno's findings when he asked subjects to extemporize
emotions; when rage was chosen, the incidents of which one
accused the other were not entirely fictitious, but had an
origin in the behavior of one of the two persons. Balidu had
no case against the pig which ate those taro seeds. But he
and Yahalijo were nevertheless angry about the taro seeds.
They had a sense of aggrieved virtue as they themselves
blinded their pig so that it would not be a menace to the
village. They could mention this grievance under the guise of
ceremonial hostility. Thus, ceremonial hostility acts in two
ways: it whets the energy of the opposing sides to greater
activity, and it drains off antipathies and grievances in socially
harmless ways.)

A little later Balidu came up and gave some areca nut to
Nyelahai, the formal indication that the hostility was ceremonial and not real. Nyelahai said that his side had been
called Dog, they had nothing to contribute and probably he
and his had better go to their places in the bush. But Balidu
told him to stay.

A little later Ombomb fastened a pig, which had been living
in the Alitoa half of the village. He performed every step of
the task with an air of the greatest momentousness.[131] The
pig's throat was held by a man sitting on it. It was then fastened to a pole, carried to the other end of the village, and
laid on the ground behind Ombomb's house, where it was
to remain until he gave his feast. A palm leaf mat was stood
up to shelter the pig from the sun.

### BALIDU'S FEAST:
### THE FOOD GIVEN BY THE DOGS (3)

After fastening the pig, which was incidental to Balidu's
feast but was too important for other events to compete with
it, the contributions of the Dogs of the Alitoa half were arranged in the central Alitoa plaza by Matasues, Wabe, Bi-

---

[131] The fastening of a large pig never fails to fill the Arapesh
with awe and excitement. They simply cannot take calmly the sight
of so much meat.

schu, Wutue, and Sinaba'i. Nyelahai and Ulaba'i had actually not been called Dogs in this feast at all, but in his speeches as *buanyin*, Nyelahai was assuming that he was identified with the Dogs, who were ceremonially opposed to Balidu. Actually, Matasues was the organizer of the Dogs. He made the largest contribution which was arranged first. The raw foods were arranged in round piles, taro with the sprouts out (the women came forward and cut off any shoots which had been overlooked), with a ring of coconuts outside, yams piled on top of the taro, and packets of sago arranged about them. Each pile was called an *aliman*[132] regardless of the actual number of objects it contained.

The group of donors here were all acting as *Uyebis*, although Matasues himself was a *gwai'oyen*, as was Wabe. Sinaba'i was included because the father of Matasues and Wabe had married his widowed mother and partially brought him up. The receiving group were all one effective generation of *Toto'alaibis*.

## DIAGRAM OF ARRANGEMENT OF FOOD GIVEN BY MATASUES AND HIS GROUP TO BALIDU AND HIS GROUP (MARCH 7)

*Gogo'wilis*[133]

| FROM | ESTIMATED[134] AMOUNT AND KIND OF RAW FOOD | To |
|---|---|---|
| Matasues | Unit 1 90 pounds of yams and taro 160 pounds of sago, a few yams | Balidu |
| Matasues | Unit 2 50 coconuts | Balidu |
| Sinaba'i | Unit 3 60 pounds of taro | Balidu |

[132] This is a final unit in Arapesh counting and may represent a variety of numbers, depending upon the scheme employed. Fortune, 1942, pp. 58–60.

[133] The vomit of the Dogs, who are returning what they have been given in the past.

[134] Estimates made by Dr. Fortune and myself on the basis of considerable experience in weighing yams, taro, and sago which were customarily purchased by the net bag full.

| FROM | ESTIMATED AMOUNT AND KIND OF RAW FOOD | To |
|---|:---:|---|
| Wabe | Unit 4 | Balidu |
| | 70 pounds taro and yams | |
| Wabe | Unit 5 | Balidu |
| | 60 pounds of taro | |
| Wabe and Bischu | Unit 6 | Balidu |
| | 40 coconuts | |
| Wabe | Unit 7 | Kule |
| | 40 pounds of taro | |
| Matasues | Unit 8 | Baimal |
| | 30 pounds of taro | |
| Bischu | Unit 9 | Baimal |
| | 30 pounds of taro | |
| Bischu | Unit 10 | Baimal |
| | 30 coconuts | |

After all the food was spread out, the young men, Baimal, Kule, La'abe, Maigi, Badui, Pidjui, and Gerud, of the Walinuba side came up at a jog trot and ran around the food, shouting the ceremonial acceptance, the *Gu Gu Gu Gu*, known as "killing the mud hen." Balidu walked up more slowly behind and took no part in either the running or shouting. Ombomb stood aside and took no part whatsoever, indicating that he was reserving all his energies for the feast for which he was responsible. Then everyone stood about rather aimlessly, until Bischu, shy and embarrassed, made a speech in which he was continually prompted by the others, telling who had given each little pile. The receivers again shouted *Gu Gu Gu Gu*, without running around. Then Balidu went over to his piles, stacked the yams together, and called out formally for all of his female grandchildren to come and carry them. The same set of girls, Una, Anibal, Anim, Miduain, Wabisu, Anyuai, etc., who had originally carried the food out onto the plaza, gathered the taro into net bags and carried it to Walinuba. The yams and sago were carried by the men and boys. After they had carried the taro the girls returned to carry the coconuts which were piled on the ground near the coconut cylinders; the other food was stored under Balidu's big house.

## BALIDU'S FEAST:
### RETURN FEAST OF COOKED FOOD (*Wileis*) (4)

As soon as the raw food was piled up in Walinuba, the people at that end of the village set to work, preparing a return feast of cooked food. This feast was spoken of as given by Balidu and Kule to the Dogs. It included coconut croquettes made by the men, a pot of coconut milk also squeezed by the men, jellied sago made by the women, and a pot of boiled game. Part of it was disposed on flat wooden plates and the remnants were on the large green leaves used in lieu of plates.[135] The plates and leaves were arranged empty on the plaza in front of Balidu's house (Fig. 1), then they added the croquettes, the jellied sago, meat which had been cut into small pieces weighing about 2 ounces each and was used to garnish each plate; the coconut milk was poured over the croquettes.

## SETS OF FOOD GIVEN BY BALIDU AND KULE TO THE DOGS

(Each plate held about twice as much as the leaves which were about 8 by 18 inches)

### Unit

1. Two plates croquettes, one leaf croquettes, one leaf sago, to Sinaba'i
2. Three plates croquettes, five leaves sago, two leaves sago, to Matasues
3. Two plates croquettes, one leaf sago, one leaf croquettes, to Wabe (for Welima's share)[136]
4. One plate croquettes, one leaf sago, two leaves croquettes, to Wabe (for Temos' share)

[135] Even when they know a feast is in progress, there are often not enough plates in one place. Leaves are also used for smaller units of food which could not be served courteously on a plate.

[136] Note that Wabe had arranged the contributions from his two wives' gardens separately, an arrangement explicitly recognized in the return feast.

5. Three plates croquettes, two leaves sago, two leaves croquettes, to Wutue[137]
6. One plate croquettes, two leaves sago, one leaf taro, to Bischu
7. One plate croquettes, two leaves sago, one leaf croquettes, to Ombomb[138]

After the feast was spread out, Balidu summoned Matasues and explained to him to whom each serving belonged. The others were then called to view the spread feast. The women folk then carried it away and distributed the plates informally to everyone in the Alitoa end of the village.

Everyone now had a fairly clear picture of the events that were to transpire and their sequence.[139] They said:

March 8. Tomorrow. Sumali and Baimal will arrange their contributions.

March 9. Monday. The *tamberan* will go to Alipinagle to release the taboo on coconuts there, and Liwo will bring their contributions.

March 10. Tuesday. This day is not very clear in anyone's mind.

March 11. Wednesday. The feast to Wihun.

March 12. Thursday. Ombomb's feast.

March 13. Friday. Payment for Yabenas, the wife of Anop.

While the return feast was being cooked, Wabe, Madje, Bunitai, Temos, and Me'elue went to meet the Waginara people who were bringing coconuts for the feast. Aden's whole household arrived. Ulaijo brought Nyelahai a big net bag of yams which he took home with him.

[137] As the old man of *Uyebis*, who had doubtless made a good contribution, although he did not appear officially.
[138] For an informal contribution of taro yesterday.
[139] Compare this with the actual sequence:
March 8: Part of Liwo contribution arrived.
*Tamberan* went to Alipinagle and returned to Alitoa.
Sumali and Baimal brought their meat contribution, some Liwo contributions.
March 9: More Liwo contributions.
March 10: The actual feast to Wihun.
March 11: Ombomb's feast. Payment for Yabenas. Scrap with Wihun. Arrival of Maguer sorcery delegation.
March 12: La'abe's payment for Imale. (This had not been planned for.)

Kule and Baimal left for Mogiligen to get their hunter's contribution. The doctor boy and the *tultul* of Kobelen arrived to visit La'abe, whose gift friends they were.

Inoman and his wife and three children and Agilapwe and his three children arrived. Anop and Matasues' wives and children and Wamu'um's children (except Bunitai) had all returned to Mobilinigum, as did Nigat (sister of Anop, and her Numidipiheim husband) after they had eaten their share of the return feast.

Maginala and Iwamini came over in the afternoon to make arrangements about the *tamberan's* going to Alipinagle.

The two Plainsmen and their little girls were still here, the little girls very gay and unfrightened.

In the late afternoon Ombomb fastened a second pig.

Welima cut the hair of Bischu whom she calls "brother."

The party who had gone to meet the Waginara people got back after dark.

MARCH 8: A party of Liwo people arrived with informal contributions from those classified as affinal relatives but who had no formal place in the feast program and so were accepted without ceremony.

### BALIDU'S FEAST: LIWO CONTRIBUTIONS (5)

| FROM | WHAT | To | RELATIONSHIP |
|------|------|-----|--------------|
| Polip | Two big packets of sago<br>One large rat | Maigi | Brother-in-law |
| Wabinole | One sago<br>Two phalangers | Maigi | Helping Polip |
| Eniga (a woman) | One cluster of areca nuts | Baimal | Classificatory grandfather |
| Sagapen | Four bandicoots, taro, and greens | Maigi | Cross-cousin |

The Liwo people simply set down their loads, rested for a little while, and started back again. Meanwhile, everyone in Walinuba was busy cooking for the arrival of the hunters from Mogiligen. Everywhere coconuts were being scraped, and big pots of taro boiled, or taro was being mashed with taro pounders, on pieces of *limbum* spathe.

BALIDU'S FEAST: CONTRIBUTION OF THE HUNTERS (6)

A little after noon the Mogiligen people arrived. In the party were Sumali, Manum, Gobonarra, Baimal, Kule, and Alis, and their wives and children. Everyone was dressed up; the small girls particularly were loaded down with ornaments. The women carried the taro in net bags and the men came in last, carrying the meat in one big bundle, suspended like a pig from a carrying pole, and decorated with streamers of green and red crotons.[140] They came in at a trot, shouting, and set their bundle down in the center. Then Sumali arranged piles of taro, from that which the women had brought and some which was already stored in the village. Sumali strutted and postured, in a brand new, very wide stiff belt. Balidu stood quietly aside and said nothing.

### ARRANGEMENT OF THE CONTRIBUTIONS OF TARO, ETC., FROM SUMALI AND BAIMAL

| UNITS | AMOUNT AND KIND | AS FROM: |
|---|---|---|
| 1 | 120 pounds of sago and 75 pounds of taro | Sumali |
| 2 | The Meat: 3 tree kangaroos, 1 cassowary, and a variety of small game | |
| 3 | 55 pounds of taro | Manum |
| 4 | 10 coconuts, 20 pounds of taro, and a kangaroo | Amito'a, to Ombomb for his feast |
| 5 | 45 pounds of taro | Sumali |
| 6 | 45 pounds of taro | Budagiel |
| 7 | 50 pounds of taro | Gerud |
| 8 | 35 pounds of taro | Midjulumon |
| 9 | 50 pounds of taro | La'abe (given him previously by Homendjuai, his sister and wife of Manum) |

[140] This bundle of meat was decorated, except for the absence of a mask, in a fashion very similar to the method of decorating and carrying large yams among the Abelam, as photographed by Dr. Fortune.

Kule, Maigi, Badui, and Pidjui ran around this food and shouted the ceremonial acceptance.

During this display, Honali arrived from Wihun and Whoiban from Liwo. After Sumali had made a speech about his hunting, Honali and Whoiban each made a brief speech, as befitted them as big men. The food was then taken away, and a feast of cooked food, similar to the one for Matasues' group, was served.

### BALIDU'S FEAST: THE ENTRY OF THE *Tamberan* (7)

After the feast, a few women were sent ahead to Alipinagle to help with the cooking there. Then Maigi and Maginala were sent off with the flutes which had been hidden the night before. The whole party of men finally reached Alipinagle, blowing the flutes on the road.

Meanwhile, in Alitoa the women clustered about, quietly expectant of the return of the *tamberan*. When its voice sounded on the road, we all ran quickly but unfrightened, down the steep road at the Alitoa end of the village which led to Moholigum. This was farther away from the Walinuba *tamberan* house which the *tamberan* would enter. The little girls stayed with their mothers. The small boys went off with Bischu and Wutue, who had not gone to Alipinagle, because their coconut palm trees had previously been released from the taboo. Everyone settled down comfortably on the hillside, laughing and chatting, and asking me if I didn't think the *tamberan's* voice was sweet. No one showed any fear, until I began to ask about the size of the *tamberan* and suggest that if it was so big how could it get into that small house. Here everyone began to look apprehensive, and Me'elue—poor, ringworm-covered, emaciated, unhappy Me'elue—hugged her thin little daughter close and muttered, "Don't talk like that. We must not think about the *tamberan*. It belongs to the men." "Yes," agreed the other women. "It is theirs. We must not talk about it, lest we die."

Along the Alipinagle road, the flutes could be heard approaching, played inexpertly but melodiously. Once there was a false alarm that we were to return, but then small boys came shouting to us that we were not to return yet. Finally, we were summoned back and returned to the village to find the flutes, accompanied by *garamut* beating, sounding forth lustily from the little *tamberan* house. Lovely as the flutes had sounded, unaccompanied and at a distance, their notes rose like a sharp wail above the incessant and not very skilled beating of the *garamuts*. The mere sound, continuous except for about three hours in the forenoon when the *tamberan* is supposed to sleep, has no doubt some relation to the tense atmosphere which prevails during a big feast.

That evening occurred an incident which illustrated another way in which the *tamberan* can contribute to the tenseness of a crowded village. The village was already crowded, and the women were hurriedly preparing the evening meal. A great number of people were gathered in the Walinuba end of the village right near the *tamberan* house. I myself was sitting in one of the little shelters which Balidu had built for Nalaijo, located on the opposite side of his big house from the little *tamberan* house. Suddenly, Balidu announced oratorically that the *tamberan* had received enough food in Alipinagle and would not be fed again that evening.[141] Immediately from the interior of the *tamberan* house came sounds of protest, whistling, and pounding on the floor. A lighted fire stick or so came hurtling out into the crowded plaza. The *tamberan* was angry. People paused; children clung closer to their mothers; the women stood worried, tensed for flight. Then there was another great clatter from the inside. This was construed, and meant to be con-

---

[141] To the women and children this signified a refusal to feed the *tamberan,* the supernatural monster. When it was pointed out to them that perhaps some of the food was eaten by men, the women agreed, shying away from the subject. The food was for the monster, that was as far as they were supposed to think. To the men, however, it meant a symbol of defiance directed at the only organized group of males which the community recognized, for only in this connection did the men ever consider themselves a group. In this particular case, it also means that the hosts (Balidu, Baimal, and Kule) did not mean to give a second feast to the Alipinagle and Kobelen and other Beach people who were clustered inside the house beating the *garamuts*. The *tamberan* had come from the Beach, only very recently, and the Beach people could regard this as a kind of insult, individual insubordination against the men's group, and particular churlishness on the part of the Alitoa hosts.

strued, as the *tamberan's* threat to emerge and kill all the women and children. Headlong and in disorder they fled from the village, gathering up the children as they ran, forsaking the paths, running down every part of the steep slope. Budagiel grabbed my hand, and with Moul holding fearfully to the other, pulled both of us down the slope.

It was all over in a minute. There were shouts of "Come back!" "It's all right." "It's finished." Breathless, disheveled, briar-torn, we climbed up again, to the sound of the children's frantic wails. In the plaza, all was confusion; everyone was rushing about, shouting, arguing. It was too dark to see clearly what was happening. The sudden tropical night had fallen, just as that last clattering threat had forced us all into flight.

And then Baimal, volatile, excitable, tiny, and indomitable, dashed forward, holding a piece of elephant grass cane in his hand, and beat furiously on the front roof of the *tamberan* house, "You would, would you? You would threaten to come out? You would frighten our women and children, and send them slipping and stumbling. You would send them into the dark, into the wet. You would chase our children away, would you? YOU. Take that, and that, and that."[142]

In a sense, Baimal's protest also expressed a difference in ethos between the Beach, which had accepted more of the *tamberan's* role as a discipliner of women, and the Mountain attitude toward the *tamberan* as protector, always careful, if possible, never to chase the women in the rain or in particularly bad weather. Also of course it was a rebuke issued by the hosts to the visitors who had overreached themselves.

Baimal then sent several plates of food into the *tamberan* to atone for his insult to the institution.


### BAIMAL'S QUARREL WITH AMITO'A (2)

Everyone was now preparing to dance; the young boys were putting leaves in their armbands and making fancy bustles; the girls were getting out their red and white cloth danc-

[142] This is a free translation of the report given me afterwards. He shouted so that I didn't get any text at the time.

ing shawls.[143] Amito'a had a touch of fever; she had been working furiously all day. Baimal was still excited from his encounter with the *tamberan*. He told Amito'a that she was sick and should not dance. She rebelled at once and announced her intention of dancing all night. To this Baimal replied that she was too old to bedeck herself like a young girl; cold and furious, she defied him and went on dancing.

\* \* \*

The dancing outside the *tamberan* house began about nine o'clock and lasted all night. It is phrased as "The women dance with the *tamberan*, outside the *tamberan's* house. The men dance, some inside and some outside." Throughout the night, the men slipped in and out of the *tamberan* house; its entrance had been masked with two big palm leaf mats. There were always seven or eight men inside, for fear that the women would count and decide that it was really only men playing the drums. Towards the end of the week, every man who was taking part in the drum beating and flute playing looked haggard from lack of sleep. Gerud and Anop, although uninitiated, were welcomed gladly enough as extra recruits in the laborious business of fooling the women for their own sakes.[144]

MARCH 9: Aden, Nyelahai, Ulaba'i, La'abe, and Wabe had slept in Alipinagle. This morning they made a small feast of cooked food there. Their women folk went over this morning and brought back the coconuts which the *tamberan* had released.[145]

---

[143] Cloth is still only an element in decoration among the Arapesh. Besides this use for dancing shawls, cloth streamers are beginning to replace the dyed sago fiber streamers which ornament the pillows, spears, taro pounders, etc.

[144] The welfare twist which the Arapesh had given to the *tamberan* observance in the attitude towards children and women robbed it of the touch of mischief and malice which did much, I believe, to keep up the spirits of its executants in other cultures. Where bullying the young boys, making definite exclusion points against the uninitiated, and pursuing the women at all hours were all barred, it became a rather heavy, highly virtuous, and dull business.

[145] Dr. Fortune conducted all the research into the *tamberan* observance from the inside. I merely record here events apparent to both men and women, from the standpoint of Alitoa.

Meanwhile more contributions to Balidu's feast arrived:

| From | What | To | RELATIONSHIP OF RECIPIENT TO DONOR |
|---|---|---|---|
| Nagawe | Taro and a wallaby | Balidu | Father-in-law |
| Balili | Taro | Baimal | Cross-cousin |
| Yamogwai | Taro and one phalanger | Kule | Cross-cousin |

Liwo Contributions

| | | | |
|---|---|---|---|
| Whoiban | Taro | Kule | Second generation cross-cousin |

Badui's affinal relatives brought eight packets of sago, and the relatives of Gerud's betrothed wife brought two packets of sago to Sumali.

## BAIMAL'S QUARREL WITH AMITO'A (3)

While these gifts were being informally received, Baimal and Amito'a came to blows, the culmination of the argument of the preceding night.[146] In the scuffle, Baimal hit her with a stick, the back of her hand was bitten, and Kule arrived just in time to restrain her from hitting Baimal over the head with an ax. Kule delivered a smart blow or so, before he ended the fight. Amito'a retired, weeping, to one of the little lean-to shelters where Winam was cooking. She sat there, feverish, miserable, tying a piece of vine into knots for the number of times that Baimal had beaten her. He came in to exhibit his wounds and glare at her. She announced that she hated all men and was going to live with her brother in Liwo. Balili and Unabelin stood about, remarking that it would be a good thing if she did, that no one wanted such a quarrelsome woman about, and Unabelin retold the story of her elopement years ago and her attack on his aging uncle.[147]

\* \* \*

[146] I find that in my account of these incidents, Mead, 1935b, pp. 152–153, I telescope the time here, making it appear that Baimal and Amito'a had fought immediately after the argument about her dancing. Actually a night intervened.

[147] For text, see Mead, 1935b, pp. 149–151.

At the other end of the village, Ulaba'i arranged his contribution, one packet of sago, 45 pounds of taro, and 12 coconuts, a miserable amount, indicative of a fact that everyone recognized that Ulaba'i was going downhill rapidly. But, despite the small size of the contribution, Balidu received it in style, and even shouted the *Gu Gu* himself.[148]

The Liwo women were given a feast and sent home.

Soon afterwards, a big party from Numidipiheim arrived, which included the affinal relatives of Aden, Bischu, Ulaba'i, La'abe, and Ombomb. All brought slight contributions to someone. Ombomb's Dunigi relatives arrived with more dry coconuts. Wabe's Bonaheitum gift friend arrived, empty-handed, as a spectator.

In the afternoon, Agilapwe's relatives from the distant village of Malis brought food and presented it formally. These included sons of Agilapwe's daughter and her Malis husband. At the same time, taro from the wife of Belatau was presented to Baimal (she is his cross-cousin), and four packets of sago and a phalanger were given to Maigi by Agilapwe's daughter's husband, his "brother-in-law." Some other Malis people, whom Agilapwe called cross-cousins, also came with this group. Agilapwe, who had been sleeping in Maigi's little house, took the group with him and moved up into one of Aden's houses.

La'abe's baby was ill during the afternoon; the cause was alleged to be a melon which had been sold to us and which had been previously charmed by Walawahan. Walawahan blew in the child's ear to exorcise the charm.

The village was now full to overflowing. The *tamberan* was singing noisily and lustily, and ceremonial hostility of some sort was plainly called for. Balidu made a long speech[149] in which he commented on the fact that Aden

---

[148] Ulaba'i was his real *buanyin,* a relationship which, as Ulaba'i failed more and more, had been taken over by Aden, Ulaba'i's brother-in-law, who had originally been the *buanyin* of La'abe's father.

[149] During a feast, it is said that the young men, fearing the results of these ceremonial speeches which the old men feel bound to make, beat the *garamuts* and blow the flutes as loudly as possible to drown out their trouble-breeding words, for the young men love peace, and the old men do not care.

had not helped him with this feast, that he was in arrears with his returns on meat, and that when he brought his new *garamut* (the one which Wabe was having made for him) into the village, he would have to fasten a pig at the same time.

## BALIDU'S FEAST: THE *Balagasik* FEAST ITSELF (8)

MARCH 10: This was the day for the feast itself, for which all this activity had been merely preliminary. Actually, the intralocality preparations are socially more important than the big conspicuous display.

Cooking began at dawn, everyone making croquettes and turning sago. The women boiled the meat in big pots covered with leaves. The little pig which Baimal had brought was the only pork there. All the raw food was piled up in front of Balidu's big house in one pyramid which the Arapesh call by the word for mountain. Taro and small yams formed the base; packets of sago were ranged in a double ring around the outside, large yams were arranged to make a crown, on the top of which great green sprays of areca nut were laid, and crowning it all was a smoked tree kangaroo. This heap and two trees about which coconuts had been fastened formed the whole contribution. The coconuts were fastened in pairs, by tying strips of the outer husk together, and tying this either to an areca palm or to the coconut palm center.[150]

The food was now all cooked; there was no sign of the Wihun people. Meanwhile, a sharp wind started to blow, the sky was overcast, and rain threatened. Banana leaves were placed on top of the mound of food to protect it from the rain. Finally, Honali and Nigi arrived alone and marched around the pile shouting *Gu Gu Gu Gu*. After this, there was another long wait. Many of the Wihun women had arrived outside the village, but still they waited. People shouted, "Go and drag the Wihun people here. Force them to come."[151] Plates of croquettes were laid out on the plaza. Finally, the Wihun people all came up the path together. The women

150 See photographs in Mead, 1934b, pp. 377–388.
151 This was, I think, extemporaneous, as is so much of the ceremonial hostility.

were decorated and wearing specially patterned and beautiful new net bags over their heads.[152] All of the women marched formally around the pile and then went and sat down underneath Balidu's big yam house. Then the men filed in and rushed about with axes and adzes, breaking the coconuts, both those on the pile and those fastened to the trees. When this activity subsided, Balidu made a speech. He held up a bunch of *ti* leaves which represented the quantity of meat, saying that now that he had made this feast for Badui, they, as his mother's brothers, must care for his health. Balidu concluded by throwing the leaves into the group of Wihun men. One of them caught them. Nigi took the leaves. But Honali made the return speech, filled with ceremonial hostility: the feast represented only women's work, the yams were scarce and small, mostly taro, hardly any meat, no pigs, etc. He also mentioned the failure of Aden and Nyelahai to help. Afterwards, people said that he had overdone his depreciatory remarks, but that was the way of Nyelahai and Honali, they were always overemphasizing their bravado.[153]

Then the Wihun people demolished the pile. While the women were carrying the food away from the mound, the men stood in front of the coconut cylinders, swinging their adzes and shouting, before cutting them down. Honali and Nigi distributed the nuts among them. Ombomb made a short, self-conscious speech to the Wihun people, announcing that he was going to give a feast the next day, but that it was absolutely none of their business and did not concern them in any way.[154]

The Wihun people were then feasted in relays as there were not enough bowls, and leaves could not be used for

[152] The use of new carrying bags as women's feast costumes occurs sporadically all over this region. It is a pretty bit of economic symbolism.

[153] Actually Nyelahai and Honali were merely acting in accordance with their temperaments. They were aggressive, domineering, loud-mouthed men; they were not able to distinguish between a natural expression of these attitudes and their ceremonial imitation required by Arapesh culture. *See also* Mead, 1935b, p. 147, for further discussion of this point.

[154] This was mere bluster, as this was one of the preparatory feasts for his big intralocality exchange with Belagomini of Wihun.

such a formal occasion. A pouring rain descended in the middle of the feast and people huddled together miserably under the houses.

* * *

### QUARREL BETWEEN ADEN AND AGILAPWE

That night Aden and Agilapwe had a quarrel. Agilapwe had taken all of his connections to sleep in Aden's houses, so that they were full; he himself was also in one of the houses. Aden called out formally to Agilapwe, "Grandfather,[155] come down from the house. You and I will sleep below and let the guests sleep above." This infuriated Agilapwe. He threw down a whole shower of sparks from the fireplace in the house where he sat and burned the people underneath. He then emerged and feinted, as if he were leaving the village, announcing that he was not going to stay any longer, he would go home that night, he would go at once, he was not going to stay and help with Ombomb's feast next day. Aden replied that he should stay, and he subsided.[156]

Then Aden made a long formal conciliatory speech to Balidu. He said that it was true that he had not helped him with this feast, as the Wihun people had claimed.[157] It was true. He had been angry about the accusations concerning Sumali's house burning. His sore had been bad.[158] He had moved away. He had left them. But now his heart was feel-

[155] This is the child-of-cross-cousin term.

[156] Here again it is very difficult to draw the line between real and ceremonial hostility. When we first went to Arapesh, we took all these episodes at their face value, as genuine quarrels, but a subsequent analysis shows that most of them actually aired genuine grievances on occasions when this sort of behavior was culturally required. That Aden was not in a bad humor that evening was shown clearly by his subsequent behavior. Agilapwe's bad humor was merely chronic. But tomorrow Agilapwe was going to undertake rather extensive obligations to Ombomb, giving him a chance to make threatening remarks about accepting those obligations.

[157] Wihun had claimed that they were really angry, because the pig which Aden owed Balidu and which would have come to them in the feast was missing.

[158] His sore had begun to improve about four or five days before, and at this time he believed that it was really getting well.

ing kindly again; later, when people returned pigs to him for his big feast, he would fasten two of them and give them to Balidu.

Baimal answered this speech by shouting histrionically, "Never mind. Never mind, you and your pigs. Never mind your sago and your help. We have now made the feast without your help."

On this note, the village slept, as best it could. Through the night there was a constant uneasy stir, creaking of houseboards, low-voiced conversations, crying of children, and the insistent music of the *tamberan*.

MARCH 11: The morning began with the customary oratory which marked the day as part of a great occasion.

### RECONCILIATION BETWEEN BALIDU AND ADEN

Aden, staff in hand, marched formally up to Balidu's plaza and sat down. Sumali made a speech in which he said that all the accusations and counter-accusations, the house burning *wishan*, the anti-pig fastening magic, should all die.

Balidu pantomimed the *wawawa* which he would shout later when Aden fastened a pig. He then made a bundle of sticks from miscellaneous rubbish which he picked up in the plaza, threw down three, four, five, six, in front of Aden. Then he got two extra sticks, threw them down and stood right over Aden in a threatening attitude, shouting, then he pushed all but three sticks away. These three, which represented three pigs which had not been returned, he pushed towards Aden.

Aden then picked up all of the sticks, danced about, threw down one stick at a time, right under Balidu's nose (Balidu was now seated), naming as he did so the occasion on which he returned the pig in question. He finally kept three sticks in his hands and said, "Yes, these three have not been returned, but they will be, they will be." He ended his harangue with the accusation that, after all, Balidu did not help him with *his* feast.

Balidu (now put on the defensive about the very matter on which his offensive started the argument), "And you! You did not help me with this feast. You gave no yams, no taro, no sago."

Aden, "The yams, the taros, the sago remain.[159] But I was angry because of your lying talk before."

Balidu, "All right. The quarrel is over. You make a feast; then I can permit the quarrel to finish. If you do not make a feast, I cannot permit it."

Aden (but this time without standing up to answer), "Two pieces of pig which you gave me, I gave to all (of my helpers in the former chain feast). Later, pigs will appear and I will return them."

Balidu (jumping up and waxing oratorical again), "You would like to try (test the strength of) your father, wouldn't you? Your father was my *buanyin*. You are only my child. If you like, you can make a feast to me. I am always giving you food and all of your young men eat it. None of them helped me with this feast."

Aden (remaining seated), "All talked angrily to me last night. I told Agilapwe. I said to sit underneath the house. Agilapwe threw away fire. He was angry." (He says this as an aside, in a low pained voice.)

Balidu (sitting down), "You fastened a pig to the people of Numidipiheim. They all came. They ate. All your young women! All your young men! They ate it up. And you gave me no sago for this feast."

Aden (sitting down), "The sago is still there. But I had no one to cut it. I had a sore. I couldn't go about. I couldn't cut it."[160]

Balidu (gently), "All right. All lied before. Never mind. I let it pass. I talk now of the food which I have given you. This should be returned."

---

[159] That is, "It is not because I didn't have food with which to help you, that I did not help." This remark is merely to reinforce his next statement.

[160] With Balidu's comment that Aden is only a member of the child generation, Aden more and more makes the appeal to pity. Balidu has given him an opening through which he can emerge, sick and sore, and he is no longer required to stamp and shout and pretend beyond his means.

## Whoiban's Speech Threatening Non-Cooperation

As soon as it was clear that Aden and Balidu had finished talking, Whoiban of Liwo stood up and began to talk. Whoiban was a close connection of Balidu through Balidu's Liwo mother; he was also the most active leader in Liwo, a young man just taking over that position. He loved oratory and made a speech at virtually every feast he attended, in whatever capacity. This speech, of which I give an abbreviated version[161] here, is a typical feast speech; the emphasis is on the dichotomy between sorcery and feasting.

"Ipagu is ill. He is sorcerized. Aden and Nyelahai know about this. They understand about this. They must make it straight. All the time, all the time, you people of Alitoa, you are the receivers of exuviae. All the time, all the time, you pass the exuviae on. This is a bad fashion. If you thought about feasts, if you talked only of feasts, that would be better. This talk of sorcery is evil. You fasten pigs, you put on paint. But you are not important men. Your backs are not black,[162] for all that. I, I don't like this sorcery talk all the time. Be-

---

[161] The records of these speeches were jotted down hastily, while I attempted to attend to the whole movement of events. Sometimes I missed several sentences and had to depend entirely on someone's hastily whispered account of what had been said. In so doing, I missed another couple of sentences. I always checked my record afterwards with interested bystanders so as to be sure that no essentials had been omitted. As our boys became better trained to sit beside us and fill in gaps or explain unfamiliar phrases, our records of oratory improved immensely of course. In Manus, Dr. Fortune found that a text given after the event did not retain the flavor of the oratorical moment as well as a partial text taken down, phrase by phrase, and somewhat mutilated, as the speeches were made. But the proficiency with which one can get such speeches down depends upon trained assistants, familiarity with the events discussed, and the extent to which the speech conforms to known oratorical forms. The Arapesh lack of feeling for form and their use of the most remote, dream-like associations, owing to which new subjects were continually being introduced without warning, made some of their speeches, or formal accusations, exceedingly difficult to follow.

[162] I.e., you do not have a crowd of men who stand behind you as supporters.

fore, your ancestors killed my ancestors.[163] As for me, I have come to help with this feast. All of us have not come. Some of them are sick.[164] But I came. However, if you make this man die, if you fail to go to the Plains and save him, then all our dealings with you are finished. You can make the feast to Magahine alone. We will not help you."[165]

A Wihun man then made a speech in which he repudiated any thought that anyone in Wihun had ever passed on the exuviae of anyone in Liwo. This speech was filled with allusions which only Liwo and Wihun understood.

## OMBOMB'S FEAST

Ombomb was to make a second feast, called *tapa'as nubat,* in the series of feasts through which he was organizing a big pig exchange with Wihun, in the course of which a new pair of flutes,[166] children of the Alitoa pair, were to be given to Wihun. Belagomini was his *gabunyan.* He and Ombomb had already exchanged a pig. Ombomb had eaten his and given half to Baimal and half to Wabe and Matasues. He had also given his *gabunyan* a large named ring.

[163] This is a frequent phrase, which always assumes that the present cooperation between two localities is a new blessing which had superseded hostility.

[164] A patent appeal for pity, as he conjures up the image of a willing helper, lying stricken by the evil machinations of the very people whom he might have helped.

[165] This is the speech of a good and responsible man who uses the threat of non-cooperation to stop sorcery, whereas irresponsible people like Yauwiyu and Tapita (see above, p. 188) use the threat of sorcery to enforce their rights or fancied rights.

Whoiban's father was a *buanyin* of Pailit. It was he who warned the Manuniki people when they came to attack Agilapwe and enabled them to repulse the attack, Mead, 1935b, pp. 159–160, and above, p. 186. Wabe, the son of Pailit, had been reared to be Whoiban's *buanyin,* but had been too sulky and misanthropic to continue. He always depreciated Whoiban and now remarked, *sotto voce,* that Whoiban was a big mouth and never kept his promises anyhow.

[166] For the theoretical treatment of this feast type, see above, p. 112.

## FIRST SERVING

| FROM | To | EXPLANATORY COMMENT |
|---|---|---|
| Matasues | Nyelahai | His *buanyin* |
| Matasues | Henalian | Who helps Nyelahai, his "sister's son" |
| Matasues | Sinaba'i | Foster brother |
| Matasues | Bischu | Gens brother |
| Wabe | Bischu. Then Bischu passed them on as follows: To his brother-in-law in Numidipiheim To the doctor boy of Waginara,[167] his cross-cousin To Whoiban (said to be in recognition of the old *buanyin* relationship with Pailit) | |
| Baimal | Balidu | Father's younger brother, who gave it to Sinue, *wa'en* |
| Baimal | Kule | Younger brother to Balili, *wa'en* |
| Baimal | Badui | Father's brother's son |
| Baimal | Sumali | Father's younger brother |

## SECOND SERVING

| Wabe | Sinaba'i | Who passed it on to Agilapwe Who passed it to: |
| --- | --- | --- |
| | Yauwiyu | His adopted son |
| | A cross-cousin from Malis | |
| | Another cross-cousin from Malis | |
| Baimal | Doctor boy of Liwo | Cross-cousin[168] |

[167] This is the same cross-cousin with whom Bischu went into the Plains on the sorcery hunt before, and in which Wabe had also assisted.

[168] As both types of cross-cousin appear in this and similar records I have not distinguished between maternal and paternal cross-cousins. In my original notes these were, however, distinguished until their non-significance was fully ascertained.

| Baimal | Ipagu of Liwo | Brother-in-law (Amito'a's brother) |
| Baimal | Sumali | Who gave it to Whoiban, cross-cousin |
| Baimal | Kule | Who gave it to Yamogwai of Yapiaun, his cross-cousin |

On this occasion, he fastened three pigs. He gave one to Baimal, one to Wabe, and one to Matasues, each of whom was to act as an intervening link in the composite chain.[169] Ombomb had fastened each pig slowly and pompously. Early this morning they were butchered by Nahomen, cut up, and cooked.

The taro croquettes and pieces of cooked pork were spread out in two servings, each time in three sets of plates. Ombomb was not dressed up at all. He merely walked up to the plates —which were spread from the lower end of Balidu's plaza down the path between La'abe's and Ombomb's house—and said quietly, "Baimal," "Wabe," "Matasues." Then these three, or sometimes the individuals with whom they had arranged to take the plates, came and took them. Baimal's group of receivers came and squatted over their plates without demonstration. Agilapwe and Yauwiyu, the receivers from Wabe through Sinaba'i, shouted, *Gu Gu Gu*. Agilapwe picked up a croquette and savagely bit off a piece, letting the rest fall, while Yauwiyu carried off the plates, yelling at the top of his voice. No one approved of this demonstration. There were muttered remarks of, "Bad man!"

The three principal receivers redistributed the plates of food as shown on p. 282.

After this distribution was completed, Belogomini, Ombomb's *vis-à-vis* from Wihun, made a speech. He was a huge fat man, covered with *tinea*, and strong as an ox.[170]

---

[169] Note that all three of these men were older than Ombomb, and that Baimal comes from the side with which he usually co-operated, Wabe and Matasues from the opposite side.

[170] He was the fat *tinea* type; I saw only one other middle-aged man of his physique, and that was on the upper Sepik, in the village of Jambon.

"We[171] are your *gabunyan*. You are making this feast now so that later you can fasten pigs and send them to us and we will return them. Take your time about it. If you are hungry eat of your food yourselves. If you have pigs, bring them. If you have no pigs, never mind, wait. Before the *tamberan* devoured the young boys in your village we sent taro and pigs. You returned them. Now the *tamberan* abides with us[172] and we will return any feast you make."

At noon, Madje spied a red phalanger in a tree across from our house. Dr. Fortune shot it and gave it to him, for first sight.

After Ombomb's feast, everything quieted down in the Walinuba end of the village. Those who had come specially for his feast mingled with the Wihun people. But there were too many people. The contrast between the feast food carried away by the participants in Ombomb's feast and the much simpler fare which was all Balidu could afford to give his guests was not conducive to contentment. Also, there was really nothing for anyone to wait for. They sat about, trying to make up their minds to go home, gossiping aimlessly.

## THE PAYMENT FOR ANOP'S WIFE (1)

Meanwhile, the center of interest shifted to the Alitoa end, where preparation was under way for the formal payment for Yabenas, the daughter of Nahomen, who was married to Anop. The food for the feast was prepared in the central section of the house of Wabe and Sinaba'i. The young people themselves both helped. Yabenas peeled and cooked the taro;

---

[171] "We" here refers to the fact that, for the final feast, there are two contracting pairs, Ombomb and Belogomini, and Kule and Wambibi. Kule has not started to make his series of feasts yet.

[172] Reference to the fact that one set of flutes had already been purchased by Wihun from Alitoa. The principals in this purchase were Baimal and the brother of Soatsalamo of Wihun. This is also a symbolic way of saying that the people of Wihun had a plentiful supply of food, because those who have the *tamberan* are abundantly blessed. Note the absence of hostility in this speech. Intralocality events are all supposed to be peacemaking; the hostility within the locality is deemed necessary to prevent too much peace and lack of effort.

Anop split and grated the coconuts. The wife of Matasues and Nigat, the half sister of Anop who was married in Numidipiheim, helped with cooking the taro for the croquettes. Nigat's sick husband, Ombaligu, sat in the corner.[173]

The children of Sinaba'i and Matasues played about the room. Yabenas was wearing a specially pretty sago apron, but she was not otherwise dressed up. It was a pleasant, unhurried domestic scene.

Then Matasues came in and summoned Wabe, Bischu, and Amau, son of Matasues' sister Nalaijo, to discuss the rings. The old Dunigi man, who was called "crocodile-skinned" man because of his heavy skin infection of *tinea*, sat in the corner and watched. He was called "grandfather" by everyone in Alitoa, in memory of the former Dunigi progenitors of

## ARRANGEMENT OF PAYMENT FOR THE WIFE OF ANOP

| OBJECT | GIVEN BY | EXPLANATORY COMMENT |
|---|---|---|
| String of shell money | Matasues | Elder foster brother of Anop and head of the family |
| Ring | Balue of Wihun | Cross-cousin (*wa'en*) |
| Ring | Nalaijo to Matasues | Nalaijo is Matasues' older sister, married in Numidipiheim |
| Ring | Matasues | |
| Ring | Wabe | Brother of Matasues; acting as an adopted member of *Uyebis* gens to which Anop belongs |
| Ring | Aden | Aden is mother's brother's son of Matasues, and also his mother subsequently married the father of Anop |
| Ring | Nalaijo to Amau | Amau is her son. (This payment is one of two instances only where I found any insistence upon a contribution being regarded as a wom- |

[173] Ombaligu's illness, which was a kind of wasting away with bad tropical ulcers, comes up later in one of Gerud's hunts for exuviae (pp. 301–302).

| Object | Given by | Explanatory Comment |
|---|---|---|
| | | an's. Nalaijo was the senior member of the group of *Toto'alaibis* members [she was older than Matasues] and was a widow and a woman of very strong personality) |
| Ring | Nigat | Nigat is Anop's half sister |
| Ring | Bischu | Father's father's brother's son of Anop |
| Knife | Wabe | As brother of Matasues, and gens brother of Anop |
| Head ornament of dog's teeth | Anop himself | |

the gens of *Toto'alaibis*. Wabe remarked to him that he came and got food all the time; why didn't he contribute a ring. The "crocodile man" only grunted unpleasantly and sat on staring.

Matasues spread the rings in a long line, away from him, commenting upon who had contributed each. When he had spread out seven rings, one headband of dog's teeth, and one string of shell money, he said, "This is enough." Wabe and Bischu both pounded on the floor, shouting in angry oratorical tones, "It is not enough. We must pay more." Then both stamped out of the house, registering rage. Bischu returned with another ring and Wabe with a big knife. For the final arrangement on the floor, see above.

Then Matasues opened his little ring bag and showed the others that he had five rings left and two strings of shell money. He said, deprecatingly, with a shy hesitant smile, "These must remain to watch over my skin." The others chorused an answer, "Yes, yes, those must remain to watch over your skin, to guard you from sorcery."

Matasues then tied little pieces of cord about four of the rings, the return rings which were to be given back at once, as their donors needed them. When Yabenas' kin accepted these rings, it would be with the understanding that immediate repayment was due. Then Matasues fastened them all together in a long single string. While he was doing this, La'abe came in and sat down to inspect the rings. Matasues said gently, "You should make a payment for Imale. You have not paid enough for her." La'abe sighed and looked worried. "I know," he answered, "but I haven't enough. All that I pay have to stay a while[174] and I haven't enough. I have only four rings and a knife."

The little family conference concluded, the men went to help with making the croquettes. Nigat mashed the taro, Anop shaped it into balls which Matasues and Bischu rolled in the grated coconut. Yabenas was sent out to get pepper catkins and did not get back until the whole ceremony was over.

\* \* \*

### THE FRACAS BETWEEN WIHUN AND NUMIDIPIHEIM

When the croquettes were about half finished, there was a great shouting from the Alitoa plaza. I was inside the house where the cooking was going on and ran out with the others. All the Wihun people were rushing around with sticks; there seemed to be a state of suspended or mimic warfare. Honali had a spear poised belligerently; now and again someone would deal someone else a glancing blow; then nothing would happen for a moment. Bischu rushed in and began taking sticks away from people and throwing them to the edge of the village. I walked right out into the midst of it, trying to decide what it was all about. It was impossible to believe that it was really a fight. The long pauses, the suspended motion, while everyone watched one person deliver a blow, had all the unreality of a slow motion picture. But the women were huddling to one side, and people shouted to me to go to the side. Dr. Fortune walked out from the house and stood in the center of the fracas, which finally calmed down. Finally, the Wihun crowd marched back to the other end of the village.[175]

[174] He cannot demand immediate repayment.
[175] I obtained the background of the stick fight from informants afterwards. The Wihun people had been sitting in the Walinuba

RETURN OF THE MAGUER SORCERY DELEGATION (6)

The Numidipiheim and Alitoa people sat down and pretended to talk about the weather until there was another diversion, as the now familiar figures of the Maguer sorcery delegation marched up, in line, the leader carrying a large green nettle leaf. All had black paint on their foreheads.

Everyone wore black paint, except Ramon, who was the gift friend of Baimal and Kule; he wore white paint to show that his presence in the group was conciliatory. He was the oldest man in the group and the Host of the Path. Balidu had remained in the Alitoa end after the Wihun people left. Agilapwe was also there, seated alone under one of Aden's houses. The Maguer people sat down and a few preliminary remarks were exchanged, as they asked for fire and lighted cigarettes.

---

end of the village, at loose ends. Kule's brother-in-law, the brother of Soatsalamo, began to meditate on how annoyed he was with his brother-in-law, his other sister's husband. This other brother-in-law was in the Alitoa end of the village; he had come up with the Numidipiheim people who came to help with the marriage payment and was now seated near the fire on the plaza, with several other Numidipiheim men, talking to Aden and Nyelahai. Nigi and Honali had wanted these two, the brother of Soatsalamo and his Numidipiheim brother-in-law, to help with the feast which they would return to Balidu, but the Numidipiheim men had refused. He pointed out that his wife, in whose name all this help was asked, was still very young, still growing on his food. She was not old enough to be much help with the work. It was not as if he were Kule, whose wife Soatsalamo was full grown and able to work.

The more he meditated on this, the angrier the Wihun man became, until he finally roused all his Wihun associates to go with him to the Alitoa end of the village, where he took a stick and started to beat up his brother-in-law who was seated by the fire. Then a general fracas started. A week later, this was spoken of as a battle; people shook their heads and said only our presence had prevented many deaths. This, in terms of everyone's temper at the time, especially the Alitoa people's determination to prevent a fight in the middle of their feasts, seems extremely unlikely to be a true statement of what would have occurred.

Then one of the Maguer men stood up and spoke:

"We made an oven.[176] We heated the stones. We named the trees. The fire went. The tree which stood for Manuniki alone was unburnt.[177] We now know that it is Manuniki."

Agilapwe (jumping up and stamping and shouting), "I know nothing about it. I tell you, I know nothing about it. All my young people are dead. If they planted it (i.e., the exuviae), I know nothing of it. I have searched and I can't find anything. I sent my tobacco to the sick man and you yourselves say his sore did not throb. His sore did not grow worse. So it was not I. Come to Manuniki and look tomorrow. See if you can find anything. If you can, take it out."

He sat down, panting. Balidu remarked, addressing the Maguer men, "I have heard all I want to hear about this matter. You brought me a message leaf.[178] What for? I had nothing to do with it. My skin has become heavy with this matter (i.e., I am sick of it). I have heard it completely (i.e., all that I want to hear)."

Maguer spokesman, "We know the road (i.e., that the exuviae took). We understand all about it. It came through Bita and Sausa of Bugabihiem. They passed it on. But they run away. They deny it. But we know. That was the road it took. And it came to Manuniki."

Agilapwe (standing up, as before), "There is no large taro there. Before, the people of But came about this and they flogged me. I took some out. Before, they gathered a lot of it (the wild taro) into a box and took it to Wewak and threw it into the sea. They made it cold. There is no large taro left. I am tired of the matter. Come and look if you like."

Kule (from the side lines and in a cool practical tone to the Maguer man), "You had better boil a lot of *wamebil* bark

[176] A divinatory oven. This method of divination is discussed in Mead, 1940, p. 345. And the details of a similar oven made for Aden are described below, p. 440.

[177] The trees named after the innocent places are consumed in the fire; only the tree of the guilty place, which is itself *hot* with sorcery, can withstand the flames.

[178] This refers to the last visit of the Maguer men when they left a *tangget* of nettle leaves in Balidu's house, serving notice on him that they expected him to take an interest in the matter.

and pour it on all the taro. There *is* only a little left. You can make it all cold."

No one made any more speeches. Everybody sat about sulkily, and I returned to Wabe's house to observe the progress of the marriage feast preparations.

* * *

### THE PAYMENT FOR ANOP'S WIFE RESUMED (2)

The feast was arranged on four bowls and four leaves. Matasues called out for Nahomen, the father of the bride, who came and sat beside the food. Selalimi (Wabe's father-in-law), Walawahan, as a member of *Uyebis,* and a son of Amambut were also present. Matasues held up the rings in one hand and then laid them in front of him. The two objects, a ring and a dog's teeth headdress, which had been set aside for Nahomen, were given to him, and Ulaba'i picked them up. Matasues pointed out the four rings which were to be returned at once and Selalimi commented on that fact. The rest of the rings with the knife were handed to Sinaba'i. He feinted handing them to his wife to put away. Just then Baimal, Kule, and Maigi came up. The rings were called back again. Then the food was distributed. Kule received one plate and one ring, and Baimal one plate and three rings. These four rings were to be returned at once. Maigi received a plate. Ulaba'i went off with two leaves of food and came stamping back and threw down the headdress, shouting that he didn't want it, he only wanted rings. Sinaba'i put the headdress away. Then Maigi took a ring, Amambut's son, a ring, Sumali, a ring. One leaf of food was given to Agilapwe who took the string of shell money. Matasues returned to Anop the dog's teeth headdress which nobody wanted.[179]

After all the refusals and rearrangements, the payment had been distributed as follows:

[179] The introduction of other objects, in addition to rings, into any of the symbolic payments is always dangerous and likely to arouse opposition. As the payments are all symbolic and must be returned in kind, special objects, like this headdress, put a greater strain on the recipient than does a standard article like a ring.

| To | NUMBER OF RINGS | COMMENT |
|---|---|---|
| Baimal | 1 | Later he also returned Maigi's and Sumali's |
| Sumali | 1 | |
| Kule | 1 | Kule's wife Ilautoa is the younger sister of the dead wife of Nahomen. This also explains Baimal's participation |
| Ulaba'i | 2 | Foster brother of Nahomen |
| Sinaba'i | Knife | Acting here with *Dibatua'am*, of which gens Nahomen is an adopted member |
| Maigi | 1 | |
| Nahomen | 1 | |
| Agilapwe | 1 | Which he finally took instead of the string of shell money |

Nahomen then presided over the small feast at which all of his party ate.

\* \* \*

Madje took the phalanger Dr. Fortune had shot and cooked it for the Maguer delegation.[180]

In the evening, Ulaba'i made a formal speech in which he said that it was true that he had not helped with Balidu's feast to any extent, but that now he was glad he had not. What kind of affair was this in which the Wihun people, who were the guests of Walinuba, come marching up in full force, to his end of the village, and start beating his brother-in-law[181] who was sitting by his fire.

Then another big man of Numidipiheim, who was the brother-in-law of the man who had been attacked, made a mild speech, saying that the poor man was useless and no good at work anyway. How could they have expected him to help with a big feast?

That evening, the Maguer men persuaded Kule and Baimal to bring up to the village Welanue, the sister of Nyelahai, and the widow of Maigi's dead brother Wankole, whom they

[180] If interpreted as done by the village, this was a very conciliatory act; actually, it was a piece of exhibitionism on Madje's part for which, however, no one would criticize him.

[181] Only in the sense that Ulaba'i, being married to a Numidipiheim woman, was likely to refer to any Numidipiheim man as his brother-in-law.

suspected of having buried the exuviae. This suspicion was
based on the accusation of the daughter of the dead man of
Magahine who was supposed to have committed the original
theft of the piece of G string. She claimed that she had seen
it given, with a tomahawk, one ring, and one other valuable,
to Bita of Bugabihiem.

Welanue, when hard pressed, admitted that her husband
had buried the exuviae which he had gotten from Bita, his
"cross-cousin" (*mehinen* type), who had gotten it from the
dead Magahine man, who wished to kill the father of Tam-
apwa, because of a rivalry relationship towards him. She said
her husband did not tell her where it was, as a woman cannot
go near a place where sorcery is being executed.[182]

MARCH 12: At dawn next morning the village was buzzing
with the news of Welanue's confession of Wankole's burial of
the Maguer exuviae. Welanue had already left the village and
gone back to *Suabibis*.

## LA'ABE'S PAYMENT FOR HIS WIFE (1)

But immediate interest in the Maguer situation was damp-
ened by La'abe's announcement that he meant to pay for
Imale.[183] He made the payment on Balidu's plaza, with his

---

[182] I did not hear about this interview until after the events of
the next morning. I never found out whether Welanue confessed,
after she had been told they knew that it had gone through Bita,
nor could I tell whether she supplied any of these details, or merely
corroborated them, as "Yes, Wankole did say something about getting something from Bita." I am inclined to think that she supplied
only vague corroboration, but I am not sure.

[183] This was a sudden decision, inspired by what Matasues had
said to him the day before. This illustrates perfectly how much the
field worker is at the mercy of chance and how much depends
upon getting around among the people, quickly, so as to be able to
link one event with another. A week later it would have been utterly impossible to learn from anyone, including Matasues and
La'abe, why La'abe had decided to make that payment. People
would have shrugged and said, "I think he found he had enough
rings" or, "He thought of his father-in-law and he thought he
would pay." They would probably not even have mentioned the
fact that his father-in-law Selalimi had been present the day before at the payment for Anop's wife, especially since Selalimi had
not taken any rings in that transaction. In field work in which the

few valuables, four rings and one knife, in a wooden bowl placed in front of him. He presented them all to Selalimi, who passed them on as follows:

| To | Object | Explanatory Comment |
|---|---|---|
| Balili | 1 Ring, 1 knife | *wa'en* |
| Sinaba'i | 1 Ring | *wa'en* |
| Wena | 1 Ring | *wa'en* |
| Walawahan | 1 Ring | Brother-in-law |

After this, Sumali made a speech in which he remarked that he had previously marked Imale for Gerud, but that she had grown too fast and so he had relinquished Gerud's claim in favor of La'abe.

Then Agilapwe came up from the other end of the village in an obviously bad temper, and made a very noisy, hostile, stamping speech, saying that he had helped pay for Imale's mother, and asking why he had not received anything.[184] He concluded his remarks with a fine burst of ceremonial sarcasm, "I am, of course, not asking for anything. I am not asking for a knife or a ring. I am just talking meaninglessly. I am a little unimportant man and you are a big man." La'abe replied that he wasn't giving anything to Agilapwe, because when he had previously given Agilapwe rings to pay for Taumulimen, Alis' wife, Agilapwe had not repaid them properly, but had sent them about in Liwo and Numidipiheim.[185]

---

worker is attempting to connect events so as to have some fair idea of the precipitating incidents in any sequence, long time, low tempo work cannot be substituted for very intensive work and never gives the same results. As it is, one gets only a section of the actual event sequence; while I was listening to Matasues tell La'abe he ought to pay for Imale, Balidu was probably saying something equally important at the other end of the village. But even this partial account, if pursued with sufficient vigor, does give some insight into the functioning of the society, a kind of insight which we have no other technique at present for obtaining.

[184] Agilapwe was the widower of Imale's mother's older sister.

[185] This was not, of course, why La'abe had not paid Agilapwe. He had never had any intention of paying him. Agilapwe was acting out of bad temper, and because La'abe's payment was small he wished to call attention to it. Although he got nothing for himself,

This interchange of hostilities started everyone making speeches. In these, Agilapwe was soundly berated by various members of *Toto'alaibis* for his dilatory methods of returning rings.[186]

## DISCUSSION ABOUT THE BETROTHAL OF KUMATI

In the course of these remarks, Sumali said, "Let Maigi pay more for Sagu before there is any more talk of Kumati."[187]

Silisium, the brother-in-law of Sumali, had been sitting inside Sumali's house, and he shouted out, "Well said."

Balidu to Agilapwe, "You have Sagu; that is enough."

Silisium, "Let me have her in return for Amito'a.[188] Sumali's daughters cannot marry my sons. There remains only Kumati."[189]

---

later in the morning he did sting La'abe into making a further payment for Imale.

[186] Notice how the circle goes. Maguer accused Agilapwe of sorcery, he angrily quarrels with La'abe, whose group in turn now charge him with behavior about which they would not ordinarily make such a fuss.

[187] Kumati, the daughter of Balidu, had been betrothed to Maigi, and Sagu, his older daughter, had been married to Maigi's elder brother. When the brother died, Sagu married Maigi. Kumati was tentatively betrothed to the son of Agilapwe who was away at work.

[188] Amito'a (usually called Gowais), daughter of Silisium, was betrothed to Badui.

[189] As Sumali's wife was Silisium's sister, Sumali's children and his children were cross-cousins. Amus, the daughter of Baimal, was already betrothed to Mai, the son of Manum, Silisium's brother. Baimal would not marry another daughter in the same direction. There did remain only Kumati, if there was to be an exchange. On the other hand, while Ilautoa and Sagu had been a sister-exchange, Taumulimen had married Alis and been paid for, so if one were talking of exchanges, Agilapwe had given *Toto'alaibis* two women and they had given his group only one. The Arapesh do not pay much attention to such exchanges, except for purposes of legalistic argument, to propose or defend some course of action which they wish to pursue for quite different reasons. Here Balidu was exasperated with Agilapwe and wished to express his exasperation. Sumali, on the other hand, was anxious to help his brother-in-law, whom he liked, to get as much as possible from his brother, whom

Balidu, "I don't want Kumati to marry and go far away. I want her to stay here and look after me in my old age. I want her here to help with feasts. We fastened a pig to you (Agilapwe) and you didn't return it."[190]

Baimal (looking mischievous and simply enjoying the argument), "That's right! Talk strong! Talk strong! Arouse my desire; and by and by, they will get up and offer many rings and many pigs. And Agilapwe, you return some of those rings we paid for Taumulimen before you talk."

\* \* \*

## MAGUER SORCERY DELEGATION (7)

Here the members of the Maguer delegation who had been sitting, sulking under a house, interrupted. They had been told that no one could go to Manuniki until the rain cleared, but there was now only a faint drizzle. All this time, everyone, except Agilapwe who had been stamping about in the rain, had been speaking from under the shelter of the houses. Now one of the Maguer men said insistently, "Let's go to Manuniki."

Balidu, "Yes, do! Hurry up! Go to Manuniki! Finish this hunting for exuviae so that the *tamberan* can go to Manuniki and taboo the coconuts. We haven't any meat to keep the *tamberan* here. If we had meat, it could stay a long time. But we have no meat; it must go."

Agilapwe (very pathetically), "It's no use your coming to taboo my coconuts. I shall have to go to jail for this sorcery. And it is none of my doing at all. But these are all young men. They like putting people in jail."[191]

---

he disliked. And Silisium saw that this was a good chance to argue his case.

[190] This is a reference to a pig which Matasues gave when they cut the sago bark apron of the widows of the dead brother of Maigi. Agilapwe had had a large share of this pig, which had never been returned.

[191] Clashes between work boys and natives who have never been to work are not frequent in Arapesh, but Agilapwe was the sort of man who could make a grievance out of anything. If he had thought the Maguer people were going to fight, he would have ac-

Ramon of Maguer (he was the gift friend of Baimal and Kule and the conciliatory member of the party), "We are not going to put anyone in jail. That is the Magahine fashion. It is not ours. We just want to find the exuviae, that's all."

Kule (who has been practical and resourceful throughout this visit), "What you should do is this: Go and tell Ulaba'i (the brother of Welanue) to make a feast for his dead brother-in-law (Wankole, the brother of Maigi), put it in an open place and ask the spirit of Wankole to come and direct him to find the exuviae. If you look only (i.e., without special direction) you won't find it. (Someone was sent to ask Ulaba'i if he would do this; he replied that he had no food, i.e., that he could not.)

Agilapwe, "I don't know anything about it. If it's there (i.e., in Manuniki) perhaps we can find it."

Balidu, "Yes, it would be proper to make a feast for a ghost. It would be better if Nyelahai and Ulaba'i did something about this matter. Before, the sick man was a friend of Nyelahai. Nyelahai and all his people are accustomed to go to Maguer and they are well received there. They are given food and areca nut. Maguer fastened a pig and sent it to Nyelahai. And when you come here, he doesn't come up. He runs away. He hides from you.[192] We, only, we feed you."

The talk then shifted to comments on Nyelahai's failure to return pigs which he owed; the Maguer men prepared to go to Manuniki. In good histrionic manner Agilapwe uttered one parting shot, as he left, "I am not a hunter. But I can fasten a domestic pig later, when I have one."

Meanwhile Yabinigi had killed a pig. Dr. Fortune now distributed it against future payments of sago. Nyelahai came up to look at the pig, but he went away again immediately, without seeing the Maguer people. The pig was accepted by Baimal and Kule, Bischu, Matasues, Ombomb, Sinaba'i, La'-

cused them of being insubordinates who did not realize that the Government was now here.

[192] The current theory of Nyelahai's recalcitrancy now was that he was angry because he was accused of the death of the child of the *tultul* of Maguer. This seems to be some remote and random accusation, now remembered to explain his conduct.

abe, Balidu, and Ulaba'i. Inoman cut it up and received the jaw in recompense.

Now Ulaba'i tried to get Sinaba'i to accompany the Maguer men to Manuniki. It was a long wet trip in the rain and a job which obviously everyone disliked. But Sinaba'i was helping Wabe make croquettes to feed the *tamberan* for having tabooed the coconuts of Bischu and Wabe before, and he refused. Finally, Ulaba'i, in a bad temper, went with them. Dr. Fortune accompanied them and recorded that Nyelahai met them there and, with Agilapwe, made a most perfunctory search among the wild taro.

\* \* \*

### FURTHER PAYMENT FOR LA'ABE'S WIFE (2)

While they were away, La'abe made a further payment for Imale. He did this very informally, seated in front of his own house where his father-in-law sat with him. His mother-in-law sat across the narrow road, with her children about her. Imale wasn't there. La'abe had placed the tortoise shell armband and one ring on a small wooden plate. Lomaijo[193] took the plate from La'abe's hand, carried it over, and handed it to Imale's mother. There were no speeches.

\* \* \*

### RETURN OF THE PAYMENT FOR ANOP'S WIFE (3)

Just after this, Balidu, Baimal, Amito'a, and Amus, looking very formal and important,[194] marched up together to the Alitoa end of the village.

The representatives of Anop's side, Matasues, Wabe, Amau of Numidipiheim, and Bischu stood about. Baimal

[193] Here is another instance of one wife's being substituted for the other (as above, p. 234) when it was Ibanyos who was sent to get pepper leaves for Whasimai's (her co-wife's) brother.

[194] There is an enormous difference in bearing between people engaged in ceremonial and those who are not. The self-conscious stride, the formation of the group, the gaze fixed and straight ahead, the rigidly composed face, all indicate to all onlookers that *something formal is going to be done*.

arranged six rings in pairs. Then he said, "These are yours. They are bad. These are ours. They are good." The rings had been matched as nearly as possible.[195]

Matasues said, "It is well." He took one of the three rings himself and gave two to Aimau to return to his mother Nalaijo. Baimal remarked that Kule's rings were all in Mogiligen and he wouldn't be able to return his until he went back there. The occasion then lapsed into informality. Balidu chatted away, saying that the *tamberan* will stay until tomorrow. (It could now be heard, awake, and resounding through the village.[196]) He also remarked that he was dissatisfied with the rings which he received for Bwao'o and he meant to hold fast to his two younger daughters.

As the *tamberan* was not to taboo coconuts that day, Wabe made a small feast for his own group, with the croquettes which were already prepared and the piece of pig which he had obtained from us.

At the other end of the village a child had a temper tantrum. This annoyed the *tamberan*, who does not like the sounds of women and children to intrude upon it. Its rage was expressed with poundings and hurled sticks. Kule was sent in with some propitiatory food.

The Maguer party returned empty-handed, having decided to employ Gerud to divine the whereabouts of the exuviae.[197] Gerud was informed of this and went to look for the special herbs which he needed.

Aimau, Sinaba'i's baby, had a long crying fit. This was attributed to the anger of the ancestors over the quarrel that morning between Ulaba'i and Sinaba'i. Ulaba'i sent for Aimau and blew in the child's ear.

In the Walinuba end, Balidu's group were feasting on the piece of pig which Aden had bought from us and had sent

[195] Matching, not improving on, the given ring is always the aim, but the fear that the ring which is returned will not be so good as that which is given is marked by the boastful overstatement.

[196] It must be remembered that, with the exception of the early morning hours, the *tamberan* has been sounding steadily throughout all the last few days.

[197] Gerud, who had learned from Alis, had not before tried out his powers.

immediately to Balidu as earnest of his good intent to end the quarrel. Balidu returned a knife and a small feast of croquettes.

## GERUD'S FIRST DIVINATION[198] (1)

Well after dark, Gerud started to divine. His procedure was typical of all his divinations thereafter; he did not vary his style. He began by standing rather stiff and still in the center of the plaza, chewing a bone (of Baimal's brother) and his magical herbs, and muttering to himself. Suddenly, with a shout, he began to run. He tore up and down the village, beating on houses, knocking over children, rushing about, in apparent disregard of obstacles. Then he dashed down the hillside and began to dig. Meanwhile, people followed him as closely as possible, trying to see what he was doing, and record his find. It was understood that he himself was possessed and would have no knowledge afterwards of what had happened. He reported two finds, a piece of very rotten bamboo, which was seized on at once by Wabe and identified as belonging to Wegul of Alipinagle, and a second piece of bamboo, which he kept. He further tried to dig in a place which was too hard. Matasues followed him closely at this point and said that it was the exuviae of his brother-in-law Ombaligu, and that he would dig and get it in the morning. After this Gerud returned to the Alitoa plaza, fell on the ground, supine, and proceeded to talk jerkily in a faraway voice. Except when he talked, as he sometimes did, for effect, shouting out some unmentionable thing to prove the genuineness of his possession (see below, p. 419), he talked so indistinctly that one had to lean over him to catch his words.

He identified the second find as belonging to the mother of Sa'omale, Badui's Liwo wife. He did not say who put it there.

Wabe declared that the first find belonged to Wegul and asked Gerud if it wasn't Wegul's, explaining that he had had

[198] I have a very poor record of this divination. It was a dark cloudy night. We had no idea of what to expect, everyone was nervous and elusive, and we got no record of what Gerud said during his prostrate trance.

a swollen leg for some time and had dreamt continually about the Alitoa village-steep. Gerud concurred in this theory and also was believed to concur in Wabe's assertion that the exuviae had been put there by Henalian, whose wife Wegul had taken.[199] Gerud also said that the exuviae which the Maguer men wanted was in Manuniki and that he would go and get it in the morning. He then came to.

The village buzzed with conversation for some time. Henalian, who was in the village, denied having put Wegul's exuviae there and said that a Liwo man had probably done it.

The affair of the mother of Sa'omale was also canvassed. Suspicion fell on Peshuhol, a Liwo man of poor character, who had wanted to marry her when she was left a widow.[200]

At the end of the evening, Ulaba'i made a big speech, asking the Maguer men why they had come here with black paint on their foreheads. If the people of this place had known anything about the exuviae, they would have taken it out long ago.

## MAGUER SORCERY DELEGATION IS ACCOMPANIED BY GERUD (9)

MARCH 13: Gerud and the Maguer men set out at dawn and returned triumphant at about eight o'clock, carrying a great piece of taro root which they deposited in the middle of the plaza.[201] Close examination revealed that this was a palpable forgery; a cleft had been cut in the old root and a wedge-shaped new piece of taro inserted. But Gerud looked very proud and everyone seemed quite pleased. Wabe boiled water and poured it over the root to make it cold. The theory was that the piece of G string itself had rotted long ago, but that this was the root in which it had been deposited.

Balidu then brought out a *tangget* (mnemonic device) and the sorcery message nettle leaf which the Maguer men had

---

[199] For account of this affair, see above, p. 190.

[200] Note that this woman was not ill at all. Gerud had merely selected a likely source of trouble, something which he was very adept at doing.

[201] Mead, 1938, Fig. 15.

left with him. He also brought the rings and tomahawk received for Gerud's former divination the night before. He declared these to be insufficient and returned the tomahawk, saying that he wanted a pig. Ombomb brought up the rings which the Maguer man had left here before and pronounced them poor. Wabe brought out a good ring to exhibit the kind of rings which they liked. The Maguer men were very conciliatory and promised adequate satisfaction, if the man recovered.[202]

Word was sent to Wegul that his exuviae had been found and that he should bring a good pot to pay Gerud. To this, Wegul sent back word that he thought Budagiel had buried some of his exuviae by mistake, thinking that it belonged to her former husband, Kamil of Liwo.[203]

Meanwhile, Matasues went privately and dug in the spot indicated by Gerud the night before, for the exuviae of his brother-in-law Ombaligu. He found another piece of bamboo and poured *wamebil* brew on it to cool it.[204]

Ombomb took the cooled exuviae to Numidipiheim and confronted Inyau with it. He confessed to having buried it

[202] These demands for payment seemed to have several roots: part of the demand was a pallid imitation of the blackmail behavior of the Plainsmen, the other half was desire for compensation for all the trouble and discomfort of these sorcery hunts, for feeding the delegations and bearing with their accusations. There was also, in this case, a lot of sheer conceit over Gerud's skill and a desire to capitalize it. While Ombomb was the source of most of the demands for payment for Gerud, Balidu, who was pretty close-fisted in his own way, was nothing loath to cooperate with him. Gerud himself, like his father Sumali, was a very acquisitive person.

[203] This accusation served a double purpose. By it Wegul said, "I have done nothing to deserve to be sorcerized. I do not believe that Henalian, my mother's brother and my wife's former husband, is responsible, because that quarrel is healed. I believe that Budagiel, Gerud's sister, buried this dirt of mine by mistake. In that case, the family of Sumali are responsible and I do not have to pay Gerud anything."

[204] Ombaligu had had a quarrel with a *buanyin* of his, Inyau of Numidipiheim. The *buanyin* had climbed Ombaligu's coconut palms which were planted on his place and taken all of the nuts without permission. Then the mother of this *buanyin* died, and Ombaligu was accused of his death; his present illness was regarded as a reprisal.

there, in revenge for his mother's death. Ombomb told him he was pretty foolish to have buried it in the place of his victim's brothers-in-law who were sure to find it. Ombomb then took the exuviae to Ombaligu and demanded a good plate for Gerud.[205]

Meanwhile Balidu had sent word to Peshuhol to come and answer the charge that he had buried the exuviae of Sa'-omale's mother, whose name was Talumen. Late in the morning Peshuhol arrived with the doctor boy of Liwo, the *luluai* of Liwo, Whoiban. Peshuhol was a miserably emaciated man, sour and unhappy looking. When his adopted brother, the former *luluai* of Liwo, died he wanted to marry his widow Talumen, and she rejected him contemptuously. He had then made an attempt to keep her small son, and had insulted him when he wanted to return to his mother with the worst language an Arapesh can use, "Go and mouth your mother's vulva."

### PESHUHOL'S DEFENSE AGAINST SORCERY ACCUSATION

Peshuhol was already speaking when we arrived at that end of the village. The ensuing conversation was recorded in the

[205] This was all Ombomb's account of what transpired. Inyau never came to Alitoa. The story was highly unconvincing because, as a rule, when revenge is attempted, the person desiring reprisal tries to get revenge in kind. Yet here, for a death, only a type of sorcery which could produce a sore was attempted. What does happen sometimes is that if a man had buried exuviae belonging to one person, and is later accused of having buried that of another, the hypothesis of original error may be introduced, as in Wegul's accusation of Budagiel above. During the next few months, Gerud took a great number of suspicious looking pieces of bamboo and tin cans out of the steeps of Alitoa. Undoubtedly, many of them were meaningless, but it seems unlikely that so many could have been. It must also be remembered that Gerud's accusations were based on a pretty shrewd knowledge of events, of existing hurt feelings, and desires for revenge. Owing to our presence in Alitoa, it had become a particularly good place for the practice of this mild form of sorcery, because during the house building or, when a whole group came to trade with us, no one's presence and motives were scrutinized as they would have been under more normal circumstances.

same way as those already discussed. Balidu was sitting under his house, looking very magisterial.[206]

Peshuhol, "I don't come to this village. True, the *luluai* (Ulaba'i) is my brother. His mother was the elder, my mother was the younger. I only journeyed through here. I went to the Plains, looking for some exuviae belonging to a But person. I came when the house was built.[207] But that's all. When I came I only carried this little net bag." Here he holds up a small net bag, half opened, as if for inspection. "How could I conceal anything in this?"[208]

Balidu, "You people of other localities are to stop burying exuviae here. I am tired of receiving *tanggets*. I am tired of people from other places coming here and asking questions about sorcery, like those Maguer people who come up here all the time. I don't like it. I won't have it."[209]

Peshuhol (already close to hysteria), "I didn't do it. I didn't put it there. I don't come here."

Balidu, "How do I know that you didn't do it? Anyway, you killed Bauwan before. You took his exuviae and you sent it to the Plains. It was a fish bone you took. And he came back here and stayed only two years and he died. It was you that did it."[210]

---

[206] It will be remembered that only two days before, Whoiban had been leveling accusations against Alitoa in the matter of the illness of the doctor boy's father. This swift countercharge against Liwo was probably not a mere coincidence.

[207] He is building up his character as good: he goes to search for the exuviae of others, he helps with our house.

[208] This is a standard alibi. See below, Me'elue's defense, p. 415.

[209] The high price demanded in all the sorcery finds would not, of course, discourage the perpetrators; it would only tend to discourage any casual accusations.

[210] This was one of the many unproved theories of why Bauwan, the former doctor boy and Baimal's younger brother, had died. It will be remembered that Tapita was also said to have claimed this death, an accusation that had been taken seriously (p. 188). But when one accusation comes up, all the long-discarded old theories are also revived to strengthen the villainy of the accused, just as a prosecuting attorney will try to produce evidence of former arrests of a defendant, even if they did not lead to conviction. A burden of guilt is built up in the minds of the audience; at least the defendant has put himself in a position before where he has been suspected of a similar crime.

"They wanted to give me the hat to look after sorcery.[211] But I didn't want it. I took it for my young men instead."[212]

Whoiban, "A man wouldn't put exuviae in another place like this. If he puts it in another place, how can the spirit of the victim come to it? If he puts it in his own place, by and by the spirit of the victim can come and he will die."[213]

Peshuhol (with hysterical repetitiousness), "I don't come here, I say. I didn't do it. I don't come here. I don't even come to see the *luluai*."[214]

Balidu, "I have understood this matter, now. It is true, this accusation against you. I have understood it."[215]

[211] I.e., "appoint me as *luluai* to act with the Government in suppressing the practice of sorcery." The Government of the Mandated Territory, as well as the Government of Papua, takes sorcery seriously as a crime. See Fortune, 1932a, Appendix III, for a discussion of the effects of this attitude on the part of the Government. *See also* Hogbin, 1935b.

[212] This statement has a double implication. It says in effect, "I am, of course, the senior member of this community and the Government offered me the position of *luluai* to stop this sorcery traffic. But I myself dislike having even that much to do with the nefarious business. So I took the Government appointments for my young men who are, of course, subject to my authority."

[213] This is pure debate and invokes the Plains method of sorcery in which it is necessary to catch the *mishin* of the victim embodied in an insect. There is no theory of wild taro magic which demands that the spirit of the victim go anywhere near the exuviae. The theory is that as the exuviae rots in the taro, the flesh of the part from which the exuviae was taken will rot; or, according to another theory, each wild taro spot produces a sore in a special place and can be so identified. Whoiban was just drawing a red herring across the trail here.

[214] This is a statement of fearfulness, i.e., "I am so aware of the hostility of this place toward me, that I don't come here even to see my mother's sister's son. I would never venture to bury exuviae in such a hostile place." The importance of this claim lies in the frequency in which habitation in a place is used as a proof that an accused person has probably buried exuviae there. So, in the Maguer case, Bita gave the exuviae to Wankole, his cross-cousin. In the matter of Wegul's exuviae, it was Henalian who came frequently to his sister's son's, the *luluai's* house, who was accused. So Peshuhol wants to prove that he does not come here, even to his relative's house.

[215] There is no English tense which renders the completeness of the native phrasing, which is well rendered by the P. E. *Me savee finish*, with a heavy accent on the *finish*.

Peshuhol, "I didn't do it. I ask help from Nyelahai and Aden. Let them come and talk.[216] And let me sit down close by and hear it said again (by Gerud) that I did it."

Whoiban, "Don't you talk about that woman (Talumen). Wahale[217] made a man of our place die. Your hamlets have taken plenty of our *tanggets* (asking about sorcery). My belly is full of this talk of sorcery."

Sumali, "You people of Liwo can make your feast to Magahine by yourselves. We won't go. You, you that is all, can fasten pigs. We will stop here. We won't help you."[218]

Whoiban, "I live on the road.[219] *Tanggets* go through my hands all the time. I don't like it. They (the men of Magahine) killed all of Ninyubeb (a small place near Umanep) and we aren't in the habit of walking about there.[220]

Peshuhol, "You keep talking about this quarrel over this woman. But that was a long time ago. This talk died long ago. If I hid exuviae, I hid it in my own place."

Whoiban, "He (Peshuhol) came here one day. Did he put it here or not? I don't know."[221]

---

[216] In other words, "Send for the other big men of this place, your *buanyins* and ceremonial opponents and see whether they will support you in this charge."

[217] Reference to an old accusation against an Alitoa man now dead.

[218] Here he returned Whoiban's non-cooperation threat of two days before. See above, pp. 280–281.

[219] There is a covert threat in this statement. Whoiban not only lives on the road; he in a sense controls the road to the Beach, along which all desirable things come. In mentioning the road, he takes a leaf out of the Plainsman's book, just as the Plainsman, threatening, will say, "This is my road. This is the road I always travel." But where the Plainsman threatens sorcery if there is no feasting, Whoiban, as a Mountain man nearer the Beach, threatens no feasting if there is sorcery.

[220] This is overtly friendly, i.e., Magahine is a hostile place and we are afraid to go there without friends.

[221] Here Whoiban is again aligning himself on the side of law and order. If Peshuhol is guilty, his own place will not defend him but will be the first to turn against him and compel him to stop his sorcery practice, as bringing trouble and disrepute upon the locality. Such an attitude is, of course, particularly applicable in this instance, where the intended victim is a Liwo woman.

This remark of Whoiban's was too much for Peshuhol. He felt utterly deserted and burst into tears as he screamed, standing now, "I, I all alone. I give you the lie. I give you the lie."

He sat down and started to sob.

Balidu (uncomfortably), "I don't like this fashion. I don't like it. It is not good making people die in other places and my having all the talk come to me."

At this point La'abe brought up the piece of bamboo with a half-chewed areca nut quid inside it. He took it over and pushed it under the hysterical Peshuhol's nose.

La'abe, "You look at this. Who put it here? A man or a ghost? Do you think a ghost put it?[222] I think a man put it."

Peshuhol, "My net bag was too small to have hidden that bamboo. Everybody saw my net bag. Plenty of people saw my net bag."

La'abe, "You are the only man who is angry about this woman. Nobody else is angry about anything. You go back home and don't bring your angers here. We are tired of taking the blame. Before, we fought your ancestors. You made sorcery against Wegul.[223] Idupihi (the sick man of Maguer), shall not die."

Peshuhol, "My anger was over long ago. The woman is long since married. My quarrel belongs to the past and this is a new bamboo."[224]

La'abe, "This is your quarrel. You are always quarreling about this woman. You never stop quarreling about her. Before, you quarreled about a pot."[225]

Peshuhol, "I wasn't angry about the woman. I was angry about the child. The child runs away all the time, from one

[222] This is typical of Arapesh attitudes toward ghosts as hardly existent. Here La'abe sneers at a ghost like a modern detective, as much as to say, "Will you deny the evidence of your five senses?"

[223] A past accusation, in other words, *"We* do not deal out death."

[224] Again the appeal to circumstantial evidence.

[225] Formerly, enraged that she refused to marry him, Peshuhol had smashed a cooking pot in which Talumen was cooking. La'abe brings the point up to refresh everyone's mind on the details of the long-standing quarrel.

mother's brother to another. I wanted to keep him. I wanted to keep him near me, near his father's palms, his house site, his sago, so that when he grew up his inheritance would be correct. So that there would be no dispute about it."[226]

La'abe (ignoring the emotional appeal), "Yes, you are angry and you try to put the blame on us. You think Alitoa will take the blame and all Liwo will sleep snugly, eh? You put things where you like in your own place. Your ancestors killed all the people of Maguer (by sorcery)."

Peshuhol, "I didn't do it. I passed through quickly. I did not stop."

La'abe, "Last night this thing was spoken. When I heard it, I said, 'Yes, this is true, this belongs to this quarrel. This is correct.'"

Peshuhol, "If a man saw me with his eyes, putting it (the exuviae), he could talk. I am sick to death of these accusations. I am always being accused. This accusation isn't worth anything. The *kiap*[227] wouldn't listen to it."

La'abe, "This isn't going to the *kiap*. But we have sent for you to talk to you. We are tired of these quarrels."

Peshuhol, "Yes, Sumein and But are always coming and accusing me. I am tired of these quarrels too. You are many and I am one."

Whoiban (coming to the rescue of Peshuhol), "We have heard all about you from the *tultul* of Magahine, about this sorcery against Maguer, and we don't like it."

Balidu, "It is true that they talked about a cross-cousin of mine (Wankole). But he is dead. He who buried the exuviae is dead. It has nothing to do with me. I know nothing about it."

Yahalijo (suddenly interrupting vindictively), "Yes, beat them until they urinate, until they urinate and defecate."

Whoiban (pacifically), "My two brothers, they were too strong. They held fast to the woman."

---

[226] This is a clever appeal to the audience. Peshuhol recites the high-sounding phrases with which every Arapesh defends the claim of the patrilineal kin on the child of a dead man.

[227] The District Officer. This is an attempt to shake La'abe in his official capacity as *tultul*. Has he a case? asks Peshuhol.

Yahalijo, "You don't belong to the Beach people. You are one with us.[228] Why didn't you come and talk?"

Peshuhol, "When I hear anything about it, I come. If I know, I come."

Yahalijo, "The child of Talumen (Sa'omale, Badui's betrothed wife) stays here with only a little pay, as she is still a child. You should not kill the mother. Let her live until her daughter menstruates and I will send pay for her. We have sent no pig, no ring for her yet. Let her mother live to receive these when she gets old."

Peshuhol, "I didn't put this thing here. I only came on my own affairs, going to the Plains, and to build the house."

Whoiban (grandiloquently), "The thing for you people of Alitoa to do is this. Keep strangers out of here. Let your friends come. Let those who have business here come. Keep other people, who are walking about without apparent errands, out of your place."

The group dissolved into desultory conversation. Baimal talked with Peshuhol and his companion. The doctor boy of Liwo talked with Balidu and left a ring with him to be taken to Dunigi by Baimal to look for exuviae, in case his father gets any worse. In a few minutes Balidu handed some tobacco to Peshuhol. The suspect bamboo was simply thrown away, without pouring any hot water on it, as the victim had shown no signs of illness. The Liwo people left.

\* \* \*

When I got back to the other end of the village, Aden was just concluding negotiations with his Magahine friend who had come up with the Maguer men and stayed behind. Aden gave him an eight-day counter made of a large fern, as a date for the delivery of some sago. Then he and Aden also departed.

The Alitoa end of the village was deserted, except for Wabe and Inoman. From the Walinuba end, the *tamberan* sang rather fitfully. The women had scattered for food and firewood.

[228] This represented an attempt on Yahalijo's part to be friendly with Peshuhol and indicated that they would have backed up his claims. She was apparently ashamed of her furious outburst.

Imale went home to Ahalesimihi with her father. Me'elue went down with Bischu, who announced that he had had enough of fights and accusations of sorcery and was returning to the peace of his small place. Soatsalamo and her baby returned to Mogiligen.

In the middle of the afternoon, a party of Nugum men arrived, selling pots. They were friends of Baimal's and Kule's. Kule bought a pot for trade beads (obtained from us), and then an elder arrived and disapproved of the sale. Kule got very angry and put all their pots out in the plaza. Ombomb, from his house, threatened to break all the pots of these people whose prices were too high. Baimal intervened, calmed the storm, and took them all back into his house. He made a feast inside his house for Nagawe, Manum, and Silisium.

## BIRTH OF OMBOMB'S BABY (1)

Meanwhile, early in the evening, Sauwedjo's labor pains began. She spent the early evening in the new ground house which Ombomb had built, standing up and walking about, groaning in a low stylized way which seemed to indicate discomfort rather than any acute pain. It had been decided by Ombomb and La'abe that Lomaijo was to act as midwife. It was a cold, drizzly night; the thermometer registered 70° F., which is very chilly in Arapesh. The *tamberan* flutes wailed throughout the night. Dr. Fortune and our boys were developing photographs. Whenever I returned to the house for any purpose, the boys were full of questions, hoping to learn something about this mystery from which they were excluded.

I shall give here a full account of this birth, which those readers not interested in the details of delivery can skip.

Lomaijo started to make the delivery receptacle. With a piece of *limbum* spathe, she made a three-sided container by gathering one end into three folds.[229] This was set up below the edge of the slope near Me'elue's house. A stout pole about 2 inches in diameter was braced against the turned-up end; the two other poles were placed on each side. At about

[229] This is the same kind of container that is used to pound taro for making croquettes.

8:30, about half an hour after her first pains, Sauwedjo and Lomaijo went down; Sauwedjo took her place on the bark seat. Imale and Me'elue were both away. Sagu, who had borne a child, and Budagiel, who had not borne a child, came for a while; Temos and Welima arrived a little later, the latter to stay overnight and take care of Lomaijo's children. They built a very small fire to keep themselves warm and to light cigarettes. I had a flashlight, but at first they were very distrustful of my using it. Lomaijo still carried Kamowon on her shoulders and came and went between the scene of the birth and her own house. Sauwedjo wore her ordinary sago aprons and a string of beads around her neck. After her first trip for supplies, Lomaijo returned with a handful of nettle leaves with which she rubbed Sauwedjo's back and abdomen. She brought these leaves down in a bundle and dropped them on the ground; during the next three hours, they were always getting lost and having to be sought with the help of a firebrand. At 9:10, Sauwedjo began to cry out rhythmically, every four minutes. When this series of rhythmic cries began, Lomaijo tied a piece of bark string about Sauwedjo's body, just under the breasts. Once or twice she pressed on it; and once it became unfastened. Lomaijo sat behind Sauwedjo holding her between her knees; when Sauwedjo writhed, she grasped her about the waist, while Sauwedjo pressed her foot against the end pole, or squatted and leaned forward on her knees, pressing her hands down on Lomaijo's two knees. She maintained this position for a moment or two, then relaxed. Lomaijo would jump up and run up to the house for some magical herbs which she needed, for a coconut shell to heat water in, for a pair of tongs with which to lift the hot stones. She seemed to have a general idea of what she needed, but absolutely no system about collecting the things. One set of the leaves she brought, the *yaluho'a* leaves, were steeped in hot water and given to Sauwedjo to drink. From time to time, Sauwedjo would seize a firebrand and examine the bark seat closely.[230] There was some liquid there at 9:40.

All this time Ombomb and La'abe had sat quietly by a fire

---

[230] This was her second child; the first had died when it was two months old.

in front of La'abe's house (Fig. 1, No. 23). At 10 o'clock Ombomb retired to his own house. La'abe, however, continued to sit by the fire. They both talked to Lomaijo and to me if we went past them.

Between 9:30 and 10:15 Sauwedjo groaned and writhed a little, but there seemed to be no rhythm in the pains. Then from 10:15 to 10:45 she cried out regularly at five-minute intervals. A second magical brew of *me'abe* bark was given Sauwedjo to wash herself in after a second larger discharge at 10:45. Welima had now taken the children to bed. Sagu and Budagiel had left. Sauwedjo stopped in the midst of her low formalized cries at 10:55 and said she didn't like the place where they were sitting. The bark receptacle and the posts were taken up and moved up right under Me'elue's house, where Sauwedjo could hold on to the house posts. The fire was moved, and the nettles were gathered up for the tenth time.

This brought us too close to La'abe, who sat there throwing more wood on his fire. The women told him to leave, but he sat on. Then they told me to go and tell him that the party had moved nearer to the village on my account and that he should go to bed, which I duly did. La'abe growled that the women had no right to come so close to the village and risk defiling it. If they did come as close as this, then he had a right to sit in front of his house and watch; nevertheless, he gathered up his fire and climbed sulkily into his house.

The *tamberan* had stopped sounding. Everyone seemed to be asleep. Sauwedjo's cries came rhythmically now. Her back was towards me when the delivery came, but it was less than a minute from the time that, squatting, she loosened her apron, and the time the child fell on the bark. Lomaijo merely held the mother; she did not touch the child, nor did Sauwedjo, until the afterbirth came some five minutes later. Sauwedjo squatted over the child, who lay with a membrane partly over its face and the cord wound tightly around its neck, but visibly breathing. After the afterbirth came away, Lomaijo ran away in the dark, and returned with some wilted leaves with which Sauwedjo was to handle the baby. She could not touch it yet with her hands. Sauwedjo picked the child up by one arm—a common trick with babies—and they cautioned her "easy." She turned it over to discover its sex, and they all (Sagu had just returned again) said in chorus, "A female." Ombomb stuck his head out of his house door and said succinctly, "Wash it,"[231] and disappeared for the night.

There was another pause while Lomaijo ran about looking for a stick with which Sauwedjo could remove the membrane from the child's head. She finally broke off a piece of sago bark and gave this to Sauwedjo. Meanwhile, the hemorrhage had half submerged the child's face in blood. After removing the membrane from the child's face with the sliver of bark, Sauwedjo loosed the cord from its throat and the child cried lustily. Then there was another long pause of eight minutes, while Lomaijo hunted for a piece of bamboo to make a new knife. Finally, this was found. Sauwedjo cut the cord, leaving about an inch of stump. This was not fastened in any way and was severed very carelessly, so that the child's leg was cut a little. Then there was another eight-minute pause, while Lomaijo climbed 100 feet or so down the slope with only a firebrand in her hand to pick a handful of green leaves with which the mother could wash the baby. Then they got a coconut shell, picked up from under the house where it had been thrown after the meat was removed, tilted some water into it, and this was held near the mother while she gave the child a superficial washing. The eyes and nose were simply washed as part of the face, but the mother put her finger inside and washed out the mouth. The body was slightly washed. Then the mother squatted, holding the baby, with the head in her spread hand and the legs inclining over the elbow, away from her body. Lomaijo then departed again to get some native cord to tie up the bark receptacle. Sagu brought two fresh pieces of *limbum* spathe, one of which had been used during the week to mash taro. This was turned over and the side which had rested on the ground when it was a taro receptacle was turned up to receive the mother. She stood up, walked a few steps to urinate, returned, and squatted over the new piece of bark. Lomaijo devoted the next 10 minutes to gathering up every spot of blood and every bit of debris connected with the birth, and putting them into

[231] Thus he gave his formal approval that it should live.

the bark receptacle which she made into a bundle and tied up under the house, to be deposited in a distant tree at dawn.

Meanwhile the mother trembled with cold. The baby had cried only when it was washed. It now lay in its mother's lap, with eyes closed, making random movements with hands and legs. Finally, the important task of removing all traces of the birth completed, the women turned their attention to Sauwedjo. She stood up, a clean piece of bark was placed over the blood in the former piece, and she lay down to sleep in front of Me'elue's house, the child on her arm, giving it the breast. It suckled feebly, and grasped the breast with both hands. The women kindled the fire higher and sat down to watch until dawn. It was just 12 o'clock.

## CEREMONIES FOR OMBOMB'S BABY (2)

MARCH 14: At dawn, Sauwedjo got up and carried her baby into the new ground house (Fig. 1, No. 26). There she sat all morning, without food, holding the child, who slept and showed no interest in suckling. Sauwedjo had not eaten since noon the day before. Ombomb, also forbidden to eat or smoke, sat beside her. Ombomb said that he was angry at its being a girl, but he was very gentle with Sauwedjo. Lomaijo, Welima, and Temos were still in attendance. The women were alarmed that the baby refused to suckle and kept waking it up and giving it the breast. It yawned prodigiously and opened its eyes, only to shut them again. One eye opened a little wider than the other. Its hands were tightly clenched, except when Sauwedjo held it to her breast, when it grasped at her breast. It was very dirty by now; its finger nails were caked with dirt, and all the creases of its body from which the blood had not been washed off were filled with dirt. The village children ran in and out admiring the baby.

At 10:30 Ombomb went to bathe and returned, bringing leaves for the child to lie on. Meanwhile Sauwedjo had been mending a small old net bag. She laid the leaves in the bag and fitted the baby in, Ombomb directing the whole procedure in a kindly and superior fashion. Then, while he went out again, Sauwedjo stood up, folded the piece of *limbum* bark on which she had been sitting, so that the blood wouldn't show, and tucked it in the roof. She hung the baby on a projection from the wall and went out alone to bathe in the pool on the Manuniki side. She bled slowly as she walked, but took no notice of the drops that fell. While she was away, Ombomb got tobacco and areca nut ready. Temos cooked in Sauwedjo's house for the small feast which was to be made at noon. When Sauwedjo returned, Temos brought her one small roasted yam fruit which she ate. Ombomb came back with a package in a banana leaf, and a coconut shell full of water in which *mauto'a* bark had been steeped. He opened the banana leaf, revealing about 12 pieces of yam fruit which had been cut in half. He named each one after a small boy of the place, then Sauwedjo, from her end, named them after small girls, naming a boy or so also. Ombomb then drank from the brew in the coconut shell.

Now Temos and Lomaijo carried in four large plates of food. Ombomb had a large bunch of tobacco: he broke this in half and gave half to Sauwedjo. He then handed her an areca nut. Both chewed areca nut. Lomaijo went away to get some pepper catkins. Ombomb gave one plate to Lomaijo and one to Temos. He called Ilautoa and she came in with a Nugum child visitor. He gave each of them a plate and some tobacco. He then threw the coconut shell of charmed water and the named bits of yams in the steep place behind the house—the part which belonged to the *marsalai*. He then went out to exchange tobacco for some areca nut. Sauwedjo took this opportunity to stand up and scrub away the blood on the bark beneath her, using her feet. Temos then brought in a long peeled rod. Ombomb came back bringing a piece of coconut palm sheath. Temos brought a bunch of leaves. Sauwedjo took the baby out of the net bag and cleaned it with the leaves. It poured rain, as Temos filled the pipes of the father and mother, who could not yet fill them with their own hands. They smoked. Ombomb laid a palm leaf mat and his carved wooden pillow on the other side of the fire from Sauwedjo and lay back and smoked. When the rain slackened, they called in Souato'a and Temos, and Ombomb took the baby and held it back to back with each of them. Then he took the peeled rod, held it against the baby's back and against theirs, handed the baby back to Sauwedjo, broke the stick into six-inch lengths, reciting the charm for backs,[232] and tied it into a bundle. This would be hung in the house later.

After this there was a pause; then food was brought to Ombomb and Sauwedjo, who ate taro, holding it carefully in wilted taro leaves. After this the baby was washed with warmed water, the mother using leaves.

\* \* \*

The rest of the village was still somewhat preoccupied with the Nugum visitors. Two of the elders had gone down to see Sinaba'i, but the rest stayed about. Wabe sent food formally to Ombomb and Sauwedjo.

In the afternoon, Amus had a bad earache. She threw off her apron and writhed and screamed in the dirt. Amito'a made a poultice of leaves and also gave the suffering child her dry breast. Maigi was ill with an acute attack of indigestion. It rained hard all afternoon, and the *tamberan* wailed fitfully.

Ulaba'i, Ibanyos, and Anyuai returned from planting taro.

In the evening Souato'a had a bad temper tantrum, when it was proposed that she should again sleep with Welima, and announced that she would sleep with her father and mother, or nowhere.[233]

MARCH 15: Temos and Welima[234] were still taking care of Sauwedjo. Ombomb and Sauwedjo were still under taboo; they could not touch food or tobacco with their hands.

\* \* \*

Baimal, Badui, and La'abe left with the Nugum people to try to purchase an extra pig for rings in Dakuar. This was done, it was said, at the insistence of Nigi.[235]

[232] This charm and the rest of the ritual content of the birth ceremony are described in Mead, 1940, p. 416.

[233] The whole proceeding of the birth of the new baby seemed to have a traumatic content for her. Her jealousy of her father had been increasing in the last few weeks, and now the repetition of Kamowon's birth seemed to increase her tension.

[234] Note here that it is the wives of her husband's own brother who take care of her, while in the case of Bischu's wife, it was the wife of a working partner.

[235] Note that Nigi had done none of the loud-mouthed demanding of more; that had all been done by Honali, yet when they tried

The women of Balidu's household made a small feast of croquettes and sent it to Aden as an acknowledgment of the piece of pig which he had sent Balidu.

Lomaijo and Amito'a set out for Wihun to carry sago and yams, part of the feast which the Wihun people had not been able to carry to Wihun.

### GERUD'S FIRST DIVINATION (2)

Lomaijo saw Wegul in Alipinagle and brought back word that Wegul said that Budagiel had given his exuviae, mistaken for Kamil's, to Ombomb[236] to bury. She also said that Wegul said he would come tomorrow and pay Gerud the pot. Ombomb sent back word that it was a lie and that when Wegul came to pay the pot he would fight him. Kule, still sore from yesterday's altercation with the Nugum potters, added that they would smash the pot. Earlier in the day, La'abe suggested that it was probably Gobonarra who had buried the exuviae, because Wegul, whom Gobonarra called cross-cousin (*mehinen*), had worked some of his sago without his approval. By this time, everyone began to agree that that was probably what had happened. They sent for Gobonarra, but when he arrived they decided to wait for La'abe's return. Everyone now spoke as if Gerud, in the course of the divination, had said that Gobonarra was responsible.[237]

Souato'a greeted her mother's return with another crying fit. Budagiel was taking care of Kamowon and Amus. Maigi was still ill, but there was as yet no hypothesis of sorcery; instead, people said it was the fashion of feasts for people to fall ill.[238]

---

to get more, they said it was done at Nigi's request, quietly pushing the too vociferous Honali out of the picture.

[236] This was plausible enough, as the cause of the quarrel had been between Ombomb and Kamil, and Ombomb had taken Budagiel away as part of his revenge on Kamil. See above, p. 166.

[237] As the crime was thus fixed on an *alomato'in,* everyone breathed a sigh of relief. In a sense, it meant the end of conflict, for such people are not held responsible.

[238] This was certainly true, and castor oil came into full play during this week.

Sumali, his two young sons, and Oiyale returned with Yabinigi, and a kangaroo, which Sumali had trapped, and a long tale against Yabinigi because he had failed to help Sumali catch a phalanger.[239]

Welima had a headache. Fastening a string around her forehead she paraded the length of the village. Then she and Temos cooked a small feast to go with a piece of phalanger which Kule had given Ombomb. With this Ombomb made a small "thank-you" feast, a *bai'*, for Wamu'um's children Bunitai and Ke'ali for helping him with his feast.

Yapul was here with both her children; Balidu also made a small "thank-you" feast.

Sinaba'i was harvesting yams.

Bischu had gone to plant taro. His dog disappeared into the bush to die there.

Ombomb went to Numidipiheim to tell Ombaligu he must pay a good plate to Gerud.

At night all the *tamberan* players were so exhausted that Ombomb broke his couvade taboo in order to go in and help them.

Honali's son, a boy of 12 or so, turned up from Liwo, alone.

Ulaba'i, Ibanyos, and Anyuai were back in the village.

MARCH 16: Although the *tamberan* still played and there were more than the usual number of people in the village, the feast aspect was disappearing.


### CEREMONIES FOR OMBOMB'S BABY (3)

At noon, Ombomb and Sauwedjo ceremonially "washed their hands." Lomaijo steeped *wanubahas* leaves in water in a coconut shell, using hot stones to heat the water. Ombomb steamed his hands first, then Sauwedjo. Then with tongs, Ombomb threw out the stones and washed his hands and arms. Sauwedjo then did likewise. Now they were free

---

[239] Upon examination, this proved to have been Yabinigi's way of avoiding Sumali's greed. Knowing that Sumali would claim the whole phalanger, he had refused to shoot it, but instead had tried to catch it in his hands, as the native without a dog does when an animal has been startled out of a tree.

to touch food and tobacco with their hands. Me'elue and Yauwito'a were present at this ceremony.

\* \* \*

Wabe had an attack of indigestion and made up his quarrel with our boys. There had been a coldness between them since Wabe accused Wadjubel of running after our boys. He had beaten Wadjubel, who left at once, and this was the first I had heard about it.

Agilapwe came up to the village and exchanged areca nut with Aden.

Amito'a's hand swelled up where Baimal bit her, or, more probably, where her hand came in contact with Baimal's teeth. But now reconciled to Baimal, she says that she pricked herself with elephant grass.

### BALIDU'S FEAST: DETAILS (9)

Nigi arrived and made a speech about the pig which was to be given him.

Iwamini and Maginala came in to help with the *tamberan*.

Balidu made a small public speech about the need for plenty of men to stay with the *tamberan* until it left the village. The men have been worried now for the last few days, for fear the women would see that the *tamberan* slept when the men slept.

Matasues was away working sago to repay our pig.

### CEREMONIES FOR OMBOMB'S BABY (4)

MARCH 17: Today Sauwedjo performed the ceremony of baking the false vegetable pudding. Two kinds of magical leaves were brought to her by Lomaijo; Temos helped her with cooking them. They were wrapped in banana leaves; then three hot stones, previously heated in flames, were put inside with a breadfruit leaf on top. This package was cooked in the hot ashes, while no one paid any attention. It was later thrown where the pigs could find it. That evening Ombomb and Sauwedjo, now purified, entered their house.

## BALIDU'S FEAST: DETAILS (10)

Kule and Wabe left to meet Baimal on the road. The party returned without a pig. They reported that the *tultul* of Dakuar had tried to shoot one with an arrow, but it had escaped. At word of their failure to find a pig, Nigi went into the Plains to see if he could find one.[240]

\* \* \*

Budagiel and Kumati went to Meloten for taro.

Balidu's widowed sister came from Ahalesimihi.

The Alipinagle people have all gone again.

Gobonarra arrived to answer sorcery accusation, but no discussion of this today.

A party of Dunigi men passed through on their way to the Beach.

Anop and Bunitai were back again to help with the *tamberan*.

Maigi was better.

MARCH 18: Kule was ill this morning, believed it was malaria and asked for quinine.

The wife of Matasues brought sago up, in return for the piece of pig given to Matasues and Bischu.

## CEREMONIES FOR OMBOMB'S BABY (5)

Sauwedjo's breast swelled up, said to have been caused by a charm belonging to Inoman and Wupale. Inoman had gone to Liwo, and they planned to get him to charm when he returned.

Later in the day, after the *tamberan* had gone to Alipinagle and returned, Inoman refused to recite exorcism for Sauwedjo's breast. He simply sulked, and no one knew what to do with him. His sulkiness was due to Wamu'um's behavior recorded below. Finally La'abe said he would try to

---

[240] This is typical Arapesh logic. Originally the theory was that Balidu owed Nigi a pig; then there came to be a general expectation of a pig; and finally, if Balidu's side could not find a pig, Nigi decided that he would go and look for one.

exorcise the evil charm, if Kule would help him. But Kule said
he didn't know it. Only Baimal knew it, and he was not here.

\* \* \*

## BALIDU'S FEAST: DETAILS (11)

In the night, La'abe had gotten up to go to the *tamberan*,
but Souato'a had such a severe crying fit that he stayed at
home.

During the morning everyone sat about, waiting for news
as to Nigi's success in his search for a pig.

At noon all the women were chased outside the village, and
the *tamberan* went to Alipinagle. Sumali and Agilapwe and
Balidu did not go. They were caught by a severe rain
there,[241] and the Alipinagle people tried to get them to leave
so that their women could come in out of the rain. But the
*tamberan*, i.e., the Alitoa people, were intransigent.

## GERUD'S FIRST DIVINATION (3)

While the *tamberan* was at Alipinagle, the matters brought
up in Gerud's divination were further discussed. Wegul paid
Gerud a pot. Gobonarra was accused. When he started to
deny his guilt, Henalian summarily told him to keep quiet.
Wegul then mentioned that now that he came to think of it,
the food which Gobonarra had given him in the past had always made him feel queer.

Wegul came over in the evening to help with the *tamberan* and reassert his solidarity with the Alitoa people.

## BALIDU'S FEAST: DETAILS (12)

In the evening, all the Alipinagle people came over to sing
with the *tamberan*. Balidu and Sumali made speeches expressing their opinion of the other half for running away to
their gardens instead of staying to help with the *tamberan*.
No public answer was made, but a little later Ulaba'i went up

[241] For this brief account of events in Alipinagle I am indebted
to Dr. Fortune who accompanied the *tamberan* there.

and sat down with Balidu. Balidu further announced that if they didn't want their coconut palms tabooed, the *tamberan* would just taboo his own trees and then go away; later, they could bring their own *tamberan* and taboo theirs.[242] The Alitoa end of the village was deserted, except for the household of Ulaba'i, including Henalian's wife and child, and Wabe, still feeling ill, and his two wives, and Gobonarra.

In the Walinuba end, everyone was there, except Alaijo, Minya, Soatsalamo, and Walipin. Imale had gone to Alipinagle and returned. Lomaijo went to the gardens in the morning and returned.

The *tamberan* feast, inside the *tamberan* house, revealed that Ombomb and Anop had gone fishing the night before and secretly brought in the fish.

Word had been brought in during the day that Wamu'um was very angry at both Inoman and Nahomen. He had been ready to fence when the Walinuba feast began. Matasues and Nahomen were both concerned in aspects of the ceremonies; Inoman came as a spectator. Wamu'um had been urged to come, but he said he had no meat, he was an old man, and he would stay in his place. He had sent up word that he was going to expel Inoman and Nahomen and that Matasues would have to make him a feast if he wanted to stay. Inoman was angry about this, but the others took it as a sign of Wamu'um's disgruntlement at being an old man. Wabe remarked that he thought he would have to find rings for a wife for Bunitai for Wamu'um was too old to walk about and find rings.

MARCH 20:[243] The Nugum visitors of Baimal left early in the morning. Baimal, Kule, Amito'a, Ilautoa, and Budagiel accompanied them to the far end of the village. Just as they left, a Nugum man picked up a firebrand from the *Uyebis* plaza and carried it off. This was a sign that he would return. The Alitoa people accompanied them to the very edge of the village and shouted after them that when the next moon rose they would come to visit them and get pots.

[242] This would entail a great deal more expense on their part.

[243] Another hiatus in my dating, but the sequence, as marked by days of the week, seems correct.

## BALIDU'S FEAST: FINAL CEREMONY (13)

Next, there was a long wait during the cooking for the final feast. Bischu and Wutue did not appear, but Matasues sent up his unfavorite wife to help with the cooking. All the Alipinagle people were here: Wegul stayed with Wabe[244]; Henalian and his wife with Ulaba'i; Iwamini with Aden; Maginala and Ga'olen in Walinuba. Agilapwe was still staying with Sagu. Wabe tabooed one of his palms with a palm leaf to show that he stood with Bischu, who was not having his trees tabooed. Everyone was angry with Bischu for running away. All sorts of hypotheses were afloat: that Bischu was angry because he didn't get a ring for the pig which Wabe distributed to Balidu and Baimal, although it had been his pig which he had given Ombomb when it was small; that Bischu was angry because earlier, when he and Wabe had prepared a feast for the *tamberan* (see above, p. 298), Balidu had decided not to have the coconuts tabooed that day. Everyone had forgotten that Bischu had said that he left (see above, p. 309) because he disliked the quarreling.

Wabe finally carried his contribution up to the Walinuba end and the big feast for the women and children was made. There were 50 plates and serving leaves in all. A partial account of the distribution was: three to Ulaba'i's wives; two to Wabe's wives; six to Maigi and Agilapwe[245]; three to Inoman; two to Baimal; one to Wegul; one to Alis; two to Balidu's women; one to Kule; 11 to Henalian, Maginala, Iwamini, Ga'olen, and Wegul. Sumali and Balidu and Ombomb did not partake of this feast. It consisted of the kangaroo Sumali had caught after the feast and a few odds and ends of smoked meat and shellfish. The women for whom the feast was made could not eat the tree kangaroo meat, but the children could.

After this feast for the women, Wabe, La'abe, and Om-

---

[244] Note that it was Wabe who had been so zealous in identifying Wegul's exuviae.

[245] When men's names were called it was understood that this was a feast for the women and children of their households.

bomb made a small feast, inside of Ombomb's house, of 13 plates of croquettes for the Alipinagle men.

When the *tamberan* was ready to emerge, it began to wail vigorously with strong *garamut* accompaniment. The women and children ran away to the usual spot, the hill overlooking Moholigum. The *tamberan* went through the village tying bands of leaves about the coconut palms and decorating all the important houses in the village, including ours, with bright-colored leaves. The *tamberan* then left the village. The women were told that it went to the Beach. The men knew that it went to Alipinagle.

After the *tamberan* left, everyone was miserably at loose ends. In the evening the Alitoa end brightened a little, and Ulaba'i and Aden sat about a big fire and laughed and talked.

Word came up that Ombomb's mother was ill, and he sent Me'elue down to look after her.

Sumali and Balidu talked formally about previous times when Wihun had not met their obligations to Bugabahiem, and Liwo wondered if the feast would ever be repaid.[246]

MARCH 21: By morning, everyone had left, except the households of Sumali and of Baimal and Kule. They were packing pots, pillows, spoons, extra net bags, bits of seed, feather ornaments, and hand drums, and getting ready to return to their small places.

La'abe, with Daulap, his Wihun sister's son, had left at dawn to work sago to repay the piece of pig obtained from us.

Wabe went hunting with Yabinigi; his two wives went to their gardens.

Ulaba'i's whole household went to their gardens.

Balidu's household was planting taro.

Finally the last stragglers departed, Ite'epe, a thin little mite of about six, carrying Eweluen on her back. Baimal and

---

[246] And here my diary carries the entry, "Blessed peace, combined with the realization that ethnology was about over." It was true that more of the life of the people was visible during that feast week than we were ever to see again. But I had known that and had prepared for two months before to follow as many of the events and personalities as possible. Where one is dealing with a seminomadic or nomadic people this method of preparing for a couple of months for a big event at which many facets of life will be shown seems to be a rewarding one.

Amito'a took Ibal, the daughter of Agilapwe, with them, and Badui went along to plant one coconut on Baimal's house site.

Yabinigi, at the request of Manusa, the *tultul* of Numidi-piheim, had gone to his hunting bush to try to shoot a male domestic pig which had gone wild. Instead he shot a female domestic pig by mistake. Wabe, who had prudently gone along to see that Yabinigi was not imposed upon, told Manusa it was his own fault. The domestic pig was also black and had not had its tail cut. He told Manusa to come and carry it away[247] and pay it to his creditors in Wihun.

It poured rain all afternoon. In the afternoon, La'abe and both wives, Wabe and his wives, and Ulaba'i and his wives returned to the village. Me'elue was still with Ombomb's mother who was ill.

## CEREMONIES FOR OMBOMB'S BABY (6)

Ombomb and Sauwedjo made the small feast of payment to the midwife, called the *dal ama'abis*, garnished with a very small piece of meat.

MARCH 22: Kumati, Pidjui, and Nigimarib came up to the village to sleep, leaving their parents in the garden.

La'abe and Lomaijo worked sago. Daulap stayed about doing nothing. Imale had a bad boil and a headache and stayed about, taking care of Kamowon, who cried less than usual and showed more initiative.

Ombomb stayed with Sauwedjo, whose breast was abscessing. He attempted to treat it with hot poultices. Me'elue was still with Ombomb's mother.

Balidu and his family were all planting taro.

Ulaba'i, his wives, his sister, and all three children were working in the new garden. Welima was helping them.

Wabe and Temos were making a taro garden.

Aden, both wives and Sauisua and Miduain, helping them carry areca nut, came up at night. Iwamini and Maginala had gone to the Beach, but Iwamini's wife and baby were with Aden.

[247] This is always done when another man's pig is killed, either by accident or if it has been trespassing in the gardens or bush of another.

Kule, Baimal, and Alis were said to be harvesting some yams.

Sumali was harvesting a second lot of yams.

Yabinigi shot a small pig. The major portion was accepted by Ombomb who said that he could eat pig now because the moon was straight over head.[248]

MARCH 23: Baijo and Anyuai went for firewood. Ulaijo had gone to help Nyelahai.

Welima was menstruating and went down to Moholigum. She and Temos had no menstrual hut in Alitoa.

Ulaba'i and Ibanyos worked in their taro garden. Whasimai and the baby stayed in the village. The baby Nemausi was being weaned and had frequent attacks of crying.

Wabe and Temos worked in the morning in Wabe's new garden.

La'abe, Lomaijo, Imale, and children all went to work sago.

Yahalijo came up and took all the children back to work with her.

Ombomb and Sauwedjo, taking the new baby, went to get taro slips.

In the afternoon, there were shouts that the Dunigi crowd was returning from the Beach. Aden came up with them to the village and Wabe and Temos came up from work. Wabe expressed great disgust with their coming just now, when there was no food. Bischu came up for a moment.

Ombomb came back, after having paid a visit to his mother and said that he thought she wasn't going to die, and that anyway she was not sorcerized, for they had gotten back her exuviae long ago. It had been taken by a Yimonihi man and Manum had paid a plate for it.[249]

[248] This was a spur-of-the-moment rationalization, but Ombomb was not tremendously interested in his baby girl and did not take very adequate precautions for her safety.

[249] Instances in which exuviae are actually gotten back like this are rarer than the occasions in which the Plainsmen hold them for further payment. Note also how much more willing the Arapesh are to attribute illness to sorcery, if they know that there are exuviae outstanding. Furthermore, Ombomb's mother was a very old woman with a large abdominal tumor. When she died, her death would be tacitly classified as from old age. Theories about her tumor varied; one was that she had had it from birth, owing to her mother's hav-

MARCH 24: Ombomb and Sauwedjo, her breast a little improved, have gone to plant some taro in Matasues' new garden. La'abe was here all day, making a palm leaf mat. His wives worked in the gardens.

Wabe sent a big ring by the Dunigi man, with the demand that the Biligil sorcerer should now return the exuviae altogether, that they had received enough pay. Temos and Anyuai went to burn off Wabe's new clearing.

Ulaba'i and Ibanyos came back at noon. Whasimai and Nemausi were here all day, except for an excursion for water and firewood. A Liwo friend of Ulaba'i's, with his family, was here overnight.

MARCH 25: Wabe and Temos went to help Balidu fence. La'abe was preparing a taro patch in this same garden of Balidu's.

Ombomb and Sauwedjo were still planting in Matasues' garden.

Inoman came in with a load of foodstuffs to sell, to get a tin of meat from us, to make his peace with Wamu'um.[250] He spoke of it as to "pay for the fence," which he had not been there to build.

Sumali and Budagiel stopped in to inquire after Midjulumon whom we had sent off several days ago with Biagu to Karawop for mail. The Dunigi men had brought the news that no ship had come in.

Ulaba'i's whole household went to help Aden in his new garden and to plant there.

Wabe came back with a piece of aerial root from which he planned to make a plate, his first plate.

Ombomb returned with word that Manusa was very angry about the pig which Yabinigi had shot and was demanding five shillings from Yabinigi and a ring from Wabe. Everyone

---

ing eaten food from a *marsalai* place; another group insisted that it had appeared after she had married and was the result of accepting food from some Plainsmen who had been responsible for her brother's death by sorcery. (This latter theory is the familiar widespread idea that eating in the "place of blood," i.e., in a place connected with the death of a relative, produces a swelling in the body.)

[250] For his quarrel with Wamu'um, see above, p. 321.

talked obstreperously of how they would beat up the Numidi-piheim people if they dared to come up and demand such a thing, and Ulaba'i beat the *garamut*, very lightly so that there was no danger of its being heard in Numidipiheim. Yabinigi returned in the late afternoon to report that he had wounded a large pig, but it was so dark that search for it was postponed until the morrow.

Iwamini returned from the Beach at dark, bringing word that there had been no ship. Sumali decided to go to the Beach and bring back Midjulumon.

March 24: (Date corrected.) Wabe, Ombomb, and La'-abe went to search for the pig which Yabinigi thought he had wounded. They didn't find it.

Matasues and Inoman were fishing to make a feast to Wamu'um to pay for the fence.

Sumali and Mindibilip left for Maguer.

Balidu brought his three younger children up and left them here, returning himself to his garden for the night.

Maigi and Sagu were in Manuniki; Badui and Sa'omale, who had joined him there, were still in Mogiligen.

In the evening Wabe worked at carving a plate.

A group of *Kaboibis* men, relatives of Kamil, the former husband of Budagiel, came through here and tried to sell us some very poor taro. They were very rude about the price and generally aggressive and disagreeable. Balidu treated these Plainsmen, who had no ties in Alitoa, in a very gingerly manner.

Ulaba'i, accompanied by Ibanyos, was building a small yam storehouse at Aden's new place.

Lomaijo went to Mogiligen to get maize. She took Kamo-won with her.

Wabe, Welima, La'abe, Ombomb, Imale, and Sauwedjo went to Alipinagle to build a yam storehouse in Welima's garden.

Wadjubel, Menala, and her baby came up, carrying a little pig from Sinaba'i's sow which had just cast a litter. They were taking this little pig to Aden.

Anop passed through on his way to join Bischu.

Budagiel, Kumati, and Kubi,[251] a small boy from Umanep, who turned up at Sumali's last night, returned to Malupit.

MARCH 25: Yam house building was still going on in Alipinagle.

Baimal, Kule, Amito'a, Ilauto'a, Amus, Minya, and Mausi came down from Mogiligen. Baimal, Amito'a, and all the children stayed here.

Ulaba'i, Ibanyos, and Segenamoya came back from their house building at Aden's.

A Wanimo police boy arrived with a message from the District Officer.[252]

Nigimarib was here with Pidjui, feeling very abused. In the morning, he had a fight with Kubi, the little *tinea*-covered stranger from Umanep, and in the evening he attempted to fight Pidjui.

## DEATH OF THE WIFE OF TAPITA

MARCH 26: The wife of Tapita died in Alipinagle. The news reached the village at dawn. There was considerable discussion about whether or not she should be buried in the official graveyard, in Alitoa, which was supposed by Government order to contain the dead of the whole locality. But she was a Plainswoman, a runaway from Ybonimu, and the people felt her as a strange and unfriendly ghost to have about. Baimal rushed about declaring, "We want no strange Plains ghosts here. Let them keep her in Alipinagle."

Although Dr. Fortune set off for Alipinagle the minute the news reached us, she would have been buried by the time he arrived[253] if there had not been a delay over the question of who was to handle the corpse; for the feeling which was expressed in Alitoa as "Don't bring that strange corpse here," was expressed in Alipinagle by a refusal to han-

---

[251] His mother had been a Liwo woman. He was an orphan and *tinea* covered.

[252] He had been sent to us out of Government courtesy, so that we could do a little exploratory work with him, pursuant to deciding whether Wanimo would be a good place to do our next field work.

[253] The Arapesh custom is to get a burial over immediately, with as little fuss as possible.

dle the strange corpse. Tapita himself was virtually bedridden.
She had died in the night and was found with her sago apron
burned off. Finally several women had to help with the
corpse.[254]

\* \* \*

The house building in Wabe's garden continued.

Imale was menstruating and returned to Alitoa. Lomaijo
was still in Mogiligen.

In the evening, Yahalijo publicly admonished Sagu because
she had returned from Manuniki tired and refused to help her
mother carry taro. "What?" demanded Yahalijo, "What do
you stay here for, close to your father and mother? For nothing? No, to look out for food, to help with the work. I am
an old woman, I need help. I am sick with work." Sagu made
no reply.

I worked with the Wanimo police boy and decided that
Wanimo would not be a very good field. Its population was
too small to justify the time necessary for working on what
appeared to be a phonetically difficult language.

## Liwo Fight (1)

News came that the wife of the *tultul* of Liwo, the widow
of the former *luluai*, had run away with Yelegen, a Liwo
man, but that there has as yet been no confrontation of the
injured parties.[255]

[254] I am merely summarizing here from Dr. Fortune's notes.
[255] Tapik's history had been a long and stormy one. She was a
Numidipiheim girl, originally betrothed to Pidjui of *Hamiebis*, the
sister's son of Balidu, now dead, after whom his own son Pidjui was
named, and whose heir Badui was. When Pidjui died, she wanted to
marry La'abe, but he disliked her and refused to keep her, although
suspecting her of having taken some of his exuviae during her brief
stay. She was then married to Gobonarra, of *Hamiebis*, a dunce and
an *alomato'in*. With Gobonarra, she used to make frequent trips to
Liwo to visit his brother, who had moved there permanently. Here
the former *luluai* of Liwo saw her, his sister acted as a go-between,
and Tapik, who loathed Gobonarra, ran away to the *luluai*. Ombomb organized a rescue party and there was a stick fight in Liwo,
for which a number of Alitoa and Liwo people were put in jail.
When the *luluai* of Liwo died, he left two widows, Tapik and

MARCH 27: The house building group returned from Alipinagle about nine o'clock. Welima remained in Alipinagle.

Soon after they got back, word was shouted over by Aden's
wife that Tapik had eloped with Yelegen, and that the doctor
boy of Liwo had been badly mauled by a bush pig.

Later, Kule, who had heard the news and gone to Liwo
to see the doctor boy, returned with Polip, Unabelin, and another Liwo man, all of whom showed slight scratches from
an encounter with Yelegen, during which they had disarmed
his party. They were bound for the Government office to open
a court case, and wanted certificates from us that they had
genuine wounds, as they knew well enough that none of the
dreadful scratches would be even visible by the time they
reached Wewak. We sent them off with a non-committal
note to the District Officer.[256]

Meanwhile people had gathered in the village to hear the
news of the fight. Kule reported the doctor boy badly
wounded by the bush pig.

## MAISOA'S HUSBAND'S ATTEMPTS TO REGAIN HER (1)

Nyelahai then introduced a new topic of controversy. The
Numidipiheim husband of Maisoa, the stupid sister of Nyelahai and Ulaba'i, had sent word that he wanted his wife
back again. Ibanyos and Ulaba'i talked at length on the neglect which this husband had meted out to her. They said
they didn't want her to go back.

## GERUD'S SECOND DIVINATION (1)

Then Nyelahai announced that he had lost a knife the
day before and wanted Gerud to work his divination stunt

---

Talumen, the heroine of the quarrels with Peshuhol and Gerud's
divinatory finds. Tapik was inherited by the *tultul* of Liwo, who was
a member of the *Suabibis* division of Liwo. This had happened
about a year before.

[256] I did not get the whole account of why Yelegen had eloped
with Tapik until August, when Unabelin told it as part of another
story. According to this account, Yelegen had taken Tapik away because he was angry over his quarrel with his son-in-law Unabelin.

to find it. Wabe then announced that if Gerud divined, he would ask him who had fastened up a bandicoot bone and so ruined his hunting. Kaberman said he meant to ask whether Inoman had hidden a phalanger bone the night he had eaten in the boy's house.[257]

## WABE'S JEALOUSY (1)

Meanwhile, in the afternoon, Welima returned without a load of taro which Wabe had told her to bring from Alipinagle, and Wabe beat her. Poor Welima, sore, bruised, and hurt, could not understand what had happened. Her offense had been very slight in proportion to the punishment. But Temos had told Wabe that someone had tried to break into her house the night before, when she was sleeping with Anyuai. Wabe was beside himself with fear and jealousy, but he did not dare beat Temos,[258] so he beat Welima instead. But Welima did not know this until evening. All of her talk, as she lay huddled into a miserable ball inside her own house, attended by Anyuai, was of Wabe's general unfairness and preference for Temos. Ombomb and La'abe had heard about it, however, and were worried as to possible complications, as they realized that Wabe's suspicions, originally aroused over Wadjubel, would point to our house boys.

[257] This method, by which people announced in advance what they meant to ask made it a great deal easier, of course, for the diviner, and also for us. During dinner we talked at length about the dire consequences of fixing any charge of sorcery on Inoman. Yabinigi would have to be discharged, if his brother was accused of sorcery; there would be no meat; after this no one else's brother would be allowed in the boy's house; this kind of thing made us weary of buying good native food, etc.

[258] The theory is that if you suspect that your wife has been unfaithful to you, you must not beat her then, or she will only lie. If she lies, your yam crop will continue to suffer from infidelity. Wabe was particularly sensitive to the effects of infidelity upon his yams. It was the point which he stressed previously in Menala's infidelity. (In other words, it was the familiar clinical picture in which the jealous person, having identified his wife with himself, feels himself —as symbolized here by the yams—attacked and invaded by the man who copulates with his wife.)

### GERUD'S SECOND DIVINATION (2)

In the evening, Gerud fell almost immediately into a trance, as he had not been asked to look for exuviae this time, but to answer questions.[259]

The questions were directed at Gerud very rapidly and he

[259] It was interesting to note how the pattern of the divination became fixed. In Gerud's first seance, he was asked to find exuviae of the Maguer man and he found exuviae of three other people besides. This time, Nyelahai set the tone with his inquiry about the knife. As a result, three other knives were mentioned, two of which, those of Kule and Gerud, had disappeared before the last divination. Wabe had wanted to ask Gerud to divine for some time, so he could ask about his hunting luck, but he thought it was necessary to have meat first, which had been the custom with the old ghost divination. In this new *sagumeh* form, the custom was to pay afterwards.

Wabe's hunting had been bad for some time. Before, he had caught two tree kangaroos and had given one to Balidu and one to Matasues, both members of his patrilineal group. Tapita, whom he called "father-in-law," was angry that he did not receive one. He was an old man, almost bedridden, and needed what help he could get. Later, when Tapita made a feast to Numidipiheim, Wabe did give him a phalanger. At this time Tapita had said to Wabe, ungraciously, "Why do you only help at feasts and give me nothing that I can eat between times?" Now Wabe suspected that Tapita had taken the bone of that phalanger and fastened it up to spoil his hunting.

At intervals, for some time, Wabe had been remarking that presently he would get Gerud to divine for him. Suddenly, the bone shifts from a phalanger to a bandicoot bone without any explanation, for Gerud was adept enough not to accuse Tapita who had had only phalanger which he could have fastened. (In addition to the pot, a ring, and a string of dog's teeth, Gerud paid Alis, from whom he learned his divinatory art, the dog's teeth and Baimal, Alis's older brother, the pot. These additional payments came up for discussion now, when Wabe discovered that meat was not necessary.) Furthermore, Me'elue was sick, although her patient, Ombomb's mother, was getting better. Ombomb was not very much concerned about Me'elue's illness, but he was worried about the possibility of trouble over Temos' accusation. This worry carried over and as long as there was a divination, he decided to ask about Me'elue. In fact, somewhat of a bargain-hunting spirit developed: here was a ready-made divination; anyone could ask anything he liked; if the answer was profitable, he paid, if not he didn't.

muttered the replies. I will present a systematic summary of the questions and the answers he gave:

1. Where was Nyelahai's knife? His little son had been using it and had accidentally buried it.

2. What did Inoman do with the piece of phalanger bone which Kaberman had seen him secrete? Threw it under the house. Phalanger was taboo to him because of some obscure charm.

3. Where was Biagu's knife? It had been thrown over the cliff, mixed with the refuse of cooking leaves.

4. Who had stolen Gerud's knife which Biagu had lost at Karawop? A boy from the next language group.

5. Who (asked La'abe) had tried to open Temos' house door, a man or a ghost?[260] The ghost of the dead wife of Tapita, who was angry because Temos had not gone to mourn her.

6. Who stole Kule's knife long before? The wife of the discharged Umanep shoot boy.

7. Why was Me'elue sick? From sorcery.

8. When would the angry Numidipiheim men come to talk about the pig? The day after tomorrow.

9. Who hid the bandicoot bone which was ruining Wabe's hunting? Welima, who had put it in a piece of bamboo inside her house.

10. Why had Welima been sick? Sorcery.

After the tenth point, Dr. Fortune remarked, experimentally, that the ground was very wet and Gerud would undoubtedly get sick if he lay on it longer without a mat. Gerud, supposedly in a trance, revived at once.

## WABE'S JEALOUSY (2)

Wabe immediately burst into a storm of accusation at Mindibilip, utterly ignoring Gerud's or rather La'abe's, ghost story. Biagu reported that he had gotten up to leave the house, just before Temos cried out, that he had stirred the fire and seen Mindibilip there. In the course of the dis-

[260] Note that La'abe gives Gerud an obvious lead here.

cussion, it developed that the Wanimo police boy, about whom everyone had forgotten, was absent when Biagu stirred the fire. Dr. Fortune sent Wabe to see if Mindibilip had any matches in his bag (the intruder into Temos' house was accused of having struck a match). No matches were found. This bit of circumstantial evidence, combined with the suggestion of the police boy, was enough.[261]

Mindibilip was very much frightened and lied stupidly, saying that the police boy had confessed to him, after he had previously eagerly argued for the ghost alibi.[262]

Gerud had said that he would find Wabe's bandicoot bone the next day, then privately asked permission of us to leave at dawn to visit his father.

In the trance he had given many corroborating details.

6. He said Mausi had seen the wife of the shoot boy take the knife.

9. He said Welima had put the bamboo in the wall of her house nearest the road.

8. He said the Numidipiheim men had retained a *sagumeh* man from Suapali, named Palao'i,[263] to fasten Dr. Fortune's wind so that they could fight without his interference. Gerud's control, Bauwan, also reported that he heard the Numidipiheim people talking and saying that people in Alitoa were just boys, really insects, and not equal to them in a fight.

\* \* \*

After the divination, I found that Ibanyos had come up

[261] This was the only unfortunate experience which we had with a police boy, but it is obvious that coming from tribes with very diverse standards of sexual morality and themselves often equipped with a good deal of authority, police boys quartered in native villages can precipitate a good deal of trouble.

[262] It is interesting to note here another example of the Arapesh indifference towards ghosts. The wife of Tapita had just died. Had this been Manus or Samoa instead of Arapesh, her presence would have been a naturally accepted event. But the Arapesh have actually very little faith in or fear of ghosts.

[263] Note how naturally Gerud, just learning his new art, in which he had had no masters, still resorts to the worldwide trick of bringing other magicians to the scene to contribute further supernatural verisimilitude.

late, accompanied by Wabisu, Una, Anim, and Anyuai, all carrying yams.

MARCH 28: Nyelahai, who had stayed overnight, left with Kule, to hear the news of the Liwo quarrel.

Me'elue was still ill. Ombomb had not gone down to see her yet, but said that he would go and see her tomorrow. He added that her illness must be due to her exuviae's having been taken when she was a child, over some quarrel which involved her parents. This would account for her *tinea* and her failure to grow. Bischu had come in yesterday afternoon with a big bag of yams for Ombomb and a request for some meat to feast Anop and Wutue who had been helping him build a garden house. Now, Ombomb went hunting with Yabinigi in the hope of finding this meat.[264] Ombomb's dog took sick. This was the last dog alive in Alitoa. It had gone with Ombomb to Alipinagle, where one dog was dying at the time.[265]

Nigimarib had another quarrel with Pidjui, followed by a crying fit. Balidu came up and took him down to the garden. (This was a setback in the process of weaning him from his over-dependence on his father.)

La'abe and Imale worked sago.

Lomaijo was still in Mogiligen.

Gerud, Midjulumon, and Manum, who had been here since the day before yesterday, went to Malupit.

Sauwedjo helped Whasimai and Maisoa take out taro.[266]

Ulaba'i went to Magahine to get areca nut, accompanied by Ibanyos and Anyuai.

\* \* \*

Nyelahai went to Numidipiheim to hear what was happening about the pig, and to get more details of the intentions of the husband of Maisoa.

\* \* \*

[264] This meant that Ombomb would take Yabinigi hunting in his bush and that the added interest of Ombomb in finding game would spur Yabinigi along.

[265] When a dog affected by this disease died, he ran around and around in narrowing circles, and finally dropped dead.

[266] This was a working combination which now occurred for the first time in the second month.

## GERUD'S SECOND DIVINATION (3)

Welima was ill. Imale gave her a dose of *ashup*, the anti-sorcery emetic, on the strength of Gerud's statement the night before that she was sorcerized. Wabe said that perhaps she was ill because of sorcery, or perhaps it was from a fight she had had with Temos in Alipinagle before, in which the dead wife of Tapita had helped Temos beat her and wounded her back.[267] Wabe searched hard inside Welima's house, but could find no trace of the bone of which Gerud had spoken.

He worked at carving his plate, and Temos went for food.

## LIWO FIGHT (2)

Balidu came up again, without Nigimarib, and went to get a ring from the wounded doctor boy of Liwo, whom he calls *wa'en*.[268]

MARCH 29: Wabe and Ombomb went to help Bischu build his ground house.[269]

La'abe, exhausted after yesterday's work, did nothing. Imale went for firewood.

Whasimai and the baby were here. Welima sulked and slept. Temos worked in the sago patch. Everyone else was away.

Gerud returned from visiting his father, who had made a small feast for him.

---

[267] The dead wife of Tapita has now become a useful alibi for the living. This is one of four hand to hand fights which occurred between women within the locality while I was there. The others were two between the two wives of Nyelahai, see below, p. 366, and one between Temos and Welima.

[268] Balidu had given a ring to him previously; now, as *mehinen*, he could hope for a return, although he could not, of course, have asked for a payment for the shed blood as a *wa'en* could.

[269] Anop and Wutue had already worked on this ground house, but the work included getting all new materials and making new thatch.

## LIWO FIGHT: FURTHER REPORT (3)

Balidu returned from Liwo, without mentioning any ring, and went straight to his garden.

Nyelahai returned from Liwo with a lurid account of the fight over Tapik, reporting on the dreadful crimes which had been committed by the *tultul's* party; how Peshuhol and Yelegen had been beaten, when they had offered no resistance; how Peshuhol's wife, who had been returning with a load of firewood, had endeavored to egg them on to greater bravery, saying "Our ancestors fought bravely. Are we, their descendants, to sit down and be defeated?" She had then tried to attack Polip with a stick of firewood; he had knocked her down and thrust a piece of bamboo into her vulva which, according to Nyelahai, had penetrated as far as her chest. Gerud and Badui reported that Sumali had seen the woman and said that she hadn't even bled, that there merely had been a little horseplay on Polip's part.[270]

Yelegen, Peshuhol, Talumen, and Tapik, taking the *tultul* of Bugabihiem as their interpreter, all went off to present their case to the District Officer.[271]

Reports were also brought in that it was now understood that Yelegen was responsible for the wounding of the doctor boy because Yelegen had paid the Plainsmen to have Polip injured, by *wishan,* by a pig so that Polip, who was a strong fighter, would be out of the way during the fight. But the sorcery misfired. After all, it was only the very inaccurate *wishan,* there were no exuviae of Polip or of the doctor boy involved, and the pig had bitten the doctor boy instead. Yelegen was not admitting this; he was said to be too much ashamed about the doctor boy's injury.[272]

---

[270] This later proved to be true. The whole incident is a splendid instance of Nyelahai's tendency to exaggerate the sadistic and conflict elements in any situation.

[271] When local officials are concerned in a quarrel, getting an interpreter for the non-official side is often difficult, and the case of the innocent is lost because of the greater pidgin facility of the official party.

[272] The various events leading to Tapik's elopement, either directly or indirectly, were as follows:

1. Tapik had never wanted to marry the *tultul* and had only done

Defendants of the *tultul's* side of the case now said that the *tultul's* party had gone to get back the *tultul's* child; they were not interested in revenge. The *"tultul's* child" was actually Tapik's child by her former husband, but the *tultul* had fed it for over a year.

---

so after a court appeal had been made to the District Officer. (Such appeals are not very often made, except by native officials who think it becomes them to follow the litigant's path whenever possible. But, if no court case had been made of it, the consensus of the community might also have forced Tapik to a marriage she disliked, as it had before in making her marry Gobonarra.)

2. Yelegen had been trying to get Tapik for some time. He had copulated with her once before, and the *tultul* had found out and had remonstrated.

3. At pressure brought to bear by the doctor boy, Balidu and Sumali had forced Yelegen to go into the Plains to recover the exuviae of the sick father of the doctor boy. Research had shown that the original theft had been made by the wife of the sick man (now dead) who had given it to her brother (away at work) who had given it to Yelegen. (Note how very often a dead person is invoked as the major criminal.) A counter theory claimed that it had been given to Yelusha, a close associate of Yelegen's who had given it to Wabimani of Dunigi. Both theories insisted that Wabimani had the exuviae. Aden, who was a trade friend of Wabimani, helped reinforce this belief; in other words, he acted as a link in the blackmail chain. He said he had heard Wabimani had it, but he couldn't go walking about for fear that his sore would get worse. Whichever of these theories was correct, Yelegen did go into the Plains and returned with some exuviae which he showed to Balidu and Sumali, in proof of his good faith.

4. The wife of Tapita died.

5. The doctor boy of Liwo was attacked by a bush pig.

6. Yelegen eloped with Tapik.

Now, said local opinion, all of these events occurred at once, so there must be a connection between them. It was known that Yelegen had gone into the Plains. Furthermore, he had been a little too willing to go and too successful in bringing back the exuviae. While he was there, he must have paid the Plainsmen for *wishan*, which would make Tapik elope with him, and which would have Polip injured so as to get him out of the way. But the Plainsmen had to have some time set for all of these events to take place. So, he knew that the wife of Tapita was going to die from sorcery set in motion by her husband, from whom she had eloped two years before. They said to Yelegen, "The day after the wife of Tapita dies, Polip will be injured by the pig and you can run away with Tapik."

It will now be clear why events which are coincidental are re-

(For the theory held by Unabelin three months later, see *"The Record of Unabelin,"* now in preparation.)

MARCH 30: This was a thoroughly nasty day; pouring rain began at 10 o'clock. La'abe and Wabe were fencing for Bischu, Imale helping them.

Ombomb and Sauwedjo went to Wamu'um's place to plant taro shoots. They stopped to see Me'elue and decided she would recover.

Lomaijo was here all day. Welima spent the day with Lomaijo, her health and spirits recovered.

## LIWO FIGHT (4)

Kule, Alis, Mausi, and Naguel came in the afternoon and stayed overnight. They reported that Baimal had gone to Liwo to see the doctor boy. Baimal came in with a ring which he had been given to take into the Plains. He called for Balidu to come up and go with him. (Balidu was a cross-cousin of the doctor boy.) When Balidu came up he and Baimal developed a new theory, that the illness of the doctor boy of Liwo was due to the malice of "crocodile-skinned" man, Sai'ole, the old Dunigi man covered with *tinea* who had been here for the feast. At Ombomb's feast he had held out a leaf to Baimal for a piece of meat and Baimal had delayed giving it to him. Later, Baimal had offered it to him and he had refused it in a pet. Now the theory was that Sai'ole had paid to have a pig bite Kule, the doctor boy of Alitoa, and the sorcery had miscarried and gotten the doctor boy of Liwo instead.[273]

---

garded as interrelated through the potent agency of Plains sorcery. This means that anyone who goes into the Plains on any errand good or bad is subsequently at the mercy of chance events, as was Nyelahai and Matasues (above, p. 188) when Matasues went to pay for Ombomb's illness, and Sumali's house burned down directly afterwards.

[273] The miscarriage theory had been originally introduced to explain why the doctor boy, against whom Yelegen had no grudge and who was not concerned in the Tapik incident, should have been wounded just as Yelegen returned from the Plains and eloped. If the original assumption is granted, that simultaneous events must be related, then the reasoning followed is explicable. But by the

## BEGINNING OF KULE'S ILLNESS (1)

Soon after this conversation, Kule began to feel very ill. There followed some desultory remarks that Liwo was saying that Alitoa was responsible for the doctor boy mishap.[274]

Feeling ill, Kule with his family stayed overnight. They had just finished taking out their yams.

Winam, Midjulumon, Bopugenon, and Eweluen came in the evening.

MARCH 31: Wabe and his two wives, Temos sulky because she disliked Alipinagle, left to take out the yams which Wabe had planted there. Ombomb, Sauwedjo, and the infant went to help. La'abe was to have gone, but he had a swollen finger.

Whasimai and the children went to Aden's.

## LIWO FIGHT (5)

Whoiban arrived from Liwo, and he and Balidu and Baimal went to Wihun to pass the ring and sorcery quest on to Wambibi, the brother-in-law of La'abe and the *buanyin* of Balidu's brothers-in-law. Wambibi's wife, married daughter, and small daughter arrived here in the afternoon to take Daulap back to Wihun.

\* \* \*

usual Arapesh method of free association, they started with a very minor premise in the original argument, which they now made their major premise, namely, that the accident to the doctor boy was due to a miscarriage of sorcery. So the argument now ran: The doctor boy of Liwo, who has no exuviae outstanding and was not disliked by Yelegen, must have been injured by accident, that is, by a miscarriage of Plains sorcery. Yelegen disowns having made any arrangement for anyone to be hurt by a pig. What other routes could a miscarriage take? A conspicuous aspect of the doctor boy's personality is that he is a doctor boy. Kule of Alitoa is also a doctor boy. Kule has exuviae outstanding. Therefore, probably the sorcery was really meant for Kule.

[274] Such accusations were merely normal returns on the accusations against Peshuhol. But they turned the thought of the Alitoa people on themselves, and being guiltless they became immediately fearful.

Kule and his family left to return to Mogiligen, Kule feeling somewhat better.

## Exorcism of *Marsalai* Anger

Outside the village, in his *marsalai* place, an exorcism of his *marsalai* was performed by Nyelahai on behalf of Me'elue. Ombomb had accepted the original theory that she was ill from old childhood sorcery, until Nyelahai inquired from her parents, who reported that there was no record of her exuviae ever having been taken. Me'elue was then pressed to remember whether she had violated any *marsalai* taboo. She finally remembered that she had been passing by Nyelahai's place after dark and she had felt the spirits chasing her, and had fallen, with Yauwito'a in her arms. So Ombomb, Sinaba'i, and Nyelahai himself contributed rings. They strung them up with *walawahik* leaves, a pig skull, and the empty wrapping of a sago packet in the *marsalai* place. Then Nyelahai made a speech to the ancestral spirits and a butterfly lit on the rings, in token of acceptance. Nyelahai then took them to Me'elue and passed them about her head, and the rings were returned to their owners.

April 1: Ulaba'i had returned from the Beach, but had stopped at Aden's. This was reported by Ibanyos who came up to the village and went back to Aden's.

Madje and La'abe left to help Yabinigi hunt cassowary.

## Kule's Illness (2)

About 10 o'clock a call came from Manuniki that Kule was very ill, down near the Sulum, and would Gerud come immediately. He left at once. Then a few minutes later came a call that Kule was dead. Gerud was recalled. Dr. Fortune left with him. La'abe, Madje, and Yabinigi, Baimal, Balidu, and Whoiban were all out of calling range. However, shout after shout was sent forth in every direction, the shouts being repeated and carried on from hilltop to hilltop. *Garamuts* were beaten in Alitoa and in surrounding hamlets. Everyone in the place left at once, except La'abe's old widowed sister, who stayed to continue the shouting and to wait for La'abe. Matasues and Sinaba'i came through the village. They stopped to shout to Alipinagle men, "Come and help us carry his body home. If he were alive and you were dead, he would carry you."

They passed on. Nahomen came through just after them. Inoman came up and sat down in the village and refused to go any farther. The children of Matasues and Inoman stayed in the village and went about muttering, "Sorcery! Sorcery!" in low frightened tones. Then came another call saying that Kule was not dead, but had some breath left.[275]

Gerud returned with a note from Dr. Fortune asking for medicine, as he had left thinking Kule was dead. Then it turned out that Ulaba'i, Aden, and Anop had not yet started, but were merely gathered in Aden's small place. Nyelahai and Henalian were still in Alipinagle. Wutue, Bischu, Ombomb, Wabe, Iwamini, and Maginala, Maigi, and Badui arrived there at about the same time as Dr. Fortune.[276] Ilautoa had been crying genuinely, as had Amito'a, but Dr. Fortune reported that Soatsalamo had difficulty even in squeezing out formal tears. Naguel had a temper tantrum, but Mausi did not grasp what was happening. When the men arrived, all the women except Amito'a retired. Hysterically, she repeatedly said, "If he dies, we will put him in Baimal's beautiful new house which he helped to build." This was an earnest cry of great affection, for the house was new; they had not begun to live in it casually themselves, and it would probably have been destroyed afterwards.[277]

When Dr. Fortune arrived, Kule was conscious and was

[275] The Arapesh have great difficulty in determining death. There are accounts of people who were dead but who simply would not stop breathing, so their mourners finally buried them and stamped on the earth until the breath stopped. This is done in all innocence. The term breath was used because when Dr. Fortune reached Kule he was only unconscious, and Dr. Fortune told them that he was still breathing, as proof that he was still alive. Only women were with him, and they were convinced that he was dead.

[276] As for all other accounts of events outside the village which Dr. Fortune recorded, I am indebted to his report for these details.

[277] Houses are usually, but not always, destroyed after death; in most cases the corpse lies in the house that it once owned.

able to speak only after a dose of aromatic spirits of ammonia. Gerud brought back the version that he had been dead and Dr. Fortune had revived him. This theory was enthusiastically received by Kaberman. (He and Gerud seemed to think it paid an obscure tribute to *sagumeh*.) To judge by the symptoms, Kule seemed to have been suffering from acute indigestion or ptomaine poisoning. He vomited profusely, which set the women all mourning again, for they regard vomiting as almost equivalent to death. Dr. Fortune gave him a dose of calomel.[278]

About six in the evening, the absent six returned from Wihun, very tired and hungry. They had shot the cassowary twice, but failed to come up with it. They had heard the *garamuts* and thought that the doctor boy of Liwo was dead, until they reached Alipinagle and learned the truth. They came into our house and decided to wait until Dr. Fortune returned before making their next move. Baimal, wearily and bitterly, counted the futile payments which had already been made on behalf of Kule to the "crocodile-skinned" man who still did not produce the exuviae: five rings, one string of shell money, one knife, one little pig, one piece of pig.

Then Dr. Fortune returned. On his way he had met a crowd of Liwo people who had gotten as far as Aden's place. He reported that Kule was better, that the theory in Mogiligen was that the "crocodile-skinned" man had revived Kule's exuviae which had been stolen by Yauwiyu at the time of the quarrel over Wasijo (see above, p. 188). Later in the evening, two new theories were developed:

1. That when Yelegen and Peshuhol went into the Plains to recover the exuviae of the father of the doctor boy of Liwo, they also paid two rings, one to make Tapik elope with Yelegen and the other to make Kule die.

2. That two young men of Liwo of Kule's age group had died recently, and this was Liwo's impersonal revenge for

---

[278] In the light of the threats and fears about sorcery, of the fact that Kule had begun to feel ill as soon as the miscarriage theory of the Liwo doctor boy's trouble was developed, it is pertinent to ask, What was the matter with Kule? He was certainly very sick. He had not been sick before the development of the theory, i.e., his illness had not given it impetus, but followed it.

which they had paid the Plainsmen. In this connection, it was cited that of all the nearby places only Liwo and Alitoa had lost men who wore hats (i.e., were Government-appointed officials). This was felt to bind Liwo and Alitoa in some way, as well as to define the malice of other places.

There was no mention of the old miscarriage theory because Kule had been so ill that only genuine sorcery, that is, sorcery performed on his own exuviae, could be suspected.[279]

Everyone waited in the village, expecting to bring Kule in the morning. Ulaba'i, Anop, and the Liwo men came down late in the evening. Inoman, Nahomen, Matasues, Balidu, and La'abe were here. Lomaijo had stayed in Mogiligen.

APRIL 2: In the early morning it was shouted that they were bringing Kule in. Everyone waited to receive him. He walked in, merely supported by the other men, and was about exhausted when he arrived (it was a good two hours' walk), but he looked better than he had the day before. All the men sat around him on the Walinuba plaza looking very serious. The women and children stayed in the background, marking it a solemn occasion. Ilautoa, whose pregnancy had become very obvious, looked terribly spent and haggard, as did Amito'a.

Wabe was very glum because he had been interrupted in

---

[279] Analysis of these theories showed that there were three different Dunigi men involved:

1. Nidiagu, a classificatory father of Anone, the wife of Yauwiyu, who had originally received the exuviae stolen by Yauwiyu. He was now dead, but he had received the pay for Ombomb's exuviae. The "crocodile-skinned" man was believed to have inherited this stock of exuviae, including that of Kule and Badui. Yauwiyu himself was not mentioned in the present discussion.

2. The "crocodile-skinned" man was discussed as acting on his own initiative, but with the old exuviae, because he was angry at Baimal's slowness in serving him at the feast. He was now said to have been heard to mutter, "A strong young man will die without being sick," a remark which, strangely enough, no one had thought of before.

3. Wabimani, the Dunigi friend of Aden and the brother of the "crocodile-skinned" man, was supposed to have been approached directly by Yelegen.

In other words, they knew that Kule's exuviae was in Dunigi. This fact now took precedence over the coincidence with the Liwo events, but some effort was still made to connect the two series.

the middle of his Alipinagle yam harvest, and by now the yams would probably have all run away, for they would say, "If those men had stayed with us, we would have stayed, but they have run off, so we will run off."[280] Wabe, in a great burst of grief over Kule's supposed death, had said, "Never mind the yam harvest, we will go." Now, after all, Kule was not dead, and his generosity had only injured himself.

It was finally decided that Matasues, Baimal, and Badui would go to Dunigi in search of the exuviae. Then Ombomb and Wabe and their wives and Anyuai returned to the neglected harvest. La'abe went hunting with Yabinigi. Matasues, Nahomen, Inoman, and Anop all went home, as did the Liwo people.

## A Sorcery Search Party

In the late afternoon Dr. Fortune decided to join the sorcery search party. This created a great sensation and arrangements were made to add more recruits to the party to act as carriers.

April 3: The search party left at dawn, its numbers augmented by Matasues, Bischu, Sinaba'i, Maigi, La'abe, and our boys, Yabinigi, Biagu, and Mindibilip. There was some argument about who was to carry. Balidu came up and stamped about Alitoa, saying that later it would be their turn to carry to Karawop for us.

\* \* \*

Kule, Ilautoa, and their two children were left in the village, as well as Amito'a, Alaijo, Amus, and Minya. Soatsalamo, Pidjui, Kumati, Nigimarib, and Bopugenon were in Balidu's house. Ulaba'i, Menala, Wadjubel, and Danue, the wife of Bischu, and her children were here. The nine-year-old Dubomagau had gone to Dunigi with Sinaba'i. Menala and Danue went to help with Wabe's yams. Wadjubel kept the two elder of Bischu's children. Sumali, Midjulumon, and the little *tinea*-covered Kubi came in at noon.

---

[280] It is taboo for harvesters to leave the garden after the harvesting is begun or the yams will be offended and run off.

Later in the day, Whehonali, an old man with a very grand manner, wearing a fringe of beard in the Plains fashion, arrived to call on us. With him were his wife and sister and sister's child, all carrying yams, taros, and pawpaws. He made a long speech, made a fern *tangget*, naming one half of the individual cuts after our possessions and one half after his, repeating yams and taro several times, because his ran short compared with ours, which he desired. In his speech, he declared that we were to be his friends and to stay here and give everyone medicine so that they would not die and also bring in European goods so as to save his people the long and wearisome walk to the Beach. I had a group of children drawing. He watched them with interest, so I asked him if he would like to draw. He said, "Yes," and set to work very solemnly. On one big sheet he drew a picture of a man, himself, and on the other side, a picture of his son who was away in Salamoa, and whom he wanted us to summon home, and on another sheet, one side of designs and the other side notation of the white property which he desired. This he left as a *tangget* for Dr. Fortune.

## BALIDU'S FEAST: DETAILS (14)

Just at dusk, Nigi and Honali, four other men, two women, and some boys arrived from Wihun, with a pig in return for the one given them at the feast. The pig was left fastened until Baimal returned, when it would be cut and a feast made. They also brought one large net bag of taro. The evening was filled with speeches in which the ceremonial hostility was not excessive. The pig had been purchased in Yimonihi.

APRIL 4: The village was unusually full of children. They had started to gather when the alarm about Kule came through. Now with so many fathers absent in the Plains, they stayed there.

Lomaijo and Imale went to help with Wabe's yams.

Ulaba'i, Ibanyos, and Segenamoya went to their taro garden, accompanied by the wife of Gobonarra, who came in last night.

Amito'a and Alaijo got firewood. Ilautoa and Mausi went to gather bamboo sprouts.[281] Kule was steadily improving.

Wadjubel and Menala did nothing.

Danue took the new baby and went for food for her pig.

Nigi was still here and came and asked for some of the same medicine which so effectively banished the sorcery from Kule.[282]

Sumali and Kule expressed strong disapproval of some of the remarks which Whehonali, the mother's brother of Honali and Nigi, had made the night before. It seemed that he had referred to our house as if he had helped build it, and had also remarked on the fact that Yabinigi was feeding us from game shot in his bush.

A traveling party of four young Abelam men came through, accompanied by a middle-aged Plainsman who spoke both languages. They were very shy and friendly, and I did a little work on their language through the interpreter who was a gift friend of Kule's. They stayed in his house that night. They were carrying packages of tobacco for sale on the Beach.

In the evening the children played games. This was one of two occasions when there were enough children in the village and no adult events to hold their interest so that games were played.

APRIL 5: Aden brought up 16 pounds of sago and sat down to await Dr. Fortune's return. He loved trading so that he never was willing to miss any part of the transaction.

## LIWO FIGHT (6)

The party of the *tultul* of Liwo came over and reported that they had got Tapik back, and that she had said it was *wishan* which took her.[283]

---

[281] These are a delicacy. Going for them now was a way of saying the household was at loose ends, waiting for news from the sorcerers.

[282] After this episode, everyone wanted calomel. It is a wise precaution to take some harmless sugar pills, which look like any stringent drug which must be given with some care.

[283] Only later did I discover how they got Tapik back. The *tultul* had found the child alone and enticed him to himself and borne

I asked them about their theory of the wound of the doctor boy of Liwo. They said that it had miscarried from Kule's sorcery.

At noon, Ombomb, Sauwedjo, Whasimai, Anyuai, the baby, Lomaijo and her baby returned from Alipinagle and reported that Wabe and his wives would not be back until the day after the next.

In the evening, just at dusk, there were *garamut* calls simultaneously from Liwo and Alipinagle. Everyone got very excited and speculated wildly: a white man was coming, a police boy was coming, the doctor boy of Liwo was dead. Finally, by calling over to Aden's place, they decided that it probably meant that the doctor boy of Liwo was dying.

### ILLNESS OF HENALIAN'S CHILD (1)

The Alipinagle call was first interpreted as meaning that Tapita was dead, then that Henalian's child, which had been reported ill earlier in the afternoon, was dead. When they kept quiet long enough to listen to his attempt to call to them, they found that Henalian was calling that he would bring his sick child over in the morning.

APRIL 6: Welima came over early in the morning and went to look for the little pig which had disappeared and which she was feeding for Ombomb. She reported that the child would be brought over later.

Ulaba'i went to Wihun with Whehonali. Whasimai went to her garden, and the baby, after some crying, was left with Maisoa.

Dr. Fortune returned at noon. He had met the Abelam men outside the village. When he inquired whether they had seen me, they reported that I had refused to speak to them or to buy any of their tobacco.[284] Closely following him came a party of Ybonimu men with sacred carvings which Dr. Fortune had arranged to buy. There was a Wihun

him back to the *Suabibis* hamlet in triumph. The next day, Tapik followed her child back, and explained that she had not left of her own volition, but because of *wishan*.

[284] We finally decided that this was just tact.

party here also to sell material culture objects. Henalian brought over his sick child, a youngster of about four.

Dr. Fortune reported that Dunigi and Biligil were in a state of feud over the death of the killer of Lui's brother,[285] and that the "crocodile-skinned" man had said that Kule would wash in two days.[286]

### KOBELEN FEAST: FIRST DETAILS (1)

A Kobelen man, a brother of Kaberman, came up to ask for help with the big Kobelen feast in which they were going to purchase the dance called the *shené* from Dakuar.

### LIWO FIGHT (7)

He brought word that the doctor boy of Liwo was very ill indeed, and Sumali set off to visit him.

* * *

Wabe and Temos returned also.

### ILLNESS OF HENALIAN'S CHILD (2)

The child had a high fever. Its illness was attributed to the effects of a *sagumeh* charm on his father's tree. Manusa, the *tultul* of Numidipiheim, had purchased with his *sagumeh* a charm for protecting coconut palms. Henalian had gotten him to put this on his palm trees. Then, when he had wanted to climb them, he had asked Manusa to come and remove the charm, but Manusa had failed to come, so he had climbed it anyhow and now his child was sick.[287]

APRIL 7: Before the Ybonimu men departed, they were formally exhorted by Balidu to tell their old men that Alitoa was not responsible for the sale of their sacred carvings.

---

[285] Lui was a particularly striking Dunigi man, who had been an assistant boss boy in Rabaul. He figures later in gossip about Imale, see below, p. 399.

[286] That is, he would be well in two days.

[287] This is typical. The Arapesh seemed incapable of systematically handling the idea of protective magic, the type of conditional curse magic so familiar in surrounding areas.

Everyone in Alitoa was very disturbed about the purchase. They were afraid to have the carvings in the village. They had insisted that they be put in the *tamberan* house and not be left in our house to make me and the boys ill. They were also afraid that the old men of Ybonimu would be angry and would work sorcery against them.

People were loitering in the village, not quite sure what was going to happen or why they were there.

### ILLNESS OF HENALIAN'S CHILD (3)

Early in the morning Matasues who owned the yam protective charm which produced a sick stomach exorcised Henalian's child.

I worked over Henalian's child. After bathing it for a couple of hours with alcohol and water, I reduced its temperature and got it to take some castor oil. Henalian was one of the most superstitious of the Arapesh. He was very little impressed with the child's improvement. I left it sleeping. When I returned to look at it in the late afternoon I found it unaccountably much worse again. It then developed that Henalian had gotten Budagiel to give it a potion of herbs which accompanied a charm which Magiel (now away at work) had formerly brought home. The potion worked as an emetic and the child was wretchedly ill again.[288]

Word came that Nagawe had killed a bush pig and would give a feast the next day to pay for building a new yam house.

[288] Magiel had taught this charm to Gerud and Budagiel, his half brother and sister. He had taught it to Wena also. Formerly, when Ombomb had been ill, he had drunk it and paid a ring and recovered. However, Henalian did not pay Budagiel anything, and "so it only made the child worse, for this was the kind of charm which only works with pay." The Arapesh can understand the idea of a rite or ceremony that only works when there is meat, but beyond this they have difficulty in comprehending the connection between magic and payment. The garden magician works without payment; charms are handed about among themselves without payment; the exorcist who removes the damage done by a conditional curse placed on his yams works without payment. It is only in the case of recently introduced magic, for which the introducer himself has paid a fee, that a fee is demanded.

## BALIDU'S FEAST: DETAILS (15)

Baimal cut the pig which Nigi had brought and distributed it with plates of croquettes to everyone here except Whoiban. These were small courtesy amounts, in acknowledgment of the help rendered at the feast.

## GERUD'S THIRD DIVINATION

At the request of Wabe, whose little pig had been missing for three days, Gerud divined in the evening. Wabe paid him a ring in advance. This time he reverted to his former pattern of rushing about, up and down the steeps, searching frantically, now in one spot, now in another. Gerud found an old fish tin full of earth, which everybody immediately pronounced to be Wegul's exuviae. Gerud afterwards added the information that half of it belonged to the wife of Iwamini. After he fell down prostrate, he made the following points, in answer to questions:

1. The tin contained the exuviae of Wegul and of the wife of Iwamini. They were both put there by Aden. Aden had put Wegul's exuviae there on behalf of Gobonarra, and that of Yinauwhat, the wife of Iwamini, because he was still angry about his old quarrel over her.[289]

[289] The wife of Iwamini was not even ill, but her recent stay with Aden, while Iwamini went to the Beach (see above, p. 247) had stirred up comment on the old story and it was fresh in everyone's mind. Also, both she and Wegul belonged to Alipinagle. She was the only Alipinagle person besides Wegul against whom anyone had a grudge at the moment. It also gave Gerud a chance to involve Aden. He had not by any means relinquished the theory that Aden had been responsible for his father's house burning down and all his rings being destroyed. Furthermore, after the former accusations against Gobonarra, which were not made by Gerud in his seance (p. 299), but were later proposed by La'abe (p. 316), Wegul (p. 316) had countered with the accusation that Gerud's sister Budagiel had put the exuviae there. Finding that everyone accepted Gobonarra's guilt, Gerud was now shifting the suspicion from one accomplice to another. There would have been no need to have posited an accomplice, if Wegul had not complicated the issue with the original theory that Budagiel had been responsible, mistak-

2. Wabe's little pig had been killed by a *Lahowhin* snake. Gerud claimed that he had found the little dead pig during his trance, had lifted it up and thrown it away. The snake had acted as a result of the talk of Nahomen[290] who was angry because Sinaba'i had just given a little pig to Aden.[291]

3. Kule would be all right.

4. Henalian's child was only sick, not sorcerized.[292]

5. (This was spontaneous and not in answer to a question, as was also number six.) Badui would be ill from sorcery later, but would drink medicine and recover.

6. Henalian would be ill from sorcery later, but would drink medicine and recover.

---

ing his exuviae for Kamil's. Wegul's theory had been developed against Gerud, in an attempt to evade paying him for his unasked services. This was also a reason for finding *more* of Wegul's exuviae. Here the crowd seized upon the idea, by a sort of stupid free association, and Gerud merely followed their lead.

[290] When something happens as a result of the "talk" of a person, this means that he has invoked the help of his ancestral spirits and the associated *marsalai*.

[291] The causes of Nahomen's anger were various, as discovered later. Gerud, talking over the seance afterwards, said that Welima had fed Sinaba'i's pig (the mother of the lost pig in question) when he had no wife, and he had given Wabe this small pig in acknowledgment. (This touch, "because Sinaba'i had no wife," is typical Gerud, for very often a man's wife does not, in any event, feed his pigs, but Gerud believed that property should be kept near its owner.) From the next litter, Sinaba'i had given Aden a small pig which Nahomen wanted; so now Nahomen had made Wabe's pig die.

This was all Gerud knew about it, besides vague rumors that Nahomen had actually been angry. His anger was, however, based on better legal grounds. Nahomen's wife had fed the mother of Sinaba'i's pig, the grandmother of Wabe's lost pig. When Sinaba'i had fastened a daughter of this original pig (the aunt of Wabe's pig) to Numidipiheim, he had not given Nahomen any share, in recognition of his wife's having fed the mother. Then Nahomen had asked for a small pig later. And from this last litter Sinaba'i had given one to Aden, one to Henalian, and kept two. So Nahomen had killed an earlier descendant of the pig grandmother in whom his rights were not being recognized. Also, of course, Wabe and Sinaba'i lived together and were very closely associated economically.

[292] Here Gerud supported the magical ministrations of his sister, against the alleged potency of Manusa's *sagumeh* charm.

7. Bischu's hunting had been spoiled by Walawahan, who had taken a phalanger bone and hidden it in his hearth ashes. Walawahan was angry about the way in which Bischu had abused him over the landslide in his garden.[293]

8. Wabe's hunting bone (mentioned in the earlier divination) was still hidden in Welima's house.

9. Yabinigi's shooting had failed today because an old man in Boinam, who had asked for a pigeon as Dr. Fortune's party came through, had not been given one. He had gotten a bone of the pigeon and a pig bone and fastened them together.

He then reverted to accusations against Nahomen over Wabe's pig, closing the divination on the matter for which he had been retained.

APRIL 8: People woke up early. There was a long, semi-formal conversational speechmaking, berating Sinaba'i[294] for

[293] Gerud, after the seance, supplied the whole series of events upon which this accusation was based. Walawahan had been hunting alone in the *marsalai* place, the hunting bush of the gens of *Diboaibis,* Bischu's garden. Walawahan had killed a phalanger there and gave Bischu part of it. Now, although Walawahan lived in Ahalesimihi, he did not belong to *Diboaibis;* he had no right to hunt in the *Diboaibis* bush unaccompanied by a *Diboaibis* man. So the *marsalai* was angry; a great rain had come, made a landslide in Bischu's garden and buried part of his yams. In return, Bischu, in obscene language, had abused Walawahan for his carelessness in inciting the anger of the *marsalai.* Walawahan and Bischu both belonged to *Uyebis,* so the attack of the *marsalai* could be regarded as having come through the phalanger bone and as having fallen upon the trespasser and his gens who shared his path. It was then, said Gerud, that Walawahan had taken one of the phalanger bones and buried it to injure Bischu's hunting. This again is typical of Gerud, jealousy over hunting grounds. He was particularly concerned over the future of the hunting grounds of *Diboaibis,* over which he hoped to hunt with the sons of Manum and Silisium. Other people merely made the point that Walawahan should have had someone with him, of course, but not that he had no right on *Diboaibis* land. Everyone agreed that Walawahan had been careless, Bischu had suffered, and yet that Walawahan might well be angry about the language that Bischu had used on the subject.

[294] The expressed disapproval was not for Nahomen but for Sinaba'i who might have been more careful, because he had angered such a socially irresponsible person as Nahomen, from whom everybody knew one could expect only bad behavior.

angering Nahomen about the pig. Now Anop's pig was dead and Wabe's lost and there would be no pigs to meet Ombomb's obligations.

## NAGAWE'S FEAST IN AHALESIMIHI

It was announced that Nagawe was going to give, not a house building feast as originally planned, but the first feast, the *abiat* in a series of "dog" feasts, to organize food to pay to Magahine. Nagawe, assisted by Silisium and Gabunyan, was the "trunk," and Baimal, Kule, and Badui were the "dogs." Ulaba'i, Baimal, Kule, Ombomb, Badui, and their respective women and children set off early for Ahalesimihi.[295]

I had to collect the details of this feast from informants. They are sketchy.

Baimal was the "dog." He received the pig, and distributed it. Baimal gave his pieces to Whoiban (Liwo), Ombomb, Ipagu (Liwo), Yelegen (Liwo), La'abe, La'abe's sister in Numidipiheim, and a foreleg to Sumali, which was received by Budagiel in Sumali's absence. La'abe accepted the piece for his sister. Kule gave one leg to Amito'a to give her brother Ipagu (Liwo),[296] one piece to Sinaba'i. Badui received the jaw, which he gave to Ulaba'i, his *buanyin*. Lomaijo returned, ahead of the party, carrying the piece of pig to her sister-in-law in Numidipiheim.

## ILLNESS OF HENALIAN'S CHILD (4)

Henalian took the sick child back to Alipinagle early in the morning. Later, Manusa appeared in Alitoa and called out for Henalian to bring the child over to be exorcised. Henalian did not respond.

\* \* \*

[295] Nagawe was the big man of Ahalesimihi and the husband of Yapul, Balidu's daughter.
[296] All the people here represented came from one division, that in which Whoiban and Yelegen were leaders, so there were no persons belonging to the opposed party present.

## LIWO FIGHT (8)

Meanwhile Balidu and Sumali went to Liwo to see the sick doctor boy. Balidu got back about four o'clock. He reported the doctor boy of Liwo recovering and that Yelegen had gone to recover[297] the exuviae which had been sent to the Plains, so that Kamil would not have to go to jail. Kamil, it was now admitted, had taken the exuviae because the doctor boy, following a borrowed fashion he had learned as a work boy, had forcibly seduced Kamil's wife, who was the doctor boy's gens sister (while the doctor boy was away at work).

Baimal, Kule, and La'abe stayed in Ahalesimihi to help Nagawe build his yam house.

Budagiel was sick after the feast and was wakened by a nightmare. She had been sleeping with Kumati and Sagu, and now called for Gerud and the other boys to come into the house and protect her.

APRIL 9: Baimal, Kule, Badui, and La'abe, with Amito'a, Il-autoa, and Imale, were still in Ahalesimihi. Lomaijo stayed in Numidipiheim overnight. Winam, Midjulumon, and the two youngest of Sumali's children returned to their hamlet. Balidu went to his garden.

## WABE PUTS UP A PUBLIC NOTICE

Meanwhile Wabe was dealing with the death of his pig. Outside the door of his main house—the one which he shared with Sinaba'i—he erected a public notice[298] that Welima should be allowed to feed no more pigs. Into a piece of *limbum* sheath, out of which pigs are fed, he thrust a spear and several broken arrows, points uppermost. To the spear he

[297] Yelegen had maintained very close connections with the Plains, ever since his adoption of Kamil long ago, when he was a small, neglected, half-starved boy, whom he found outside of *Kaboibis* and brought home. Later, he had exchanged rings with the *Kaboibis* men, and remained fast friends. He was the only man who usually succeeded in getting exuviae back from the Plains. To do this, it needed a real affinal tie, or one which was regarded as close as an affinal tie, as was this.

[298] Mead, 1938, Fig. 9.

tied an old piece of yam, on which pigs are fed. Welima, to relieve her feelings, tied a *tangget* that she would give no more food to Inoman and Nahomen.[299]

Wabe then put black paint on his forehead[300] and, accompanied by Maginala and Ga'olen, his cross-cousins, he set out for Liwo to try to buy a pig.

Welima went to Alipinagle.

Ombomb and Sauwedjo left for work.

By late afternoon, no one was left in the village except the children of Balidu, Budagiel and Bopugenon, Ulaba'i and his wives, Temos, and Sinaba'i and his children.

* * *

APRIL 10: Wabe returned, sulky and subdued, without a pig.

The people helping Nagawe in Ahalesimihi were said to be still there.

Lomaijo and her baby returned from Numidipiheim.

Budagiel and Bopugenon left for the bush.

## LIWO FIGHT (9)

It was reported[301] that the doctor boy was still improving and that Yelegen was bringing back the exuviae.

[299] For the forms of these notices, see Mead, 1938, pp. 194–195.
[300] Black paint is the sign of warfare, therefore, the sign of anger, and to Wabe, to whom grief and anger were synonymous, the appropriate paint to use, even when he was setting out on an apparently peaceful mission.
[301] When I merely say *report*, it is because I had decided that it was futile to try to discover the source of the rumor. An episode will illustrate this kind of futility. I was dressing sores one morning when a commotion broke out at the other end of the village. I asked Wabe, who came along at that moment, what was happening. He listened a minute and then said, "Whoiban has come from Liwo to tell Balidu that unless he does something about the sickness of the father of the doctor boy, when Alitoa carries a pig to Magahine they needn't go through Liwo." This was familiar material, the sound of speech-making had stopped, so I finished the dressing before going up. In Walinuba, I found only Yahalijo. "Where is Whoiban?" "In Liwo, I suppose." "Wasn't he here?" "No." Still hopeful of training informants, I marched back and confronted Wabe with this information. "Why did you tell me that?" "Well, if

Ombomb and Sauwedjo returned in the late afternoon.

A party of Liwo people, no one immediately concerned with the quarrel, came through to sell us bananas.

APRIL 11: The Liwo people stayed overnight in one of Balidu's houses, and left this morning early. Wabe worked on his plate. Welima took taro to Bunitai—a present from a mother's brother to a sister's son. Ulaba'i and Ibanyos came back to the village.

### RETURN OF THE MAGUER SORCERY DELEGATION (9)

Biagu returned from a mission for us, bringing with him a Maguer youth who came to report that the sore was no better and to demand back the pay.[302] Nyelahai was sent for and he came up immediately. Three rings and a knife were sent back; one ring and one knife were kept, on the theory that part of the sore, which had dried up, had belonged to this place, and that the rest belonged to Bugabihiem. This was merely a one-sided decision, however. Sinaba'i had the rings, and they would be taken to Maguer later.

### LIWO FIGHT (10)

Biagu brought word that Yelegen had returned to Liwo with the exuviae of the doctor boy.

\* \* \*

Dr. Fortune worked with Ombomb on his charms, including the yam protective charms of which Ombomb was very much afraid. The shoot boy killed two hornbills and one of these was given to Ombomb in payment for his magical information.

---

he had been here, that is what he would have said," said Wabe reasonably. Where minds worked like this, it was often hopeless to probe for sources of rumors.

[302] It is characteristic that when a life was at stake, a whole party of Maguer men came up, but when it was merely a matter of collecting property, they sent a youth alone, except for the accident of Biagu's presence. It was also characteristic of Nyelahai that he came right up when a matter of pride was involved.

## MAGUER SORCERY DELEGATION (10)

APRIL 12: Nyelahai and Sinaba'i left with the Maguer boy to return the rings. Now that this place was no longer under suspicion, relations were much improved and Nyelahai was willing to be helpful and pleasant again.[303]

## ILLNESS OF HENALIAN'S CHILD (5)

Henalian called over to ask where Sumali was. The child was ill and he had concluded that the illness was due to another set of yams, as the exorcism of Matasues was unsuccessful.[304]

Wabe and his wives were in Alipinagle, fencing a new garden.

La'abe and Imale left Ahalesimihi yesterday and went to make a new taro garden. Lomaijo joined them today.

Baimal, Kule, Badui, Amito'a, Ilautoa, Mausi, and Naguel returned from Ahalesimihi. Amus had a sore foot and had been left with Balidu's widowed sister in Ahalesimihi. Ombomb and Sauwedjo were both sick. The sickness was attributed to Ombomb's magic having gone into the hornbill which he had received in payment for it on April 12 and then eaten.

## LIWO FIGHT (11)

Polip, Unabelin, and Siakaru of *Suabibis*, Liwo, came over in the late afternoon but were recalled by a *garamut*. A police boy had come to take them to Wewak.

\* \* \*

A party of Ybonimu men came to sell us a large image.

[303] Nyelahai loved to boast of sorcery practice, but deeply resented any accusations originating from others.

[304] Such orthodoxy as that, only the person who put the charm on the yams can remove the illness caused by them, is only resorted to as an alibi. As a rule, anyone who owns the same charm can pronounce the exorcism.

### A *Tangget* Asking for Aid against Sorcery (11)

A Malis man, Agilapwe's father's son by a Malis mother, who had been present at Ombomb's feast, came to leave a sorcery *tangget*. His elder brother was ill and the exuviae were believed to be in Bonaheitum where Ombomb's brother Wabe had friends. Ombomb and Wabe call the sick man *babuen* (child of cross-cousin) "because they call Agilapwe *babuen*." The *tangget* was left with Balidu and Baimal as Wabe was not here.

April 13: Early in the morning, Baimal and Balidu marched formally up to the Alitoa end of the village, to deliver to Wabe the *tangget* which the Malis man had left.[305] Wabe set off almost at once for Bonaheitum, alone, but arranged for Temos to join him. He went, grumbling quite justifiably because the Malis man had brought no property which he could use to fee the sorcerer.

* * *

A large party came up from Kwobilisi to meet a group from Ahalesimihi and carry back yams which were being sent by Wena to his mother, the wife of Wamu'um. From Kwobilisi came Nahomen, Inoman, Wawehai, and all of the children old enough to carry, including Keali and the deaf boy, whom I had never seen before. They arrived in the morning and sat down to wait. Ulaba'i took Segenamoya and Dubomagau and went to look for pepper catkins for the assembled crowd. He found a large nest of edible caterpillars. Here was a dilemma, for he had no desire to feed this little bit of meat to Nahomen and Inoman. So when he returned to the village he gave the caterpillars to Balidu, his *buanyin*, as represented by Baimal and Kule. Thus his fortunate find was banked, not cast away into the insatiable mouths of *alomato'im*.

Inoman and Matasues' children all had a slight fever. They had Wabe's sick dog with them.

[305] This shows the real usefulness of a *tangget:* it compels formal action. If the Malis man had merely left an oral message, there would have been no such formality.

The Ahalesimihi party included Wena, his wife, his sister, Naushe'e, his wife, the children of Silisium and of Silisium's dead brother. This repayment was formal, as Wena had previously formally borrowed yams from his mother when his child was born (see above, p. 232). They all returned at once to Ahalesimihi, while the Kwobilisi party remained.

Ombomb and Sauwedjo both recovered, after large doses of castor oil, and left at noon for their gardens to get food.

Belagomini arrived from Wihun at dusk, and in the absence of Ombomb, his *gabunyan*, stayed with Baimal.

In the evening, Sumali, Midjulumon, and Ite'epe came in, as did Aden.

La'abe went with Yabinigi to hunt for a marauding pig and they stayed out overnight.

## Liwo Fight (12)

April 14: Kule and Matasues went to Liwo to hear how the fight altercation was progressing. They did not return to the village at all.

\* \* \*

## Illness of Henalian's Child (6)

Sumali heard that Henalian had been shouting for him and called out to him to come and have his child exorcised. No answer.

Laden with their yams, the Kwobilisi delegation returned, except for Nahomen and his children who remained in Alitoa. Ulaba'i and his family promptly packed up and the women went to Moholigum, he and Segenamoya to Aden's place with Aden.

Ombomb and Sauwedjo were still away, as were La'abe and his wives. Maigi and Sagu were gardening in Manuniki.

Baimal and Amito'a prepared to return to Mogiligen, but I tempted them to remain by a promise of food, as Amito'a had said she meant to dye sago aprons and I wanted to see it done. Amito'a knew how to make the particularly handsome type of apron called a *wulus*.

Silisium and Wena came in, Silisium to bring food to Gerud, and Wena on his way to see his mother.

Wutue and his family came in, as did Bischu and his children. Yabiok stayed. Ulaba'i returned with Sauisua, Kubi,[306] and Segenamoya. His wives came up from Moholigum.

Ilautoa had a small sister of Nagawe with her. Amus was still in Ahalesimihi.

Wadjubel was staying with Balidu and was reported to have said she meant to stay on there.

A Bonaheitum party passed through, going to the Beach to purchase Tridacna shell.

The *luluai* of Bonaheitum, a very dignified old man, stayed with the *luluai* of Alitoa; the rest went on to the Beach.

### Return of the Maguer Sorcery Delegation (11)

Nyelahai, Sinaba'i, Miduain, and the Maguer delegation—in full force again—returned from Maguer. They had found half of the sore dried up, and so had returned only the second payment, keeping the first as fee for Gerud's finding the exuviae in Manuniki. A Bugabihiem man had been to Maguer and given a theoretical route for the exuviae, which was from the dead *luluai* of Magahine to his brother-in-law, the *tultul* of Waginara, to the doctor boy of Waginara (an ex-Bugabihiem man), to Senaru, an old man of Bugabihiem, and from him to Alitoa. The delegation, however, paused with Senaru, whom they now believed to be the sorcerer. They asked to have Gerud go with them to Bugabihiem on the morrow and find the exuviae in the *marsalai* place. They agreed at first, then everyone began to think of the great number of deaths which had been laid to that place (a quicksand), and finally they decided that Gerud should do his divining here in Alitoa at night.

\* \* \*

[306] This little *tinea*-covered boy, child of a classificatory sister of the *luluai* married to a Umanep man, kept turning up, now with one person, now with another. The other children disliked him because of his *tinea*, and never really accepted him as a member of the community. He spent most of his time with adults.

The Maguer men also brought news of the death of a man named Genedu, of Magahine. This news was shouted to the neighboring hamlets. Agilapwe beat the death *garamut* for the next two hours.[307]

## GERUD'S FOURTH DIVINATION

That evening Gerud divined. He rushed about from one slope to another. Finally, after digging furiously in a hole and finding a piece of bamboo, he fell down. The counts of the divination were:

1. The boy's lost knife, which he had formerly said had been thrown away with the cooking leaves (see above, p. 333) had been in the hole where he had tried to dig, but it had cut his hand, so he had desisted.[308]

2. The piece of bamboo contained the exuviae of a sick man of Nibau (Malis) and had been placed there by the son-in-law of Agilapwe.[309]

3. He gave details of the location of the exuviae of the Maguer man in Bugabihiem. It lay in the Anigelu river, under a stone, on top of which the *marsalai*, Anigelu, was coiled.

4. The Magahine man, Genedu, who had just died, had died from sorcery made in Bonaheitum.[310]

5. Gerud outlined the course which the exuviae of the

---

[307] It was one of Agilapwe's pleasant customs to beat the death *garamut* in situations where, as he had no immediate reason to be grieved, the suspicion always was that he was beating it for joy.

[308] Kaberman looked in the hole later and said there was no knife there.

[309] The illness of the Malis man, about which Wabe had gone to Bonaheitum, was, of course, in everyone's mind.

[310] Now note: Bonaheitum had behaved very badly on the recent trip into the Plains. A *tangget* had been left with Wabe, accusing Bonaheitum of the sorcery of a man related to Alitoa people. The *luluai* of Bonaheitum was in the village, alone, and had been formally reproved by Dr. Fortune that afternoon, which may have emboldened Gerud to attack Bonaheitum. Gerud also knew that after Dr. Fortune's trip into Dunigi, which had included the unpleasant reception at Bonaheitum, we had definitely decided not to try to move our camp into the Plains. My personal diary for April 6 carries the entry: "Decision not to go *kunae* (Plains)."

Maguer man had taken, agreeing with the route which the Bugabihiem man had given, but having the trail end at Bugabihiem.

The Maguer men had to rest content with this until the next day. Otherwise there was nothing in the divination which interested anyone very much.

## CEREMONIAL DYEING

During the night, Amito'a, Ilautoa, and I dyed sago leaves to make the special *wulus* aprons. They needed a big pot for these; they got me to help them carry Lomaijo's most cherished cooking pot out to use, so that I could share the responsibility afterwards. The work was done in the little ground house which Kule had rebuilt for the feast. It took all night, first to cut the various herbs and leaves into small bits with a knife and then to dye the successive layers of skeined sago leaves. The wind blew furiously; the little house was full of smoke and very chilly. The men had been ordered to stay away and modulate their voices, but they refused to take this, "the women's *tamberan*," very seriously. Kule took his children to bed with him, but Badui and Pidjui laughed aloud, and it was said to be because of this that one skein caught fire. Amito'a thoroughly enjoyed the whole occasion; the exclusion and partial subjugation of the men, the night, the coziness of the little hut, the leaping flames under the black pot and the bubbling crimson liquid oozing out under the covering flannel-like leaves fastened over the top of the pot. "It is good," she said. "Two by two we go for firewood; two by two we bring up water; two by two we dye our aprons."

Meanwhile, reflecting the structurally involved sex antagonism and dichotomy, Baimal sat up with Dr. Fortune and told him a long series of war tales out of the past, imputing ferocities to the male sex.

A howling gale arose during the night, and broke down a ground house of Aden's.

APRIL 16: The morning dawned very bright, but with the wind still raging. The gaily dyed skeins of sago leaf were spread out on the low roofs to dry in the sun. The mishap to Aden's ground house was laid to the great *marsalai*, Behebil, the *marsalai* of *Kanehoibis,* who was angry because Ulaba'i had cut some trees on his ground yesterday. Although no one else took any notice of possible danger from the high wind, Ulaba'i kept his family in all morning, afraid that a tree or a branch would fall on one of their heads.[311]

## Maguer Sorcery Delegation (12)

Early in the morning, Baimal, Balidu, Kule, and Badui marched militantly up to the Alitoa end of the village, where the Maguer men were staying, to disavow publicly a charge brought by the Maguer men that Badui had been offered some exuviae when he went through Maguer with Biagu. Although Badui was said to have refused this exuviae, they nevertheless wanted the whole charge withdrawn. The burden of their defense was that no one ever entrusted exuviae to boys as young as Badui.[312]

And immediately following this came a deputation from Walinuba, to say that the Bugabihiem *marsalai* was too dangerous and that Gerud should not be permitted to go. If his father were here to go with him, it would be different, but to go alone was unsafe. He had divined the night before and located the exuviae and that was sufficient.[313]

The Maguer men argued, but in vain. Disappointed, they prepared to leave. They had made several calls in Bugabihiem but the Bugabihiem people had simply evaded them. They had hoped, as they said frankly, that by engag-

[311] It will be remembered that formerly Ulaba'i's lounging shelter had blown down, again because of the anger of Behebil, because Iwamini had cut wood there without asking permission. Now Ulaba'i cuts trees, and it is Aden, a member of *Kanehoibis,* who is punished. But this time there was more rationale in the theory, because Aden should have gone with Ulaba'i. On the whole, however, the explanations which connect disasters caused by wind and rain with particular acts are very tenuous and unsystematic.

[312] In the discussion afterwards, it seemed that their anger at some new sorcery accusation involving Alitoa and their panic when the sorcery traffic was attributed even to young boys was about evenly divided.

[313] Note the confusion here between the supernatural and the real danger to a young boy going into a hostile community to accuse one of its members of sorcery.

ing Gerud, they could enlist a party of Alitoa men to go with them and make the Bugabihiem people pay attention. They looked very forlorn and dispirited as they sat there, hunching their shoulders under their carrying bags.

As if in compensation for not letting Gerud help them, Baimal and Nyelahai made violent speeches of sympathy. They seized the nettle banner and the sorcery *tangget* and stamped and shouted. Nyelahai pointed out how he had arranged for the death of a Dakuar man to avenge the death of a cross-cousin[314] and that he was quite equal to killing more people. Baimal mentioned the name of a man of Bugabihiem, recently dead, and said that if Bugabihiem wanted to lose more men, just let them keep this Maguer exuviae, just let them allow the Maguer man to die. Afterwards Baimal remarked to me, with a dramatic gesture, "We talk big and many people die. If we talk easy, they remain alive."

The Maguer people then set out alone for Maguer, feeling sure that there was no use now in stopping again in Bugabihiem.

The old Bonaheitum man, his hands busy twisting bamboo into ring cutters, followed the arguments about, as they shifted from the Alitoa end to the Walinuba end, for the final set of speeches against Bugabihiem. During these latter speeches a party of Liwo people passed through and they could be guaranteed to pass them on.[315]

[314] It is boasting scenes like this that start the rumors as to actual complicity in a death, very often without any other foundation.

[315] Alitoa had been on very poor terms with Bugabihiem since the death of Pailit, who it was believed had been sorcerized by his last wife, the mother of Sinaba'i. This breach had been partially healed by the marriage of Balidu's eldest daughter to a Bugabihiem man. Then both of them had gone away to work for the white man and never returned, and this had not improved community relationships. Furthermore *Suabibis* were on very bad terms with Bugabihiem at present, and Alitoa were on good terms with *Suabibis*.

### ILLNESS AND DEATH OF NYELAHAI'S BABY[316] (1)

Just after this, the two wives of Nyelahai came up. Natun, the younger, was frantic because her baby was in a coma. She was wailing as if it were dead. I found it was only unconscious. While I went to get restoratives, Natun handed the baby to Ombomb, her sister's husband, to hold, and became involved in a hand to hand fight with Nyalamidju, Nyelahai's old pig-keeping wife.[317]

Natun was accusing her of having caused her baby's death. Nyelahai was doing nothing. Amito'a separated the two women. I revived the baby. After Gerud had been called in to charm it, beating its back with *walehik* leaves and blowing on it, I gave it castor oil and returned it to its mother, who gave it the breast, but without apparent conviction that it was alive. She went on, accusing her old co-wife of having carried a contagion to it from a child she had visited in Numidipiheim and which had died recently.[318] Then she mentioned that she had gone with the child near a tree inhabited by a tree spirit and had heard a tree spirit call out,[319] and then Nyelahai said they would take the child to Sumali who knew the exorcism for this illness. I protested but in vain.

### LIWO FIGHT (13)

From Baimal, I learned that when he had gone into the Plains, he had heard of the location of the doctor boy's exuviae in Dunigi and he had sent the word to Liwo as to who had sent it—Kamil's wife. Then she had sent food to the doctor boy; the sore had pained worse when he ate her food,

[316] It is worth noting here that Henalian's child did recover, despite its haphazard treatment.

[317] This vigorous old woman was the mother of Talumen, and the grandmother of Sa'omale, Badui's betrothed.

[318] The Arapesh experienced some sort of epidemic a few years before (probably influenza) and recognize that contagion exists in what they call cases of "a cold in the stomach."

[319] These tree spirits play a very minor role in Arapesh; this was the only time I ever heard one invoked to explain illness.

proving the exuviae she had taken was responsible, and then
Yelegen had gone into the Plains to get the exuviae.

Lomaijo returned and discovered that her big pot had
been used for dye. She flew into a terrific rage at Amito'a.
In the course of the altercation, in which Amito'a and Ilautoa
in self protection dragged my name in as often as possible,
Lomaijo retaliated by saying that she did not mind her pot's
being used to dye an apron for me, but that it should have
been used to dye aprons also for Sagu, Budagiel, Wadjubel, . . . ! Her Ahalesimihi brother was in the house with
her. Balidu, whether tactfully or not, I never knew, picked
up Wadjubel's name and began demanding that more rings
be paid for her by Amambut, Lomaijo's titular father and the
father of Wadjubel's absent betrothed. Not another word
issued from Lomaijo's house.

## MAISOA'S HUSBAND'S ATTEMPTS
## TO REGAIN HER (2)

A party of Numidipiheim men, brothers of Maisoa's husband, arrived to regain Maisoa who had never been paid for
properly. The formalities were postponed until the next day.
They all remained as guests of Ulaba'i, who was very busy
making a bamboo shelf to match the tireless industry of the
Bonaheitum man.[320]

\* \* \*

Ombomb returned from ostentatiously taking a net bag
of yams to Me'elue.

Before Nyelahai left, Yabinigi got him to remove the ad-
verse talk which he had made to the ancestors. Nyelahai had
been in good spirits, fraternizing with everyone, so that this
seemed a propitious moment. Nyelahai took the shotgun and
called on the names of his ancestral spirits, asking them to
disregard his previous talk and let Yabinigi find game.

\* \* \*

APRIL 17: At dawn the payment for Maisoa was spread out
on Ulaba'i's plaza: four rings, a tortoise shell armband, and a

[320] This is a good illustration of Arapesh suggestibility. I had
never seen Ulaba'i do a single piece of concentrated work before.

net bag of yams. Baimal, Wabe, and Gerud took the rings for future return.[321] The Numidipiheim men stayed about for a couple of hours and then Maisoa left with her brothers-in-law. She was passive and lumpish as always, saying nothing, and giving no indication of her feelings in the matter.

La'abe and Imale returned and left for Kwobilisi to get coconuts.

### ILLNESS AND DEATH OF NYELAHAI'S BABY (2)

Nyelahai and Natun returned from Sumali's, where the child had been exorcised. It had another convulsion on the way back. Now they sought a new diagnosis, either the *abuting* charm owned by Ombomb or the *yaboluh* charm owned by Maigi. Both Ombomb and Maigi exorcised the child. The other wife had gone home yesterday. Today, the mother of Natun came from Wihun to see the child.[322]

Ombomb's sister's daughter and son came up from Numidipiheim to see him.

### A *Tangget* ASKING FOR AID AGAINST SORCERY (2)

Wabe returned from Bonaheitum, reporting no success in his search for the sorcerer of the Malis man. People had called out that he was coming. Agilapwe and the two Malis men were here to receive him and hear the news. People said privately that Agilapwe himself was suspected. The party went away quietly, without any speech making.

Ulaba'i, with Whasimai, the three children, and the

[321] Previously one ring, one plate, and a piece of pig had been paid.
[322] Now I learned that all of Nyelahai's children, except his one stunted child, had died of convulsions. Then I told the parents that, although I could pull the child through an attack if I was on the spot, it would probably never be strong, and they made no further attempt to have it doctored, either naturally or magically. There is a genuine feeling against bringing up handicapped individuals.

*luluai* of Bonaheitum, all went to Liwo.[323] They were taking Anyuai back to her betrothed's household. Ibanyos went to Moholigum. Nyelahai stayed in Ulaba'i's house.

Wabe enlarged on a tale, the first rumor of which had been brought by the Bonaheitum *luluai*. A Wihun party had gone to Biligil to inquire about some sorcery. Daulap, La'abe's little thirteen-year-old nephew, had tackled a big man, shouting that he would have him jailed.[324] The Biligil man had beaten Daulap; Daulap's elder brother had then attacked the Biligil man with a club, and a Biligil man had thrown spears. No one had been hurt.

Sagu came into the village with a great lot of edible caterpillars (*oshogu?*). Menala had also gathered a lot of them. Midjulumon and Bopugenon reported another treeful seen on the way.

In the evening, Ulaba'i complained bitterly that he had no food: first Maguer, then the Bonaheitum people, then this hurricane wind directed against him, and then Numidipiheim people had brought yams which he could not eat.[325]

Nigi came in from Wihun with wooden carvings to sell us.

APRIL 18: Early this morning Mindibilip, Bopugenon, and Midjulumon went for the edible caterpillars they had seen. Miduain and Welima also went for caterpillars.

A group of Ybonimu people came here to sell us some carvings, then went on to Alipinagle to collect a pig from Tapita in payment for his wife's death. Wabe, Welima, and Temos also went to Alipinagle, ostensibly to get food, really to see this pig transaction.

Nyelahai and his wife and children remained here.

Ombomb and Sauwedjo planned to go back to their gar-

---

[323] This trundling of guests about from place to place, and even from household to household, is very common.

[324] Children are usually not taken on such trips, just because they are likely to act in this way and precipitate trouble. All of the violent talk and gesturing which accompanies talk of sorcery searches, at a distance, appeals to a child as a real image of the behavior which is to come, whereas the actual behavior of the search party becomes milder and milder until, confronted with the sorcerer or his representative, Dr. Fortune reported, they actually pat him caressingly.

[325] As they were from former *abullu* seed of his.

dens, but as it rained they postponed it until the next day.[326]

Everyone in Balidu's household was away gardening. Kule and Baimal and their household had returned to Mogiligen.

La'abe and Imale prepared to go to Wihun to hear more about the fight, but his Wihun relatives came to see him and he postponed going until the next day.

Nyelahai and his family went home, expressing resignation about the sick baby.

Matasues came up and went back with Nyelahai.

Ulaba'i returned from Liwo, leaving Anyuai there.

APRIL 19: La'abe left for Wihun with his relatives. Yabinigi went with him to see his brother-in-law. Ulaba'i went to Wihun, with Ibanyos and Segenamoya to borrow[327] some taro.

Whasimai and the child were at Aden's.

Until noon there was no one in the Walinuba end of the village when Me'elue came up on an errand and to ask if I would treat her *tinea*. She looked frail and miserable and had become doubly self-conscious about her skin. I started to treat it, but warned her that it would have to be done regularly, not at long intervals. She went back down to Moholigum.

Ulaba'i returned late at night. Temos came back at night from Alipinagle, leaving Wabe and Welima there.

## DEATH OF NYELAHAI'S BABY (3)

APRIL 20: Nyelahai's baby died in the night. Ibanyos, Whasimai, and Me'elue went to help bury it. It was buried soon after dawn; none of the men went. The comment was that Nyelahai's children always died, and in the next breath, "What had that woman been eating which made the child die?"

[326] Ever since Ombomb had become ill, as he believed from reciting his own charms, he was avoiding us and avoiding staying in the village as much as possible.

[327] When one relative makes a specific request from another for food, not connected with a feast or with ordinary hospitality, this is regarded as a loan which should be repaid. It was such a solicited loan that Wena was repaying (above, p. 359).

Lomaijo, Imale, Badui, and Midjulumon and Bopugenon who were at Balidu's had all gone to Sumali's.

Balidu and Yahalijo came up to pack up more things which they needed for a longer stay in the garden.

Ulaba'i went to Aden's place to see the Bonaheitum men, as they passed through. Then he took some taro down to Nyelahai. His wives and Aden's wives also took taro for the small family death feast which was to be made on the morrow.

## THE THEFT OF MAGINALA'S SISTER[328] (1)

Ombomb came back and called repeatedly for Wabe in Alipinagle, but got no answer. He concluded that he had gone in an attempt to get back Maginala's sister Weamale, who had eloped or been carried off, nobody knew which.

Sauwedjo and infant had stayed with Bischu. News came that the father of the doctor boy of Liwo had killed a bush pig which had been a very bad garden thief and was planning to send it to Nagawe who would smoke it and send it on to Magahine. Lomaijo, Imale, and the children went on to help with the pig, to carry it to Ahalesimihi.

Aden came up for a few minutes in the morning and went back.

APRIL 21: Ombomb, Yabinigi, and Yabenas, the wife of Anop, left for a hamlet near Magahine to get some dry coconuts from a gift friend. The day count had been sent before by Bischu.

During the day Danue (the wife of Bischu), Yabiok, and the new baby which had now been named Yabijo, passed through to join Matasues.

Temos left for Alipinagle.

Wabe returned, after a vain hunt for Maginala's sister.[329]

[328] Maginala's sister was a full-grown girl. She had been married before to a Umanep man, but had run away when there were 10 rings and two pigs outstanding. Her father's brother, who lived in a small place beyond Wihun, tried to marry her to an older man there, but she refused. Now the same group were said to be trying to marry her to a man in Numonihi, and Wabe and Ombomb were to help Maginala get her back.

[329] She was later returned to her brother.

He brought his elder brother Wupali, who lived permanently in Wihun, his wives and children and a Boinam gift friend with him.

Then Ombomb's party returned from the Beach; the people who were to have met them on the road with the dry coconuts had not come. He heard from Temos that Sauwedjo had complained about her breast again. He got Wupali to charm a leaf and took it away with him to apply to her breast.[330] Me'elue went down to Moholigum.

Balidu, Yahalijo, Kumati, and Sa'omale came back for the night. Badui and Nigimarib were in Mogiligen with Baimal, and Pidjui was with Sagu and Maigi in Manuniki.

La'abe was said to be back from Wihun, but did not answer when Ombomb attempted to call him. His wives were at work on a new planting.


## WABE'S INCREASING DISGRUNTLEMENT

Temos returned again from Alipinagle. This infuriated Wabe. After dark he beat her with a stick and she fainted. He left her lying on the Alitoa plaza and Mindibilip stumbled over her, thinking she was a log.

Just at dusk a group of emissaries from a Roman Catholic Mission school marched into the village, carrying banners, wearing shirts. They came to recruit children for the Mission school. Everyone was very uncomfortable and embarrassed. Ulaba'i protested that they had no children, that the other division had plenty and could provide children for the school. They fed the emissaries.

Nyelahai had made a small death feast for his baby that day.

APRIL 22: The Catholic emissaries left.

The Wihun people left at noon for Liwo.

Wabe took all of his plates and pots from Temos' house and put them in Welima's. He expressed his wholehearted disapproval of her entire behavior and threatened to give her to

[330] Wupali's magic had been one of the original hypotheses about Sauwedjo's breast.

a police boy.[331] Welima went about looking happy for the
first time since we had come to Alitoa. At noon Wabe packed
up both wives and went off to Alipinagle. He announced that
he was going to the Beach in search of rings, for there was a
plan on foot to use our house as a *tamberan* house after we
left. In that case, Wabe would receive rings from Bunitai, as
his sister's son, and he was beginning to worry where he could
get the rings to return them.[332]

\* \* \*

A party of Ybonimu people bound for Aitape stopped to
sell carvings to us and brought word of the date when a
Ybonimu party would come to conclude the death exchanges
for the wife of Tapita.

Winam, Budagiel, Midjulumon, Bopugenon, and Eweluen
came in. Moul, aged four, and Ite'epe, aged six, had stayed
with Sumali. Mindibilip had confessed to Dr. Fortune the
day before that Budagiel wanted to marry him. He was in a
fine flutter of excitement and apprehension, as were we, for
Mindibilip was a poor *parti*, from the Alitoa standpoint; he
was young, had no relatives, and lived in a poor and distant
village. Furthermore Budagiel was betrothed to Monau and
there was already trouble enough between Sumali and
Aden.

## RETURN OF THE MAGUER SORCERY
### DELEGATION (13)

In the afternoon the Maguer delegation, including the
*luluai* of Maguer, Mindibilip's mother's brother, the boy who
had always taken the lead before, and the ubiquitous Magahine man, arrived. They had been to Bugabihiem where a
Bugabihiem man had resorted to the old method of divining. He had chewed a magical root and dreamt about the

[331] This is a kind of bogie man threat now frequently used
among the Arapesh to keep the women in order. It aptly sums up
their opinion of the police boys, as able to deal with recalcitrant
women by rape in a way in which they cannot.
[332] This was an event at least two years distant. His premature
interest in it now merely expressed the state of anxiety in which
Wabe lived.

matter. This dream had given a new path for the exuviae, from the mother of the *tultul* of Waginara[333] to an old man of Umanep (whom Mindibilip of Maguer called *babuen*), to Whoiban of Liwo, to Bischu. A call was sent out for Bischu. Balidu, in private conversation with the Maguer men, disclaimed all sorcery for his division, but raised his eyebrows over Bischu's character.

Unabelin and his two young brothers came over and worked with me for the first time. They had gotten off with only a few informal strokes for their fight over Tapik.

APRIL 23: The whole day was taken up with Maguer affairs. Senaru of Bugabihiem had gone to Maguer and accused the *luluai*. Now the poor old man had had to walk all the way up here, lest he be accused of murder if the man died.

Bischu came striding in with Anoan on his shoulder; Balidu marched, staff in hand, up to the *Uyebis* plaza. Then there was a long conversation. Bischu disclaimed the accusations. Balidu disclaimed all accusations. The Magahine man threatened and blustered. Bischu was reminded of a pig's jaw and two rings which he had received lately and declared they had been brought to him by his cross-cousin from Waginara to take into the Plains on a sorcery search (see above, p. 233). Then conversation turned to Gerud's powers, which were unique and powerful as they combined some real Rabaul magic with *sagumeh*. Gerud suddenly, as if affected by all this praise, remarked that he had had a dream the night before, and rushed off and brought back an old piece of bamboo with a piece of areca nut quid in it, fastened in with earth. He did not say whose this was.

At noon it rained. La'abe's two wives returned to the village and Yabinigi returned. The Maguer men sat about and talked. There was no hostility this time, as the Maguer delegation were not relatives of the sick man, but merely canny older men, judicially investigating a case and clearing themselves. Their tactful attitude aroused no hostility in Alitoa. An example of the difference in tone was Balidu's confidential

[333] See above, p. 361, for previous route.

comment to them, his age mates, about Bischu, who was young and headstrong.

## GERUD'S FIFTH DIVINATION

In the evening Gerud was asked to divine again. He put on a fine show:

1. Tearing down two banana trees in great excitement, declaring the exuviae would be at their base. In the end he had to admit it was lost and found only a piece of elephant grass stalk. He then said he would find it in the morning.

2. He then fell prostrate and said that the exuviae had been moved here by Agilapwe and Debinitai of *Suabibis*. La'abe suggested Wankole (the dead brother of Maigi whose wife had formerly confessed his complicity), and Gerud agreed. He further said that Henalian had worked with Agilapwe and that the exuviae had been buried at the time that Yauwhut had died and all of his possessions had been hung on a pole.

3. The part of the exuviae which had been in the Bugabihiem *marsalai* place had been taken out by Peta of Bugabihiem and given to Imedu of Liwo to hide in the Liwo *tamberan* house instead. Imedu was helping Tapio' of Umanep, who wanted to avenge his brother's recent death upon a man of the same age and status in another village.[334] Peta had removed the exuviae from Bugabihiem at the time that they tried to catch him on an accusation concerning the illness of Nyegu of Liwo[335] (Kubi's father).

4. Tapio' of Umanep had also sent three rings via Wena to Yelegen to take into the Plains to find some filed exuviae of the Maguer man and have him killed quickly.[336]

5. Bischu was not guilty. That was all a lie.

[334] This is the impersonal revenge motive in which age, sex, and status are the requirements and there need be no hostility. This was invoked as one explanation of Kule's illness, see above, pp. 341–345.

[335] Gerud ignored here the fact that in his previous divination he had said that the exuviae was still in Bugabihiem and now put the removal back many months.

[336] The introduction of Plains sorcery here as a hypothesis means that there is a growing fear that the sick man will die. In case of death, no *marsalai* place or *tamberan* house magic is sufficient to explain it; it must always have been Plains sorcery.

Then he was asked by the *luluai* of Maguer:

6. Where was the exuviae of the wife of the *luluai* of Maguer? There was a long pause. Then he said that it was in the *marsalai* place of Waginara and had been given to him by Menau, and put there by Lopas, a Waginara woman previously married to the dead son of the *luluai* of Maguer, because her former mother-in-law had interfered with her marrying a younger brother of her deceased husband.

When Gerud had been tearing up the banana trees, Madje had called upon Bauwan to make him stop and come up on the plaza, because he was alarmed at their destruction.

After the divination there were a series of speeches by Balidu. Balidu emphasized: a, that that exuviae had been buried by Wankole, who was dead, and that it was, therefore, none of their affair;[337] b, they had said that *sagumeh* lied, but Gerud had additional magical powers obtained from Magiel, his half brother, who had brought them from Rabaul.

APRIL 24: Sumali joined his family and they all returned to the bush.

La'abe, Bischu, and Ulaba'i went to Liwo, accompanying the Maguer delegation. Balidu and Yahalijo announced their annoyance at Badui's staying so long in Mogiligen and said they would do nothing until he returned. Wadjubel, Kumati, and Sa'omale were with them. Then Balidu, Wadjubel, and Kumati went to Manuniki to help in Sagu's garden. Yahalijo and Sa'omale went to Mogiligen to bring back Badui.

Sinaba'i and his family came up. Ombomb came up and reported that the abscess on Sauwedjo's breast had burst. Me'elue came up with Yauwito'a and stayed here.

La'abe returned from Liwo; both his wives were here. He reported that no one had come to talk with them at Liwo, but had just claimed that it was all untrue. They had looked in the *tamberan* house at Liwo indicated by Gerud and had found nothing. Yelegen denied that he had taken any rings to the Plains to procure the death of the Maguer man. Bischu had gone straight back to his garden.

---

[337] Actually, Gerud had named two living persons, Agilapwe and Henalian, and had merely grunted assent to La'abe's tactful insistence on Wankole.

Menala, Welima, and Whasimai went to help Silisium harvest and bring back yams.

La'abe, Imale, and the children remained in the village, while Lomaijo went to the garden.

Ombomb went hunting with Yabinigi.

Me'elue and Yauwito'a remained in the village.

Ulaba'i and Dubomagau and Madje were here all day.

Yauwiyu and Wasijo, and Yelegen and his family came to trade food with us.

Lomaijo returned from the garden to find Kamowon crying and La'abe chagrined that he had not been able to soothe her. He scolded Lomaijo because there were no yams cooked for Kamowon who disliked taro, and he told her to cook at once. When she refused, he beat her. Lomaijo retired into her house and took a piece of firewood with which she broke up a yam or so, and then threw a fusillade of yams out of the house at La'abe where he was sitting down below.[338]

Balidu, Wadjubel, Kumati, and Nigimarib came back in the evening.

Word came that Yelusha had been visited by the punitive *tamberan* in Liwo.

APRIL 26: In the village there were only La'abe and his family, Balidu's household which had returned the night before, and Sinaba'i and Dubomagau.

---

[338] During the preceding days Imale had been menstruating, and La'abe had been paying much more attention to Lomaijo. Now his interest in Imale had revived, and he found himself on uncomfortably friendly terms with Lomaijo, which he terminated by this quarrel. In the past week there had also been a temporary shift in position between Temos and Welima and between Sauwedjo and Me'elue. This may have been an accident, but one event may have, to some extent, influenced the others. Husbands feel worried and anxious over the possible sorcery which will arise from neglecting their marked wives in favor of later comers, and the sight of one husband conciliating a neglected wife sometimes has a stimulating effect on another.

The day before a trade friend of Amambut's had sent word by Bischu and Anop to Lomaijo to bring a plate to him. This meant that La'abe would have had to go. He had been demurring about it; the gift friend was on the Beach near Kuminum; it was a long trip. Quarreling with Lomaijo was a way of pushing this demand into the background.

Sauwedjo returned with her baby. She walked the length of the village carrying it on her extended arm and displaying her breast for sympathy.

Ombomb and Yabinigi returned with no hunting luck.

## THE *Tamberan* ATTACK ON YELUSHA (1)

In the middle of the morning, Balidu came to get me, and took me to his house in great excitement. There sat Yelusha of Liwo, who had been chased away by the *tamberan*, and his newly inherited wife Talumen, the mother of Sa'omale, and, therefore, the *ashi'* of Balidu. They had run away to Yelusha's cross-cousin (*wa'en*), Balidu. Although this attack had taken place in Liwo, all of the actors were so closely involved with Alitoa that tremendous excitement reigned here. Yelusha's two wives, one of whom was a sister of Amito'a, the other, Talumen, the sister of Yelegen, had gotten into a fight, and the other wife, Niewap, had used obscenity to Yelusha. The *buanyin* of Yelusha, the doctor boy of Liwo, and his brother gathered the men, brought the *tamberan*, and attacked the place. They had cut down trees, strewn the place heavily with leaves and even dumped out the earth of the fireplace. Yelusha repeatedly emphasized this point—they had dumped out his fireplace.[339]

He further kept remarking that he and the other wife had quarreled over a pig, just a little pig, because he had given it to Yelegen, and his other wife, Yelegen's sister, hadn't wanted him to do so.[340]

[339] This is a particularly ferocious form of *tamberan* attack; everybody commented upon it. Such an attack is made when a community wishes to be rid of a man forever. It was said that it had been done here because Yelusha had no pig, but no one felt that this was a sufficient excuse.

[340] Yelegen had used this pig to pay blackmail in *Kaboibis* for the life of Soguliwali, a big man of Bugabihiem.

The relationships to Alitoa of the persons involved in this affray were as follows:

1. Yelusha was the father's sister's son of Balidu; his mother had belonged to *Toto'alaibis*.

2. The doctor boy, the *buanyin* of Yelusha, and Whoiban, were the mother's brother's sons of Balidu.

3. Yelusha's first wife, Niewap, the one who used obscenity to-

Sumali arrived in the evening and made a great speech, welcoming Yelusha and declaring that now he and Talumen should stay here forever, and never go back to Liwo.[341]

* * *

In the afternoon, Lomaijo took both children and threatened to run away. La'abe followed her and brought the children back. She went to weed her garden for the rest of the afternoon.

At dusk, Nigimarib had a fit of hysterics when he was refused food. His mother did not get back with Badui until well after dark.

---

ward him, was the classificatory sister of Amito'a, being, like Amito'a and Ombomb, the child of a *Kanehoibis* mother. (As both Yelusha and Niewap had Alitoa mothers, people in Liwo sometimes spoke of them as *atip awhilap,* one gens, because their mothers came from the same place. This equation of gentes in a distant place is very common. I found it also in Manus where observances which applied to the gens of the betrothed within one's own village applied to the whole village of the betrothed, if the betrothed came from elsewhere. It seems to be associated with localized gentes in which the concepts of descent and residence are inextricably combined.) This relationship involved Ombomb, Amito'a, and Baimal somewhat with the opposite party.

4. Talumen, the inherited wife of Yelusha, with whom he had taken refuge in Alitoa, was sure of a welcome here because her mother was married to Nyelahai and her daughter was betrothed to Badui. Furthermore, the Alitoa people had only recently busied themselves in her behalf in the sorcery accusations against Peshuhol.

It is also significant that Yelegen and Yelusha had been involved in the recent illness of the doctor boy, helping Kamil, who had been responsible for the injury. The doctor boy, just recovering from his wound, was delighted to have an excuse for attacking them, as he was the weaker, and the accident of the quarrel with his wife made it Yelusha who caught the onus of his revenge.

It is incidents of this sort which prevent the *tamberan* punitive expeditions from becoming really useful social sanctions. The provisions that the man must first become vulnerable and that the mechanism be set in motion by an individual both defeat rather than further the ends of justice.

[341] In that event there would have been a real issue about the three young children of the other wife who had remained with their mother. But this was customary oratory and not to be taken seriously. It was meant to make Yelusha feel less ashamed and more at home.

Sinaba'i went to meet Menala and the other yam-carrying women who had gone to Ahalesimihi, and they all went straight to Moholigum.

Anop passed on his way through to join Bischu on a trip to Kuminum to purchase a new kind of pig-hunting magic.[342] He was carrying a bow and arrows as they expected to pass through a deep, uninhabited belt of bush. Lomaijo had again been nagging La'abe to go with them, but he had definitely decided not to go.

APRIL 27: Balidu's household was here all day. Sumali stayed with Midjulumon and Bopugenon, on much warmer terms with Balidu than was usual. Yelusha and Talumen sat about, like people of note who have recently been bereaved and so must receive special consideration.

Ombomb went off to see Bischu about his projected trip. He took Me'elue and Yauito'a along and left them in Bischu's garden. He had returned the night before to Sauwedjo's house.

La'abe strung dog's teeth[343] for gifts for the Kobelen feast.

Lomaijo shaved her head and put on a new sago apron. Imale was in Alipinagle, helping Welima.

Sinaba'i and Menala came up to the village.

Ulaba'i, both his wives, and two children, and Kubi were here.

## KOBELEN FEAST (2)

A big man of Kobelen arrived to talk about the dog's teeth and feathers which his friends Ulaba'i and Aden were to contribute to the purchase of the *shené* dance complex. He shouted as he entered the village, but afterwards there was no ceremony at all. Ulaba'i entertained him.

\* \* \*

Dubomagau had a crying fit at dusk.

APRIL 28: Ombomb and all the young boys played the

---

[342] Described in Mead, 1940, Pt. 3, p. 448.
[343] Mead, 1938, Fig. 59, p. 275.

first top game of the season early in the morning on the Walinuba plaza.[344]

Ulaba'i left to help clear a big garden tract for Aden. Iwamini, Maginala, and Ga'olin also went.[345] La'abe, who had started to Alipinagle to ask Maginala to help with the Kobelen show, met him on the road, delivered the message, and then turned back. He later set out for Ahalesimihi with the same message. The Kobelen man stayed here all day, very quietly. Lomaijo was mildly ill, no temperature.

Ulaba'i returned in the evening with Segenamoya. Ibanyos and Anyuai had been working in Moholigum, in his old garden.

Sumali went back to Wihun, leaving his two small boys here.

Sagu and Maigi were still in Manuniki, but Pidjui had come back.

A party of Wihun boys arrived late at night, on the return trip from the Beach.

APRIL 29: In the Alitoa end of the village there was only Menala, and her baby, Anyuai, Wadjubel, and Dobumagau. Ulaba'i had gone back to Aden's. Sinaba'i was in his garden.

Balidu and Yahalijo had gone to work with Badui, on part of Aden's garden for which Badui was taking the responsibility. Yelusha and his wife went with them to work on the fence, but people were saying now that soon Yelusha would be going back to Liwo.

Ombomb and Sauwedjo were away fencing a taro patch.

In the afternoon, Sumali returned from Wihun. Wabe, Maginala, and Ga'olin came back from helping Aden fence. He had given them a small feast of soup and croquettes, but no meat.[346] Wabe said that Maginala and Ga'olin, his

---

[344] Mead, 1938, Fig. 89; Mead, 1940, p. 430.

[345] This was said to be done because Iwamini was a *gwai'oyen*, therefore, he and all of his adopted gens had to help his original gens.

[346] This absence of meat here is significant, for the reader may think that the number of pigs which have been mentioned in the preceding pages contradicts my statements about the scarcity of meat. Yet for a feast here, Aden, a big man, had no meat. Each of the pigs listed has been distributed to an enormous number of people.

*mehinis,* patrilineal cross-cousins, were helping him, because
he was Aden's *mehinen,* paternal cross-cousin.[347]

Sagu and Maigi came over for a short time and went back.
Yapul and her baby also came for a brief visit.

Nyalamidju, Nyelahai's pig-keeping wife, came up to see
her daughter Talumen; the whole quarrel was discussed
again, with the party which had returned from Aden's.

Ulaba'i came home at night, with Whasimai and the baby.

### END OF MAGUER SORCERY SEQUENCE (14)

APRIL 30: The news was drummed through the mountains that the Maguer man with the sore was dead.

\* \* \*

The Kobelen man left.

Menala and Whasimai went to Moholigum to plant taro.

Ulaba'i joined Ibanyos at Aden's. He and Sinaba'i would
go to Maguer for the mourning, it was said. Balidu had had a
slight fever four days ago for which he had taken quinine.
He had not yet washed, although he had been walking about
quite unconcernedly. But now he remembered it again and
said that he could not go to Maguer.

\* \* \*

Badui, Pidjui, and Yelusha were fencing in the new garden.
Yahalijo, Kumati, Wadjubel, Sa'omale, her mother and grandmother, all went to work in the old garden.

Sumali and the two little boys returned to the bush.

It was said that Nagawe was giving his house-thatching
feast that day.

Anyuai, Nemausi, and Dubomagau were alone in the
Alitoa end of the village.

In the afternoon, Nigi and Honali and their wives and
children arrived to sell us things. They stayed overnight with
Balidu.

---

[347] Note that this morning, when Wabe had not been known to
be included in the group and so did not need to be included in the
theory, La'abe had said that Maginala and Ga'olin were helping Iwamini. This illustrates the looseness of the forms of relationship obligation.

Wutue and Yanyibis came through. His wife was at Aden's place, preparing the ground for taro.

Sinaba'i and Menala came back to their house; with them was Miduain, just returned from helping Wamu'um, her father-in-law.

Budagiel arrived, accompanied by a small girl cousin of about 14, from Liwo.


## KABERMAN'S MEDITATIONS ON WOMEN

Our boys were very much excited by the presence of Budagiel and Wadjubel, who were obviously out to attract them. They hung about inside the house, too coy to go out and face the girls. After dinner, Kaberman, whom Wadjubel fancied, came and talked for a long time about how danger-ous women were, especially Mountain women married to more Beachward boys. "Women from inside keep too rigor-ous taboos and they are too cold. If we marry one, we must taboo also, lest the coldness of the women fasten on our skins, lest we be not able to find game easily or plant yams well. If we plant yams, pigs will go inside the garden and the yams will run away. We call these women from the Moun-tains, *ulahait mokwot,* dead logs."

"Our own women are not so cold. If they menstruate and menstruate again, once, twice, we can marry them. But in the Mountains they must taboo meat, taboo cold water, plant yams, and hunt for a year first. When our women have men-struated two or three times we try them. Then, if we can find game, all right. If we can find pigs, in our traps and in the rain, if cassowaries fall into our deadfalls, if our dogs catch phalangers, if the yams that we plant stay in the garden and fill the house to the ridge pole, we say, 'It is all right.' But if our yams fail, if our hunting fails, we rid ourselves of the coldness of the new woman. We wash with bark and leaves in the wood and set the woman afar off. We call her as a sister or a mother. We plant food. She cooks and gives us food, but the woman sleeps in one house and the man in the other. The woman sleeps with her sister-in-law or her mother-in-law, the man with his brothers. Then when a year has passed and the man has grown plenty of yams and found plenty of meat, then the two can sleep together. When we marry a woman from the Mountains, all caution us 'Such a woman is cold. Do not sleep with her quickly.'"

He added that the talk of the old men about all the foods that made one sick was probably all untrue and was only meant to keep young men in order.[348] But the talk about the dangerousness of women to a man's powers of hunting and gardening—THAT was true. And he went away to hide in the boy's house, afraid that Wadjubel would find him.

MAY 1: Gobonarra came in the morning.

Menala was sick.


## THE *Tamberan* ATTACK ON YELUSHA (2)

The doctor boy of Liwo came over to Balidu's. Everyone sat about in semi-formality. He first showed his wounds; his leg was healed, but his hand was hopelessly crippled into a knot. He admitted the plunder, but denied that he had thrown out the fireplace. He admitted that he had been angry at Yelusha over his father's illness and his failure to go quickly and get the exuviae back. There were no hostile speeches.

A party of Alipinagle people led by Wabe, who now considered himself a member of Alipinagle rather than of Alitoa, came over.

Wabe announced that he meant to stay in Alipinagle. He had started to make a garden with Balidu, but then his pig had died. Now he feared that the big pigs of La'abe and Balidu would eat all of his taro, so he planned to stay in Alipinagle where there were *no big pigs*.[349]

Ulaba'i came back at night. So did Sinaba'i. There was no more talk of anyone's going to Maguer. Ibanyos stayed at

---

[348] Note that Kaberman had been away to work and had the advantage of comparative discussions with members of other cultures. I never found a boy who had not been away who dared to voice such a skeptical note.

[349] It is interesting to compare Wabe's symbolic statements which have almost the complete affective association characteristic of dream symbols.

Aden's. Nahomen and his baby came in and stayed at Ulaba'i's.

Wadjubel and Budagiel were around all day; they cooked special food for the boys, and generally tried to make an impression. The boys' main response was fright: after all, Wadjubel and Budagiel were both big girls, older than they, and Budagiel had even been married once.

Nigi and the Wihun people had left in the morning.

MAY 2: Every single soul was gone from the village, except Nahomen. Gerud and Mindibilip had gone to Gerud's.

Aden came in with Ulaijo's Wihun son at noon.

## HONALI AND NIGI CAPTURE A GIRL (1)

In the afternoon the news was called over that there had been a big fight. Honali and Nigi had carried off the daughter of Salawasimi—she was a big girl—and her party had gone yesterday and severely beaten up Honali and Nigi.[350] Now they were summoning Badui to go and help his mother's brothers. But Badui had gone to Ahalesimihi to help his brother-in-law Nagawe finish thatching his yam house. Aden took the call and made the answers. He added that he wanted a ring in return for the one which Honali and Nigi had claimed from him when he was injured by Wankole.[351]

[350] Note that Nigi and Honali's children had most considerately brought us a lot of food just before this happened.

[351] This was a quarrel dating back many years. Aden had been jailed over the fight over Tapik. His wife Baijo had gone to stay with her sister Welenue, the wife of Wankole. No one knew when the people who were in jail would come back. No one else had ever gone to jail from Alitoa, except Amambut, who had been taken all the way to Rabaul as a witness in the case of the murder of Lomaijo's mother. After several months, Baijo decided that Aden must be dead, and she began to live with Wankole. Everyone knew about this. Aden had no brother old enough to claim her.

Meanwhile, in jail Aden dreamed continually that his net bag was being gnawed by rats. He said to himself, "What is going wrong in Alitoa. Who is sleeping with my wife and endangering my yams." When he returned to Alitoa, he and Wankole fought, and Aden was wounded. Then, after peace was restored, Honali and Nigi, the mother's brothers of Badui, Aden's *buanyin*, took advantage of this *buanyin* relationship and called for the payment

Meanwhile Balidu came up from his garden and announced his intention of going to join Honali and Nigi. Baimal came through just then, on his way to Ahalesimihi to help with Nagawe's house, but decided to go to the fight instead.

Ulaba'i and his wives and children came back in the evening.

Badui returned at nightfall.

MAY 3: Very little was known here yet about the fight. Balidu, Baimal, Badui, Pidjui, and Wabe had gone to see Honali and had been joined by Iwamini, Maginala, and Henalian.

Sinaba'i and his family came up, Miduain bringing Anim with her.

Aden stayed here all day to listen to any fight news. Matasues came up to hear about the fight. Ulaba'i stayed also.

Temos and Welima came over with some Boinam people and cooked food for our boys to show their sorrow at their leaving.[352]

There were *garamuts* going at *Suabibis'* small place. Whoiban had killed a wild pig. He had sent for Sumali; the two of them had taken it to Polip, Whoiban's brother-in-law of *Suabibis,* and from there the whole party took it to a *gabunyan* of Polip's in Suapali.


## HONALI AND NIGI CAPTURE A GIRL (2)

Balidu returned in the afternoon with a circumstantial account of every detail of the fight. While Nigi was here in Alitoa, May 2, Honali had carried off a girl named Yakop, the stepdaughter of Salawasimi, the grand old man who had called on us in April and who was the mother's brother of Nigi and Honali. This girl had been betrothed for a long time. Honali had marked her for a boy named Sha'atamau, a club-

---

for blood. At this time Aden had given them a ring. Now, some years later, these same men are said to be injured, and using the same path that they used, but as a *mehinin,* sister's son, able only to ask for a return, he demands a ring.

[352] At this time we were planning to leave in a few weeks, a plan which was changed later.

footed youth, the son of Honali's eldest brother, Whehonali. The girl objected to marrying a club-footed man. Honali paid five rings. She did not come. They paid three pieces of pig. Still she did not come. Then they asked to have the rings returned, but nothing happened. So now Honali had carried her off. The rescue was organized by her own brother Whehalowhin. He enlisted the help of Amambut of Ahalesimihi, always a ready trouble maker, whom he called *ya'en*, as a brother-in-law of his dead father. Amambut had enlisted Walawahan. The brother was also helped by all of the members of his own gens, Bausen, Ashugu, and Ambauimen. This party of five went up to Honali's place, beat up Honali, Nigi, and Honali's son. The captured girl came up during the fight and ran away with her own party! Just as they were leaving, reinforcements from another Wihun gens came up to help Honali and Nigi. Walawahan ran away. The fight was renewed. Belagomini of the reinforcing party fought Bausen, Nigi hit Amambut, etc. Details were given of each blow. The attacking party had also beaten a woman, the wife of one of the reinforcing party. They departed with most of the honors.

Amambut took the girl home with him and went into Ahalesimihi to report what he had done. Everyone was most unenthusiastic about being drawn into a quarrel which was none of their business, and they told him to take the girl back. He said the fight was over now anyway, and they would exchange rings and make peace.

Then on May 3, the Alitoa party had arrived. They challenged the girl's side to a return engagement, but they refused. They said they had fought enough, they had been angry about having the girl carried off, their anger was appeased. They would now send the girl to Honali.

Now Honali and Nigi would have to give a big feast, kill pigs, and send rings to all their *wa'en's*, and all their *wa'en's buanyins*, etc.[353] Balidu was quite convinced that the other

[353] Honali and Nigi had been particularly active in collecting rings in previous encounters. When Ombomb had been injured in the fight over Tapik, they had asked for a ring through a complicated path, and now Ombomb was asking for this back.

side would not have to make any such heavy payments; they had not started the trouble.

Baimal and Badui had gone to Ahalesimihi, although the feast was held yesterday.

Bischu and Anop had now set out for the Beach, on their search for hunting magic.

Matasues left in the evening, but the households of Sinaba'i, Ulaba'i, Aden, and Balidu stayed overnight.

MAY 4: It poured rain most of the day.

Matasues came in and went to Numidipiheim on a collecting trip for us.

He left his wife Wahewai and children here.

Anyuai, Kumati, and Aden's little *mehini'* from Numidipiheim went about with entwined arms all day. Then they were joined by three little girls from Ahalesimihi who came in with Wena's sister carrying net bags of yams.

*Garamuts* were sounding in Suapali for the pig feast.

Ombomb was here in the morning and left to do some fencing.

Me'elue then came up with some food for Matasues' household.

MAY 5: A fine day. No one here in the morning, except Balidu, his younger children, and Wadjubel.

*Garamuts* still sounding from Suapali.

At noon, Nagawe and the whole house-building party came over to sell things and dance the *tangeba* dance so that I could see it. They put on the *tangeba* costume, the special armlets of red wickerwork and *nassa* shell, and the bird-of-paradise feathers in their hair, and danced for us on Balidu's plaza, gracefully and with no fuss. Then it poured and they gathered in our house and called their genealogies. This was spur of the moment festive ending for the house-building which had occurred to someone and been taken up by the group.

## LIWO FIGHT (14)

At dusk, Polip arrived from *Suabibis*, saying that they were bringing a piece of pig to Aden to wipe out the shame of their previous encounter with the government, when Polip had received several blows from a semiofficial cane. Aden was their maternal cross-cousin. This meat was said also to wash the mud off their feet after all the journeying about, incidental to the quarrel over Tapik.

This news was called out to Alipinagle.

MAY 6: The Ahalesimihi delegation stayed overnight. The next morning, while waiting for the arrival of the Liwo party, they danced again. Walawahan and his men arrived to join them.

Then the party from Liwo marched in: Polip, Unabelin, the *tultul*, Siakaru, Whoiban, followed by Madjeke himself.[354] Madjeke made the presentation speech. The whole Liwo delegation sat down in the Alitoa end. The mothers of Yelegen and Madjeke both made informal speeches saying what they thought of women who ran about, especially Tapik.

Infected by the atmosphere and perhaps a little piqued that he had no part in it, Baimal made a speech to Walawahan, his *buanyin*, demanding rings for Walawahan's share in the recent Wihun fracas.[355]

### ILLNESS AND DEATH OF LA'ABE'S "BROTHER" (1)

Then came a call that Wambiali, a "brother" of La'abe who was domiciled with the gens of *Ashue'bis*, a gens closely associated with *Suabibis*, was ill, and the whole Liwo delegation went home.

The doctor boy of Waginara brought up a little European pig to Ombomb.

Maginala and Ga'olin caught two female wallabies. Ga'olin gave his to Wabe, his *wa'en*, who gave it to Aden, his *wa'en*. Maginala gave his to Balidu.

MAY 7: Sumali caught a tree kangaroo yesterday, and he and Budagiel brought it down.

[354] Madjeke was the big man of *Suabibis*, the father of Polip and Unabelin. This was the only time I ever saw him. He was a fine specimen of a man, tall and spare, with hawklike features and a fine arrogance.

[355] In the course of his speech, I discovered that the youth who started the fight was the same one who started the quarrel with Numidipiheim at the Alitoa feast.

### ILLNESS AND DEATH OF LA'ABE'S "BROTHER" (2)

La'abe went to Liwo to see his sick brother and reported him very ill.

\*    \*    \*

### THE NEW *Garamut* (4)

Now that Aden had meat, he was prepared to bring in the *garamut* which Wabe had had made for him. There was a crowd in the village, especially of Alipinagle people, on behalf of Wabe, waiting to help with this. The Ahalesimihi people had all gone home, and Baimal and Kule had returned to Mogiligen.

### DEATH OF LA'ABE'S "BROTHER" (3)

MAY 8: Word came at dawn of the death of La'abe's brother. Everyone was very concerned as to what was to be done about the *garamut* feast. It seemed that he had been a sick old man of no importance. La'abe gave permission for the *garamut* feast to go on.[356] Furthermore, he announced that his brother had told him that he dreamt all the time of Manuniki and that he suspected Yauwiyu. Ombomb exhorted him to fight Yauwiyu, if he came to the funeral. La'abe left for Liwo.

The dead man was the child of La'abe's father by a Liwo mother. When the father of La'abe had died in Wihun, leaving La'abe there with his mother's people, this half brother had returned to *his* mother's people. He and La'abe had always continued connections with each other, but he had never known well, or kept in touch with, the rest of the *Toto'alaibis* gens. The dead man was a widower with a son of 12. There would be no important mourning, the son was too young. The Arapesh think that mourning is for the sake

---

[356] This is a good illustration of Arapesh humanization of taboo. It was not forbidden to feast if there was a death; it was forbidden to feast if it offended living persons who were relatives of the dead.

of the living, not for the dead. He had been failing for some time and no one had ever gone to look for his exuviae, which is equivalent to the community's saying, "Well, this man is sick and useless and he might as well die." Although La'abe talked a little about sorcery now, that was mere form. Everyone knew that nothing would be done about it.

\* \* \*

## THE NEW *Garamut* (5)

Meanwhile, there was much worrying because there were not enough men to haul the *garamut* into Aden's place. They called to Mogiligen and Ahalesimihi to come and help. They decided that they would have to use boys and, therefore, there would be no bull-roarer. It began to pour almost as soon as the *garamut* party left, an evidence of the anger of Behebil over having the *garamut* taken away from his bush. Nyelahai, Henalian, and Matasues appeared after the party had left and did not go. Later, Aden's wife came down and complained bitterly that there were not enough men. They offered, in apology, that Gobonarra had told them that Ahalesimihi had come, which turned out to be untrue, for only Gabunyan had gotten off before the rain.

They finally pulled the *garamut* as far as Aden's place and then came into Alitoa for the feast. There were 35 plates and bowls of food, soup, and peeled taro and croquettes, garnished with the wallaby from Wabe, the tree kangaroo from Sumali, and the pieces of pig from Liwo.[357] Balidu garnished one large plate with a smoked rat and sent it down. There was no formality. Aden merely indicated whose plate was whose. The plates were arranged in little clusters and given to Balidu, Sumali, Nyelahai and his mother, Matasues, Agilapwe, Belatau, and Henalian, and these men distributed the plates to their younger relatives.

[357] This is a good illustration of the way meat is assembled for a minor occasion. The *garamut* was finished; everyone knew it. Then Wabe was given a wallaby which he gave to Aden when he heard that Polip was bringing the pig, and Sumali, finding a tree kangaroo at the same time, added it. The determining trigger was a bush pig killed accidentally.

In the evening, Aden made a speech saying that his helpers should not think that he had eaten the choice internal organs of the pig, the *Suabibis* people had done that.[358]

Late in the afternoon Nyelahai reported to us that the Numidipiheim people had killed his pig and so we were not to allow them to carry anything for us.[359]

MAY 9: The day opened with speeches. Balidu demanded pigs from the doctor boy of Liwo, on account of his wound, and Yelusha because he had been insulted.

Iwamini had gone up at dawn to start beating the new *garamut* which should have been beaten all night, but nobody cared to stay up. Its tone was very bad, Baimal said, because the men who had hauled with him had slept with their wives the night before. Wabe said it was because they did not have enough men to cut a big enough slit.

A party of Bonaheitum men passed through and left a sorcery *tangget* in the Government rest house. This meant, "We have the exuviae of someone in this village. Better come and find out about it."

La'abe reported that Yauwiyu had offered food to all the mourners at his brother's funeral, and he had accepted it and not vomited, so Yauwiyu was not guilty.[360]

Salawasimi was here in the evening and made a speech to Baimal about an *abullu* which he was going to make. He was an old man, and soon he would be dead, but anyway he was going to make an *abullu*. Baimal answered his speech: he too would make an *abullu;* they both stamped about in fine style.

MAY 10: At dawn, just before leaving, Salawasimi made a speech to Balidu, saying he had better come and take out the

---

[358] Later, the *Suabibis* people explained that *they* had not done it, but the *women* had been hungry and so had eaten the entrails. This was regarded as adequate explanation, for women are not socially responsible.

[359] This represented a fine confusion between native and white ideas. One of the sanctions in native life is to refuse to let a hamlet help in carrying a pig; the labor is slight and the feasting good. Carrying for the white man is difficult and usually disliked, but here Nyelahai had assimilated it to the same pattern.

[360] This is the usual result. A man accuses another vigorously, but when he takes his food, he does not vomit, and so acquits him.

yams which Balidu habitually planted in his garden. He was an old man and he was tired of looking after them. Balidu replied smoothly that of course he would come and harvest his yams, but, no, he couldn't think of breaking the old tie, so that he would come and plant them again next year. Then Salawasimi departed.[361]

That morning we sent a whole party of carriers down to the Beach with material culture: Wabe, Ombomb, La'abe, Ulaba'i, Gabunyan, Naushe'e, Pidjui, Badui, Madje, Iwamini, Mai, Midjulumon, Sinaba'i, Nigimarib, Naguel, Dubomagau, Temos, Welima, Wadjubel, and Kumati. This exodus effectively disorganized village life for the next few days. In addition, I had a bad attack of malaria; as a result the *Diary* for May 11 and May 12 is worthless.

Lui of Dunigi was here the evening of May 12.

MAY 13: The carrying party got back and scattered to their gardens.

Gabunyan killed a pig which was nearly dead and brought it over to Baimal, his *wa'en,* who gave it to Ombomb, who had it cooked, to take to Wihun. Dr. Fortune planned to go into the Plains.

MAY 14: Ombomb, Sauwedjo, and Miduain took the cooked pig to Wihun.

Dr. Fortune left for the Plains, accompanied by Sumali, Naushe'e, Gabunyan, Maigi, La'abe, Gerud, Henalian, and Maginala, and Ombomb joined the party at Wihun. Wabe did not go because he had a bad foot.

In the village, there were only the households of Sinaba'i and Balidu, and the wives and children of Ulaba'i, La'abe, and Sumali. Yapul and her two children came over to stay at Balidu's.

News came that three Bugabihiem men had been summoned to Wewak, charged with sorcery against the Maguer man who was dead.

Balidu and his household left in the evening to sleep in the garden.

[361] This had been a kind of test visit under the guise of ceremonial speech making, covering a rapprochement between Balidu and Salawasimi, who had been involved on opposite sides of the Honali-Nigi fight.

MAY 15: There was a general exodus from the village. Sumali's family left. Sinaba'i, his family, La'abe's two wives, all went to Ahalesimihi to help with Nagawe's house.[362] They were joined by Baimal's family on the way.

Ulaba'i went to the Olem River.

Baimal painted bark paintings for us. Badui fell ill. He had been helping Baimal.

A party of Ybonimu men passed through, carrying a note from Dr. Fortune to the District Officer. They were on their way to report a very brutal murder of a Plainsman by the Abelam people who, they said, had enticed the man there, set on him, cut him up, and buried him in several ant hills.

MAY 16: Balidu and his family were back. Badui was still ill.

Welenue and her children, Yabenas and Nigat, the sister of Anop, passed through on their way to Mobilinigum.

Biagu brought word that the Bugabihiem men had not been put in jail.

Ulaba'i returned at dusk and said that he had heard the *kiap's garamut* in Liwo.

Unabelin came back with Sagu and Sa'omale who had been helping with the yam harvest of Unabelin's father.

There began to be a fear that Badui was ill from a *sagumeh* charm.

MAY 17: About nine in the morning shouts came from Alipinagle that Dr. Fortune had been attacked in the Plains. The whole village immediately began to mourn at the top of their voices, "Alas, the poor master, he is dead." With some difficulty—I never learned to understand the peculiar pronunciation used in the shouted communication—I found out that a messenger had arrived in Alipinagle with a letter, and that Iwamini had already left Alipinagle with it. I sent Biagu off to meet him. While the village mourned, I tried to calculate how help could be got in. Biagu and Iwamini returned, saying that Dr. Fortune had been attacked with a tomahawk in the arm and head, and had been carried into Kaboibis. They handed me the tobacco tin which con-

---

[362] Note how very slowly a house which is built ceremonially is put together.

tained the message which read, "Please send me more tea
to keep negatives, and some lamp mantles." It was headed
"Ilapweim," and undated. I talked it over with the natives,
who agreed that the rumor of hurt was probably a lie, as
only the message and no Alitoa man had come. There was
also the rumor that the Ybonimu men had brought which
might have been responsible. Reassured, but still very much
in the dark, I sent tea, mantles, and bandages, which were
taken on by a Bonaheitum man passing through Alipinagle.
There was no further news all day. The *garamut* in Liwo
was beating for the coming of a white man, later identified
as a master from Salamoa.

## PRESENTATION OF A PIG

In the late afternoon, Matasues, accompanied by Anop
and Nigat, brought up a fastened pig and gave it to Badui.
He presented it with very little ceremony, but with the following speech:

"I give this pig to you. If you want to give it to your *buanyin*, do. If you want to give it to your *gabunyans*, do. Aden
gave me a piece of pig from his feast. So I made a pig trap.[363]
The pig that I gave to my sister (Nigat) when it was very
small, this pig went inside. She fastened it. I was angry. I
said, 'Why did you hurry up? Why did you fasten him? I
wanted him for a feast in the future.' She cried. So I said,
'Never mind. I will take it to Badui.' I wanted them to save
this pig, but they caught it. They fastened it."

Badui took it on in to Honali and Nigi.

MAY 18: The next day was disorganized by the presence
of carriers, first the Liwo carriers and then the need for Alitoa

[363] This whole procedure illustrated the confusion between wild
game and domestic pigs—the domestic pig was uninjured, but once
inside the trap it was treated as a wild animal. It also illustrates the
function of having several exchanging partners. Badui could not
give the pig to Aden, his *buanyin*, for Aden was already in arrears.
But he did owe one pig to Nigi, so he could use it in that way.
Meanwhile, Matasues had banked his pig against the future, not
quite as effectively as if the original were still alive, but even that
pig would have been subject to possible accidents at any point.

carriers. The master from Salamoa, the late Mr. L. F. Exton,[364] was on his way into the Plains, recruiting for the gold fields.

Sumali and Maigi arrived at dusk, with a note from Dr. Fortune, reporting everything all right, and they started a rumor that we were going into the Plains. They were simply intoxicated with the trading possibilities, and Sumali talked in lyric terms of the amount a few beads would buy.

## THE AFFAIR OF SILISIUM AND HIS BROTHER'S WIFE

Word arrived in the evening that Manum had discovered that his wife had been seduced by his younger brother Silisium. The affair was reported with great circumstantiality and not a little laughter, for both Manum and Silisium were thick-set, middle-aged men, and Homendjuai was a worn mother of adolescent children. Dr. Fortune had refused to take Silisium into the Plains with him, because he had claimed that he was too ill to carry anything heavier than a lamp. Silisium had returned to Ahalesimihi and met Homendjuai, his elder brother's wife, on the road and copulated with her. Manum spied on them, came up to the village, accused Silisium, who denied it, and promptly ran away with his own wife to his wife's brother's garden. Then Lomaijo, whom Homendjuai called "younger sister," as "younger brother's wife," and whom Manum called "daughter," obtained a confession from Homendjuai. There had been three previous incidents: when Homendjuai took yams to Belal in Wihun, Manum saw enough to make him suspicious; when they all slept at Awidibigemi, on the way back from Wihun, here Manum also suspected; once in Ahalesimihi. Now this had occurred, and Manum had declared himself weary of the whole business and ready to fight Silisium, or else he wanted a ring to soothe his feelings.[365]

Manum had gone home to beat Homendjuai, but her "mother" and sister were there helping her with the garden.

---

[364] Mr. Exton was killed a few months later by a group of natives nearer the Sepik River.
[365] Mead, 1935b, pp. 131–132, for the text of one of the accounts which I received. The above account is a summary of several.

If he had beaten her, there would have been no one to cook for them and entertain them, so he didn't beat her.

The comment in the village that night was all amusement and slightly salacious gossip. There would be no fight. Everyone was sure of that. "Were Manum and Silisium not brothers?" "If it had been another man, they might have fought. But these are brothers." "It is all one gens, they will quickly make peace." "Within one gens there will be no fight."

### Kobelen Feast (3)

MAY 19: About 9:30, the *tultul* of Kobelen who was: the elder "brother" of our boy Saharu, the father of Kaberman's betrothed wife, and the gift friend of La'abe, arrived, accompanied by a Kobelen man named Konaligu. They carried a ceremonial spear, topped with cassowary feathers which formally summons promised contributions to a feast. They set the spear in the ground in front of La'abe's door. People called out to Aden and Nyelahai to come and receive them also, but neither appeared. The Kobelen men took the staff and placed it in front of Ulaba'i's door also, calling out to him that they counted five days now to the feast. The staff was finally returned to La'abe's doorway.

The messengers sat about all day, cooked for by Sumali's household, gossiping with Sumali and Balidu. At dusk, some children saw a firefly light on the spear and they told Balidu. He and Sumali sent for La'abe and told him that the firefly had probably been the ghost of his father, who had come to warn him that he was being sorcerized and he had better go and get some medicine from me.[366]

Balidu was still ill and I gave him calomel.

[366] A firefly is always interpreted as a ghost. Any unusual occurrence which seems tinged with the supernatural can be interpreted as a warning about sorcery. Now note that Balidu was ill, but the only treatment he was receiving was my medicine. When La'abe is warned, he is, therefore, told to drink my medicine also. This tendency to take the clue for the next action from the most recent event rather than to follow any definite plan is one of the most characteristic aspects of Arapesh lack of a fixed structure.

MAY 20: A call came from Alipinagle that Henalian had
fastened a pig. He got Madje and Wabe to help him carry it
to Wihun, where he gave it to Honali and Nigi.

Only women and children were left in the village, when a
huge party of Plainsmen arrived at the Government rest
house. They asked for food, and hastily, worriedly, the
women sent food out to them. There was a general atmosphere of panic until they left.

MAY 21: Dr. Fortune got back with his first Plains collection. The day was devoted to unpacking and the evening to
developing photographs. The village life was still disorganized by the carriers' return.

From now on I will give only events, and will no longer
record the presence or absence of every person in the village.
I think an adequate sample of this sort has now been presented to the reader.

## KOBELEN FEAST (4)

MAY 22: Events centered about La'abe's house. First, there
was a discussion as to whether La'abe should or should not
fasten a pig for the Kobelen show.[367] La'abe had only two
pigs and one was already promised to Wambibi, his brother-
in-law. La'abe asserted that he wouldn't take his only pig, he
wouldn't go at all, no one from Alitoa would go, everyone
would be too ashamed to take only feathers and tobacco
with no pigs.

\* \* \*

## ACCUSATION OF ADULTERY AGAINST IMALE (1)

This was followed by a quarrel between Lomaijo[368] and

[367] This pig was one which he owed Kobelen for the *midep*
dance which he was helping to purchase. Kobelen was calling in all
their small outstanding debts, so as to meet the big payment for
the *shené* next week.
[368] Lomaijo possessed a curious streak of social responsibility
which she always seemed to use to aggravate her relationships with
La'abe. Whenever he was failing to meet some obligation, there
was pretty sure to be some form of quarrel with Lomaijo.

Imale. Ombomb and Sauwedjo had brought back a tale about an encounter between Imale and Lui, the big Dunigi man, on the road. When La'abe had gone into the Plains before, on the sorcery hunt for Kule, he had sent Imale and her mother to Wihun to take some yams. On the road, they had met Lui and another Dunigi man. Lui had thrust his hand inside Imale's apron and had threatened to copulate with her, but her mother was there and nothing had happened. Sauwedjo had told this tale to La'abe, who questioned Imale and seemed satisfied with her answers. But Lui had once wanted to marry Imale, and La'abe was not quite convinced. He told Imale that if her garden work suffered he would beat her. This had happened yesterday. Now, today, Lomaijo brought it up again, accusing Imale of all sorts of delinquencies and laziness in gardening. La'abe made another speech in which he said that when he met Lui he would confront him with his behavior and would say, "What? Should our women go and marry you Plainsmen? True, your women envy the ornaments our women wear and run away to us. But if one of our women went to marry one of you Plainsmen, she would become an ugly looking wreck with no proper ornaments."[369]

Souato'a sat with her father and hung her head during the quarreling between the two women.

### KOBELEN FEAST (5)

MAY 23: This was the day set to go to Kobelen. Dr. Fortune had decided to organize a party and go. La'abe, at the last moment, decided to fasten his pig, and he sent for Nyelahai, and he and Ombomb and Dr. Fortune started off ahead, to follow the formal path that a pig must take.[370]

[369] Lui was very sensitive about belonging to the backward Plains. He himself had paid a pig to the old men, so that he could continue to wear a loin cloth, and he had married his wife in the Mountain fashion and refused the Dunigi custom of the long honeymoon seclusion. So La'abe knew that any speech referring to the inferiority of Plains custom would hurt.

[370] From here on, I shall merely record the reverberations in the Mountains of the Kobelen feast.

All of our boys left with Dr. Fortune, except Mindibilip, who stayed to cook for me.

Only Balidu and women and children remained in the village, as the people gradually left for a long breathing spell. Wena, Amambut, and Silisium's son came over to pick some of Wena's coconuts. Imale went back to Ahalesimihi. Lomaijo had gone to the Kobelen feast with La'abe.

Later in the day, Sumali, Baimal, and Kule took rings and went to Kobelen too.

MAY 24: Balidu and his family left for their gardens.

The only people in the place were Welima and the children of Matasues. The wife of Nigi and some Dunigi friends of Aden's passed through.

Sumali's family, except Budagiel and Ite'epe, came down in the evening.

MAY 25: The village was empty. I had an attack of malaria.

MAY 26: Unabelin came over, and I worked with him all day. In the afternoon some Ahalesimihi people came in, including the young wife of Gabunyan. She reported the last act in the seduction by Silisium of his brother's wife. Silisium had returned to Ahalesimihi and paid Manum a ring and Manum had said, "The talk can die now."

MAY 27: Ombomb, Ulaba'i, and Sumali got back from Kobelen, very hungry. Those who had close friends in Kobelen had stayed, because there had been food for them. Sumali was feeling additionally discouraged because Manum and La'abe had decided to plant their yams together, and not to plant with him. He had heard about the ring which Silisium had paid Manum.

There was some gossip over recent events.

## HONALI AND NIGI CAPTURE A GIRL: CONCLUSION (3)

The girl had been sent to Honali and Nigi, but she had refused point blank to marry the club-footed nephew. Then Nigi had proposed that he marry her himself. Honali did not approve of this; Nigi was too old. She had been paid for for a member of the younger group. Nigi had made a special trip to Balidu's garden to find out what he thought. Balidu had approved of Nigi's plan. But then the girl had objected again; they had finally married her to the brother of her original betrothed.

## THE *Tamberan* ATTACK ON YELUSHA: CONCLUSION (3)

After fencing with Aden and Balidu, Yelusha had returned to Liwo without making any propitiatory payment to his *buanyins* who had instituted the attack.[371]

## DEATH OF WENA'S BABY

The baby had died the night of the 23rd (the day Wena had come to Alitoa for coconuts), and the news had only just now reached Alitoa. After some talk, it was decided that Gerud should divine for the cause of the baby's death.

## GERUD'S SIXTH DIVINATION

Gerud ran around and found a piece of bamboo with an areca nut in it, which he said was Aden's, but about which he made no further accusation.

Then he fell down and said:

1. Wena's child had died from sorcery. Halesiu, the Boinam wife of Balili, had put its exuviae in the Yapiaun *tamberan* house.[372]

2. Honali's pig had gone wild because Salawasimi had sent rings to an old man in Boinam to make *wishan* against it.

---

[371] This is the stubborn way in which the Arapesh evoke a certain amount of form from their amorphous culture. The doctor boy should not have emptied out the fireplace, and when he did, Yelusha refused to obey the rule that a man so banished must pay a pig before he returns.

[372] Halesiu was here pictured as taking the part of her sister's husband Nagawe, who had grown Wena. When he returned from work, Wena had gone to live with Manum and Silisium instead of with Nagawe. Any contact with the *tamberan* is enough to kill an infant. A woman's approaching the *tamberan* was explained by her being a Plainswoman not afraid of Mountain *tamberan*.

Salawasimi had paid rings when he went to Boinam to mourn the death of the father of the *tultul*.[373]

3. Sinaba'i had been sorcerized.[374]

4. Dubomagau had been sorcerized.[375]

5. Ombomb had been sorcerized.[376]

6. Wena had been sorcerized.[377]

Then he was asked by a little Maguer boy who was there with Mindibilip:

7. Who entered the boy's house about three weeks before, when Kaberman had said he saw a ghost? Gerud answered: Lomaijo.[378]


## Visit of Nugum Potters

MAY 28: The village was empty again, except for Balidu's children, and Alaijo, Minya, and Amus. Toward evening a party of Nugum potters came through and sought hospitality from Alaijo, but she was afraid of them. She said she had no food and told them to sleep in Kule's house. She and the children then left for the bush. They did so, but were so angry that they burned up part of the door for firewood.[379]

---

[373] Gerud knew about this trip, and it gives just the right circumstantial touch. This Boinam man had died just before Dr. Fortune's second trip into the Plains. It was, of course, inevitable that any accident to Honali's pig should be attributed to Salawasimi after the recent fracas.

[374] He had been ill just before the Kobelen feast.

[375] This was gratuitous free association; Dubomagau, Sinaba'i's small son, had not been ill.

[376] Ombomb had been ill on the trip into the Plains and had returned with all his hair shaved off.

[377] More free association from Wena's baby's death.

[378] Whether Gerud made this pointless accusation to divert attention from Wadjubel, who would have been the obvious suspect, because any accusation against Wadjubel would have turned everyone's mind to his own sister Budagiel, or whether this was just carelessness, I do not know. This was Gerud's poorest and least interesting divination.

[379] This incident illustrates why, whenever Baimal and Amito'a threatened to separate, Baimal's brothers always remonstrated with him, that he could not afford to lose Amito'a who knew her part in life, while Alaijo did not.

A party of *Suabibis* people came from Liwo to trade and tell about the big dry coconut exchange feast they were going to give Suapali.

### KABERMAN'S RETURN TO ALITOA

In the afternoon, Kaberman returned, tired out. Besides his usual duties as cook, he had had to act as informant for Dr. Fortune on Kobelen personalities and relationships; the undue mental strain had exhausted him. The double role of being a member of his own village and a white man's servant within it had also been new and trying. He went straight to the boy's house. There he heard the tale that Gerud had said Lomaijo had come into the boy's house to see him. They also told him that Ombomb had added the detail that Kaberman had struck a match and seen who it was. Almost simultaneously with hearing this tale a centipede bit Kaberman. He came over to me, much agitated, between the pain of the bite, his rage and fear at the accusation, and a general sense of loneliness and betrayal. "Everyone is angry at me. I did not see anyone. I only heard. Ombomb lies when he says I struck a match. They all lie. They all lie and they all believe the lies. Now everyone will work sorcery against me. I cannot stay here. I must go home at once. This place is full of anger against me." I sent for La'abe, who very sensibly said that he was not angry and that he knew it was nonsense. I pointed out that Gerud's ghost always lied about sex affairs. Gerud was summoned and came in looking pale and wan. He said he must have eaten something to spoil his divination. He was tired of it. They had asked him and his control ghost had lied to him. It was the Maguer boy's fault for asking the question. Amity was restored and La'abe contributed the final touch. The centipede which had bitten Kaberman was a ghost that was angry because he and Kaberman, who really belonged here now, had been away so long.

* * *

Nyelahai returned from Kobelen, and the next day he and Matasues and Ulaba'i planned to set out for Boram to meet

Monau, as a message had come through that Monau had landed there with a great deal of property.

La'abe and Baimal also returned from Kobelen.

After the scene with Kaberman, La'abe made another speech about what he was going to say to Lui about the Imale incident.

MAY 29: Nyelahai, Matasues, Iwamini, Madje, Sumali, and Ulaba'i set off in high good spirits to bring Monau home.[380]

La'abe was here all day, while Lomaijo went to the garden. In the afternoon they left to help Amambut harvest his yams. Imale was still in Ahalesimihi.

Sinaba'i was here, sick for no apparent reason, except the feast and the alternating hunger and food.[381]

Badui, Baimal, Pidjui, Balidu himself, Gerud, and Mindibilip fenced Balidu's taro garden.

MAY 30: Balidu, Baimal, Sagu, Maigi's youngest sister, Yahalijo, and Kumati all went to Wambibi's small place in Wihun to collect some taro which Wambibi owed Balidu, as part of a preliminary payment for the big pig.

Menala went down to Moholigum, Sinaba'i remained here, exhibiting his illness. The village was deserted, except for Pidjui, Nigimarib, and Dubomagau who stayed with Sinaba'i.

Balidu decided not to go all the way to Wihun, but turned back wearily to Alitoa.

Menala returned in the evening.

Some Wihun people came to sell things to me.

MAY 31: Balidu's party returned from Wihun.

## A SYMBOLIC THEFT

Agilapwe and a party of his affinal relatives from Malis came to sell me food. It was all poor, wormy, not worth buying. As I refused one article after another, I could see sullenness mounting in the eyes of the strangers. Out of the corner of my eye I saw a box of trade matches lying on a far table at

---

[380] Their relationships were: sister's husband, brother, half brother, betrothed wife's father, and sister's husband, respectively.
[381] And, of course, Gerud's divination.

the edge of the verandah. When the party had left I found the matches had disappeared. We used these matches as small change; there were hundreds of them about and no chance of identifying them. But I walked up to the Walinuba end, where the party was sitting with Balidu, and demanded stormily, "Who stole my matches?" A young man of Malis, a returned work boy, took the box from his net bag and handed it to me, saying seriously, "I didn't steal them, I just took them." People talked of this dreadful theft for weeks afterwards. Every new caller would bring up the subject and express his indignation.[382]

Late in the afternoon, Sinaba'i and his household left for Moholigum.

JUNE 1: I let Gerud go with his father to help him fence. The boy was still looking wan and ill, and insisting that he had inadvertently eaten something which he should not.[383]

The Nugum visitors passed through on their way home. Balidu stayed in his house and did not greet them as they passed. This was the punishment which he had said he would mete out to them, when he heard of their damage to Baimal and Kule's property. After a ferocious speech of disapproval, I had asked him what he was going to do with them. He answered, as if he were promising them six months in jail, "When they pass through again, I shall sulk."

The village was deserted all day, except for Balidu. In the late afternoon a call came across the hills from *Suabibis* saying that three Government officials, one of them a doctor, and Dr. Fortune were coming, and everyone in the locality was to muster in Alitoa. There was frantic beating of *garamuts*. Later, Ulaba'i and his party came in saying that Yabinigi had reported that Monau was not at Boram, and that Dr. Fortune

[382] I consider this a good example of pathological stealing, that is, theft which was merely symbolic. The party felt hurt and rejected. I had bought nothing of all they had carried so far. The boy took the matches compulsively, out of his need. That would explain his returning them at once, and, at the same time, denying the theft. He was a sophisticated work boy and knew I could never identify a box of matches.

[383] The inevitable Arapesh expression of guilt.

had told him to return here because the District Officer[384] was coming.

People began to stream in. Their whole behavior was in marked contrast to their behavior during some affair of their own, when everyone was busy and preoccupied and it was almost impossible to get anyone to answer a question. Here no one had anything to do. Some of the children had been painting with paper and paint which I provided; in the evening, the men came in and also painted. No one had any important court cases; no one was frightened by the coming visit of the District Officer; it was simply an external event to be lived through with as little boredom as possible.

La'abe and Ombomb were both a little skeptical of the rumor. La'abe had had to leave Amambut's yam harvest in the middle. Badui and Gerud returned, breathless, after having cut only one tree for Sumali's fence.

JUNE 2: In the morning they did a little desultory work on the road; Yauwiyu started to rebuild Aden's ground house that had blown down long before. Dr. Fortune arrived at noon with the news that the rumor was entirely false, Ulaba'i had misunderstood. As he passed through Kobelen he had seen that they were giving a feast to wash their hands that day.

It then transpired that yesterday Matasues' big pig had disappeared and his wife had traced it to Belatau's pig trap which showed signs of having been recently used. Matasues then got Bunitai, newly initiated into the practice of divining, to divine; he said that Belatau had killed the pig. Ombomb, Matasues, and Ulaba'i went over and forcefully dragged a confession out of Belatau and his wife.[385] Agilapwe, who had received none of the pig, came back and spent the day here to reaffirm his solidarity with Alitoa.[386]

---

[384] Throughout this account I shall use the term District Officer for brevity, although actually there was only an Acting District Officer stationed at Wewak during this period. From the standpoint of the natives, however, he functioned as a full District Officer.

[385] This antisocial, sly behavior was characteristic of broken-down places like Manuniki, full of the old and the degenerate.

[386] People said if he had eaten a piece of the pig, he would have been too ashamed to come.

People started to disperse, grumbling mildly.
In the evening, Lui of Dunigi came to sell us a mask.

### ACCUSATIONS OF ADULTERY AGAINST IMALE: CONCLUSION (2)

In the evening, La'abe charged Lui with the Imale affair. His accusation, however, was very mild. Lui got out of it by saying that he had really been talking to Imale about another woman. He further made a few remarks about, "Would I talk thus to a woman on my hereditary path? This is the path I value. I always travel on it. My father traveled on it. It is the path of pigs and of wealth. It is the path to the sea. I would not talk lightly to a woman here. Surely no one would think I would talk so *on my Path*."[387]

La'abe very eagerly and easily accepted all of his excuses.
JUNE 3: The village was again deserted.
Kule, Baimal, and Balidu went to the Suapali feast which was still in progress.
Sumali's and Kule's families remained here.
La'abe came back late at night with a great roll of sago bark for walling Nagawe's house.
JUNE 4: The village was quiet, with everyone away. Baimal, Balidu, and Ulaba'i returned at night. La'abe and Baimal were in Ahalesimihi helping Nagawe.
JUNE 5: Empty village. Kule, Badui, and Pidjui returned from Suapali. Kule's family had already gone home and he followed them.
JUNE 6: Village deserted.

### YAPIAUN FEAST (1)

It was said that Balili, helped by Mogiligen men, was hunting meat for the Yapiaun feast.
Nagawe was walling his house. Wabe was planting a small garden. Ombomb was helping Aden fence his garden.
Sumali had gone into the Plains, and returned with a dog he had purchased in Kaboibis.

[387] The old threat of sorcery.

JUNE 7: Village still deserted.

In the evening Bischu and Iwamini and their wives brought up their babies for castor oil.

### YAPIAUN FEAST (2)

JUNE 8: Village deserted. News shouted that Sumali had killed a wild pig and given it to Balili for his coming feast.

JUNE 9: Kaberman came down with fever.[388]

At dusk, Miegelian, the wife of Wamu'um and the mother of Wena, came up to the village with Wabisu and the deaf child and announced that she was leaving Wamu'um forever and going to live with Wena. They slept in Bischu's empty house.

JUNE 10: The next morning Ombomb returned from clearing land. The wife of Wamu'um talked to him at some length and now merely announced that she was going to stay with Wena until after the harvest.[389]

Then she left for Ahalesimihi.

About noon, people began to come into the village. La'abe and his wives and Amambut came in, La'abe from working on Nagawe's house, Lomaijo from helping Amambut store his yams.

[388] This fever attacked everyone in our household, a heritage from the Kobelen feast. The Arapesh, quite accustomed to epidemic following a feast, explained it by the belief that each dance is accompanied by disease-bringing charms. This fever somewhat resembled dengue; there was no abatement in the temperature from the time it set in. It was epidemic at this time all along the coast as far as Wewak.

[389] Ombomb gave me the background of the quarrel. He had given a little pig to feed to Keali, the adolescent daughter of Wamu'um and Ombomb's dead sister's daughter. One day when Keali had gone to weed taro and only Miegelian was at home, a hawk had got Keali's pig, but had not got Ulaba'i's little pig which she was looking after. Later, Ombomb had told Bunitai that Miegelian was responsible for the death of the pig. Bunitai went home and accused her. She retaliated by saying it was foolish to give a pig to feed to a girl whose breasts weren't fully up. Wamu'um took his daughter's part and beat his wife, the stepmother. She took Wabisu and the deaf boy and left, saying that she was going to her son permanently but that later the children should go back to the stepfather who had adopted them.

There was much shouting all day about Balidu's pig which had wandered away.

Ulaba'i's family returned at dusk.

Ombomb was preparing to go to Aitape to get a pig, accompanied by Anop, Bunitai, and Ga'olin.

Ulaba'i, La'abe, Nyelahai, and Amambut were preparing to go along the coast towards Wewak on a trading trip to buy baskets.[390]

They shouted out for Bunitai to come and divine over Aden's sore which was worse again.[391] He did not come.

### BUNITAI'S FIRST DIVINATION

However, Bunitai had divined the night before Wena had sent yams and tobacco to him, asking him to work on the cause of his baby's death.[392] Bunitai said that Manum was responsible, that he had taken the infant's exuviae and put it in a tobacco tin and hidden it in the ashes of his fire, because he and Silisium did not want Wena's children to grow up and inherit their hunting grounds as co-inheritors with their children. He represented Manum as saying: "Why should he stay here on my land and beget sons to grow up strong and tall like him, to take the land from my children.

[390] Both of these proposed trips were following up friendships made in work boy days. They were non-traditional and, in a sense, extra-legal paths, followed under the Pax Britannica.

Note that now that this group had harvested their yams and given their feast, there came a period of free wandering. It was also now very good weather, bright, with little rain.

[391] Aden's sore had opened again and he now was thinking continually of the piece of exuviae which Gerud had found at the beginning of his last divination, see above, p. 401. He was said to have handed it to Ombomb. What had Ombomb done with it? Had he given it to Sumali and Balidu? Had they hidden it again? Probably. Aden had been thinking about Sumali and Balidu all the time and at night he dreamt about them.

This is a good illustration of two common points: 1, the tendency to worry most about a known piece of exuviae regardless of the question of motives; 2, the tendency to revert to one's own suspicions, in most cases, one's own hostilities, rather than to rely on such formalities as divination.

[392] Bunitai and Wena were stepbrothers.

I have many sons to divide this bush. This is not his place. It is arrogance on his part to come here. Let him go back to Alitoa where he belongs. Then if he begets children they can live.[393]

[393] Now there are several interesting points about this interpretation. Bunitai had followed Gerud's lead; it was because Wena was living in a foreign place that the trouble had come. But Bunitai wanted to get Wena back to Alitoa, whereas Gerud merely wanted to send him back to cooperate with Nagawe in Ahalesimihi. Furthermore, there was probably a spice of rivalry in Bunitai's blaming Gerud's mother's brother for the deed, in this, his first divination, where he worked on the same problem as Gerud. This rivalry became clearer in later divinations.

Later, I discussed this death of Wena's baby with Wabe, asking him who had killed it. "Manum, by *sagumeh*. (Manum knew no *sagumeh*, by the way.) Bunitai had said so." "But," I objected, "Gerud's ghosts said something different." "Then Gerud's ghost had lied." "Why?" Wabe thought a while. "Had Wena paid Gerud to divine?" "No." "Ah, well, that was the reason. Gerud had not been paid and so his ghost had lied. Now Bunitai had been given food and tobacco and so the ghosts had told the truth." This showed how faith in Gerud was waning, for two months ago Wabe had believed Gerud without having paid a retaining fee.

But no one ever did anything about this accusation against Manum, who never even troubled to deny it. Manum knew no *sagumeh*; Arapesh people did not sorcerize each other's babies. Gerud had been within the bounds of possibility when he accused the Plains wife of Balili; the Plains people were, after all, death-dealing sorcerers. But in the mountains infants died because their mothers ate from *marsalai* places, or from the accidental effects of protective charms placed on food, not from black magic of the sorcery type. Furthermore, it was true, as Gerud had said, that Wena was actually working for Manum when he should have been working for Nagawe. The whole accusation was stupid. People were beginning to shrug their shoulders over this divining. Gerud had been falling down, then with Bunitai's entrance, his stupidity reacted on Gerud. The term, "the ghost must have lied" came up oftener.

Actually, no form of divining lasts very long in Arapesh because of the impossible demands that the diviner should find exuviae and that the sores affected should immediately recover. Compared with the Admiralty Island Manus requirement, a diagnosis in a case of malaria, a confession, repayment, and the recovery of the patient, the Arapesh requirement is impossible to maintain. And combined with the impracticability of their pattern of divining, they have a greater skepticism and preference for detective methods and for following the lines of their own suspicions.

JUNE 11: Saharu came down with the fever.

Village empty.

JUNE 12: Ombomb left for Aitape by himself; La'abe, Nyelahai and Ulaba'i for the Wewak coast.[394]

Salawasimi passed through, taking a pig to Whoiban, a classificatory brother-in-law.

JUNE 13: Village deserted, except for Balidu's household, and Lomaijo and her baby. Unabelin was here working with me.

JUNE 14: Sinaba'i and Menala and the children came back to the village at night.

Whasimai passed through on the way to Aden's. Unabelin still here.

Wabe and Temos came up at night.[395]

JUNE 15: Polip called over, through Maigi (at Manuniki), to tell Unabelin to come home and help carry a Wihun pig which Whoiban was giving them.[396]

In the morning, while Wabe was still here, Wegul beat a *garamut* furiously in Alipinagle because someone had started a rumor that Belagomini had said that Wegul was going to adopt one of his children.[397]

This started people talking about a rumor that Whoiban meant to come and talk strongly to Balidu about Aden's newly aroused suspicions about the piece of exuviae which Gerud had found. Whoiban was expected to threaten noncooperation over the Magahine feast, that unfailing sanction which could be produced at every new quarrel. But Whoiban, busily engaged with his pig, did not come. In the after-

---

[394] These two traveling parties had each lost an average amount of their projected personnel.

[395] It was this evening that I discussed with Wabe the causes of Wena's baby's death, the gist of which I have incorporated above.

[396] This was the same pig which Salawasimi had carried through here on the twelfth.

[397] I never did get an adequate explanation of why this had made Wegul so angry, except that it was not true. In fact, far from adopting other people's children, Wegul had arranged to have his adopted. Wabe was planning to adopt one and Maginala the other. But it was a characteristic of the Arapesh to react furiously against any false accusation. (Compare the American and English libel law in this respect.)

noon, however, Balidu got angrier and angrier the more he thought about it and finally he stood up in Walinuba and shouted a lot of disagreeable remarks to Maigi, who was in Manuniki, accusing him and Agilapwe of circulating the rumor about this new piece of exuviae.[398]

Yapul brought over some yams, and Badui and Pidjui went back with her to help Nagawe to harvest yams.

Wabe left again to finish fencing a small yam garden.

## Wupali's *Abullu* (1)

Ibanyos and Sauwedjo returned from Wihun, where they had gone to see Wupali, and reported that he had many, many yams and would make an *abullu* when Ombomb got back.

Sinaba'i, Menala and the baby, Gerud, and Dubomagau went to help Sumali fence.

In the evening Ibanyos went to Aden's and Sauwedjo to Bischu's.

Kaberman's brother, his brother's wife, and his betrothed, came up to see him from Kobelen, having heard of his illness and believing that he had been sorcerized.

Balidu received them very formally and courteously, he and Yahalijo coming up to the Alitoa end of the village to sit with them. The women were wearing the new tassel earrings which had been one of the new styles imported with the *shené*.

June 16: The village was again deserted.

Balidu's family all went to Manuniki to help Maigi.[399]

Mindibilip and the little Maguer boy were sent to Matasues' place for food. They reported that there had been a quarrel between Matasues and Inoman, because Inoman had taken his young son out bird snaring, and when they snared a hornbill, he and his little son had gorged it alone. Ombaligu,

[398] Maigi had left Alitoa right after the feast and had only been back for short intervals since. He, who had been almost a part of Balidu's household, had become a stranger. Agilapwe was up to his old game of making trouble between Aden and Balidu, a pastime of which he never tired.

[399] To heal the breach made yesterday.

Matasues' brother-in-law, had passed by and seen them.[400]

Me'elue and her child came up to get something from Sauwedjo's house and went down again.

In the evening Iwamini and Madje came in to sleep. Sauwedjo and her baby slept here.

Mindibilip came down with the "Kobelen" feast fever, as we had come to call it.[401]

JUNE 17: The village was again deserted.

A group of Boinip people passed through, including a woman, wearing clothes, who wanted to buy from us as if we kept a store.[402]

Gerud returned. When questioned about Bunitai's divining, he said that it was probably a lie.

JUNE 18: Balidu was here all day; in the evening, Maigi moved over, prepared to help him plant his yams. It turned out that Balidu was going to plant his yams without any magic whatsoever. Only Ombomb and Baimal knew the sea shell magic, and both were away: Ombomb had gone to Aitape and Baimal was hunting somewhere in the bush with Balili. But it did not matter very much, Balidu said. Those who had the magic used it; those who did not, just planted their yams anyway. If a man knew how to plant yams[403] they came up.

JUNE 19: Empty village again.

A party of Ybonimu men were here to sell us *badul* masks.

Two men from Webogulu, a village near Ilapweim, came through and proved good informants.

JUNE 20: The Ybonimu people left the next morning with a big party of Devunogu people, on their way to the Beach to buy pigs. There were women as well as men in this group; the women wore very tiny aprons, the men were naked.

[400] This offense was doubly heinous because Inoman, already an *alomato'in* himself, was training his son to be the same kind of person by his evil example.

[401] The boys had accepted this explanation; even Kaberman, after his worry over Gerud's accusations in the divination, did not think he was being sorcerized.

[402] No woman among all of the Mountain people wore any cloth, but here was a Plainswoman who had been away with her husband and come back from the white man, in clothes, to rejoin a totally naked people.

[403] Thus successful experience supersedes magic.

They were off their Road, and passed through in hurry and apprehension.

In the afternoon Baimal, Amito'a, and Gabunyan's wife and sister came from Ahalesimihi with yams. These were the share which Baimal and Kule had in the harvest of their sister's son Gabunyan. They stayed overnight.

## WAGINARA FEAST (1)

JUNE 21: Whoiban came early in the morning to announce that Apo of Umanep was going to make the feast of Brushing Away the Ashes, for his brother's death, in a hamlet near Waginara. The *tamberan* was to come and there was to be a big exchange of pigs, much bigger than anything that had ever been known for a feast of this sort. Baimal left with him to take the news to Matasues. Amito'a stayed. The Ahalesimihi people went home. Sagu came in during the day. Sauwedjo was here with her baby. Ibanyos came up in the afternoon.

## THE SORCERY ACCUSATION AGAINST ME'ELUE (1)

Late in the afternoon, all these women were sitting chatting on the Walinuba plaza, when Me'elue, her child on her back and accompanied by Una (the daughter of Matasues), burst in upon them, panting, tearful, to deny an accusation of sorcery which Sauwedjo had been circulating against her.[404]

[404] This was the first I had heard of this accusation. It seemed that on June 16, when Sauwedjo had slept here, she had discovered, or so she said, that a piece of Ombomb's headband had been cut, and she also heard that Me'elue and her child had been here during the day and had entered her house. Then she seized her chance and began surreptitiously accusing Me'elue of having cut the headband. She did it very cunningly. She claimed that she did not want to make a fuss, because then Ombomb would discover that she had left his net bag unguarded and beat her. But alas, that such a little phalanger of a woman, all covered with *tinea*, one who had always practiced sorcery (had she not, years before, hidden a piece of taro skin in the roof, and if Ombomb had not found it, he would have died), alas, that such a one should make a big strong man like Ombomb die. So her poisonous calculated words ran on. And finally Madje had heard the gossip, and sympathizing with Me'elue, un-

Me'elue burst forth, "Sorcerize Ombomb! Why should I do such a thing? I am his wife, his wife! He grew me. He paid for me. I have borne him children. Am I an inherited wife, am I a stranger, that I should sorcerize him? I am his own wife, the wife whom he grew."

Sauwedjo sat nursing her baby, the net bag in front of her, its contents spread out, the headband with the missing cord placed significantly on top.

Amito'a acted as a kind of referee, scolding now one side, now the other.

"Why did you enter the house?"

"To get the dog's teeth. He told me, Ombomb told me to come and get them."

"Did you take Yauito'a up with you into the house?" asked Amito'a.

"Me? No, I left her below," answered Me'elue.

"And entered alone the house of your co-wife! Silly!" Amito'a slapped her on the wrist with one of the spread-out necklaces.

At this Me'elue cried harder than ever. "He does not give me food. He never looks at me or takes food from my hand. I and my child go hungry. We eat the food of others. This stranger woman is always angered at me. If he makes a garden for me, if he cuts down trees and fences my garden, she is angry. She is too strong. She eats meat, and I and my child, we stop without anything."

From Sauwedjo, bent over her child, came a contemptuous, "Oh, I eat meat, do I? Tcha!"[405]

Amito'a now spoke more gently to Me'elue, "You are not a woman who came here after you were grown that we should suspect you of sorcery. You were but a little thing when you came, when we paid for you."

Thus encouraged Me'elue burst out again, "Am I a stranger? Am I a late-acquired wife? Now I have borne him a child, a daughter. She remains! Why should I sorcerize him? He came down to me. He said, 'Go and get the dog's

---

fortunate like himself with her *tinea* skin, he had gone down the night before to warn her.

[405] This scornful repetition of an accusation is a familiar form of rhetoric used in disputes.

teeth. Fasten them on the neck of our child.' So I did so."
And then she added, as a final point, "And her water bamboo.
She says I broke that too. Madje, he said so."[406]

Sauwedjo shook this accusation aside with a wave of her
hand, "I did not say so. The water bamboo, that is mine. I
alone broke it."

Here Sagu interrupted pacifically, "A stranger, another
must have cut the string. There are always Plainsmen coming
to Ombomb's house. One of them must have entered and
done it."

But Sauwedjo would have none of this. "There have been
people in the village all the time. The master's boys have
always been here. They would have seen if a Plainsman had
entered the house. She, that one, alone entered. Of you only,
have they spoken."

Me'elue, getting more tearful and less controlled all the
time, "Always, always she scolds me. They two, they stay
always together. He does not treat me like a wife. Those
dog's teeth were mine."

Here Amito'a again decided to be judicial, "But they were
in Sauwedjo's house," she said. "So now there is gossip."

Sauwedjo, caustically, "Let him make her work.[407] I shall
go back to Dunigi." She had been quietly suckling her baby
all the time.

Me'elue stood up, her poor thin little body looking both
wizened and child-like. "I shall take my yams, my baskets. I
shall go down below altogether. I carried only a little basket.
When I returned I emptied it. I emptied the little rubbish
within it. It was not a big basket to hold hidden sorcery
things. When I emptied the basket all would have seen it.
Lately, the pigs ate my taro. I said 'Never mind! I have no
husband, I have no husband to look after me, to clear the
ground and to plant. I am the wife that he paid for as a child.
I am not a stranger.'" She turned and went down the hill.[408]

[406] Here again the unbearableness of an untrue, any untrue accusation is demonstrated.

[407] This is a reference to Me'elue's lack of strength.

[408] There is a simplified, compact account of this whole affair,
Mead, 1935b, pp. 112–120. Here I shall merely record the events
as they occur among other incidents in the *Diary*.

Sauwedjo went back to her house. I stayed to listen to the comments. The women shrugged their shoulders. The headband had been cut. But by whom? Perhaps by Sauwedjo herself. After all, she was the stranger, the Plainswoman. She was jealous when Ombomb even spoke to Me'elue. On the other hand, who could blame Me'elue, declared Sagu. "Ombomb deserved to be sorcerized for treating his wife so." "Who knows," added Amito'a, "Perhaps Sauwedjo just did it, so she could say Me'elue did it." Everyone's comments concentrated on the incident as a fight between the two women, not as a matter which might really lead to sorcery and death.

Yabinigi and Gerud went on a three-day hunting trip.

JUNE 23: I came down with the "Kobelen" fever.

La'abe and his party returned from their trading trip.

JUNE 24: Ombomb got back in the afternoon. He had purchased and lost a little pig on the way, so aside from payment from us, for whom he had brought some beads, his whole trip had been wasted.

## ADEN'S ILLNESS (1)[409]

JUNE 25: Sumali and Balidu made big speeches about Aden's suspicions and also referred to a time before when Aden had paid two rings to a man in Sublamon to sorcerize Iwamini's wife, and public pressure had made him get the exuviae back. Sumali had said first that if it weren't for Gerud's being here he would never come here. They concluded by saying how peaceful everything would be after Budagiel and Monau were married.[410]

Yabinigi and Gerud returned with only a hornbill. Gerud left to work with his father.

JUNE 26: A Liwo crowd came to sell us things; Unabelin and Siakaru remained afterwards.

[409] The details of Aden's illness will be treated as a separate sequence from now on. For other aspects, see Gerud's and Bunitai's divinations.

[410] This whole situation between Aden and Balidu should be regarded as a confusion between ceremonial and real hostility. Given the ceremonial hostility, when troubles like Aden's sore arose, they had a natural path to flow in, and in the end, both parties were left confused and angry, and not knowing where they were.

## Waginara Feast (2)

Matasues came through on his way back from the Waginara feast. He reported that it had been inspired by the Kobelen feast and that afterwards Waginara had made a mnemonic device of coconut ribs and handed them to Kobelen and said, "Beat this if you can." He said that all the villages near the Beach had gone, and 70 pigs had been exchanged.[411]

June 27: Wabe and Ga'olin passed through, returning from the Waginara feast.

It was reported that Nagawe had decided not to make an *abullu*, but to help his brother-in-law Balili with his feast.

## The Sorcery Accusation against Me'elue (2)

Ombomb was back in the village. He had not seen Me'elue and was paying no attention to the sorcery accusation about which La'abe had told him.

I asked La'abe what he thought about the charge against Me'elue. He said, "Bischu and I are tired of looking after her and feeding her. She is always getting food from us. It is not as if she were a widow with no husband. I have told her to go back and get food from her father and brothers." When I asked Ombomb if he meant to send her away, he replied emphatically that he did not, "No, indeed. She will just stay down there with Anop, and work there as I say. If she had sorcerized me, of course, I would chase her off home. If not, she will stay and work as I say."

June 28: Deserted village.

June 29: At Madje's request Gerud was to divine about Aden's sore.

[411] This was probably a gross exaggeration, but there was no way of checking up on it. The feast would go down in native lore as having had 70 pigs anyway.

## GERUD'S SEVENTH DIVINATION

It was a very dark night, and all our flashlight batteries were exhausted, so we had great difficulty following Gerud about. At our boys' request we had made a good many warning remarks about bringing up points which would involve them, and Mindibilip had a stick with which he announced he would fight anyone who asked any embarrassing questions. Furthermore, Gerud himself was subdued and distrustful of his own powers. There was no one there, except Sinaba'i, La'abe, Badui, Madje, Unabelin, and our boys.

Gerud dashed about, found a little piece of rotten bamboo, and then began digging under our back steps. When I got there, I found a controversy going on among our boys which stopped when I arrived. Gerud rushed back to the plaza and fell down. First he muttered a little of his *sagumeh* charm in a dreamy voice. Then he kept saying over and over, "Stones, stones." Unabelin said very loud, "He is talking of the cooking stones of Aden. They were not scraped and so were used for sorcery."[412] Gerud paid no attention to this remark. Suddenly he exclaimed, "They are blowing the bamboo flutes at Yapiaun." This was the familiar blasphemy which showed he was possessed. As there were no native women or children there, no one was chased away."[413]

Then Madje said, indicating the piece of bamboo in Gerud's hand, "What have you here?"

Gerud, "A piece of areca nut kernel."

Madje, "Is it Aden's?"[414]

Gerud, "Yes."

[412] Cooking stones on which meat juice has fallen and dried can be used for sorcery.

[413] When they were present, the men were always on the alert, lest Gerud start to talk about the *tamberan,* when women and children were promptly chivied away.

[414] Gerud's procedure in always finding so much exuviae where he divined was in keeping with the old pattern of dreaming, except that in the old pattern the exuviae was supernaturally transported to the dreamer's village, but Gerud had adopted the more difficult task of explaining how so much exuviae got into his neighborhood by human agency.

Madje, "Who put it there?"

Gerud, "Yauwiyu. He did it in revenge for Aden's taking the exuviae of Iwamini's wife."[415]

Madje, "Is this all?"

Gerud, "Yes, I took out a piece before." Then he fell to more muttering about stones.

Sinaba'i asked, "What injured my pig yesterday?"

Gerud, "A falling tree branch."

Badui, "Sa'omale is sick. Is she sorcerized?"

Gerud, "No, she only has a cold, that's all."

Then more about "Stones, stones under the house of the master, stones to fasten them here."

At this point, the whole thing degenerated into a storm of comment from our boys, who it seems knew perfectly well what this talk of stones was about. They were stones which had been buried under our back steps to keep us here so that we would never get back to the Beach. Wabe and Naushe'e[416] had put them there. Mindibilip and Saharu both got very much excited. Unabelin resisted the whole idea, saying that magic would not work on white people. To which our boys retorted that he was trying to hush the matter up because he wanted us to stay too. Kaberman took it more casually. Mindibilip said that people had buried stones under the District Officer's porch, and he had never come. Saharu insisted that because of the stones we had all been sick. Mindibilip said that before, when Gerud had divined and Dr. Fortune had been away and I had been ill, Gerud had wanted to take the stones out, but the local people had prevented him from doing so.

All this time, Gerud lay on the ground, forgotten. He finally came to and came into the house with the others. We questioned him as to how much he remembered, and as usual he talked freely about the points he had made.[417]

[415] This old attempt of Aden's had been discussed by Balidu just two days before.

[416] Hauled in to explain this use of a Plains type of sorcery. Naushe'e had lived for years in Ilapweim.

[417] I have reported this divination a little differently from the others, for with the smaller crowd it was easier to follow. The points were:

1. A piece of areca nut belonging to Aden, put there by Yauwiyu,

Our boys added that Ombomb had offered his new baby girl to Kaberman as a wife, and had suggested to Mindibilip that he marry Miduain, so plainly the Alitoa people were trying to hold us fast there forever. They dug under the steps and found nothing.

## YAPIAUN FEAST (3)

JUNE 30: Dr. Fortune left with Kaberman, Gerud, Badui, Unabelin, Madje, and Sinaba'i for Balili's feast.[418]

The village was deserted, except for Menala and her baby who returned to sleep here.

JULY 1: Some Alipinagle women came over in the morning to sell food. They reported that Wabe and Temos had gone to Balili's feast and Welima had gone to Ahalesimihi. There was also a rumor again that Nagawe was going to make an *abullu*.

JULY 2: Anop and Yabenas passed through, on their way to help Bischu make a new yam garden. Anop stopped and chatted. He said he had only felled the trees of the border and cut the bush of his new garden. Me'elue had gone to see her father. When she returned, Anop would go up the standing trees and Me'elue could work at the foot. "Yes," he added, "I suppose she has taken the exuviae to her father, and he has sent it to the Plainsmen. By and by, Ombomb will die. If he had kept his wife with him, she would not do this. But he leaves her around and he leaves his things around, carelessly. Now he will die. I am tired of looking after her garden. It is

to avenge Aden's old attempt to sorcerize his sister-in-law, the wife of Iwamini.

2. Stones under our verandah put there by Wabe and Naushe'e to keep us in Alitoa.

3. Sinaba'i's pig had been killed by a branch.

4. Sa'omale only had a cold, no sorcery.

It will be noted that here Gerud had gone to the other extreme from his last divination, made only a few points, only one spontaneous one, and no miscellaneous statements about sorcery.

[418] As for all non-Alitoa events attended by Dr. Fortune, the details are from his notes.

not as if she were a widow. She has a husband who should look after her."[419]

## ADEN'S ILLNESS (2)

After they left, Baijo came in, ostensibly to sell us something, and really to question our boys very minutely about the place from which Gerud had taken the piece of bamboo so that they could bring an exorcising brew to make the place cold. Mindibilip said it was dark and he did not know where the place was.

Baijo said that Aden was very, very sick and that they had sent for Iwamini to come and build him a special little ground shelter as is customary for the very sick.[420]

## YAPIAUN FEAST (4)

Wegul came with some food and said that Balili had postponed his final distribution of food until the next day. Balili was said to be starving all his guests, waiting for a pig from Wihun. It was hinted that Balili had overreached himself in trying to give this feast. The ridge pole of his new house was very low. He and his wives had had to put it up alone. His place was too small for the crowd. There was nothing to eat.

JULY 3: The village was quiet in the morning. Shuisha and Anyuai came in with some papayas to sell. Menala, Miduain, and the baby were here all day. Temos came over from Alipinagle with Welima's younger sister to get something from her house. Welima was in Ahalesimihi helping her father harvest his yams. Temos and Wabe had just returned from Wihun from helping Wupali harvest his yams.

[419] When I presented this theory of Me'elue's whereabouts to La'abe, he only shrugged, "It's something which is the affair of the two women. Sauwedjo is always taking all the food and meat. Did she cut it off just to make a quarrel? She comes from the Plains. Anyway, it's her own business."

[420] For sickness, like birth and menstruation, is unclean and should not occur at the raised house floor level.

## YAPIAUN FEAST (5)

In the afternoon, everyone came through from the Balili feast. The pig had finally come, given to Balili by Belal of Wihun, who was the maternal half brother of Yamogwai of Yapiaun.[421]

*   *   *

Two Ybonimu men came through and reported that in three days the District Officer was coming in to investigate the murder in the Plains.

## ADEN'S ILLNESS (3)

Mindibilip went over in the afternoon to see Aden and returned to report him much recovered again. As soon as herbs could be poured into the hole from which Gerud had taken the exuviae, he would be all right.

## THE SORCERY ACCUSATION AGAINST ME'ELUE (3)

In the evening, I talked with Ombomb again about what he meant to do about the Me'elue incident. He had been told about it by La'abe, but had persisted in regarding it as a

---

[421] Other economic details reported from the Balili feast and discussed generally in Alitoa were:

Nagawe had distributed a pig on a second series of dog feasts. His first has been described above, p. 354.

Baimal started a series of dog feasts, in anticipation of a future feast exchange with Numonihi.

Baimal gave a piece of his pig to Aden, a further healing of the *buanyin* quarrel.

Nyelahai had called out for a piece of pig from Walawahan on the ground that previously Nyelahai had given him a little pig which Walawahan had later fastened and given to his *buanyin*. Walawahan gave him a piece of pig and later promised a bigger return.

These items give a fair account of how other people took advantage of Balili's feast to give small feasts of their own, just as various small matters were provided for in the Alitoa feast.

woman's quarrel and La'abe's interest in it as an attempt to get rid of Me'elue, because she was a burden on La'abe and Bischu. So he had emphasized that from now on she was to work with Anop and stay with his, Ombomb's, mother in Moholigum where Anop usually stayed also. Now, I asked him, who had cut the string. "Well," he answered, "Had anyone?" "Why yes," I said, "I saw the cut string myself." At this he got very much excited. Apparently he had never half believed the story. He went home, demanded the cut headband from Sauwedjo, who took this opportunity to convince him that Me'elue had undoubtedly taken something of hers also.

The conversation which followed was an interesting comment on the elaboration of rumor. Ombomb, Mindibilip, Gerud, and Sinaba'i sat on our verandah and talked the case over. Sinaba'i asked Ombomb why he had not believed it before. Why, Gerud, in his last divination, had said Me'elue cut the cord. At first Mindibilip contradicted this, but when Sinaba'i insisted, Mindibilip agreed, "Yes, I forgot. Gerud said it." Gerud sat by and said nothing. He was not required to remember what he said during divination. But he did add, "Yes, my ghost said that Me'elue did the sorcerizing."[422]

Furthermore, Ombomb recanted his previous statement when he first heard about it, for then he had supported Me'elue and said that he had told her to come and get the dog's teeth. Now he took this back and said that he had merely told his child in her mother's hearing that she could have the dog's teeth which were in his net bag. And, he added with great conviction, Me'elue would not have entered Sauwedjo's house alone unless she had wanted to sorcerize someone.[423]

JULY 4: Ombomb went down to Moholigum to fasten a *tangget* on Me'elue to say that unless she brought back the

[422] Actually this matter had not been mentioned in the last divination.

[423] It is important to note here that if Me'elue was motivated merely by a desire to take something of Ombomb's away from Sauwedjo, this symbolic act, which would be interpreted in very simple psychological terms, would be almost equivalent in Arapesh to sorcerizing, for here, angry, one takes part of the body of the person who had rejected one, and so puts that person in danger.

piece of his headband and the piece of Sauwedjo's necklace—which she had now discovered was also missing—he would chase her back to her parents and, as soon as her child was weaned, would take the child back. He said, previously, when she had fastened up the piece of taro skin before Sauwedjo came, she had been put up to this by her parents, who were angry because he had not paid better for her. He found Me'elue gone; she had taken all her yams. He left word with Matasues to take her to her parents with the *tangget*.

A great storm came up at noon. The village was deserted. Ombomb returned and he and Sauwedjo left.

Sumali and Budagiel and Midjulumon came down and spent the night.

JULY 5: Gerud was ill with a kind of influenza. Sumali immediately declared it was sorcery and gave him a drink of *ashup*, the bitter sorcery emetic, declaring that this was the work of Kamil, over the old quarrel over Budagiel (p. 166).

Gerud poured the *ashup* out surreptitiously, supported by Ombomb who said that it was not sorcery, because his legs pained as well as his head and there were no leg exuviae outstanding.[424]

Ombomb also decried any accusation against Aden on the subject, evidently realizing that such accusations would be made by somebody else.

The village was beginning to fill up again with people coming to meet the District Officer.[425]

In the afternoon La'abe beat a *garamut* furiously and shouted abuse at Alipinagle because Temos had told Ulaba'i

[424] The belief that the illness must attack the part of the body from which the exuviae came is one of those convenient, sometimes accepted rationalizations, which can be used in an argument, as in this case, but is never pushed to its logical conclusions.

[425] I have cited the various rumors and false alarms connected with the proposed Government visit in the past, not as a criticism of Government but as a good illustration of the amount of time which the natives waste because of faulty methods of communication and calculation of time. The waste is the more conspicuous when the rumor concerns a non-existent Government visit because it affects everybody, but similar false alarms about illness, death, fights, pigs, etc., always influence people to move about in directions in which they would not otherwise go.

that she had overheard Welima's father's other wife and the
wife of Wegul saying that two years before La'abe had seduced the Boinam wife of Maginala. La'abe, with tears of
rage, announced that tomorrow he would go over and beat
both women. He further remarked, and everyone agreed with
him, that the Boinam wife of Maginala had delusions that
every man she met seduced her.[426]

JULY 6: The village was crowded with people waiting for
the District Officer.

Bunitai came up, apparently recovered from his illness,[427]
but without his herbs which he had been asked to bring.

## ADEN'S ILLNESS (4)

Nyelahai began the morning with a threatening speech,
"You who have buried the exuviae, take it out quickly. I
have just been into the Plains. I have just seen Nyakanara. He
said to me: 'I know. I understand completely about this
exuviae of Aden's. There are only two reasons for quarreling,
the dispute over his brother's wife and the squabble over the
pig which was sent to Kobelen. These are the quarrels. These
are the people responsible. If Alitoa has deposited the exuviae,[428] let them kill him. If Manuniki has deposited the
exuviae[429] let *them* kill him! If it was the big place, let them
kill him! If it was the small place, let them kill him! Just let
them! Aden is no friend of mine, eh! Aden is no relative of
mine, eh! Aden never gave me food when I traveled, I suppose? Let them kill him? Then others will die.' "

[426] This wife was a runaway from the interior. I never had an
opportunity to know her. She was not popular in Alipinagle, and
several men had had this same experience with her. Temos' tale-
bearing was a reaction against living in Welima's village which she
hated.

[427] This illness was laid to the fact that he and Inoman had
killed three *lauwan* snakes in one day, an unusual number, so they
must have been *marsalais*, or connected with *marsalais*.

[428] On account of the pig quarrel, here brought forward publicly
for the first time.

[429] Iwamini's wife belonged to Manuniki, and to the quarrel
over her.

## THE SORCERY ACCUSATION AGAINST ME'ELUE (4)

Early in the morning the two wives of Nyelahai had a quarrel which began over a pig of Natun's which had gotten into Nyalamidju's garden, went on to recriminations about the death of Natun's baby, until finally Natun said that presently Nyalamidju would go and weep at Ombomb's funeral when he died and semen appeared on his phallus.[430] This was regarded by everyone as an admission by Natun that her parents (the parents of Me'elue) now had the exuviae and were going to kill Ombomb.[431]

A little later, Me'elue's parents appeared to answer the sorcery charge. The mother sat down with her loving son-in-law Nyelahai, and he gave her areca nut. Ombomb produced the cut headband and Sauwedjo's necklace and demanded that they be returned. The father of Me'elue remarked that many men had worn that headband,[432] that undoubtedly Sauwedjo had cut it herself to throw suspicion upon Me'elue, that Sauwedjo treated Me'elue very badly, and anyway Me'elue was innocent. He then retired, growling, and sat down. At this point Me'elue came up with Yauito'a on her back. This was the first time that she and Ombomb had met since he had returned from Aitape. Ombomb hurled himself toward her like a lance, demanding why she had entered the house, why she had cut the headband, why she had cut the necklace, what she had done with the exuviae, etc. Except for a whispered denial or so, she barely answered, stand-

[430] Nyalamidju was a titular "mother" of Ombomb's. This sign after death meant that the individual had been sorcerized through the use of genital secretions. See Mead, 1940, for list of such signs.

[431] No one paid the slightest attention to the discrepancy between death from a headband which, according to the theory Ombomb had been promulgating vigorously the day before, should only affect the head, and death from genital secretions which was indicated by Natun's speech.

[432] This alibi of another victim is sometimes used both to clear an accused person and also to explain an otherwise inexplicable illness or death. An example of the latter was Wegul's theory that Budagiel had taken his exuviae, thinking it was Kamil's, see above, p. 316.

ing rueful and resigned beside her own parents to whom she felt sure she would have to return. The big group of by-standers exclaimed over the evidence of the cut ornaments. Sauwedjo stood by Ombomb's side and made a few hostile exclamations. Then La'abe stepped forward and presented Me'elue with a *tangget*, a red-green croton leaf, tied in the middle. As he gave it to her he said, "I charge you not to work this sorcery against Ombomb." Both father and mother repeated emphatically that they did not traffic in sorcery.

Nyelahai took this occasion to reiterate his earlier speech, restate his talk with Nyakanara, and remark that if Aden died, Ombomb would undoubtedly die too, because Nyakanara had access to Ombomb's previous exuviae, which was held in Kairiru by Imala.[433]

Here Ombomb cited Natun's remark, and Nyalamidju was just ready to repeat it, when Nyelahai leaped up with a stick and silenced the two women, saying they had just been quarreling about pigs. Matasues said pacifically, why all this talk, later a diviner would work and the truth would be known. Me'elue and her parents left and slept that night at Aden's place.

After they left, the two wives of Nyelahai got into another quarrel inside Ulaba'i's house. Nyelahai went in and beat Nyalamidju, and Ulaba'i announced his intention of beating Natun, but he couldn't find a stick.[434]

There was a brief respite, and then Matasues made a speech asking why Ulaba'i had given Anyuai to the *Suabibis* people, when he had been given no exchange for her. Now Una was to marry Magiel (Ulaba'i's foster brother) and who would there be to give in exchange? No one answered this; so Matasues then made a speech ordering Yauwiyu to go and

---

[433] This was actually a very hostile speech. Here Nyelahai put Ombomb's life into the hands of everyone present, by announcing exactly where his exuviae was filed, and that in the hands of a professional sorcerer who was thoroughly venial. Indirectly, there-fore, under the guise of taking Aden's part against a member of Balidu's party, Nyelahai was supporting his parents-in-law against Ombomb.

[434] Very prudently, for he would have had to pay her afterwards, if he had beaten her. Kule had paid a knife to Amito'a for the time in which he interfered between her and Baimal.

get Agilapwe and Belatau and make them come and answer
the charges of sorcery against them. Yauwiyu left the Alitoa
end where Matasues was speaking and moved up and sat
down in the Walinuba plaza.

The wives of Selalimi and Wegul came over to answer
La'abe's anger about their accusations. They said they knew
nothing about it except what the wife of Maginala had told
them, and she had subsequently run away to her brother.
Maginala remarked *sotto voce* that she might stay there
forever, for all he cared.[435] Temos and Lomaijo made vitu-
perative speeches about the absent woman.

## ADEN'S ILLNESS (5)

Just before dark, Agilapwe came up, and a big series of
speeches started about sorcery and Aden's sore.

Matasues, "You people of the other side had better take
out this exuviae, and take it out quickly. Later, if Aden dies,
he has many friends. Who gives food to the Plainsmen?
Aden! Who gives rings and knives to them? Aden! If he
should die, if later some of you should die, it would not be
we, the brothers of Aden,[436] who had sent the rings. There
will be no need to accuse us. But his Plains friends will be so
angry that they, they themselves, the Plainsmen, will avenge
him, they will kill the men of the side which killed him."

Balidu, "It's Agilapwe's taro which holds the exuviae. The
wife of Agilapwe went to see Aden and the sweat rose on his
face. His sore pained terribly. It is the wild taro of Manuniki
that is responsible."

Agilapwe, "That is a lie. The sweat did *not* rise when my
wife went to see Aden."[437]

Matasues, "Why is Agilapwe angry? Because he is alone.

[435] Ombomb told us later that this woman had been lured away
from Boinam by La'abe and Wabe's love magic, had successively
accused everyone in the village of having seduced her, and had
twice been beaten in a disciplinary fashion, once in Wihun and
once in Numonihi for her false accusations.
[436] The use of the term "brother" here is in the dual organization sense, a sense in which it seldom occurs. Actually, Matasues
was much more a "brother" of Balidu.
[437] The truth of this charge was never ascertainable.

Because he has no brothers and no sons. But let him think of Aden. Aden calls him father."[438]

Balidu, "They accuse me of being angry about this pig. They say I wanted to hold on to this pig. But this is empty talk. But Aden's sore belonged to the long past. This quarrel about the pig is recent. Over a trouble before, yes, I could have been angry. But this pig is a new trouble. The sore is an old sore."

Agilapwe, "I am one, that is all. I am alone. I stand alone. I deny it. I give you all the lie. Where is it that Aden's spirit goes when he dreams? To Alitoa!"

Balidu, "Now, Agilapwe! You accuse me. You go to Aden and hear his dreams. You go about vilifying me. You talk of the piece of areca nut which Gerud found." (Here Agilapwe called for Yauwiyu and Maigi to come and join the discussion.) "But you, you have the exuviae. You gave it to your daughter to take to Nibau[439] and put in the *tamberan* house. You go, follow it up, get it, Aden is my *wauwen*. He is not another man. He is my *wauwen*. I stand on the boundary. Aden inherits from *Hamiebis*. Badui inherits from *Hamiebis* from Pidjui who died. I stand on the boundary.[440] I would not sorcerize him."

(Maigi and Yauwiyu came up and sat down with Agilapwe.)

Agilapwe, "For what should I be accused? Am I an evil man? Am I a witch[441] that I should do that?"

Balidu, "I stayed down by the water. Only the children were here."

"What did they do? What did Maigi and Yauwiyu do? What became of that piece of areca nut that Gerud took out?"

[438] Because, after Aden's death, the mother of Aden had married the father of Agilapwe.

[439] Near Malis. This is a brand new theory which had not been broached before. It was an indirect way of saying to Agilapwe: "After all, you needn't talk so much about your close ties to Aden. You really have most of your ties in that faraway place of Malis, full of strangers. Even your daughter is married there."

[440] This means, I am closely related to him and his concerns.

[441] Agilapwe's mother had been a witch, and some people said he was one.

Sumali, "I don't know. I gave it to Ombomb. Someone go and ask Ombomb what he did do with it."

Yauwiyu, "I went to see Aden. I gave him areca nut, I put it under his arm pit and between his loins. His sore did not throb. Sweat did not come up on his skin. If I had been guilty of the sorcery, when I do this, while I am yet on the road, their sores throb, and the sweat pours out.[442] I am not guilty. I have proved it."

Maigi, "What, am I an old man, that I should sorcerize? Does my father live that he should help me? All are dead. I am but a young boy. I could not make it."

Sumali, "*Hamiebis* belongs to us too. We look after their possessions.[443] Later we give Budagiel to the brother of Aden. There is no quarrel."

La'abe, Matasues, and Nyelahai (all talking together), "Before this was not so . . . Aden's sore was practically dried up . . . Tuag[444] fastened it up . . . . It was going to get well . . . . Only a little stopped . . . . Then we carried this pig to Kobelen . . . . When we returned, we found Aden's sore had gotten much worse . . . . This is not a meaningless sore. Sumali is trying to avenge the burning of his house."

Matasues, "And Aden dreams of Alitoa all the time."

Agilapwe, "If this were a taro sore, it would spread and much matter would come out of it. It would stink. This is a small sore. It does not spread. It does not suppurate. It does not stink. It does not belong to taro. It is exuviae, buried where? In a *tamberan* house or where? Before I tried to kill a man of Nugum. I put the exuviae in my wild taro. The man did not die."[445]

Ulaba'i, "If Aden dies, you people who have killed him, you can fasten the pigs which he owed to Magahine and lift them up and carry them there."[446]

---

[442] Yauwiyu's irresistible desire to pose as a sorcerer himself *in other cases.*

[443] Badui had charge of the *ginyau* of *Hamiebis.*

[444] The Arapesh name for a white woman which was sometimes used to me.

[445] The owner of a sorcery patch crying-down his wares.

[446] I.e., what a great economic loss Aden's death would be.

Nyelahai, "If you want to, kill him. Go on, kill him. Kill him! His Plains friends understand all about it. Do *you* give rings to them? Do *you* give knives to them? Do *your* wives hasten to set food before them? No, your bats[447] hang up inside the house and you yourselves sit down outside empty-handed."

Sumali (to Agilapwe), "How about the quarrel over the fire in Aden's house? Before you slept in Aden's house. He quarreled with you. You scattered the coals through the floor. You said, 'You quarrel with me over your house, do you? Later, you will sleep in a ground house.[448] Later still, you will be better.'"

Agilapwe, "Who says they heard me say that?"

Sumali, "Now I know about my house firing. When I went into the Plains with Tuag[449] they revealed it. When Magahine came and danced over the Tereba, there were many Plainsmen there. I gave them no food. They were angry. They burned my house. They revealed it. They told me when I went with Tuag."[450]

Kaberman (aside, to himself), "It was the same in Kobelen. Many Plainsmen were given no food. Later, some evil will befall us. Will the *shené* burn perhaps?"

Agilapwe, "When his father died, he and his brother lived with me. I cared for them. I cared for their property. They grew. When Aden was grown he knew everything[451] about which were his sago palms, his coconut palms, his yams. He said 'I stayed here long enough.' He left. I did not hold on to him. He came to Alitoa. He built houses here. He married his wives. We have always been quarrelsome. If we were angry over sago, over coconuts, over yams, we did not talk quietly. We shouted. If one talked, the other shouted the reply. This is our fashion. This accusation is brought against me vainly. I

[447] Figurative for wives.

[448] Where a sick man sleeps.

[449] Dr. Fortune.

[450] Sumali says, therefore, I no longer suspect Aden of having burned my house and, therefore, would not have sorcerized him.

[451] That is, I kept good count and taught him carefully, as his father would have done.

am not guilty. *Wha'a no'a no inab.*[452] Why don't you accuse other places?"

Sumali, "When the piece of areca nut was taken out, I gave it to Ombomb. It was completely dark. I don't know what he did with it."

Alis (returning from having asked Ombomb), "They made it cold with *wambibil* leaves."

A chorus of, "When?"

Alis, "The next day."

Sumali (emotionally), "Take out his exuviae. Take it out. He is helpless. He can't do his gardening. He only sits down. Half of his seeds have sprouted. Take it out. He is the trunk of the feasting to come, but he can do nothing. He cannot bring feast things to us when he is ill. All his yams are gone. only taro remains. Let him recover that he may fill up the cook pots and bake with cooking stones."

Balidu, "He is the trunk of the *Midep* (dance complex). Let him get well. Let the *Midep* come and let us dance it. He is the trunk of the Magahine feast. Let him get well and we will all carry pigs to Magahine and share in the feast. He will sit down. He will not eat. He will give it all to us."[453]

Nyelahai, "You make it emerge. You reveal it. You recover it, or by and by Ombomb cannot recover. He will die. Maigi and Agilapwe, however you have made it. In wild taro? In a *tamberan* house? Or in true sorcery, reveal it, or the Plains will avenge. They will make it their affair. They will avenge Aden. Ombomb will die."

Kule, "We went up. We asked Aden, of what do you dream? He said, 'Always of Alitoa.' 'At what does your sore throb?' 'For the wife of Agilapwe only.'"

Agilapwe, "It is not so. It is all a lie. He dreams of Alitoa, yes, that is true. I sit down. You are all too full of words, too arrogant. Before, the father of Aden died. I cared for his children. We quarrel. True. We shout. It is nothing. I have not done this."

---

[452] This is an obscure reference to the *loh*, the bone tubes placed in the tubes of blood for novices and is used here as a strong assertion of innocence.

[453] As is the fashion of a giver of a feast.

Ulaba'i (wearily), "Stop talking. It is of no use. If he dies, well, he dies."

Balidu, "Let the talk go to other places. You accuse us. We are guiltless. It is not a running taro sore. It is the kind of sore which comes from *tamberan* houses."

Sumali, "Before, all Maguer accused us. They accused Bugabihiem. But it was Numonihi that killed Milio of Maguer. Not taro, but true sorcery. The taro was nothing. At Balili's feast they told me. Taro did not kill him. Sorcery did. Before, I wanted Kamias of Liwo to die. I sent talk. He died and I paid nothing. I did not give the Plainsmen rings and they fired my house."

Balidu, Baimal, and Kule together, "Our hands are cold. If we bury exuviae, sores do not come up."

\* \* \*

I have quoted this scene in such detail because it so perfectly sums up not only the whole problem of sorcery among the Arapesh, but also reveals so many of the personalities who have appeared in this narrative. The Arapesh have handled the problems of illness and death by thrusting them outside their borders; an instant's ill temper on the inside opens the way for prolonged and greedy persecution from the Plains sorcerers, the outsiders. But by a malicious twist of fate, the theory of sores had not been included, but had been left within the community. And before this evil which they themselves were supposed to be causing, not merely to have caused in a moment's irremediable bad temper, but to be continually causing, they were helpless, baffled, angry, and accusing each other, always without real conviction.

Each man appears here acting true to type: Nyelahai blustering and threatening; Balidu, cautious, reasonable, and appealing to motives of prudence and calculation; Agilapwe, violent, but protesting that his bark is worse than his bite; Matasues, judicial, worried, grave; Ulaba'i, discouraged; Yauwiyu, foolishly, maliciously boastful; Sumali, practical and invoking actual events; Agilapwe, dwelling on the past; Sumali and Balidu, on the future; Ulaba'i, defeated and weary.

Here for all of the mutual accusations, they are one family.

There are no outsiders present. One of their number is ill, and who, who has betrayed him?

JULY 7: Everyone still gathered waiting for the District Officer. Balidu left in the morning for his garden and returned saying that it was Sinaba'i's pig which was eating his yams. (He had previously said it was Agilapwe's.) There was a heated conversation in which the women of Balidu's household said that when the pig was fastened they would demand a share of the return feast because the pig had grown fat on their yams.

The two wives of Nyelahai continued quarreling. Nyalamidju declared that her hand had been held unfairly, so that she had not been able to return Natun's blows. If she had been allowed to return the blows, her feelings would have been assuaged, but this way, she must be given a ring. (Later Nyelahai did give her one, privately.)

People said that before Nyelahai had wanted to get rid of Nyalamidju, but that Ombomb, Bischu, and La'abe had all protested. "When we have a feast, it is she who comes and helps. You, yourself, asked her to come and marry you when they made that yam feast in Liwo. Now you can just keep her and look after her. She has been good to us."[454]

News came through, in the late afternoon, that the District Officer was sleeping in Umanep.

Dr. Fortune suggested to Nyelahai that Natun might be gotten back for Yabinigi.

JULY 8: The Acting District Officer and a medical assistant arrived in the morning. When the medical inspection was made, the *framboesa* cases included: Wamu'um, his wife Miegelian, her daughter Wabisu, Wamu'um's son Bunitai and his daughter Ke'ali, Belatau and his *tinea*-covered son, Agilapwe and his daughter, Aden, Inoman and his daughter, Sinaba'i and his daughter Miduain, Badui, and Naushe'e's small child.[455]

The inspection also showed a great deal of hookworm, also four pregnant women, Ilautoa, Ibanyos, the wife of

---

[454] Instance after instance proved that a woman's best security lay in the men of her husband's group; if they approved of her, they upheld her claims on her husband.

[455] The clustering of relatives here is striking.

Amambut, and the older wife of Matasues. The Government officers spent the night here. They brought word of a dysentery epidemic in Aitape.

JULY 9: It rained hard and carrying was impossible, so the official visit was prolonged another day.

Meanwhile, it seemed that Dr. Fortune's casual remark to Nyelahai that he would appeal to the District Officer and get Natun back for Yabinigi had been having results behind the scenes. Yabinigi consulted Ombomb on the possibility of putting this into effect. Ombomb was then reported to have consulted Natun, who said that, after all, she was Yabinigi's lawful wife and would go back to him if the District Officer so ordered.[456] Ombomb then approached Nyelahai to see what action he would take. He flew into a towering rage and said that Natun was his wife, and if she was taken from him, he would cut down his trees, break down his house, throw away all his possessions, and leave Alitoa forever. Ombomb immediately moderated his tone. He and La'abe agreed that it would be dreadful no longer to have Nyelahai to help them with their feasts. In commenting on the case, Ombomb and La'abe said that they would have helped Yabinigi before, but he did not stay in Alitoa, with his own people. He was always running off to Wihun and staying with his sister's husband. If he stayed with them, then they would help him.

But meanwhile, Yabinigi's hopes had been stirred, and there was no telling what he, in the erroneous belief that he had Dr. Fortune's support, might not accomplish.[457]

So Ombomb and La'abe put their heads together and considered. And then they appeared with a most surprising suggestion: how about getting Yabinigi's other wife back? We had never even heard of this wife, but it seemed that she had been lured away by two Sepik natives who had settled down in Suapali on their way home from working for the white man. This suggestion calmed Yabinigi, and also, fortunately, appealed to the District Officer who happened to be particularly annoyed by trouble made by foreign natives who moved

---

[456] I am inclined to think that this was a fabrication on Ombomb's part. At any rate, she later denied it.

[457] What nobody realized, of course, was that Dr. Fortune had simply wearied of the sound of Nyelahai's boasting voice.

into local communities. The whole group was summoned. Yabinigi's wife (a poor spectacle of a girl covered with a skin disease[458]) was returned to Yabinigi, and the two Sepik intruders, together with their Suapali supporters, were severely scolded. They were warned that if they caused any more trouble, they would have to go out of the District, back home where they belonged. They went away sulkily.

JULY 10: The Government party left for the Plains.

People all left for their hamlets; village empty.

## WUPALI's *Abullu* (2)

JULY 11: Sinaba'i and Ombomb went to Wihun to help Wupali harvest his yams.

\* \* \*

Baimal was helping Balidu plant.

Kule went to help Yamogwai in Yapiaun.

La'abe's household were in the village.

JULY 12: Dr. Fortune left for the Plains, a plan which had been arranged with the District Officer. With him went Anop, Wabe, Iwamini, Gobonarra, Yabinigi, Mindibilip, and a newly come Maguer boy, Wanaka.

La'abe left for Ahalesimihi to plant his yams with Manum. Sumali had now decided to join Manum also, after Manum had forsaken him.

Balidu was still planting yams. Ombomb had planted the yams he harvested in late January. These which La'abe was now planting came from that same harvest.

## THE THEFT OF MAGINALA's SISTER (2)

In the afternoon, news came that Aimau and Manusa of Numidipiheim had carried off the sister of Maginala, Weamali, while she was gardening with Temos. They said she had been single too long, and if Maginala would not arrange

---

[458] Called in P. E. *kuskus,* a combination of scabies and penicillium.

for her marriage, they would.[459] It was whispered that Nyelahai was responsible for this.

Balidu and Baimal came back from the yam planting.

Maigi and Sagu came in late in the evening.

JULY 13: Ombaligu, the Numidipiheim husband of Nigat, sister of Anop, came up early in the morning to learn how the capture of Maginala's sister was being taken by this community. Balidu came up to the Alitoa plaza and made a loud speech about the virtues of paying openly for wives in the plaza, and the evils of sneaking and surreptitious violence. Ombaligu left contented, convinced that there was to be no fight.

* * *

Agilapwe passed through, limping badly, on his way to Ahalesimihi.

## NAGAWE's *Abullu* (1)

Balidu and Baimal and their households left for Nagawe's *abullu*, in Ahalesimihi.

## WUPALI's *Abullu* (3)

In the afternoon, Ombomb, Sinaba'i, Sauwedjo, Menala and the baby, and Miduain returned from Wihun, where they had been helping Wupali plant his yams. They said that the actual *abullu* would not take place for some time.

## THE SORCERY ACCUSATION AGAINST ME'ELUE (5)

Me'elue was still down with Ombomb's mother. Ombomb said she could just stay there for the present, until her child was weaned. Then he would take the child and send her home. She wouldn't dare do anything now after being given the *tangget* publicly.[460] Already Wambibi, *luluai* of Wihun,

[459] She had been betrothed to Iwamini, but his wife objected. Maginala wanted her to marry within the village to strengthen Alipinagle.
[460] I had some difficulty in understanding why this constituted such a sure precaution, but it seems that if later Ombomb fell ill,

had said in a public speech that if they had the exuviae they must let it rot. If Ombomb fell ill, they would be forced to pay for the return of the exuviae.

Whasimai, her baby, and Miduain went to Liwo to take some coconuts to Anyuai, who had gone back there only two days before.

## NAGAWE'S *Abullu* (2)

JULY 14: Nagawe made his *abullu*. Everyone in the village left early to attend it. In the evening Ulaba'i, Nyelahai, Sumali, Madje, and Sinaba'i returned from the *abullu*, reporting that Nagawe had made two mounds, one in the name of each wife.

Miduain returned with Yabinigi's new wife. She reported that there had been two births in *Suabibis*. Polip's wife had a daughter, and the wife of Kwanemit, the brother of Gobonarra, a son.

JULY 15: Ombomb and his wife returned at noon. Ulaba'i and Ibanyos were here.

## THE THEFT OF MAGINALA'S SISTER (3)

Henalian and Maginala had wanted her for an adopted son, but had paid nothing for her. Maginala reported that she was weeping.

After they left, both Ulaba'i and Ombomb were noncommittal. It was something Nyelahai and Manusa had arranged. Aimau himself, to whom the girl was to be given as a wife,[461] didn't particularly want her. But Nyelahai and Manusa had said he should take her, and Aimau was a mild and compliant young man. Temos had been in the plot and

---

Me'elue and her parents would have all Wihun against them, as they had been publicly enjoined.

[461] In cases such as these and even where the elopement is planned by the parties concerned, the last thing the prospective husband would dare to do would be to copulate with the stolen woman. There was no surer way of signing his own death warrant in case she did not remain. This one fact gives the theft of women a very different context among the Arapesh than in many primitive societies.

had lured her to the distant garden. Ombomb, as a relative
of Aimau, was mainly concerned with the girl's being sickly
and very little good for work.

* * *

Matasues and his wife, and some of Wamu'um's children
were here all afternoon.

Agilapwe passed through, returning from Nagawe's *abullu,*
which he said was over.

Badui and Maigi are preparing to go to Wewak with Kule
for new medical supplies.

JULY 16: Kule, Badui, Maigi, and Naushe'e left for Wewak,
taking a load of material culture with them.

Baimal and Amito'a returned from Nagawe's *abullu* with
a load of painted yams.

A message came through that a recruiter was coming in
from the coast.

Alo, the wife of Nagawe, and her daughter accompanied
them to help them carry.

ADEN'S ILLNESS: THE DIVINATORY OVEN (6)

(This account was given me by Mindibilip and Madje.)

Present were Aden, Ulaba'i, Madjeke (the big man of
*Suabibis*), a *wa'en* of Aden's, Madjeke's son Polip, whom he
also called *wa'en*. Madjeke presided over the proceedings.

The "oven" consisted of a circle of *kotoesilu* plants, which
have heavy green leaves and large bulbous roots. As many
of these are brought as there are suspected places. In this
case there were seven, named Alitoa (the place itself),
Agilapwe, Maigi, Yauwiyu, the *marsalai* of Bugabihiem, the
*tamberan* house of Ahalesimihi, and the *tamberan* house of
Yapiaun. Madjeke contributed the blood from the phallus
which had to be sprinkled among the magical ingredients.[462]
Two ancestral stones were brought from the deserted hamlet
of *Kanehoibis,* Buluguhip.

The principle of the oven is that the insects placed inside
the covering smell the blood on the guilty roots and cluster
there, and because of the heat of the sorcery which the guilty

[462] For a full account of this formula, see Mead, 1940, p. 435.

roots symbolize, the heat of the fire remains powerless. The food about these roots is raw and the insects are still alive. After the stones had been heated and put in their places, Ulaba'i and Madje talked to their ancestors, "Tell us. What place took the exuviae? What place has the exuviae? Let the guilty part of the oven remain raw. We wish to know."

Three roots showed clusters of insects and uncooked bananas: Ahalesimihi, Yapiaun, and Bugabihiem. They fastened *tanggets* for all three places, and decided to ask Ahalesimihi and Yapiaun first and Bugabihiem later.

JULY 17: The village was empty, and I had an attack of malaria. At noon a recruiter (Mr. Joseph Hoddinott) arrived, having met Ombomb previously on the coast, and been assured by him that there were plenty of boys to be had in the Plains. Ombomb was sent for. He collected several people, who promised to carry as far as Wihun in the morning.

JULY 18: The day began with pouring rain. The natives said the rivers would be flooded and refused to go in. Mr. Hoddinott decided to postpone his trip until the next day and stay on in the Government rest house. I borrowed his Suwein boys and did some comparative work with them.

Ombomb said that Lui was inaugurating a new *buanyin* relationship and that he wanted to carry a pig to Dunigi the next day to help him.

Dr. Fortune returned just after dark, with news of the proceedings in the Plains and of a new fight between Dunigi and some more inland villages. The District Officer was still reconnoitering the position, and the whole area was in an uncertain state. Dr. Fortune himself had gone down into Ulup, and people had come in from the Abelam villages below and brought him a wealth of small material culture—incised coconut shells, cassowary bone daggers, coconut shell whistles, etc. Some of this he brought back with his own carriers, and the larger part of the collection, about 100 large bark paintings from the facades of old *tamberan* houses and yam houses, were brought in the next day by Plains carriers.

JULY 19: Mr. Hoddinott was ill, and I was down with fever. Under Dr. Fortune's advice and because of his own health, Mr. Hoddinott decided against going farther into the interior.

## THE THEFT OF MAGINALA'S SISTER (4)

Ombomb and those whom he had collected to go with him dispersed. Wabe went to Numidipiheim to discuss the case of Maginala's sister.[463]

Wabe was an ideal envoy here; he was at present living in, and identified with, Alipinagle, and he was Aimau's mother's brother.

JULY 20: Manusa took back Maginala's sister, saying that Aimau did not like her, and that he disliked all the talk that was going on. It was said that this was Wabe's doing. The whole matter, like so many of Nyelahai's gestures, ended in nothing.

\* \* \*

JULY 21: Dr. Fortune accompanied Mr. Hoddinott part of the way out and stopped to investigate the *marsalai* place of Bugabihiem, a quicksand with the water filled with vegetable oil. I had fever.

News came of the death of the child of Sumali's sister, in Wihun. The husband of this sister, the father of the dead child, had helped Yabinigi before against Suapali in his attempt to get his wife back. Now, when Yabinigi did succeed in getting her back, this old participation was revived. It was said that previously the father of Yabinigi's wife had given exuviae to the Suapali people, and they had now paid for death to be worked with it.

[463] There were undoubtedly a good many details in this case which, what with my own illness, that of Mr. Hoddinott, and the excitement of Dr. Fortune's return with the big collection, were missed altogether. Afterwards, as is usually the case, I could not recapture them. I am giving the details of white interruption here because otherwise the paucity of details of native life would be out of context. The combination of Government, carriers, comings and goings, and a season when everyone was normally away in the gardens, did make very little news, but some of that I missed. I would omit this section altogether, except for the fact that a certain sequence is preserved throughout, in terms of the major themes of Arapesh life at the moment.

JULY 23: I had fever. No entries in the *Diary*.[464]

JULY 24: Word arrived from Mr. Cobb that he was leaving for Sydney on the next boat (the "Mirani"). As we expected six months' cargo on that boat, which was to be stored at Karawop until we left for the Sepik, it was necessary for Dr. Fortune to go down and receive it, as Mr. Cobb was not to be there.

No entries.

JULY 25: Village empty.

JULY 26: Village empty.

JULY 27: Dr. Fortune left at dawn, accompanied by Mindibilip, Yabinigi, Badui, and Maigi; Sagu and Nigimarib went along to see off Pidjui, who had run off to Karawop and signed on as a work boy for some distant spot. Nigimarib's face was swollen almost beyond recognition from some infection unknown to the people and which he had picked up in the Plains. Although some people said Bischu's charm might be applicable, no effort had been made to find Bischu, and the swelling was not going down.

## WUPALI'S *Abullu* (4)

JULY 28: Village empty.[465] Everyone had gone to Wupali's *abullu* in Wihun.

## GERUD'S EIGHTH DIVINATION

JULY 29: In the evening Bischu came up to the village with Wabisu, the daughter of the wife of Wamu'um, and her deaf brother. The deaf boy's leg was swollen. Bischu asked Gerud to divine about the cause of this swelling, but the boys suspected that he really wanted to know what was the matter with his hunting without making a point of it.

---

[464] This means that nothing conspicuous happened, or Dr. Fortune would have recorded it.

[465] During this entire period, my boys and I worked separating the bark paintings from the insect-ridden, rotting back frames, reframing the best ones with new wood. This was a good-sized task, but the beauty of the paintings, no sample of which has been collected before, justified a heavy expenditure of effort.

Gerud took out no exuviae. He ran around a little, and then fell prostrate in the Walinuba end of the village (something he had never done before).

1. Gerud said that the boy's leg was swollen from the *sagumeh* magic of the Suapali people who were angry about Yabinigi's wife.[466] La'abe had been sick in Ahalesimihi, also as a result of the anger of the Suapali men.

2. Bischu then asked, "What is spoiling my hunting?" Gerud, "Ombomb and his wife have fastened up a cassowary bone. They are angry about Badui's feast."[467]

3. Gerud then said dreamily, "The 'Mirani' will come tomorrow. I can see the masters all sitting down to dinner now at Karawop."[468]

4. Kaberman asked him whose was the death *garamut* which had been heard yesterday from the Beach. He said it was for a big man of Aotogi—which everyone had said it was—and that the ghost was under the *tamberan* house, and he could see its eyes.

At this announcement everybody huddled a little closer.

5. Sagu, who had returned, asked if the people of her former husband from whom she had run away had any of her exuviae. Gerud answered, "No, none."

6. Gerud announced that everyone was dancing at Wupali's *abullu*, and that the son of Wambibi was playing, i.e., copulating with his wife.[469]

7. Finally, he volunteered that Aden's exuviae had been removed from Manuniki to the *tamberan* house in Ahalesi-

---

[466] It was the practice now to attribute every disaster to Suapali. The rain which had spoiled Ombomb's garden and the death of Sumali's child in Wihun had already been so attributed by popular gossip. As the former husband of Yabinigi's wife was a strange work boy, the attribution of *sagumeh* powers was also perfectly consistent.

[467] Angry because Bischu had run away and refused to have his coconuts tabooed at that feast. This was a very old and slight quarrel.

[468] The steamer "Mirani" had come two days before, but word had not reached us yet.

[469] This is the type of remark which is supposed to give the touch of authenticity to possession. Only a possessed man would refer to such an intimate detail with names.

mihi.[470] Bischu asked him who put it there and he said he didn't know.[471]

JULY 30: Village empty again, except for Sinaba'i and his wife.

Unabelin and a party of *Suabibis* people came through, returning from Wihun.

JULY 31: Village empty. Sinaba'i's family gone.

AUGUST 1: Baimal and Amito'a and Amus came in. Baimal was planning to go and get some sago from Nagawe. Finally Alaijo and Minya arrived, and they set out.

Badui, Maigi, and Nigimarib returned with the news (untrue) that Dr. Fortune was going to stay and run the plantation.

AUGUST 2 : Ombomb and Sauwedjo and child came in early in the morning. Welima was with them.

Ulaba'i and Ibanyos and Segenamoya here.

## PRESENTATION OF A PIG TO BALIDU (1)

AUGUST 3: Isobai, the Wihun husband of Yabinigi's sister, brought word that the people of Boinip had fastened a pig to Wambibi who was going to give it to Balidu. He called out for Balidu, who came up from his garden and summoned carriers for the pig, Kule, Baimal, Sinaba'i, Badui, and Maigi. While they were preparing to set off, two men came from Magahine to announce a big *abullu* which they had just made, 10 mounds in the great garden which they were asking for the feast which was to come later. The party to Wihun was postponed till the morrow.

AUGUST 4: The party set off for Wihun to bring back the pig. Village empty.

AUGUST 5: Balidu and his party returned. The pig was presented to Maigi for his sister's husband in Magahine. All

---

[470] In this announcement he was following his father's lead of a *rapprochement* with Aden, and also the lead given by the divinatory oven, which had pointed to Ahalesimihi and not to Manuniki.

[471] On July 31, when I was working up the account of this divination, I asked Gerud again who he had said had put the exuviae in Ahalesimihi, and Gerud replied in a cocksure way, that he had said that Tapita or Agilapwe gave it to Selalimi.

the women of the households involved had arrived to help cook and carry the pig.

Ilautoa arrived with the new baby, which was flourishing.

* * *

A party of Nugum Plainsmen, without an interpreter, passed through.

The *tultul* of Bonaheitum came through, reporting that Mr. Cobb had not gone to Sydney but had returned to Karawop and that there was a quarantine on account of the spreading dysentery.

## WUPALI's *Abullu* (5)

People began coming through on their way back to Wihun to carry off the yams.[472]

AUGUST 6: Biagu ran away. Having been sent to Liwo on an errand, he just didn't come back.

## PRESENTATION OF A PIG TO BALIDU (2)

The pig cooking went on and Balidu himself prepared to go to Magahine with the party which took it. This plan was well known to everyone.

AUGUST 7: Dr. Fortune left at dawn for the Beach.

Balidu, Maigi, Kule, Baimal, Badui, and their women, except Ilautoa, left to carry the pig to Magahine. Ilautoa returned to Mogiligen. Naguel stayed with Madje.

## BUNITAI's SECOND DIVINATION (1)

In the evening, there was no one in the village except Ulaba'i, Madje, the two little girls, Kumati, Sa'omale, and the two smaller boys, Naguel and Segenamoya, our boys, and myself. Suddenly, without any warning, Bunitai and his young brother arrived. They spoke to no one. The first an-

---

[472] During the previous part of the *abullu,* they had merely danced and feasted, but had left the mound of yams standing for all to admire.

nouncement of their presence[473] was the low, ghost-calling whistle given by Bunitai as he stood in the Alitoa plaza. Kaberman, who was in our cook house, heard this whistle and rushed out, calling to me as he ran. It was a dark night, and Bunitai was running in circles around and around the plaza, striding and stamping. (He did not bang at things as much as Gerud had.) After about three minutes of this, he rushed down the slope behind Ulaba'i's house and came up around Bischu's house and beat on the sago bark walls of Bischu's house.[474] Then he rushed up to the other end of the village and into the *tamberan* house, knocking down flutes and masks and making a tremendous clatter. Kaberman went in with him (it was pitch dark) and swore that he saw him take something out of the hole of a flute. He came out with this piece of exuviae clutched tightly in his hand. Madje grabbed it out of his hand for safety.

Bunitai went down the village, beat on the walls of La'abe's house, then up, and beat again on the walls of Bischu's house, stamped about in a circle six times on the plaza, rushed back to La'abe's house and knocked the ladder down. Then he returned to the Alitoa plaza, stamped in a circle again, and fell down.

Meanwhile, Ulaba'i, Madje, and Gerud examined the find. It was the most explicit exhibit which I saw, a small piece of pus-stained bandage, wrapped in a banana leaf and tied with a bit of string, the whole thing tied inside a bamboo.[475] Everyone emitted low whistles of horror.

Meanwhile Bunitai began to speak in a gasping, labored voice. No one asked him any questions. They merely stood around him and listened.

"Agilapwe put it in the flute. Before, when he quarreled

[473] Balidu's absence had been well advertised. Bunitai had been repeatedly asked to come and divine and had refused. Now he came when he expected the village to be empty.

[474] This beating on house walls was pattern behavior and was supposed to indicate where other objects tinged with sorcery lay. Once before, when Gerud had beaten on Whasimai's house wall, she had reported that she found a phalanger bone hidden in the thatch when she looked next morning.

[475] Beside this specimen, all Gerud's rotted, ambiguous pieces of bamboo and empty tins looked very doubtful.

with Aden about the house. At Badui's feast. . . . He took the bandage. He cut it in half. He gave half to Silisium to put in the _tamberan_ house in Ahalesimihi.[476] There is none in Yapiaun. If Aden dies, it will be because of the pig that La'abe gave him to send to Kobelen for the _midep_. Everyone is angry about this and they have made Agilapwe conceal the place where the exuviae was. . . . There's a bone in Bischu's house. . . . I found the piece of bandage in the mouth of the flute." (Here there was a hasty survey by on-lookers. Any children about? Where were Naguel and Sege-namoya? Asleep apparently. Any of the women? No. Kumati and Sa'omale had evidently huddled within doors, too shy to come out.) "The quarrel was about sleeping in the house. Agilapwe threw down the fire. All the people of this place have made Agilapwe stubborn. By and by Aden will die. . . . The other piece of the bandage is in one of the rafters of the _tamberan_ house in Ahalesimihi—La'abe has been sor-cerized also."

Bunitai and his brother then left without any conversation. I asked Gerud why he hadn't found this exuviae. He said that he had banged the outside of the _tamberan_ house—this was true—but that his ghost control had not told him to go inside.

AUGUST 8: Ombomb came in this morning, carrying a net bag of yams. He said that probably Bunitai had waited until Balidu left, and then added the information that Ulaba'i had brought Bunitai, something which my boys had not known the night before.

## LIWO INVALIDATES THE _Shené_

Unabelin was here. He brought news that Yelusha and another Liwo man and their two wives had gone to Murik, walking all the way, and had returned with the very latest Murik styles, much newer than the _shené_. The men had birds-of-paradise feathers for their hair, armbands, and a new kind of belt, and chains for their necks with rings on them.

---

[476] This was Bunitai's second attempt to involve Manum and Silisium in sorcery charges. I never got any light on this antagonism, unless it was an indirect way of fighting Gerud.

The women had a new kind of apron, short in front and long behind. They had brought Murik baskets, and they refused to carry their babies in net bags any more but carried them in these instead, as they had seen the Murik women do. They were so proud that they wouldn't sit on the ground, but sat on wooden pillows all day long.

Everyone was furious. Kobelen sent up word that they were coming to fight them. At one stroke, much of the value of the *shené* had been demolished, and Yelusha, probably without planning it, had taken a fine revenge on everyone.

## The Killing of the *Suabibis* Pig

Later, when Unabelin was out hunting for ethnobotany for me, he met his father and Polip carrying a pig to Aden. This pig had been killed by the *tultul* of Bugabihiem for invading his gardens (which he had made, incidentally, on *Suabibis* land) and left lying a whole day before they notified Madjeke. It was their biggest pig and had been saved for Aden's feast to Magahine.

Agilapwe's little girl was here with some yams to sell. She stayed and talked awhile with Sa'omale and Kumati.

The pig-carrying party got back from Magahine, but did not come to Alitoa, scattering to their gardens.

August 9: Unabelin left early to go and take part in the pig quarrel.[477]

## Bunitai's Second Divination (2)

In the afternoon, Wabe, Iwamini, and Waginala passed through, returning from a call on Aden. They heard all about Bunitai's divination from him. Wabe said that he had not

---

[477] The father of the *tultul* of Bugabihiem had been permitted, by the ancestors of Unabelin, to garden on *Suabibis* land. Now he felt so secure that he killed all of the *Suabibis* pigs which got into his garden. And he did not make good fences. About seven months before he had killed one of their pigs, and Unabelin had cut down some of his yams and smashed about his house and said, "If he stays here he will finish off all our pigs. We had better chase him away." But Madjeke had refused to do this, why I never understood, unless he felt that Unabelin was talking out of turn.

divined before because he was angry that he had not been invited to the *garamut* pulling feast.

\* \* \*

### THE ELOPEMENT OF THE DAUGHTER OF WHEHONALI

But they were more immediately interested in the elopement of the daughter of Whehonali. This woman was famous because she had been the wife of the Umanep man who had started the Messiah-cult[478] rumors among the Arapesh. She had originally shared in the lies which her husband told, hiding with him in the bush and saying that she had been to the land of the spirits. Afterwards, when the messianic prophecy collapsed, she had confessed, and her brothers had taken her back to show their contempt for her lying husband.

Meanwhile, Suli, an old man of Wihun, had paid for her younger sister, who had died. She was sent to marry Suli. But he was an old man, he never paid anything for her, he sent no meat to her relatives, and she suspected him of sorcerizing her, so she had now run away to Aimau, of Numidipiheim.[479]

Wihun had summoned Wabe to come and answer for the elopement, but he did not intend to go. He said that she had run away of her own accord, because she disliked Suli, and she had been shamed by her former lying husband.[480]

Wabe then went off to Alipinagle to plant his yams there.

### YAHALIJO'S EXUVIAE (1)

A little later, Soasalamo, the wife of Maginala, back again from the Plains, came to sell me something and to get a

---

478 A nativistic cult of the Wewak coast.

479 The chain of events here is obvious. She was the parallel cousin of Maginala. When Wabe had gone to get back Maginala's sister, he had been able to promise his own and Maginala's connivance in getting Aimau another wife.

480 This reference to her former husband was a red herring. It did not in any way explain why she should be allowed to elope, but Wabe introduced it into the argument as if it did explain and justify it.

piece of cloth which she had lost and Sa'omale had found. Sa'omale gave it to her.

Later, Yahalijo came up to the village and announced that a piece of bandage which had her blood on it, from the wound she had received when Nigimarib threw the firewood at her, had later been wrapped up with that piece of cloth. She was horribly upset and came up and appealed to me to help her get it back.

Yapul and her children and the daughter of Amambut also arrived. Maigi and Sagu came back.

Yabinigi returned, saying he had wounded a cassowary.

At dusk there was a great drumming from Liwo, and our boys went up to Aden's place to hear the news. They returned to say that it was a summons from the medical assistant for the hill people to come down to the Beach, where he was stationed maintaining a dysentery quarantine at Matapau. They had stopped to gossip with Badui on their way back.

AUGUST 10: Balidu household still here, without Balidu.

## YAHALIJO'S EXUVIAE: CONCLUSION (2)

Sa'omale and Kumati, backed up with a stern message from me, went to Alipinagle and got back Yahalijo's bandage.

## BUNITAI'S SECOND DIVINATION (3)

AUGUST 11: This was four days after Bunitai's divination, and still no public action had been taken about it.

Balidu came up to the village early in the morning and sat down in front of his house. A little later Baimal and Henalian came up and sat down with Balidu, talking excitedly; in a few moments, Balidu burst forth in a great speech. Baimal had just told him what had happened.

This was one of the most illuminating events in Arapesh, so I shall trace it in some detail, since it stands in such close opposition to the societies in which children are professional tale bearers and in which troublemaking is everyone's profession.

On the evening of the divination, Ulaba'i, Madje, Kumati,

Sa'omale, Gerud, and our boys knew about it. When Om-bomb passed through the next morning he knew about it. Agilapwe's little girl came in to sell me yams that morning, and she stopped and talked with Kumati and Sa'omale. They told her about it, and she took the tale home to Agilapwe. Yet, when Yahalijo came up in the afternoon, Kumati told her nothing about it.[481] That afternoon, our boys stopped to see Badui on their way back from inquiring into the cause of the Liwo drums, and they told Badui. But no one told Balidu. It was one thing to carry tales about little bits of slander, but everyone was frightened here of the quarrel which might result and of Balidu's being angry at Bunitai. And there is a saying, "When the old men talk quarrelsomely the young men drown out the sound with dancing." None of the children wanted a quarrel.

Meanwhile, from Manuniki the news had finally reached Amito'a, always spoiling for a fight; she had told Baimal, and he and Henalian, who was with him, had gone at once to Balidu. Baimal was the first responsible adult member of Balidu's side to hear about it. Ulaba'i, Wabe, and, it later turned out, Ombomb also, were ranged on the other side.

To return to Balidu's speech, he spoke at the top of his voice, but sitting down, as there was no opponent in the village. Baimal, Henalian, Maigi, Badui, and Sinaba'i, who had just come up, were sitting about. Winam and her baby sat on the plaza in front of Sumali's house, and Balidu addressed most of his remarks in her direction. She acted as a kind of Greek chorus to his words, nodding her head and uttering exclamations at dramatic points. Yahalijo and Yapul were seated under the big house; Sagu sat alone under her little house.

When I arrived, Balidu was saying: "What is he, another man, that this accusation should lie heavy upon me. He is my cross-cousin. He calls me *wauwen*. When he dies pigs and rings must come to me before they bury him. If they do not come he can lie (unburied) and stink. Who is it that accuses me?"[482]

---

[481] Kumati and Sa'omale claimed that the excitement over Yahalijo's lost bandage had driven everything out of their heads.

[482] This was a hostile and spurious speech. Balidu was only Aden's cross-cousin by a most remote course, through Balidu's iden-

Baimal, "He, Aden, that's all. He says, 'The father of
Balidu and Sumali killed my father and now the sons are killing me.'"[483]

Balidu, "Oh, he does, does he? I'll chase him out altogether
to *Suabibis*.[484] He accused this *tamberan* house, this new
house. I built it. I built it for Badui. I arranged food. I arranged meat. I cut sago. I made a feast. I built it for
Badui.[485] It is not a *tamberan* house, that it should work

[483] This was a new accusation. There had been an old quarrel
between the father of Balidu and the father of Aden. There had
been an accusation that the father of Balidu had paid the Plainsmen to smoke exuviae stolen by the people of Manuniki.

[484] This is by association with the fact that Kwanemit had already moved to *Suabibis*.

[485] It was said that Balidu could afford to have a big house
built for him because he had meat. On inquiry, it turned out that
he had meat because his son-in-law Nagawe had a good hunting
dog and kept him well supplied, and also that between himself and
his brother Sumali yams were often supplied in return for meat.
The statement that Balidu could afford a big house really meant
that he himself was a good gardener, had good hunting connections, and was a leader whom people would be glad to help, in return for which he feasted them. He built the house for Badui to use
at the *balagasik* feast (pp. 275–276). Wabe, La'abe, and Agilapwe
were formal assistants (that is, the assistants who justified the giving
of a feast), and Badui, Maigi, and Pidjui worked as members of the
household itself. Nagawe actually provided all the meat, and
Balidu's own household worked sago. Wabe received one phalanger, one bandicoot, and sago. Agilapwe and La'abe each received
half a phalanger. Wabe did the decorations of sago bark on the
back of the house and Agilapwe those on the front. The thatch was
done in four divisions, by Wabe, La'abe, and Maigi. Yapul came
to help her mother cook for the builders. Agilapwe was helped by
his sons.

In this house Balidu housed his yam harvest just before the big
feast. There were about 1200 pounds of yams, of which 700 were

tifying himself with his dead sister's son, Pidjui of *Hamiebis*, who
had been a genuine *wa'en* of Aden's. His claims to rings on the
basis of such a relationship would have been so tenuous as only to
be honored if there were no other better-qualified *wa'en*. Aden's
relatives were so few that his only true mother's brothers were the
two wasters, Gobonarra and Kwanemit, and it might well be that
if everyone were friendly, Balidu's remote claim rather than theirs
would have been honored. To mention such a claim here was
merely a way of referring to Aden's death, which at the moment
there was no doubt Balidu was really angry enough to desire.

sorcery. By and by, I will get firewood and burn it to the ground. Who dares to come and make sorcery in it?[486] It is the wives of Aden (who are to blame for his sore). The two wives of Aden. He does not sleep apart from his wives. The old sore from the previous attack was kept open, and someone got pus and put it in the wild taro. I warned him. I said, 'Cross-cousin, sleep away from your wives and the sore will dry.' But he would not listen. Ulaba'i, look at him. He stayed away from his wives and the sores dried up.[487] This man Aden! He thinks only about sorcery. He doesn't think about feasts and dances and good things.

"They made the divinatory oven. The stone broke.[488] By and by he will die. If the stone had not broken he would not be going to die."

Henalian, "Yes, the stone crumbled to bits and he will die."

Badui, "They got one of the ancestral stones from the old place of *Kanehoibis* and *it* crumbled into little bits."

Balidu, "He is my cross-cousin. He is not another man. And yet he accuses me. Have we quarreled over sago, over a house site, over a garden? No. Have we quarreled over coconut palms or areca nut palms? No. Have we quarreled over my holding fast to his exuviae? No! Nothing. It is true that we argued over a sago tree. He was obstinate. I was obstinate. Finally, he cut it. I said, 'Very well. Later when you have a sago tree ripe for cutting Badui shall go and cut one.' This was not a quarrel. This was a friendly argument."

(Here someone said something about the pig which

---

quite small. These were assorted into 30 piles inside the house. The house itself was not used during the feast; it stood there proudly housing the yams, and the guests sat underneath it.

486 Here he shifts from a defense of the house itself, which is not a tenable position, to an accusation against some outsider who has entered his house.

487 This was a reasonable accusation. Sores could not get well unless intercourse was rigidly abstained from, and Aden was the only man in the community who was definitely believed to be too uxorious. The same claim had been made against him in the past when his pig had died. He could not keep away from his wives.

488 This was the first report of the breaking of the stone. It had not impressed Madje or Aden at the time.

*Suabibis* had brought to Aden. Balidu had not heard any-thing of that either.)

Balidu, "So *Suabibis* brought a pig to Aden, did they? And to whom did he give it?"

Henalian, "One part to Wihun, two to Nyelahai, two to Numidipiheim."

Balidu, "Later on, he will die because he did not taboo women."

The loud-voiced conversation dropped off.

\* \* \*

Isobai of Wihun came through on his way from the Beach and stopped for gossip.

Me'elue passed through on her way back from Wihun to Moholigum.

Henalian set off for Alipinagle.

\* \* \*

ADEN'S ILLNESS: FURTHER INCIDENTS (7)

Wutue came up late in the morning. He had been staying with Aden for the last month, planting part of his garden there, an unusual move for the solitary Wutue. He sat down with Balidu who again burst into loud speeches, telling Wu-tue to tell Aden the following, "Go and tell all the wives and the sisters and the brothers of Aden. I am not coming near him. He has accused me, his cross-cousin, of sorcery. Very well. When he dies they can pay me rings and pigs. They can give a *gaba*[489] to me. But I, I shall not go near him. If he should die and I hear anyone accuse me of his death, I shall take a spear and kill him. Never mind if I hang for it. I shall kill the accuser. And I shall not go near Aden."

Wutue (talking in a low voice), "What other people say, I don't know. I don't hear their talk. I stay on the hill with Aden. What Aden says, I know. He says, 'Fine days and rainy days, Balidu climbs up to his garden in Nugum. When it rains, he does not shelter in my house.' I say, 'Why does he not come and sit down in my house, by my fire? Must it

[489] The ceremonial name for the rings paid to a *wa'en* at death.

not be that he knows who is sorcerizing me and is ashamed?'
This I know Aden says, for I sit down with him and hear it."

And Wutue got up and went back to Aden's.

* * *

Maigi and Sagu took home their little pig, a gift from
Maigi's sister in Magahine. Balidu had bought two little pigs
in Magahine. His whole family went to their garden.

AUGUST 13: It was a squally, rainy day. Yabinigi returned
from the *Suabibis* bush off which he had been obscenely
warned by Heagul, his brother-in-law, the husband of Welenue. Balili and his women brought food to sell.

Then Ombomb and Sauwedjo came in, full of news.

La'abe, said Ombomb, was going to stay in Ahalesimihi
until Aden got well. This he had told Ombomb at Wupali's
*abullu*.[490] If Aden died he meant to take sides against Balidu
as responsible. He was angry because Aden, who was really
his *buanyin*, had been treated so badly.[491]

Ombomb announced that he would stand with La'abe in
this.

The second matter in which Ombomb was interested was:

## THE SKIN DISEASE OF YABINIGI'S WIFE

This girl was a deplorable spectacle; now it seemed that
she had not had this skin infection when she had run away
from Yabinigi. She had run away right after the first menstruation feast, and Nahomen, sly, irresponsible, and malicious, had suggested to his younger brother that he take the
*walowahine* yam, half of which she had eaten, into the Plains
and have her sorcerized. Yabinigi docilely had done so. Now

---

[490] Later proved to be untrue. It was only after he fell ill and
Bunitai linked his illness with Aden's in the same divination that
La'abe began feeling so strongly on the subject.

[491] Aden had been the *buanyin* of La'abe's father and had been
given to Balidu as his *buanyin* by La'abe's father. But Aden was
helping La'abe purchase the *midep*, and in the course of trans-
ferring the pig to Kobelen for the *midep*, if Aden was not to pay
that pig to Balidu, to whom he owed it, he had to assert that he
and La'abe were really *buanyins*. This was all highly irregular behavior, and La'abe was naturally not feeling very comfortable about
it.

he had his wife back, covered with an infection, for which he was sure his act was responsible. When Dr. Fortune returned he was going to ask for a leave of absence and go into the Plains and get it back.[492]

Dr. Fortune arrived in the evening with the news that the Beach villages would carry us down the next week.

AUGUST 14: Ombomb and his wife left to go fencing. He was going to stop and see Aden.

AUGUST 15: We packed. No events.

## ADEN'S ILLNESS (8)

AUGUST 16: Ulaba'i made a short speech saying that if Aden died, he would fasten *tanggets* and they would not be loosened, nor would his side have anything to do with Balidu's side, until peace was made as after a fight, with exchange of pigs and rings. No one answered this.

No one paid much attention to this, however, as there was a new matter to be attended to.

## LOMAIJO'S CONFESSION OF SEDUCTION

La'abe, when he came to plant his yams, had again been impressed with how poor they were, and his old suspicions of Lomaijo had revived under the impetus of Gerud's accusation. Furthermore, he had been ill, he was worried about the quarrel over Aden. Finally, two days before, in Ahalesimihi, La'abe beat Lomaijo, accusing her of an affair with Kaberman, in which he did not really believe. Lomaijo stoutly denied this, but finally confessed that months before, when La'abe had gone to Wewak and left her working sago with Nahomen, he had entered her house and seduced her. She added that she thought he had taken some exuviae and was now making sorcery against her.[493]

[492] This is the only instance I have of the use of the *walo-wahine* meal. Ombomb, in discussing this incident with me, stressed the fact that Nahomen and Yabinigi were neither very intelligent nor stable people. People like that sometimes did use it, he said.

[493] This accusation was based on the fact that several years before there had been a quarrel between Nahomen and Maigi, his brother-in-law, on one side and Nagawe, Wena, and Amambut on the other. Soon afterwards, the wife of Nahomen had died, and this

On August 16 a huge crowd was gathered in Alitoa, preparatory to our departure. La'abe and Lomaijo returned from Ahalesimihi, and Nahomen was summoned to come up and answer the charge.

Baimal stood up at his end of the village and made a long and threatening speech to Nahomen, who sat all alone in the middle of the Alitoa plaza. Baimal's speech was mainly shouts and abusive terms. Then Lomaijo walked up to the plaza, La'abe following a little behind her. She sat down a little way from Nahomen, looking sulky and ashamed, but mainly sulky. Nagawe prowled about, not sitting down. Amito'a stood on the edge of the scene and interrupted occasionally. Ulaba'i walked about near his house, carefully dissociating himself from Nahomen. Kule sat down on the other side near Aden's house, and played his usual role of representing the common-sense point of view of disinterested public opinion. Nahomen had a little fire beside him, as if to warm himself in the hostile atmosphere.

Lomaijo, "You did it. You came in. You lay on my legs. I slept with my child. I tried to cry out. In vain. You, brother! You came and played with me. I did not want you. The next day you came and tried to talk with me. I did not want it. I came up on top."

She said this in a low, vigorous, accusing voice, and at intervals while she spoke, Nahomen, surlily, "You are lying. . . . I did not do such a thing. . . . You are lying."

Lomaijo, "You lifted up my apron. You held a firestick. I saw you. It was you!"

Nahomen, "*Ipa!*[494] Miduain and the wife of Sinaba'i were sleeping in the next house. How, if I came as you say, did you not call out to them?"

Lomaijo (stubbornly), "It was you. I saw you."

Nahomen, "You went up on top. I did not say anything to you. It is a lie."

---

quarrel had been invoked in the discussion. Therefore, Nahomen might have seduced Lomaijo merely to avenge his wife's death. Furthermore, as soon as a sex offense was tinged with a sorcery motive, that became primary in everyone's eyes, which was always useful in distracting attention.

[494] A common exclamation, literally, "you" (plural).

Amito'a, interjecting, to Nahomen, "You paid for her, eh. You paid for her and wished to consummate the marriage. *Ipa!* And now you have sorcerized her. *Ipa!*"

Nahomen, "How should I wish to kill her?" (to Amito'a). (To Lomaijo), "Why didn't you cry out then, and say 'Brother, I don't want this.'"[495]

La'abe, "Come on, talk, confess. Why didn't you come up quicker?"

Nahomen (to Lomaijo), "By and by you will die. And I, I will be accused. I do not come up here. I stay in my place."

Lomaijo (still being circumstantial), "Afterwards I came up here. Balidu asked me, 'Where is the sago?' I said, 'There is none. I just came on top.'"

Nahomen, "Inoman, too, was there. Why could you not have called out, 'Brother, he has taken my exuviae for sorcery'? The sago, true, we were working it together. La'abe had gone away. He left you there. We worked sago. Everyone can watch me. If I send a knife or a tomahawk into the Plains, then they can talk."[496]

Lomaijo, "It is true. You have sorcerized me."

Nahomen, "You can talk if you see a knife or a tomahawk go in. You can talk later."

Amito'a, "Her sister (of Lomaijo), formerly she died of sorcery. Now you wish to make her die."[497]

Nahomen, "I? I am not a maker of sorcery."[498]

Amito'a, "What are you doing, going about lifting up women's aprons, sister's aprons? This is the bad fashion of all Kwainigil."[499]

Anop strolled on the scene from the direction of Sinaba'i's house, staying at a distance. La'abe stood against a palm near Aden's house, with both hands behind his back.

[495] While pretending to argue merely that he couldn't have done as she says, he is slyly insinuating that she accepted him. This was probably true. Lomaijo was thoroughly disgruntled at La'abe, but later, because of the fear of sorcery, had turned against Nahomen. This is the form that guilt usually takes.

[496] Here he reverts to the sorcery charge which he fears.

[497] This is one of the points which are forever being brought up, as if there was a curse over each family line.

[498] This remark was merely formal and said without conviction.

[499] Inhabitants of Alitoa. Amito'a has reverted for a moment to talking as a member of Liwo.

La'abe (to Lomaijo), "Did he copulate with you? Speak."

Nahomen, "If a man copulates with a woman, will he forget it? No."

La'abe (to Nahomen), "Why didn't you care for your own wife and keep her alive to copulate with? Instead you get into quarrels and you lost her. This fashion is no good. This is my wife, not yours."

Nahomen (to Lomaijo), "And you, why didn't you call out to Ulaba'i? (Also sleeping some distance away but within hearing.)

Kule (dispassionately, to Nahomen), "Go on. Make the thing straight. Confess and pay up."

Nahomen, "No! No! I will not pay."

La'abe, "It is true!"

He walked across the plaza, revealing a light switch held behind him. With this he beat Nahomen lightly four or five strokes, after which Nahomen seized a piece of elephant grass stalk and made a feint of hitting him back. La'abe walked back to his original post. No one else stirred.

La'abe, "You, you didn't look after your own wife. You ate here and there. You quarreled with people. You did not look after her. By and by I'll have you put in jail."

Nahomen, "NO! NO! I did not copulate with her."

La'abe, "The woman has confessed. Now you confess too."

Nahomen, "If it were so I would confess that I had copulated with her."

Nagawe, "What is true? Did he copulate with her or only lift up her apron?"

La'abe, "If you don't confess I'll have a law case against you."

Ulaba'i, "You know it's true. Come on, confess."

Nahomen, "NO! NO! I say."

Amito'a, "Her sister. She is dead. *She* only remains."

La'abe, "Many times I have gone away and left my wife with you. The *luluai* is not strong. It is always I who must walk about. All right. Now I am through. I am going to stay at home and other people can walk about.[500] The *luluai* can walk about."

---

[500] La'abe's familiar slight sense of self-pity is rising now. While he did the people's work, his brother betrays his trust.

Kule (to Nahomen), "Go on, get something, and give it to the woman to give to her husband."[501]

La'abe, "You pay, and you get the exuviae back. Quickly. Or I'll go to Wewak."

Kule, "Come on, confess and pay it."

Amito'a, "You get back the exuviae. Wash it and crumble it up and throw it away."

La'abe, "Manum asked me (when she confessed), 'How often have you left her with him?' I replied 'Often! I went to the Beach this time and I left her to cut sago.' I left my wife and in the night you sorcerize her."

Amito'a, "We call them our children, and the wives of our children.[502] This is an evil fashion, this."

La'abe, "Stop hiding this. Confess. I beat Lomaijo and she confessed."

Amito'a, "Before, when her sister died, I said to Lomaijo, 'Sister-in-law, now you must look after yourself very carefully, so that you will remain.' She said, 'Oh, I shall remain. If any man attempts me, I'll stab him with my knife.'"[503]

Nahomen said no more. The group melted away, and Nahomen got up and walked out of the village.

Wabe commented, "I'd divorce that woman. I had one like her and I divorced her. If one copulates and confesses, she can stay with me, but a woman who conceals her sins will ruin a man."

Nothing more would be done about this unless Lomaijo fell ill, when Nahomen would again be accused. But he was an *alomato'in*, insensible to all the arguments which moved other men, and it would not matter very much. There was nothing to be done with him. He remained to menace the community.

AUGUST 17: The carriers gathered and took us down from Alitoa, leaving Aden's fate and so the relative tranquillity of the little community still undecided.

---

[501] A symbol of repentance was all that La'abe was demanding.

[502] She refers to the fact that Baimal calls Nahomen and his brothers, child.

[503] This was pure malice on Amito'a's part and meant to convey her lack of faith in Lomaijo's unwillingness.

# TABULAR AND ANALYTICAL TREATMENT OF ALITOA DATA

## CENSUS LIST FOR REFERENCE

This list is designed for ready reference to the members of Alitoa locality, for readers who wish to place in context anecdotes which appear in other papers in this series. The names of the heads of households are arranged alphabetically, and each household has been given a serial number. The head of the household is lettered A. The wives appear in order, with the names of the children of each wife indented under her name, and carrying the same letter, so the first[1] wife is B and her children are B1, B2, etc.; the second wife C and the third wife D. Later letters indicate other members of the households, exclusive of wives and children of wives, and their exact status is explained in the comment column. A deceased wife will not be included unless she has children still resident in the household; in this case, her name will appear in parentheses, and her children will be indicated by the letter which precedes her name.

1 That is, the wife who is now resident in his household and has been longest married to him of his present wives.

SAMPLE FORM

| Serial Number | A Name of Householder<br>B Name of first wife<br>  B1 Eldest resident child of this wife: sex; age<br>  B2 Next oldest resident child of this wife: sex; age<br>C Name of second wife<br>D Name of third wife<br>E, F, etc. Other residents in the household | Gens<br>Gens or locality[2] | Resident Hamlet | Comment |
|---|---|---|---|

[2] When a woman comes from another locality, her locality is substituted for her gens when she is mentioned.

| SE-RIAL NUM-BER | NAME | GENS | RESIDENCE HAMLET | COMMENT |
|---|---|---|---|---|
| 1 | A Aden | Kanehoibis (Alitoa branch) | (1) Alitoa (2) Alipaba | |
| | B Baijo | Dibatua'am | | Sister of Nyelahai and Ulaba'i |
| | B1 Sauisua: f; 2–3 | | | |
| | C Ulaijo | Dibatua'am | | Sister of Baijo (widow of a Wihum man) |
| | E Madje: m; 17–19 | Kanehoibis-Uyebis (alapwen) | | Son of Aden's mother and Anop's father |
| 2 | A Agilapwe | Labinem (sole representative) | Manuniki | Chronic yaws sore on leg |
| | B (Taromano) | Dibatua'am | | Sister of Nyelahai |
| | B1 Ibal: f; 7–8 | | | |
| | B2 Yuwalen: f; 5–6 | | | |
| | B3 Wapial: m; 3–4 | | | |
| | C Malasua | Banyimebis | | Widow of a Uyenehas man; pig keeper |
| 3 | A Alis | Toto'alaibis | (1) Mogiligen (2) Nebihitali | Just married |
| | B Taumulimen | Uyenehas | | Sister of Maigi |

| | | *Diboatbis* | | *Ahalesimihi*[3] | |
|---|---|---|---|---|---|
| | | Numomihi | | | |
| 4 | A Amambut | | | | |
| | B No'abis | | | | |
| |   B1 A'ati: m; 12–14 | | | | |
| |   B2 Tchaho: f; 4–5 | | | | |
| | D Mother of No'abis | | | | Widow of a Liwo man, who joined her daughter and married Amambut but also |
| | | | | (1) Moholigum | Young man, just married, uninitiated |
| | | | | (2) Kwobilisi[4] | Daughter of Nahomen |
| | | *Uyebis* | | | |
| 5 | A Anop | | | | |
| | | *Dibatua'am* | | | |
| | | Wihun (regarded as Kanehoibis because widow of father of Aden) | | | |
| | B Yabenas | | | | |
| | E Mother of Anop | | | | |
| | | *Kanehoibis* | | | |
| | F Muliwen | | | | Mother of Matasues, Ombomb, Wabe |
| | G Wadjubel: f; 18–20 | | | | Sister of Anop (betrothed to absent son of Amambut) |
| | | *Toto'alaibis* | | | |
| 6 | A Baimal | | | | |
| | | | | (1) Mogiligen | |
| | | | | (2) Walinuba | |

[3] I lack sufficient complete data about garden hamlets in Ahalesimihi to make it worth while to include any of them.

[4] New hamlet of Matasues and Wamu'um.

466

| Serial Number | Name | Gens | Residence Hamlet | Comment |
|---|---|---|---|---|
| | B Amito'a | Liwo (daughter of a Kanehoibis mother) | | Runaway wife of a Liwo man |
| | B1 Amus: f; 4–5 | | | |
| | C Alaijo | Numidipiheim | | Widow of dead brother Bauwan |
| | C1 Minya: f; 9–10 | | | Daughter of Bauwan |
| 7 | A Balidu | Toto'alaibis | Walinuba | Big man of Alitoa |
| | B Yahalijo | Wihun | | |
| | B1 Baduï: m; 18–20 | | | Just initiated, marriage not consummated |
| | B2 Pidjui: m; 15–16 | | | |
| | B3 Kumati: f; 11–12 | | | Formerly betrothed to Maigi, now returned to her father |
| | B4 Nigimarib: m; 8–9 | | | |
| | E Sa'omale: f; 12–13 | Liwo Biegilipim | Yapiaun | Betrothed wife of Badui, 3 Mother's brother's son of Baimal (6-A) and Kule |
| 8 | A Balili | Wihun | | |
| | B Suamaile | | | |
| | B1 Adainyamea: m; 6–7 | | | |
| | B2 Taimani; f; 3–4 | | | |

| | | | |
|---|---|---|---|
| C Malidjua | Numomihi | | A very old man |
| D Halesin | Boinam | | |
| 9 A Belatau | Uyenehas | Manumiki | |
| B Uwaidjo | Biegilipim | | Covered with *tinea* |
| B1 Walaminia: m; 23 | | | |
| B2 La'amen: m; 10–11 | | | |
| 10 A Bischu | Uyebis | (1) Alapihi (2) Alitoa | Taken by *Uyebis* as a very young child |
| B Danue | Numidipiheim | | |
| B1 Yabiok: f; 4–5 | | | |
| B2 Anoan: m; 2–3 | | | |
| B3 Wabijo: f; born Jan., 1932 | | | |
| 11 A Gabunyan | Diboaibis | Ahalesimihi | Widowed mother of Gabunyan, sister of Balidu |
| B Malasamum | Wihun | | |
| D Nigilowe | Toto'alaibis | | |
| 12 A Gobonarra | Hamiebis | (1) Malupit, Alitoa (2) Dunigi | Only survivor of his gens in Alitoa, *alomato'in* |
| B Culumen | | | Runaway woman from Dunigi |
| B1 Sauedjo: f; 13 | | | Daughter of 12-B by Dunigi husband |
| B2 Mogoabil: m; 5–6 | | | Son of 12-B by Dunigi husband |

| SERIAL NUMBER | NAME | GENS | RESIDENCE HAMLET | COMMENT |
|---|---|---|---|---|
| 13 | A Henalian | *Maliebis Dibatua'am* | Alipinagle | Joined his brother-in-law Selalimi |
| | B Hano | | | |
| | B1 Apelehenum: m; 7 | | | |
| | B2 Tuagisa: m; 4 | | | Child whose illness is discussed in Record of Events |
| | B3 Mwaikina: m; 2–3 | | | |
| | E Manuwai | *Maliebis* | | Father's sister of Henalian. Mother of Nyelahai and Ulaba'i |
| 14 | A Inoman | Born *Wihun*, foster child *Dibatua'am*, *gwai'oyen* to *Toto'alaibis* | Kwobilisi[5] | |
| | B Domau | Born *Uyebis*, adopted *Maliebis* | | |
| | B1 Oiyale: m; 9–10 | | | |
| | B2 Gisoman: f; 5–6 | | | |
| | B3 Mag'a'a: m; 1–2 | | | |

[5] Old hamlet of La'abe's father, but new hamlet of same name now being made by Matasues.

| | | | |
|---|---|---|---|
| 15 A Iwamini | | Alipinagle | |
| B Yinauwhat | Born *Kanehoibis*, *gwai'oyen* to *Banyimebis* | | |
| B1 Ibanyos: f; 1–2 | *Uyenehas* | | |
| 16 A Kule | *Toto'alaibis* | (1) Mogilligen | Younger brother of Baimal; doctor boy |
| | | (2) Alitoa | |
| | | (3) Nebihitali | |
| B Ilautoa | *Uyenehas* | | Sister of Maigi; formerly betrothed to Baimal |
| B1 Naguel: m; 6–7 | | | |
| B2 Mausi: f; 3–4 | Wihun | | Widow of dead brother Bauwan |
| C Soatsalamo | | | Child of Kule |
| C1 Walipin: m; 1–2 | *Toto'alaibis* | Alitoa | *Tultul*, Government-appointed interpreter |
| 17 A La'abe | *Diboaibis* | | Inherited by La'abe from a cross-cousin |
| B Lomaijo | | | |
| B1 Souato'a: f; 4–5 | | | |
| B2 Kamowon: f; 2–3 | *Banyimebis* | | Formerly betrothed to Gerud but grew too fast |
| C Imale | *Banyimebis* | | |
| 18 A Maginala | Boinam | Alipinagle | |
| B Soasalamo | | | Woman with delusions |

| SE-RIAL NUM-BER | NAME | GENS | RESIDENCE HAMLET | COMMENT |
|---|---|---|---|---|
| | C Aga'amwi | Dumigi | | Runaway woman from Plains |
| | C1 Infant girl un-named | | | |
| | E Ga'olin: m; 23–24 | | | Brother of Maginala, unmarried, tinea |
| | F Weamali: f; 20–21 | | | Sister of Maginala, unmarried, held to attract new recruits to Ali-pinagle |
| 19 | A Maigi | Uyenehas | (1) Manumiki (2) Alitoa | |
| | B Sagu | Toto'alaibis | | Daughter of Balidu, widow of Maigi's brother |
| 20 | A Manum | Diboaibis | | |
| | B Homendjuai | Toto'alaibis | Ahalesimihi | Sister of La'abe |
| | B1 Mai: m; 14 | | | Betrothed to Amus, 6-B1 |
| | B2 La'atowin: m; 11 | | | |
| | B3 Kubi: m; 8 | | | |
| | B4 Naipa'um: m; 4 | | | |
| | B5 Anuli: m; 0–1 | | | |

| | Born Toto'alaibis, gwa'oyen to Uyebis | (1) Mobilinigum (2) Kwobilisi (3) Alitoa | |
|---|---|---|---|
| 21 A Matasues | | | |
| B Minago'a | Maliebis | | Originally betrothed to Abugil, Matasues' elder absentee brother. Betrothed to Magiel |
| B1 Una: f; 11-12 | | | |
| B2 Anamen: m; 5-6 | | | |
| C Wahewai | Numidipiheim | | Runaway from a Numidipiheim man |
| C1 Ashuga: m; 4-5 | | | |
| C2 Shu'ite: m; 1-2 | | | |
| 22 A Menyul | Toto'alaibis | Hidden away in bush near Malupit | Mentally unbalanced brother of Balidu and Sumali |
| B Madjuamal | Numonihi | | Lame |
| B1 Salagiel: f; 2-3 | | | |
| 23 A Nagawe | Kanehoibis (Ahalesimihi branch) Biegilipim | Ahalesimihi | Big man of Ahalesimihi |
| B Alo | | | |
| B1 Anau: m; 10-11 | | | |
| B2 Malagi: f; 5-6 | | | |
| C Yapul | Toto'alaibis | | Daughter of Balidu |
| C1 Maleheu: f; 3-4 | | | |
| C2 Otamai: m; 0-1 | | | |

| SERIAL NUMBER | NAME | GENS | RESIDENCE HAMLET | COMMENT |
|---|---|---|---|---|
| 24 | A Nahomen | Born Wihun, adopted Dibatua'am Uyenehas | Kwobilisi[6] | Widower and *alomato'in* |
|  | B (Dead wife, sister of Maigi) B1 Anim: f; 11 B2 Mi'a'inyu: m; 3 |  |  |  |
| 25 | A Naushe'e | Kanehoibis (Ahalesimhi branch) Ilapweim | Ahalesimihi | Has lived many years in Ilapweim |
|  | B Weyal B1 Ame': m; 3–4 B2 Moshesh: m; 0–1 |  |  |  |
| 26 | A Nyelahai | Dibatua'am | (1) Tereba (2) Moholigum | Big man of Alitoa end |
|  | B (Dead wife, sister of Aden) B1 Hadjatuk: m; 12 |  |  |  |
|  | C Nyalamidju | Liwo |  | Widow of a Liwo man; old woman, pig keeper; mother of 7-E |

[6] New place of Matasues.

| | | | |
|---|---|---|---|
| D Natun | Wihun | | Originally betrothed to Yabinigi; sister of Me'elue |
| D1 Infant which died April 22, 1932 | | | |
| E Bwanai: f; 5 | | | |
| 27 A Ombomb | Toto'alaibis Wihun | Alitoa | Adopted daughter of Nyalamidju |
| B Me'elue | | | Sister of 25-D |
| B1 Yauito'a: f; 2–3 | | | |
| C Sauwedjo | Dunigi | | Runaway wife from Plains |
| C1 Infant girl born March 12, 1932 | | | |
| 28 A Selalimi | Banyimebis Wihun | Ahalesimihi | Domiciled in Ahalesimihi |
| B Samanuai | | | |
| B1 Iwatien: m; 12–13 | | | |
| B2 Ilawen: m; 7–8 | | | |
| B3 Manawam: f; 4–5 | | | |
| C Sa'i'o'o | Wihun | | Widow of brother, remains in Alipinagle |
| C1 Tamil: f; 5–6 | | | Child of 28-C by dead husband |
| 29 A Silisium | Diboaibis Numonihi | Ahalesimihi | Brother of Manum |
| B Ya'umen | | | Betrothed to Badui, 7-B1 |
| B1 Gowais: f; 12–13 | | | |
| B2 Nautal: f; 9–10 | | | |
| B3 Malipim: m; 2–3 | | | |
| B4 Infant girl | | | |

| SERIAL NUMBER | NAME | GENS | RESIDENCE HAMLET | COMMENT |
|---|---|---|---|---|
| 30 | A Sinaba'i | *Dibatua'am* | (1) Alitoa (2) Moholigum | |
| | B (Dead Dumigi wife) | | | |
| | B1 Miduain: f; 11–12 | | | Betrothed to son of Wamu'um |
| | B2 Dubomagau: m; 8–9 | | | |
| | C Menala | Wihum | | Formerly married in Wihun, then wife of Wabe |
| | C1 Aimau: m; 0–1 | | | Child promised to Wabe in return for Menala |
| | | | | Brother of Balidu |
| 31 | A Sumali | *Toto'alaibis* | (1) Malupit (2) Alitoa | Sister of Silisium and Manum |
| | B Winam | *Diboaibis* | | Formerly married in Liwo, now betrothed to Monau, brother of Aden, away |
| | B1 Budagiel: f; 20–21 | | | Chief diviner, one of our boys |
| | B2 Gerud: m; 18–19 | | | |
| | B3 Midjulumon: m; 12–13 | | | |

| | | | | |
|---|---|---|---|---|
| | B4 Bopugenon: m; 10–11 | | | |
| | B5 Ite'epe: f; 7–8 | | | |
| | B6 Moul: m; 4–5 | | | |
| | B7 Eweluen: m; 1–2 | | | |
| 32 | A Tapita | *Diboaibs* | Alipinagle | Domiciled in place of dead *Banyimebis* wife |
| | B Adule | Ybonimu | | Died in March, 1932 |
| 33 | A Ulaba'i | *Dibatua'am* | (1) Moholigum | Government appointee, *luluai*, brother of Nyelahai |
| | | | (2) Alitoa | Sister of Aden |
| | B Ibanyos | *Kanehoibis* (Alitoa branch) | | Runaway from a Numidipiheim man |
| | C Whasimai | Numidipiheim | | Betrothed to a *Suabibis* boy, in Liwo |
| | C1 Anyuai: f; 10–11 | | | |
| | C2 Segenamoya: m; 6–7 | | | |
| | C3 Nemausi: f; 2–3 | | | |
| 34 | A Wabe | Born *Toto'alaibis*, *gwai'oyen* to *Uyebis* | (1) Alitoa | Brother of Matases and Ombomb |
| | | | (2) Alipinagle | |
| | B Welima | *Banyimebis* | | Daughter of Selalimi, sister of Imale, 17-C |

| SERIAL NUMBER | NAME | GENS | RESIDENCE HAMLET | COMMENT |
|---|---|---|---|---|
| | C Temos | *Uyebis* | | Daughter of the brother of Wutue. Betrothed to Yauwiyu, then to Sinaba'i, exchanged for Menala, 30-C |
| 35 | A Walawahan | Born *Uyebis* | Ahalesimihi | Domiciled in his dead wife's place |
| | B (Dead *Diboaibis* wife) | | | |
| | B1 Sala'a: m; 14 | | | |
| | B2 Sauiadjo: f; 9–10 | | | |
| | C Suamali | Wihun | | Formerly married to dead brother of Agilapwe |
| | C1 Infant boy | | | |
| 36 | A Wamu'um | *Maliebis* | (1) Moholigum (2) Kwobilisi | Domiciled with his dead wife's brother, Matasues |
| | B (Dead wife, Malihiyau, sister of Matasues) | | | |
| | B1 Bunitai: m; 19–20 | | | Not initiated, a *sagumeh* diviner |
| | B2 Keali: f; 15–16 | | | Betrothed to Numidipiheim boy, away |
| | C Miegelian | *Diboaibis* | | Sister of Nagawe, widowed mother of Wena |

| Individual | Spouse / birthplace note | Name | Remarks |
|---|---|---|---|
| C1 Aniyolin: m; 14–15 | | | Deaf. Child of Wena's father fostered by Wamu'um |
| C2 Wabisu: f; 11–12 | | | Child of Wena's father fostered by Wamu'um |
| C3 Ta'onae: f; 4–5 | | | Child of Wena's father fostered by Wamu'um |
| 37 A Wegul | Born Liwo, brought home by *Banyimebis* father | Alipinagle | Suspected of being a witch |
| B Mo'onen | *Wihun* | | Formerly wife of Henalian, eloped with Wegul |
| B1 Infant girl | | | |
| 38 A Wena | Born *Uyebis*, domiciled in Ahalesimihi, with mother's brother Nagawe | Ahalesimihi | |
| B Ma'omen | *Wihun* | | Formerly betrothed to Bischu, given to Wena |
| B1 Infant girl | | | |
| 39 A Wutue | *Uyebis* | (1) Ategini (2) Alitoa | |
| B Mela | *Kanehoilbis* | | |
| B1 Shuisha: f; 10–11 | | | |
| B2 Yanyibis: m; 5–6 | | | |
| B3 Ui: m; 2–3 | | | |

| Serial Number | Name | Gens | Residence Hamlet | Comment |
|---|---|---|---|---|
| 40 | A Yabimigi | Had no household, formerly married to Natun, 26-D, and to Wihun girl. Our shoot boy | | |
| 41 | A Yamogwai | Biegilipim Numonihi | Yapiaun | Brother of Balili |
| | B Ulahaiyu | | | Old father of Yamogwai and Balili |
| | E Sama'a | | | Mother of Yamogwai, wife of 41-E |
| | F Maguenai | | | Mentally unstable |
| 42 | A Yauwiyu | Born *Suabibis*, adopted by *Labinem*, who married his mother | Manuniki | |
| | B Anone | Dunigi | | Runaway wife, from Plains |
| | B1 Magidai: f; 4–5 | | | |
| | B2 Infant girl: 0–1 | | | |
| | C Wasijo | *Maliebis* | | Daughter of Wamu'um and dead sister of Matasues and widow of brother of Maigi |
| | C1 Selandjim: m; 3 | | | Child of former husband of Wasijo |

# CHECK LIST, GENS MEMBERSHIP

*Banyimebis*
Ga'olin
Iwamini
Maginala
Selamini
Tapita

*Biegilipim*
Balili
Sama'a
Yamogwai

*Dibatua'am*
Nahomen
Nyelahai
Sinaba'i

Ulaba'i
Yabinigi

*Diboaibis*
Amambut
Gabunyan
Manum
Silisium

*Hamiebis*
Gobonarra

*Kanehoibis*
Alitoa branch
Aden
Madje

Ahalesimihi branch
Nagawe
Naushe'e

*Labinem*
Agilapwe
Yauwiyu

*Maliebis*
Henalian
Wamu'um

*Toto'alaibis*
Alis
Baimal
Balidu
Inoman

Kule
La'abe
Menyal
Ombomb
Sumali

*Uyebis*
Anop
Bischu
Matasues
Wabe
Wutue

*Uyenehas*
Belatau
Maigi

## HAMLET CHECK LIST

| NAME | CHIEF MAN | ASSOCIATED GENTES | NAME | CHIEF MAN | ASSOCIATED GENTES |
|---|---|---|---|---|---|
| Alapihi | Bischu | Uyebis (Kanehoibis)[7] | Kwobilisi I | (La'abe)[10] | Toto'alaibis |
| Alipaba | Aden | | | Inoman | |
| ALITOA[8] | Ulaba'i | Uyebis and Dibatua'am (Kanehoibis) | Kwobilisi II[11] | Matasues and Wamu'um | Maliebis<br>Uyebis and Maliebis |
| | Wabe | | | (Nahomen) | |
| | Bischu | | | (Inoman) | |
| | Aden | | | (Bunitai) | |
| Amoloegali | (Anop)[9] | Uyebis (Dibatua'am) | Maloten[12] | Wamu'um (Matasues) | Maliebis |
| | Sinaba'i | | | | |
| | Ombomb | | | | |
| Ategini | Wutue | Uyebis | | | |
| | (Ombomb) | | | | |
| | (La'abe) | | | | |
| | (Bischu) | | | | |

7 This is Aden's new place. The old place of Kanehoibis was called Bulubuhip.

8 Large places in capital letters.

9 Place of Anop's father, and Anop will be regarded as its chief owner.

10 Place of La'abe's father, but had now been permanently given to Inoman, a gwai'oyen to Toto'alaibis from Dibatua'am.

11 This is a new hamlet just being started by Matasues and Wamu'um and to it they have given the old name of the former Kwobilisi which is now almost deserted. When Kwobilisi is mentioned in the Diary, it is this new Kwobilisi that is meant.

12 This was an old Maliebis site, at which Matasues had joined Wamu'um, while Wamu'um's wife, Matasues' sister, was still alive. They were now deserting it for the new Kwobilisi, just keeping a small garden near there.

| NAME | CHIEF MAN | ASSOCIATED GENTES |
|---|---|---|
| Malupit | (Nyelahai)[13] | (Dibatua'am) |
| MANUNIKI[14] | Sumali, Gobonarra | Toto'alaibis |
|  | Agilapwe | Labinem |
|  | Belatau | Uyenehas |
|  | Maigi | (Kanehoibis) |
| Meigum[15] | Balidu | Toto'alaibis |
| Mobilinigum[16] | Matasues | Uyebis |

13 This place had belonged to Nyelahai before, and Aden had lived there with him. Now given to Sumali entirely in return for his taking over Gobonarra.
14 Manuniki was still regarded as a decayed village, not as a small hamlet.
15 New garden of Balidu's which seemed likely to be turned into a small hamlet; Ombomb and Wabe and La'abe there gardening.
16 Old hamlet, now close to abandonment.

| NAME | CHIEF MAN | ASSOCIATED GENTES |
|---|---|---|
| Mogilligen | Baimal | Toto'alaibis |
| Moholigum | Ulaba'i | Dibatua'am |
| Nebihitali[17] | Kule | Toto'alaibis |
| Tereba[18] | Nyelahai | Dibatua'am |
| Yaugen[19] | Balidu | Toto'alaibis |
| Walimuba[20] | Balidu | Toto'alaibis |
|  | Baimal |  |

17 Mogilligen is their hamlet, and this is a very small center, where Kule and Alis garden.
18 New place which Nyelahai founded after leaving Malupit.
19 Gardening hamlet of Balidu being replaced by Meigum.
20 Half of the village of Alitoa.

It will be noted that Wabe is the only man of any importance who had founded no small hamlet of his own. He planted with Balidu, with Bischu, with Wupali in Wihun, and with Maginala and Ga'olin on Welima's father's land in Alipinagle. He was nowhere host and everywhere guest, which accounts in part for his restless discontent and his final attempt to establish himself permanently in Alipinagle and be counted as a member of that community with a place of his own. He had, it is true, a house site in Alitoa, but he had had no gardening site.

## MARSALAI PLACES OF ALITOA

| Name of Marsalai | Name of Place | Gens | Embodiment | Sacred Features and Peculiarities | Special Powers |
|---|---|---|---|---|---|
| Behebil | Behebil | Kanehoibis | Two-headed lizard | An abó tree. Death for anyone who sees him[21] | Hurricane |
| Tuamolin Ebapin | Diaship Tagapen | Banyimebis Biegilipim | Two-headed snake Rat with phosphorescent buttocks | A forbidden stream Appears as an omen of death of a member of the gens | Rain and wind Rain and wind |
| Awheugupen | Alubunup | Toto'alaibis | Two-headed lizard | An atien tree. This marsalai is the son of Behebil | Rain and wind |

[21] On p. 51 of Mead, 1933a, this reads as if the abok tree were personalized and itself meant death if seen. This misstatement was due to an error of punctuation.

| | | | | | |
|---|---|---|---|---|---|
| Dagmulin | Uwebun | *Hamiebis Dibatua'am* | Two-headed lizard | (1) Mounds which look like bandicoot mounds; if these are touched they release whirlwinds<br>(2) A special variety of tree fern, *nyumeis*, to touch meant death | Whirlwind |
| Bagalin | Wahamep | *Diboaibis* | A kangaroo | *Mohulugas*, a bamboo grove of Plains type, which symbolized the members of the gens. If anyone cuts one a man of the gens will die | Rain and wind |
| Bubu[22] | Buté | *Uyenehas* | Two-headed lizard | Gens death omens by showers of stones down into Sulum River | |
| Nigiauwen | Milaib | *Labinem Uyenehas* | Two-headed *lahó* snake | An *ulu'* tree | Wind and rain |

22 Bubu and Behebil were said to be the fathers of all the other *marsalais*.

## SAMPLE OF COCONUT PALM OWNERSHIP IN WALINUBA PART OF ALITOA

| OWNER OF HOUSE SITE | NUMBER OF TREES | OWNER OF TREE | GENS | OWNER OF TREE CALLS OWNER OF HOUSE SITE |
|---|---|---|---|---|
| Sumali | 4 | Sumali (inherited) | Toto'alaibis | |
| Sumali | 1 | Wutue | Uyebis | Classificatory father's brother (ya'en) |
| Baimal | 1 | Kule | Toto'alaibis | Elder brother (asho'en) |
| Baimal | | Gabunyan | Diboaibis | Mother's brother's son (wau'en) |
| Baimal | 1 | Mai (planted by Manum for his son) | Diboaibis | Mother's father's brother's son's son (wau'en) |
| Baimal | 1 | Bischu (planted by father of Bischu) | Uyebis | Classificatory brother (ashoe'en) |
| Baimal | 1 | Ombomb | Toto'alaibis | Father's brother's son's son (niganin) |
| Balidu | 1 | Wupale (who now lives in Wihun) | ex-Toto'alaibis | Father's brother's son (asho'en) |
| Balidu | 1 | Manum | Diboaibis | Wife's brother (mewhen) |
| Sumali | 1 | Alis | Toto'alaibis | Father's younger brother (ya'en) |
| Baimal | 1 | Balidu | Toto'alaibis | Father's younger brother (ya'en) |
| Baimal | 1 | Ombomb | Toto'alaibis | Father's brother's son's son (niganin) |
| Baimal | 1 | Balili | Biegilipim | Father's sister's son (mehinen) |
| Balidu | 1 | Bischu | Uyebis | Classificatory father (ya'en) |
| Balidu | 1 | Wena | Uyebis | Classificatory grandfather (babu'en) |

OMENS AND PORTENTS BELONGING TO DIFFERENT GENTES OF ALITOA

| Gens | Omen<br>Saginin, Saginis | Comment |
|---|---|---|
| Toto'alaibis | Dream of many sago trees being cut and of falling down, breaking | |
| Uyebis | If the *sigavelu*, the black parrot, cries in the night | This gens came out of bamboos and had an omen bird, *siaule'*, whose cry directs hunters |
| Dibatua'am | If the *kumun* bird is seen with best view of the beak, and one bird only | |
| Diboaibis | Dream of the *abulowhi* fruit being cooked | |
| Kanehoibis and Hamiebis | If the *kumun* bird (hawk) is seen in pairs, and tops of heads showing best | |
| Toto'alaibis and Uyenehas | If *kwain* (parrot) is seen, One for Uyenehas, Two for Toto'alaibis | |
| Biegilipim | If the *ebapin*, the rat *marsalai* with the phosphorescent buttocks, is seen | This gens came out of bamboos and has an omen bird, *siaule'*, whose cry directs its hunters |

## OWNERSHIP OF CHARMS[23]

| | |
|---|---|
| Yams | Balidu, Nyelahai, Baimal, Ombomb |
| Hunting | Sumali, Alis, Maginala, Bischu |
| Domestic pigs | Nyelahai, Maigi, Aden |
| Protective magic producing stomach ache | Walawahan, Matasues, Sumali |
| Protective magic producing swelling of breasts | Inoman |
| Protective magic producing vomiting | Ombomb, Matasues, Nyelahai |
| Protective magic producing headache | Balidu, Agilapwe |
| Love magic | Wabe, La'abe, Ulaba'i |
| *Sagumeh* | Sinaba'i, Alis, Gerud, Bunitai |
| Prolonging the night | Wegul |

[23] This list does not include the census of those who knew charms connected with the *tamberan*. It is merely a census of common knowledge.

# ANALYSIS OF ALITOA MARRIAGES

| HUSBAND | | WIFE |
|---------|---|------|
| Aden | A (1) | Baijo (1) betrothed to Aden as a child |
| | | Baijo of *Dibatua'am* exchanged for Iban-yos, sister of Aden who married Ulaba'i, brother of Baijo | |
| | B (2) | Ulaijo, sister of Baijo, who came as a widow | B Ulaijo (1) betrothed as a child and married to a Wihun man. He died and left her with one small son |
| | | | (2) She married Aden, her sister Baijo's husband |
| Agilapwe | A | A betrothed *Kanehoibis* wife who died | A Betrothed to Agilapwe. Died |
| | B | A *Suabibis* woman, mother of Yauwiyu, who ran away | B (1) She married a man of Ilawhainamit, and he died |
| | | | (2) Married Agilapwe |
| | | | (3) Ran away to a Liwo man |
| | C | Talomen, the sister of Yabinigi. She died | C (1) To Agilapwe and died |
| | D | Malasu inherited from a *Uyenehas* man | D (1) Married to a man of *Uyenehas* |
| | | | (2) Inherited by Agilapwe |
| Alis | A | Taumulimen, betrothed to her just as she reached puberty | A (1) Betrothed to a brother of Yabinigi who died at But, and lived before puberty in Nahomen's household, with her older sister, Nahomen's wife |
| | | | (2) Given to Alis just before puberty |

| Husband | | Wife | |
|---|---|---|---|
| Amambut | A A *Kanehoibis* woman, now dead | A | (1) Betrothed to a Liwo man who died |
| | | | (2) Married the elder brother of Amambut. He died |
| | | | (3) Married Amambut and she died |
| | B No'abis | B | (1) Betrothed for Silisium |
| | | | (2) Married Amambut |
| | C Mother of No'abis | C | (1) A Numonihi man and bore No'abis |
| | | | (2) Followed her daughter and married her daughter's husband |
| Anop | A Yabenas, betrothed to him as a child | A | (1) Betrothed to Anop as a child |
| Baimal | A A *Banyimebis* woman, betrothed as a child, who died | A | First betrothed husband |
| | B Nemilu, a *Kanehoibis* woman | B | (1) Married to a *Suabibis* husband, ran away to Baimal. Died in childbirth |
| | C Ilautoa, betrothed to him as a child | C | (1) Betrothed to Baimal, many years her senior, preferred |
| | | | (2) Kule, brother of Baimal and was permitted by Baimal to marry Kule |
| | D Amito'a, ran away to him from *Suabibis* | D | (1) Betrothed as a child to a *Suabibis* man who died |
| | | | (2) Inherited by an old man of *Suabibis*. Ran away to |
| | | | (3) Baimal |

E Alaijo, inherited from his dead brother Bauwan

E (1) Betrothed to a Numidipiheim man, who was crippled from a fight. Ran away at adolescence[24]
(2) Married Bauwan
(3) Inherited by Baimal

Balili:[25]

A Suamaile, betrothed as a child

A (1) Betrothed to Balili

B Malidjua, seduced while work boy husband was away

B (1) Betrothed to a Wihun man who was away at work when she grew up
(2) Seduced by Balili

C Halesiu, ran away to him

C (1) Betrothed to a Boinam man, but he had another wife
(2) Ran away to Balili

Belatau

A Uwaidjo, betrothed as a child

A (1) Betrothed as a child

B A *Dibutua'am* woman who ran away

B (1) Married to Belatau. Ran away to a
(2) Numidipiheim man

Bischu

A Ma'omen, but later gave her to Wena

A (1) Betrothed to Bischu, but he meanwhile got Danue and so gave her to Wena
(2) Wena

B Danue

B (1) Betrothed as a very small child to a Numidipiheim youth, no pay and so given to Anouel, as a small child
(2) Betrothed to Wabe
(3) Matured too fast and given to Bischu

24 His other wife Welene, the sister of Yabinigi, also ran away from him and married the brother of Maigi, and afterwards Heagul of Liwo.

25 This may be incomplete as Yapiaun affairs were not so well known in Alitoa, and I did not get this information from Balili himself.

| Husband | Wife |
|---|---|
| Gabunyan | A Malasamum, betrothed as a child | A (1) Betrothed as a child |
| Gobonarra | A Tapik, inherited from his dead parallel cousin Pidjui, to whom she had been betrothed. She ran away | A (1) Betrothed to Pidjui of *Hamiebts* |
| | | (2) Tried to marry La'abe but he refused her |
| | | (3) Given to Gobonarra |
| | | (4) Seduced from Gobonarra by the *luluai* of Liwo. He died |
| | | (5) Inherited by the *tultul* of Liwo |
| | B Gulumen, a runaway with three children, from Dunigi | (6) Carried off by Yelegen but returned to the *tultul* |
| Kule | A Betrothed to a girl who died | A (1) Betrothed to Kule and died |
| | B Ilauto'a, originally betrothed to his elder brother Baimal | B (1) Betrothed to Baimal, but favored Kule |
| | C Soatsalamo, inherited from his dead brother Bauwan | (2) Married Kule |
| | | C (1) Betrothed to Bauwan, who died just after she reached puberty |
| | | (2) Inherited by Kule |
| La'abe | A Lomaijo, whom he inherited from an Ahales-imihi cross-cousin | A (1) Betrothed to a youth who died just as she reached puberty |
| | | (2) Inherited by La'abe |
| | B Episode with Tapik, whom he refused to marry | B Tapik's history given above (see Gobonarra) |
| | C Imale, who was given to him because she grew up too fast | C (1) Betrothed to Gerud but she grew faster than he did |
| | | (2) So given to La'abe before puberty |

| | | |
|---|---|---|
| Henalian | A Betrothed to an Ahalesimihi girl who died young and childless | A (1) Betrothed to Henalian and died |
| | B Betrothed to Hano, his present wife | B (1) Betrothed to Henalian and married him |
| | C Mo'onen of Wihum who ran away to him and from him | C (1) Betrothed and married to a Boinam man, who had another wife. Ran away to |
| | | (2) Henalian, and ran away from him to |
| | | (3) Wegul, his sister's son, so that the pair had to flee to Liwo for a period |
| Inoman | A Domau, betrothed as a child | A (1) Betrothed to Inoman and married him |
| Iwamini | A Betrothed to Weamali, the sister of Maginala, then given Yinauwhat and gave up Weamali | A (1) Betrothed to Iwamini, and given up when Yinauwhat objected |
| | | (2) Carried off to Aimau and returned — Not yet one consummated marriage |
| | B Yinauwhat | B (1) Betrothed to Monau. He stayed away so long that she was |
| | | (2) Married to Iwamini |
| Maginala | A An Ahalesimihi girl, betrothed in childhood and died in childbirth | A (1) Betrothed, and died in first marriage |
| | B Soasalamo of Boinam who ran away to him | B (1) Married to Numonihi man, who found her lazy and chased her away[26] |
| | | (2) Married Maginala |

[26] This statement that a man drove a woman away occurs very seldom, but by all accounts this woman was unstable, with fantasies of rape, directed against all sorts of unlikely people. See *Diary*, pp. 427–428.

| HUSBAND | WIFE |
|---|---|
| C Aga'amwi of Dunigi who ran away to Wihun, and Wihun people gave her to Maginala | C (1) Married to a Dunigi man who gave her no food. Ran away to Wihun and they sent for Maginala |
|  | (2) |
| Manum A Homendjuai, elder sister of La'abe. Betrothed as a child, and she bore one child and died | A (1) Betrothed as a child, married and died |
| B Nigisiman, who changed her name to that of her elder sister Homendjuai, whom she replaced | B (1) Married her dead elder sister's husband and took her name |
| Matasues A Betrothed wife who died before puberty | A Died before puberty |
| B Wahewai of Numidipiheim whom his sister helped to elope to him | B (1) Betrothed to a Numidipiheim man[27] who had another wife who took all the food. Her sister-in-law Nalaijo helped her to escape to her brother |
|  | (2) Matasues |
| C Minago'a who had been betrothed to Abugil | C (1) Betrothed as a child to Abugil, Matasues' elder brother, who stayed away at work |
|  | (2) Married to Matasues with Abugil's consent |
| Menyul A Madjuamal who ran away to him | A (1) Betrothed to an old man, she herself a cripple. Ran away to |
|  | (2) The unstable Menyul |

27 This Numidipiheim man's present wives were still quarreling over meat. See Diary for January 29 (pp. 214–215).

| | | | | | |
|---|---|---|---|---|---|
| Nagawe | A | (1) | Alo of Yapiaun, betrothed as a child | A (1) | Betrothed and married |
| | B | (1) | Yapul of *Toto'alaibis*, betrothed as a child but left with her parents | B (1) | Betrothed and married but always spent much time with parents[28] |
| Nahomen | A | (1) | Elder sister of Maigi, *Uyenehas*, betrothed as a child, bore children and died | A (1) | Betrothed to and married Nahomen |
| Naushe'e | A | (1) | Weyal, of Ilapwein, married her while he was living there | A (1) | Betrothed and married to Naushe'e |
| Nyelahai | A | (1) | Sister of Aden, betrothed as a child, died without children | A (1) | Betrothed as a child, died childless |
| | B | (1) | Daughter of Amambut, who died, only one child survived, others died of convulsions | B (1) | Betrothed as a child, married Nyelahai, died |
| | C | (1) | Nyalamidju, an old woman, inherited from a distant Liwo relative as a pig keeper | C (1) | Betrothed to a man who died |
| | | | | (2) | Inherited by his brother |
| | | | | (3) | Bore children in old age to Nyelahai |
| | D | (1) | Natun of Wihun, who had been betrothed to his younger brother | D (1) | Betrothed as a child to Yabinigi, disliked his deafness, and taken by |
| | | | | (2) | Nyelahai right after puberty |
| Ombomb | A | (1) | Me'elue, betrothed as a child, and married her after puberty | A (1) | Betrothed as a child to Ombomb |
| | B | (1) | A Liwo girl, not yet pubescent, who ran away to him and was reclaimed by Liwo | B (1) | Betrothed to a man with another wife, ran away to Alitoa and taken on by Ombomb |
| | | | | (2) | Returned to her previous husband |

28 This is a common result of the anomalous practice of betrothing two girls to one youth. Badui's other betrothed, Gowais, stayed with her parents, and Yapul, even after she bore children, stayed at home almost as much as with her husband.

| HUSBAND | WIFE |
|---|---|
| C Sauwedjo, who ran away from Dunigi to Wihun, and was given to Ombomb by Wihun relatives | C (1) Married by Plains custom to a Dunigi man, who was a poor provider and beat her |
| | (2) Ran away to Wihun, with Aga'amwi, wife of Maginala, and was given to Ombomb |
| Selalimi A Samanuai, inherited betrothed of his dead brother | A (1) Betrothed to elder brother of Selalimi who died before she reached puberty |
| | (2) Married Selalimi |
| B A *Banyimebis* woman who was betrothed to him. She died | B (1) Betrothed to him, died after marriage |
| C Saido'o, inherited from his brother, and refused to leave Alipinagle[29] | C (1) Married to brother of Selalimi |
| | (2) Inherited by Selalimi but staying in Alipinagle |
| Sema'a A Majuenai of Wihun, betrothed to him as a child, and his only wife | A (1) Betrothed as a child and lived till old age with his wife |
| Silisium A A Numonihi girl inherited from his cross-cousin. She died also | A (1) Betrothed to a cross-cousin of Silisium, who died |
| | (2) Married Silisium and died |
| B Ya'umen who had been betrothed to him as a child | B (1) Betrothed to and married Silisium |

[29] Selalimi belonged in Alipinagle but had moved to Ahalesimihi to work with his brothers-in-law by wife B.

C A Numonihi girl betrothed, and bore him one child but driven away by Ya'umen and married a cross-cousin of Silisium's

   C (1) Betrothed to Silisium but came into a household with a first wife who hated her
     (2) Driven out and married a cross-cousin of her husband's who kept her and the child[30]

Sinaba'i

A A Numonihi girl who was betrothed to him but who ran away before adolescence

   A (1) Betrothed to Sinaba'i, but ran away before adolescence to a Numonihi man and
     (2) Married this Numonihi man

B A Numidipiheim girl, betrothed but also ran away as she was adolescent

   B (1) Betrothed to Sinaba'i, ran away at adolescence
     (2) Married a Liwo man

C A Dunigi woman, inherited from his brother who bore him three children and died

   C (1) Betrothed and married in Dunigi, ran away to Alitoa
     (2) Married Sinaba'i's brother who died
     (3) Married Sinaba'i, bore him three children and died

D Temos, betrothed only, as she was prepubescent, when she was given to Wabe

   D (1) Betrothed to Yauwiyu, ran away before puberty, disliking his flightiness and his other Dunigi wife
     (2) Betrothed to Sinaba'i
     (3) Given to Wabe in exchange for Menala

E Menala, whom he seduced from Wabe

   E (1) Betrothed to a Wihun man, who meanwhile took another wife and failed in affinal duties, so her brothers connived to give her to

[30] This last fact is proof of the attitude of Ya'umen, who did not even want the other wife's child in the house.

| HUSBAND | WIFE |
|---|---|
| **Sumali** | |
| A  A sister of Sinaba'i; betrothed and died childless | A (1) |
|  | (2) Wabe, from whom she was seduced by Sinaba'i |
|  | (3) Betrothed to Sumali, died |
| B  A Wihun woman, betrothed, and chased away by Winam | B (1) Betrothed to Sumali, chased away by his inherited wife, and ran away and |
|  | (2) Married a Numidipheim man |
| C  Winam, inherited from a cross-cousin | C (1) Betrothed to and married Salami of *Uyebis* and bore Magiel |
|  | (2) Inherited by Sumali, quarreled and ran away |
|  | (3) Married a man in Malis, returned a year later to visit and was got back by |
|  | (4) Sumali. Chased away other wife, and bore seven children |
| **Tapita** | |
| A  A *Banyimebis* woman, betrothed and married her and moved to her village. She died | A (1) Betrothed to Tapita, married him and died |
| B  Adule, a Biligil woman whom some of the young men brought back from a feast in the Plains | B (1) Married to an Ybonimu husband, seduced into running away by Wabe and La'abe, given to |
|  | (2) Tapita |
| **Ulaba'i** | |
| A  Ibanyos, betrothed as a child, exchanged for Baijo | A (1) Betrothed as a child and married Aden |

B Whasimai, ran away to him from Numidipiheim where she was married to his mother's brother

B (1) Betrothed to a Numidipiheim, who was already an old man, and she ran away at adolescence to Ulaba'i

   (2) Ulaba'i

Wabe

A Danue, betrothed as a child, but she grew up fast and was given to Bischu instead

A (1) Betrothed to Wabe but

   (2) Given to Bischu

B Welima, betrothed as a child, and married him

B (1) Betrothed and married to Wabe

C Menala, whose brothers persuaded him to capture her, and who was then seduced by Sinaba'i

C (1) Betrothed to Wihun husband. Captured by Wabe, seduced by and married to

   (2) Wabe, seduced by and married to

   (3) Sinaba'i

D Temos, who was given him in exchange for Menala

D (1) Betrothed to Yauwiyu, ran away before puberty

   (2) Betrothed to Sinaba'i

   (3) Given to Wabe

Walawahan

A An Ahalesimihi woman, betrothed and married her and moved to her village. She bore two children and died

A (1) Betrothed as a child and married Walawahan and died

B Suamali, who had been chased away by brother of Agilapwe because she had *tinea*

B (1) Betrothed and married to brother of Agilapwe who chased her away because she had *tinea*

   (2) Married Walawahan

Wamu'um

A Malihiyau, sister of Matasnes, betrothed as a child, and bore him several children, died as mature woman

A (1) Betrothed as a child and married Wamu'um

| Husband | Wife | |
|---|---|---|
| B Miegelian, the widow of the father of Wena, and adopted[31] her children | B | (1) Betrothed to the father of Wena, and bore him all his children. He died |
| | | (2) In her old age she married Wamu'um |
| **Wegul** | | |
| A Married to a Liwo woman who bore him three children and died | A | (1) Betrothed, married, bore three children and died |
| B Mo'onen, wife of his "mother's brother" who was herself a runaway from Boinam | B | (1) Betrothed and married to a Boinam man who had another wife. Ran away to |
| | | (2) Henalian. Seduced from him by |
| | | (3) Wegul |
| **Wena** | | |
| A Ma'omen, who was originally betrothed to Bischu, his father's brother's son, and then given to him | A | (1) Betrothed to Bischu and then when Bischu was given Danue, she was |
| | | (2) Given to Wena |
| **Wutue** | | |
| A A *Diboaibis* girl who was betrothed to him and died | A | (1) Betrothed to Wutue and died young |
| B A *Toto'alaibis* girl, betrothed and died | B | (1) Betrothed and died |
| C Mela, inherited from his brother | C | (1) Betrothed to and married brother of Wutue, bore two children |
| | | (2) Married Wutue and bore him children |
| **Yabinigi** | | |
| A Natun, betrothed to him as a child, disliked his deafness and taken by Nyelahai | A | (1) Betrothed to Yabinigi, rejected his deafness |
| | | (2) Married to Nyelahai |

31 That is, he was no relation to the dead man, but only, through Matasues, a close associate of his throughout his life.

B Wihun wife, betrothed as a child and carried off by Suapali, and later gotten back

    B (1) Betrothed to Yabinigi
       (2) Carried off right after puberty by Sepik men domiciled in Suapali
       (3) Gotten back for Yabinigi by appeal to Government

Yamogwai
Yauwiyu

A Ulahaiyu, betrothed as a child

    A (1) Betrothed as a child to Yamogwai

A Temos, betrothed as a child, but she rejected him before puberty

    A (1) Betrothed to Yauwiyu but disliked him and his Dunigi wife
       (2) Betrothed to Sinaba'i
       (3) Married to Wabe, in exchange for Menala

B Anone, a runaway Dunigi woman

    B (1) Betrothed and married in Dunigi, ran away to
       (2) Yauwiyu

C Wasijo, inherited from dead brother of Maigi

    C (1) Married to the brother of Maigi, he died and she was inherited by
       (2) Yauwiyu

# ILLUSTRATIVE DEATH PAYMENTS

### (As of the winter of 1932)

## THE FATHER OF MAGINALA

Salihan was the son of a *Banyimebis* father and the sister of Pailit, who was sent by Alitoa to end the old feud between Alitoa and Alipinagle. He was the father of Maginala, Ga'olin (who was *tinea*-covered and unmarried), and Weamali, an unmarried daughter. His wife was dead.

When he died, the *tamberan* of *Toto'alaibis* tabooed all the coconut palms and all the areca nut palms of Alipinagle. The areca nut taboo was released in 1931 and the nuts paid to the maternal cross-cousins. Part of the coconuts were released for the *balagasik* feast in March, 1932, but then the *Toto'alaibis tamberan* returned and put the taboo on again, to last until the big final feast, when pigs would be paid.

The payments made at the time of death were as follows:

| To Wabe | 1 Ring | wa'en (cross-cousin) |
|---|---|---|
| To La'abe | 1 String of dog's teeth | wa'en (cross-cousin) |
| To Balidu | 1 Ring | wa'en (cross-cousin) |
| To Nyelahai | 2 Rings | wa'en (cross-cousin) |
| To Manusa | 2 Rings | mehinin (cross-cousin) |

All of the mother's brothers were dead, and the payments were made to the eldest acting son of each mother's brother. So Sumali, Baimal, Ombomb, and Ulaba'i received nothing.

He was buried by Wabe, Maginala, and Ga'olin.

## THE BROTHER OF BAIMAL

Bauwan, the younger brother of Baimal, died five years ago. He was buried by Baimal and Kule, each of whom inherited one wife, Baimal the older wife Alaijo, and Kule, the younger wife Soatsalamo. He left only one child, a girl of four or five, Minya, the daughter of Alaijo. Baimal, in taking Alaijo, became responsible for Minya also.

The rings were supplied by Baimal, Kule, and Sumali, father's younger brothers of the dead man. They were given as follows:

Four rings to Balili, *wa'en*, mother's brother's son of Yapiaun

Two rings to Yamogwai, *mehinin*, father's sister's son of Yapiaun[32]

Two pigs to Balili who gave a piece to Yamogwai

Mogiligen was a new hamlet and had no mature coco-nuts, so they were not tabooed.[33] His house site stood vacant until five years later, when Ombomb built a ground house on it.

### THE SISTER OF OMBOMB

Malihiyau was a younger daughter of Pailit, married to Wamu'um of *Maliebis*. She was buried by Matasues, her elder brother, who had lived with her husband, and by Ombomb, her youngest brother. She was buried in Maloten, her husband's place. The payments for her death were made to Ombomb "because he was the youngest brother and she was the youngest sister."[34] Ombomb distributed the payment as follows:

| | | RELATIONSHIP TO THE DEAD |
|---|---|---|
| 1 Plate | Balidu | Father's brother's son |
| 1 Plate | Sumali | Father's brother's son |
| 1 String dog's teeth | Agilapwe | Mother's mother's brother's son |
| 1 Ring | Inoman | Father's father's brother's son's adopted son, re-adopted into gens of dead woman |
| 1 Plate | Monau[35] | Mother's brother's son |

[32] Note that with brother and sister exchange, which happens not infrequently among the Arapesh, the two kinds of cross-cousins will be in the same place; in a large death feast, where the emphasis tends to be upon payment to a *place*, this tends further to confuse the proper distinctions between mother's brother's son and father's sister's son.

[33] I.e., there was no plan to make a really large feast.

[34] This was a ready rationalization of the facts which were that Matusses was too closely linked up with Wamu'um to be a proper receiver, and Wabe now worked with Matasues. Therefore, Ombomb was the best route through which to pay the dead woman's gens.

[35] Here the idea of the junior line was carried out, so Ombomb, in recounting these events, said, "When Nalaijo dies, Aden will get something," i.e., Nalaijo is Ombomb's eldest sister and Aden is Monau's senior.

| 1 Plate | Wupali | Elder half brother by different mother |
| 1 Plate | Nahomen[36] | Father's father's brother's son's adopted son |
| 1 Plate | Nyelahai[36] | Father's father's brother's son's son |

## DEATH OF THE INFANT OF NYELAHAI

This was a girl infant. She was buried by women, the mother's sister, Natun, and Nyelahai's brother's wife. Nyelahai made a small feast for them and paid three rings and one string of shell money to his brother-in-law, Natun's Wihun brother.

If other than the immediate kin of the dead perform the burial, they must be paid a feast, washing their hands, before the maternal and affinal kin can be paid. So when Maigi's brothers died, Ombomb and Bischu, distant relatives, buried them and were paid for their services by relatives of the widows, from the payments

[36] Nyelahai was the son of Yelehiu, the brother of the dead woman's father, who had been given as an *alapwen* to *Dibatua'am*. It was in ways like this that the *awelahem* tie was kept perpetually alive.

which were made by the inheriting husbands of those widows.

Similarly when the wife of Tapita died (p. 328) she was buried by strangers, and her own relatives from the Plains had to pay rings to "wash the hands of the grave diggers" before they could collect the pig that was due to them.

In the first instance when Maigi's brothers died, the payments of the inheriting husbands were used by the kin of the dead, from which to pay the mother's brother of the dead, Kunagen of Liwo. When there is a widow involved, the inheriting husband always pays the kin of the dead husband first, and only in later years makes symbolic payments to the kin of the woman herself. In the case of an elopement, the same pattern is followed, the former husband is paid first by the new husband, and later the kin of the wife. So Aimau, the child of Sinaba'i and Menala (see above, p. 181), who was being given back to Wabe, Menala's former husband from whom Sinaba'i had seduced her, was legally equivalent to an *alapwen*, the first child born to the widow who remarries outside her husband's gens, and which is returned to that gens in lieu of any other payment, in return for their having originally grown the widow.

## INSTANCES IN WHICH THE MOTHER'S BROTHER'S CURSE WAS USED IN ALITOA

Gobonarra, the worthless mother's brother of Aden and Ibanyos, cursed Ibanyos because he was given no rings when Ibanyos married Ulaba'i. Ibanyos had two children who died, and then Gobonarra boasted of his feat. A ring was paid to him, and Aden, the brother of Ibanyos, ceremonially removed the curse with the *limbum* spathe and fire tongs. This is an interesting example because it shows, first, the familiar event of Arapesh culture presenting perfectly good paths which can be used by an ill-natured person, and second, the formlessness of Arapesh conceptions which permits one person to put a curse on and another to take it off. The payment of the one ring to Gobonarra, however, did preserve a certain sense of form, but they did not trust him to remove the curse properly, even so.

In the past, Wabe was playing a part in one of Aden's preliminary distributions and expected to redistribute the plates in his share to Matasues, Henalian, Sinaba'i, and Bunitai, and Bunitai failed to appear. Bunitai was Wabe's dead sister's son. Wabe cursed Bunitai with the curse for males which meant that he would become lazy and worthless. Bunitai, according to Wabe, became hope-

lessly lazy, his hunting failed, his gardening went to pieces. Later, he importuned Wabe with a gift of meat, and Wabe spat upon ginger, and talked again to the ancestors and the results of the curse were taken off.

When the husband of Ulaijo, the sister of Nyelahai and the present wife of Aden, died, Ulaijo returned to Alitoa with her small son, and Nyelahai and Ulaba'i gave the child food until finally the orphan flourished and grew tall. Then Wambibi, a brother of the deceased husband, demanded him back. Nyelahai and Ulaba'i demanded two pots and a ring to pay for the food that they had given him. Wambibi failed to do this, and Nyelahai cursed the boy, his sister's son, after which Wambibi paid the pots and ring and the curse was removed.

In this instance, Nyelahai was using a legitimate device. The price that he demanded could not have covered the cost of feeding his nephew for two months, and he had fed him for six years. But it was fair that this food expenditure should be recognized, and this Wambibi had been too churlish to do.

Whasimai was married to the mother's brother of Ulaba'i, her present husband, to whom she eloped. Her husband cursed Ulaba'i and one of their children died. Then after the outraged husband died, Wamu'um, his brother, took the curse off.

Here the curse was one of vengeance and so could not be removed with a payment, and Ulaba'i was well outside the law in marrying his mother's brother's wife. The only other case of a man's marrying a mother's brother's wife was that of Wegul of Alipinagle, who married a woman who had previously eloped to his mother's brother, Henalian. Here Henalian invoked the *tamberan* instead of the curse, which illustrates very nicely the way in which one is an elaboration of the other. Ulaba'i's mother's brother lived in Numidipiheim, and the *tamberan* is essentially a method that is used within the locality to exile someone from it temporarily, so that it was not a method that was open to him. Wegul, furthermore, did not really belong in Alipinagle which was his mother's place. Henalian was the older and more powerful man, and Wegul and his wife were forced to flee to Liwo, Wegul's father's place, and live there for five years.

Consideration of these instances shows that the least legitimate use of the curse was made by Gobonarra and Wabe, the ne'er-do-well and the temperamental misfit, and the two other users in Alitoa were Nyelahai and Henalian, both bad-tempered people. Nyelahai, furthermore, used the elder brother curse on Yabinigi to spoil his hunting because Yabinigi's gardening was all done in Wihun.

## EXAMPLES OF SPONSORSHIP

### In Making an *Abullu*

| MAKER | SPONSOR |
| --- | --- |
| Ombomb and Wabe | Nyelahai |
| Ombomb and Bischu | Nyelahai and Henalian |
| Sinaba'i and La'abe | Anouel, Ulaba'i, Nyelahai |
| Brothers of Whasimai | Ombomb, Matasues, and La'abe |

### For Fathers of First Children

| NEW FATHER | SPONSOR | RELATIONSHIP |
| --- | --- | --- |
| Matasues | Nyelahai | *Buanyin and awalahen* brother |
| La'abe | Sumali | Gens brother |
| Ombomb | Wupali | Paternal half brother |

## MEN WHO HAD MADE ABULLUS

| Name | Number |
|---|---|
| Balidu | A great many |
| Wupali | 4 |
| Nyelahai | 3 |
| Ombomb | 2 |
| Wabe | 2 |
| Sumali | 2 |
| Baimal | 2 |
| Sinaba'i | 1 |
| La'abe | 1 |
| Ulaba'i | 1 |

It is said: "Baimal made one to Balidi, his *wa'en* (cross-cousin) and he will make the next to Nagawe, a father's cross-cousin's son." Here the *abullu* is slipping more and more into the *rite de passage* economic pattern.

## CENSUS OF EXUVIAE

The whereabouts of the exuviae, whether any exuvia was outstanding, and, if so, where it was filed, was of the greatest importance in judging the strength of a community. This was so for several reasons: (1) It determined the amount of blackmail which the community was continually paying. (2) It determined the tone which Plainsmen could take in the community. (3) It determined the quality of intracommunity quarreling because it was more complicated to devise theories of newly stolen exuviae than to postulate Plainsmen malice, and if no exuviae were known to be outstanding, new malice had to be imputed.[37] (4) Indirectly, this is an index of the health of various members of the community. For every sickly person, some exuviae will be believed or claimed to exist in the Plains, while if a man is consistently healthy, in time the best-substantiated claims of the Plains blackmailers are disallowed and the exuviae are said to have rotted. (5) It determines in some degree the amount of watchfulness which a man must maintain, for if his exuvia is already filed where anyone can get it without the risk of stealing it, there is less fear of theft of new exuviae (this is qualified by the nature of the exuviae; if the filed exuvia is only *adu'iss*, then there is still ever present danger of the theft of *simadip*). (6) It determined a man's vulnerability to threats for no threat was idle if exuviae were outstanding.

[37] Here lay the crux, although due to another cause, of the Aden difficulty; because it was a sore it could not be blamed on the Plainsmen, and, therefore, the community had to be torn by suspicion and accusation.

| Name | Exuviae[38] Outstanding | Kind | Where | Comments |
|---|---|---|---|---|
| Aden[39] | Skin infection (diagnosed by presence of sore) | Unknown | Unknown | Unknown. Recent |
| Agilapwe | Skin infection type (presence of sore) | Unknown | Waginara *marsalai* place | Taken by dead gift friend years before |
| Alis | Potential death (knowledge of possibility and neurasthenia) | Semen | Unknown | Seduced woman believed to have taken it, was dead. No blackmail |
| Anop | None | | | |
| Badui | *adu'isi*, potential death | A bandicoot bone | Dunigi | Stolen by Yauwiyu over quarrel about Wasijo |
| Baimal | None | | | |
| Balidu | None | | | |

[38] The distinction between exuviae deposited in *marsalai* places and in *tamberan* houses, on the one hand, and exuviae in the hands of the professional sorcerers of the Plains, on the other, is a functional one and is not distinguished in terminology. I shall, therefore, use the terms *potential death* and *potential skin infection* to cover the two.

[39] Aden had formerly had some *adu'isi*, part of a yam, outstanding in Nugum, taken by the sister of Silisium who had run away from Agilapwe to him and wanted to marry him. Aden had refused her saying, "You are my father's wife," which showed how he felt about Agilapwe (cf., Agilapwe's claims to have brought Aden up, *Diary*, p. 432). She had stolen a piece of food, but Sumali had got it back by paying four rings and one tomahawk.

| | | | | |
|---|---|---|---|---|
| Bischu | No exuviae. Bone to spoil hunting (diagnosed by bad hunting and Gerud) | Bone | Taken by Walawahan | |
| Gobonarra | None. Had a tumor attributed to his taking food from men who had killed his father | | | |
| Kule | Potential death | Bone | Kairiru[40] | Taken by Yauwiyu over quarrel about Wasijo. Blackmail paid: 5 rings, 1 string of shell money, 1 little pig, 1 knife, 1 piece of pig |
| Inoman | None | | | |
| La'abe | Potential death | *simadip* Semen | Kairiru | Taken by Tapik when she temporarily married him after death of Pidjui of *Hamiebis*. Sent to Ubohon, in Nugum, and got back to Dunigi by Waliba, a Kairiru man, brother-in-law of La'abe's sister's Wihun husband Wambilbi. Cost of getting it back into this language group: 4 rings, 1 knife |
| Maigi | None | | | |
| Matasues | None (?) | | | I could get no account of any, but Matasues showed considerable anticipation of black-mail |
| Nahomen | None | | | |

[40] Small place near Dunigi. Works with Dunigi.

| NAME | EXUVIAE OUTSTANDING | KIND | WHERE | COMMENTS |
|---|---|---|---|---|
| Nyelahai Ombomb | None | | | |
| | Potential death | *adu'isi* Areca nut quid *simadip* Semen | Kairiru | Taken by Yauwiyu over Wasijo quarrel. Held in Kairiru. Blackmail paid: 1 ring, 2 plates |
| Sinaba'i | Potential death | *adu'isi* Bone | Dumigi | Taken by a previous Dumigi wife, now dead |
| Sumali | Potential death but so old that it is believed to have rotted | *adu'isi* Bone | Dumigi | Taken by a runaway wife whom Winam chased away |
| Ulaba'i | Potential death | *adu'isi* Bone | Ybonimu | Taken years before by Amambut, in anticipation of a quarrel. Blackmail paid: 3 rings, 3 knives |
| Wabe | (1) Potential death | *adu'isi* Bone | Ybonimu | Seven items of blackmail |
| | (2) Potential death (Suspected from Bonaheitum *tangget*). Bone which spoiled hunting | Bone | Alitoa (?) | Welima accused by Gerud |
| Wutue | None | | | |

There are several interesting points here: Balidu had no exuviae out (in spite of the fact that he was a big man) nor had Nyelahai, Baimal, or Sumali, but all the younger men, just beginning to play a part—Wabe, Ombomb, La'abe, Kule, Ulaba'i, Sinaba'i, Badui, and Alis—had. As the fear and suspicion of the local community probably are more accurate than the Plains blackmail which waits upon the expression of these suspicions, it might be said that it was the death of this group which was most feared. The older men, if they had survived so far, were believed to be strong enough to last until old age. It is also striking that exuviae are stolen by irresponsible men, and they themselves have no exuviae outstanding.

## HERBS PLANTED IN ALITOA

The following list was made with the assistance of young boys. I made it once when the village was deserted and did not have an opportunity to repeat it. It, therefore, represents only what the young—such as Madje and Gerud—know, but may, nevertheless, be taken as a fair sample of the variety of herbs, with ceremonial and practical uses, which are to be found in an old village.

| LOCATION[41] | ARAPESH NAME | DESCRIPTION | USES |
| --- | --- | --- | --- |
| | alouhin | Red hibiscus | Recently imported, used as casual ornamentation |
| | omaliuh | Shrub with decorative flowers | Imported from Beach, casual ornamentation |

[41] We started just behind the old *tamberan* house, now used as a boys' house, proceeded along the edge of the village to Wabe's house, then into the graveyard, back in front of the house of Sinaba'i and Wabe, along the other edge of the village, around Balidu's house, and back to our own. Location will be indicated only in a few instances in which I thought it might be significant.

| Location | Arapesh Name | Description | Uses |
|---|---|---|---|
| | so'wib | Plant with small bright leaves | Put in grave when someone is buried |
| | lisu | Yellow-flecked croton | Yam magic |
| | wanyal | Yellow croton | Yam magic |
| | usegeha | Dracaena | Used in tanggets; put in boy's pierced septum |
| | duanabehu | Small plant with dark purple patches on leaves | Phalanger hunting magic |
| | yabuloh | Decorative leaves | Planted on places where there has been a fight. Used in preparation for a fight. Now used in football matches |
| | wehiten | Low bush | In rite de passage |
| | agup | Tree with small fruit | Eaten |
| | talulip | Bush with variegated leaf | Phalanger hunting magic |
| | a'oh | Tree | Against the trunk men let blood ceremonially from the phallus |
| | bagun | Tree | Bark is used to make G strings |
| | unali'yalih | Croton | Hunting cassowary magic |
| | banong | Pale pink hibiscus | Hunting phalanger magic |
| | nih | Bright red dracaena | Fighting magic and tanggets put in graveyard[42] |
| | walahi' | Dracaena | Offering to ghosts in marsalai place; tying tanggets to break off relations |

[42] Government-established graveyard.

| | | | |
|---|---|---|---|
| aun[43] | Big red-leafed *dracaena* | | *Tanggets* |
| mamub | Narrow-leafed red and green *dracaena* | | *Tanggets* |
| uluban | Limbum palm | | Flowers used for broom, spathe for cooking, sago working, etc. |
| malibis | Wild taro | | Sorcery to produce sores |
| sani[44] | Tree with pods containing easily crushed red seeds | | Recent import. Used as face paint |
| Garden plot in front of Sinaba'i's house | ulainyil | Red *dracaena* | Decoration |
| | nibu | Small plant | Yam magic |
| | namo | Small plant | Eaten for *sagumeh*[45] possession, also for success in fastening pigs |
| Passing along end of village | vogisab | Decorative croton | Yam magic |
| | aluiohis | Red hibiscus | Only worn by big men in time of fighting |
| | alibin | Small plant | Made into a brew fed to pigs to make them fat |

[43] In graveyard were also *usegeha*, *aiowhin*, and *so'wib*.

[44] This is an example of a recent import which had received no name. It was merely called by the word for "decoration on wood."

[45] Sinaba'i, during his widower days, had tried to use the *sagumeh* form of possession now used by Gerud.

| LOCATION | ARAPESH NAME | DESCRIPTION | USES |
|---|---|---|---|
| | *mehalop* | Tree | Against the trunk small pre-adolescent boys let their blood to make themselves grow big |
| | *yamwe* | Small plant | Leaves used for blood letting in phalanger hunting magic, juice mixed with lime to make white face paint |
| | *solo'win tanum* | Edible banana Plant | In divinatory oven |
| | *dilibuh* | Shrub | Leaves used in *rite de passage*, phalanger and bandicoot hunting magic; Potion of bark and leaves fed to short-winded pigs and also to short-winded men |
| | *elibin* | Cactus-like shrub with huge stem, spiked and small ellip-toid leaves | Fighting magic.[46] Leaves mixed with bone dust, held in hand of warrior makes his blows crippling; enemy will either grow crooked arms and legs, or limbs will swell |
| | *magas* | Common beech tree | Leaves used to make cigarettes; bark used to put on the snare for cassowary. (The leaves are curly and will make the rope curl about the cassowary's foot) |

[46] The frequency of fighting magic might suggest a greater emphasis on war than exists, but war magic and love magic were always being brought home by young men in the hope that they could be articulated with the culture.

| | | | |
|---|---|---|---|
| Special plot belonging to Ulaba'i | *ton*, P.E. *y shauwep* | Nut-bearing tree | Kernels are eaten, after being steeped in water |
| | *bolobidan* | Plant with purple-patched leaves | Phalanger hunting magic |
| | *nauitog* | Little plant with green, tooth-edged leaves | Phalanger hunting magic |
| Continuing along edge of village | *bulienalelehas* and *basholibihas* | Plants with broad leaves | Not planted but have sprung up here from garbage. Used as vegetable greens |
| | *'ai'ato'a* | Plant with bulbous root | Gives yellow color used to paint net bags and sago aprons |
| | *tapuwal* | Small plant | Leaves used to season the greens called *bishas* |
| | *amade'u* | Plant | *Rite de passage* |
| | *baugwap* | Plant | Leaf pressed between hands after handling corpse; divinatory oven |
| | No name, P.E. *muli* | Lime | Just planted for eating. Seed from Wihun[47] |
| | *boboiyohas* | Pawpaw | For eating |
| | *bagabisuh* | Vegetable green | A bush growing green which is eaten but not planted; self-sown |

[47] Note this instance of irregular seed diffusion. This comes from the Coast, but Wihun got it first.

| LOCATION | ARAPESH NAME | DESCRIPTION | USES |
|---|---|---|---|
| | iluh | Breadfruit tree | Seeds eaten; bark used for G strings. Associated with ancestral ghosts |
| | bishaulog | Tree which spreads horizontally after growing just a short distance, dams flooding streams by catching drift | Taro magic[48] (for the taro called *nugalo*) |
| | amatogo | Very slender bamboo | Stalks used for arrow-shafts for shooting small birds |
| | uman, P.E. *alan* | Red edible fruit | Fruit eaten. Branches used to man the inner frame for sago bark walls |
| | dishu | Plant | Yam magic |
| | waudo' | Shrub | Leaves put in grave under corpse |
| | bilia | | Leaves on which coconut meat is scraped and in which it is baked before it is made into oil[49] |
| | bul | Plant | Leaves eaten to give one the ability to learn and remember songs |
| | ugulas | Vegetable leaves | A bush green, self-sown |
| | mishubin | | Given to a dog to make it find game |
| | milip | Tree? Leaves with red, heart-shaped leaves | Put in the mouth of an emerging adolescent girl or a novice |

48 Is used in the new Liwo fish magic.

49 The Arapesh make very slight use of coconut oil, and it was not made during my stay in Alitoa.

| | | |
|---|---|---|
| 'wabu' | Tree with very tiny leaves sparsely placed on branches | Yam magic |
| butugulin | | Magic for fastening pigs |
| dogumenuhas | Vine with edible leaves | Planted for greens |
| auloh | Shrub | Bark-made potions for men or pigs with colds. Leaf held in hand to show peaceful intent, disavowal of war or black magic |
| washeh | Croton | Yam magic |
| amatubeh | Palm with reddish, yellow leaves | The juice of the young coconut is mixed with leaves good for phalanger hunting magic, and mebun,[50] cooked, the juice drunk, and husk replaced at foot of palm. Next day hunter observes taboos, must not look up at tall trees, must keep eyes on ground. Next day goes hunting and phalangers show up like the red leaves of the coconut |
| wanume' | | Leaf is chewed with areca nut, first part spit out, second half eaten to release the taboo on eating meat at dal a mambis meal |
| malino | Nettle | Cassowary hunting magic, put on snare because its leaves are curly |
| tanum | Green-leafed variety | Rite de passage herb |
| minanahip | Shrub | Berries used for blue dye in net bags. Brought from Plains and not used by women here |

[50] Mebun, scented earth, probably flowers of sulphur.

| LOCATION | ARAPESH NAME | DESCRIPTION | USES |
|---|---|---|---|
| | *ashup* | Tree | Bark used as an emetic against sorcery |
| | *biligab* | Plant with long-ribbed leaf | Plains use the stalk in ears and nose. Here it is planted, but not used for anything |
| | *mal* | Croton | Yam magic |
| | *a'abiluh* | Vegetable green | Planted to eat |
| | *alipein* | Coconut with very small orange coconuts | Hunting magic |
| | *tchehih* | | Leaves upon which counter-curse and counter-love magic can be breathed to banish ghosts who have been invoked. Chewed with areca nut by one who takes off a curse he had laid |
| | *yabuloh* | Different plant of same name | Fed to pigs to make them fat |
| | *mushas* | Tree | Leaves used as substitute for betel pepper leaf in pepper chewing |

# A CLUE TO THE LAST GENERATION

In attempting to reconstruct the interrelationship of individuals in a former generation, the field worker is very much at the mercy of accident. If number or class of feasts made is an accurate estimate, or if number of war counts won or battles fought can be equated with personality, well and good, but when these fail, it is sometimes extremely difficult to find an index. The best index I could discover to the last generation in Alitoa was the disposal of the bones of the dead; the ceremonial significance of these bones has already been discussed.[51]

| NAME OR RELATIONSHIP TO LIVING | BONES | GIVEN TO | CALLED BY DEAD |
|---|---|---|---|
| Pailit of *Toto'alaibis* (father of Matasues, Wabe, and Ombomb). A good hunter, strong in a fight, and able to talk | Upper arm bone | Sinaba'i | Adopted son; *niganin* |
| | Upper arm bone | Wamu'um | Daughter's husband; *nigauwin* |
| | Shoulder blade | Matasues | Third son, who was given away in adoption; *niganin* |
| | Shoulder blade | Ombomb | Fifth son; *niganin* |
| | Thigh bone | Wupali | Eldest son |
| | Thigh bone | Nyelahai | Classificatory son; *awalahen* |
| | Skull and jaw bone | Wabe | Fourth son, but acting eldest son |
| | Breast bone | Ibedu of Numidi-piheim | Daughter's husband; *nigauwin* |
| | | Father of Manusa of Numidipiheim | |
| | Rib | | Brother-in-law; *mewhen* |

51 Mead, 1940, pp. 432-433.

| Name or Relationship to Living | Bones | Given to | Called by Dead |
|---|---|---|---|
| | Rib | Anouel, father of Anop | Wife's sister's husband; awanin |
| | Lower arm bone | Silisium of Ahale-simhi | Mother's sister's son; awanin |
| | Lower leg bone | Belagomini of Wi-hun | Mother's brother's son; wauwen |
| | Lower leg bone | Walawahan Aden | Classificatory niganin |
| | Lower arm bone | | Wife's brother's son; mehinen |
| Maulimen, father of father of Baimal, father of Balidu and Sumali. A good man but not a distinguished one. Killed in Dunigi. His bones brought back by Sa'alie (p. 156) of Dunigi | Bones | Father of Baimal, the eldest son. He gave one bone to Sumali.[52] Balidu had none | |
| Father of Aden, died very young | Bones not taken | | |
| Yelehiu, father of Nyelahai and Ulaba'i | Two upper arm bones | Ulaba'i | Second son |
| | Jaw bone | Nyelahai | Eldest son |
| | Rest of bones | Henalian[53] | Sister's husband |
| | Yabinigi had none | | |

[52] When Ombomb built his house (p. 221) he found it and kept it.

[53] Henalian was particularly fond of bones, he liked to collect them, ornament them with woven bands and fragrant herbs, and wear them.

| | | | |
|---|---|---|---|
| Anouel, father of Anop. Matasues, his adopted son and heir, said, "Never mind about his bones, he was too big-mouthed," but Anop and So'oepin took them out | Head and one upper arm bone | Matasues | Adopted son |
| Father of Magiel and adopted father of Ulaba'i | One shoulder blade | Ombomb | Wife's sister's son; *niganin* |
| Father of Bischu, "Only a hunter!" | One shoulder blade | So'oepin | Son |
| | Bones not taken | | |
| Father of Wena, good arguer and talker, no hunter or pig fastener | Bones not taken. Hair cut and given to Bischu who used it for divination | | |
| | Took a few bones | Wena | Own son |
| Father of La'abe, died in Wihun, buried there | One upper arm bone | Bischu | Brother's son |
| Father of Maigi, had been dead 3 years, good hunter and gardener, did not make feasts | One upper arm bone | | |
| | Never got his bones | | |
| | Will take out some bones | | |

The indications from this material are that the dominant personality in the last generation was Pailit, the father of Wupali, Abugil, Matasues, Ombomb, Wabe, Nalaijo, and the deceased wife of Wamu'um. His bones are well scattered through the community and were used by Sinaba'i; Alis, Gerud, and Bunitai in their *sagumeh* divining. Furthermore the breach with Bugabihiem over Pailit's death had never been really healed. Next in importance came the father of Balidu, the father of Nyelahai, and the father of Anop. These findings are borne out by other accounts.

## OUTSTANDING ECONOMIC OBLIGATIONS

It has become apparent from the *Diary* that economic events planned ahead play a definite part in keeping Arapesh life focused, at least to some extent. It is therefore worth while to list the known events in the future toward which Alitoa life was already organized:

### BIG EVENTS

Magahine Feast of Exchange of Pigs from all who were initiated there 15 years ago.[54] Aden was the only Alitoan represented in this feast, and had made the second of a set of chain feasts to his helpers in Alitoa and Numidipheim.

Coconut Exchange Feast with Wihun, of which Ombomb and Kule were the Alitoa "trunks," and Belogomini and Wambibi of Wihun the *vis-à-vis*.

Payment for the *midep* to Kobelen; here La'abe and his newly revived *buanyin*, Aden, were the "trunks."

Coconut Exchange between Ahalesimihi and Numonihi. Of this Nagawe was the "trunk," and so would involve all *Toto'alaibis* and *Uyebis*.

Death Feast for the Father of Maginala, in Alipinagle. This was scheduled for about two years ahead. This was the only feast which Alipinagle was directly planning.

Possible Death Feast for Bauwan, who had been dead five years, but whose bones had not been taken out. There was division of opinion on this; Baimal said he was an arrogant bombastic fool and should be left in his grave, for his bones would be of no use to anyone.

[54] This is far longer than these feasts are usually allowed to run, but disturbances due to adjustments to white contact had postponed this one several times.

Possible Undertaking of a Great Initiation Feast by Alitoa. In reply to the goading remarks made by Wihun at the Yapiaun feast, Balidu had taken up the challenge and announced that they would build a big initiatory enclosure in Alitoa.

To these events, especially to the last one if it were realized, the planting of gardens, the raising of pigs, the economical consumption of sago, the abstention from eating coconuts would all be directed.

# FIFTY MINUTES OF VILLAGE LIFE IN ALITOA

SCENE: In front of Balidu's place, February 9. Fair day after a rainy one. A few days before the giving of the big *Toto'alaibis* feast.

| TIME | PERSONS[55] | BEHAVIOR |
| --- | --- | --- |
| 8:00 A.M. | Balidu, Kumati, Amito'a, Nigimarib, Amus, Wasijo and her baby | Balidu is just sitting. Wasijo is trying to get her fretting baby to nurse. It frets and refuses the breast. Amus lolls in her mother's lap. Nigimarib sits with his hands behind his head and bumps his elbows together. Kumati just sits |
| 8:05 | La'abe, Souato'a, the *luluai* of Wihun (La'abe's brother-in-law), Daulap, son of the *luluai*, and Lamein, the 10-year-old betrothed wife of Kaberman, join the group | *Luluai* sits down and remarks that he is going now. Souato'a sits down beside Amus, who crawls out of her mother's lap and looks doubtfully at Souato'a. Balidu passes a few casual remarks to *luluai*. Amito'a plays with Souato'a's ears and remarks that they ought to be pierced, Amus' were at her age. Lamein sits down beside Kumati and whispers to her. Daulap stands and leans against a post. Souato'a plucks her chin. Amus bumps her lips. La'abe tells Souato'a to scratch his back |

[55] See Guide List of Personal Names for ages, sex, etc. (p. 525).

| Time | Persons | Behavior |
|---|---|---|
| | | Balidu remarks they have gone to get wood to make a drum. Baby of Wasijo still frets. She says it is sick and can't wash. Amito'a says it is sick. Wasijo tries her breast, gives it to child, tries it again, gives it to child. Lamein continues to whisper to Kumati |
| 8:10 | Wabe passes with a group of Nu-midipiheim men, all with axes | |
| 8:13 | Baimal, husband of Amito'a, comes over and joins the group | They remark that he won't go anywhere today. La'abe says he is going to build a ground house and stay there until it is finished. Baimal remarks that he is going to work Sumali's sago patch. Amus goes back to her mother's lap. Souato'a bumps her mouth |
| 8:15 | Lomaijo, wife of La'abe, comes up with her baby and stops at a distance, about 15 feet, holding baby on her lap | La'abe and Souato'a take no notice of her. She gives the baby the breast, child plays with it, pulls the nipple, nurses a little, stops, pulls at her grass skirt, mother lifts her up, rubs noses, kisses her neck, etc. This goes on until Ombomb's baby comes later. Lamein has persuaded Kumati and the two little girls, followed by Nigi-marib, to run off and get the kittens. Each brings one. Sit and play with kittens, snuggle them against chin and nose, then give them to mother cat to nurse. Balidu, Baimal, La'abe nod approval. I ask about parentage and am told whom the cat belongs to, where found, and that the kittens were fathered by a Wihun cat. This cat was taken there for the purpose |
| 8:19 | Amito'a, Amus, and Baimal get up and walk off, go into house | Balidu tells children to put the kittens away. They do and Lamein and Kumati do not come back |

|  | | |
|---|---|---|
| 8:24 | Son of Ulaijo passes and *luluai* of Wihum gets up and joins him. Boy wields a stick to corral two dogs. Lamein comes back | La'abe and Balidu sit still. Remark on collecting the dogs. Lamein comes back and sits down. Nigimarib finds a seed and plays with it desultorily |
| | | Souato'a sits with crossed arms and does nothing. Daulap still stands, and cracks his fingers |
| 8:27 | Gerud and Madje come up | Gerud sits down and Madje stands. Gerud cadges some tobacco. Orders Nigimarib, his first cousin, to come with him to the bush. Nigimarib ignores order |
| 8:30 | Gerud and Madje set off. Kaberman, Bopumogau pass by after them | Wasijo puts her baby in a net bag. It cries harder than ever |
| 8:35 | Amito'a and Amus return, having eaten a baked breakfast | Amito'a tells Wasijo not to cover the child's head. Wasijo says the other net bag is better, but makes no move to exchange the child and her things |
| 8:38 | Sauwedjo passes on the way to her garden, alone | Her puppy strays behind. She calls and Lamein runs and picks it up and gives it to her |
| 8:39 | La'abe gets up and goes toward his end of the village | Souato'a remains and bubbles her lips. Nigimarib loses his fruit and tells the two little girls to get it. Amus gets it. He tells them to stay there and throw it to him, but they silently refuse and go back to plucking their lips |
| 8:42 | Balidu leaves group to micturate | Wasijo's baby continues to cry. She finally gathers it up, shouts out that she is going |
| 8:43 | Balidu returns and Wasijo sets out for Manuniki, alone | Nigimarib begins to play ball with Daulap. I join in. Souato'a laughs, then begins prodding her lower lip with her tongue. Amus bubbles hers |

| TIME | PERSONS | BEHAVIOR |
|------|---------|----------|
| 8:44 | Ombomb's baby toddles up and sits down beside Lomaijo | Lomaijo's baby gets off her lap and goes and sits by Ombomb's baby. Then gets up and sits on other side of Lomaijo. Ombomb's baby follows. (Note that these two children were co-nursed.) This is kept up for some time, then Lomaijo's baby gets in mother's lap |
| 8:47 | Ulaijo, Ibanyos, Anyuai, Segenamoya, Sauisoa, and Nemausi go by on way to plant taro, in garden | Daulap says he is tired of ball playing and wanders off. Nigimarib breaks the seed in half and drops it. The two little girls pick it up, and begin crumbling it to bits |
| 8:50 | I leave group | |

# GUIDE LIST OF PERSONAL NAMES
# IN ALITOA

This list has been prepared to enable the reader to place individuals in the original discussion of personalities (pp. 1–195) and on the census (pp. 462–478), thus providing a ready reference for age, sex, household position, and, for adults, personality description.

# GLOSSARY[1]

This glossary contains only Arapesh and pidgin English (P. E.) words that are used more than once and without a parenthetical explanation.

*abullu,* yam harvest ceremony of the Beach and Mountain Arapesh

*abuting,* long yams

*alapwen,* a child who is given in adoption to the gens of its mother's former husband

*alomato'in,* men who fail to maintain their adult male ceremonial life, lit., "male woman," P. E. "man no good"

*ano'in,* a poorly conceptualized institutionalized relationship between men who have declared themselves to be rivals, or between their children, or between people who are born on the same day

*ashup,* an emetic taken by those who are afraid they have been sorcerized

*baik,* a small feast made by the men of a hamlet to their women folk who have helped in a large feast

*balagasik,* feast given to the mother's brothers of a just initiated boy

*buanyin,* hereditary male feasting and exchange partner

*exuviae,* emanations of the body used for sorcery practices

*gaba,* the term used for rings cut from *tridacna* shell, the typical *rite de passage* valuable, when used in mortuary payments

*gabunyan,* a ceremonial exchange partner in an intervillage exchange; used of the principals in such an exchange

*garamut* (P. E.), a wooden slit gong, which usually lies horizontal

*ginyau,* one moiety of the set of moieties which regulate feasting. See *iwhul.* Second meaning, heirloom to which some sanctity is attached

*gwai'oyen,* a child which is adopted into a gens to keep up gens strength

*iwhul,* one moiety of the set of moieties which regulate feasting. See *ginyau*

*kiap* (P. E.), general term for administrative officers of the Australian administration, specifically the District Officer

*kumun,* one moiety of the set of moieties in which membership is strictly hereditary, functions at initiation, lit., hawk tabooed by all members. See *kwain*

*kunae* (P. E.), applied to the grass which covers New Guinea plains, in Sepik-Aitape District also used to denote the interior which is characterized by such grass-covered plains

*kuskus* (P. E.), a form of scabies complicated by penicillium

*kwain*, one moiety of the set of moieties in which membership is strictly hereditary, functions at initiation, lit., cockatoo, tabooed by all members. See *kumun*

*laplap* (P. E.), loin cloth, knee length, of trade cloth, conventional costume of work boys and culture contacted natives; cloth

*luluai* (P. E.), Government-appointed village head

*marsalai* (P. E.), supernaturals which inhabit various unsavory sections of the bush, especially water holes, and are embodied in snakes, lizards, crocodiles, etc. Arapesh, *walin walinab*

*mehinen*, primary meaning, sister's son. For extensions, see kinship lists (pp. 29, 30)

*midep*, a dance complex which Alitoa was preparing to purchase from Kobelen, said to come from Mushu Island

*oshogu*, edible caterpillars, a delicacy

*ponkol* (P. E.), sago palm petioles

*sagumeh* (P. E.), a form of combined sorcery and divination, associated with pointing bones, burial of exuviae, and possession by a spirit of the dead; contains many work boy elements and was rapidly diffusing through the returned work boys on the Madang Aitape coast

*shené*, a dance complex sold by Dakuar to Kobelen, in 1932; said to have come from "Murik," a loose designation for villages near the mouth of the Sepik

*tamberan* (P. E.), the supernatural guardian of the adult male group, usually impersonated by a musical instrument or sound-making device such as the bull roarer, flutes, etc.; not used in the other pidgin English sense of "soul of a dead man"

*tangeba*, a dance complex which had been imported by the hamlet of Alitoa called Ahalesimihi, from Sublamon (Magahine) just previous to 1931

*tangget* (P. E.), mnemonic devices used to convey messages or make records

*tinea, tinea embricata*, a form of ringworm

*tultul* (P. E.), Government-appointed village interpreter between native language and pidgin English

*wabul*, place, used with attributives to indicate hamlet, locality, etc.

*wawen* or *wa'en*, primary meaning is mother's brother. For extensions, see kinship lists (pp. 28, 29)

*wishan*, a form of sorcery in which the sorcerer uses the exuviae of one member of a community in order to bring misfortune, but not death, upon some other member of that community whose exuviae he does have in stock

# BIBLIOGRAPHY

Bateson, Gregory
    1932 "Social Structure of the Iatmül People of the Sepik River,"
*Oceania*, 2:245–291; 401–453.
    1935 "Culture Contact and Schismogenesis," *Man*, 35:178–183.
    1936 *Naven: A Survey of the Problems Suggested by a Composite Picture of the Culture of a New Guinea Tribe Drawn from Three Points of View.* Cambridge: Cambridge University Press; 2nd ed., 1958, SP21. Stanford: Stanford University Press.

Earthy, E. Dora
    1933 *Valenge Women.* London: Oxford University Press.

Edel, May M.
    1937 "The Bachiga of East Africa." In *Cooperation and Competition,* editor Margaret Mead. New York: McGraw-Hill; reprinted 1961. Boston: Beacon Press.

Elkin, A. P.
    1935 "Kinship in the Admiralty Islands," *Oceania*, 5:490–493.

Fortune, Reo F.
    1932a *Sorcerers of Dobu: The Social Anthropology of the Dobu Islanders of the Western Pacific.* London: Routledge; reprinted 1963, D 119. New York: Dutton.
    1932b *Omaha Secret Societies.* Columbia University Contributions to Anthropology, Vol. 14. New York: Columbia University Press.
    1933 "A Note on Some Forms of Kinship Structure," *Oceania*, 4:1–9.
    1935 *Manus Religion: An Ethnological Study of the Manus Natives of the Admiralty Islands.* Philadelphia: American Philosophical Society; reprinted 1965, Bison BB303. Lincoln: University of Nebraska Press.
    1939 "Arapesh Warfare," *American Anthropologist*, 41:22–41.
    1942 *Arapesh.* Publications of the American Ethnological Society, Vol. 19. New York: Augustin.
    1943 "Arapesh Maternity," *Nature*, 152:164.
    1947a "Law and Force in Papuan Societies," *American Anthropologist*, 49:244–259.

1947b "The Rules of Relationship Behavior in One Variety of Primitive Warfare," *Man,* 47:108–110.

Gifford, Edward W.

1929 *Tongan Society.* Bernice P. Bishop Museum Bulletin 61, Honolulu, Hawaii.

Hocart, A. M.

1927 *Kingship.* London: Oxford University Press.

Hogbin, H. Ian

1935 "Sorcery and Administration," *Oceania,* 6:1–32.

Junod, H. A.

1927 *The Life of a South African Tribe.* London: Macmillan.

Lowie, Robert

1927 *The Origin of the State.* New York: Harcourt Brace.

Mead, Margaret

1930a *Growing Up in New Guinea.* New York: Morrow; reprinted with new preface 1962, Apollo A58. New York: Morrow; 1968, Laurel 3270. New York: Dell.

1930b *Social Organization of Manua.* Bernice P. Bishop Museum Bulletin 76, Honolulu, Hawaii; reprinted 1969.

1932a *The Changing Culture of an Indian Tribe.* New York: Columbia University Press; reprinted with new introduction 1966, CAP 266. New York: Capricorn Books (Putnam).

1932b "An Investigation of the Thought of Primitive Children, with Special Reference to Animism," *Journal of the Royal Anthropological Institute of Ireland and Great Britain,* 62: 173–190.

1933a "The *Marsalai* Cult among the Arapesh, with Special Reference to the Rainbow Serpent Beliefs of the Australian Aboriginals," *Oceania,* 4:37–53.

1933b "More Comprehensive Field Methods," *American Anthropologist,* 35:1–15.

1934a *Kinship in the Admiralty Islands.* Anthropological Papers of The American Museum of Natural History, New York, 34, Part 2.

1934b "How the Papuan Plans His Dinner," *Natural History,* 34:377–388.

1934c "Tamberans and Tumbuans in New Guinea," *Natural History,* 34:234–246.

1935a Review of *The Riddle of the Sphinx,* by Geza Roheim. *Character and Personality,* 4:85–90.

1935b *Sex and Temperament in Three Primitive Societies.* New York: Morrow; reprinted with new preface 1963, Apollo A67. New York: Morrow; 1968, Laurel 7777. New York: Dell.

editor. 1937a *Cooperation and Competition among Primitive Peoples*. New York: McGraw-Hill; enlarged ed. 1961, BP123. Boston: Beacon.

1937b "A Reply" to Review by R. C. Thurnwald of *Sex and Temperament in Three Primitive Societies, American Anthropologist*, 39:558–561.

1938 *The Mountain Arapesh. I. An Importing Culture*. Anthropological Papers of The American Museum of Natural History, New York, 36, Part 3; reprinted 1970 as *The Mountain Arapesh*, Vol. II. *Arts and Supernaturalism*. AM Science Books B 19b. Garden City, N.Y.: Natural History Press.

1940 *The Mountain Arapesh. II. Supernaturalism*. Anthropological Papers of The American Museum of Natural History, New York, 37, Part 3; reprinted 1970 together with I. *An Importing Culture*.

1949a *The Mountain Arapesh. V. The Record of Unabelin with Rorschach Analyses*. Anthropological Papers of The American Museum of Natural History, New York, 41, Part 3; reprinted 1968. AM Science Books B 19a. Garden City, N.Y.: Natural History Press.

1949b *Male and Female*. New York: Morrow; reprinted 1967, Apollo A160. New York: Morrow; 1968, Laurel 5176. New York: Dell.

1956 *New Lives for Old: Cultural Transformation, Manus 1928–1953*. New York: Morrow; reprinted with new preface 1966, Apollo A 124. New York: Morrow.

1963 "The Bark Paintings of the Mountain Arapesh of New Guinea," in *Technique and Personality in Primitive Art*. ("Museum of Primitive Art Lecture Series," 3.) New York: The Museum of Primitive Art, 8–43.

1964 *Continuities in Cultural Evolution*. New Haven: Yale University Press; reprinted 1966, Y154. New Haven: Yale University Press.

Radcliffe-Brown, A. R.

1924 "The Mother's Brother in South Africa," *South African Journal of Science*, 21:542–555.

Thurnwald, Richard C.

1916 *Banaro Society*. Memoirs of the American Anthropological Association, No. 3. Lancaster: American Anthropological Association.

Tregear, E.

1904 *The Maori Race*. Wanganvi, N.Z.: Willis.